AW

HOUGHTON MIFFLIN

English

Authors
Robert Rueda
Tina Saldivar
Lynne Shapiro
Shane Templeton
C. Ann Terry
Catherine Valentino
Shelby A. Wolf

Consultants
Jeanneine P. Jones
Monette Coleman McIver
Rojulene Norris

HOUGHTON MIFFLIN

BOSTON

Acknowledgments

For each of the selections listed below, grateful acknowledgment is made for permission to excerpt and/or reprint original or copyrighted material as follows:

Published Models

"Ananse the Spider in Search of a Fool" from *Ashley Bryan's African Tales, Uh-huh*, retold and illustrated by Ashley Bryan. Copyright © 1998 by Atheneum Books for Young Readers. Copyright © 1972 by Ashley Bryan. Reprinted with the permission of Atheneum Books for Young Readers, an imprint of Simon & Schuster Children's Publishing Division.

From "Cold-Blooded Reptiles" from *Snakes* by Eric S. Grace. Copyright ©1994 by Eric S. Grace. Reprinted by permission of Sierra Club Books for Children.

"Forecast: Hot and Hotter!" by Samantha Bonar from *3-2-1 Contact* Magazine, June 1996 issue. Copyright ©1996 by Children's Television Workshop. Reprinted by permission of Children's Television Workshop. All rights reserved.

Acknowledgments are continued at the back of the book following the last page of the Index.

ISBN: 0-618-31002-9

11 12 13 14 15 16 17 18 – DCI – 09 08 07

TABLE OF CONTENTS

Part 1

Grammar, Usage, and Mechanics

Unit 1   The Sentence 31

Part 1

Unit 2 Nouns 83

Part 2 Writing, Listening, Speaking, and Viewing

Unit 9 — Writing to Persuade 396

SECTION 2 Explaining and Informing

Unit 10   Writing to Compare and Contrast 440

SECTION 3 **Narrating and Entertaining**

Unit 12 **Writing a Personal Narrative** 524

Unit 13 · Writing a Story 551

Part 3

Tools and Tips

Listening, Speaking, and Viewing

A Day in the Life of a Student

Abuela, I just HAD to tell you about my birthday party. It was so much fun!

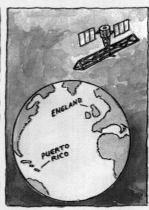

It must be important. Tell me everything, dear.

It sounds like we got different results growing our seeds than you did.

We'll aim the camera at our plants so you can see them.

Then the mummy sits up and says, "Is there any pizza? I haven't eaten for six hundred years!" It was a great movie!

SCHOOL BUS

Will you come speak at Career Day? We'd love some free samples!

Chef Louis looks doubtful

It would only take about an hour. I think the students would find your job fascinating.

Learning from Each Other

Each of you is unique. You have your own personal experiences, talents, knowledge, opinions, and observations. That makes you valuable resources for each other. As individuals you're like one-of-a-kind books, full of information and ideas to share. Together as a class, you're a whole encyclopedia!

Together, we can grow giant vegetables, write Chinese characters, save a game, and splint a broken bone!

By sharing what you know and learning from others, you can make school—and life—easier and much more fun! You can rely on each other to solve problems, to think of new ideas, and to offer encouragement. How? SPEAK, LISTEN, and VIEW! Speaking lets you share what you know. Listening and viewing let you learn from others. Here are some of the major purposes for speaking, listening, and viewing.

Speaking	Listening and Viewing	Examples
to entertain	for enjoyment	telling or listening to a story, admiring a painting, participating in friendly conversation
to inform	to get information	asking for or giving directions, scanning the lunch choices, reading someone's body language
to persuade	to form an opinion	recommending a book, listening to a movie review, watching a commercial

Think and Discuss

- Look back at the pictures on the previous page. What is each person's purpose for listening, speaking, or viewing?
- At what other times do you rely on listening, speaking, and viewing during the day?

Discussion Breakdown

These students are trying to pick a service project to perform for their school. They are not using good listening and speaking skills. What are they doing wrong?

Think and Discuss

- What is each student doing wrong in this discussion?
- What could the students do to improve their discussion?

Discussion

Breakthrough

The students are still planning their school service project. How have they improved their listening and speaking skills?

Think and Discuss

- What has each student done to improve his or her listening or speaking skills?

Being a Good Listener and Speaker

Remember to use these basic guidelines for listening and speaking with others, whether you are in class, on the playing field, at the mall, or with your family.

When You Listen

▶ Get rid of distractions. Turn off the music. Close the door.
▶ Make eye contact with the speaker.
▶ Listen attentively. Don't make noise or let your mind wander.
▶ If you get confused, repeat what was said in your own words. Check that you've understood.
▶ Silently summarize what you hear.

When You Speak

▶ Participate, lead, and listen. Vary your role occasionally.
▶ Don't interrupt! Wait your turn.
▶ Don't have side conversations.
▶ Make eye contact with your listeners. Speak slowly, clearly, and loudly enough to be understood.
▶ Ask others what they think of your ideas. Say what you think about theirs.
▶ If you disagree, politely explain why.
▶ Stick to the subject being discussed.
▶ Summarize the main points of the discussion from time to time.

Try It Out Choose one of the statements below. Decide whether or not you agree with it. Discuss your opinions in small groups.

● Professional athletes should not advertise products, such as sneakers and soft drinks.
● Everyone should study music and art at school.
● First-aid certification should be required for everyone over age ten.

Being a Good Viewer

Seeing is not the same as viewing. When you see, your eyes simply pick up images. When you view, you learn through your eyes. What information can the people in these pictures gather by viewing?

When You View

Viewing the World Around You

▶ First, take in the big picture. Notice all that you can.

▶ Then, focus. Where is your eye drawn? What are the most important parts of what you're viewing?

▶ Then refocus. What interesting or important details do you see?

Viewing Others

> You must have done well on the math test!

▶ Pay attention to body language. People often use their hands to demonstrate or to add meaning to what they are saying. A smile, a frown, a blush, a yawn, or another expression is a clue to how someone is feeling. Observing body language can also help you figure out how people are reacting to what you say and do.

Viewing Still or Moving Images

doggie

▶ Notice where your eye is drawn. What is the main focus of the image? What techniques did the person who created this image use to get your attention?
▶ Decide what message, if any, the image sends.
▶ Identify the target audience. Is it meant for children? adults? sports-lovers? Think about how different audiences might react to this image.
▶ Think about the purpose of the image. Is it meant to entertain? to inform? to persuade?

Try It Out In small groups, create a silent scene, using actions, facial expressions, and hand gestures. Perform your scene in front of the class. Once you've finished, have your classmates guess what was happening.

The Writing Process

A Day in the Life of a Student

What Is the Writing Process?

The writing process helps you move step by step from a blank sheet of paper to an interesting piece of writing. The writing process gives you many chances to improve your writing.

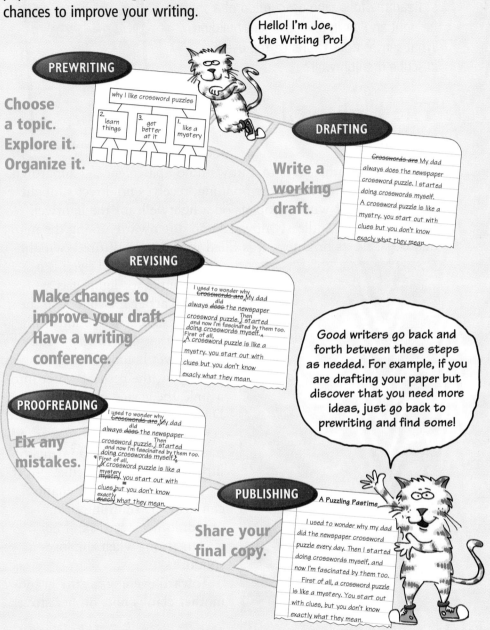

Hello! I'm Joe, the Writing Pro!

PREWRITING

Choose a topic. Explore it. Organize it.

why I like crossword puzzles

2. learn things 3. get better at it 1. like a mystery

DRAFTING

Write a working draft.

Crosswords are My dad always does the newspaper crossword puzzle. I started doing crosswords myself. A crossword puzzle is like a mystry. you start out with clues but you don't know exacly what they mean.

REVISING

Make changes to improve your draft. Have a writing conference.

I used to wonder why Crosswords are My dad did always does the newspaper crossword puzzle. Then and now I'm fascinated by them too. doing crosswords myself. First of all, A crossword puzzle is like a mystery. you start out with clues but you don't know exacly what they mean.

Good writers go back and forth between these steps as needed. For example, if you are drafting your paper but discover that you need more ideas, just go back to prewriting and find some!

PROOFREADING

Fix any mistakes.

I used to wonder why Crosswords are My dad did always does the newspaper crossword puzzle. Then and now I'm fascinated by them too. doing crosswords myself. First of all, A crossword puzzle is like a mystery mystry. you start out with clues but you don't know exactly exacly what they mean.

PUBLISHING

Share your final copy.

A Puzzling Pastime

I used to wonder why my dad did the newspaper crossword puzzle every day. Then I started doing crosswords myself, and now I'm fascinated by them too.
First of all, a crossword puzzle is like a mystery. You start out with clues, but you don't know exactly what they mean.

Looking Ahead In this section, you will learn about the writing process as you write a description. To get ready, you will first read a description that was published in a book.

Read the following description of a shaft for light and air in an apartment building. What senses does Laurence Yep use to describe the lightwell?

The Lightwell

by Laurence Yep

My grandmother lives in a tiny studio apartment in Chinatown. Her home, in the rear of the building, receives no direct sunlight even though her window opens on a lightwell; for the lightwell seems to stretch endlessly upward and downward among the many buildings. At its brightest, it is filled with a kind of tired twilight.

Although the lightwell is a poor source for light, it is a perfect carrier for sound. In the mornings it carries sound from all the other apartments—the slap of wet laundry being hung in a window, the rush of water into a sink, the crying of a baby. During the afternoons, bits of conversation float into my grand-mother's home like fragments of little dramas and comedies—just as, I'm sure, the other tenants can hear the shuffling of my grandmother's cards and her exclamations when she loses at solitaire.

Toward evening, as my grand-mother clanks pots on her stove,

Go to www.eduplace.com/kids/ for information about Laurence Yep.

I can hear matching sounds from the other apartments as her neighbors also prepare their meals. And the smell of my grandmother's simmering rice and frying vegetables mingles with the other smells in the lightwell until there are enough aromas for a banquet.

Side by side, top and below, each of us lives in our own separate time and space. And yet we all belong to the same building, our lives touching however briefly and faintly.

Reading As a Writer

Think About the Description

- What sights, sounds, and smells does Laurence Yep describe?
- In the first paragraph, what exact words does the author use to describe the light in the lightwell?
- What details help you imagine the sounds from other apartments?

Think About Writer's Craft

- In the second paragraph, what comparison does the author use to describe the bits of conversation?

Think About the Picture

- Look at the illustration on page 10. Why do you think the artist used soft lines and patches of color rather than hard, connected lines and distinct objects and people?

Looking Ahead

Now you are ready to write your own description. Starting on the next page, you will find many ideas to help you. As you go along, you will see how one student, James M. Glover, used the writing process to write a description of a walk in the woods.

Using the Writing Process

What Is Prewriting?

Prewriting has three parts: choosing your topic; exploring your topic; and organizing, or planning, your writing.

Start thinking about **audience** and **purpose** right away. What kind of paper will you write? Who will read or listen to your writing?

Think about how you are going to **publish** or **share** your paper. This may affect how you write it.

How Do I Choose a Topic?

Here are a few ways to find an idea to write about.

Ways to Think of Topics		
Try this!	**Here's how.**	
Remember your experiences.	Once you got lost in a large shopping mall.	• Write a **personal narrative** about what happened. • **Describe** the mall or a store you visited there.
Listen to other people.	You heard a family member talk about immigrating to the United States.	• Write a **story** about someone's first day in this country. • Write a **research report** on immigration.
Read a book.	You enjoyed a book about Greek gods and heroes.	• **Persuade** your friends to learn more about Greek mythology. • **Compare and contrast** an ancient hero with a modern sports star.
Reread your journal.	You wrote a journal entry about sleeping late on Saturdays.	• Write an **opinion essay** about how you love sleeping late. • **Compare and contrast** mornings on school days and on weekends.
Use your imagination.	What would it be like to be in a hurricane?	• Write a **research report** on hurricanes. • Write a **story** about experiencing a hurricane.

Write a Description

Choosing a Description Topic

Learning from a Model James wanted to write a description to submit to an Internet site that publishes student writing. He made a list of ideas and then thought about each one.

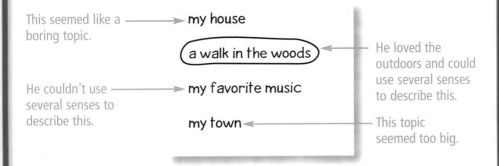

This seemed like a boring topic. → my house

(a walk in the woods) ← He loved the outdoors and could use several senses to describe this.

He couldn't use several senses to describe this. → my favorite music

my town ← This topic seemed too big.

▶ **Choose Your Topic**

As you choose your topic, think about your **purpose**, your **audience**, and how you will **publish** or **share** your description.

❶ **List** five topics, such as a pet, a favorite place, an interesting person, or a special occasion. Use the chart on page 12 to help you think of ideas.

❷ **Discuss** your topics with a partner. Which ideas does your partner like best? Why?

❸ **Ask** yourself these questions about each topic.

- Is this topic about a single person, place, or thing?
- Have I seen this or done it myself? Can I think of interesting details?
- Can I use at least three senses to describe it?
- Which topic would both my audience and I enjoy?

❹ **Circle** the topic you will write about.

📁 Keep all your work for your description in one place, such as a writing folder.

Tech Tip
See page H47 for ideas for using a computer during the writing process.

What Is Exploring?

Exploring is the second part of prewriting. Explore by recalling events, gathering facts, and thinking of details to elaborate your topic.

How Do I Explore My Topic?

This chart shows different strategies you can use to explore a topic.

Exploring Strategies	
Try this!	**Here's how.**
Brainstorming a list	Delia's Log Cabin thick round logs whispering pines color of honey smoky wood stove
Clustering	hot weather CANOE TRIP tipped over campfire dinner
Making a chart	Pine Trees Touch | flexible needles, prickly points Smell | sharp, tangy
Drawing and labeling	Happy Birthday! The party was a total surprise.
Interviewing with a partner	What's your dog's favorite thing to eat?
Asking *Who? What? When? Where? Why? How?*	The Day of the Flood **What?** Cannon River rising over its banks **Why?** too much rain in a week—ten inches
Freewriting	I love sleeping late—really, really late. What's so great about it? I don't know—hiding under covers, warm sheets, no one bothering me, all by myself.

 See page H59 for more graphic organizers.

Exploring a Description Topic

Learning from a Model James used an Observation Chart to help him brainstorm details about taking a walk in the woods. He focused on the senses that were important to his topic.

Sound	Sight	Touch
squirrel chattering	green trees	leaves on my face
wind in treetops	squirrel near a tree	water falling on my hands
water falling from branches	light through trees	cold air

▲ **James's Observation Chart**

▶ **Explore Your Topic**

❶ **Picture** what you are describing. What do your readers need to know to help them clearly imagine it?

❷ **Write** down as many details as possible. Use an Observation Chart.

❸ **Use your five senses** to brainstorm sensory words and details to add to your chart. Use the sensory words listed below or think of your own.

Sight	Sound	Smell	Touch	Taste
misty	jingle	smoky	velvety	nutty
immense	shrill	flowery	moist	fruity
scamper	slurp	musty	furry	briny
gleaming	gurgle	piny	greasy	bitter
glisten	crunch	stale	spongy	spicy
ivory	scratch	vinegary	rubbery	savory
droopy	rumble	fresh	brittle	peppery
bushy	hum	moldy	silky	tangy
ragged	bellow	acrid	mushy	tart
spindly	thunder	burnt	flinty	sugary

If you can't think of many sensory words, try another topic.

What Is Organizing?

Organizing is the third part of prewriting. You select the ideas and details that you want to include. Then you group the ones that belong together and put the groups in order.

How Do I Organize My Writing?

Group facts, events, or ideas. Put related details into separate groups, such as what happened first or second or the steps for doing something.

Choose an organization. Present the groups of details in an order that fits your purpose. It often helps to chart, diagram, or outline your plan.

Ways to Organize	
Try this!	**Here's how.**
Chronological order First Next Last	Tell events in the order they happen.
Spatial order	Describe things in the order they are arranged in space, such as from top to bottom, right to left, or far to near.
Comparison and contrast	Tell likenesses and then differences, or tell them the other way around.
Order of importance LEAST MOST MOST LEAST	Tell the most important reason first and the least important reason last, or tell them the other way around.
Question and answer Q? A . . . Q? A . . .	Ask a question and tell the answer. Then ask another question and answer that.
Logical order	Group related details and present the groups in an order that makes sense.

Organizing a Description

Learning from a Model James needed to order the details in his Observation Chart. He decided to use a flow chart.

- He chose to tell details in the order they happened on his walk.
- He circled details from each part of his walk in different colors.
- Next, he made a flow chart showing each part of his walk.
- Then he added groups of details in chronological order.
- Finally, he added more details.

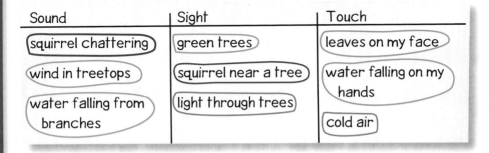

Sound	Sight	Touch
squirrel chattering	green trees	leaves on my face
wind in treetops	squirrel near a tree	water falling on my hands
water falling from branches	light through trees	cold air

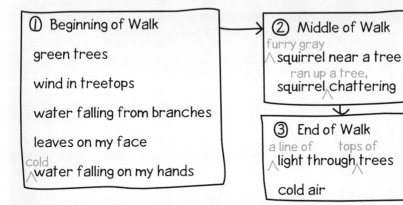

① Beginning of Walk

green trees

wind in treetops

water falling from branches

leaves on my face

cold
water falling on my hands

② Middle of Walk

furry gray
squirrel near a tree
ran up a tree,
squirrel chattering

③ End of Walk

a line of   tops of
light through trees

cold air

▲ James's flow chart

▶ Organize Your Description

❶ **Group** the details about your topic that belong together.

❷ **Make** a flow chart. Show your details in the order you will tell them.

❸ **Add** any more details you think of. Use exact words.

What Is Drafting?

When you draft, get your ideas on paper. Don't worry about mistakes. You can fix them later because this is a **working draft**.

- Think about your purpose and your audience as you write.
- Add more details as you go along. Good ideas can come at any time.
- If you change your mind, don't start over. Cross out what you don't want, and keep writing!

How Do I Draft My Paper?

Write sentences and paragraphs. Start with the plan you made when you organized your ideas. Turn the words and phrases into sentences. Each section should make at least one paragraph. Most paragraphs will need a topic sentence. The **topic sentence** tells the main idea.

Write a beginning and an ending. Write an interesting beginning that introduces your topic. Write an ending that tells an overall impression or makes a final comment about your topic.

Make transitions. Use transitional words and phrases to tie your sentences and paragraphs together.

Ways to Make Transitions	
Try this!	**Look at these examples.**
Use time clues.	before, after, finally, then, next, until, when, often, soon, since, meanwhile, at last, afterward, yesterday, at night, Monday
Link causes and effects.	because, as a result, so that, therefore, if . . . then, thus, due to, in response to
Use place clues.	above, around, down, here, there, beside, inside, outside, over, under
Signal likenesses and differences.	however, although, in contrast, similarly, unlike, instead
Introduce another idea.	also, too, another, in addition, furthermore
Show degree of importance.	above all, better, best, equally important, most important, worse, worst, strongest

Drafting a Description

Learning from a Model James wrote his working draft. He began with the first group of details in his flow chart. He thought of a good topic sentence about first entering the woods. Then he turned the sentence into a question to grab his readers' attention. He used the details in his chart to write his other sentences and paragraphs. He didn't worry about mistakes yet.

Have you ever been in the woods after a rain? I went one afternoon. The woods dripping trees looked like standing dollar bills. then I saw as I walked, leafs occassionally brushed my face and dropped cold water on my hands When the wind blew, it shook water from the branches and rustled the leaves.

I saw only one animal, a furry gray squirrel. It ran up a tree, where it sat chattering at me.

I saw a line of light slanting through the tops of the trees like a stairway. After a few minutes all the stairways of light faded, and I felt cold. It was getting late and time to go home.

▲ James's working draft

▶ Draft Your Description

❶ **Write** an interesting beginning that introduces your topic.

❷ **Use** your flow chart to write the rest of your paper. For each paragraph, think of the main idea and write a topic sentence. Write other sentences to fill in the details about the main idea. Don't worry about mistakes. Just write!

❸ **End** by telling an overall impression or making a final comment about your topic.

What Is Revising?

When you revise, you make changes to your draft to make it clearer or more interesting. Ask yourself the Big Questions. Don't worry about fixing mistakes yet.

How Do I Make Revisions?

Don't erase! Make changes right on your draft. Don't worry if your paper looks messy. You can make a clean copy later. Here are ways to make your changes.

Revising: The Big Questions
- Did I say what I wanted to say?
- Did I elaborate and use details?
- Did I organize the facts, events, or ideas clearly?
- Did I write in a way that is interesting and appropriate to my audience?

It's wise to revise!

Ways to Mark Your Revisions

Try this!	Look at these examples.
Cross out parts that you want to change or take out.	She wore ~~very~~ unique emerald earrings.
Use carets to add new words or sentences.	stealthy, slow-moving My ∧ cat stalked the birds at the feeder.
Draw circles and arrows to move words, sentences, or paragraphs.	(It will save gasoline.) Ride a bike instead of asking someone to drive you somewhere. ∧
Use numbers to show how sentences should be ordered.	① Put the wheel back on the bike. ③ Then tighten the brakes. ② Tighten the axle nut so the wheel doesn't fall off.
Use attachments to add sentences that won't fit on your paper.	I smelled something burning. ∧ I found the eggs all black in the pan. When I dashed into the kitchen, I saw smoke, and

Revising a Description

Learning from a Model James reread his working draft. To help readers picture his walk in the woods more vividly, he elaborated by adding exact words and sensory details.

Have you ever been in the woods after a rain? I went one
afternoon. The woods dripping trees looked like standing dollar bills.
were an intense green,
sopping wet
then I saw as I walked, leafs occassionally brushed my face and
splattered
dropped cold water on my hands When the wind blew, it shook
more
I thought I must be on a bridge with a clear stream
water from the branches and rustled the leaves. trickling under me.

▲ **Part of James's revised draft**

▶ Revise Your Description

Reread your description. Use the Revising Checklist to help you evaluate your description and make changes. Use a thesaurus to find lively, colorful words. Don't worry about mistakes yet.

Revising Checklist

- ✔ Did I introduce my topic in an interesting way?
- ✔ Did I write clear topic sentences?
- ✔ Did I add details that support the topic sentence in each paragraph?
- ✔ Did I order the details in a way that makes sense?
- ✔ Where do I need to add sensory words or details?
- ✔ Did I write an ending that tells an overall impression or makes a final comment?

📖 See the Thesaurus Plus on page H96.

> Remember to use transitional words to connect your sentences and paragraphs.

What Is a Writing Conference?

In a writing conference, a writer reads his or her paper to a partner or a group. The listeners tell what they like, ask questions, and make suggestions. Your conference partners might be a classmate, a small group, your teacher, or someone who knows about your topic.

How Do I Have a Writing Conference?

In a writing conference, you will be either the writer or the listener. Use these guidelines to help you do your best in either role.

Guidelines for Having a Writing Conference	
When You're the Writer . . .	**When You're the Listener . . .**
• Read your paper aloud. • Pay attention to your listeners' comments and suggestions. Keep an open mind. • Take notes to remember any compliments, questions, or suggestions. • Reread your paper after the conference. • Use your notes. Make any other changes you want.	• Look at the writer. • Listen carefully. Don't let your thoughts wander. • Retell what you have heard. • Then tell two things that you like about the paper. • Next, ask questions about things you don't understand. • Finally, give one or two suggestions to help the writer. • Always be positive and polite.

Having a Writing Conference

Learning from a Model James had a conference with his classmate Jessica.

▶ **Have Your Writing Conference**

❶ **Find** a partner or a small group, and have a writing conference. Use the guidelines on page 22.

❷ **Use** your conference notes to make any other changes you want.

What Is Proofreading?

When you proofread, you correct spelling, capitalization, and punctuation. You also check that you have used words correctly, written complete sentences, and indented paragraphs.

How Do I Proofread?

Use these tips to help you proofread.

- Use proofreading marks.
- Proofread for one skill at a time.
- Circle words that might be misspelled. Check spellings in a dictionary.

Proofreading Marks		
Try this!	**Here's when.**	**Look at these examples.**
¶	to begin a new paragraph; to indent the paragraph	¶The green dragon guarded his hoard. Chests of gold were stacked on top of each other.
∧	to add letters, words, or sentences	My cat love s to tease our two dogs.
∧,	to add a comma	Red orange and yellow leaves swirled in the air.
⌄" ⌄"	to add quotation marks	"Yes," he said cheerfully.
⊙	to add a period	Nora built the cabinets⊙Then she painted them.
╭	to take out words, sentences, and punctuation marks; to correct spelling	A huge dog, a German shepherd, barked at me.
/	to change a capital letter to a small letter	How many Mothers and Fathers were at the meeting?
≡	to change a small letter to a capital letter	Her name is mrs. Murgatroyd.
∿	to reverse letters or words	Siezе the day!

Proofreading a Description

Learning from a Model James made more changes to his description after discussing it with Jessica. After James revised his paper so that it read the way he wanted, he proofread it.

¶Have you ever been in the woods after a rain? I went one ^late

afternoon. The ~~woods~~ dripping trees looked like standing dollar bills. ^were an intense green, ^broccoli

~~then I saw~~ as I walked, ~~leafs~~ occasšionally brushed my face and ^sopping wet leaves

dropped cold water on my hands⊙When the wind blew, it shook ^splattered ^more

water from the branches and rustled the leaves. ^I thought I must be on a bridge with a clear stream trickling under me.

▲ **Part of James's proofread draft**

▶ **Proofread Your Description**

Proofread your description, using the Proofreading Checklist below. Use the proofreading marks shown on page 24.

Proofreading Checklist

Did I
- ✔ indent all paragraphs?
- ✔ use complete sentences?
- ✔ use capital letters and punctuation correctly?
- ✔ use the correct form of adjectives when comparing?
- ✔ use correct forms of nouns and verbs?
- ✔ correct any spelling errors?

Use the Guide to Capitalization, Punctuation, and Usage on page H64 and the Spelling Guide on page H80 for help.

What Is Publishing?

When you publish your writing, you share it with your audience.

How Do I Publish My Writing?

Here are some ideas for sharing your writing.

Write It Down

- Send your paper as a letter or an e-mail to friends or family.
- Send your paper to a magazine that publishes student writing.
- Create a collection of writing with your classmates.
- Submit your paper to the school newspaper.

Talk It Up

- Read your paper aloud from the Author's Chair.
- Record your paper on audiotape. Send it to a friend or a relative.
- Present your paper as a speech or an oral report.
- Read your paper as part of a panel discussion or debate.

Show It Off

- Illustrate your writing with photographs or drawings.
- Read your paper aloud on a video "broadcast."
- Make a poster and attach your paper to it.
- Show slides about your topic to the class while reading your paper aloud.

Tech Tip

Make an electronic multimedia presentation. See page H53 for ideas.

How Do I Reflect on My Writing?

Reflecting is rewarding! You'll get new writing ideas, and you'll realize how much you've learned from the writing you've done.

When you reflect, you think about what you have written. You can think about what you did well, what you could do better next time, and what your goals are for your next writing assignment.

 You might want to keep a collection of some of your writing, such as favorite or unusual pieces.

Publishing a Description

Learning from a Model James used e-mail to send a final copy of his description to an Internet site that publishes student writing. He attached a photograph of the woods where he walked.

James M. Glover

In the Woods
by James M. Glover

Have you ever been in the woods after a rain? I went late one afternoon. The dripping trees were an intense green, like broccoli. As I walked, sopping wet leaves occasionally brushed my face and splattered cold water on my hands. When the wind blew, it shook more water from the branches and rustled the leaves. I thought I must be on a bridge with a clear stream trickling under me.

> I can almost hear this sound myself.

I saw only one animal, a furry gray squirrel. It kept rolling an acorn around in its tiny paws. Then it scampered up a tree, where it sat chattering at me.

As I walked on, I saw a line of light slanting through the tops of the trees. It was so bright and straight, I thought I could walk on it like a stairway. After a few minutes there were stairways of light everywhere. Then they faded, and I felt cold. It was getting late and time to go home.

> As I walked on links these two paragraphs well.

> Well done! You finish with the end of your walk.

▶ **Publish Your Description**

Make a neat final copy of your description. Give your description an interesting title. Publish or share your description. Look at page 26 for ideas.

 Will you keep this description? Use the paragraph on page 26 to help you reflect on your writing experience.

Grammar, Usage, and Mechanics

What You Will Find in This Part:

Informal Language

When you're talking with family or friends, you might use informal language that may not follow all the rules of standard English. All that matters, though, is that everyone understands each other.

Similarly, when you write journal entries, notes, or other personal writing, it doesn't matter whether every word or punctuation mark is correct.

MARCH
29
fishing with Grandpa—
6:00AM

Formal Language

However, in class and in many life situations, formal English is often expected—when you apply for a job, for example, speak with people in a workplace, or write for an audience.

This section of the book will help you develop your ability to use formal language when you need it.

611 Acorn Circle
Peterstown, MD 12345
February 19, 2001

...mmunities were
...me families were
...in their homes; but they are struggling
...out heat, electricity, or water. My classmates and
I would like to do something to help out the storm
victims. Will you allow us to have a food and clothing drive
in the town hall?

We would like to hold this event this Saturday.
Most of the students have already talked to their
parents and to the local merchants about the drive.
Everyone seems excited, and we think it will be a very
successful event. Please let us know if we can go ahead
with our plans.

Thank you for considering our request.

Yours truly,

Albert Collier

Albert Collier

The Sentence

Is everyone ready? What a great show we have! Smile for the kiddies. They are going to love you.

1 Kinds of Sentences

Which sentence asks a question? Which one makes a statement? What might the next sentence say if it were an exclamation? an order?

"Do you mean a present?" Sarah stared at him wide-eyed, not believing her ears.

—from *Mama's Going to Buy You a Mockingbird,* by Jean Little

- A **sentence** is a group of words that expresses a complete thought. All sentences start with a capital letter.

- A sentence that makes a statement is a **declarative sentence**. It ends with a period.

    We bought a package of wrapping paper.

- A sentence that asks a question is an **interrogative sentence**. It ends with a question mark.

    What are you going to wrap?

- A sentence that gives a command or makes a request is an **imperative sentence**. It ends with a period.

    Help me. Please hold the box.

- A sentence that shows excitement or strong feeling is an **exclamatory sentence**. It ends with an exclamation point.

    This is a wonderful gift! How clever you are!

 Tip

If you overuse the exclamation point, it will lose its impact.

Try It Out

Speak Up What punctuation mark should end each sentence? Is the sentence declarative, interrogative, imperative, or exclamatory?

1. How many pennies are in the bowl
2. The contest deadline is tomorrow
3. Write your answer in the box
4. What an interesting guess you made
5. Do you think I'll win a prize

Enter the penny contest.

Summing Up

- A **declarative sentence** makes a statement.
- An **interrogative sentence** asks a question.
- An **imperative sentence** gives a command or makes a request.
- An **exclamatory sentence** shows excitement or strong feeling.

On Your Own

Write each sentence. Add the correct end punctuation, and write what kind of sentence it is.

Example: What fun this trip will be
What fun this trip will be!   exclamatory

6. I am really looking forward to this trip
7. Have you ever climbed this mountain
8. Look at my great new hiking boots
9. Please give me the bug spray
10. Did you pack a map
11. Two pairs of socks should be enough
12. How careless of me to forget my soap
13. These snacks will give us some energy
14. Do we have everything
15. What a lot of stuff we have
16. Hiking can be hard work
17. Help me carry our backpacks to the car
18. Will your lotion really block the sun's harmful rays
19. You won't be too hot or too cool if you bring layers of clothing
20. Be careful not to pack more than you can carry
21. I have the compass and the flashlight
22. Do we have enough water
23. How much film should I bring
24. How exciting it will be to reach the top of the mountain

more ▶

25–36. Write the twelve sentences in this part of a script. Add the correct end punctuation for each sentence. Then write what kind of sentence it is.

Example: Hiking is not a sport for everyone

Hiking is not a sport for everyone.   *declarative*

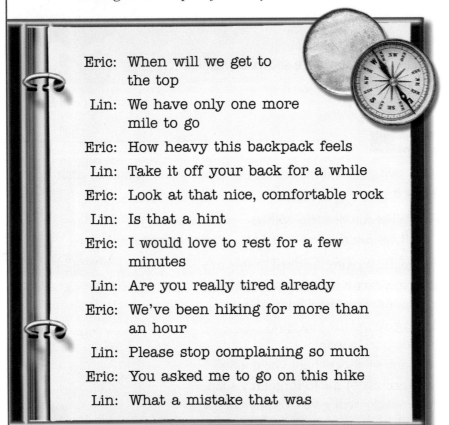

Eric: When will we get to the top

Lin: We have only one more mile to go

Eric: How heavy this backpack feels

Lin: Take it off your back for a while

Eric: Look at that nice, comfortable rock

Lin: Is that a hint

Eric: I would love to rest for a few minutes

Lin: Are you really tired already

Eric: We've been hiking for more than an hour

Lin: Please stop complaining so much

Eric: You asked me to go on this hike

Lin: What a mistake that was

Writing Wrap-Up

WRITING • THINKING • LISTENING • SPEAKING

CREATING

Write a Skit

Write a brief skit about an outing, such as a hike, a train trip, or a museum visit. Create two characters. Use all four kinds of sentences. Ask classmates to take parts and read your scene aloud. Encourage them to use their voices to show what kinds of sentences they are reading.

2 Complete Subjects and Predicates

Play "S and P Go Shoe Shopping." Take turns being S and P. When you are S, suggest a beginning for a sentence. When you are P, finish the sentence. For example,

S: The wingtips in this shoe store
P: flew off the shelves

How many silly shoe-shopping sentences can you build?

- Every sentence has two parts, a subject and a predicate. The **subject** tells whom or what the sentence is about. The **predicate** tells what the subject does, is, has, or feels.

- All the words in the subject make up the **complete subject**. All the words in the predicate make up the **complete predicate**.

Complete Subject	Complete Predicate
Green sneakers	are on sale.
Who	wants a pair?
My friend	does.
Everyone in school	is wearing bright shoes.

Try It Out

Speak Up In each sentence what is the complete subject? What is the complete predicate?

1. Judy Hart took a bus.
2. The bus stopped at Bill's Computer Store.
3. Bill Woo is the owner of the shop.
4. The salesclerk smiled at Judy.
5. Bright lights glowed.
6. Large screens flashed messages at Judy.
7. Other customers were trying out the computers.
8. Software of all types lined the shelves.

more ▶

Try It Out continued

9. The sales staff was courteous, helpful, and knowledgeable.
10. What captured Judy's attention most?
11. Color animations make her research more fun.
12. Someone in the shipping department will help her.

Summing Up

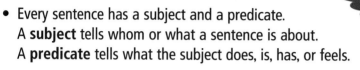

- Every sentence has a subject and a predicate.
  A **subject** tells whom or what a sentence is about.
  A **predicate** tells what the subject does, is, has, or feels.

- A **complete subject** contains all the words in the subject.

- A **complete predicate** contains all the words in the predicate.

On Your Own

Write each sentence. Draw a line between the complete subject and the complete predicate.

Example: Fireworks have existed for hundreds of years.
Fireworks | have existed for hundreds of years.

13. A new year begins.
14. An explosion of color fills the sky in many cities.
15. Dozens of holidays are celebrated with fireworks.
16. Celebrations for the Fourth of July include fireworks.
17. The Orange Bowl Festival in Miami features them.
18. Canada sets off fireworks on Canada Day.
19. Italians light fireworks during a springtime holy day parade.
20. The ancient Greeks used fireworks.
21. The Chinese developed the technique.
22. People do enjoy fireworks.
23. Little children are enchanted by them.
24. The different colors pop out of the sky in a burst.
25. A sudden boom combines with an explosion of color.
26. Everyone sighs in approval.

more ▶

27–46. Write the twenty sentences in this news report. Draw a line between the complete subject and the complete predicate in each sentence.

Example: The fireworks will begin soon.
The fireworks | will begin soon.

Fireworks De-Light Crowds

The Fourth of July fireworks are starting. Hundreds of people are waiting here at the waterfront. Everyone in the crowd sang earlier during the holiday band concert! Some folks stood up for patriotic songs.

We hear a loud pop now. A shower of lights is exploding above our heads. Babies in strollers cry out with pleasure. Adults cheer. Vendors are selling flags, balloons, food, and beverages. Young children wave their flags proudly. They parade across the grass. Eager puppies are following them. Brilliant fireworks sparkle against the dark sky. Different colorful patterns fill the air. Music accompanies these fireworks. It is a technological feat. You should listen carefully to the notes. Engineers are coordinating the fireworks with this original music. The final display fades at last. Small white stars remain in the sky.

Writing Wrap-Up

WRITING • THINKING • LISTENING • SPEAKING

DESCRIBING

Write a Journal Entry

What have you seen recently that made an impression on you? Describe it to a partner. Then write a journal entry about it, describing what you saw and heard. Work with your partner to be sure each sentence has a subject and a predicate.

3 Simple Subjects and Predicates

The cute little <u>puppy</u> <u>loved</u> the toy.
Take turns changing the underlined words. One person changes *puppy* to another word, and the next changes *loved*. Keep taking turns changing the words. How many different "stories" can you tell by changing the words in those two positions?

- You have already learned about complete subjects and complete predicates. The *main* word (or words) in the complete subject is called the **simple subject**.

- The main word (or words) in the complete predicate is called the **simple predicate**. The simple predicate is made up of at least one verb, a word that shows action or being. The main verb may have one or more helping verbs.

Simple Subject	Simple Predicate
The doorbell	rang.
The frisky brown puppy	jumped at the noise.
Bob Smith from New York	was visiting at the time.
He	has been playing with the puppy.
New York	is Ann's home too.
Ann's dog	has grown large.

Try It Out

Speak Up In each sentence what is the simple subject? What is the simple predicate?

1. Marty Shaw heard the bulldozer.
2. The bulldozer moved slowly.
3. Its big scoop had been pushing piles of sand.
4. Marty's eyes sparkled with delight.
5. Piles of sand disappeared.

more ▶

6. The dark sand looked moist.
7. A pool of water was evaporating in the sun.
8. This one child was studying the construction crew.
9. Marty noticed everything on the site.
10. He could hear the bulldozer's horn.
11. The small boy's dream appeared before his eyes.
12. The driver of the huge bulldozer waved to Marty.

Summing Up

- A **simple subject** is the main word (or words) in the complete subject.

- A **simple predicate** is the main word (or words) in the complete predicate. A simple predicate is made up of at least one verb.

On Your Own

Write the simple subject of each sentence, and underline it. Then write the simple predicate of the sentence, and underline it twice.

Example: Three customers had entered the bicycle shop.
          customers *had entered*

13. The owner of the bicycle shop smiled.
14. Customers were filling the shop.
15. A tall blond girl had been studying one bicycle.
16. It was standing in front of the other bicycles.
17. A shiny silver bell hung from its handlebar.
18. Julie's sister was buying some reflectors.
19. Uncle Bert examined a mountain bike.
20. A boy has bought a book on bicycle repair.
21. Todd Mitchell from Dallas asked about a tandem.
22. He wants a bicycle with seats and pedals for two riders.
23. Crowds of curious customers have been staring at the unicycle.
24. This unusual, awkward vehicle is an antique.

more ▶

25–38. This part of an encyclopedia entry has fourteen simple subjects. Write the entry. Underline each simple subject once. Then underline the simple predicate twice.

Example: Races among bicyclists became a popular sport worldwide.
Races among bicyclists *became* a popular sport worldwide.

Bicycling (continued)

People have been riding bicycles for about 150 years. The first official race on bicycles was held in France in 1868. Races in the United States began in 1878. Olympic games have included bicycle races since 1896.

European riders raced on country roads at first. Britain's roads were in poor condition, however. Cyclists were suffering immensely from rocks, broken pavement, traffic, weather, and bumps.

Indoor tracks gained popularity then. Many enthusiastic, loyal fans could watch the race from the comfort of their seats under one roof. Bicyclists could enjoy the safety, convenience, and consistency of indoor tracks. Madison Square Garden in New York became one of the first important sites for bicycle track races.

Interest in road races has spread to nearly every country today. It is quite popular in France, Italy, and Belgium. The world of bicycles flourishes!

Writing Wrap-Up
WRITING • THINKING • LISTENING • SPEAKING

COMPARING / CONTRASTING

Write an Editorial

How does riding a bicycle compare with riding in a car or a bus? Write an editorial about bicycles. Tell how a bicycle ride is better than riding another vehicle. Also tell how it is worse. Read your editorial to a partner. Does your partner agree with you? Then reread your editorial, and have your partner identify each simple subject and simple predicate.

   For Extra Practice see page 75.

4 Imperatives and Interrogatives

Make me a sandwich, please.

Poof! Are you a sandwich yet?

Both sentences in the joke have the same subject. What is it? What words other than *sandwich* would fit this joke?

- You know that an imperative sentence gives a command and an interrogative sentence asks a question. Can you find the subject of these imperative sentences?

   Forget about the crowds in the subway. Please call a taxi for me.

- The subject of an imperative sentence is always *you. You* is usually understood rather than stated.

   (You) Forget about the crowds in the subway.
   (You) Please call a taxi for me.

> **HELP**
> **? Tip**
> Remember that an interrogative sentence ends with a question mark and an imperative sentence ends with a period.

- In an interrogative sentence, the subject is always stated, but it does not begin the sentence. You can usually find the subject of an interrogative sentence by rearranging the question into a statement. Then ask *who* or *what* does the action.

Question	Will the taxi get to the airport on time?
Statement	The taxi will get to the airport on time. (Simple subject is *taxi*.)

Try It Out

Speak Up What is the simple subject of each sentence? Is the sentence imperative or interrogative?

1. Did Paula find her seat?
2. Watch that first step.
3. Can you climb aboard the bus?
4. Should we sit here?

more ▶

5. Sit next to me.
6. Please take any seat as quickly as possible.
7. Will the bus driver stop here at the corner?
8. Do we get off soon?
9. Please hold this shopping bag for a minute.
10. Can you read the next street sign?

Summing Up

- The subject of an imperative sentence is always *you*. *You* is usually understood rather than stated.

- To find the subject of most interrogative sentences, rearrange the question into a statement. Then ask *who* or *what* does the action.

On Your Own

Write the simple subject of each sentence.

Example: Does the car need water? *car*

11. Check the water and the oil.
12. Does the car need oil?
13. Do I change the fluids monthly?
14. Write the mileage on the invoice.
15. Is someone cleaning the rear window?
16. Replace the windshield wiper blades.
17. Will you check the tires?
18. Is the pressure the same in all four tires?
19. Did this tire wear out too fast?
20. Do you hear a rattle in the muffler?
21. Inspect the hoses of the air conditioner.
22. Please give me five gallons of gas.
23. Don't fill the tank.
24. How much do I owe?

more ▶

25–42. This part of a safety manual has eighteen sentences. Write the simple subject of each sentence. Then label the sentence *imperative* or *interrogative*.

Example: Always look both ways.   *(You) imp.*

 # Tips for Pedestrians

- Walk on the sidewalks.
- Is the street clear of cars? Wait for the light anyway.
- Are you going out at night? Wear light colors.
- Is a friend talking to you? Are the sights interesting? Don't forget to watch for cars.
- Always cross the street carefully, please.

 # Tips for Bicyclists

- Do you bicycle on city streets? Ride in the same direction as the car traffic.
- Stay as close as possible to the right edge of the roadway.
- Do you see the traffic signals and stop signs? Obey all traffic signs.
- Are other bicyclists performing stunts or racing? Do not take any safety risks on your bicycle.
- Use a hand signal for all right turns, left turns, and stops.
- Ride in a single file.

Writing Wrap-Up   WRITING • THINKING • LISTENING • SPEAKING

EXPLAINING

Write Safety Tips

What do you do that requires special care? skate? build things? ride the subway? Write safety tips for the activity. Use imperative and interrogative sentences. Then read your tips to a partner, and ask what he or she learned.

5 Compound Subjects

Whom or what is this sentence about? What connecting word joins the subjects?

Doris and Geraldine went to rehearsal with a stone wall of silence between them.

—from *Mama, I Want to Sing*, by Vy Higginsen

You already know that every sentence has a simple subject.

The students in the band play well.

Some sentences have more than one simple subject. When a sentence has two or more simple subjects joined by the connecting word *and* or *or,* the subject is called a **compound subject**.

Why do Joan and Carol practice so often?

My brother or my sister will sing tomorrow.

Parents, relatives, and friends may attend.

Beautiful music and lively dances will be performed.

Try It Out

Speak Up What is the compound subject in each sentence? What connecting word joins the simple subjects?

1. Handbags and wallets can be made from plastic.
2. Plastic, steel, and aluminum are building materials.
3. Is aluminum or steel stronger?
4. Coal, gas, or oil can be used to make plastic.
5. Is plastic or glass better for lenses?
6. Cheap plastic and expensive steel can be used together in the same product.
7. Cars and trolleys are made from plastic.
8. Computers and cameras have some very strong, lightweight, and sturdy plastic parts.

more ▶

9. Plastic tools and machines do not break easily.
10. Plastic pots and pans are easy to clean.
11. Plastic skis, bikes, and snowshoes are expensive.
12. Is plastic or aluminum cheaper?

Summing Up

- A **compound subject** contains two or more simple subjects. They are joined by a connecting word such as *and* or *or*.

On Your Own

Write the compound subject of each sentence. Then write the connecting word that joins the simple subjects.

Example: Large companies and small businesses produce plastic.
　　　　　companies　　businesses　　connecting word: and

13. Glass or plastic may be used to make bottles.
14. A dish or pan of plastic is light.
15. Many containers and tools for the kitchen are plastic.
16. Are plastic counters or wooden tables more practical?
17. Does your watch or your headset have plastic parts?
18. Completely plastic houses and cities do not exist yet.
19. Homemakers, businesspeople, and children use plastic.
20. Don't TVs, VCRs, and phones have plastic parts?
21. Is Kent, Ike, or Bea Davis buying plastic dishes?
22. Cold sandwiches and salad can be wrapped in plastic.
23. Bea and her classmates learned more about plastic.
24. A book or an encyclopedia is a good place to find information.
25. Boys and girls in the class divided into teams.
26. Bea and her team watched a film about plastic.
27. Casey, his team, and the librarian searched in magazines.
28. Books, magazines, or films were used by each team.

more ▶

29–38. This public-service radio announcement has ten sentences. Write the compound subject of each sentence. Then write the connecting word that joins the simple subjects.

Example: When did scientists and technicians develop plastic?
scientists   *technicians*   *connecting word: and*

Planet Earth: Treat with Care

A bottle or a jar may be made out of glass.

A fall or a blow may just smash it, alas.

Good trees and their wood are becoming so rare.

What will carpenters or builders use to make a chair?

Then inventors and scientists made something fantastic.

Many bottles or chairs are now formed out of plastic!

Yes, plastic and other such things saved the day.

The problem and the worry is how to throw them away.

Some plastic and some chemicals can spoil land and air.

So you, I, and others must not toss them everywhere!

PLEASE RECYCLE!

Writing Wrap-Up   WRITING • THINKING • LISTENING • SPEAKING

PERSUADING

Write a Public-Service Announcement

What is an issue that bothers you? traffic? endangered animals? a dirty lake? What do you want people to do about it? Write a public-service announcement about it. Include at least three sentences with compound subjects. Also use rhyme, if you like. Read your announcement to a small group, and discuss the message.

6 Compound Predicates

splashed	dripped	poured	drizzled
sprinkled	flowed	flooded	gushed
ran	walked	dashed	waited

Take turns making sentences about a rainstorm. In each sentence use two of the verbs above, joined by *and* or *or*.

You have learned that a sentence can have more than one simple subject. A sentence can also have more than one simple predicate. When a sentence has two or more simple predicates joined by a connecting word such as *and* or *or*, the predicate is called a **compound predicate**.

Children in the park jumped, played, or ran.

Al and I will walk fast and stop at Jim's house.

People opened umbrellas, hopped on buses, or dashed into stores.

Try It Out

Speak Up What is the compound predicate in each sentence? What connecting word joins the simple predicates?

1. Visitors to the museum buy a ticket and enter.
2. They can tour the galleries or watch slides.
3. A guide was wearing a suit of armor and telling dragon stories.
4. We looked, asked questions, and learned.
5. Children and adults will eat lunch or rest.

more ▶

6. Leon and Angel saw and appreciated the exhibits.
7. Leon walked upstairs and found the animal room.
8. Everyone went to the gift shop and bought post cards.

Summing Up

- A **compound predicate** contains two or more simple predicates. They are joined by a connecting word such as *and* or *or.*

On Your Own

Write the compound predicate of each sentence. Then write the connecting word that joins the simple predicates.

Example: Jim will visit a science museum and see every exhibit.
will visit   see   connecting word: and

9. Our group had joined a tour and followed the guide.
10. People studied coins, saw jewels, or examined ancient tools.
11. Berto and Ana observed, inspected, and tried everything.
12. A guide was holding a snake and describing it.
13. She answered questions and explained reptiles.
14. Everyone touched the snake or held it.
15. Emily saw and used a television camera.
16. A few were making faces or dancing in front of the camera.
17. Some computers played games or taught math.
18. One computer talked in different languages and sang songs.
19. Water in a tank rocked and splashed.
20. Big waves grew fast, crashed heavily, and faded.

more ▶

21–32. This flyer has twelve sentences. Write the compound predicate in each sentence. Then write the connecting word that joins the simple predicates. Remember to check the title.

Example: Parents will visit a classroom or tour the school.

will visit   tour   connecting word: or

Come and see the Oakwood School Science Fair this Friday, March 22.

★ Students at Oakwood study and work hard on their science projects. Some stay late or visit the library. Now parents and grandparents can come, visit, and see the results. Visitors enjoyed and valued last year's fair. Students gave reports, made posters, or built models. Others explained experiments or showed displays. Dozens of booths filled classrooms and covered the gym. Families looked, learned, and felt proud. This year's fair will surprise and impress them even more.

★ Our cafeteria will serve free food and provide soft drinks.

★ Judges will view all displays and award prizes.

Writing Wrap-Up   WRITING • THINKING • LISTENING • SPEAKING

INFORMING

Write a Flyer

Think of a special event in your school or town. Then write a flyer announcing the event. Use at least three sentences with compound predicates. In a small group, take turns reading your flyers aloud. Then work in pairs to find the compound predicates.

Writing Good Sentences

Combining Sentences: Compound Subjects You can make your sentences sound less repetitive by eliminating extra words. Try combining similar sentences that have different subjects. Connect them with a conjunction, such as *and* or *or,* to make a compound subject.

The science teacher is organizing a trivia game for the science fair. Her students are organizing a trivia game for the science fair.

} The science teacher and her students are organizing a trivia game for the science fair.

Apply It

1–4. Revise this answer key to a trivia game. Combine similar sentences, using the conjunction *and* or *or* to join the compound subjects.

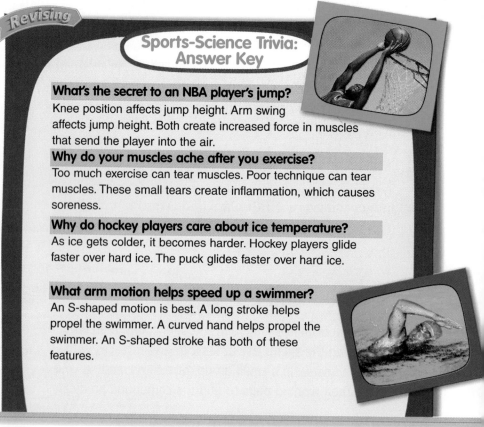

Revising

Sports-Science Trivia: Answer Key

What's the secret to an NBA player's jump?
Knee position affects jump height. Arm swing affects jump height. Both create increased force in muscles that send the player into the air.

Why do your muscles ache after you exercise?
Too much exercise can tear muscles. Poor technique can tear muscles. These small tears create inflammation, which causes soreness.

Why do hockey players care about ice temperature?
As ice gets colder, it becomes harder. Hockey players glide faster over hard ice. The puck glides faster over hard ice.

What arm motion helps speed up a swimmer?
An S-shaped motion is best. A long stroke helps propel the swimmer. A curved hand helps propel the swimmer. An S-shaped stroke has both of these features.

Combining Sentences: Compound Predicates Here's another way to smooth out your writing. Combine two or three simple sentences into one sentence with a compound predicate. Connect the predicates with a conjunction, such as *and, but,* or *or.*

On the Web site, students explore.
On the Web site, students discover.
On the Web site, students learn.

On the Web site, students explore, discover, and learn.

Apply It

5–8. Revise this Web page. Use compound predicates to combine each set of underlined sentences. Choose conjunctions that express your meaning.

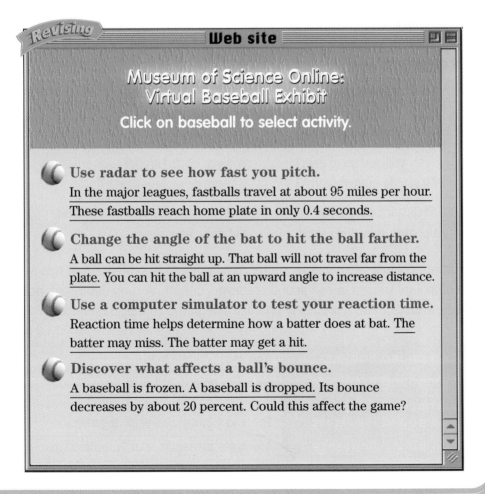

Revising

Web site

**Museum of Science Online:
Virtual Baseball Exhibit**
Click on baseball to select activity.

Use radar to see how fast you pitch.
In the major leagues, fastballs travel at about 95 miles per hour. These fastballs reach home plate in only 0.4 seconds.

Change the angle of the bat to hit the ball farther.
A ball can be hit straight up. That ball will not travel far from the plate. You can hit the ball at an upward angle to increase distance.

Use a computer simulator to test your reaction time.
Reaction time helps determine how a batter does at bat. The batter may miss. The batter may get a hit.

Discover what affects a ball's bounce.
A baseball is frozen. A baseball is dropped. Its bounce decreases by about 20 percent. Could this affect the game?

7 Compound Sentences

Which sentence has a compound predicate? Which sentence is two sentences joined by a connecting word?

The ground was frozen rock hard, and it was impossible to bury the mummy. A heavy snowfall could cover the summit and make recovery impossible.

—from *Discovering the Inca Ice Maiden: My Adventures on Ampato*, by Johan Reinhard

- So far you have studied only simple sentences. A **simple sentence** has a subject and a predicate and expresses a complete thought. Sometimes two simple sentences can be combined into one sentence called a **compound sentence**. The simple sentences are joined by a comma and a connecting word like *and, or,* or *but.*

Simple Sentences	Compound Sentences
Jo is a scientist.	Jo is a scientist, and
She travels often.	she travels often.
Will you go to Peru?	Will you go to Peru, or
Will you do more research?	will you do more research?
Prehistoric people had no alphabet. They drew signs.	Prehistoric people had no alphabet, but they drew signs.

- Do not confuse a compound sentence with a simple sentence that has a compound subject, a compound predicate, or both. A compound sentence has a subject and a predicate on *each* side of the connecting word.

Compound Subject	Ann and I do research.
Compound Predicate	We write reports and read them aloud.
Compound Subject and Compound Predicate	She and I study and work together.
Compound Sentence	Ann types the report, and I proofread it.

Speak Up Which sentences are compound sentences? Which are simple sentences with compound subjects or predicates? What is the connecting word that joins the parts of each compound sentence?

1. Ancient people in Peru made long lines, and they drew huge pictures of animals.
2. Oversized images were drawn, but they are a mystery.
3. Some lines are forty miles long, and some pictures are the size of two football fields.
4. Dirt, rocks, and stones were cleared from a dark layer of earth.
5. A sandy layer showed up clearly, and it still shows today.

Summing Up

- A **compound sentence** is made up of two simple sentences. The simple sentences are joined by a comma and a connecting word like *and, or,* or *but.*

On Your Own

Write each compound sentence, and underline its two simple sentences. If the sentence is not compound, write *not compound.*

Example: The drawings in Peru are old, but they remain clear.
The drawings in Peru are old, but they remain clear.

6. Ancient people drew these pictures but probably never saw any of them whole.
7. The pictures are seen best from the air, and now people take photographs of them from airplanes.
8. Are the markings a calendar, or do they mean something else?
9. Most of the pictures are in Peru, but other countries have some too.
10. Scientists have studied these pictures, and many books have been written about them.

more ▶

11–18. This page for a travel Web site has eight sentences. Write each sentence. If the sentence is compound, underline its two simple sentences. If the sentence is not compound, write *not compound*. Don't forget the title.

Example: Peru's beaches and resorts attract many tourists.
Peru's beaches and resorts attract many tourists.
not compound

Travel-Web

Europe and Asia are wonderful, but have you seen PERU?

★ Peru excites the eye and opens the mind.

★ You will float down the Amazon River, and you will climb the Andes Mountains.

★ The colorful city of Cuzco and the ruins of Machu Picchu are unforgettable.

★ A plane will fly you to Nazca, and you will gasp at the huge figures scratched in the earth. The figures cannot be seen on the ground, but they become clear from the plane. Take pictures, or just enjoy the view.

Our helpful travel agents will answer your questions and make all your reservations for beautiful Peru today.

Writing Wrap-Up

WRITING • THINKING • LISTENING • SPEAKING

EXPRESSING

Write a Travel Brochure

What city, museum, park, or other place have you enjoyed visiting? Write a travel brochure about the place. Use some compound sentences. Find a partner, and read your brochures to each other. Have your partner tell you which detail about your place is most memorable.

54 **Unit 1:** The Sentence

For Extra Practice see page 79.

8 Conjunctions

Will Carl swim? sail? dig in the sand? nap? Take turns making sentences about Carl at the beach. Each sentence must have the word *and, but,* or *or.*

The connecting words *and, or,* and *but* are called **conjunctions**. You can use conjunctions to make subjects, predicates, and sentences compound. The conjunction that you use depends on your purpose.

HELP

 Tip

Remember to use a comma before the conjunction in a compound sentence.

Use *and* to add information.   I can swim and dive.
Use *or* to give choice.   Does he sail or swim?
Use *but* to show contrast.   I swim, but Lee sails.

Try It Out

Speak Up Choose the better conjunction.

1. Shall we sail now (but, or) wait until later?
2. The wind is strong, (or, and) the waves are high.
3. We might tip over (but, or) freeze out there!
4. Sailing is a joy (but, and) not in bad weather.
5. We could water-ski, (but, and) the sea is rough.
6. You (and, but) I should shoot baskets instead.
7. I want to swim, (or, but) I am cold.
8. Do you like sailing (but, or) is hiking better?

Summing Up

- The words *and, or,* and *but* are conjunctions. Use *and* to add information, *or* to give a choice, and *but* to show contrast.

Write *and, or,* or *but* to complete each sentence.

Example: Now the weather is better, _____ we can sail.   *and*

9. John, Sue, _____ I can steer.
10. Help us raise the sail _____ pull up the anchor.
11. I brought the picnic lunch, _____ I forgot the juice.
12. We can sail to that island _____ stop now for a swim.
13. John _____ Sue both want to go there.

14–20. This weather report is missing seven conjunctions. Write the weather report. Supply the best conjunction to fit each sentence.

Example: The sky will clear Monday, _____ the sun will shine.
       The sky will clear Monday, and the sun will shine.

WTHR

Hail Without Fail!

Skies are clear, _____ that will change. We forecast high winds _____ low visibility. Rain and hail will arrive soon _____ will become fog. Don't swim _____ drive. Close windows _____ doors. Stay inside _____ be safe. The hail may be the size of baseballs, _____ this thunderstorm will be severe.

Writing Wrap-Up   WRITING • THINKING • LISTENING • SPEAKING

DESCRIBING

Write a Weather Report
Think of a day when the weather was perfect for you. Write a weather report for your town or city for that day. Use compound sentences and sentences with compound subjects and compound predicates. Take turns with a partner reading your reports to each other. Are your ideas of a perfect day similar or different?

9 Complex Sentences

Which words in the list make sense in the sentence?

before	while	until	when	after
because	unless	if	as	

Does a baby snake cry _____ you take away its rattle?

- You have learned that simple sentences can be joined by the words *and, or,* or *but* to form a compound sentence. Simple sentences can also be joined by other words to form a **complex sentence**.

Simple	I spotted the snake. It slid away.
Compound	I spotted the snake, and it slid away.
Complex	After I spotted the snake, it slid away. I spotted the snake before it slid away.

- The words *and, or,* and *but* are **coordinating conjunctions**. They join sentence parts that are equal in importance, such as the parts of a compound sentence. The parts of a complex sentence, on the other hand, are joined by a **subordinating conjunction**. Subordinating conjunctions subordinate one sentence part to another. That is, they make one part less important than another.

 HELP **Tip**

If the subordinating conjunction begins the sentence, use a comma after the first part of the sentence.

Coordinating Conjunction:	I spotted the snake, and it slid away.
Subordinating Conjunction:	I spotted the snake before it slid away.
Subordinating Conjunction:	After I spotted the snake, it slid away.

Conjunctions in Complex Sentences			
after	because	since	when
although	before	unless	whenever
as	if	until	while

Speak Up Is each sentence simple, compound, or complex? If it is compound, what is the coordinating conjunction? If it is complex, what is the subordinating conjunction?

1. Consider the slow, soundless, isolated life of snakes before you judge them.
2. Snakes have no legs, but they can slither along the ground rapidly.
3. Snakes cannot move forward on glass because the surface is too smooth.
4. The number of snakes is decreasing as people build on open land.
5. Although not all snakes are deadly, humans often fear them.
6. Treatment for certain snake bites must be quick, or the person may die.
7. Snakes are solitary creatures and even hunt alone.
8. If you come upon a snake, do not disturb it.

Summing Up

- A **complex sentence** is made up of two simple sentences joined by a **subordinating conjunction**.

For each sentence, write *simple, compound,* or *complex.* For each compound or complex sentence, write the conjunction.

Example: If you ever see a python, you will recognize it.   *complex   If*

9. Pythons seem scary because they can be so large.
10. While some pythons are only three feet long, others may grow to thirty feet.
11. Most pythons swim and climb with ease in their tropical environment.
12. Although pythons do not bite, they can be very dangerous.
13. Spotted pythons can be deadly, but they can also be quite beautiful.
14. Some of these colorful snakes change from yellow to green as they grow.

more ▶

15. You may admire the python's coloring, or you may admire its size.
16. These snakes may look colorless for a time until they shed their skin.
17. Their skin is tough, and their bodies are powerful.

18–28. Varying sentence structure can make your writing more interesting. Notice the variety in the eleven sentences of this speech. Write each sentence, and label it *simple, compound,* or *complex.* Underline any conjunctions.

Example: Do not panic when you see a snake.

Do not panic __when__ you see a snake.   *complex*

For the Sake of Snakes

Many humans dislike snakes, but they should admire these creatures instead. After humans move into a place, snakes move out. However, snakes are helpful to humankind. They prey on rats, mice, and other rodents. When snakes decrease, these rodents increase.

Although snakes may look scary, they are weak in some ways. They have no ears, and they have no voice. Also, their body temperature depends on the air temperature. They cannot move until warm air heats their bodies.

People would respect snakes if they learned more about them. Unless people become educated about such creatures, some species may be forever wiped out.

Writing Wrap-Up
WRITING • THINKING • LISTENING • SPEAKING

EXPRESSING

Write a Speech
How do you feel about snakes, worms, bugs, or other creepy-crawly things? Do you feel scared? curious? amused? impressed? protective? Write a short speech about such a creature. Be sure to use strong reasons to back up your opinions. Use simple, compound, and complex sentences. Present your speech to a small group. Do others in the group agree with you?

Writing Good Sentences

Combining Sentences: Compound Sentences You can vary the
length of sentences in your writing by combining two short sentences into
a single compound sentence. Join the simple sentences with a comma and
a conjunction, such as *and, but,* or *or.*

Keeping a pet snake requires
special care. You can learn
how to keep it healthy.

Keeping a pet snake requires
special care**, but** you can
learn how to keep it healthy.

Apply It

1–6. Revise these tips for a Web site. Combine each pair of underlined
sentences to make a compound sentence. Choose the conjunction (*and,
but,* or *or*) that gives the meaning you want.

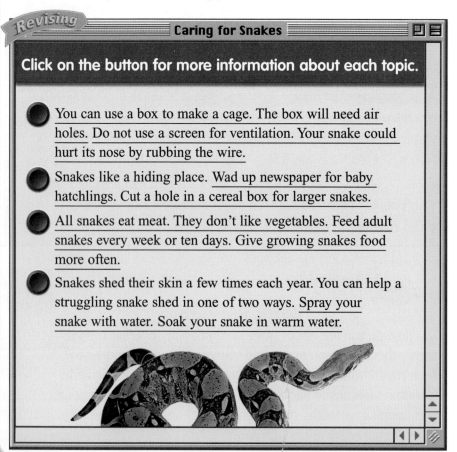

Revising

Caring for Snakes

Click on the button for more information about each topic.

You can use a box to make a cage. The box will need air
holes. Do not use a screen for ventilation. Your snake could
hurt its nose by rubbing the wire.

Snakes like a hiding place. Wad up newspaper for baby
hatchlings. Cut a hole in a cereal box for larger snakes.

All snakes eat meat. They don't like vegetables. Feed adult
snakes every week or ten days. Give growing snakes food
more often.

Snakes shed their skin a few times each year. You can help a
struggling snake shed in one of two ways. Spray your
snake with water. Soak your snake in warm water.

Combining Sentences: Complex Sentences A complex sentence has two main parts that are not equal. One part supports, or is subordinate to, the other part. You can combine two simple sentences to make a complex sentence. Use a subordinating conjunction, such as *since, after,* or *because,* to show the relationship between the parts. If the subordinating conjunction begins the sentence, separate the two parts of the sentence with a comma.

Some snakebites are fatal to humans.	People should be cautious around snakes **because** some snakebites are fatal to humans.
People should be cautious around snakes.	**Because** some snakebites are fatal to humans, people should be cautious around snakes.

Apply It

7–10. Read this part of a research report. Combine the underlined sentences to form complex sentences. Choose a subordinating conjunction *(after, because, since,* or *until)* to make your meaning clear.

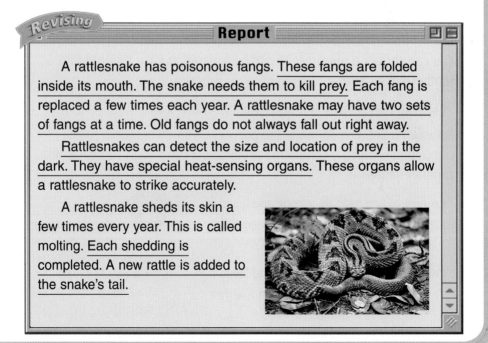

Revising

Report

    A rattlesnake has poisonous fangs. <u>These fangs are folded inside its mouth. The snake needs them to kill prey.</u> Each fang is replaced a few times each year. <u>A rattlesnake may have two sets of fangs at a time. Old fangs do not always fall out right away.</u>

    <u>Rattlesnakes can detect the size and location of prey in the dark. They have special heat-sensing organs.</u> These organs allow a rattlesnake to strike accurately.

    A rattlesnake sheds its skin a few times every year. This is called molting. <u>Each shedding is completed. A new rattle is added to the snake's tail.</u>

10 Fragments and Run-ons

Are these groups of words sentences?
How can you make them into good sentences?

Scott wrote a story. About a broken pencil.
Readers may not be interested it has no point.

- You know that a sentence must have a subject and a predicate. A **sentence fragment** is missing one or both of these sentence parts. A fragment does not express a complete thought. You can correct sentence fragments by supplying the missing sentence parts.

  Incorrect: I want to talk to you. About a summer job.

  Correct: I want to talk to you about a summer job.

- A **run-on sentence** is two or more sentences that are run together with commas or without any punctuation. Often you cannot tell where one thought ends and the next one begins.

  Incorrect: Uncle Frank is a writer Aunt Jill is one too.

  Incorrect: Ann read their book, she loved it, she will read it again, then she will give it to me.

- You can correct a run-on sentence by separating each thought into a sentence of its own.

  Correct: Uncle Frank is a writer. Aunt Jill is one too.

- Sometimes you can combine the parts of a run-on sentence into a compound subject, a compound predicate, a compound sentence, or a complex sentence.

  Correct: Ann read their book and loved it. She will read it again, and then she will give it to me.

  Correct: Ann read their book and loved it. After she reads it again, she will give it to me.

HELP

Tip

Use a variety of sentence types when you correct run-on sentences and fragments in your own writing.

Speak Up How would you correct each fragment?

1. My dad works on a pit crew. At the dirt track.
2. I stand in the pit. And watch races.
3. Waving the checkered flag.
4. Cars stop at the pit. For repairs.
5. As fast as possible.
6. I want to work on automobiles. As a mechanic.

How would you correct the run-on sentences in each item?

7. I have a different job every summer, it is fun.
8. Last year Al and I walked dogs and we fed them and we bathed them also.
9. Once Al walked three big dogs together their leashes became tangled they tripped him.
10. This summer I am working in a pet store the customers laugh at the puppies I laugh at the puppies.
11. By next year I will have had a lot of experience with animals, I want to work for a veterinarian.
12. Veterinarians are usually kind, they are helpful, sometimes they work long hours.

Summing Up

- A **sentence fragment** is a group of words without a subject or a predicate or both.

- A **run-on sentence** is two or more sentences that are run together with commas or without any punctuation.

- Fragments and run-ons can be corrected in several ways.

Rewrite these sentences, correcting the fragments.

Example: The world is full. Of interesting careers.
The world is full of interesting careers.

13. My uncle builds skyscrapers. In large cities.
14. He studied engineering. In college.
15. Cousin Rose is a different kind. Of engineer.
16. She designs machines. With moving parts.
17. A large manufacturing company.
18. My uncle's last building. Was made of granite.
19. Tons of stone were used. For the outside walls of the structure.
20. Workers drove enormous cranes. At the building site.
21. My uncle was so proud. Of the new building.
22. His creative talent and his years of experience.
23. He received an award. At the opening.

Rewrite these run-on sentences correctly.

Example: Yesterday was an exciting day my class visited a college we learned some interesting things.
Yesterday was an exciting day. My class visited a college and learned some interesting things.

24. All of us in the class went together, I sat next to Susan on the bus.
25. A professor escorted us into an auditorium people with different careers talked with us it was fascinating.
26. Susan enjoyed the forest ranger's discussion I was interested in the detective's lecture.
27. One speaker planned the diets for zoo animals she brought a lion cub she let us pet a chimpanzee.
28. The banker received the most attention, Ursula asked him about his salary, the bank is good to its employees.
29. We got a special treat from the last speaker the gourmet chef gave us baked Alaska for dessert it was great!
30. We are planning a similar class trip next month we will tour a hospital a doctor will speak to us.

more ▶

31–38. This part of an e-mail to a pen pal has four fragments and four run-on sentences. Write the e-mail correctly.

Example: I paint funny pictures on sweatshirts I give them to friends, or I sell them. At craft fairs.

I paint funny pictures on sweatshirts. I give them to friends, or I sell them at craft fairs.

Proofreading

e-mail

My brother is interested in landscape design. As a career. My father is a floral designer, my mother is a photographer all three careers are similar. In some ways. Each requires artistic talent the person also should have an eye for color. And balance.

My brother enjoys planting colorful flowers, he likes to clip shrubs into unusual shapes. He has been reading many books about trees and flowers there is so much to learn. About landscaping. He will learn it!

Writing Wrap-Up   WRITING • THINKING • LISTENING • SPEAKING

EXPLAINING

Write a Letter

Write the first part of a letter to your school guidance counselor. Tell about careers you might want to consider. For at least one career, explain the cause for your interest. What sparked that interest? Write five or more sentences. Take turns with a partner, reading your letters to each other. Then work together to make sure that neither letter has fragments or run-on sentences.

Enrichment

Sentences!

Design a Card

Imagine that you work for a greeting card company. You are asked to design a new birthday card. First, fold a piece of construction or typing paper in half. Then think of a birthday message that contains all four sentence types—declarative, interrogative, imperative, and exclamatory. Write the message on your card, punctuating it correctly. Illustrate your card with original drawings or pictures from magazines.

One human year equals seven dog years.

Challenge Make the birthday message a rhyming poem, using all four sentence types.

PYRAMID DESCRIPTION

Write a five-line pyramid description. Center each line and follow this form: Line 1—Write a simple subject. Line 2—Add a simple predicate. Line 3—Add descriptive words to the subject. Line 4—Add *and* and a verb to form a compound predicate. Line 5—Add a subordinating conjunction and another sentence to form a complex sentence.

Wind.
Wind blows.
A raw wind blows.
A raw wind blows and howls.
A raw wind blows and howls before the rain begins.

1 **Kinds of Sentences** *(p. 32)* Copy each sentence, and add the correct punctuation. Then write *declarative, interrogative, imperative,* or *exclamatory* to identify each sentence.

1. Has a circus come to your town
2. A small circus visited us in June
3. What a sight the tent was
4. Our seats were near the center ring
5. Go to the circus next week

2 **Complete Subjects and Predicates** *(p. 35)* Copy each sentence. Draw a line between the complete subject and predicate.

6. My best friend collects posters.
7. Her large collection includes twenty horse posters.
8. A poster is hanging on her door.
9. Posters cover her bedroom walls.
10. Someone from Texas gave her a giant poster of a sunset.

3 **Simple Subjects and Predicates** *(p. 38)* Write the simple subject. Underline it once. Write the simple predicate. Underline it twice.

11. Mo Jones has been reading a travel folder.
12. He has discovered Jamaica.
13. It is called the "Wooded Isle."
14. Mo's cousin rode on a bamboo raft.
15. Many tourists like the shops.

4 **Imperatives and Interrogatives** *(p. 41)* Write the simple subject. Then write *imperative* or *interrogative*.

16. May we see your new dog?
17. Please hold the leash.
18. Are beagles calm and obedient?
19. Think carefully about a puppy.
20. Will you walk your dog daily?

5 **Compound Subjects** *(p. 44)* Write the compound subject and the connecting word that joins the simple subjects.

21. Will Fran or Joe rebuild the bike?
22. Joe's brother and sister sketched a new design.
23. Orange paint or reflectors will glow in the dark.
24. Mirrors and horns will be added.
25. Mike, Pam, and Carlos will paint the bike.

6 **Compound Predicates** *(p. 47)* Write the compound predicate and the connecting word that joins the simple predicates.

26. High winds whistled, howled, or roared.
27. The captain could order the sails down or leave them up.
28. The waves rose and fell.
29. Every sailor trusted and obeyed the captain.
30. The ship outran the clouds and escaped the storm.

7 **Compound Sentences** *(p. 52)* Label each sentence *simple* or *compound*. Copy the compound sentences. Underline the simple sentences that make up each compound sentence.

31. Buses and planes bring tourists to Washington, D.C.
32. Spring is here, and it is breezy.
33. I see cherry trees and smell their sweet blossoms.
34. The Capitol has Saturday tours, but the FBI is closed then.
35. The city is a symbol of the nation's history, legacy, and unity.
36. Washington is named for George Washington, and *D.C.* stands for District of Columbia.

8 **Conjunctions** *(p. 55)* Write the conjunction in parentheses that fits the sentence better.

37. Paris (and, but) London are both capital cities.
38. Is London (and, or) Paris nicer to visit?
39. You can speak English in both cities, (or, but) it is more fun to speak French in Paris.
40. The Seine River runs through Paris, (and, or) the Thames River flows through London.
41. Take a ferry or a plane from France to England, (and, or) ride through an underwater tunnel.

9 **Complex Sentences** *(p. 57)* For each sentence, write *simple,* *compound,* or *complex*. For each compound or complex sentence, write the conjunction.

42. Both radio and television offer many job opportunities.
43. If a TV career interests you, you should first consider your talents.
44. Before you choose a career, list your best school subjects.
45. You should study books, magazines, and newspapers on the topic, but people are also valuable resources.
46. Talk with people in the radio business, and visit a local station.
47. Will you interview a writer, an editor, a technician, or a receptionist?

10 **Fragments and Run-ons** *(p. 62)* Label each group of words *sentence, fragment,* or *run-on.* Rewrite fragments and run-ons correctly.

48. Packed the moving van.
49. Last week was exciting, we moved to a new house on Monday.
50. Dad stacked the boxes carefully.
51. First the mattresses or the biggest, bulkiest furniture.
52. Then the smaller items fit onto the truck everything was organized well.
53. Markers, tape, newspapers, and packing bubbles.
54. Our lawn was full of people, no one minded, cars were everywhere.
55. Our friends will paint and then we'll put down the rug and later everyone will unpack boxes.

Mixed Review 56–65. This part of a short story has six punctuation errors, one incorrect conjunction, two fragments, and a run-on sentence. Write the story correctly.

Proofreading Checklist
Did you check carefully for:
✔ end punctuation?
✔ punctuation with compounds?
✔ choice of conjunctions?
✔ fragments?
✔ run-ons?

Proofreading

A Mind of Its Own

Ezra sat at the computer, and stared at the screen. Was he just exhausted. Were his eyes playing tricks on him! Was his sister playing tricks on him? He rubbed his eyes and then he looked again. That thing was still there

He should do something, or he didn't know what. Ezra's father might help, but he was away. In Canada. Ezra's mother and sister weren't home either he was alone. How ridiculous all this was? There was absolutely nothing to worry about. He shouldn't be frightened of his own computer because it was sending him strange messages. Ezra took a deep breath. And put his hands on the keyboard.

✓ Test Practice

Write the numbers 1–10 on a sheet of paper. For questions 1–5, read each sentence. Choose the underlined part that is the simple subject of the sentence. Write the letter for that answer.

1 Aunt Belle has eaten all of the pickles in the jar!
    A   B   C   D

2 French women wore elaborate hairdos in the 1700s.
     F   G   H   J

3 The large orange cat ignored the curious kitten.
         A   B   C   D

4 Your enthusiasm is a wonderful quality.
      F   G   H   J

5 We discussed the recent events in social studies class.
     A   B   C   D

For questions 6–10, read each sentence. Choose the underlined part that is the simple predicate of the sentence. Write the letter for that answer.

6 A funnel-shaped cloud appeared on the horizon.
                     F   G   H   J

7 Marcus put a mound of shrimp on his plate.
            A   B   C   D

8 The scientific researcher examined the unhealthy livestock.
          F   G   H   J

9 Workers were repainting the old mansion on the hill.
              A   B   C   D

10 The jury filed out of the courtroom.
           F   G   H   J

Write the numbers 11–16 on a sheet of paper. Read the underlined sentences. Then find the answer that best combines them into one sentence. Write the letter for that answer.

11 Terry ordered chips and salsa.
Margo ordered eggs.

 A Terry and Margo ordered chips and salsa and eggs.

 B Terry ordered chips and salsa Margo ordered eggs.

 C Terry ordered chips and salsa or Margo ordered eggs.

 D Terry ordered chips and salsa, but Margo ordered eggs.

12 The father penguin warms the eggs.
The eggs hatch.

 F The father penguin warms the eggs until they hatch.

 G The father penguin warms the eggs, the eggs hatch.

 H The father penguin and the eggs warm and hatch.

 J The eggs hatch until the father penguin warms the eggs.

13 Did you give an oral report?
Did you write an essay?

 A Did you give an oral report, but did you write an essay?

 B Did you give and write an oral report and an essay?

 C Did you give an oral report or an essay?

 D Did you give an oral report, or did you write an essay?

14 Put conditioner on your hair.
Rinse the conditioner out.

 F Put and rinse out the conditioner on your hair.

 G Put conditioner on your hair, or rinse it out.

 H Put conditioner on your hair, and then rinse it out.

 J Put it on your hair and rinse the conditioner out.

15 Flossing is important.
It prevents gum disease.

 A Flossing is important before it prevents gum disease.

 B Flossing is important because it prevents gum disease.

 C Flossing is important unless it prevents gum disease.

 D Flossing is important or it prevents gum disease.

16 The guests can play horseshoes.
They don't like board games.

 F The guests can play horseshoes, and they don't like board games.

 G The guests can play horseshoes, or they don't like board games.

 H The guests can play horseshoes, unless they don't like board games.

 J The guests can play horseshoes if they don't like board games.

Write the numbers 17–20 on a sheet of paper. Read each underlined pair of sentences. Then find the answer that best combines them into one sentence. Write the letter for that answer.

17 Did the dog hide under the porch?
Did the dog jump into the truck?

 A Did the dog hide under the porch or into the truck?

 B Did the dog hide or jump under the porch or into the truck?

 C Did the dog hide under the porch but did the dog jump into the truck?

 D Did the dog hide under the porch or jump into the truck?

18 I put an icepack into the lunchbox.
It would keep my sandwich cool.

 F I put an icepack into the lunchbox so it would keep my sandwich cool.

 G I put an icepack into the lunchbox but it would keep my sandwich cool.

 H I put an icepack into the lunchbox or it would keep my sandwich cool.

 J I put an icepack into the lunchbox unless it would keep my sandwich cool.

19 Bats are nocturnal creatures.
Owls are nocturnal creatures.

 A Bats are nocturnal creatures, but owls are too.

 B Bats and owls are nocturnal creatures.

 C Bats are nocturnal creatures and owls.

 D Bats are nocturnal creatures, and owls are.

20 Fiona wanted to go skating.
The forecast was for rain.

 F Fiona wanted to go skating, but the forecast was for rain.

 G Fiona wanted to go skating, and the forecast was for rain.

 H Fiona wanted to go skating, so the forecast was for rain.

 J Fiona wanted to go skating, the forecast was for rain.

(pages 32–34)

1 Kinds of Sentences

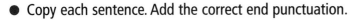

- A **declarative sentence** makes a statement.
- An **interrogative sentence** asks a question.
- An **imperative sentence** gives a command or makes a request.
- An **exclamatory sentence** shows excitement or strong feeling.

Remember

● Copy each sentence. Add the correct end punctuation.

Example: Where do crickets live   *Where do crickets live?*

1. Some crickets live outdoors
2. How do crickets chirp
3. They rub their front wings together
4. Did you hear that cricket
5. How cheerful it sounds
6. Field crickets chirp rapidly in hot weather

▲ Copy each sentence. Add the correct end punctuation, and label each sentence *declarative*, *interrogative*, *imperative*, or *exclamatory*.

Example: Look at those horses   *Look at those horses.   imperative*

7. They are draft horses
8. Watch them pull the heavy plows
9. Why doesn't the farmer use a tractor
10. Tractors and fuel are very expensive
11. Can't tractors pull more weight than horses
12. How beautiful those big horses are

■ Follow the directions in parentheses to write each new sentence.

Example: Was 1816 a strange year? (change to exclamatory)
         What a strange year 1816 was!

13. Was it a year without a summer? (change to declarative)
14. The weather was very unusual. (change to interrogative)
15. Can you find out about it? (change to imperative)
16. What a summer frost the South had! (change to declarative)
17. A blizzard hit New England in June. (change to exclamatory)
18. A volcano caused the odd weather. (change to interrogative)

(pages 35–37)

2 Complete Subjects and Predicates

Remember

- Every sentence has a subject and a predicate. A **subject** tells whom or what a sentence is about. A **predicate** tells what the subject does, is, has, or feels.
- A **complete subject** contains all the words in the subject.
- A **complete predicate** contains all the words in the predicate.

● Copy the underlined words. Then write either *complete subject* or *complete predicate* beside each group.

Example: <u>Some wonderful toys</u> are made at home.
Some wonderful toys   complete subject

1. Kim and her father <u>made a track for marbles</u>.
2. They <u>looked at different materials</u>.
3. <u>Kim's father</u> had some pieces of pipe.
4. Kim and her brother <u>found some paper tubes</u>.
5. The children <u>taped the tubes and pipes together</u>.
6. <u>Everyone</u> took turns holding up one end.

▲ Copy each sentence. Draw a line between the complete subject and the complete predicate.

Example: Many people play dominoes.   *Many people|play dominoes.*

7. The game of dominoes is very old.
8. Early settlers in this country played dominoes.
9. My little brother makes domino snakes.
10. The dominoes stand on their narrow ends.
11. One good push knocks them all down.
12. The pieces are black with white dots.

■ Write a sentence using each word group.

Example: friend writes   *My friend writes stories and poems.*

13. train climbed
14. people need
15. quarterback threw
16. light shines

17. Mike was
18. soup boiled
19. boy watched
20. girl heard

(pages 38–40)

3 Simple Subjects and Predicates

Remember

- A **simple subject** is the main word (or words) in the complete subject.
- A **simple predicate** is the main word (or words) in the complete predicate. A simple predicate is made up of at least one verb.

● Copy the underlined words. Then write either *simple subject* or *simple predicate* to identify each word.

Example: My <u>family</u> travels each summer.   *family   simple subject*

1. Sometimes we <u>sleep</u> in a tent.
2. Last summer we <u>stayed</u> in hotels.
3. One <u>hotel</u> was really special.
4. Every <u>room</u> was a railroad car.
5. All of us <u>were enjoying</u> ourselves.
6. I <u>slept</u> on a train for the first time.

▲ Write the simple subject and simple predicate of each sentence. Underline the simple subject.

Example: Ms. Brown has taught art for three years.
   <u>*Ms. Brown*</u> *has taught*

7. She has been helping my class.
8. The whole class presented a play.
9. The class play needed sound effects.
10. The art teacher had filled a can with paper clips.
11. A boy in the band shook the can.
12. The roar of a train filled the room.

■ Complete the following sentences. Underline each simple subject. Draw two lines under each simple predicate.

Example: Three tired passengers _____.

Three tired passengers boarded the train.

13. The two women _____.
14. The hat on the man _____.
15. The train _____.

16. _____ stopped suddenly.
17. The nervous passengers_____.
18. _____ continued on its way.

(pages 41–43)

4 Imperatives and Interrogatives

- The subject of an imperative sentence is always *you. You* is usually understood rather than stated.
- To find the subject of most interrogative sentences, rearrange the question into a statement. Then ask *who* or *what* does the action.

● Write the simple subject of each sentence.

Example: Look at this new bike. *(You)*

1. Do you have one?
2. Is your bike blue also?
3. Hold this wrench, please.
4. Are the handlebars straight?
5. May I ride your bike?
6. Look at me.
7. Shall we go to the park?
8. Please follow me.

▲ Write the simple subject of each sentence. Then label each sentence *imperative* or *interrogative*.

Example: Does this bus go to First Street? *bus   interrogative*

9. Does the bus stop here?
10. Put on your sneakers.
11. Can we walk that far?
12. Take the map along.
13. Wait for the green light.
14. Does the sign say *First Street*?
15. Look for Alan's house.
16. Check both sides of the street.

■ Rewrite each sentence. Make your sentence imperative or interrogative, as shown in parentheses. Then write the simple subject of the new sentence.

Example: I would like you to hold my camera. (imperative)
    Hold my camera, please. (You)

17. I wonder why we are stopping here. (interrogative)
18. Perhaps something is blocking traffic. (interrogative)
19. Someone will have to look out the window. (imperative)
20. A car broke down at the traffic light. (interrogative)
21. Everything has stopped. (interrogative)
22. You should ask the bus driver for more information. (imperative)
23. The bus will be moving soon. (interrogative)
24. You should sit down in your seat. (imperative)

(pages 44–46)

5 Compound Subjects

- A **compound subject** contains two or more simple subjects. They are joined by a connecting word such as *and* or *or*.

● Give each sentence a compound subject by adding a simple subject. Use each word from the box only once. Write the new sentence.

Example: Linda and _____ went to the park.
 Linda and Pat went to the park.

friends	Pat	uniforms
pitcher	girls	glove

1. Maria and her _____ met near the baseball field.
2. Teenage boys and _____ were warming up.
3. The helmets and _____ display the team name.
4. How do the mask and _____ protect the catcher?
5. The batter and the _____ faced each other.

▲ Write the compound subject. Then write the connecting word.

Example: Arts and crafts are often found in museums.
 arts crafts connecting word: and

6. Hopis and Navajos make silver jewelry.
7. Have pottery or sculptures been found in Mexico?
8. Ornaments and fine metal objects come from Peru.
9. Plates and utensils are carefully made.
10. Colors, shapes, and figures decorate the objects.

■ Write compound subjects to complete the sentences below. Use connecting words to join the simple subjects.

Example: _____ make good pets for children.
 Gentle dogs or cats make good pets for children.

11. _____ live in a fishbowl.
12. _____ are very unusual pets.
13. Must _____ be kept in cages?
14. _____ sleep all day.
15. _____ require space to run.
16. _____ have huge appetites.

(pages 47–49)

⑥ Compound Predicates

Remember

- A **compound predicate** contains two or more simple predicates. They are joined by a connecting word such as *and* or *or*.

● Copy the sentences. Underline the compound predicates.

Example: The Clock Museum shows clocks and sells them.
The Clock Museum <u>shows</u> clocks and <u>sells</u> them.

1. Leon walked inside and looked around.
2. Many clocks stood on the floor or hung on the walls.
3. They ticked, hummed, or turned.
4. A tall clock told time and rang bells.
5. Water clocks and sand clocks splashed or dripped.
6. Leon liked the sand clock best and studied it carefully.

▲ Write the compound predicate of each sentence.
Then write the connecting word that joins the simple predicates.

Example: Steam engines can move ships or pull trains.
can move pull connecting word: or

7. A fire boils water and creates steam.
8. Steam turns wheels or heats buildings.
9. We visited a museum and saw a steam engine.
10. People will see, hear, and smell the boilers.
11. My mother and father heard a steam whistle and smiled.
12. Some people covered their ears or left the room.

■ Complete each sentence, adding a compound predicate. Write the completed sentences.

Example: The ticket taker ＿＿＿.
The ticket taker greeted us and tore our tickets.

13. A large wheel ＿＿＿.
14. The whole crowd ＿＿＿.
15. The strange machine ＿＿＿.
16. Different voices ＿＿＿.

17. Ana and a friend ＿＿＿.
18. Several small boats ＿＿＿.
19. Children and a teacher ＿＿＿.
20. All of the children ＿＿＿.

(pages 52–54)

7 Compound Sentences

- A **compound sentence** is made up of two simple sentences. The simple sentences are joined by a comma and a connecting word such as *and, or,* or *but.*

● Write *compound* or *not compound* to describe each sentence.

Example: You know the English alphabet, but do you know any others?
compound

1. Many different alphabets exist today.
2. Our alphabet has twenty-six letters.
3. Some of the letters are consonants, and some are vowels.
4. Some alphabets are read from right to left.
5. We read from left to right, and we write that way too.
6. Alphabets are interesting, and I want to learn more about them.

▲ Write *compound* or *simple* to describe each sentence. Remember that a simple sentence may have a compound subject or a compound predicate.

Example: The Chinese language is different from the Japanese language, but the writing is similar. *compound*

7. Chinese and Japanese are written from left to right.
8. People speak different forms of Japanese, but most people understand each other.
9. The Chinese language has nine forms, but each one is different.
10. The earliest, simplest Chinese writing dates from about 1500 B.C.
11. Is it harder to read Chinese, or is it harder to read English?

■ Write compound sentences, using the subjects and predicates given below. Use commas correctly, and use *and, or,* and *but* at least once.

Example: subjects: Kate, Ben   predicates: prints, types
Kate prints her stories, but Ben types them later.

12. subjects: my sister, she   predicates: is, teaches
13. subjects: Jim, he   predicates: writes, sings
14. subjects: mother, I   predicates: builds, paint
15. subjects: Jo, we   predicates: plays, watch

(pages 55–56)

8 Conjunctions

Remember

- The words *and, or,* and *but* are conjunctions. Use *and* to add information, *or* to give a choice, and *but* to show contrast.

● Write the conjunction in each sentence.

Example: My sister Javis and I went to summer camp. *and*

1. We met other campers and made friends quickly.
2. The camp was on a lake, and the setting was beautiful.
3. Mountains and forests surrounded the lake.
4. Few people lived or worked in the area.
5. The lake was ice cold, but we swam every day.
6. We hiked and rode horses on trails through the woods.

▲ Write *and, or,* or *but* to complete each sentence.

Example: My brother Joe _____ I have a sailboat. *and*

7. One person can sail the boat, _____ two can take turns.
8. Today Joe _____ I sail together.
9. We can sail to an island _____ stay near the coast.
10. I like the island, _____ Joe likes the coast better.
11. We put the sails up _____ sail toward the island.
12. At first a strong wind blows, _____ then it dies down.

■ Write a conjunction to complete each sentence. Then write *compound subject, compound predicate,* or *compound sentence.*

Example: High diving takes courage _____ demands great skill.
        and   compound predicate

13. A diver leaps off a surface _____ plunges into deep water.
14. A brave person can jump, _____ a skillful diver must control every movement.
15. Judges study the dive _____ give points to the diver.
16. All positions _____ motions must be done the right way.
17. Are the diver's feet _____ hands pointed?
18. Is an arm _____ a leg held at the wrong angle?

(pages 57–59)

⑨ Complex Sentences

Remember

- A **complex sentence** is made up of two simple sentences joined by a **subordinating conjunction**.

● Write the conjunction in each complex sentence.

Example: Animals need care when they travel. *when*

1. You may take a pet on a trip if you plan ahead.
2. Before you leave, a vet should check the animal.
3. Give the animal water whenever you make a stop.
4. Do not fly with a pet until you check with the airline.

▲ Write *simple, compound,* or *complex* for each sentence. Then write the coordinating or subordinating conjunction.

Example: Unless you are dreaming, you will not see a unicorn.
       complex   Unless

5. Although there are many stories about the unicorn, it is only an imaginary animal.
6. Long-ago explorers had no binoculars or cameras.
7. They used their imagination when they saw a distant animal.
8. Stories spread about the unicorn, and we can still read them today.

■ Add a subordinating conjunction from the box to complete each sentence correctly. Write the sentence.

Example: Penguins could not survive _____ their bodies were special.
       unless
       Penguins could not survive unless their bodies were special.

| when | because | unless | although | whenever |

9. _____ they have a layer of fat, penguins can live in the cold.
10. _____ penguins have wings, they cannot fly.
11. They use their short wings as flippers _____ they swim.
12. Males sit on the eggs _____ females search for food.

(pages 62–65)

10 Fragments and Run-ons

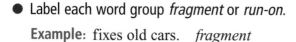
Remember

- A **sentence fragment** is a group of words without a subject or a predicate or both.
- A **run-on sentence** is two or more sentences that are run together with commas or without any punctuation.
- Fragments and run-ons can be corrected in several ways.

● Label each word group *fragment* or *run-on*.

Example: fixes old cars.   *fragment*

1. With his hammer.
2. That car is old, it is pretty.
3. Tom wants a car my sister just got one.
4. Rides like a new one.
5. One day the morning bus.

▲ Label each group of words as a *fragment*, a *run-on*, or a *sentence*.

Example: Is my friend and neighbor.   *fragment*

6. She has roller skates I have skates too.
7. We skate at the park, it has a rink the rink is free.
8. We go for an hour after school on Fridays.
9. Sometimes my older brother.
10. He is a good skater we skate together.

■ Rewrite each run-on correctly. Rewrite each fragment to make it a complete sentence.

Example: Sal was hungry he wanted a snack he loved baked apples.
       Sal was hungry and wanted a snack. He loved baked apples.

11. Luckily, a large bag of apples.
12. Tony offered his help he turned on the oven.
13. Sal got a pan he put the apples in it.
14. The smell of apples and cinnamon.
15. Would take at least an hour.
16. The apples were perfect, Sal and Tony shared them.

Nouns

Pointing his colorful biplane east, he skirted the mountains and the hot-air balloons.

1 Recognizing Nouns

What real words would you substitute for the underlined nonsense words?

Xithyd, the great <u>uckcht</u>, was filled with <u>phruvl</u>. Soon everyone in <u>Svwpblx</u> would know that he had invented a <u>btqokkz</u>!

- A **noun** is a word that names a person, a place, a thing, or an idea. When a noun names an idea, it names something that cannot be touched, such as *time, friendship, anger,* or *summer.*

    person   idea   thing   place
Gina read about the <u>history</u> of farming <u>tools</u> in the <u>United States.</u>

- A noun can be made up of more than one word.

Person	baby sitter, Jan Smith, Dr. Jones, President Adams
Place	dining room, Hill School, Pacific Ocean, New Mexico
Thing	fire engine, credit card, look-alike, frying pan

Try It Out

Speak Up Does each noun name a person, a place, a thing, or an idea?

1. microscope
2. excitement
3. fire station
4. United States
5. scientist
6. Thomas Edison
7. fun
8. Indian Ocean
9. radio
10. loyalty
11. planet
12. Houston
13. Willie Mays
14. memory
15. hide-and-seek
16. weeping willow
17. neighbor
18. decision
19. Mount Vernon
20. baby

more ▶

Which words are nouns in each sentence?

21. Inventors have special talents.
22. A clever invention can save time for a person.
23. Many years ago people hunted for food.
24. Then a hunter invented the bow and the arrow.
25. Plants from farms soon became a source for food too.
26. Families moved to villages and traded goods.
27. Now a store sells a meal in a can or a box.
28. Inventors are always creating new machines or engines.
29. Eli Whitney helped farmers in the United States.
30. His machine removed seeds from cotton.
31. The curiosity of the inventor has improved life.

Summing Up

- A **noun** names a person, a place, a thing, or an idea.

On Your Own

Write each noun in these sentences.

Example: Rubber trees grow in South America.
Rubber trees   South America

32. Drops of rubber ooze from the bark like tears.
33. People long ago made waterproof shoes from the juice.
34. Modern scientists developed new products.
35. A chemist in England made an eraser from the liquid.
36. Factories in Europe made hoses and raincoats.
37. The first items made of rubber had little strength.
38. Charles Goodyear in the United States solved this big problem.
39. The appearance of the automobile created a new need.
40. John Dunlop developed a tire filled with air for cars.
41. These inventions changed the world.

more ▶

42–66. This press release has twenty-five nouns. Write each noun.

Example: People will love this new product. *People* *product*

Zingy Results with Zilch!

To: Newspapers in the United States

Wack-O Manufacturing Company has an important announcement! Our firm is introducing a brilliant new product. Aaron A. Aardvark, our most imaginative developer, created its name—Zilch. This easy, modern device makes no sound and does no work. Zilch just attracts attention. Place Zilch in the yard or the window. Our unusual invention will bring new friends together. Passers-by will stop in amazement. Owners will become instant celebrities of their neighborhoods!

Writing Wrap-Up

WRITING • THINKING • LISTENING • SPEAKING

COMPARING / CONTRASTING

Write a Press Release

Think of a product you use often, such as a computer, an alarm clock, or a pen. Write a press release to announce this amazing new product to the world. How is it like other products on the market? How is it better than the competition? In a small group, take turns reading your press releases. Ask members to question you about anything in your release that is not clear. Then ask them to name the nouns.

For Extra Practice see page 112.

2 Common and Proper Nouns

Which words are nouns? Why are they capitalized?

The National Aeronautics and Space Administration called Dr. Franklin Ramón Chang-Díaz at the Charles Stark Draper Laboratory in Cambridge, Massachusetts, one day in May 1980.

—from *Standing Tall*, by Argentina Palacios

- Some nouns name a particular person, place, thing, or idea. These are called **proper nouns**. A proper noun begins with a capital letter. Nouns that do not name a particular person, place, thing, or idea are called **common nouns**.

Common:	city	girl	ocean	state	month
Proper:	Boston	Amy	Indian Ocean	New York	July

- If a proper noun is made up of more than one word, capitalize only the important words.

    New Jersey   Gulf of Mexico   Statue of Liberty

- When you use the word for a person in your family as a name, capitalize it. Otherwise, do not capitalize the name.

    Robert Goddard, the father of rocket science, is a hero to Dad.
    My mom took photos of the space shuttle launch.

Try It Out

Speak Up What are the nouns in these sentences? Is each noun a common noun or a proper noun?

1. Edward White was the first American to walk in space.
2. The astronaut practiced daily in an airtight room for several hours.
3. Astronaut White walked in space above California.
4. Could White see the Gulf of Santa Catalina?
5. The astronaut did not want to return to the spacecraft immediately.

more ▶

6. His pilot convinced White to come back.
7. The spacecraft orbited Earth before the flight ended.
8. A crew and a ship waited patiently in the Atlantic Ocean.
9. Aunt Mattie, Mom, and my grandfather watched his trip on television.

How would you capitalize these proper nouns?

10. cape of good hope
11. nile river
12. baltimore
13. karen gerber
14. new hampshire
15. fourth of july

Summing Up

- A **common noun** names any person, place, thing, or idea.

- A **proper noun** names a particular person, place, thing, or idea.

- A proper noun always begins with a capital letter.

On Your Own

Write the proper noun in each pair correctly.

Example: egypt—country   *Egypt*

16. thursday—day
17. ohio river—river
18. island—isle of wight
19. governor—pete wilson
20. world trade center—building
21. teacher—ms. goldrich
22. athlete—jackie robinson
23. may—month
24. mars—planet
25. memorial day—holiday
26. state—wyoming
27. white house—building
28. continent—africa
29. emily dickinson—poet
30. bay of fundy—bay
31. mountain—mount fuji

more ▶

32–42. This movie review has eleven capitalization errors in nouns. Write the review correctly.

Example: Captain Wan is played by ethel chou.
Captain Wan is played by Ethel Chou.

Proofreading

Review in the Dark

Space Serenade in Perfect Tune

The new Movie *Space Serenade* opened at the Colony Cinema last night. The action takes place on a spacecraft headed for mars. Inside are six crew members and two robots named Paulie and sally. At first, things seem normal on the ship, which looks as big as the Pacific ocean. Then someone talks about missing the fourth of July in New england.

Suddenly Paulie bursts into a Song about home, and the crew joins in. What began as a typical space movie has turned into a Musical! The singing and dancing heat up as the ship rocks its way through Space. Back here on earth, people in hollywood must be dancing too, for this movie is a winner. Dance your way to the Colony to see it!

Writing Wrap-Up WRITING • THINKING • LISTENING • SPEAKING

EVALUATING

Write a Review

What movie, TV show, or other performance have you seen lately? Did you enjoy it? Why or why not? Write a review. Be sure to state the reasons behind your personal opinions. Include proper nouns. Then read your review to a partner. Does he or she find it convincing? Work with your partner to check that you capitalized all the proper nouns.

For Extra Practice see page 113.

Writing with Nouns

Elaborating with Appositives Remember that an appositive is a word or group of words that comes right after the noun it explains. Appositives are usually set off from the rest of the sentence by commas.

Try adding an appositive to a sentence when you want to elaborate or make your meaning clear. An appositive can help your reader to picture, hear, taste, smell, and feel what happened!

1. I bought a Red Ruby at the park.
2. I bought a Red Ruby, a sweet and crunchy candied apple, at the park.

Apply It

1–5. Revise this advertisement. Add at least five appositives that elaborate or tell more about the nouns.

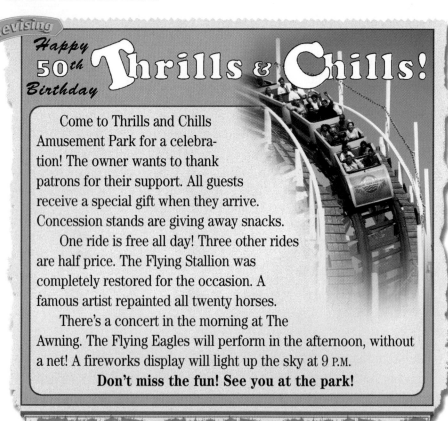

Revising

Happy 50th Birthday

Thrills & Chills!

Come to Thrills and Chills Amusement Park for a celebration! The owner wants to thank patrons for their support. All guests receive a special gift when they arrive. Concession stands are giving away snacks.

One ride is free all day! Three other rides are half price. The Flying Stallion was completely restored for the occasion. A famous artist repainted all twenty horses.

There's a concert in the morning at The Awning. The Flying Eagles will perform in the afternoon, without a net! A fireworks display will light up the sky at 9 P.M.

Don't miss the fun! See you at the park!

Combining Sentences with Appositives Do you sometimes use a noun in one sentence and explain it in another? Consider combining the sentences, using an appositive.

Karl and Francie wrote cartoons for the newspaper.
Karl and Francie are students at my school.

Karl and Francie, students at my school, wrote cartoons for the newspaper

Apply It

6–10. Combine each set of underlined sentences in this cartoon by using appositives.

3 Singular and Plural Nouns

One-Minute Warm-Up

Retell the event, making the underlined nouns plural. Then ask someone else to tell what happened next, using one or more plural nouns.

The <u>chef</u> made <u>turkey</u> and <u>potato</u> for the <u>man</u> and <u>woman</u> at the garden <u>party</u>. Then some <u>fox</u> ran out of the <u>bush</u> and . . .

- A noun that names one person, place, thing, or idea is a **singular noun**. A noun that names more than one person, place, thing, or idea is a **plural noun**. In most cases, you can change a singular noun to plural by adding *-s*.

HELP ? Tip

Use your dictionary to find the plural spellings of nouns.

| **Singular:** | truck | plant | letter | noise | Jane |
| **Plural:** | trucks | plants | letters | noises | Janes |

Many nouns do not become plural according to the regular rules. Study the chart below and on page 93.

Forming Plurals		
Singular Ending	**Plural Form**	**Example**
s *ss* *ch* *sh* *x* *z*	Add *-es.*	Thomas—Thomases boss—bosses porch—porches bush—bushes fox—foxes waltz—waltzes
consonant + *o*	Add *-es.* (Some add only *-s.*)	potato—potatoes veto—vetoes echo—echoes (Eskimo—Eskimos) (solo—solos) (piano—pianos) (cello—cellos)

Forming Plurals		
Singular Ending	**Plural Form**	**Example**
vowel + *o*	Add *-s.*	radio—radios studio—studios
consonant + *y*	Change *y* to *i* and add *es.*	baby—babies party—parties country—countries
vowel + *y*	Add *-s.*	day—days turkey—turkeys
f or *fe*	Sometimes change *f* to *v* and add *-s* or *-es.*	life—lives half—halves wolf—wolves roof—roofs chef—chefs

- Some nouns have the same spelling in the singular and the plural.

    moose—moose   salmon—salmon   deer—deer

- Other nouns are spelled differently in the plural.

    child—children   woman—women   tooth—teeth
    man—men   goose—geese   mouse—mice

Try It Out

Speak Up For each pair of words in parentheses, choose the correct plural form.

1. The new (puppies, puppys) have sharp (tooths, teeth).
2. The gardener weeded the berry (patchs, patches) and planted (tomatos, tomatoes).

more ▶

Try It Out continued

3. Loggers use (axes, axs) to cut (treeses, trees).
4. The (moose, mooses) heard the (echos, echoes) of (wolves, wolfs).
5. There are four (Besss, Besses) in the (classs, classes).

What is the plural form of each noun?

6. apple
7. policy
8. hero
9. watch
10. wife

11. dress
12. studio
13. donkey
14. Ross
15. waltz

Summing Up

- Add *-s* or *-es* to most singular nouns to form the plural. Use the spelling of the singular noun to decide how to form the plural.

- Some nouns have the same singular and plural forms.

- Some nouns are spelled differently in the plural.

On Your Own

Write *singular, plural,* or *singular and plural* to describe each noun.

Example: goose   *singular*

16. piano
17. moose
18. women
19. dresses

20. Norrises
21. deer
22. lilies
23. alleys

On Your Own continued

Write the plural form of each noun. Use your dictionary if you need it.

Example: knife *knives*

24. brush
25. opera
26. couch
27. country
28. monkey

29. salmon
30. cross
31. brain
32. mouse
33. nursery

34. Diane
35. radio
36. calf
37. stereo
38. mix

39. trolley
40. tomato
41. belief
42. hero
43. child

44–55. This poem has twelve incorrect noun plurals. Write the poem correctly.

Example: The lilys bloomed in the fields.
            The lilies bloomed in the fields.

Delicious Days

We strolled through the gardens for houres,

Admiring the plantes and the flowers.

The leafs near the berrys

Were the color of cherrys,

And the rose bushs grew tall as toweres.

We spotted some mouses and some sheep,

And some childrens on a hill rather steep.

They were digging up potatos,

Munching bunches of tomatos.

Then they lay down on boxs to sleep.

WRITING • THINKING • LISTENING • SPEAKING

CREATING

Write a Poem

Write a poem. It could be about people or places, animals or food, your thoughts and feelings, or another topic. Use at least five plural nouns. You may or may not want to use rhyme. Then take turns reading your poems aloud in a small group. Read your poem again, and ask group members to list the plural nouns they hear.

4 Possessive Nouns

One-Minute Warm-Up

Which noun shows ownership in this sentence? How can you tell?

Yani's father has helped her to see pictures in her mind by encouraging her to make up stories.

—from *A Young Painter: The Life and Paintings of Wang Yani, China's Extraordinary Young Artist,* by Zheng Zhensun and Alice Low

You can change the form of a noun to show ownership, or possession. A **possessive noun** names who or what owns or has something.

Pat's coat = the coat owned by Pat

the babies' blocks = the blocks belonging to the babies

The chart below shows how to change nouns into their possessive forms.

Rules for Forming Possessive Nouns	
Singular nouns Add an apostrophe and *-s ('s)*	a woman's gloves Mr. Ross's hat the teacher's question
Plural nouns that end in *s* Add only an apostrophe (').	the students' papers the Williamses' house the girls' pens
Plural nouns that do not end in *s* Add an apostrophe and *-s ('s)*	the men's umbrellas the geese's nest the children's uniforms

Try It Out

Speak Up What is the possessive form of each noun in parentheses? Is the possessive noun singular or plural?

1. _____ toys (children)
2. the _____ apartment (Ramoses)
3. the _____ webbed feet (goose)
4. a _____ meeting (parents)

more ▶

5. _____ office (Dr. Lewis)
6. the _____ photocopies (library)
7. the _____ manes (horses)
8. the _____ theme (story)
9. _____ coat (Mrs. Jones)
10. _____ tails (bunnies)

How would you complete each sentence? Use the possessive form of the noun in parentheses. Does the possessive end in *'s* or *s'* ?

11. During her childhood, _____ dream was to become a doctor. (Elizabeth Blackwell)
12. _____ applications to medical schools were not welcomed. (Women)
13. Her hard work and persistence gained her _____ respect. (professors)
14. She helped alter this _____ view of women doctors. (country)

Summing Up

- To form the possessive of a singular noun, add -*'s*.

- To form the possessive of a plural noun that ends in *s*, add only an apostrophe (').

- To form the possessive of a plural noun that does not end in *s*, add -*'s*.

Rewrite each group of words, using a possessive noun.

Example: the shirts of the bowlers   *the bowlers' shirts*

15. the dish belonging to the cat
16. the croaking of the frogs
17. the cages for the mice
18. the wings of the birds
19. the club for women

20. the tools of the plumber
21. the pencil belonging to Mr. Lane
22. the desk that Nicholas has
23. the health of the Harrises
24. the speeches by the boss

more ▶

25–34. This entry from an online encyclopedia has ten groups of underlined words. Write the entry, changing each group of underlined words to include a possessive noun.

Example: Dr. Susan Steward ignored <u>the expectations of society</u> for women.
Dr. Susan Steward ignored society's expectations for women.

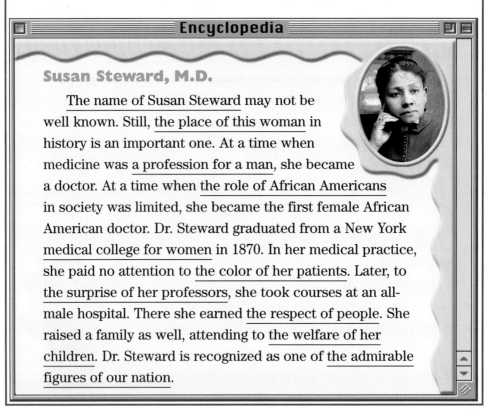

Encyclopedia

Susan Steward, M.D.

<u>The name of Susan Steward</u> may not be well known. Still, <u>the place of this woman</u> in history is an important one. At a time when medicine was <u>a profession for a man</u>, she became a doctor. At a time when <u>the role of African Americans</u> in society was limited, she became the first female African American doctor. Dr. Steward graduated from <u>a New York medical college for women</u> in 1870. In her medical practice, she paid no attention to <u>the color of her patients</u>. Later, to <u>the surprise of her professors</u>, she took courses at an all-male hospital. There she earned <u>the respect of people</u>. She raised a family as well, attending to <u>the welfare of her children</u>. Dr. Steward is recognized as one of the admirable <u>figures of our nation</u>.

Writing Wrap-Up

WRITING • THINKING • LISTENING • SPEAKING

SUMMARIZING

Write an Encyclopedia Article
Write a brief article telling about someone you admire. Choose either a person in your life or a famous person. Describe what the person has done that is admirable. Include factual information as well as qualities. Use possessive nouns. Then find a partner, and read your articles to each other. You may want to compile a class *Encyclopedia of Admirable People.*

                     For Extra Practice see page 115.

Writing with Possessive Nouns

Combining Sentences: Possessive Nouns A possessive noun can take the place of a phrase or a sentence. If you use possessive nouns to combine sentences, your writing will sound less repetitive.

Elizabeth Blackwell received a medical degree.

This medical degree made her the first woman doctor in the United States.

Elizabeth Blackwell's medical degree made her the first woman doctor in the United States.

> Remember, to make a plural noun possessive, write the apostrophe after the final -s.

Apply It

1–5. Revise these questions for a mock interview with Dr. Blackwell. Use possessive nouns to combine each pair of underlined sentences.

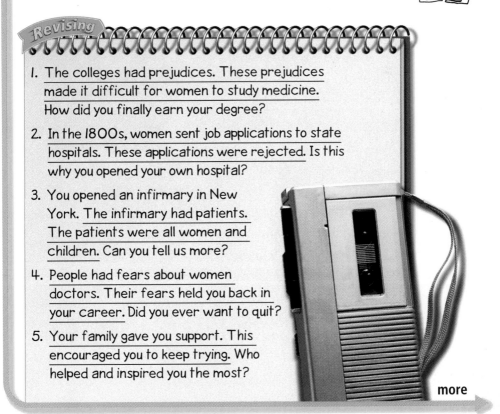

Revising

1. The colleges had prejudices. These prejudices made it difficult for women to study medicine. How did you finally earn your degree?

2. In the 1800s, women sent job applications to state hospitals. These applications were rejected. Is this why you opened your own hospital?

3. You opened an infirmary in New York. The infirmary had patients. The patients were all women and children. Can you tell us more?

4. People had fears about women doctors. Their fears held you back in your career. Did you ever want to quit?

5. Your family gave you support. This encouraged you to keep trying. Who helped and inspired you the most?

more

Combining Sentences: Appositives with Possessive Nouns

You can make your writing more concise even when you have a lot to say! Instead of writing two sentences, try using a possessive noun to turn one of the sentences into an appositive.

Elizabeth Blackwell graduated at the top of her class.

She was the first female student at Geneva Medical College.

Elizabeth Blackwell, Geneva Medical College's first female student, graduated at the top of her class.

Apply It

6–10. Revise this introduction for the mock interview. Use appositives with possessive nouns to combine each pair of underlined sentences.

Revising

Introducing Elizabeth Blackwell

Prejudice kept women out of medical school in the 1800s. One woman broke through this barrier. Elizabeth Blackwell earned her medical degree in 1849. She was the first woman physician of the country.

State hospitals refused to hire Blackwell, so she opened her own. Her patients were cared for by an entirely female staff. Her patients were the poor of New York City. It was the first hospital of its kind. Emily Blackwell helped run the hospital. Emily was the sister of Elizabeth. They worked well together. They also founded a school in New York. It was a medical college for women.

It's time to meet Elizabeth Blackwell and hear more about her life. She is the guest for this evening. Let's give this pioneer a round of applause!

5 Plural and Possessive Nouns

—from *The Wright Brothers,* by Russell Freedman

Which nouns in this sentence are plural? Which is possessive? both?

For weeks he had heard rumors about the Wright brothers' flying machine, and being a curious fellow, he wanted to investigate the miracle for himself.

You have learned how to form plural nouns and possessive nouns. Do not confuse possessive nouns with ordinary plural nouns. Most plural nouns end in *s (two pilots).* If a noun is possessive, you will find an apostrophe (') before or after the *s (one pilot's uniform, four pilots' opinions).*

Forming Plural and Possessive Nouns		
Kind of Noun	**Ending**	**Example**
Plural (more than one) Most singular nouns	Add -*s* or -*es.*	two boys the Lewises
Singular Possessive (belongs to one) Most singular nouns	Add -*'s.*	a boy's shoe Kim Lewis's key Jess's locker
Plural Possessive (belongs to more than one) Plural nouns ending with *s*	Add '.	two boys' shoes the Lewises' key
Plural Possessive (belongs to more than one) Plural nouns not ending with *s*	Add -*'s.*	the mice's teeth the women's ideas the men's team

Speak Up Is the underlined word plural, singular possessive, or plural possessive?

1. six <u>wolves</u>
2. <u>wolf's</u> tail
3. three <u>boys</u>
4. two <u>boys'</u> shoes
5. one <u>boy's</u> socks
6. <u>Gus's</u> pencil
7. three <u>Guses</u>
8. the <u>Joneses'</u> dog
9. the <u>child's</u> shirts
10. the <u>children's</u> sneakers

Summing Up

- Do not confuse possessive nouns with plural nouns.
- Most plural nouns end in *s*.
- Possessive nouns have an apostrophe before or after the *s*.

Write the noun in parentheses in its correct plural, singular possessive, or plural possessive form.

Example: Twenty hot-air _____ will race. (balloon)   *balloons*

11. Balloon _____ have become popular. (race)
12. Several _____ are supporting this race. (airport)
13. An area is reserved for _____. (spectator)
14. One _____ son is in the race. (spectator)
15. The occasion is a _____ delight. (photographer)
16. Will all the _____ please climb aboard? (passenger)
17. Many _____ cameras click rapidly. (photographer)
18. All the _____ friends wave goodbye to them. (passenger)
19. Soon they cannot hear their _____ voices. (friend)
20. The balloons soar over one _____ house. (passenger)

more ▶

21–28. These tongue twisters have eight incorrect plural or possessive nouns. Write the tongue twisters correctly.

Example: The chiefs children chose chunky cheese for their chili.
The chief's children chose chunky cheese for their chili.

Proofreading

The World's Best Tongue Twisters

- Chuck's child chews Stu's shoe's.
- Patty potted Peter Pipers pickled peppers.
- Two geese's gosling's grew green.
- The seven sisters sixth sheep shall sleep soon.
- Cyril seized the five thieves skis.
- Betty's brother better butter Brads bread better.
- Bobby bought big batch's of boxed biscuits.
- Mr. See had a saw, and Mr. Soar had a seesaw, so See's saw sawed Soars seesaw.

Writing Wrap-Up WRITING • THINKING • LISTENING • SPEAKING

CREATING

Write Tongue Twisters

Write three tongue twisters. Use a plural noun in one, a singular possessive noun in another, and a plural possessive noun in the last. Exchange papers with a classmate, and try repeating each other's sentences rapidly. Then read your work aloud, and have your partner spell the possessive nouns you used. Did you agree with each other on the spelling?

For Extra Practice see page 116. Plural and Possessive Nouns **103**

Using Exact Nouns

When you write, you use nouns to name people, places, and things. Choose exact nouns that will help your readers understand precisely what you mean.

Less exact noun: Maria wore shoes to walk on the beach.
More exact noun: Maria wore sandals to walk on the beach.

Apply It

1–6. Rewrite the message on this post card. Use a more exact noun in place of each underlined noun.

Revising

Dear Aunt Mim,

    Dad and I spent the entire afternoon at the beach. Some <u>people</u> put on <u>stuff</u> so that they could swim under the water and study the fish. Other tourists were renting <u>equipment</u>. I just wanted to float in the water, so I rented a <u>thing</u> to float on.

    We were surprised to see a lot of <u>stuff</u> growing on the beach. Lots of people sat under the trees, but many were collecting <u>things</u> along the shore.

    We'll be home again next week.

Love,
Cara

Place
Stamp
Here

Enrichment

Nouns!

Proper Places

Players: 2 or more

Materials: You need a timer, index cards, and a dictionary to check spelling. Each player chooses two common nouns such as *holiday* or *mountain*. The players then write each noun on a separate index card.

To play: Mix the cards, and place them facedown. Someone draws a card and sets the timer to three minutes. Players write as many proper nouns as possible for that common noun. Then exchange papers to check answers. Another player draws a card to repeat the process.

Scoring: 5 points for each proper noun; 2 extra points if the noun is spelled correctly. The player with the most points wins.

Challenge Vary the game by using only geographical names.

Appositive Interview

Interview a classmate. Write your questions first, including some that will have the names of people, places, or things in the answer.

Use facts from the interview in an informative paragraph. Include appositives, such as the ones underlined below. Write possessive nouns correctly.

Angela Perkins, <u>a sixth-grader</u>, lives on Maple Street. Angela's main interest is pets. She has pet chickens and takes care of Goldy, <u>her family's cat</u>. She also walks two neighbors' dogs.

Extra! Collect the interviews and turn them into a class newspaper.

1 **Recognizing Nouns** *(p. 84)* Write the nouns in each of the sentences below.

1. This diner belongs to Sid Newman and his family.
2. Sid works behind the counter in the summer and on holidays.
3. The T-shirts for his staff have green stripes.
4. Dr. Jones often eats tuna fish or cottage cheese for lunch.
5. Many friendships have sprung up over meals in the restaurant.
6. Soon Sid will open a diner near Spring Lake in New Jersey.

2 **Common and Proper Nouns** *(p. 87)* Write each noun. Underline the common nouns once and the proper nouns twice.

7. Linda Chu and her family live in Fort Wayne, Indiana.
8. On weekends Linda and her mom catch fish in Lake Michigan.
9. Mrs. Chu ties the hook to the line.
10. Many people catch trout, catfish, and bass in the lake.
11. In July and August, Jim Dobbs sells tackle from his van.
12. Jim is known throughout the area for his knowledge about fish.

3 **Singular and Plural Nouns** *(p. 92)* Write the plural forms of the nouns in parentheses.

13. Our city _____ have many _____. (park, bench)
14. Sometimes _____ hide in the _____. (fox, bush)
15. You can hear _____ of _____ from the bandstand. (echo, waltz)
16. Are _____ good places to grow _____? (city, potato)
17. The _____ honked during the late summer _____. (goose, day)
18. The _____ hung next to the small green _____. (berry, leaf)

4 **Possessive Nouns** *(p. 96)* Write the possessive form of each noun in parentheses.

19. A _____ career can sometimes change. (person)
20. Good salespeople know all their _____ names. (customers)
21. An aircraft _____ job is very detailed. (mechanic)
22. Several _____ groups have held workshops. (women)
23. All of the _____ children became farmers. (Curtises)

5 **Plural and Possessive Nouns** *(p. 101)* Write the correct plural or possessive form of each noun in parentheses.

24. One of _____ hobbies is folk dancing. (Carlos)
25. He knows dances from many _____. (country)

Go to www.eduplace.com/tales/hme/ for more fun with parts of speech.

26. Each _____ dances are different. (country)
27. Carlos went to a folk dance at a _____ house. (friend)
28. Some of his _____ parents know dances from other lands. (friends)
29. _____ Polish grandmother remembers dances from her childhood. (Phyllis)
30. Her _____ favorite dance is a Polish Polka. (grandmother)
31. The _____ favorite dance is the Salty Dog Rag. (grandchildren)
32. _____ played ragtime and danced rags in the 1920s. (American)
33. _____ favorite rags included the Twelfth Street Rag. (Americans)
34. Folk dance _____ are held all over the world. (festival)
35. This _____ New England Folk Festival will attract thousands. (year)
36. For many _____ the festival has featured music, dance, crafts, and other folk arts. (year)
37. The _____ best moments are when they taste foods from their native land. (Morrises)

Mixed Review 38–48. This part of a feature article has three errors with common or proper nouns, six errors with plural nouns, and two errors with possessive nouns. Write the article correctly.

Proofreading Checklist

Have you written these correctly?

✔ proper nouns
✔ plural nouns
✔ possessive nouns

Back Yard Garden Booms

Tony Valenti stands in his yard in Middlebury and smiles. Usually Spring arrives late in vermont, but this year seems different. It is only june. Still, the air has been warm for days, and leafs are unfolding in the trees. Like many homeowners Tony is thinking about bushs, lilies, and tomatos.

Tonys' gardens are not like other homeowners' gardens, however. Other peoples' plants don't grow as big or as full as his plants do. Tony has the gardener's special touch. Flowers, vegetables, and trees seem to obey him. On weekends familys come to admire his work. Even babies and childrens love the lush, colorful yard. Tony doesn't mind the human visitors. He is bothered only by the deer and the mouses that can damage his plants.

✔ Test Practice

Write the numbers 1–6 on a sheet of paper. Read each group of sentences. Choose the sentence that is written correctly. Write the letter for that answer.

1 A The Queen of England has little real power.

B Long ago Queens and Kings had total control over their subjects.

C Queen Elizabeth must have attended many official ceremonys.

D The queens jewels are very beautiful and expensive.

2 F Brightly wrapped boxs covered the table at the birthday party.

G All the guest's expressed best wishes to the birthday girl.

H Beth's little cousin gave her three big birthday kisses.

J The event was put on by a company called party magic.

3 A Wolfs live and hunt in family groups called packs.

B Humans first tamed dogs over 10,000 years ago.

C Did you know that red foxs will eat almost anything?

D A obedient dog will follow its masters commands.

4 F Dramatic photographs showed the tornados path.

G All hurricanes' names are listed in this reference book.

H The two mens' boats were damaged by the waves.

J The insurance companys must pay for the hail damage.

5 A Sophies grandmother lives just down the street.

B Sophie loves to explore her grandmothers' attic.

C Once she found a beautiful pair of womens' gloves there.

D Delicate green leaves were embroidered by hand on each of the gloves.

6 F Memorial Day is an important holiday in our Town.

G The parade begins on Maple avenue.

H The Boy Scouts march every year.

J After the parade, everyone gathers for a lunch of Pizza and ice cream.

Now write the numbers 7–12 on your paper. Look at each underlined part of the paragraph. Find the correct way to write the underlined part in each numbered line. Write the letter for that answer. If the part is already correct, write the letter for the last answer, "Correct as it is."

(7) People dance for many reasons they dance in many styles.

(8) In some traditional societys, people dance to please the gods.

(9) In other cultures, people dance to tell stories. In india dancers

(10) hand movements have specific meanings. is called mime.

(11) Waltzs are dances that people do just to enjoy music with a

(12) partner. Johann strauss of vienna wrote music for the waltz.

7 A reasons? They dance
   B reasons. they dance
   C reasons. They dance
   D Correct as it is

8 F societees, people
   G societies, people
   H society's, people
   J Correct as it is

9 A In India dancer's
   B in india dancers'
   C In India dancers'
   D Correct as it is

10 F This mixture of acting and dance is called mime.
   G is called mime in our country.
   H is called mime and is a mixture of acting and dance.
   J Correct as it is

11 A Waltzs are Dances
   B Waltzes are dances
   C Waltzes are dancies
   D Correct as it is

12 F partner, Johann Strauss of vienna
   G partner. Johann strauss of Vienna
   H partner. Johann Strauss of Vienna
   J Correct as it is

Unit 1: The Sentence

Kinds of Sentences *(p. 32)* Write the sentences with correct end punctuation. Write *declarative, interrogative, imperative,* or *exclamatory.*

1. Where did I put my glasses
2. I took them off to swim
3. How cold that water is
4. Swim with me, please
5. Can you do a butterfly kick

Subjects and Predicates *(pp. 35, 38)* Write each sentence. Draw a line between the complete subject and the complete predicate. Underline the simple subject once and the simple predicate twice.

6. The roses blossomed first.
7. Susan had watered them every day.
8. Her whole family loves flowers.
9. Susan's flowers grow every spring.
10. She will study plants in school.

Imperatives and Interrogatives *(p. 41)* Write the simple subject of each sentence. Then write *imperative* or *interrogative* to label the sentence.

11. Hold on to the railing.
12. Where does this bridge go?
13. Shall we walk across it?
14. Turn left here.
15. Does John know the way?

Compound Subjects and Predicates *(pp. 44, 47)* Write the compound subjects and compound predicates in these sentences. Write the connecting words.

16. Terry and Fran went to the park.
17. They rode their bikes or walked.
18. Terry saw Kim and ran to her.
19. Sue and Joe have ridden horses.
20. John and Lee dismounted, fed carrots to their ponies, and relaxed.

Compound Sentences, Conjunctions *(pp. 52, 55)* Combine the simple sentences into a compound sentence. Use a comma and *and, or,* or *but.*

21. My sister lives at college. She comes home every other weekend.
22. She needed shelves. Cal built them.
23. Should I paint them white? Does this stain look better?
24. Cal will put biographies on the top shelf. Sue will put mysteries here.
25. Does Sue read novels? Does she prefer nonfiction?

 See www.eduplace.com/kids/hme/ for a tricky usage or spelling question.

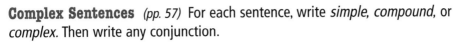

Complex Sentences *(pp. 57)* For each sentence, write *simple, compound,* or *complex.* Then write any conjunction.

26. Because we were late, we hurried.
27. Is Doug's watch slow or fast?
28. I hear the train, but I can't see it.
29. Dad will help if we miss our train.

Fragments and Run-ons *(p. 62)* Write a sentence from each fragment. Rewrite each run-on sentence.

30. Three brushes and a can of paint.
31. May I help may I hold the ladder?
32. Early tomorrow afternoon.
33. Mom will paint the door, I'll paint this wall, Dad will do that one.

Unit 2: Nouns

Common and Proper Nouns *(pp. 84, 87)* Write each noun. Label it *common* or *proper.*

34. Norman Rockwell was an artist.
35. New York City was his birthplace.
36. His paintings appeared on the cover of the *Saturday Evening Post.*
37. Rockwell studied at the Chase School of Art.

Singular and Plural Nouns *(p. 92)* Write the plural form of each noun.

38. crutch   40. worry   42. alley   44. wolf   46. potato
39. piano   41. wax   43. glass   45. moose   47. child

Possessive Nouns *(p. 96)* Write the possessive form of each noun in parentheses.

48. Some careers were once _____ jobs. (men)
49. Any job can also be a _____ work. (woman)
50. A _____ job is very dangerous. (firefighter)
51. Tugboat _____ training takes seven years. (pilots)
52. _____ dream is to be an astronaut. (Dolores)

Plural and Possessive Nouns *(p. 101)* Write the correct form of the noun in parentheses.

53. Charles _____ Atlantic flight took place in 1927. (Lindbergh)
54. Everyone waited for _____ of his plane. (report)
55. His _____ name was *Spirit of St. Louis.* (plane)
56. His flight captured _____ imaginations all over the world. (people)

(pages 84–86)

1 Recognizing Nouns

• A **noun** names a person, a place, a thing, or an idea.

Remember

● Write the noun that names the word in parentheses.

Example: Benjamin Franklin was born in Massachusetts. (person)
Benjamin Franklin

1. Young Ben Franklin worked in his father's shop. (place)
2. Later he published a newspaper for his half-brother. (thing)
3. Ben then went to Philadelphia to try his luck. (idea)
4. Later he went to London to buy printing equipment. (thing)
5. He returned to Philadelphia in 1726. (place)
6. Ben Franklin was interested in politics. (idea)

▲ Write all the nouns in the sentences below.

Example: Benjamin Franklin became an ambassador representing the
American colonies in Great Britain.
Benjamin Franklin ambassador colonies Great Britain

7. During the Revolution, Ben Franklin became a leader.
8. Few people had hope that the two countries could be friends.
9. Ben Franklin gave advice to George Washington.
10. Mr. Franklin also was a member of the committee that wrote the
Declaration of Independence.
11. A printer, a writer, a thinker, and a leader, Benjamin Franklin was
also a great citizen and a patriot.

■ Write your own nouns to complete the following sentences. Use the type of
noun shown in parentheses.

Example: I visited the birthplace of _____. (person) *John Adams*

12. _____ and _____ were great Americans. (persons)
13. They worked hard for _____ and _____. (ideas)
14. My favorite American was born in _____. (place)
15. I read about this person in a _____. (thing)
16. One of the presidents of the United States was _____. (person)

(pages 87–89)

2 Common and Proper Nouns

- A **common noun** names any person, place, thing, or idea.
- A **proper noun** names a particular person, place, thing, or idea.
- A proper noun always begins with a capital letter.

Remember

● Write the proper noun in each sentence.

Example: My cousin Jay is a pilot. *Jay*

1. This man lives in the city of New York.
2. My cousin made many trips in April.
3. One trip began at Kennedy Airport.
4. His plane flew to England that day.
5. My cousin returned home on a Tuesday.

▲ Write the nouns in these sentences.
Underline the common nouns once. Underline the proper nouns twice.

Example: Willa Brown was a young pilot who lived in Chicago.
Willa Brown pilot Chicago

6. One day this woman visited an editor named Enoch Waters.
7. This man worked for a newspaper called the *Chicago Defender*.
8. Willa wanted to let people know about African Americans who were flyers.
9. Students from the Coffey School held shows at the Harlem Airport.
10. The reporter wrote articles, and crowds came to the shows.
11. Does Aunt Louise remember those articles?

■ Rewrite each sentence by supplying a proper noun to replace each underlined group of words.

Example: The pilot had a mission. *Al Grant had a mission.*

12. The mission was to cross the ocean.
13. The hard part would be to cross it by tomorrow.
14. The trip had to be taken during this month.
15. The pilot wanted to start from a certain city.
16. My dad read about the trip in the newspaper.

(pages 92–95)

3 Singular and Plural Nouns

- Add *-s* or *-es* to most singular nouns to form the plural. Use the spelling of the singular noun to decide how to form the plural.
- Some nouns have the same singular and plural forms.
- Some nouns are spelled differently in the plural.

● One of the underlined words in each sentence is a plural noun. Write the plural noun.

Example: The <u>students</u> in Adam's <u>class</u> took a trip.   *students*

1. They visited a <u>farm</u> where <u>potatoes</u> grew.
2. <u>Boxes</u> of potatoes were piled on the <u>porch</u>.
3. Two <u>women</u> were reading a <u>list</u>.
4. Many <u>cartons</u> were loaded on a <u>train</u>.
5. Some were going to <u>stores</u> in the <u>country</u>.
6. Some were delivered to <u>chefs</u> in the <u>city</u>.

▲ Write the plural form of each noun in parentheses.

Example: Dawn's school has two music _____. (studio)   *studios*

7. One room has two _____. (piano)
8. One wall is covered with _____. (shelf)
9. Last week several _____ gave a jazz concert. (class)
10. People never looked at their _____. (watch)
11. Some concerts are like _____. (party)
12. _____ of the music remained in the air. (Echo)

■ Write one sentence for each pair of nouns, using the plural form of both nouns. Underline the plurals.

Example: hat, dress   *My sister bought two <u>hats</u> and several <u>dresses</u>.*

13. brush, tooth
14. boot, foot
15. man, sheep
16. knife, tomato
17. mouse, cage

18. zoo, monkey
19. train, whistle
20. worker, factory
21. glass, dish
22. bus, ticket

(pages 96–98)

4 Possessive Nouns

Remember

- To form the possessive of a singular noun, add -'s.
- To form the possessive of a plural noun that ends in s, add only an apostrophe (').
- To form the possessive of a plural noun that does not end in s, add -'s.

● Write the correct form to complete each sentence.

Example: One of the (nations, nation's) space heroes was a chimpanzee.
nation's

1. The (animals, animal's) name was Ham.
2. (Hams', Ham's) trip made him famous.
3. The (rocket's, rockets') speed was almost six thousand miles per hour.
4. (Peoples, People's) understanding about space travel grew.
5. Other (chimp's, chimps') flights have been useful too.
6. (Scientist's, Scientists') photographs show (animal's, animals') behavior during space flights.

▲ Rewrite each phrase. Use possessive nouns.

Example: quiz for the student   *the student's quiz*

7. job of my sister
8. hoof of the horse
9. antler of the moose
10. book belonging to Chris
11. dog of the Harrises
12. tails of the mice
13. smile of Louis
14. bike belonging to two brothers

■ Rewrite each sentence by using a possessive noun instead of the underlined phrase.

Example: The field trip of my class was interesting.
My class's field trip was interesting.

15. The faces of the monkeys made Kim laugh.
16. The children of the Joneses wanted to rest.
17. The friends of Jess took her picture.
18. The den of the fox was a deep hole.
19. All the voices of the children sounded excited.
20. The students of Mrs. Brown wrote reports.

(pages 101–103)

5 Plural and Possessive Nouns

- Do not confuse possessive nouns with plural nouns.
- Most plural nouns end in *s*.
- Possessive nouns have an apostrophe before or after the *s*.

● One noun in each sentence matches the description in parentheses. Write the noun described in parentheses.

Example: Dan is very interested in airplanes. (plural)   *airplanes*

1. Look at these pictures. (plural)
2. That plane's design is very old. (singular possessive)
3. Hang gliders first appeared in the nineteenth century. (plural)
4. Is there a hang gliders' club? (plural possessive)
5. He flies silently below the clouds. (plural)
6. There is no engine's roar. (singular possessive)
7. The pilots' friends watch. (plural possessive)

▲ Write the correct form of the noun in parentheses. Then write whether it is plural, singular possessive, or plural possessive.

Example: Did you hear the (teachers, teacher's) instructions?
      teacher's   singular possessive

8. The museum (guides, guides') spoke to us.
9. This (week's, weeks') topic was helicopters.
10. (Helicopters', Helicopters) hover noisily.
11. (Pilots, Pilots') voices cannot be heard over the noise.
12. Other (museums', museums) show movies.
13. There is the (visitors', visitors) lobby.
14. (Pams, Pam's) mother bought T-shirts for us.

■ Write a sentence for each noun, using the form shown in parentheses.

Example: pilot (plural possessive)
      The pilots' flight paths were the same.

15. cloud (plural)
16. pilot (singular possessive)
17. propeller (plural)
18. astronaut (singular possessive)
19. rocket (plural)
20. crew (plural possessive)

In one smooth move, she
leaps, flies, flips, falls,
and lands.

Verbs

1 Action Verbs

What words are action words, or verbs, in this sentence?

Urchins feed with the aid of a complex, five-toothed jaw that resembles the part of an electric drill that grips the drill bit.

—from *Shell,* by Alex Arthur

- You know that a verb is the main word in the predicate of a sentence. An **action verb** tells what the subject *does* or *did.*

  We walked on the beach.

  We ran toward the ocean.

- Sometimes an action verb tells about an action that you cannot see.

  We want seashells.

  I wonder about the tides.

Try It Out

Speak Up Find the action verbs.

1. I found a sand dollar on the beach.
2. Dad and I studied the sand dollar carefully.
3. I touched the pattern on its surface.
4. I brought the sand dollar into the house.
5. It fits in the palm of my hand.
6. Dad placed it on the windowsill in the sunlight.

Summing Up

- An **action verb** tells what the subject of the sentence does or did.

Write the action verb in each sentence. Then label the action *visible* or *invisible*.

Example: Sand dollars bury themselves slightly in sand.   *bury   visible*

7. I collect seashells and sand dollars.
8. Feel the slots and notches all over this sand dollar.
9. Sand moves through these notches.
10. The sand dollar eats shellfish and plants.
11. Artists appreciate the beauty of its five-point star.
12. They paint pictures of sand dollars and other sea creatures.
13. I love paintings of the ocean.

14–18. These laptop notes for a student report have five action verbs. Write the notes. Underline the action verbs.

Example: Sand dollars usually eat tiny plants.
Sand dollars usually eat tiny plants.

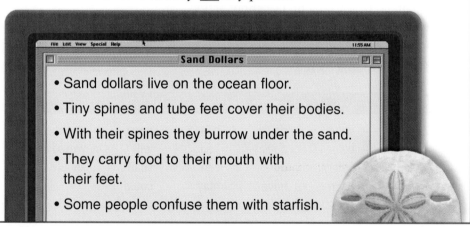

File Edit View Special Help   11:55 AM

Sand Dollars

- Sand dollars live on the ocean floor.
- Tiny spines and tube feet cover their bodies.
- With their spines they burrow under the sand.
- They carry food to their mouth with their feet.
- Some people confuse them with starfish.

Writing Wrap-Up   WRITING • THINKING • LISTENING • SPEAKING

INFORMING

Write Report Notes

What do you know a lot about? the bus route? basketball? rock groups? Write four or five sentences of notes on the topic. Find a partner and read your notes to each other. Compare the topics you wrote about. Then work together to list each other's action verbs.

Main Verbs and Helping Verbs

One-Minute Warm-Up

What words can you think of, other than *will*, that work with *walk* in this sentence?

We <u>will walk</u> with Willie in the woods on Wednesday.

- You know that every sentence has a verb in the predicate. The verb can be one word or several words.

  Kenneth walked home.

  I will be going home soon too.

- A verb that is made up of more than one word is called a **verb phrase**. It contains a main verb and a helping verb or verbs. The **main verb** expresses action or being in the sentence. The **helping verbs** work with the main verb, but they do not show action.

  Bill Moore has arrived home.

  The door has been locked.

Common Helping Verbs					
am	were	do	has	must	might
is	be	does	had	will	would
are	being	did	can	shall	should
was	been	have	may	could	

- Sometimes the helping verb in one sentence is the main verb in another. Be sure to read the whole sentence before you identify a main verb and its helping verbs.

Verb	Main Verb	Helping Verb
did	I did my homework.	I did wait for you.
has	Bob has it.	Bob has taken it.

- Questions are often formed with helping verbs. In questions the main verb and its helping verbs may be separated by the subject of the sentence or by other words.

  Should we leave now?

  Will the show start early?

Tip

To find the verb in a question, turn the sentence into a statement.

Try It Out

Speak Up Find the verb phrase in each sentence. Which words are main verbs? Which are helping verbs?

1. In 1803 land between the Missouri River and the Rocky Mountains was sold.
2. The land was bought by the United States.
3. Would anyone explore the land?
4. Meriwether Lewis and William Clark were chosen by President Thomas Jefferson.
5. They had lived in the wilderness.

 Summing Up

- The **main verb** expresses action or being.
- A **helping verb** works with the main verb.
- A **verb phrase** is made up of one or more helping verbs and a main verb.

On Your Own

Write each verb phrase. Underline each helping verb once and each main verb twice.

Example: A Native American woman may have saved the Lewis and Clark expedition.   *may have saved*

6. Sacajawea was born in Idaho around 1787.
7. She had been kidnapped from her tribe.
8. In 1805 her husband was hired as a guide for Lewis and Clark.

more ▶

9. Would Sacajawea go with them?
10. Could they cross the Rocky Mountains on foot?
11. Horses would be needed for that part of the trip.
12. The woman must have helped the explorers.
13. She did know the land along their route.
14. She could act as interpreter too.
15. Without her, the expedition might have failed.

16–28. This magazine advertisement has thirteen verb phrases. Write the advertisement. Underline each helping verb once and each main verb twice.

Example: Sacajawea will be seen every week.
Sacajawea <u>will be</u> <u><u>seen</u></u> every week.

Sacajawea Stars in Saturday Series

Sacajawea has been given a great compliment. She has been made the hero of a cartoon! History books have viewed her as a star for years. Now TV is recognizing her star quality. Every Saturday morning at 8:30, Sacajawea will be featured in the cartoon adventure series *The Guiding Princess*.

Families can enjoy this new series together. They will laugh; they will cry; they will learn.

The creators of the series have studied history. Do they tell the story accurately? Yes. Can the true story entertain you? Yes. Should you watch? Definitely!

Writing Wrap-Up WRITING • THINKING • LISTENING • SPEAKING

PERSUADING

Write a Press Release

What person in history or in the world today would *you* choose as the subject of an animated TV series? Write a press release for the series that will convince the public to tune in. Use at least four verb phrases. Read your press release to some classmates. Were they convinced?

3 Direct Objects

Take turns answering this question: What did you see at the science museum?

Your answer can be true or fanciful, but be sure to repeat all the answers others have given before adding your own.

- An action verb is often followed by a noun or a pronoun that tells *who* or *what* receives the action.

  Fran and I visited a museum of science.

  One exhibit showed a mummy from Egypt.

  The adults and the children loved it.

  The museum guide described Egyptian pyramids.

- The word that tells *who* or *what* receives the action is called the **direct object**. To find the direct object, first find the verb. Then ask *who* or *what* receives the action. A direct object can be a noun or a pronoun, a word that takes the place of a noun.

  The guide helped Maria. *(The guide helped whom?)*

  The skeleton of a whale amazed everyone in our group. *(The skeleton amazed whom?)*

  Luke had studied fossils. *(Luke had studied what?)*

  Please notice them in the rock. *(Notice what?)*

- In some sentences the direct object is compound.

  This display featured plants and animals of the desert. *(This display featured what?)*

  Visitors enjoyed the computers and the rockets. *(Visitors enjoyed what?)*

  Some people bought cards and books in the museum shop. *(People bought what?)*

Direct Objects **123**

Speak Up Find the verb in each
sentence. Then find the direct object.
The direct object may be compound.

1. We attended a show on electricity at
   the science museum.
2. A huge generator produced light and energy.
3. Then we saw a model of an Apollo spacecraft.
4. We examined it closely.
5. Lauren and Rodrigo watched a film about rockets.
6. Later we visited the exhibit on natural history.
7. I like the stuffed giraffes and elephants best.
8. My friends preferred the dinosaurs and other prehistoric animals.

Summing Up

- A **direct object** is a noun or a pronoun that
  receives the action of an action verb.

- Some direct objects are compound.

- To find the direct object, find the action verb,
  and ask who or what receives the action.

Write the action verb and the direct object in each sentence. The direct
object may be compound.

Example: Sir Francis Drake planned a voyage around the world.
action verb: planned   direct object: voyage

9. The Queen of England encouraged Drake in 1577.
10. Sir Francis treated the members of his crew well.
11. He won their respect and loyalty.
12. Drake commanded five ships at once.
13. Two smaller ships carried supplies.

more ▶

14. They visited many ports in South America.
15. Drake's great voyage benefited England.
16. The British people greeted the weary sailors.
17. The Queen knighted Sir Francis Drake.
18. She praised him and the entire crew.

19–30. This guessing game has twelve action verbs. Each verb has at least one direct object. Write the game. Underline the action verbs once and the direct objects twice. Remember to check the title.

Example: I encouraged writers and artists.
      I encouraged writers and artists.

Discover my name. Use these clues.

- I made many speeches, and crowds cheered me.
- The whole world knows me by my first name.
- I have an important title. However, people seldom use it.
- Many kings and princes proposed marriage to me.
- I knew William Shakespeare and Sir Francis Drake.
- I spoke several languages.
- I ruled my nation for forty-five years.
- Later on, another queen of my country was given my name.

Answer: Elizabeth I, Queen of England

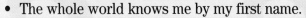

WRITING • THINKING • LISTENING • SPEAKING

DESCRIBING

Write Clues to "Guess Who"

Think of a well-known person, such as a historical figure or someone in the news. Write at least five clues about the person, starting with *I* and using action verbs and direct objects. See whether a partner can identify your mystery person. Then ask which clue was most helpful.

4 Transitive and Intransitive Verbs

Which verb has a direct object? Which verb does not?

Then, two days before my birthday, a delivery company brought a box to our house. It was wrapped in brown paper.

—from "What the Princess Discarded," in *Birthday Surprises*, by Barbara Ann Porte, edited by Johanna Hurwitz

- A **transitive verb** is an action verb that sends its action to a noun or pronoun in the predicate. The receiver of the action is the direct object. An **intransitive verb** has no direct object. The same verb can be transitive in one sentence and intransitive in another.

Verb	Transitive	Intransitive
speak	The students speak French.	They speak well.
study	We study grammar.	We study hard.

- Some action verbs are always intransitive. They never have direct objects.

Intransitive Verbs: Her eyes twinkled.

Carla will listen to her carefully.

Try It Out

Speak Up Find the verb or verb phrase in each sentence. Which are transitive, and which are intransitive? If the verb is transitive, find the direct object.

1. Ann's family bought her birthday present.
2. They chose a watch with an orange band.
3. Ann wore her new watch to school.

more ▶

4. Now she will know the correct time.
5. She talks about her present all the time.
6. The second hand sweeps around the numbers.
7. The watch's colorful face gleams brightly.
8. Ann keeps the watch in its case at night.
9. The numbers glow in the dark.
10. Can Ann tell the time without a light?

Summing Up

- A **transitive verb** is an action verb that sends its action to a noun or a pronoun that is its direct object.
- An **intransitive verb** has no direct object.
- Some action verbs are always intransitive. Some can be either transitive or intransitive.

On Your Own

Write the verb or verb phrase in each sentence. Label it *transitive* or *intransitive*. If it is transitive, write the direct object.

Example: Your silly riddle pleased Rory. *pleased   transitive   Rory*

11. We laughed at the joke about the flea.
12. Maria explained the joke to them.
13. Berto introduced a new riddle to us.
14. Will his sisters remember the rhyme?
15. Mrs. Garcia chuckled very softly.
16. She smiled at us.
17. We delighted the Garcias with Granddad's funny story.
18. A good clown can tell jokes without any words.
19. Maria played the guitar after dinner.
20. Everyone listened to the beautiful music.
21. The applause surprised Maria.
22. Then Mr. Garcia also played.   more ▶

23–34. Write the sentences in these jokes. Underline the twelve verbs or verb phrases once. Label each *transitive* or *intransitive*. Then underline any direct object twice.

Example: What kind of person steals soap? (A dirty crook)

What kind of person <u>steals</u> <u><u>soap</u></u>? transitive

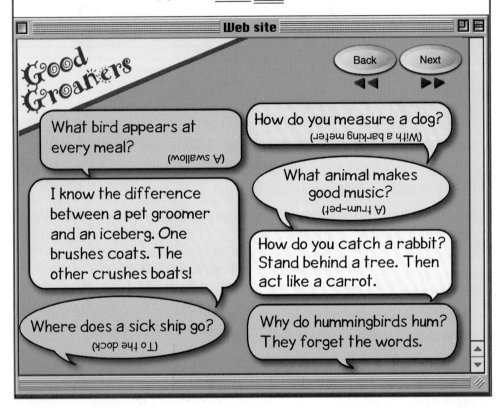

Web site

Back   Next

Good Groaners

What bird appears at every meal? (A swallow)

How do you measure a dog? (With a barking meter)

I know the difference between a pet groomer and an iceberg. One brushes coats. The other crushes boats!

What animal makes good music? (A trum-pet)

How do you catch a rabbit? Stand behind a tree. Then act like a carrot.

Where does a sick ship go? (To the dock)

Why do hummingbirds hum? They forget the words.

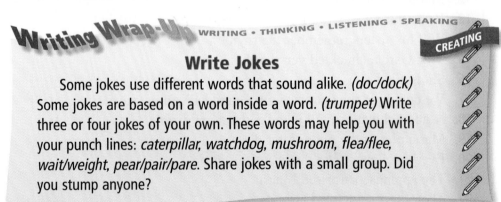

Writing Wrap-Up   WRITING • THINKING • LISTENING • SPEAKING

CREATING

Write Jokes

Some jokes use different words that sound alike. *(doc/dock)* Some jokes are based on a word inside a word. *(trumpet)* Write three or four jokes of your own. These words may help you with your punch lines: *caterpillar, watchdog, mushroom, flea/flee, wait/weight, pear/pair/pare.* Share jokes with a small group. Did you stump anyone?

For Extra Practice see page 169.

5 Being Verbs and Linking Verbs

Make as many sentences as you can from the words below. Add *the*, *a*, and *an* as you need them.

mountains	Rockies	big	is
beautiful	ancient	are	
seem	appear	look	

- Some verbs do not show action. They show what the subject is or is like. Verbs called **being verbs** show a state of being.

  Mr. Wong became our principal. He seems kind.

HELP Tip

Linking verbs never have direct objects.

- A being verb is often a **linking verb**. It links the subject of the sentence with a word in the predicate that tells more about it.

  Mr. Wong *feels* happy.   He *had been* a teacher for twenty years.

Common Being Verbs and Linking Verbs							
am	are	were	be	been	look	feel	smell
is	was	seem	being	become	appear	taste	

- Linking verbs link the subject with a word in the predicate. The word can be a **predicate noun** or a **predicate adjective**. A predicate noun renames the subject. A predicate adjective describes the subject.

  Predicate Nouns: Ms. Ide is our coach. *(Ms. Ide = coach)*
                            She has become my friend. *(She = friend)*

  Predicate Adjectives: Mr. Hill was friendly.
                            He appeared shy to strangers.

- Some verbs can be either linking verbs or action verbs.

  Action: Mr. Hill looked at the student murals.

  Linking: The designs looked colorful and creative.

Speak Up What is the linking verb in each sentence? What is the predicate noun or predicate adjective?

1. The Black Hills are really mountains.
2. Thunderhead Mountain is part of the Black Hills.
3. Someday the mountaintop will become a huge statue.
4. The statue will be a profile of Chief Crazy Horse.
5. Chief Crazy Horse was a Sioux Indian chief.
6. The statue is rough now.
7. The work on it seems slow.

Model for Crazy Horse Statue

Summing Up

- A **being verb** is a **linking verb** when it links the subject of a sentence with a predicate noun or a predicate adjective.
- A **predicate noun** renames or identifies the subject.
- A **predicate adjective** describes the subject.

Write each sentence. Underline the linking verb. Draw an arrow from the simple subject to the predicate noun or predicate adjective.

Example: The Iroquois are Native American peoples in New York.

The Iroquois <u>are</u> Native American peoples in New York.

8. Six groups eventually became part of the Iroquois nation.
9. One group was the Mohawks.
10. The Mohawks were enemies of another Iroquois group.
11. Hiawatha was a powerful chief of the Mohawks.
12. Hiawatha appears heroic in a poem by Longfellow.

more ▶

13. This poem is *The Song of Hiawatha.*
14. Hiawatha felt unhappy because of the wars.
15. The chances for peace looked hopeless.
16. Hiawatha became a peacemaker.
17. The Iroquois were powerful around 1570.
18. Their power was great for more than one hundred years.
19. Their constitution became a model for other governments.

20–26. This electronic manuscript for part of a textbook has seven linking verbs. Write the textbook part. Underline each linking verb once. Underline the words it links twice.

Example: Peace was very important to Hiawatha.
Peace was very important to Hiawatha.

≡≡≡≡≡≡≡≡≡≡≡≡ **Web site** ≡≡≡≡≡≡≡≡≡≡≡≡

The Iroquois League

Around 1570 five Native American groups became the Iroquois League. Hiawatha and Dekanawidah were the founders. To them, a league appeared stronger than one group alone. In fact, the league seemed very successful. It was the most advanced culture in the Eastern Woodlands region of New York. The Iroquois felt powerful, and their future looked very bright.

Writing Wrap-Up

WRITING • THINKING • LISTENING • SPEAKING

EXPRESSING

Write an Editorial

Are there cliques, or exclusive groups, in your school? What are the advantages and disadvantages of belonging to a clique? Write an editorial stating your opinion. Use predicate nouns and predicate adjectives. Find a partner, and read your editorial aloud. Does your partner feel the same way?

For Extra Practice see page 170. Being Verbs and Linking Verbs **131**

6 Simple Verb Tenses

Which verb or verbs tell about something in the present? in the past? How could they be changed to express the future?

That circular track, which still exists at the back of Lincoln Park and became a fixture of my teenage years, is unconventional.

—from *A Kind of Grace,* by Jackie Joyner-Kersee

- The **tense** of a verb tells when the action or the state of being takes place. The word *tense* comes from the Latin word for time. The words *present, past,* and *future* all refer to time. The present, past, and future tenses are called simple tenses.

- The **present tense** tells that something is happening now.

  Present Tense: The dancers perform outdoors. The gardens are lovely.

- The **past tense** tells that something has already happened. Usually the past tense of a verb is formed by adding *-ed.* The past tense of the verb *be* is *was* or *were.*

  Past Tense: The audience applauded. The play was wonderful.

- The **future tense** tells that something is going to happen. It is usually formed with the helping verb *will* or *shall.*

  Future Tense: Gail and Tim will be late.

  We shall save the seats for them.

Rules for Forming Verb Tenses	
Present Tense When the subject is singular, add *-s* to most verbs to make them singular.	run—Luis runs.
To make a verb that ends in *s, x, z, ch,* or *sh* singular, add *-es.*	watch—He watches.
To make a verb that ends in a consonant and *y* singular, change the *y* to *i* and add *-es.*	cry—Aki cries.
When the subject is plural, do not change the form of the verb.	hurry—They hurry.

Rules for Forming Verb Tenses *(continued)*

Past Tense	
For most verbs, add *-ed.*	talk—talked
When a short verb ends in a consonant, double the consonant and add *-ed.*	bat—batted
When a verb ends in *e,* drop the *e* and add *-ed.*	hope—hoped
When a verb ends in a consonant and *y,* change the *y* to *i* and add *-ed.*	try—tried
Future Tense	
Use the basic form of the verb with the helping verb *will* (or *shall*).	hop—will hop fly—shall fly

Try It Out

Speak Up Is the tense of each underlined verb present, past, or future?

1. The Olympic games <u>started</u> in ancient Greece.
2. Today's Olympics <u>developed</u> from Greek festivals.
3. Until the seventy-seventh festival, the games <u>lasted</u> only one day.
4. Now they <u>last</u> for two weeks.
5. Olympic athletes <u>become</u> heroes to the public.
6. Thousands of people <u>will attend</u> the next Olympics.

Summing Up

- The **tense** of a verb tells when the action or the state of being takes place.
- The **present tense** tells that something is happening now.
- The **past tense** tells that something has already happened.
- The **future tense** tells that something is going to happen.

Write each verb. Then write the past tense and the future tense of the verb.

Example: push *pushed* *will (shall) push*

7. plant
9. rent
11. call
13. decide
8. subtract
10. move
12. invite
14. clean

15–22. These headlines have eight verbs. Write the headlines. Underline each verb. Then write its tense.

Example: Athletes Arrive for Olympics

    Athletes <u>Arrive</u> for Olympics *present*

Olympic Games Will Begin Tomorrow

Mayor Marcos Will Greet Officials

City Speeds Through Last-Minute Preparations

Desperate Fans Wait in Line for Spare Tickets

Volunteers Staffed Box Offices

Opening Ceremonies Will Start at 7:00 P.M.

Last Runner Will Light Olympic Flame

City Rehearsed Its Emergency Plans Yesterday

Writing Wrap-Up

WRITING • THINKING • LISTENING • SPEAKING

INFORMING

Write Headlines

Write five headlines about an event in your school, your town, or the world. Use verbs in the past, the present, and the future tenses. Remember to capitalize important words. Ask a partner to listen to your headlines. Then read them again, and have your partner name each verb and its tense.

7 Perfect Tenses

Find the verbs below. Which parts are helping verbs? main verbs?

By next week Jay will have owned his tuba for a year, but he never had cleaned it until today. Finally, he has discovered a great new cleaner. It is a tuba toothpaste!

Principal Parts

- You have already learned about the present tense *(ask)*, the past tense *(asked)*, and the future tense *(will ask)*. Verbs have other tenses too. All the tenses of a verb come from four basic forms. These basic forms are the **principal parts** of the verb.

Principal Parts of Verbs			
Verb	**Present Participle**	**Past**	**Past Participle**
work	(is) working	worked	(has) worked
share	(is) sharing	shared	(has) shared
cry	(is) crying	cried	(has) cried
hop	(is) hopping	hopped	(has) hopped

- The present participle and the past participle are always used with a helping verb.

- Remember, when a verb ends with a consonant and *y*, change the *y* to *i* before adding *-ed: cried.* When a one-syllable verb ends with a vowel and a consonant, double the consonant before adding *-ed: hopped.*

Try It Out

Speak Up What are the present participle, the past, and the past participle of the following verbs?

1. hike
2. wait
3. drop
4. ban
5. dry
6. walk

Forming and Using the Perfect Tenses

- You have learned the three simple tenses of verbs—present, past, and future. For each simple tense, there is also a perfect tense—**present perfect**, **past perfect**, and **future perfect**. Each perfect tense is formed with the helping verb *have* and a past participle. The chart below shows the forms of *have*.

Subject	Forms of *have*
Singular	
I	have, had
you	have, had
he, she, it, and singular nouns	has, had
Plural	
we	have, had
you	have, had
they and plural nouns	have, had

- In the perfect tenses, the past participle form of the verb stays the same. The form of the helping verb changes to show the tense.

The Perfect Tenses	
Use the **present perfect tense** to express action that took place at an indefinite time in the past. The action may still be going on.	The band has played two songs.
Use the **past perfect tense** for an action in the past that was completed before another action took place.	The band had played two songs before you arrived.
Use the **future perfect tense** for an action that will be completed before another action in the future.	The band will have played many more songs before the concert ends.

Speak Up What is the tense of the underlined verb in each sentence?

7. Kate <u>had learned</u> that music before.
8. She <u>has practiced</u> it over and over.
9. By the time she performs it, she <u>will have rehearsed</u> it a dozen times.
10. <u>Had</u> you ever <u>listened</u> to the piece before Kate played it?

What are the present perfect, past perfect, and future perfect forms of each verb below? Use *he* or *she* for the subject.

11. climb   13. bury   15. copy   17. reply
12. press   14. stop   16. rub   18. plan

Summing Up

- The **principal parts**, or basic forms, of a verb are the verb, the present participle, the past, and the past participle.
- The **perfect tenses** are made up of a form of *have* and the past participle.
- Use the **present perfect** for an action that took place at an indefinite time in the past. Use the **past perfect** for an action completed before another past action. Use the **future perfect** for an action that will be completed before another action.

Write the correct form of *have* for the tense shown in parentheses.

Example: People _____ played trumpets for centuries.
          (present perfect)   *have*

19. In 2000 B.C., Egyptians used a trumpet as a battle signal. Many types of trumpets _____ appeared since then. (present perfect)
20. By the Middle Ages, trumpets _____ reached a length of six feet or more. (past perfect)

more ▶

21. The trumpet _____ included valves since the 1820s. (present perfect)
22. Who knows what changes trumpeters _____ invented a few hundred years from now? (future perfect)
23. _____ music _____ changed drastically by then? (future perfect)

24–32. This part of an e-mail has nine perfect tense verbs. Write the letter. Underline each perfect verb form and label it *present perfect, past perfect,* or *future perfect.*

Example: Have you ever played the drums?
          Have you ever <u>played</u> the drums?   present perfect

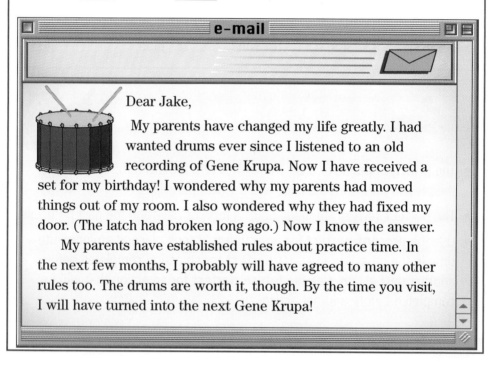

e-mail

Dear Jake,

My parents have changed my life greatly. I had wanted drums ever since I listened to an old recording of Gene Krupa. Now I have received a set for my birthday! I wondered why my parents had moved things out of my room. I also wondered why they had fixed my door. (The latch had broken long ago.) Now I know the answer.

My parents have established rules about practice time. In the next few months, I probably will have agreed to many other rules too. The drums are worth it, though. By the time you visit, I will have turned into the next Gene Krupa!

Writing Wrap-Up   WRITING • THINKING • LISTENING • SPEAKING

EXPLAINING

Write a Letter

Write a letter to a friend. Tell about a change that happened in your life recently. Identify the cause and the effects of that change. Tell how you felt. Use all three perfect tenses. Read your letter to a classmate. Has he or she had a similar experience?

          For Extra Practice see page 172.

8 Regular and Irregular Verbs

What's wrong with the verbs in these sentences?
How can you fix them?

Clara Nette lended me her drawing of the school band.

Have you saw the book *A Fife's Life*, by Windham Reed?

- You have learned to use the principal parts of verbs to form all the tenses. Most verbs have past and past participle forms that are formed by adding *-ed*. These verbs are called **regular verbs** because they follow this pattern.

- Remember, when a regular verb ends with a consonant and *y*, change the *y* to *i* before adding *-ed*. When a regular one-syllable verb ends with one vowel and a single consonant, double the consonant before adding *-ed*. When a regular verb ends with *e*, drop the *e* before adding *-ed*.

> **HELP**
> **? Tip**
> Use your dictionary when in doubt about spelling.

  cry–cried   hurry–hurried   hop–hopped   file–filed

- The past and the past participle of some verbs are not formed by adding *-ed*. These verbs are **irregular verbs**. The best way to learn the principal parts that you do not know is to memorize them.

Principal Parts of Some Irregular Verbs			
Verb	**Present Participle**	**Past**	**Past Participle**
be	(is) being	was	(has) been
blow	(is) blowing	blew	(has) blown
do	(is) doing	did	(has) done
drive	(is) driving	drove	(has) driven
fly	(is) flying	flew	(has) flown
freeze	(is) freezing	froze	(has) frozen
have	(is) having	had	(has) had
lend	(is) lending	lent	(has) lent
make	(is) making	made	(has) made
ring	(is) ringing	rang	(has) rung

Principal Parts of Some Irregular Verbs (continued)

Verb	Present Participle	Past	Past Participle
see	(is) seeing	saw	(has) seen
speak	(is) speaking	spoke	(has) spoken
steal	(is) stealing	stole	(has) stolen
swim	(is) swimming	swam	(has) swum
take	(is) taking	took	(has) taken
tear	(is) tearing	tore	(has) torn
throw	(is) throwing	threw	(has) thrown
write	(is) writing	wrote	(has) written

Try It Out

Speak Up What are the principal parts of each verb? Is the verb regular or irregular?

1. steal
2. ring
3. mail
4. tear
5. love
6. do

What is the correct verb for each sentence? Is the verb regular or irregular?

7. Have you (took, taken) art classes?
8. Randy has (study, studied) art since kindergarten.
9. My instructor (be, was) a portrait painter for years.
10. What (made, make) this work of art better than the others?
11. I have (saw, seen) oil paintings and watercolors.
12. I have (wrote, written) about the paintings.

Summing Up

- When the past and the past participle of a verb are formed by adding -ed, the verb is **regular**. When the past and the past participle are formed in some other way, the verb is **irregular**.

- Many commonly used verbs are irregular. You need to memorize their principal parts.

Write the correct form of each verb in parentheses.

Example: A bus (drove, driven) us to the art museum. *drove*

13. Our art class has (did, done) good work.
14. Our teacher (spoke, spoken) to us about our work.
15. Have you (took, taken) art classes?
16. I have (wrote, written) captions for my drawings.
17. Each student has (make, made) a clay sculpture.

18–24. This list of captions for drawings has seven incorrect past participles. Write the captions correctly.

Example: I writed captions for my seven drawings.
   I wrote captions for my seven drawings.

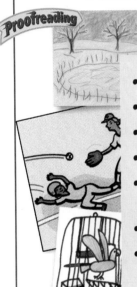

Proofreading

- Manuel has rang the bell for dinner.
- Who has taked the bird out of its cage?
- Late as usual, Ariana flied down the hall.
- The boy seed a duck, but it swam away quickly.
- Zeke has tore the newspaper into strips, and the children have made funny hats with them.
- The little pond has already froze for the winter.
- She had stole the base even before he threw the ball.

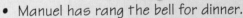

Writing Wrap-Up

WRITING • THINKING • LISTENING • SPEAKING

CREATING

Write Captions

Using stick figures, draw four small sketches. Write a caption for each on the back. Use a past or a past participle form from the chart in each caption. Trade sketches with a partner, and write captions for each other's sketches. Read both sets of captions aloud. How similar or different are they? Work together to check your irregular verbs.

Writing with Verbs

Using Tenses Correctly Using tenses correctly will help you communicate clearly. When you write about something that takes place completely in the present, stick to the present tense.

Incorrect: Our family is going to the arts festival today. We <u>wanted</u> to see Lionel's painting. He is proud of it.

Correct: Our family is going to the arts festival today. We want to see Lionel's painting. He is proud of it.

The same idea applies to other tenses. When action takes place entirely in the past, make sure to put your verbs in the past tense. Future action should be written in the future tense.

Apply It

1–6. Rewrite these captions for a newspaper layout. Decide which tense is best for each caption. Revise any incorrect verb tenses.

Revising School Weekly

RECTO

Lincoln School Arts Festival: What a Success!

The crowd enjoyed the paintings and the drawings. Students in the school show their creative talent, and they will take a lot of pride in this display.

The sixth grade presented its sculpture garden. The display will be in front of the school and is really impressive. Students made the clay figures in art class.

NEXT YEAR

Next year we will have another festival. There is a bigger exhibit of art. Students will paint a mural for the cafeteria, and they invited a speaker.

In some paragraphs you may need to discuss things that happen at different points in time. You can change verb tenses carefully to make your meaning clear without confusing your reader.

The following paragraph is mainly written in the past tense, but present and future tenses are also needed for it to make sense.

> Maine painters of the past century had distinct styles. Many made the sea their primary subject. When you visit the coast of Maine, you will see why. The colors of the water change moment by moment. The painters captured these hues on canvas.

> The present tense shows something that is happening right now or something that goes on continuously.

Apply It

7–14. Rewrite this part of a friendly letter. Revise the verbs as needed, using correct tenses.

Revising

Dear Grandma,

Our class went on a field trip to an art museum. I will be writing to tell you about an amazing coincidence. I go around a corner, and I see these paintings. I thought that they are yours! They looked like the ones you paint last summer. The paintings were done by the artist Winslow Homer. One showed people in a sailboat. The sailboat was leaning on its side, and it will be giving the people an exciting ride.

Have you heard of Winslow Homer? He painted many pictures of the sea. My teacher says to me that Mr. Homer lived in Maine, just as you do.

I'll tell you more about the pictures when I saw you.   Love,

                    Trey

Winslow Homer
—"*Breezing Up*"—

Writing with Verbs   **143**

9 Subject-Verb Agreement

Which three verbs are incorrect? How would you fix them?

Farmer: I will water the horse now.

Visitor: What do you mean?

Farmer: The horse are thirsty for a drink of water. Where am you going with that milk?

Visitor: I are going to milk the cat.

- A verb and its subject must agree in number. Use a singular verb with a singular subject and a plural verb with a plural subject. A compound subject joined by *and* usually takes a plural verb.

  Singular: The boy calls.   **Plural:** The boys call.
  The girl races.   The boy and the girl race.

- Singular verbs in the present tense usually end in *-s* or *-es*. However, when the singular subject is *I* or *you*, the singular verb does not end in *-s* or *-es*. Plural verbs in the present tense do not usually end in *-s*.

  Singular: I laugh.   **Plural:** The girls dance.

- The verb *be* does not follow the usual rules.

Agreement with the Verb *be*		
Subject	**Verb**	**Sentence**
I	am (present)	I am well today.
	was (past)	I was sick yesterday.
he, she, it, and all singular nouns	is (present)	It is raining now. The cat is playful.
	was (past)	She was hungry.
we, you, they, and all plural nouns	are (present)	We are cousins. The coach and the carpenter are friendly.
	were (past)	They were teammates. You were on that team last year.

Speak Up Choose the correct verb in parentheses.

1. Horses and ponies (is, are) important to people.
2. Often a horse and a rider (become, becomes) good friends.
3. In many different jobs, a horse (work, works) hard.
4. Some farmers (plow, plows) their fields with horses.
5. Horses (is, are) helpful to ranchers.

Summing Up

- A subject and its verb must agree in number.
- If the parts of a compound subject are joined by *and,* use a plural verb.
- The verb *be* does not follow the usual rules. You need to memorize its forms.

On Your Own

Write the correct present tense form of the verb in parentheses to complete each sentence.

Example: Many types of horses _____ in the world. (live)   *live*

6. Horses _____ different in size, color, strength, and speed. (be)
7. The largest horses _____ six feet tall. (stand)
8. A very large horse _____ a weight of up to two thousand pounds. (reach)
9. A pony _____ a horse under fifty-eight inches tall. (be)
10. The workhorse and the racehorse _____ special abilities. (have)
11. A workhorse often _____ extremely heavy loads. (pull)
12. A racehorse _____ faster than thirty miles an hour. (run)
13. The coats of pintos _____ splashed with color. (appear)
14. For this reason, people _____ them "paints." (call)

more ▶

15. Often police officers _____ horses in their work. (ride)
16. Ranchers _____ great distances on horseback. (cover)
17. A horse _____ good and bad treatment. (remember)
18. A good rider _____ a horse with patience. (treat)
19. These animals _____ people in many ways. (help)

20–30. This part of a book review has eleven incorrect verb forms. Write the book review correctly.

Example: This book are excellent.   *This book is excellent.*

Book Corner

Velvet and Pie Make a Hit

National Velvet, by Enid Bagnold, are definitely a book for horse lovers. However, if you am not a horse lover, it does not matter. This book appeal to everyone.

Velvet Brown are a fourteen-year-old girl. She wins a horse and fall in love with it. "Pie" is unruly, but to Velvet he are a champion. She and a jockey friend enters him in an important race, but she decides to ride him herself. The adults laughs, but Velvet pay no attention. People am not always right. Velvet and the reader learns some important lessons.

Writing Wrap-Up   WRITING • THINKING • LISTENING • SPEAKING

SUMMARIZING

Write a Book Review

Write a review of a book you remember well. The book can be one you enjoyed, did not enjoy, or had mixed feelings about. Use the present tense for most verbs as you summarize the story. Find a partner, and read your reviews to each other. Compare your reactions to your books.

10 More Subject-Verb Agreement

is were
was

The owl is thinking of some words. Which one of these words will *not* complete the sentence correctly? Why not?

Either Jonas or Dina _____ looking for a big book on owls called *Whooooo's Whooooooo*.

You know that the verb in a sentence must agree with the subject. You have also learned that when the parts of a compound subject are joined by *and*, the verb is plural.

- When *or, either . . . or*, or *neither . . . nor* is used to join the parts of a compound subject, the verb may be singular or plural. Use a plural verb if both parts of the subject are plural.

  Books or magazines were always on the table.

  Either carrots or apples are in the refrigerator.

- Use a singular verb if both parts of the compound subject are singular. If one part is singular and one part is plural, make the verb agree with the subject that is closer to it.

  Neither Jim nor Sally is ever without a good book.

  Neither Ted nor his friends like mystery books.

  Either the twins or Maria belongs to a book group.

- The verb in a sentence beginning with *here* or *there* must also agree with the subject. *Here* or *there* is never the subject of a sentence. To find the subject, ask, *Who or what is here?* or *Who or what is there?*

  Here is the index. *(What is here?)*

  Here are the sisters. *(Who is here?)*

  There are Ms. Ryan and Mr. Knox. *(Who is there?)*

  There are the online catalogs. *(What is there?)*

Speak Up Which verb in parentheses is correct?

1. Either our school library or the city library (is, are) open.
2. There (is, are) the dictionaries.
3. Either books or magazines (is, are) excellent references.
4. Neither the atlas nor the dictionary (is, are) on the shelf.
5. Here (is, are) an atlas and a map.
6. Either the librarian or the online catalogs (is, are) available.

Summing Up

- If a compound subject is joined by *or, either . . . or,* or *neither . . . nor,* make the verb agree with the subject that is closer to it.

- In sentences beginning with *here* or *there,* first find the subject, and then make the verb agree with it.

On Your Own

Write the verb in parentheses that correctly completes each sentence.

Example: Here (is, are) many old cars.   *are*

7. There (was, were) no cars before the late 1800s.
8. Either trains or horses (was, were) used to go places.
9. There (is, are) a model of the first car in this museum.
10. Here (is, are) an old Model T and a Maxwell.
11. Either the Model T or the Oakland (was, were) purchased by many.
12. There (was, were) also Hudsons on the road.
13. Either steam or electricity (was, were) used for cars.
14. Neither steam cars nor electric cars (was, were) fast.
15. There (was, were) no trucks or buses at first.
16. Neither tolls nor a speed limit (was, were) in use.
17. Neither cars nor roads today (looks, look) like early ones.

more ▶

18. Either my great-grandmother or my great-grandfather (remembers, remember) the Stanley Steamer.
19. Either horse-drawn carriages or buggies (was, were) popular before the invention of the car.
20. Now cars or buses (is, are) used for most travel.
21. American cars or foreign cars (is, are) popular today.

22–30. This part of a student essay has nine incorrect verb forms. Write the essay correctly.

Example: Here is the new houses.   *Here are the new houses.*

Proofreading

A Missing Playground

My family and I have lived in our house for ten years. Neither the house nor the neighborhood are still the same. At first there was only my house and my friend Ian's house. The open field or the woods was our playground. Neither a bus nor a car were ever in the street. Then, five years ago, there was a big change. Either a crane or bulldozers was always at work. A new house or a store were built each day. Now there is many people and cars. Neither the woods nor the field exist. Are progress or change always good?

Writing Wrap-Up   WRITING • THINKING • LISTENING • SPEAKING

COMPARING / CONTRASTING

Write an Essay

Write a short essay in which you compare and contrast something old with something new, such as an old and a new pair of shoes or your former and present schools. Use *here, there, or, either . . . or,* and *neither . . . nor* in some sentences. With a classmate, take turns reading your papers aloud. Work together to check all your verb forms.

11 Contractions

One-Minute Warm-Up

Which words are contractions? What two words does each combine?

> Did you ever put a stone into a campfire? It doesn't melt, does it? But inside the Earth's mantle it's hot enough to melt rock!
>
> —from *Geology Crafts for Kids,* by Alan Anderson, Gwen Diehn, and Terry Krautwurst

- A **contraction** is a word formed by combining two words and shortening one of them. An apostrophe takes the place of the letter or letters left out.

- Sometimes the verb is shortened.

  we're = we are   they've = they have

  I'll = I will   I'm = I am

 Tip

Beware of words easily confused with contractions.
you're = you are
your = belonging to you

- An apostrophe and *s* (*'s*) can stand for *is* or *has*. Read the whole sentence for clues to the meaning.

  He's measuring the water. *(He is)*

  It's been two minutes. *(It has)*

- Often a verb and *not* are combined. Most contractions with *not* are formed by using an apostrophe to replace the *o* in *not*.

Contractions Formed with *not*	
isn't (is not)	can't (cannot)
aren't (are not)	couldn't (could not)
wasn't (was not)	shouldn't (should not)
weren't (were not)	wouldn't (would not)
won't (will not)	doesn't (does not)
don't (do not)	hasn't (has not)
didn't (did not)	haven't (have not)

- Only the part of a contraction that is a verb is part of a verb phrase. The word *not* and the contracted form *n't* are never part of a verb phrase.

He'll mix the chemicals carefully. *(verb phrase = will mix)*

Kenneth shouldn't add too much acid. *(verb phrase = should add)*

Try It Out

Speak Up What words make up the contraction in each sentence? What words make up each verb phrase?

Scientist with fossil

1. I'm working with a group of scientists.
2. They're studying the history of the earth.
3. They've already looked at the earth of the present.
4. Now they'll imagine the earth a million years ago.
5. They won't publish their research for several months.

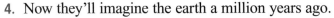

Summing Up

- A **contraction** is the shortened form of two words. Dropped letters are replaced by an apostrophe.

- In contractions made with a verb and *not,* the *n't* is not part of the verb phrase.

On Your Own

Write each contraction. Write the words that form the contraction. Then write the verb phrase.

Example: They've worked as a team.

They've   They/have   have worked

6. The scientists haven't completed their project.
7. They're studying a damaged forest in Washington.
8. We've seen the volcano nearby.
9. It's throwing ash onto the trees of the forest.

more ▶

10. Now the trees aren't looking very healthy.
11. One scientist hasn't taken samples of the soil yet.
12. Another one can't finish his research.
13. The problems couldn't be solved easily.
14. They'll write a report about the project next year.

15–26. This story dialogue has twelve incorrect contractions. Write each contraction correctly.

Example: Our tour guide isnt sure about the nearby volcano.   *isn t*

Proofreading

"Youv'e got to see this newspaper, Ivy. You'll be amazed."

"Whats it about, Leon? I do'nt have much time. I cant stay longer than a minute."

"You are always in a hurry, and your'e always late!"

"We are'nt discussing me. Wer'e talking about an article."

"Remember the volcano we did'nt get to see yesterday?"

"Sure. The fog wouldnt lift, so we couldn't see a thing."

"Thats right. I'am afraid we missed more than we realized. Its' erupting!"

Writing Wrap-Up   WRITING • THINKING • LISTENING • SPEAKING

NARRATING

Write a Dialogue

Imagine two people who have just missed something exciting, such as an eclipse, a celebrity sighting, or a contest prize. What might they say? Write a short dialogue, including some contractions. With a classmate, take parts and read the dialogue to a small group. Then read it again, and have your classmates spell each contraction aloud. Did you all agree on the spelling?

12 *sit, set; lie, lay; rise, raise*

One-Minute Warm-Up

How would you fix the verbs the poet used incorrectly?

Ike and Ron raise healthy hens, which they keep in nice clean pens.
As the farmers wait for eggs, they set down and rest their legs.
Once the eggs are in a heap, Ike and Ron lay down to sleep.

Some verbs have related but different meanings. Three confusing pairs are *sit, set; lie, lay;* and *rise, raise.*

Verb	Definition	Sentence
sit	to rest in an upright position	I sit in the chair.
set	to put or place an object	I set the cup down.
lie	to rest or recline	I lie on the blanket.
lay	to put or place an object	I lay the book on the shelf.
rise	to get up or go up	We rise early.
raise	to move something up, to grow something, or to increase	They raise their hands. Farmers raise corn. Ed will raise his fee.

To decide which verb to use, ask yourself what the subject is doing. If the subject is placing an object somewhere, use *set* or *lay.* If the subject is resting, use *sit* or *lie.* To decide whether to use *rise* or *raise,* ask yourself, *Raise what?* If your answer names something, use *raise.* If the question has no answer, use *rise.*

Try It Out

Speak Up Which word in parentheses correctly completes each sentence?

1. You may (set, sit) next to me.
2. He will (lie, lay) that board down here.
3. You can't (lie, lay) on that.

more ▶

4. I (set, sit) the chairs here so that people can (set, sit).
5. Sarah (rises, raises) hens on a farm in Virginia.
6. She (rises, raises) early to feed the chickens.
7. The chickens come when Sarah (rises, raises) her hand.
8. Next year her family will (rise, raise) their prices.

Summing Up

- Use the verbs *sit* and *lie* to refer to a resting position.
- Use the verbs *set* and *lay* to mean "put an object somewhere."
- Use the verb *rise* to mean "get or go up."
- Use the verb *raise* to mean "move something up, grow something, or increase something."

On Your Own

Write the verb in parentheses that correctly completes each sentence.

Example: I often (sit, set) by the kitchen window.   *sit*

9. My cat is hurt! It (lies, lays) outside the window.
10. Dad can (sit, set) its broken leg in a splint.
11. I will (lie, lay) my cat on a blanket in a box.
12. We can (sit, set) the box in the kitchen.
13. I will (sit, set) next to it for a while.
14. The sun (rises, raises) early in the morning.
15. I won't (rise, raise) the window shade.
16. Then maybe my cat will (lie, lay) in its box longer.
17. If you (rise, raise) your voice, you might wake it.

more ▶

18. My brother (rises, raises) early to make breakfast.
19. He (sits, sets) a large bowl of hot oatmeal on the table.
20. I will quickly (sit, set) down to eat.
21. My brother (lies, lays) the morning paper on the kitchen counter.

22–30. These instructions have nine incorrect verb forms. Write the instructions correctly.

Example: Sit the water bowl down. *Set the water bowl down.*

Happy Puppy Pointers

- You are the puppy's parent. It should not rise itself.
- A puppy raises early. Take it outside immediately.
- A puppy will lay down a lot. Don't worry. That's normal.
- A puppy can set on command. Train it young.
- Sit clean water out at all times. Puppies drink a lot.
- Lie newspapers on the floor. Set the puppy there often.
- Your puppy will lay on your bed if you let it. Don't.
- Set with your puppy and pet it often. Let it bond with you.
- Combine love with training, and you will rise a good dog.

Writing Wrap-Up   WRITING • THINKING • LISTENING • SPEAKING

EXPLAINING

Write Instructions

Write instructions for the care of a pet. You can choose to be serious or not serious. Use *sit, set, lie, lay, rise,* and *raise.* Read your instructions to some classmates. Have them listen for the correct verbs.

13 lend, borrow; let, leave; teach, learn

One-Minute Warm-Up

What's wrong with these sentences? How can you fix them?

May I borrow your umbrella? Leave me have it, and I will learn you how to make a new word out of EDWRAWON.

(a new word)

- Here are three more verb pairs that are sometimes confused. *Lend* means "to give temporarily." *Borrow* means "to take temporarily."

   Will you lend me your boots? *(Will you give them to me for a while?)*

   May I borrow them for a hike? *(May I take them for a while?)*

- *Let* and *leave* have different meanings too. The verb *let* means "to permit." The verb *leave* means "to go away" or "to allow to remain in one place."

   My brothers let me go with them. *(They permit.)*

   Tomorrow we leave for a camping trip. *(We go away.)*

   I will leave my camera in the tent. *(It will remain.)*

- The third confusing pair is *teach* and *learn.* Teach means "to give instruction." *Learn* means "to get instruction."

   Alice will teach tennis. *(She will instruct.)*

   Babies learn very fast. *(They receive instruction.)*

Try It Out

Speak Up Which word in parentheses correctly completes each sentence?

1. Shari can (teach, learn) how to ski this weekend.
2. Her uncle will (teach, learn) her.
3. Next winter she will (teach, learn) to ski on larger slopes.
4. Her uncle will also (teach, learn) her brother.

more ▶

5. Her brother will (teach, learn) the basics.
6. Did I (let, leave) my umbrella at your house?
7. Please (leave, let) me go outside.
8. We should (let, leave) before sunset.
9. Please (lend, borrow) me your umbrella.
10. Please return it if you (lend, borrow) it.

Summing Up

- *Borrow* means "to take temporarily." *Lend* means "to give temporarily."

- *Let* means "to permit." *Leave* means "to go away."

- *Teach* means "to give instruction." *Learn* means "to receive instruction."

On Your Own

Write the verb in parentheses that correctly completes each sentence.

Example: I can (borrow, lend) you that book. *lend*

11. I must (teach, learn) myself the library's new system.
12. Do you want me to (teach, learn) you?
13. Yes, I don't think I can (teach, learn) it on my own.
14. (Let, Leave) us start at the beginning.
15. Will you (let, leave) me ask a question first?
16. May I (borrow, lend) your instruction manual?
17. Yes, I can (borrow, lend) that to you.
18. Thanks. Just (let, leave) it on the table for me.
19. Then I can (teach, learn) other people what I know.
20. Did you remember the flashlight I wanted to (borrow, lend) from you?
21. Yes, I was going to (borrow, lend) it to you and (let, leave) you keep it for a week.
22. I promise not to (let, leave) it out in the rain.

more ▶

23–30. These bulletin board notices have eight incorrect verbs. Write the notices correctly.

Example: Let the book here. *Leave the book here.*

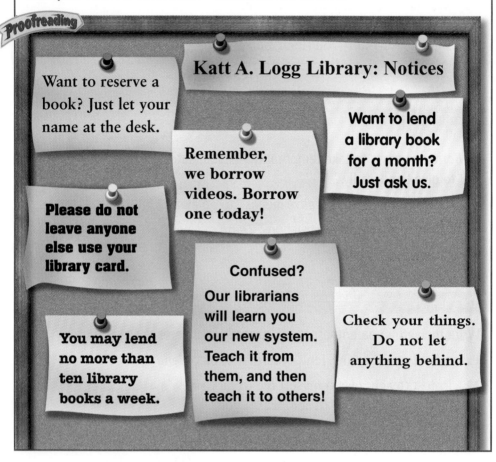

Katt A. Logg Library: Notices

Want to reserve a book? Just let your name at the desk.

Want to lend a library book for a month? Just ask us.

Remember, we borrow videos. Borrow one today!

Please do not leave anyone else use your library card.

Confused? Our librarians will learn you our new system. Teach it from them, and then teach it to others!

You may lend no more than ten library books a week.

Check your things. Do not let anything behind.

WRITING • THINKING • LISTENING • SPEAKING

Writing Wrap-Up

CREATING

Write Bulletin Board Notices

What notices are on the bulletin board at school? at the supermarket? in other places? Write six notices of your own. Be serious, imaginative, or funny, but use a different verb from this lesson in each notice. Have a classmate listen to your notices and tell you which one is most appealing.

   For Extra Practice see page 178.

Using Exact Verbs

When you write, you use verbs to tell about actions. Some verbs, such as *said,* are often overused. You can avoid repeating *said* by choosing other verbs that have similar meanings and are more exact.

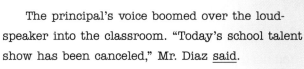

Overused verb:
"Why aren't we having a talent show?" Blake said.
"That's what I want to know," Heather said.
More exact verb:
"Why aren't we having a talent show?" Blake asked.
"That's what I want to know," Heather replied.

Apply It

1–6. Rewrite this story. Use the Thesaurus Plus in your book to replace each underlined verb *said* with a similar but more exact verb.

Revising

The principal's voice boomed over the loud-speaker into the classroom. "Today's school talent show has been canceled," Mr. Diaz <u>said</u>.

"Aw, that's not fair," several students <u>said</u> unhappily.

"What do you think happened?" others <u>said</u>.

Tanya leaned toward me, put her hand over her mouth, and <u>said</u> in my ear, "I had a feeling something was going to go wrong."

Soon everyone was discussing the situation.

Ms. Chao clapped her hands once and said, "That's enough talking. Please get back to work."

"Oh, please, Ms. Chao," Ike <u>said</u>. "Could you tell us what happened?"

"I heard that a family of skunks invaded our auditorium," she <u>said</u>.

Enrichment

Verbs!

Campaign Speech

You are the president of your class, and you're running for reelection. Write a campaign speech telling what you have done and what you will do if reelected. Use at least five different helping verbs. Underline each helping verb.

Steve Dunne for President! Steve Dunne for President!

Elect Steve Dunne, It's a Done Deal.

Steve Dunne for President! Steve Dunne for President!

A Matter of Principal Parts

Players: 2–3

Materials: You need paper, a pencil, a paper clip, and 18 index cards. On the cards write the verbs from the left-hand column of the chart on pages 139–140. Make a spinner like the one shown on the right.

To play: A player draws a card and spins. If the spinner stops on the blank, the player says *I* and the past form of the verb on the card— for example, *I flew.* If the spinner stops on *have,* the player says *I have* and the past participle—*I have flown.*

have

Scoring: A correct verb form earns one point.

Challenge Make a new spinner with *be, have,* and a blank. Make another with *I, you, he, she, it, we,* and *they.* The player draws a card and spins both spinners. He or she then uses the pronoun with correct forms of both verbs—for example, *He is taking.*

1 Action Verbs *(p. 118)* Write the action verb in each sentence.

1. I visited a computer center.
2. We saw a room full of terminals.
3. We heard computer voices.
4. The computer questions puzzled us.
5. We wrote computer programs.

2 Main Verbs and Helping Verbs *(p. 120)* Write the verb phrase in each sentence. Underline the helping verbs once and the main verbs twice.

6. Don Quixote had read the tales.
7. Could he ignore warnings?
8. He did consider himself brave.
9. His old horse had been given a special name.
10. They would conquer giants.

3 Direct Objects *(p. 123)* Write the action verb and the direct object in each sentence.

11. Carla requested information from the National Park Service.
12. She received maps and booklets.
13. Carlsbad Caverns covers several miles.
14. Mammoth Cave has many visitors.
15. Luray Caverns in Virginia contains colorful columns.
16. The details filled her with curiosity.

4 Transitive and Intransitive Verbs *(p. 126)* Write each verb. Then label it *transitive* or *intransitive.*

17. Jazz began in New Orleans.
18. Jazz musicians played by ear.
19. They played blues and spirituals.
20. Many musicians put their hearts into their music.
21. They invented new sounds.
22. People danced to great jazz bands.
23. The jazz world admired the great Louis Armstrong.
24. Armstrong mastered the trumpet.
25. We will remember his songs.

5 Being Verbs and Linking Verbs *(p. 129)* Write each linking verb and the predicate noun or the predicate adjective.

26. Ann is a newspaper carrier.
27. She feels proud of her job.
28. Her route is Main Street.
29. The blocks are hilly.
30. Ann is responsible and prompt.
31. The weather can be a factor.
32. Sometimes it is rainy.
33. Other times the air feels chilly.
34. Snow looks beautiful.
35. It becomes a problem on the ride.
36. Ann is dependable every day.
37. Her customers seem happy.

6 Simple Verb Tenses *(p. 132)* Write the correct form of the verb in parentheses. Then write its tense.

38. Last week Maggie _____ her first trophy in the rodeo. (earn)
39. Both Maggie and her brother _____ hard all last year. (practice)
40. She _____ experts daily. (watch)
41. Who _____ a flaw yesterday? (spot)
42. Tomorrow he _____ too. (compete)

7 Perfect Tenses *(p. 135)* Write the correct form of *have* for each tense shown in parentheses.

43. Aaron _____ tested his skills as a pilot. (present perfect)
44. He _____ operated the controls before. (past perfect)
45. His friends _____ noticed his knowledge. (present perfect)
46. He _____ enjoyed many helicopter rides by now. (future perfect)

8 Regular and Irregular Verbs *(p. 139)* Write the correct form of each verb in parentheses. Then label it *regular* or *irregular.*

47. The student _____ now. (write)
48. Lisa has _____ a red pen. (see)
49. Last week I _____ a test. (take)
50. Nick has _____ his best. (do)
51. I _____ tests in the past. (like)
52. Tests have _____ helpful. (be)

9 Subject-Verb Agreement *(p. 144)* Write the verb in parentheses that agrees with the subject in each sentence.

53. Teresa and her brother (take, takes) swimming lessons.
54. Two lifeguards (watch, watches) every class.
55. Teresa (was, were) in a swimming meet last week.
56. She and her brother (compete, competes) in swimming meets.
57. They (enjoy, enjoys) team races.

10 More Subject-Verb Agreement *(p. 147)* Write the verb in parentheses that correctly completes each sentence.

58. Neither Ida nor they (rides, ride).
59. Either Mo or Dan (skate, skates).
60. There (was, were) no baseballs.
61. Neither his classmates nor Mike (play, plays) soccer.
62. There (is, are) a goalie and a net.

11 Contractions *(p. 150)* Write each contraction. Then write the verb phrase.

63. They've removed the bottles.
64. Shouldn't we fill this test tube?
65. I'd added too much acid.
66. She's combined two liquids.
67. The laboratory won't be locked.
68. You're working as a team.

12 sit, set; lie, lay; rise, raise (p. 153) Write the word in parentheses that is correct in each sentence.

69. I (set, sit) in the middle row.
70. Suddenly a man (raises, rises).
71. (Lay, Lie) your package here.
72. All of us (rise, raise) early.
73. He (sits, sets) the box down.
74. Let's (rise, raise) the window.
75. Let your dog (lie, lay) there.
76. I (lie, lay) the bread down.

13 lend, borrow; let, leave; teach, learn (p. 156) Write the word in parentheses that completes each sentence correctly.

77. He will (teach, learn) the class.
78. Please (let, leave) me sit here.
79. Libraries (lend, borrow) books.
80. May I (lend, borrow) the globe?
81. Shall we (let, leave) for home?
82. Did you (teach, learn) to sew?

Mixed Review 83–92. This diary entry has ten incorrect verbs. Write the entry correctly.

Proofreading Checklist

Look for errors with
✔ verb tenses
✔ subject-verb agreement
✔ contractions
✔ confusing verb pairs

Proofreading

Surprising Mom and Dad

Yesterday my parents will celebrate their anniversary. They marryed each other fifteen years ago. Jonathan and I throwed a big surprise party for them. Mom and Dad has many friends, and they helpped us a lot. We lent chairs and other things from them, and they made tons of food.

Unfortunately it was raining, so we could'nt sit outside. That didn't spoil things though. Jennifer took pictures of Mom and Dad when they see all the people. Wow, were they surprised! There was twenty people at the party, and everyone had a great time. We did too, but we were tired afterward. Neither Mom nor Dad expect a big party again for a long time!

Test Practice

Write the numbers 1–10 on a sheet of paper. Choose the best way to write the underlined part of each sentence. Write the letter for that answer. If there is no mistake, write the letter for the last answer.

1 The pond has <u>freezed</u> solid.

  A froze

  B frozen

  C freeze

  D (No mistakes)

2 Tomorrow we <u>will visit</u> him.

  F visited

  G have visited

  H has visited

  J (No mistakes)

3 Last week Christine <u>swimmed</u> in the quarry.

  A swam

  B swum

  C swims

  D (No mistakes)

4 Sugar <u>wont</u> dissolve in that.

  F wont'

  G wo'nt

  H won't

  J (No mistakes)

5 <u>Theyr'e</u> trying to find the cause of the disturbance.

  A Theyre

  B They're

  C Theyre'

  D (No mistakes)

6 <u>Set</u> down gently in that old chair.

  F Sit

  G Sits

  H Sat

  J (No mistakes)

7 The sun <u>rises</u> early in summer.

  A rise

  B raise

  C raises

  D (No mistakes)

8 The mayor has <u>spoke</u> to the press.

  F spoken

  G speaked

  H speaken

  J (No mistakes)

9 My parents <u>flew</u> to Miami.

  A flied

  B flown

  C flies

  D (No mistakes)

10 In 1804 Haiti <u>declares</u> independence <u>from</u> France.

  F declare

  G will declare

  H declared

  J (No mistakes)

Write the numbers 11–22 on your paper. Read each item. Choose the line that shows the mistake. Write the letter for that answer. If there is no mistake, write the letter for the last answer.

11 A Let's see the natural
    B history display. Fossils
    C and bones fascinate me.
    D (No mistakes)

12 F I don't know how to knit.
    G Aunt Gerry has promised
    H to learn me next time I visit.
    J (No mistakes)

13 A When a bank borrows
    B money to a customer, it
    C charges the customer interest.
    D (No mistakes)

14 F I think the play is good.
    G Neither Jo nor her friends
    H agrees with me. They hate it!
    J (No mistakes)

15 A Baseball pitcher
    B Dennis Martinez threw a
    C perfect game back in 1991.
    D (No mistakes)

16 F The airline's are having
    G a sale on flights to Florida.
    H Do you think we can go?
    J (No mistakes)

17 A I was worried about you.
    B You was supposed to call me
    C yesterday, but you didn't.
    D (No mistakes)

18 F All six girls' uniforms
    G and softball gloves are in
    H Mrs. Jay's big silver van.
    J (No mistakes)

19 A There is Mr. Meade and
    B his dog. They often go for
    C a vigorous run at this time.
    D (No mistakes)

20 F On one side of the valley
    G lays a village. My aunts or
    H my mom takes me there.
    J (No mistakes)

21 A Marcia's father won't
    B leave her and her sister
    C go to the mall today.
    D (No mistakes)

22 F Our noisy furnace have
    G kept Jessica awake
    H all night.
    J (No mistakes)

(pages 118–119)

1 Action Verbs

- An **action verb** tells what the subject of the sentence does or did.

Remember

● Write an action verb from the box to complete each sentence.
Use each verb only once.

Example: My father _____ as a scientist. *works*

1. He _____ starfish and other sea animals.
2. Scientists _____ about many different kinds.
3. They have _____ starfish of many colors.
4. Starfish _____ in oceans.
5. They _____ many arms covered with tiny feet.
6. They _____ on their feet along the ocean floor.
7. Starfish _____ clams and oysters.

know
move
have
works
studies
eat
found
live

▲ Write the action verb in each sentence.

Example: My family took a vacation. *took*

8. We traveled down the coast of Oregon.
9. We stopped at windy beaches.
10. Big waves crashed onto the shore.
11. Huge rocks stood in the surf.
12. We explored the shore.
13. I love that big orange starfish.

■ Complete each sentence, adding an action verb that makes sense.

Example: A few kinds of jellyfish _____ people. *sting*

14. The people _____ the jellyfish by accident.
15. You can _____ jellyfish in every ocean in the world.
16. They _____ along with the ocean currents.
17. They _____ tiny plants.
18. Most jellyfish _____ no color.
19. I _____ a jellyfish at a museum.
20. Have you ever _____ a jellyfish?

(pages 120–122)

2 Main Verbs and Helping Verbs

Remember

- The **main verb** expresses action or being.
- A **helping verb** works with the main verb.
- A **verb phrase** is made up of one or more helping verbs and a main verb.

● Write the verb phrase in each sentence. Underline the main verb in each phrase.

Example: Had Lewis and Clark explored the new land? *Had explored*

1. They had taken one trip.
2. Another man, Pike, was planning a trip.
3. Was he looking for fame?
4. He did find a new mountain.
5. It was named Pikes Peak in his honor.
6. Pike and his men were taken prisoner.
7. They did return home with new information.

▲ Write the verb phrase in each sentence. Underline each helping verb once and the main verb twice.

Example: The new lands were being filled with settlers. *were being filled*

8. Pioneers were traveling in wagons.
9. They had formed wagon trains for safety.
10. Did the travelers face many hardships?
11. A scout would be riding ahead of the wagon train.
12. The scout was looking for possible dangers.
13. Many families were going to California.
14. Miners had been finding gold in the mountains.

■ Use each verb phrase in a sentence. Include at least one question.

Example: could have explored
        Could we have explored the woods behind your home?

15. would call
16. did build
17. must have scared
18. had traveled
19. would have carried
20. might have seen

(pages 123–125)

3 Direct Objects

- A **direct object** is a noun or a pronoun that receives the action of an action verb.
- Some direct objects are compound.
- To find the direct object, find the action verb, and ask who or what receives the action.

● Write a direct object from the box to complete each sentence. Make sure your choice makes sense.

Example: This morning I made my _____. *breakfast*

dishes
milk
breakfast
bread
cereal
oranges

1. First, I put dry _____ into a bowl.
2. Then I poured _____ over it.
3. Later I toasted some _____.
4. I also squeezed _____ for juice.
5. I washed the _____ after breakfast.

▲ Write the direct object in each sentence. If the direct object is compound, write *compound*. Do not include the conjunction.

Example: The Polos brought jewels and riches from Asia.
     jewels riches compound

6. In 1295 Marco Polo organized a large party.
7. He, his father, and his uncle invited many friends.
8. A man wrote a book about Marco Polo's travels.
9. In the book he described China, Persia, and Java.
10. Christopher Columbus carried a book about Marco Polo with him.
11. Marco Polo's travels inspire me.

Marco Polo

■ For each verb listed below, write a sentence that includes a direct object. Write at least two sentences that have compound direct objects.

Example: discovered *I discovered a torn map in my backpack.*

12. dug
13. bought
14. hid
15. drew
16. opened
17. counted
18. followed
19. whispered
20. wrote

(pages 126–128)

4 Transitive and Intransitive Verbs

- A **transitive verb** is an action verb that sends its action to a noun or a pronoun that is its direct object.
- An **intransitive verb** has no direct object.
- Some action verbs are always intransitive. Some can be either transitive or intransitive.

● Copy the underlined verb. Label it *transitive* or *intransitive*.

Example: Tom <u>plays</u>. *plays intransitive*

1. Tom <u>plays</u> basketball.
2. He <u>dribbles</u> skillfully.
3. He <u>shoots</u> the ball from both sides.
4. Sometimes he <u>misses</u> the basket.
5. Sometimes he <u>misses</u> badly.
6. He <u>waves</u> to the crowd.

▲ Write each verb. Label it *transitive* or *intransitive*.

Example: June finished the race. *finished transitive*

7. She ran well.
8. June drank water.
9. She drank thirstily.
10. June won a ribbon.

11. She hugged her mother.
12. Her mother smiled with joy.
13. The crowd cheered for her.

■ Write an ending for each sentence. Use a transitive or intransitive verb as shown in parentheses. Write the complete sentence.

Example: Before the game, the crowd _____. (transitive)
   Before the game, the crowd bought tickets.

14. Soon the teams _____. (intransitive)
15. The referee _____. (transitive)
16. The cheerleaders _____. (intransitive)
17. Mrs. Lewis _____. (transitive)
18. At halftime the band _____. (intransitive)
19. Outside the stadium, cars _____. (transitive)
20. No one inside the stadium _____. (intransitive)

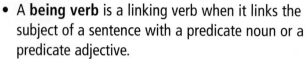

(pages 129–131)

5 Being Verbs and Linking Verbs

- A **being verb** is a linking verb when it links the subject of a sentence with a predicate noun or a predicate adjective.
- A **predicate noun** renames or identifies the subject.
- A **predicate adjective** describes the subject.

● Write the linking verb in each sentence.

Example: A checkerboard is black and red. *is*

1. Checkers was a favorite game in England in the 1700s.
2. The game of checkers appears easy.
3. Strategies are important, however.
4. Even children feel excited about this game.

▲ Copy each sentence. Underline the linking verb. Draw an arrow from the simple subject to the predicate noun or the predicate adjective.

Example: The kite exhibit at the science museum is wonderful.

The kite exhibit at the science museum is wonderful.

5. Kites became popular hundreds of years ago.
6. The Chinese were responsible for the first kites.
7. Those kites looked different from today's kites.
8. They were large leaves with twisted vines.
9. In contrast, modern kites seem fantastic.

■ Write the linking verb. Then write the predicate noun or the predicate adjective, and label it.

Example: A man named Charles Darrow was creative.
    was creative—predicate adjective

10. He became an inventor.
11. Mr. Darrow felt very good about one of his inventions.
12. It was a game about real estate.
13. Several toy companies were unwilling to make it.
14. Would Darrow's game be a failure forever?

(pages 132–134)

⑥ Simple Verb Tenses

Remember

- The **tense** of a verb tells when the action or the state of being takes place.
- The **present tense** tells that something is happening now.
- The **past tense** tells that something has already happened.
- The **future tense** tells that something is going to happen.

● Label each underlined verb *present, past,* or *future.*

Example: Rosa <u>entered</u> a four-mile race. *past*

1. She <u>will race</u> on Saturday.
2. First, Rosa <u>breathed</u> deeply.
3. She <u>stretches</u> her legs.
4. The runners all <u>start</u> together.
5. Rosa <u>ran</u> quickly.

▲ Change the tense of each underlined verb to the tense named in parentheses.

Example: The house <u>will need</u> a foundation. (past) *needed*

6. Someone <u>arrived</u> to dig the basement. (future)
7. Then large trucks <u>carried</u> the wet concrete. (present)
8. Wet concrete <u>will fill</u> the empty forms. (present)
9. The concrete <u>dries</u> for days. (future)
10. Finally, the workers <u>remove</u> the wooden forms. (past)
11. The carpenters <u>will complete</u> the house in four months. (past)

■ Write verbs to complete the following sentences. Write each verb in the tense named in parentheses.

Example: Ken _____ a secret message. (past) *discovered*

12. Ken _____ the message in a hollow tree. (past)
13. Ken _____ books on codes and symbols at the library. (future)
14. Ken and Alice _____ their own message in code. (present)
15. They _____ clues where people _____ them. (present, future)
16. They _____ a map, but they _____ where to find it. (past, past)

(pages 135–138)

7 Perfect Tenses

Remember

- The **principal parts**, or basic forms, of a verb are the verb, the present participle, the past, and the past participle.
- The **perfect tenses** consist of a form of *have* and the past participle.
- Use the **present perfect** for an action that took place at an indefinite time in the past. Use the **past perfect** for an action completed before another past action. Use the **future perfect** for an action that will be completed before another action.

● Write the four principal parts of each verb.

Example: walk *walk, is walking, walked, has walked*

1. order   3. form   5. hurry   7. spray
2. prepare   4. grab   6. trip   8. reply

▲ Write *present perfect, past perfect,* or *future perfect* to describe each underlined verb.

Example: The saxophone <u>has changed</u> the sound of music. *present perfect*

9. Antoine-Joseph Sax <u>has earned</u> a place in music history.
10. Soon the saxophone <u>will have reached</u> the age of 160 years.
11. After Sax <u>had developed</u> it, he persuaded the French army to use it.
12. By the time World War I ended, dance bands <u>had adopted</u> it.
13. Jazz musicians <u>have increased</u> its popularity over the years.

■ Write the tense of the verb indicated in parentheses.

Example: Jess _____ the saxophone. (discover—present perfect)
     has discovered

14. Jess _____ the clarinet for several years. (play—past perfect)
15. Then, after he _____ a jazz concert, he begged his parents for a saxophone. (attend—past perfect)
16. Now he _____ to study the sax. (decide—present perfect)
17. People remark on how quickly he _____ the instrument. (learn—present perfect)
18. Before the year ends, he _____ a band. (form—future perfect)

(pages 139–141)

⑧ Regular and Irregular Verbs

- When the past and the past participle of a verb are formed by adding *-ed*, the verb is **regular**. When the past and the past participle are formed in some other way, the verb is **irregular**.
- Many commonly used verbs are irregular. You need to memorize their principal parts.

● Write the basic verb form of each underlined verb. Use your dictionary if you need help.

Example: Luis <u>had chosen</u> a science project. *choose*

1. He <u>drew</u> a poster about polar bears.
2. Luis <u>took</u> two hours to draw the poster.
3. He <u>had written</u> many facts about polar bears.
4. Mr. Kraft, his teacher, <u>spoke</u> to Luis later.
5. He <u>had lent</u> Luis a book about bears.
6. Luis <u>had done</u> an interesting project.

▲ Write the correct verb form in parentheses to complete each sentence. Use your dictionary if you need help.

Example: The library (lend, lent) Beth an art book. *lent*

7. Beth (brought, bringed) the book home.
8. She (know, knew) the picture of the smiling woman.
9. Beth had (saw, seen) many pictures of the Mona Lisa.
10. An artist named Leonardo da Vinci had (did, done) it.
11. The book (gave, given) Beth other details about him.
12. He had (drew, drawn) a flying machine.

■ Write a sentence using the present participle, the past, or the past participle form of each verb below. Label the verb form.

Example: go *Jim had gone yesterday. past participle*

13. begin   15. bite   17. stand   19. read
14. drink   16. throw   18. come   20. swim

(pages 144–146)

⑨ Subject-Verb Agreement

- A subject and its verb must agree in number.
- If the parts of a compound subject are joined by *and*, use a plural verb.
- The verb *be* does not follow the usual rules. You need to memorize its forms.

Remember

● Write the verb that is correct in each sentence.

Example: The first Morgan (were, was) named for its owner. *was*

1. A Morgan's sleek coat (look, looks) dark in color.
2. Most Morgans (have, has) few white marks.
3. Their thick manes and tails (flows, flow) in the wind.
4. This rather small horse (have, has) special abilities.
5. It (are, is) known for both strength and speed.
6. It (pull, pulls) a plow or a buggy with its strong legs.

▲ Write the correct present tense form of the verb for each sentence.

Example: Today, quarter horses _____ popular. (be) *are*

7. Quarter horses _____ used in races at rodeos. (be)
8. Ranchers _____ quarter horses on the range. (ride)
9. This strong horse _____ cattle well. (herd)
10. It _____ fast over short distances. (run)
11. The horse also _____ very quickly. (turn)
12. Quarter horses _____ these skills in rodeos. (display)

■ Choose a present tense verb to complete each sentence. Write the sentences.

Example: The students _____ horses around the ring.
The students ride horses around the ring.

13. Each rider _____ the speed and the direction of the horse.
14. The students _____ the reins in the correct way.
15. Each rider's voice _____ signals to the horse.
16. The person's legs and hands _____ the horse too.
17. The horse and the rider _____ together.
18. All the riders _____ their new skills.

(pages 147–149)

⑩ More Subject-Verb Agreement

- If a compound subject is joined by *or, either . . . or,* or *neither . . . nor,* make the verb agree with the subject that is closer to it.
- In sentences beginning with *here* or *there,* first find the subject, and then make the verb agree with it.

Remember

● Write the verb in parentheses that is correct in each sentence.

Example: Neither Julio nor Dale (like, likes) mystery books. *likes*

1. Julio or Dale (is, are) fond of *The Wizard of Oz*.
2. Here (is, are) a little girl and her dog.
3. A tin man or a lion (meet, meets) Dorothy.
4. Neither the lion nor the straw man (is, are) very happy.
5. Either her friends or Dorothy (talk, talks) to the wizard.
6. There (go, goes) the wizard in a balloon.
7. Dorothy or her friends (get, gets) what they want.

▲ Write a present tense verb to complete each sentence.

Example: Either Holly or Ted _____ golden hamsters. *has*

8. There _____ hamsters in the living room.
9. Either Holly or Ted _____ the hamsters.
10. There _____ sticks for the hamsters to chew.
11. Either hamster _____ at night.
12. Hamsters or gerbils _____ easily in a city.
13. Here _____ Holly's hamster.

■ Write a sentence beginning with each group of words below. Be sure that the verb in each sentence agrees with the subject.

Example: Roller skates or bicycles _____.
 Roller skates or bicycles make wonderful gifts.

14. Either skates or a bike _____.
15. There are _____.
16. Here is _____.
17. There is _____.

18. Neither my parents nor I _____.
19. Bikes, skates, or skateboards _____.
20. Here are _____.

(pages 150–152)

11 Contractions

Remember

- A **contraction** is the shortened form of two words. Dropped letters are replaced by an apostrophe.
- In contractions made with a verb and *not*, the *n't* is not part of the verb phrase.

● Write the contraction in each sentence.

Example: Don't you know the story about Isaac Newton? *Don't*

1. Didn't an apple fall on his head?
2. That's the way he discovered gravity.
3. He'd also studied sunlight.
4. It's made of the colors of the rainbow.
5. Haven't I shown you my prism?
6. It's hanging in a sunny window.

▲ Write each contraction. Then write the verb or verb phrase.

Example: Before 1758, people didn't understand comets.
   didn't did understand

7. Edmund Halley wasn't satisfied with the explanations.
8. He'd asked questions about the comet of 1682.
9. Weren't there old records of a similar comet?
10. Didn't it appear every seventy-five years?
11. Hadn't he predicted the return of the comet in 1758?
12. It's named Halley's Comet in his honor.

■ Write a contraction for the underlined words. If the sentence contains a verb phrase, write the verb phrase.

Example: I <u>have not</u> finished my report. *haven't have finished*

13. <u>It is</u> about a recent discovery by some scientists.
14. <u>They had</u> dived eight thousand feet underwater.
15. That far below the surface, <u>there is</u> no sunlight.
16. On the ocean floor, <u>they have</u> found hot springs.
17. They <u>did not</u> expect plants or animals down there.
18. <u>I have</u> read about the unusual creatures.

(pages 153–155)

12 *sit, set; lie, lay; rise, raise*

Remember

- Use the verbs *sit* and *lie* to refer to a resting position.
- Use the verbs *set* and *lay* to mean "put an object somewhere."
- Use the verb *rise* to mean "get or go up."
- Use the verb *raise* to mean "move something up, grow something, or increase something."

● Write the correct present tense verb for each sentence.

Example: When we go hiking, we (rise, raise) early. *rise*

1. The night before, we (sit, set) our packs by the door.
2. We (lie, lay) our boots and heavy socks there too.
3. We hike for several hours before we (sit, set) down for lunch.
4. Tired hikers (lie, lay) on the grass and rest.
5. Let's (rise, raise) the number of hikes we take.

▲ If the underlined word in each sentence is correct, write *correct.* If it is incorrect, write the word that should replace it. Use the words *sit, set; lie, lay;* and *rise, raise.*

Example: Your dog can <u>lay</u> on the blanket. *lie*

6. Let's <u>set</u> on a blanket and watch the football game.
7. <u>Set</u> the picnic basket over here.
8. Before the game, a student will <u>rise</u> the flag.
9. Will Tom play, or will he <u>sit</u> on the bench?
10. An injured player <u>lies</u> on the field.

■ Answer each question by writing a complete sentence containing one of the words in parentheses. You may change the tense of the word you choose.

Example: Where is your dog? (sit, set) *Butch is sitting on the couch.*

11. I can't hear John. What should he do? (rise, raise)
12. Where did you put the flashlight? (sit, set)
13. What crops does that farmer grow? (rise, raise)
14. I am very tired. What should I do? (lie, lay)
15. At what time will you get up tomorrow? (rise, raise)

(pages 156–158)

13 *lend, borrow; let, leave; teach, learn*

- *Borrow* means "to take temporarily." *Lend* means "to give temporarily."
- *Let* means "to permit." *Leave* means "to go away."
- *Teach* means "to give instruction." *Learn* means "to receive instruction."

● Write the correct word to complete each sentence.

Example: Anyone can (teach, learn) to type. *learn*

1. (Let, Leave) me show you how.
2. You can (lend, borrow) Dion's keyboard.
3. This book can (teach, learn) you more than I can.
4. Please turn off the lights when you (let, leave).
5. The class will (teach, learn) how to fix mistakes.
6. The teacher will (lend, borrow) any student a dictionary.

▲ If the underlined word in each sentence is correct, write *correct*. If it is incorrect, write the word that should replace it.

Example: Mr. Lopez will <u>learn</u> us typing. *teach*

7. The school will <u>borrow</u> computers from a store.
8. My father will <u>leave</u> me stay after school.
9. We will <u>learn</u> touch typing.
10. A local business will <u>lend</u> us computers.
11. I wish someone would <u>borrow</u> me one.
12. We must <u>let</u> the keyboards here.

■ Use one phrase from each pair in a written sentence.

Example: lend a red sweater; borrow a red sweater
Please lend me a red sweater until tomorrow.

13. borrow a math book; lend a math book
14. leave the players; let the players
15. teach me to; learn how to
16. learn a new skill; teach a new skill
17. let her shaggy dog; leave her shaggy dog
18. borrow your radio; lend your radio

Who is this curious sea creature, peering boldly from behind that peculiar mask?

Modifiers

Adjectives

Hatchet
GARY PAULSEN

How many adjectives can you find? What are they?

He was dirty and starving and bitten and hurt and lonely
and ugly and afraid and so completely miserable that it
was like being in a pit, a dark, deep pit with no way out.

—from *Hatchet,* by Gary Paulsen

- An **adjective** describes, or modifies, a noun or a pronoun. One adjective can change the meaning of a whole sentence.

  We take exciting trips. We take boring trips.

- Adjectives can tell *what kind, which one,* or *how many.*

HELP

Tip

To decide whether a word is used as an adjective, ask yourself whether it tells *what kind, which one,* or *how many.*

What kind	We climbed steep, rocky trails.
Which one(s)	Those hikers met at this stream.
How many	Several boys carried two canteens.

- Sometimes adjectives come before the noun they describe. At other times, adjectives follow the noun they describe.

  Three hungry and tired campers stumbled home.

  Children, cheerful and noisy, called to us.

- You know that a predicate adjective follows a linking verb. A predicate adjective describes the subject of a sentence.

  Nina felt sleepy. I was anxious to get home.

- An adjective may be more than one word. When such an adjective comes before a noun, it is usually hyphenated.

  I get paid weekly at my part-time job.

  We bought three-sided tents.

Speak Up Which words are adjectives?

1. Gene builds tiny, old-fashioned houses for dolls.
2. Most people think that they are attractive and unusual.
3. Some rooms, small and bright, are empty.
4. Little electric lights shine through clear windows.
5. This miniature house includes that fifty-year-old clock.

Summing Up

- An **adjective** describes, or modifies, a noun or a pronoun.
- An adjective can tell *what kind, which one,* or *how many.*

Write each adjective. Then write and underline the word it describes.

Example: That mountain bike is beautiful.
That, mountain, beautiful   <u>*bike*</u>

6. Two salespeople showed us this green bike.
7. Other stores are selling bikes with twenty-seven speeds.
8. Good bikes are expensive.
9. Prices are high at all stores.
10. These bikes, shiny and bright, have different features.
11. This bike has handlebars with good grips.
12. Padded seats are comfortable.
13. That model is popular with many people.
14. You can go long distances with little effort.
15. Does this tri-colored bike have thirty speeds?
16. Another bike, pretty and fast, has wide tires.
17. I am happy with this new model.

more ▶

18–40. This ad from a shoe company's Web site has twenty-three adjectives. Write each adjective. Then write and underline the word it describes. (Do not check for adjectives in the blue titles or in the brand name.)

Example: Buy these incredible new sneakers!
these, incredible, new <u>*sneakers*</u>

=== Web site ===

US
FOOTWINGS

Footwings Make Sore Feet Soar!

- Do you have sore feet?
- Do you have trouble keeping up with fast-moving friends?
- Do you feel weak and clumsy?

You're lucky. You've found US!

Buy one pair of US Footwings, and you'll never have aching feet again. These sneakers, soft and light, are miraculous. Those blistered, tired feet will turn into free-floating clouds. Limp into participating stores. Float out in bouncy new US Footwings. Whoosh past several slow friends. Glide around jealous passers-by. Those two feet will never feel clunky again!

Writing Wrap-Up
WRITING • THINKING • LISTENING • SPEAKING

PERSUADING

Write an Ad
What item have you been dreaming of? What would you like to see invented? a micro homework processor? an automatic room-cleaning device? Write an ad for the item of your dreams. Use lots of interesting adjectives. Convince your reader of the importance of your product. Find a partner, and take turns reading your ads. How do your ads compare?

For Extra Practice see page 223.

Writing with Adjectives

Elaborating Sentences Help your reader "see" exactly what you want by choosing precise adjectives to describe nouns. Although adjectives are often placed before nouns, you can vary their placement to make your sentences more interesting.

Adjectives tell *what kind, which one,* and *how many.*

Adjectives before the noun	Bob's Bike Shop has three purple off-road bikes for sale.
Adjectives after the noun	Bob, helpful and friendly, knows a lot about bikes.

Apply It

1–7. Help the writer of this catalog page elaborate this description. Add adjectives to modify each underlined noun. Use what you already know about bicycles and details from the pictures.

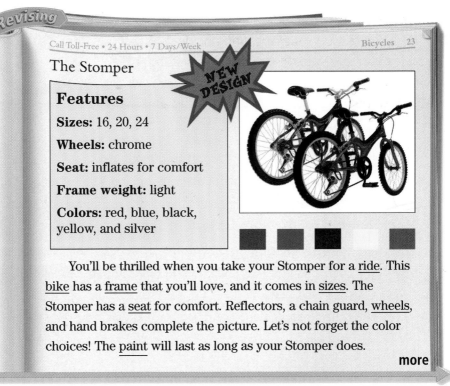

Revising

Call Toll-Free • 24 Hours • 7 Days/Week Bicycles 23

The Stomper

NEW DESIGN

Features

Sizes: 16, 20, 24

Wheels: chrome

Seat: inflates for comfort

Frame weight: light

Colors: red, blue, black, yellow, and silver

You'll be thrilled when you take your Stomper for a <u>ride</u>. This <u>bike</u> has a <u>frame</u> that you'll love, and it comes in <u>sizes</u>. The Stomper has a <u>seat</u> for comfort. Reflectors, a chain guard, <u>wheels</u>, and hand brakes complete the picture. Let's not forget the color choices! The <u>paint</u> will last as long as your Stomper does.

more

Combining Sentences As you revise your writing, see if you can combine details from different sentences to make a single sentence. Remember that you can change many other words into adjectives by using the endings *-y, -ed,* and *-ing.* This can make your writing more concise.

Too wordy
Internet auctions are fast.
They are also full of excitement.

More concise
Internet auctions are fast and exciting.

Apply It

8–12. Revise this draft of an Internet auction ad. Combine the details in each set of sentences to make a single sentence.

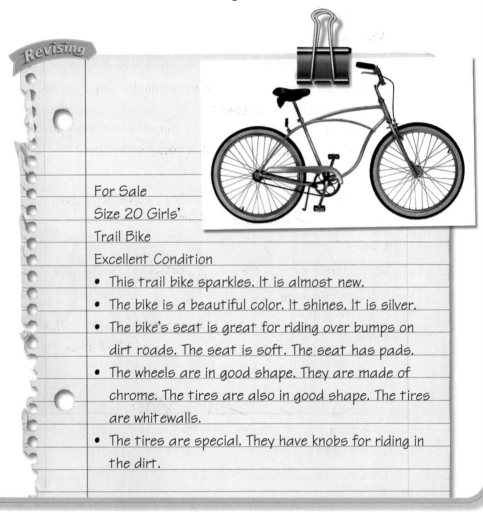

Revising

For Sale

Size 20 Girls'

Trail Bike

Excellent Condition

- This trail bike sparkles. It is almost new.
- The bike is a beautiful color. It shines. It is silver.
- The bike's seat is great for riding over bumps on dirt roads. The seat is soft. The seat has pads.
- The wheels are in good shape. They are made of chrome. The tires are also in good shape. The tires are whitewalls.
- The tires are special. They have knobs for riding in the dirt.

2 Articles and Demonstratives

Which words belong in a group with *this, those, these,* and *an?* Which come before proper nouns?

By that time, the Dutch had built a string of windmills from the Battery to Park Row.

—from *The Wind at Work: An Activity Guide to Windmills,* by Gretchen Woelfle

- The words *a, an,* and *the* are special adjectives. They are called **articles**. An article can come before a noun or before another adjective.

  The ball hit an old shed.

  A window was broken.

  A girl told the owner she was sorry.

- *The* refers to a specific item. It can be used with singular nouns *(the dog)* or plural nouns *(the cats).* A or *an* refers to any one item. Use *a* before words that begin with a consonant sound *(a country, a helicopter, a knee).* Use *an* before words that begin with a vowel sound *(an elephant, an ankle, an hour).*

- Adjectives that tell *which one* are called **demonstrative adjectives**. They point out a specific person, place, or thing.

  This book is better than that magazine.

  These stories are more interesting than those articles.

  That store sells all of those newspapers.

- *This* and *these* point out people, places, or things that are nearby. *That* and *those* point out people, places, or things that are farther away. Study the following chart.

Demonstrative Adjectives		
Singular	this	that
Plural	these	those

Speak Up Which word in parentheses correctly completes each sentence?

1. (A, The) windmill in our back yard is very old.
2. (A, The) blades still turn in (a, an) unusually strong wind.
3. (This, These) form of energy has been replaced by newer forms.
4. (That, Those) new forms create more power.

Summing Up

- *A, an,* and *the* are special adjectives called **articles**. *The* refers to a specific item or items. *A* or *an* refers to any one item in a group.
- **Demonstrative adjectives** tell *which one*. Use *this* and *these* for things nearby. Use *that* and *those* for things farther away.

Write the article or demonstrative adjective that completes each sentence correctly.

Example: I saw (a, an) amazing painting in the museum.   *an*

5. What (a, the) wonderful display this museum presented!
6. Many of (the, a) paintings show no people.
7. Do you know (this, these) artist's work?
8. Edward Hopper is (a, an) admired American painter.
9. He enjoyed painting (a, the) city streets of New York.
10. I saw Hopper's work in (the, a) Museum of Modern Art.
11. (This, That) painting over there is haunting.
12. (The, An) empty cafeterias and movie lobbies look odd.

more ▶

13. (These, Those) people in the painting over there seem lonely.
14. Hopper often uses (a, an) harsh light in his paintings.
15. Of (these, those) three paintings here, I like this one best.

16–28. This part of a letter has thirteen incorrect articles or demonstrative adjectives. Write the letter correctly.

Example: I'm painting an picture of this flowers.
I'm painting a picture of these flowers.

Proofreading

We've been in the Netherlands for a entire week now, and that country is great! I had read about a Dutch tulips, but seeing hundreds of this flowers is amazing. I'm holding an red tulip now, and that single flower is an amazing thing.

Do you remember this book we liked, with pictures of windmills? Well, that windmills were just like the ones here. I want to paint all those beautiful sights I'm seeing. I've started an painting of a old windmill and another of an tulip garden. I think this paintings will be my best work ever!

Writing Wrap-Up WRITING • THINKING • LISTENING • SPEAKING

DESCRIBING

Write a Letter

Close your eyes, and picture a place you really enjoyed seeing—a park, a mountain, a special house, a new city. Write a letter to a friend, and describe that favorite place. Be sure to tell why you enjoyed it so much. Find a partner, and read your letters to each other. Are your favorite places similar or different?

3 Comparing with Adjectives

What's wrong with the wording of this riddle? How can you fix it?

What's fastest—hot or cold?

Hot is more fast. You can always catch cold.

- You can use adjectives to compare two or more people, places, things, and ideas.

  John is hungrier than I am.

  You made the wisest choice.

  Ms. Rosa is the friendliest teacher.

- To compare two things, use the **comparative** form of the adjective. Add -er to one-syllable and some two-syllable adjectives to form the comparative. To compare three or more things, use the **superlative** form of the adjective. Add -est to one-syllable and some two-syllable adjectives to form the superlative.

  Comparative: I am taller than Cedric. *(two things compared)*

  Superlative: Peter is the tallest of all. *(more than two compared)*

- Sometimes the spelling of an adjective changes when you add -er or -est to form the comparative or the superlative.

Spelling Changes in Comparative and Superlative			
Adjectives ending in e: Drop the e and add -er or -est.	large	larger	largest
	nice	nicer	nicest
Adjectives ending in a consonant preceded by a single vowel: Double the final consonant and add -er or -est.	flat	flatter	flattest
	sad	sadder	saddest
	big	bigger	biggest
Adjectives ending in a consonant + y: Change the y to i and add -er or -est.	busy	busier	busiest
	happy	happier	happiest
	silly	sillier	silliest

Speak Up What are the comparative and superlative forms of each adjective?

1. old   3. fat   5. hungry
2. thin   4. cute

Summing Up

- Use the **comparative** form *(-er)* of an adjective to compare two people, places, things, or ideas.

- Use the **superlative** form *(-est)* to compare three or more.

- Sometimes the spelling of an adjective changes when *-er* or *-est* is added.

Write the form of the adjective in parentheses that correctly completes each sentence.

Example: Is a cheetah _____ than a horse? (fast) *faster*

6. Where is the _____ place in the world? (wet)
7. Is Spanish _____ for English speakers than Russian is? (easy)
8. What is the _____ building in the world? (tall)
9. Are blue whales _____ than right whales? (large)
10. Are animals _____ in the fall or in the spring? (hungry)
11. Do you feel _____ in the city or in the wild? (safe)
12. What conditions produce the _____ sunsets of all? (red)
13. What is the _____ river in North America? (long)
14. Is the Nile the world's _____ river? (wide)
15. Is the sailfish the _____ creature in the ocean? (fast)
16. Are there hiking trails on the _____ side of Mount Washington? (steep)
17. Is Earth the _____ planet? (small)

more ▶

18–28. This list of almanac facts has eleven incorrect adjective forms. Write the list correctly.

Example: Rhode Island is the smaller of the fifty states.

Rhode Island is the smallest of the fifty states.

Proofreading

Encyclopedia

Interact with the Facts

- The brighter star we can see is called the Dog Star.
- Arizona is dryer than India and weter than Egypt.
- The mountain K2 is highest than Denali but lower than Everest.
- China has the largeest population of any country.
- Australia is coldest in July than in January.
- Some of the hotest temperatures occur in Death Valley.
- Death Valley is also the lower place in the Americas.
- Alaska is largest than Texas. It's the biggest state of all.
- John F. Kennedy was the younger elected president.
- The bee hummingbird is the smaller bird in the world.

ALASKA

Writing Wrap-Up

WRITING • THINKING • LISTENING • SPEAKING

COMPARING / CONTRASTING

Write Almanac Facts

What facts do you know about your personal world? Is one short-cut to school faster than another? Is one flavor of juice sweeter than another? Is another class in your school larger than yours? Write a list of ten facts, important or trivial, serious or funny. Use adjectives with *-er* and *-est*. Find a partner, and take turns reading your facts. Did you both use adjectives correctly?

For Extra Practice see page 225.

4 Comparing with *more* and *most*

What's wrong with this riddle? How would you fix it?

Which is the fruit with the most saddest moods?
Blueberries

- You already know that you add *-er* or *-est* to one-syllable adjectives to form the comparative or superlative. You form the comparative and superlative of most two-syllable adjectives and all adjectives of three or more syllables by adding the words *more* and *most*.

Adjective	Comparative	Superlative
honest	more honest	most honest
dangerous	more dangerous	most dangerous
plentiful	more plentiful	most plentiful
healthy	more healthy	most healthy
comfortable	more comfortable	most comfortable

- Be sure not to combine *-er* with the word *more* or *-est* with the word *most*.

Incorrect: Peaches are <u>more sweeter</u> than lemons.
Correct: Peaches are sweeter than lemons.

Incorrect: This is the <u>most freshest</u> fish in the market.
Correct: This is the freshest fish in the market.

- When you compare things that are less rather than more, use *less* for the comparative and *least* for the superlative.

Grapes are less hearty than bananas.
Are cantaloupes Jake's least favorite fruit of all?

Peppers are less expensive than mushrooms.
Potatoes are the least expensive of all.

Comparing with *more* and *most*   **191**

- A few adjectives are irregular. They have different forms to show the comparative and superlative.

Adjective	Comparative	Superlative
much, many	more	most
little	less	least
good	better	best
bad	worse	worst

Try It Out

Speak Up What are the comparative and superlative forms of each adjective?

1. jealous
2. attractive
3. comfortable
4. generous
5. pleasant
6. comical

Summing Up

- Use *more* or *less* to form the comparative and *most* or *least* to form the superlative of most two-syllable adjectives and all adjectives of three or more syllables.

- Some adjectives have different forms in the comparative and superlative.

On Your Own

Write the form of the adjective in parentheses that correctly completes each sentence.

Example: Today's weather is _____ than yesterday's. (bad)   *worse*

7. Rubies are _____ than diamonds. (colorful)
8. In this state the _____ rain falls in August. (little)

more ▶

9. Is the Library of Congress the world's _____ library? (good)
10. The food at the picnic was _____ than last week. (bad)
11. Are mules _____ than donkeys? (stubborn)
12. Do firefighters have the _____ job? (dangerous)
13. Texas has _____ rainfall than Arizona. (much)
14. Traffic seems _____ on Tuesdays than on Fridays. (good)

15–22. These quiz show questions have eight incorrect adjective forms. Write the questions correctly.

Example: Which city has the more museums?
Which city has the most museums?

Proofreading

Quiz ? Quest

- Where do the mostest rain and the least rain fall?
- What is the most commonest word in English?
- What was the most bad storm of the 1900s?
- Which city has most tourists—Paris or Rome?
- Is the poodle a popularer dog than the collie?
- Who won the Academy Award for bestest actor in 1999?
- Is the lion or the tiger most endangered?
- Which country grows lesser rice—Japan or Thailand?

Writing Wrap-Up WRITING • THINKING • LISTENING • SPEAKING

Write Questions

What do you know? Are you curious to learn how to fly a kite? the number of windows on a bus? Write five questions of fact that use adjective comparisons with *more, most, less,* and *least.* Then take turns asking a partner your questions. Which questions inspire you and your partner to find the answer?

5 Proper Adjectives

Which word is a proper noun? Which word is made from another proper noun? What proper noun is it formed from?

First, we recovered Roman artifacts off the coast of southern Italy.

—from *Talking with Adventurers*, edited by Linda and Pat Cummings

- An adjective formed from a proper noun is called a **proper adjective**. Like a proper noun, a proper adjective is capitalized.

   Here is a Mexican silver bracelet.
   His Australian hat is made of leather.
   Did you go to the Hawaiian luau?

- The endings most often used to change proper nouns into proper adjectives are *-an, -ish,* and *-ese.* Notice the other spelling changes when the ending is added.

Proper Noun	Ending	Proper Adjective
Ireland Britain Poland	-ish	Irish seacoast British accent Polish song
Italy Brazil Canada	-an	Italian painting Brazilian leather Canadian money
Japan China Vietnam	-ese	Japanese food Chinese language Vietnamese poem

- You will find other spelling changes in proper adjectives too.

   French cooking is popular in countries other than France.
   Norwegian sweaters are famous outside of Norway.

Speak Up What proper adjective is formed from each underlined noun? Give each phrase.

1. ruins of <u>Rome</u>
2. pottery from <u>Mexico</u>
3. dances of <u>Poland</u>
4. hotels of <u>Europe</u>
5. imports from <u>China</u>
6. pyramids in <u>Egypt</u>
7. provinces of <u>Canada</u>
8. settlers from <u>England</u>
9. cars from <u>France</u>
10. cheese from <u>Denmark</u>
11. wool from <u>Iceland</u>
12. rivers of <u>Sweden</u>

Summing Up

- A **proper adjective** is an adjective formed from a proper noun.
- A proper adjective begins with a capital letter.

Write the proper adjective in each sentence. Remember to capitalize it.

Example: Some alaskan dogs are used to pull sleds. *Alaskan*

13. The dachshund, a german breed, was used to hunt badgers.
14. An english sheepdog has a long, shaggy coat.
15. Pictures of greyhounds were found on the walls of ancient egyptian temples.
16. The pug is a chinese breed that has a snub nose.
17. The australian dingo is a wild dog.
18. Our neighbors own an irish setter pup.
19. This spaniel looks like the dogs on japanese vases.
20. An afghan hound has long, silky fur.
21. The scottish terrier was originally bred to hunt woodchucks.
22. Some breeds, such as the boston terrier, are born with short tails.

more ▶

23–30. This part of a menu has eight underlined phrases. Each phrase has a proper noun. Write the underlined phrase, changing the proper noun to a proper adjective.

Example: A delicious <u>meat dish from Cuba</u>   *Cuban meat dish*

Menu
A Taste of the World

Starters
- A <u>salad from Korea</u> with cabbage and hot spices
- Pickled fish and onions, a <u>starter from Sweden</u>
- Shrimp with cocktail sauce, a <u>favorite in America</u>

Main
- Macaroni with <u>cheddar cheese from England</u>
- Sweet <u>sausages from Italy</u> in olive oil and garlic
- Stir-fried beef in the <u>style of Japan</u>
- A <u>sauce from Mexico</u> on fresh fish from the sea

Ending
- Cheesecake topped with <u>pineapple from Hawaii</u>

Writing Wrap-Up WRITING • THINKING • LISTENING • SPEAKING

CREATING

Write a Recipe
Invent a recipe that will make mouths water or smile. Include some ingredients that you have personally experienced. First, list the ingredients. Then write the step-by-step instructions. Use at least five proper adjectives. Read your recipe to a classmate. Then work together to check for correct capitalization.

   For Extra Practice see page 227.

6 Adverbs

What did Tom shout? *How* did he shout it?
What else could Tom say, and how could he say it?

"Fire!" shouted Tom alarmingly.

An **adverb** is a word that modifies a verb, an adjective, or another adverb. Adverbs that modify verbs answer these questions: *How? Where? When?* Many such adverbs end in *-ly*.

How:	Alma left quickly.
Where:	She arrived there.
When:	Then she returned.

HELP ? Tip

When you are looking for the adverb, ask *How? Where?* or *When?* about the verb, the adjective, or the adverb.

Try It Out

Speak Up Find the adverbs and the verbs they modify.

1. Yesterday we packed.
2. I enjoyed our trip immensely.
3. Mom drove carefully and well.
4. Dad always checked the maps.
5. We usually headed north.
6. Finally, we arrived safely.

Summing Up

- An **adverb** can modify a verb, an adjective, or another adverb. Many such adverbs end in *-ly*.
- An adverb that modifies a verb usually tells *how, where,* or *when.*

Write each adverb. Then write and underline the word it modifies.

Example: We enjoyed the natural beauty of Georgia immensely.
immensely, enjoyed

7. First, we toured a wildlife refuge in southeastern Georgia.
8. The Okefenokee Swamp attracts thousands of visitors annually.
9. We camped at Lake Lanier Islands next.
10. Then we drove south to the peanut farms.

11–22. This part of a science textbook has twelve adverbs. Write each adverb. Then write and underline the verb or verb phrase it modifies.

Example: Peanuts are grown oddly. *Peanuts are grown oddly.*

How Peanuts Grow

Farmers must plow the rich soil deeply. The loose soil helps the life process of a peanut. Peanut seeds are planted at about four-inch intervals. The peanut plant blossoms continuously for two or three months. The flowers wither gradually. Their stems turn downward. Next, they slowly but steadily enter the ground. There they form seed pods. Farmers carefully harvest the pods. All the pods must be fully ripened. Then the sun dries the pods naturally.

Writing Wrap-Up

WRITING • THINKING • LISTENING • SPEAKING

EXPLAINING

Write a How-To

Think of something you have watched grow: a plant, a building, your younger brother. Write a paragraph or two telling the steps in the growing. What did you observe at each step? Use adverbs. You may want to sketch the changes you saw. Read your work to a small group of classmates.

7 More About Adverbs

Which word tells how successful Mr. Goodridge was? What other words could replace this word in the sentence?

William C. Goodridge became a highly successful York businessman.

—from *Black Artists in Photography, 1840–1940,* by George Sullivan

When an adverb modifies an adjective or another adverb, it usually tells *to what extent.*

    adj.   adv.

A **very** large crowd gathered **quite** quickly.

Try It Out

Speak Up What word does each underlined adverb modify?

1. a <u>terribly</u> long way
2. <u>completely</u> safe elevator
3. reads <u>quite</u> carefully
4. <u>very</u> realistic dreams
5. writes <u>extremely</u> well
6. sings <u>very</u> beautifully
7. smiles <u>so</u> happily
8. stands <u>incredibly</u> proudly
9. burns <u>less</u> brightly

Summing Up

- Adverbs that modify adjectives or other adverbs usually tell *to what extent.*

Write each underlined adverb. Then write the word it modifies, and label it *adjective* or *adverb*.

Example: The photographer was <u>very</u> happy.   *very, happy   adjective*

10. She looked <u>very</u> thoroughly at all of her pictures.
11. One photograph had <u>especially</u> bright colors.
12. A beautiful sea scene <u>rather</u> suddenly caught her eye.
13. She thought <u>quite</u> carefully about each photograph.
14. Ms. Ramos wanted to win an <u>extremely</u> important photo contest.

15–20. These captions from a photo album have six adverbs underlined. Write each underlined adverb. Then write the word it modifies, and label it *adjective* or *adverb*.

Example: Scott looks <u>completely</u> radiant.
    completely, radiant   adjective

Andy is posing <u>very</u> carefully for the photographer.

Quite clearly, the camera caught the moment <u>extremely</u> well.

This <u>really</u> orange sunset was <u>absolutely</u> incredible!

The sky was becoming <u>quite</u> dark here.

Writing Wrap-Up   WRITING • THINKING • LISTENING • SPEAKING

REFLECTING

Write Captions

What experiences in your life do you want to remember? Draw or cut out pictures to capture those memories. For each image, write a caption. Tell why the event is important to you. Include adverbs modifying adjectives and other adverbs. Read your work to a partner, and ask which detail is most vivid.

Writing with Adverbs

Elaborating Sentences Adverbs help create a picture in the reader's mind. When you use adverbs to modify verbs, adjectives, or other adverbs, you add elaboration to your writing. Remember that you can vary the placement of adverbs.

Adverb modifying a verb	Tammy focuses her camera carefully.
Adverb modifying an adverb	Stay absolutely still while she takes your picture.
Adverb modifying an adjective	This park, especially beautiful in the spring, will make a lovely setting for this photograph.

Apply It

1–6. Help the caption writer elaborate these descriptions. Add an adverb to modify each underlined word. Use details from the photographs.

Middle School Photography Club
Photo Contest

Raymond,
<u>determined</u>
to win the
race, keeps on
swimming.

The <u>curious</u> dog
<u>digs</u> in the yard.

The <u>colorful</u> hot-air balloons
rose <u>quietly</u> into the air.

Baby Rebecca
slept <u>soundly</u>
in Grandma's
arms.

more

Combining Sentences When you revise your writing, check to see if you gave separate details in separate sentences. Try combining these sentences to make one elaborated sentence. Sometimes it helps to change an adjective to its adverb form when you do this.

Too wordy

The photograph showed the science lab. The photo was clear. Mrs. Green worked in the lab. She looked busy. She worked with care.

More concise

The photograph clearly showed the science lab. Mrs. Green worked busily and carefully in the lab.

Apply It

7–12. Revise this draft of an essay. Combine each pair of underlined sentences, using adverbs.

Remember that many, but not all, words can be made into adverbs by adding the ending -ly.

Revising | **Essay**

If I can borrow a camera, I'll take a picture of Mrs. Green, our science teacher. Mrs. Green always speaks softly. She sounds happy. I can tell that she likes teaching very much. She likes to help students. That is obvious. She assists everyone who needs her. Mrs. Green encourages us to ask thoughtful questions. Her encouragement is constant.

In class Mrs. Green presents science problems to us in a very clear way. Then we discuss the problems and try to solve them. She helps us. She is quiet.

Mrs. Green has changed the way we study science. Because of her we know how to work. We work with confidence. Her influence on us goes beyond science. She inspires us to learn and to have fun. Her inspiration is unfailing. She is an outstanding teacher!

8 Comparing with Adverbs

What do you think will happen in this race? Compare how the runners will run. Use adverbs such as *slowly, speedily, fast, quickly,* and *skillfully.*

- Like adjectives, adverbs can be used to make comparisons. To compare two actions, use the comparative form *(-er).* To compare more than two actions, use the superlative form *(-est).*

  Comparative: Dan arrived later than Sidney.

  Superlative: I arrived latest of all.

- If the adverb ends with *-ly,* add *more,* or *most* to make comparisons.

Adverb	Comparative	Superlative
skillfully	more skillfully	most skillfully
frequently	more frequently	most frequently
heavily	more heavily	most heavily

- When you compare actions or qualities that are less rather than more, use *less* to form the comparative and *least* for the superlative.

  Dan rows less often than Lian does.

  Their coach complains least often of all.

- Do not combine the *-er* ending with the word *more* or the *-est* ending with the word *most.*

  Incorrect: Lian rows more straighter than Dan.

  Correct: Lian rows straighter than Dan.

  Incorrect: Of all the crew, she worked most hardest.

  Correct: Of all the crew, she worked hardest.

- Some adverbs have irregular forms of comparison.

Adverb	Comparative	Superlative
well	better	best
badly	worse	worst
little	less	least
much	more	most

Try It Out

Speak Up Give comparative and superlative forms.

1. loudly
2. easily
3. little
4. bravely
5. badly
6. well

- Add -er to form the comparative and -est to form the superlative of many adverbs.
- If the adverb ends with -ly, add *more* or *less* to form the comparative and *most* or *least* to form the superlative.
- Some adverbs have irregular forms of comparison.

On Your Own

Write the adverb that correctly completes each sentence.

Example: Jay speaks (better, more better) than Ian onstage. *better*

7. Our cast rehearsed (more hard, harder) than last week.
8. Ian remembers his lines (more easily, easier) than Jill does.
9. We liked Oscar (less, least) of all the speakers.

more ▶

10. We performed (worse, more worse) today than yesterday.
11. Of all the students, Antonia worked (hardest, harder).
12. Unfortunately, Alex performed (worstest, worst) of all today.

13–20. This part of a character sketch has eight incorrect adverb forms. Write the sketch correctly.

Example: Grandpa visits us more oftener now than in the past.
Grandpa visits us more often now than in the past.

Grandpa's Craft

Grandpa is a small man, but he speaks more louder and more deeply than most large men. With his big voice, he tells stories best than anyone else. I listen more happily to tales about his boyhood. He builds up suspense more skillfullier than a mystery writer does. Would his pet frog jump more higher than his friend Gus's frog? While he's telling this tale, I think most about that long-ago frog than about my own cat lying on my lap. I like Grandpa's modern stories least than his old ones. Still, of all our family storytellers, he always tells his stories goodest.

WRITING • THINKING • LISTENING • SPEAKING

Writing Wrap-Up

DESCRIBING

Write a Character Sketch

Write a brief character sketch, describing how someone in your life does something—kicks a ball, cooks, tells a joke, or sings, for example. Let your reader know your character as well as you do. Use comparisons with adverbs. Read your sketch to a small group. Do you need to correct any adverb forms?

9 Negatives

Double negatives are a no-no.

Can you explain why this joke is funny?

Teacher: Give me an example of a double negative.
Student: I don't know none.
Teacher: Right!

- Some modifiers or other words mean "no" or "not." A word that means "no" is called a **negative**. A negative can reverse the meaning of a sentence.

  Sheldon is on the team.   Sheldon is not on the team.

- Some of the most common negatives are *no, none, not, no one, never, nothing, nowhere,* and *nobody.* The *n't* in a contraction is also a negative.

  Don never mows the lawn.   Sid couldn't go with us.

- Do not use two negatives to express one negative idea. Two negatives used together are called a **double negative**.

  Incorrect: I can't find nothing to wear.

  Correct: I can find nothing to wear.

  Correct: I can't find anything to wear.

- The example above shows that you can avoid a double negative by dropping *not (n't).* You can also substitute a positive word for a negative word. In the last sentence, *nothing* was changed to *anything.* Most negative words have matching positive words.

Negative	Positive
nothing	anything
neither	either
never	ever
nobody	anybody
no	any
none	some

Speak Up Which word in parentheses makes each sentence negative?

1. We will (ever, never) be ready for this storm.
2. This flashlight has (no, some) batteries.
3. (Someone, No one) has gone to the store this week.
4. Batteries are (nowhere, everywhere) to be found.
5. These wax candles (never, always) fail.

Summing Up

- A **negative** is a word that means "no" or "not."
- Avoid using a **double negative**, two negatives together.

Write the word or words in parentheses that complete each sentence correctly.

Example: Carl hadn't read (nothing, anything) about the Inca. *anything*

6. (Nobody, Anybody) had told Carl about the Inca empire.
7. This South American empire doesn't exist (anymore, no more).
8. The civilization (hasn't, has) never disappeared entirely, though.
9. Nobody could (never, ever) wipe out their customs.
10. Nobody knows (nothing, anything) definite about their early history.
11. The Inca never made (no, any) decision without careful thought.
12. The Inca (had, hadn't) no system of money.
13. They didn't have a system of writing (neither, either).
14. Carl (couldn't, could) hardly wait to find more information about the Inca civilization.

more ▶

On Your Own continued

15–24. This part of an online interview has ten incorrect negatives. Write the interview correctly.

Example: Nothing isn't really known about the Inca before 1438.
Nothing is really known about the Inca before 1438.

Interview ▢ ▤

 **CYBER CHAT**

Interviewer: Nobody doesn't know more about the Inca than Dr. Ruiz. Weren't the Inca a large group, Dr. Ruiz?

Dr. R.: No. They weren't no larger than other groups until 1438. Then they expanded. By 1532 the empire stretched out over two thousand miles. History may not never have seen a faster growth.

Int.: There wasn't nothing important about that year, was there?

Dr. R.: Yes. The Spanish invaded. The Inca couldn't never win against them.

Int.: Didn't none of the Inca survive?

Dr. R.: Yes, some did survive. Their descendants make up about half of Peru. In some mountain villages, nothing hasn't changed much. Actually, under the emperor, people couldn't go nowhere or do nothing without permission. That's not true no more, of course.

Writing Wrap-Up   WRITING • THINKING • LISTENING • SPEAKING

Write an Interview

Think of something you know or do well. It could be a hobby, a report topic, a TV show, a job. Write at least five questions that an interviewer might ask you as an expert on this subject. Include a negative in at least three questions. Then ask a classmate to interview you, reading your questions aloud to you. Answer the questions briefly. Then interview your partner, using his or her questions.

10 Adjective or Adverb?

What's wrong with these sentences? How can you fix them?

Shayla usually plays soccer good. She hurt her elbow bad yesterday, though, and today she isn't moving quick.

• Sometimes it is easy to confuse adjectives and adverbs. When an adjective and an adverb are similar, you can usually tell which is the adverb because it ends in -ly.

Adjective	Adverb
slow	slowly
quick	quickly
bad	badly
sweet	sweetly

HELP Tips

• Adjectives tell *what kind, which one,* or *how many.*
• Adverbs tell *how, where,* or *when.*

• Remember that adjectives modify nouns and pronouns. Adverbs modify verbs, adjectives, and other adverbs.

Incorrect: We walked quick through the leaves.

Correct: We walked quickly through the leaves.

• The words *good* and *well* are sometimes confused. *Good* is an adjective. It modifies a noun or a pronoun.

It is a good day to take pictures.

Carly's pictures are always good.

She feels good about her work.

• *Well* is usually used as an adverb. However, when *well* means "healthy," it is an adjective and modifies a noun or a pronoun.

Adverb: I played baseball well.

Adjective: I didn't feel well when I awoke. *(I wasn't healthy.)*

Speak Up Choose the word in parentheses that completes each sentence correctly.

1. The band played (loud, loudly).
2. They marched (bad, badly), however.
3. People waved (wild, wildly) from windows.
4. The hero was a (good, well) football player.
5. The quarterback spoke (good, well).
6. He received (great, greatly) praise.
7. The hero thanked everyone (polite, politely).
8. Later hundreds of people departed (slow, slowly) for home.
9. The events of the day had gone (good, well).

Summing Up

- Use adjectives to modify nouns and pronouns.
- Use adverbs to modify verbs, adjectives, and other adverbs.
- *Good* is an adjective. *Well* is an adjective only when it means "healthy." Otherwise, *well* is an adverb.

Write the word in parentheses that completes each sentence correctly. Then label the word *adjective* or *adverb*.

Example: That was a (good, well) story.   *good   adjective*

10. The author wrote (good, well) about an interesting character.
11. The heroine was a (good, well) leader.
12. She played her part (good, well) in the complicated plot.
13. The author planned the plot (careful, carefully).
14. He did not write the book (quick, quickly).
15. Creating such a work is not (simple, simply).
16. He must feel (proud, proudly) of his accomplishment.

more ▶

17–28. This part of a social studies report has twelve incorrect adjectives or adverbs. Write the report correctly.

Example: Joan of Arc showed tremendously skill in battle.
Joan of Arc showed tremendous skill in battle.

Proofreading

A French Hero

In 1428 Joan of Arc was about sixteen. The French army was losing slow to the English. She went quick to the aid of France. At first the French prince did not take her serious. She behaved too strange, he thought. Eventually, she commanded a group of French soldiers. They fought good and won an important battle. Joan acted brave. Her cause was well, she believed. In the end, though, the king treated her bad. She was given an unfairly trial. Joan defended herself good, but she was sentenced to death. She showed greatly courage at the end. Today the French treat her memory very respectful. She is a true national hero.

Writing Wrap-Up

WRITING • THINKING • LISTENING • SPEAKING

EXPRESSING

Write a Letter

What makes a hero? Is every hero like Joan of Arc? Give an example of what you believe it takes to be a true hero. Write your ideas in a letter to your school or town newspaper. Use *good, well, bad, badly* as well as other adjectives and adverbs. Find a classmate, and take turns reading your letters. Compare your examples of heroes.

Choosing Different Adjectives and Adverbs

Make sure you use exact adjectives and adverbs to make your writing lively and your meaning clear.

It rained lightly and a gentle wind whispered in his ear.

It rained heavily and a howling wind nearly knocked him over.

Apply It

1–10. Rewrite this story using adjectives and adverbs from the box.

loudly	easily	deafening	excitedly	dim
shadowy	distant	sheer	rapidly	hurried

Revising

The Kansas Storm

It began with the _____ sound of thunder. I saw the _____ swirl of a tornado in the distance. "Look, Mom," I said _____, pointing to the window. Looking through the _____ curtain, she _____ saw it. Then, as the wind roared in our ears, she said _____, "We'd better go downstairs." I took another _____ look at the tornado moving _____ toward us.

Later, as we sat in the shelter listening to the _____ storm, my brother and I made shapes with our hands on the _____ walls. Soon the storm had passed right by us.

Enrichment

Modifiers!

Haiku

A haiku is a poem that has three lines and seventeen syllables. The first line has five syllables, the second line seven, and the third line five. Write a haiku about something in nature. Look through magazines for ideas, or just look out your window. Use adjectives and adverbs in your haiku. Underline the adjectives in red and the adverbs in blue.

A feathery weed
pushes up through the sidewalk—
so fragile, so strong.

Movie Ad

Design a full-page newspaper ad for a movie. It can be a real movie or one you make up. On white paper write the title in big letters. Then draw a picture to illustrate it. Next, write five favorable statements by reviewers of your movie. Include adjectives and adverbs. Have some of your adverbs modify adjectives—for example, *very exciting.* Write adjectives in red and adverbs in blue.

Challenge Not everyone has the same taste in movies. Write an unfavorable review of the movie you advertised or another movie. Use negative words and the comparative and superlative forms of adjectives and adverbs.

1 **Adjectives** *(p. 180)* Write the adjectives. (Do not include *a, an,* or *the*.) Then write the word that each adjective describes.

1. Aleika is popular at parties.
2. She is a one-woman band.
3. She plays a small drum.
4. She plays two huge, flat cymbals.
5. She gives concerts, large and small.

2 **Articles and Demonstratives** *(p. 185)* Write the correct articles and demonstrative adjectives.

6. Do you own (a, an) poodle or (a, an) Irish setter?
7. I have (a, an) old mutt that is (a, an) wonderful friend to me.
8. (This, These) gray poodle is Jo's.
9. Did (the, an) dog win (a, an) award?
10. (Those, That) setters won in (the, a) annual competition.

3 **Comparing with Adjectives** *(p. 188)* Write each sentence, using the comparative or superlative form of the adjective in parentheses.

11. The _____ game was better than the earlier one. (late)
12. Even our _____ player scored. (weak)
13. It was the _____ game of all. (short)
14. It was also the _____ day of the year. (hot)
15. This season was _____ for us than last season. (happy)

4 **Comparing with *more* and *most*** *(p. 191)* Write each sentence, using the comparative or superlative form of the adjective in parentheses.

16. Is this show the town's _____ entertainment? (good)
17. Which is the _____ camera of all? (expensive)
18. This old model is _____ than an instant camera. (bad)
19. One of the _____ of all books is *Tom Sawyer.* (popular)
20. Are rubies _____ than diamonds? (valuable)
21. Do apples have _____ vitamin C than oranges do? (much)
22. Which fruit has the _____ vitamin C of all? (little)

5 **Proper Adjectives** *(p. 194)* Write a proper adjective for the proper noun in parentheses.

23. (China) vase
24. (Spain) lace
25. (Africa) art
26. (Italy) food
27. (Mexico) fan
28. (Egypt) river
29. (Russia) caves
30. (Brazil) dance
31. (Asia) travel
32. (India) culture
33. (Ireland) crafts
34. (Scotland) wool
35. (Greece) hotel
36. (Hawaii) bird
37. (Finland) aunt

 Go to www.eduplace.com/tales/hme for more fun with parts of speech.

6 Adverbs (p. 197) Write each adverb and the verb it modifies in these sentences.

38. The week passed slowly.
39. Lou waited patiently.
40. He often visits the zoo.
41. Today he ran there.
42. First, he saw the lions.
43. He usually watches carefully.
44. Then Lou studied the polar bears.
45. The bears stared back at him.
46. One bear dived deep into the pool.
47. She swam underwater playfully.
48. Lou observed peacocks next.
49. Their colorful tails spread wide.

7 More About Adverbs (p. 199) Write each adverb that modifies an adjective or another adverb.

50. Lou watched the very playful birds.
51. One bird was remarkably graceful.
52. Lou sat especially quietly.
53. His movements were extremely cautious.
54. The bird sang quite beautifully.
55. The zoo offers a completely realistic safari ride.
56. The fare is rather inexpensive.
57. Lou chose an incredibly good seat.
58. The tour guide spoke really well.
59. Herds grazed freely in absolutely quiet areas.

8 Comparing with Adverbs (p. 203) Write each sentence correctly, using the comparative or superlative form of the adverb in parentheses.

60. Gus draws _____ than Ron. (well)
61. Ron paints _____ than Gus. (fast)
62. Ruben draws _____ of all three boys. (carefully)
63. Of all the students, Kim is the _____ interested in drawing. (little)
64. Winona draws _____ than Jeanette does. (frequently)
65. I painted _____ today than I did yesterday. (badly)
66. I finished _____ than Ron did. (late)
67. Gus tried _____ of all of us. (hard)
68. He paints at home _____ than in class. (much)
69. We praise animal drawings _____ of all. (enthusiastically)

9 Negatives (p. 206) Rewrite each of these sentences to avoid double negatives.

70. Lee didn't see no clouds.
71. A wind didn't never blow.
72. No warning wasn't given.
73. She hadn't expected no rain.
74. Not none of us stayed dry.
75. We couldn't do nothing about it.

76. Wasn't Lee never upset?
77. She didn't complain to nobody.
78. The boys couldn't say nothing.
79. Lee didn't smile at neither of them.

 Adjective or Adverb? *(p. 209)* Write the correct adjective or adverb for each sentence.

80. Al likes (good, well) food.
81. He cooks (good, well).
82. He takes time to measure everything (careful, carefully).
83. He watches the stove with a (careful, carefully) eye.
84. He mixes the ingredients (gradual, gradually).
85. He brings his homemade soups to a (slow, slowly) boil.
86. He stirs them (slow, slowly).
87. He doesn't work (quick, quickly).
88. He bakes (good, well) bread with (great, greatly) flavor.
89. He also creates (delicious, deliciously) dishes of his own.
90. He can cook (wonderful, wonderfully) without following a recipe.
91. What (wonderful, wonderfully) sauces he makes!

Mixed Review 92–102. This weather report has seven errors with adjectives and four errors with adverbs. Write the weather report correctly.

Proofreading Checklist
Have you used these correctly?
✔ adjectives and adverbs
✔ articles and demonstratives
✔ comparatives and superlatives
✔ proper adjectives and negatives

This Week's Weather

Good morning! The weather has been badly, and many people have had colds. Finally it's an good morning in the Chicago area. You won't see many clouds, and the sun will shine bright all day. Unfortunately, today will be the most nice day this week. A bad storm is moving slow toward us from the canadian border. This evening, clouds will move in more quickly, and things will become worser. Rain will be most heaviest around midnight, with thunder, lightning, and violent winds.

Tomorrow, believe it or not, the weather will be even worst than tonight. Don't go nowhere tomorrow unless you have to, and drive very careful. By tomorrow night, things should be calmer. Clouds and some rain will stay with us, though, for the rest of the week.

Test Practice

Write the numbers 1–11 on a sheet of paper. Read each sentence. Find the part of the sentence that needs a capital letter. Write the letter for that answer.

1 When we were away / we got a carved german / cuckoo clock. / None
        A   **B**   **C**   **D**

2 Venice is an / italian city / full of canals instead of streets. / None
     F   **G**   **H**   **J**

3 My mother / ordered beef and noodles / at the chinese restaurant. / None
     A   **B**   **C**   **D**

4 The museum / held an exhibit / of ancient korean pottery. / None
     F   **G**   **H**   **J**

5 We ordered / dozens of dutch flower bulbs / to plant at our school. / None
     A   **B**   **C**   **D**

6 My friend Henry / has a collection / of scary Mexican masks. / None
      F   **G**   **H**   **J**

7 The russian alphabet / differs from / the one used to write English. / None
      A   **B**   **C**   **D**

8 The neighborhood / grocery store sells / norwegian goat cheese. / None
     F   **G**   **H**   **J**

9 Castles in ruins / dot the green hills / of the irish landscape. / None
     A   **B**   **C**   **D**

10 The beauty of the / Japanese cherry tree / is beyond comparison. / None
     F   **G**   **H**   **J**

11 Which african country / is larger, / Kenya or Nigeria? / None
      A   **B**   **C**   **D**

Now write the numbers 12–15 on your paper. Use the paragraph to answer the questions. Write the letter for each answer.

---

¹²A hundred years ago, women wore the most gorgeousest long dresses. ¹³Although the gowns were lovely, they were very tight, and the wearers felt uncomfortably. ¹⁴In the 1920s, clothing designer's rised the hemlines on dresses and maked the outfits simpler. ¹⁵Todays' women won't never go back to those stiff garments of the past!

---

12 Which is the best way to rewrite Sentence 12?

A A hundred years ago, women weared the most gorgeousest long dress's.

B A hundred years ago, women wore the gorgeousest long dresses.

C A hundred years ago, women wore the most gorgeous long dresses.

D Best as it is

13 Which is the best way to rewrite Sentence 13?

F Although the gowns were lovely, they were very tight, and the wearers felt uncomfortable.

G Although the gowns were lovely, they were very tightly and the wearers felt uncomfortable.

H Although the gowns were lovely, they were very tightly, and the wearers felt uncomfortably.

J Best as it is

14 Which is the best way to rewrite Sentence 14?

A In the 1920s, clothing designers raised the hemlines on dresses and maked the outfits simpler.

B In the 1920s, clothing designers raised the hemlines on dresses and made the outfits simpler.

C In the 1920s, clothing designers rised the hemlines on dresses and made the outfits more simpler.

D Best as it is

15 Which is the best way to rewrite Sentence 15?

F Today's women won't ever go back to those stiff garments of the past!

G Today's women won't ever go back to those stiffly garments of the past!

H Todays' women wont' ever go back to those stiff garments of the past!

J Best as it is

Unit 1: The Sentence

Kinds of Sentences *(p. 32)* Add the correct end mark to each sentence. Label the sentences *declarative, interrogative, imperative,* or *exclamatory.*

1. The cat and the kittens are playing
2. Would you like a kitten
3. How cute they are
4. Please keep them off the chair
5. I like the black kitten

Compound Subjects and Predicates *(pp. 44, 47)* Write the parts of the compound subject or the compound predicate.

6. Carpenters pound nails or saw wood.
7. Lori measures a piece of wood and cuts it in half.
8. Lori and Russ are very experienced.
9. My brother and I help them.

Fragments and Run-ons *(p. 62)* Correct each sentence fragment or run-on sentence.

10. I belong to a book club, I receive a new book each month.
11. I like mysteries and I like biographies and I have some of each.
12. Funny book with a good story.
13. The plot was good I liked it.
14. Solved the mystery.

Unit 2: Nouns

Plural Nouns *(p. 92)* Write the correct form of the noun given.

15. Three _____ from our street are coming to a barbecue. (family)
16. Everyone will bring two _____. (dish)
17. I sliced _____ for a salad. (tomato)
18. All the _____ play volleyball. (child)
19. We make some great _____. (volley)

Possessive Nouns *(p. 96)* Write the correct form of the noun in parentheses.

20. The _____ chair is high. (lifeguard)
21. All the _____ swimming suits are bright orange. (lifeguards)
22. The _____ instructor is late. (girls)
23. _____ lesson will begin soon. (Tess)
24. The _____ lesson will be on the backstroke. (children)

See www.eduplace.com/kids/hme/ for a tricky usage or spelling question.

Unit 3: Verbs

Main Verbs and Helping Verbs *(p. 120)* Write the verb phrase in each sentence. Underline the helping verbs once and the main verbs twice.

25. Ali has studied color photography.
26. She will need a darkroom.
27. She must have learned about light meters and lens filters.
28. She has developed her photographs.
29. Should she exhibit her pictures?

Direct Objects *(p. 123)* Write the action verb and the direct object in each sentence.

30. Today at school I learned the legend of Atlantis.
31. This mysterious island contained a great empire.
32. Earthquakes and floods destroyed it.
33. The sea swallowed Atlantis in a single day and night.
34. People have written stories about this mystery.

Transitive and Intransitive Verbs *(p. 126)* Write the verb in each sentence. Label the verb *transitive* or *intransitive*.

35. A jeweler repairs watches.
36. Mr. Milne cleaned my watch.
37. The watch ticks smoothly now.
38. The grandfather clock in the hall chimed.
39. Do you know the correct time?

Being Verbs and Linking Verbs *(p. 129)* Write each linking verb and its predicate noun or predicate adjective.

40. Peter is a student at a cooking school.
41. Someday he will become a great chef.
42. This wonderful vegetable dish seems nutritious.
43. The green vegetables look fresh.
44. The food tastes delicious.

Simple Verb Tenses *(p. 132)* Write each sentence. Use the correct tense of the verb in parentheses to complete each sentence.

45. Last year Jessie _____ her cousins in Japan. (visit)
46. Jessie _____ their history and language. (study)
47. She _____ many new foods when she was in Japan. (taste)
48. Jessie's cousins _____ to the United States next year. (travel)
49. Jessie _____ them around her country when they come. (guide)

Perfect Tenses, Irregular Verbs *(pp. 135, 139)* Write the present tense, present participle, past tense, and past participle of each verb below.

50. freeze
51. fly
52. swim
53. make
54. throw
55. tear

Subject-Verb Agreement *(pp. 144, 147)* Write the present tense of the verbs.

56. There _____ many kinds of dogs. (be)
57. Neither that poodle nor those Scottish terriers _____ very big. (be)
58. Watchdogs _____ houses and businesses from burglars. (protect)
59. This boxer and that German shepherd _____ good guard dogs. (make)
60. Either a collie or a sheepdog _____ excellent as a herder of farm animals. (be)

Contractions *(p. 150)* Write each contraction. Write each verb phrase.

61. We're studying about plants.
62. Plants can't live without light.
63. They'll bend toward the light.
64. My plants aren't getting enough water.
65. I've written my science reports.

sit, set; lie, lay; rise, raise *(p. 153)* Write the verb in parentheses that completes each sentence correctly.

66. (Sit, Set) the cartons down.
67. I will (rise, raise) them up.
68. (Lay, Lie) those papers here.
69. Please don't (sit, set) on them.
70. You can (lie, lay) on the cushion.

lend, borrow; let, leave; teach, learn *(p. 156)* Write the verb in parentheses that completes each sentence correctly.

71. I will (teach, learn) Rita.
72. (Let, Leave) the game on my desk.
73. May I (lend, borrow) your rules?
74. Rita will (teach, learn) quickly.
75. Karl will (let, leave) us play too.

Unit 4: Modifiers

Adjectives *(pp. 180, 185)* Write each adjective. Include the articles.

76. This well-known music was written by an excellent musician.
77. That famous composer writes songs.
78. Some songs are cheerful and pretty.
79. Other songs, slow and sad, are nice too.
80. Two big concerts were held in the gym.

Comparing with Adjectives *(pp. 188, 191)* Write the comparative or superlative form correctly.

81. Wheat is the world's _____ grain crop. (important)
82. Wheat fields cover _____ land than any other crop. (much)
83. Bread is one of the _____ products of wheat. (tasty)
84. Our crop is _____ this year than last year. (big)

Proper Adjectives *(p. 194)* Write a proper adjective from the noun in parentheses.

85. A _____ Blue cat has blue-gray hair. (Russia)
86. A _____ Blue cat has shorter legs. (Britain)
87. A _____ cat has a curly tail. (China)
88. _____ art shows many cats. (Egypt)

Adverbs *(pp. 197, 199)* Write the adverbs.

89. Today a storyteller told a very strange story.
90. She spoke rather softly.
91. The story was quite scary.
92. The storyteller often paused.
93. I was totally surprised at the end.

Comparing with Adverbs *(p. 203)* Write the comparative or superlative form of the adverbs.

94. The actors performed _____ tonight than last night. (good)
95. Sean said his lines the _____. (dramatically)
96. Claudia spoke _____ than Sean. (softly)
97. She was always the _____ prepared. (little)

Negatives *(p. 206)* Write each sentence to avoid the double negative.

98. There wasn't no chalk.
99. No one couldn't write on the chalkboard.
100. The teacher hadn't found none in the supply closet.
101. We hardly never use any chalk.

Adjective or Adverb? *(p. 209)* Write the correct adjective or adverb in each sentence.

102. Rose tells (good, well) stories.
103. She writes (good, well) too.
104. Her stories are (funny, funnily).
105. They end (happy, happily).
106. I listen (eager, eagerly) to Rose's stories.

(pages 180–182)

1 Adjectives

- An **adjective** describes, or modifies, a noun or a pronoun.
- An adjective can tell *what kind, which one,* or *how many.*

Remember

● Write the adjectives in these sentences.

Example: This dog was lucky. *This   lucky*

1. He was lost.
2. Two children found Moon.
3. They helped dirty, scared Moon.
4. They brought him to that excellent shelter.
5. Moon was kept in this six-foot pen.
6. We saw that big friendly dog.
7. He was white and black.
8. I liked his happy bark.
9. We gave Moon this new home.

▲ Use the following adjectives in sentences. Draw an arrow to the noun or pronoun that each adjective modifies.

Example: red-hot   *The red-hot peppers made my eyes water.*

10. twelve
11. suspicious
12. crisp
13. reckless
14. tiny
15. those
16. prize-winning
17. toothless

■ Write adjectives to complete the sentences. Use the type of adjective shown in parentheses.

Example: A castle is a _____ building. (what kind) *huge*

18. Most castles have only _____ main entrance. (how many)
19. Life inside a castle must have been _____. (what kind)
20. _____ castles had moats, _____ ones. (which one, what kind)
21. They also had _____ windows. (what kind)
22. Each castle had _____ _____ hall. (how many, what kind)
23. _____ hall must have been _____. (which one, what kind)
24. _____ guards must have stood in front of the _____ gates. (how many, what kind)

(pages 185–187)

2 Articles and Demonstratives

Remember

- *A, an,* and *the* are special adjectives called **articles**. *The* refers to a specific item or items. *A* or *an* refers to any one item in a group.
- **Demonstrative adjectives** tell *which one.* Use *this* and *these* for things nearby. Use *that* and *those* for things farther away.

● Write the correct article or demonstrative adjective.

Example: Clarence was (a, an) lion.   *a*

1. He became (a, an) movie star in 1965.
2. He starred in (the, an) film called *Clarence the Cross-Eyed Lion.*
3. Many people enjoyed (that, those) film.
4. He was (a, an) easygoing lion.
5. He later appeared in (a, an) television series.
6. (This, These) show was *Daktari.*

▲ Write each article and demonstrative adjective.

Example: That plane is a glider.   *That   a*

7. A glider does not have an engine.
8. This bigger plane will pull the glider into the air.
9. When the planes get very high, the glider lets go.
10. This glider is newer than that one.
11. Those pilots will control these gliders.

■ Write the story plot below in your own words. Use articles and demonstratives. Underline the articles once and the demonstratives twice.

Example: Mouse bothers lion.

> *Once upon <u>a</u> time, when <u>a</u> lion was asleep, <u>a</u> tiny mouse ran right up <u>that</u> lion's back.*

12. Lion catches mouse.
13. Mouse pleads for life.
14. Mouse promises to return favor.
15. Lion lets mouse go.
16. Then lion gets caught in hunter's net.
17. Mouse hears lion roaring.
18. Mouse chews net and frees lion.

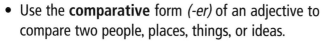

(pages 188–190)

3 Comparing with Adjectives

Remember

- Use the **comparative** form *(-er)* of an adjective to compare two people, places, things, or ideas.
- Use the **superlative** form *(-est)* to compare three or more.
- Sometimes the spelling of an adjective changes when *-er* or *-est* is added.

● Write the comparative or superlative adjective in each sentence.

Example: June has the longest day of the year. *longest*

1. June days are longer than those in the fall.
2. The shortest day is in December.
3. The coldest weather comes soon after.
4. Chicago has been called the windiest city.
5. Many cities are windier, though.
6. Miami, Florida, is warmer than Chicago.
7. One of the chilliest spots in New England is on Mount Washington.

Miami, Florida

▲ Write the correct form of each adjective in parentheses.

Example: The _____ land animal is the African elephant. (large) *largest*

8. A giraffe, however, is _____ than an elephant. (tall)
9. The _____ mammal is a kind of bat. (small)
10. Bats also have the _____ hearing of any land mammal. (sharp)
11. The _____ animal ever seen was a ribbon worm. (long)
12. A turtle is _____ than a toad. (slow)
13. A cheetah is _____ than a racehorse. (fast)
14. The _____ and _____ animal is the blue whale. (large, heavy)

■ Write a sentence for each phrase. Use the comparative or superlative form of the adjective, as shown in parentheses.

Example: a bright color (comparative)
    Red is a brighter color than gray.

15. the nice pet (superlative)
16. a hot climate (comparative)
17. the cold day (superlative)
18. the happy time (superlative)
19. the silly joke (comparative)
20. the true friends (superlative)
21. an easy book (comparative)
22. a sad story (comparative)

(pages 191–193)

④ Comparing with *more* and *most*

- Use *more* or *less* to form the comparative and *most* or *least* to form the superlative of most two-syllable adjectives and all adjectives of three or more syllables.
- Some adjectives have different forms in the comparative and superlative.

● Write the words that complete each sentence correctly.

Example: One of the (more interesting, most interesting) hobbies of all is stamp collecting.   *most interesting*

1. Collecting stamps is not the (good, best) way to get rich.
2. That is the (worse, worst) reason of all to start this hobby.
3. There are (better, best) reasons than that to collect stamps.
4. Rare stamps are (more unusual, most unusual) than people think.
5. This hobby is (less expensive, least expensive) than other hobbies.
6. It also makes trips to the post office (much, more) exciting.

▲ Write the correct comparative or superlative form of the adjective in parentheses to complete each sentence.

Example: Some animals are _____ than others. (unusual)
     more unusual

7. Which animal is the _____ engineer of all? (good)
8. Beavers are _____ engineers than mice. (good)
9. Beavers spend _____ time in water than on land. (much)
10. Gorillas may be the _____ appreciated animals. (little)
11. Gorillas are really _____ than other animals. (gentle)

■ Write the comparative or superlative form of an adjective to complete each sentence. Do not use the same adjective more than once.

Example: Which is the _____ camera?   *least expensive*

12. This is the _____ camera made today.
13. Is that a _____ camera than my old one?
14. I would like to take _____ pictures than I usually do.
15. I am the _____ photographer of all my friends.
16. Karen is _____ with a camera than Leroy.

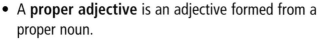

(pages 194–196)

5 Proper Adjectives

Remember

- A **proper adjective** is an adjective formed from a proper noun.
- A proper adjective begins with a capital letter.

● Write the proper adjective in each sentence.

Example: My family is Mexican. *Mexican*

1. For breakfast we had Irish soda bread.
2. I ate Scottish oatmeal.
3. We also enjoyed Italian cheese.
4. For lunch I ate Swedish meatballs.
5. Dad served them on German noodles.
6. I also had crisp Chinese vegetables.
7. With dinner we ate Swiss cheese.
8. I toasted the cheese on French bread.

▲ Write a proper adjective from each noun in parentheses.

Example: The _____ language has words from many other languages. (England) *English*

9. We have borrowed the _____ word *pronto*. (Spain)
10. The word *coupon* is a _____ word. (France)
11. When someone sneezes, we often say a _____ word. (Germany)
12. _____ people say *il weekend*. (Italy)
13. _____ citizens know what rock-and-roll is. (China)
14. Our word *hi* means "yes" to a _____ person. (Japan)
15. The _____ word for *was* sounds like the name *Bill*. (Russia)
16. The word *raccoon* is a Native _____ word. (America)

■ For each proper noun, write a proper adjective. Then write a sentence with the adjective.

Example: Scotland *Scottish Do you like Scottish bagpipes?*

17. England	20. Ireland	23. China	26. Mexico
18. Norway	21. Italy	24. Japan	27. Hawaii
19. France	22. Brazil	25. Canada	28. Alaska

(pages 197–198)

⑥ Adverbs

Remember

- An **adverb** can modify a verb, an adjective, or another adverb. Many such adverbs end in *-ly*.
- An adverb that modifies a verb usually tells *how, where, or when.*

● Write the adverb in each sentence.

Example: Yesterday Alan picked his first tomato.   *Yesterday*

1. Alan grows tomatoes anywhere.
2. He lives in the city now.
3. Alan carefully planted two plants.
4. He watered them daily.
5. Finally, he picked four ripe tomatoes.
6. He served them proudly.

▲ Write all the adverbs that modify verbs in these sentences.

Example: Five little bats hung upside down.   *upside down*

7. Susan looked at them nervously.
8. Finally, she asked if they were alive.
9. Now she and her uncle were staring at some.
10. They were sleeping quietly.
11. Bats live everywhere, but most people never see them.
12. Susan really hoped they would fly.

■ Write each adverb and the verb it modifies. Underline the adverb once and the verb twice.

Example: Ana was cheerfully washing her bicycle.

   cheerfully   *was washing*

13. Suddenly she saw a cat.
14. The cat was staring hard at a sparrow.
15. The sparrow was pecking carelessly at some seeds.
16. The hungry cat crept steadily toward the bird.
17. Ana shouted loudly at the cat.
18. The sparrow flew high into a tree.

(pages 199–200)

7 More About Adverbs

- Adverbs that modify adjectives or other adverbs usually tell *to what extent.*

● Write the underlined adverb and the adjective or the adverb that it modifies.

Example: Luis took a <u>very</u> long hike. *very   long*

1. At first he walked <u>quite</u> slowly.
2. Then Luis saw some <u>very</u> dark clouds.
3. He walked <u>more</u> quickly.
4. Luis stayed <u>really</u> calm.
5. He looked for a <u>completely</u> safe place.
6. He saw a <u>truly</u> perfect shelter ahead.

▲ Write the adverb in each sentence that modifies an adjective or an adverb. Then write the word that it modifies.

Example: Most sharks are very good swimmers. *very   good*

7. Some sharks, such as the nurse shark, are rather slow.
8. Others, including the mako shark, are really fast.
9. Sharks have an especially good sense of smell.
10. They most often eat other fish.
11. Some sharks will swallow almost any object.
12. They have eaten very old ropes and boots.
13. A few sharks are extremely dangerous to people.

■ Write an adverb to modify the adjective or the adverb that follows it. Label the modified word *adjective* or *adverb.*

Example: A magnet is a _____ important tool. *very   adjective*

14. For hundreds of years, magnets guided sailors _____ accurately.
15. A horseshoe magnet is _____ stronger than a straight magnet.
16. It is stronger because the two points are _____ closer together.
17. Nails become magnets _____ quickly.
18. You hold them _____ close to a magnet.
19. No one is _____ sure what makes magnets work.
20. Some types of magnets are _____ useful in scientific research.

(pages 203–205)

8 Comparing with Adverbs

Remember

- Add *-er* to form the comparative and *-est* to form the superlative of many adverbs.
- If the adverb ends with *-ly,* add *more* or *less* to form the comparative and *most* or *least* to form the superlative.
- Some adverbs have irregular forms of comparison.

● Write the form of the adverb that is correct in each sentence.

Example: Tuesday I ran (better, more better) than I usually do.   *better*

1. I study (best, bestest) in the library.
2. Now I worry (littler, less) than I used to about Field Day.
3. Robin always ran the (best, most best) in our class.
4. She (most frequentliest, most frequently) won the Field Day race.
5. This year I practiced (more often, more oftener) than ever before.
6. Tomorrow I want to run (more better, better) than ever.
7. What I fear (mostest, most) is the heat.

▲ Write the form of the adverb in parentheses that correctly completes each sentence.

Example: My brother Bob rides _____ than I do. (well)   *better*

8. The horses obey him _____ than they obey me. (quickly)
9. He runs the barrel races _____ than anyone else. (fast)
10. Last year he ran the course _____ than he does now. (badly)
11. He trained _____ this year than last year. (often)
12. Of all the horses, Pepper runs _____. (enthusiastically)
13. Bob and Pepper will not race _____ than any other pair. (badly)
14. I think they will enjoy themselves _____ of all. (much)

■ Use the phrases below in complete sentences.

Example: reads more slowly   *Sally reads more slowly than Liz.*

15. sings better
16. are most easily lost
17. answered most quickly
18. laughed longer
19. asked most often
20. painted most creatively
21. felt best
22. sews more skillfully

(pages 206–208)

⑨ Negatives

Remember

- A **negative** is a word that means "no" or "not."
- Avoid using a **double negative**, two negatives together.

● Write the words that make these sentences negative.

Example: Last summer nobody wanted to stay home. *nobody*

1. Mark wanted to do something he had never done before.
2. None of us had ever tried camping.
3. Dad made lists to make sure that nothing would be left behind.
4. We chose a place that was not crowded.
5. The camp was nowhere we had ever been.
6. We had no stove, and we cooked over a fire.
7. Later no one wanted to go home.

▲ Write the word in parentheses that completes each sentence correctly.

Example: Natalie didn't see (no, any) grocery store. *any*

8. No one (never, ever) bought much at the store.
9. Your store isn't (anything, nothing) like my store.
10. The store no longer carries (no, any) frozen food.
11. The store didn't (never, ever) have a bakery.
12. Natalie couldn't find fresh fruit (nowhere, anywhere).
13. This store isn't in business (no more, anymore).

■ Write each sentence correctly, avoiding double negatives.

Example: No one uses picture writing no more.
        No one uses picture writing anymore.

14. Once many people didn't use nothing else.
15. Until 1821 the Cherokees didn't have no alphabet.
16. There wasn't no way they could write certain ideas.
17. Sequoya didn't let nothing stop him.
18. Sequoya's alphabet wasn't hard for no one to learn.
19. Cherokees had never read no Cherokee newspaper before.
20. Now there wasn't nothing they couldn't read.

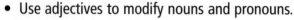

(pages 209–211)

10 Adjective or Adverb?

- Use adjectives to modify nouns and pronouns.
- Use adverbs to modify verbs, adjectives, and other adverbs.
- *Good* is an adjective. *Well* is an adjective only when it means "healthy." Otherwise, *well* is an adverb.

Remember

● Write the correct word to complete each sentence.

Example: Last year I got a (good, well) camera. *good*

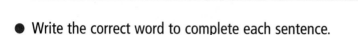

1. I (quick, quickly) learned how to use it.
2. My pictures were not (good, well), though.
3. I took pictures (bad, badly).
4. My friend Sal takes (good, well) pictures.
5. He (careful, carefully) showed me what to do.
6. I read (good, well), and I have many books.
7. I read one (good, well) book about cameras.

▲ Complete each sentence by writing the correct word: *good, well, quick,* or *quickly.*

Example: My older sister Cheryl cooks very _____. *well*

8. Someday she will be a _____ chef.
9. Last year she took a class at a _____ French cooking school.
10. Cheryl has spoken French _____ for many years.
11. She _____ learned to cook many dishes.
12. A few dishes are also _____ and easy to make.
13. I am slow, but Cheryl can create a delicious meal _____.

■ Write a sentence using each pair of phrases. Underline the phrases.

Example: good music   plays well
        Andy loves good music and plays the clarinet well.

14. slow eater   talked slowly
15. looks good   feels well
16. looked bad   threw badly
17. quick wink   quickly saw

18. bad handwriting   writes badly
19. tasted sweet   sweetly asked
20. good performer   juggles well

Capitalization and Punctuation

Spread out in all its red, white, and blue glory, the U.S. flag floated down the streets of Atlanta, Georgia, in a Fourth of July parade.

1 Reviewing End Punctuation

What sentence should I give you?

With classmates, role-play a period, an exclamation point, a question mark, and a judge. The judge asks each mark what kind of sentence it should get and why.

You know that a sentence begins with a capital letter and ends with an end mark. End marks tell whether you are making a statement (.), asking a question (?), giving a command (.), or showing strong feeling (!).

We'll select a recipe.	Please open the cookbook.
Do you take cooking lessons?	What a thin sauce this is!

Try It Out

Speak Up What are the correct end marks?

1. Am I cooking dinner tonight
2. We like cooked greens
3. Will you make the biscuits
4. Please have some pecans
5. You can shell them first
6. How tasty the chocolate garlic soup is
7. What is in the microwave
8. What an amazing cook you are

Summing Up

- Use a **period** to end a declarative or an imperative sentence.
- Use a **question mark** to end an interrogative sentence.
- Use an **exclamation point** to end an exclamatory sentence.

Write the sentences. Add end marks.

9. Heat up the pan first
10. The cooking oil is bubbling up
11. Should I pour the omelet into the pan now
12. The summer vegetables were fried earlier
13. What a skillful chef you are
14. How do you fold the omelet in half

15–22. This part of a TV script has eight punctuation errors. Write the script correctly.

Example: Look at this pizza   *Look at this pizza.*

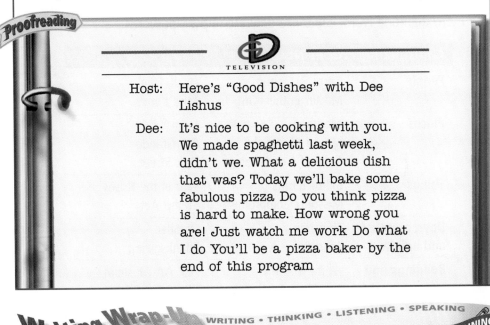

Proofreading

TELEVISION

Host: Here's "Good Dishes" with Dee
Lishus

Dee: It's nice to be cooking with you.
We made spaghetti last week,
didn't we. What a delicious dish
that was? Today we'll bake some
fabulous pizza Do you think pizza
is hard to make. How wrong you
are! Just watch me work Do what
I do You'll be a pizza baker by the
end of this program

Writing Wrap-Up   WRITING • THINKING • LISTENING • SPEAKING

EXPLAINING

Write a TV Script

What would you like to see taught on TV? cooking? dog training? basketball? the guitar? Write part of a script for a TV how-to series. Use all four kinds of sentences. Find a partner to listen to your script. Use your voice to show the different kinds of sentences. Then ask your partner what he or she learned from your script.

2 Proper Nouns and Adjectives

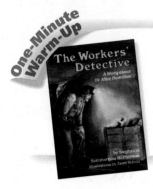

Which adjective in this sentence is formed from a proper noun? Name the proper noun.

In Brussels Alice heard noted European experts speak on all aspects of industrial medicine.

—from *The Workers' Detective: A Story about Dr. Alice Hamilton,* by Stephanie Sammartino McPherson

- You have learned that a proper noun names a particular person, place, or thing. A proper noun begins with a capital letter. If a proper noun has more than one word, capitalize only the important words.

Capitalizing Proper Nouns		
People	Carol B. Cohen Martin Luther King Jr.	Uncle Hank Miss Lopez
Places	Montana Mount Mansfield Cape of Good Hope	India Rio Grande Oak Street
Things	Bill of Rights Missouri Compromise	War of the Roses Stamp Act
Days, months, and holidays	Thursday Fourth of July	October Thanksgiving
Buildings and companies	White House Ace Shoe Company	Fisk Art Museum Clay's Food Store

- You have also learned that a proper adjective is an adjective that is made from a proper noun. You should capitalize proper adjectives as well as proper nouns.

France	French bread
Greece	Greek dances
North America	North American animals
Turkey	Turkish rugs

Speak Up Which nouns and adjectives should be capitalized?

1. Was dr. alice hamilton born in new york?
2. She entered the university of michigan in march of 1892.
3. The hamiltons had dutch, irish, and english ancestors.
4. Did dr. hamilton ever live and work at hull house in chicago?
5. She treated italian children in her clinic there.

 Summing Up

- Capitalize proper nouns and proper adjectives.
- If a proper noun consists of more than one word, capitalize all the important words.

On Your Own

Write the proper nouns and the proper adjectives. Capitalize them correctly.

Example: Alice hamilton was a kind of american pioneer.
     Alice Hamilton   American

6. This hamilton girl was born in february 1869.
7. She attended a school called miss porter's school in farmington, connecticut.
8. In 1925 she published the first book about industrial poisons in the united states.
9. She investigated factories for the bureau of labor and studied lead poisoning.
10. As part of her research, hamilton visited many german and british manufacturers.

more ▶

11. How many european trips did dr. alice hamilton take?
12. She also carried out studies for the state of illinois.
13. Was alice the first female teacher at harvard medical school?

14–28. This part of a biographical sketch has fifteen proper nouns and proper adjectives that should be capitalized. Write the proper nouns and proper adjectives correctly.

Example: Alice was born in new york and edith in germany.
Alice was born in New York and Edith in Germany.

Proofreading

Successful Sisters

Hull House, Chicago

How amazing the Hamilton sisters were! The younger one, alice, was a doctor. She studied workers' health problems for governments and the league of nations. To advance peace, she met in europe with swiss, french, and belgian women. She also helped out at Hull House, a settlement house on South Halsted Street in Chicago.

Her sister edith was not idle either. She became head of the bryn mawr school in maryland. Later she wrote famous books about greek and roman myths. Edith died in May 1963 at 95, and Alice in september 1970 at 101.

Writing Wrap-Up

WRITING • THINKING • LISTENING • SPEAKING

PERSUADING

Write an Editorial

The Hamilton sisters made a difference in the lives of many others. How can you convince students to be involved in their school and their community? Write an editorial for your school newspaper. Urge students to tutor children, to organize a park cleanup, or to volunteer at a community event. Use at least five proper nouns and proper adjectives. Read your editorial to a partner. Ask your partner which sentence is most convincing.

3 Interjections

Which word below expresses an emotion or feeling? What punctuation mark is used after it? Is this word a part of the sentence, or does it stand alone?

"Hey, I'm a hero," he said. "Tell me how to act humble. I've never had to do it before."

—from *One-Man Team*, by Dean Hughes

An **interjection** is a word or words that show feeling. If the interjection stands alone, it is followed by an exclamation point. If it begins a sentence, it is set off by a comma.

Hooray! They won the game.
Oh, I knew they would!

Oh, no! I can't believe it.
Whew, they finally scored a run.

 Tip

Do not overuse interjections in your writing.

Try It Out

Speak Up What is the interjection in each sentence?

1. Goodness! Both teams play hard.
2. Amazing! The fans love the game.
3. Well, that team won't win again.
4. Good grief! Is this a winning streak?
5. Oh, I don't think so.
6. Pow! The batter blasted that ball into the bleachers.
7. Oh, no! They won by just one run.

 Summing Up

- An **interjection** is a word or words that show strong feeling.
- Use an exclamation point or a comma to set off an interjection.

Interjections **239**

Write each sentence, correcting the punctuation. Underline each interjection.

Example: Phew She almost collided with the center fielder.
Phew! She almost collided with the center fielder.

8. Ugh The umpire really made a bad call.
9. Whack Did you hear the bat hit that fast ball?
10. Bravo Mike tagged the runner out at home plate.
11. Whoops Sarah shouldn't have swung at that pitch.
12. Uh oh their coach is replacing the pitcher.
13. All right He loaded the bases.

14–18. These comments from an electronic chat room have five punctuation errors. Write the messages correctly.

Example: Hey! are you back from the game yet?
Hey, are you back from the game yet?

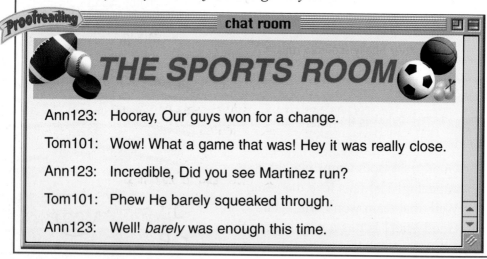

Proofreading

chat room

THE SPORTS ROOM

Ann123: Hooray, Our guys won for a change.

Tom101: Wow! What a game that was! Hey it was really close.

Ann123: Incredible, Did you see Martinez run?

Tom101: Phew He barely squeaked through.

Ann123: Well! *barely* was enough this time.

Writing Wrap-Up   WRITING • THINKING • LISTENING • SPEAKING

EXPRESSING

Write a Letter

Think of something that you are excited about. Write a letter or an e-mail to a friend. Tell what makes it so exciting. Use some interjections. Read your letter to a partner. Have your partner raise a hand for each interjection and guess the punctuation.

4 Commas in a Series

How many things does Fausto do in the first sentence? How can you tell?

> Fausto knelt, prayed, and sang. But he couldn't forget the man and the lady, whose names he didn't even know, and the *empanada* they had given him.
>
> —from *Baseball in April,* by Gary Soto

- A **series** is a group of three or more items together in a sentence.

  A fork, a knife, and a spoon came in the package.

- Use commas to separate the items in a series. Notice how commas can change the meaning of a sentence.

  I bought fruit salad, tuna sandwiches, and juice.

  I bought fruit, salad, tuna, sandwiches, and juice.

HELP ? Tip

Put a comma wherever you pause to take a breath.

- A conjunction such as *or* or *and* usually appears before the last item in the series. The conjunction connects the items.

  Do I use one, two, or three teaspoons of parsley?

  My mom taught me to ski, to scuba dive, and to play chess.

Try It Out

Speak Up Where do commas belong in these sentences?

1. Red is the color used for stop signs traffic lights and some fire hydrants.
2. Red yellow orange green and blue are five colors in the rainbow.
3. Does blue make you sleepy wake you up or help you think?
4. Colors inspire advertisers designers florists and chefs.

more ▶

Use each list of items as a series in a sentence. Where do commas belong?

5. soccer   baseball   tennis   basketball
6. cars   buses   trains   planes
7. flowers   trees   grass   bushes
8. walk   run   skip   jump
9. history   science   gym   math
10. bake   fry   cook   boil

Summing Up

- Use a **comma** to separate items in a series. The commas tell your reader to pause between items.

- Use a comma before the conjunction that connects the items.

On Your Own

Write each sentence, adding a series of items. Insert commas and a conjunction where needed.

Example: The four seasons are _____.
The four seasons are spring, summer, fall, and winter.

11. Three musical instruments are _____.
12. _____ are the three basic meals of the day.
13. In the summer people usually _____.
14. Did Stephen lose _____?
15. Four European countries are _____.
16. Did you invite _____ to the party?
17. _____ are four of the world's rivers.
18. Popular books have been written by _____.
19. For that cake do you use _____ cups of flour?
20. Have you ever vacationed in _____?
21. The best cars on the road are _____.

more ▶

22–30. This personal inventory list has nine errors in using commas in a series. Write the list correctly.

Example: I enjoy playing soccer shopping, and walking on the beach.
I enjoy playing soccer, shopping, and walking on the beach.

Proofreading

Take a Look at Me

- My closest friends are Michela Sally and Victor.
- Spaghetti, pizza, carrots and spinach are my favorite foods.
- At school this year I sang in the chorus joined the chess club, and became a crossing guard.
- Next year I may be in either the band the play, or the swim team.
- My best subjects are math, science, and spelling. Next year I will take music or French.
- I would like to travel to Kenya Egypt, Korea or China.
- In my spare time, I either play basketball read or listen to music.

Writing Wrap-Up   WRITING • THINKING • LISTENING • SPEAKING

REFLECTING

Write a Personal Inventory

Before you write, it helps to brainstorm and make lists about the topic—even when the topic is you. What are your favorite things? In what activities do you participate? Write six sentences about yourself. Use a series in each one. Find a classmate, and take turns reading your inventories aloud. Be sure to pause a little at each comma. Do you two have any interests in common?

Writing with Commas

Combining Sentences: Words or Phrases in a Series Use a series to combine two or three sentences that tell about the same thing. One smooth, elaborated sentence is clearer than several choppy, repetitive ones. The series can consist of single words or of phrases (groups of words).

The menu should be clear. The menu should be interesting. The menu should look attractive.	**Incorrect:** The menu should be clear, interesting, look attractive. **Correct:** The menu should be clear, interesting, and attractive.

Apply It

1–4. Revise the underlined sentences in this wordy menu. Use a series to combine groups of sentences that tell about the same thing. Rewrite incorrect series so that all items are stated in the same way.

Revising

Today's Specials

Appetizer: Spicy Shrimp
The shrimp are served on a bed of lettuce. Spicy sauce comes on the side. Fresh lemon and green parsley also come on the side.

Main Course: Spaghetti and Meatballs
The spaghetti has tomato sauce. It has meatballs. It is covered with cheese. The sauce is homemade. All morning the chef peels tomatoes and crushes garlic! He also chops parsley.

Dessert: Strawberry Shortcake
The strawberries are sweet and delicious. The whipped cream is sweet and delicious. The biscuit is also sweet and delicious.

Combining Whole Sentences in a Series Sometimes a related group of whole sentences can be combined in a series. Remember to separate the combined sentences in your series with commas and to place a conjunction before the last item in your series.

The math class wrote a survey.	The math class wrote a survey,
Teachers distributed it in homeroom.	teachers distributed it in homeroom,
Students filled it out at home.	and students filled it out at home.

Apply It

5–8. Revise this report. Use a series to combine each set of underlined sentences. Remember to use commas and a conjunction.

Revising

Over one hundred sixth-graders responded to our survey! We counted the responses. Volunteers entered the numbers on the computer. Our teacher helped us create a colorful bar graph. It looked fantastic!

Students shared what they like to do for entertainment. Half of them spend time with friends. One third of them play sports. One tenth of them go to the mall.

We asked students to select a fantasy vacation. A ride on the space shuttle came in first. A safari in Africa placed second. Snorkeling in Australia scored third. Nobody picked summer camp!

We highly recommend this project. Every student signed the survey. Our teacher put it in a time capsule. The principal locked it in the school safe. What will students think of us in twenty-five years?

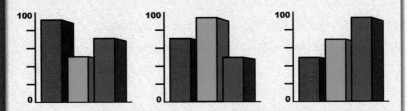

5 More Uses for Commas

How many commas are missing from this sentence? Where do they belong?

Yes Matt whales look like fish but they are mammals the largest mammals of all.

You have already learned that a comma separates the simple sentences that make up a compound sentence. It also separates the parts of a complex sentence when the first part begins with a subordinating conjunction such as *although*.

> A female whale is called a cow, and a baby whale is a calf.

> Although whales live in the ocean, they are not fish.

HELP

? Tip

Don't mistake a compound sentence for a compound predicate that has two verbs.

A whale can dive, and surface with great power.

- You have also learned that an appositive is a word or group of words that identifies or explains the noun that it follows. Commas separate an appositive from the rest of the sentence.

> Blue whales, the fastest kind, are found in all oceans.
> Mr. Gilmore, an expert on whales, works at an aquarium.

- Commas are also used to set off certain introductory words such as *well, yes,* and *no* at the beginning of a sentence.

> Yes, I have seen a finback whale.
> Well, we actually saw its spout first.

- Commas also set off a noun in direct address, the name of a person who is directly spoken to.

> From this distance, Sue, that looks like a blue whale.
> Jerry, have you read *Island of the Blue Dolphins*?

Speak Up Where do commas belong in these sentences?

1. Class who invented the first workable steamboat?
2. Yes it was Robert Fulton.
3. He was a well-known portrait painter but he became more and more interested in engineering.
4. He ran his first steamboat on the Seine a river in France.
5. No that was not the only boat Fulton built.
6. The *Clermont* another steamboat traveled the Hudson River.
7. When you visited New Orleans did you see a steamboat Kwan?

Robert Fulton's steamboat named the *Clermont*

Summing Up

- Use a comma to separate simple sentences in a compound sentence.
- Use a comma to separate the parts of a complex sentence that begins with a subordinating conjunction.
- Use commas to set off an appositive.
- Use a comma after introductory words such as *well, yes,* and *no.*
- Use commas to set off a noun in direct address.

Write these sentences, and add commas where needed.

Example: The hornet a common insect is like the yellow jacket.
The hornet, a common insect, is like the yellow jacket.

8. Paul how many parts does an insect's body have?
9. Well there are three main sections Mr. Jensen.
10. Some insects help humans but others are very harmful.
11. The honeybee a stinging insect makes honey.

more ▶

12. Because mosquitoes are blood-sucking insects they carry disease.
13. Valerie are there other insects with wings?
14. Yes Mr. Jensen moths and flies have wings.

15–26. This part of an interview for an online magazine has twelve comma errors. Write the interview correctly.

Example: Yes Jamal, ants are very social, and hard-working.
Yes, Jamal, ants are very social and hard-working.

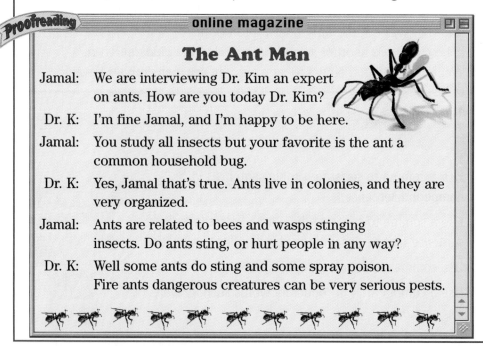

Proofreading

online magazine

The Ant Man

Jamal: We are interviewing Dr. Kim an expert on ants. How are you today Dr. Kim?

Dr. K: I'm fine Jamal, and I'm happy to be here.

Jamal: You study all insects but your favorite is the ant a common household bug.

Dr. K: Yes, Jamal that's true. Ants live in colonies, and they are very organized.

Jamal: Ants are related to bees and wasps stinging insects. Do ants sting, or hurt people in any way?

Dr. K: Well some ants do sting and some spray poison. Fire ants dangerous creatures can be very serious pests.

Writing Wrap-Up
WRITING • THINKING • LISTENING • SPEAKING

CREATING

Write an Interview
Imagine that you are an ant. Write an interview with yourself. Ask and answer questions about your work, hobbies, and dreams as an ant. Tell why you like being an ant. Use commas in the ways you just learned. Then in a small group, read your interview aloud, changing your voice for each part. Remember to pause a bit at each comma. Have one of your listeners tell you the most enjoyable part of your interview.

Writing with Commas

Combining Sentences: Introductory Groups of Words Sometimes a group of words that begins a sentence is an **introductory phrase**. To vary sentence length, you can use introductory phrases to combine a pair of sentences. Make one of the sentences into a phrase by using the present participle form of the verb. Set off such phrases with a comma.

A ladybug wears black spots on its red body. It is easy to identify.	Wearing black spots on its red body, a ladybug is easy to identify.
I saw a ladybug on a leaf. The ladybug was eating aphids.	Eating aphids, the ladybug sat on a leaf.

Incorrect:
Eating aphids, I saw a ladybug on a leaf.

> It sounds as if you ate the aphids! Make sure an introductory phrase describes the noun or the pronoun that follows it.

Apply It

1–5. Combine each pair of sentences in this brochure. Change one of the sentences in each pair to an introductory phrase.

Revising

Buy a Ladybug Kit!

- People use the ladybug spray. They can attract ladybugs.

- Curious learners read this booklet. They discover fun ladybug facts!

- Nature lovers observe ladybugs in the observation station. They learn more about this creature's habits.

- Amateur scientists use the magnifying glass to study ladybugs. They notice features that are normally impossible to see.

- People put the ladybug house outside in the fall. It provides a warm, dry shelter for hibernating ladybugs.

more

When you revise your writing, try combining related sentences to clearly link their meanings. Use a subordinating conjunction, such as *after, since, while, where, because, although,* and *so that,* to express the meaning you intend. Don't forget to use a comma to separate the two parts of the sentence.

Our class is studying insects.
We will be more aware of them. } Because our class is studying insects, we will be more aware of them.

Apply It

6–10. Revise this observation journal for the class bulletin board. Link the underlined sentences, using a subordinate conjunction from the box.

after	as	even if	while
although	because	since	

Revising

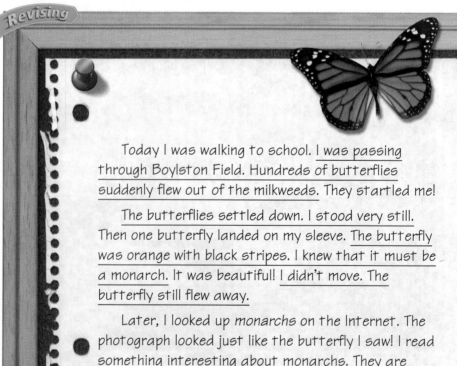

Today I was walking to school. I was passing through Boylston Field. Hundreds of butterflies suddenly flew out of the milkweeds. They startled me!

The butterflies settled down. I stood very still. Then one butterfly landed on my sleeve. The butterfly was orange with black stripes. I knew that it must be a monarch. It was beautiful! I didn't move. The butterfly still flew away.

Later, I looked up monarchs on the Internet. The photograph looked just like the butterfly I saw! I read something interesting about monarchs. They are poisonous to birds. Birds leave them alone.

6 Abbreviations

Why was the shortened term *NASA* created?

It said that the National Aeronautics and Space Administration (NASA) was looking for a new group of astronauts.

—from *Sally Ride: A Space Biography,* by Barbara Kramer

An **abbreviation** is a shortened form of a word. It usually ends with a period. Abbreviations are often used in addresses, in lists, or to save space. Study the chart of common abbreviations. Notice that not all abbreviations have capital letters or periods.

HELP ? Tip

If you need help with an abbreviation, use your dictionary.

Common Abbreviations			
Places			
Apt.	Apartment	Mt.	Mount or Mountain
Ave.	Avenue	Pkwy.	Parkway
Expy.	Expressway	P.O.	Post Office
Businesses and titles			
Co.	Company	P.D.	Police Department
Inc.	Incorporated	R.N.	Registered Nurse
Ltd.	Limited	J.P.	Justice of the Peace
Measurements			
in.	inch	hp	horsepower
ft	feet	mph	miles per hour
States			
CA	California	IN	Indiana
NY	New York	MI	Michigan
Agencies and organizations			
SBA	Small Business Administration		
NPR	National Public Radio		
NATO	North Atlantic Treaty Organization		

Speak Up How would you abbreviate these groups of words?

Fifth Avenue

1. Fifth Avenue
2. Fun Games, Incorporated
3. Garden State Parkway
4. Apartment 3-A
5. Mount Washington
6. Post Office Box 871
7. Pearly Piano Company
8. Morton Lewis, Limited
9. Drew Stanley, Justice of the Peace
10. five feet, one inch

Summing Up

- **Abbreviations** are shortened forms of words.
- Most abbreviations begin with capital letters and end with periods.

Write the abbreviation of each item.

Example: Missouri   *MO*

11. National Public Radio
12. Mount Snow
13. 55 miles per hour
14. Main Street
15. Bright Company
16. Indiana
17. California
18. horsepower
19. Brook Parkway
20. Simon and Lane, Incorporated
21. feet
22. inch
23. Madison Avenue
24. Justice of the Peace
25. Small Business Administration
26. North Atlantic Treaty Organization

more ▶

27–36. This bicycle registration form has ten abbreviation errors. Write the form correctly.

Example: Where purchased: V&W, Incorp.   *V&W, Inc.*

Department of Public Safety
Application for Bicycle Registration

Evans Pol. Dept.
342 Ames Ave.
Evans, Colo. 80620

Name: <u>Doc. Maria Fernandez</u>

Address: <u>42 Pine St</u>
          <u>Apt. 4B</u>

City, State: <u>Evans, CO</u>

Height: <u>5 ft. 6 in</u>   Hair color: <u>black</u>

Employer: <u>Tyler Medical Cor.</u>

Address: <u>PO. Box 18</u>

City, State: <u>Coralles, NMex.</u>

Make of Bicycle: <u>Speedy</u>

Color(s): <u>Blue</u>

Serial Number: <u>123456</u>

Speed limit within town: <u>10 m.p.h.</u>

Writing Wrap-Up
WRITING • THINKING • LISTENING • SPEAKING

PERSUADING

Write a Classified Ad
Write an ad to sell your bicycle or some other item that you own. Include a description of the item that will turn your readers into buyers! Include your name and address. Use four or more words that can be abbreviated. Ask a partner to listen to your ad. Then as you read it a second time, ask your partner to write abbreviations for the words that can be shortened.

7 Quotations

One-Minute Warm-Up

In these sentences who can't swim? How can you tell?

The lifeguard said I can't swim in the pool.

The lifeguard said, "I can't swim in the pool."

- When you write someone's exact words, you are writing a **direct quotation**. The speaker's words are set apart from the rest of the sentence with **quotation marks**. Begin the first word of the quotation with a capital letter. You usually place end punctuation inside the quotation marks.

  Terry said, "Let's go swimming."

  "This beach is closing," the lifeguard announced.

- Notice that a comma separates the speaker from the quotation.

- When a quotation ends in a question mark or an exclamation point, however, do not add a comma.

  "What time will the beach open?" I asked.

- A quotation is sometimes interrupted in the middle. End the first part of the quotation with quotation marks. Begin the second part with quotation marks. Use commas to separate the quotation from the speaker.

  "Do you realize," asked Rob, "that we forgot the raft?"

- If the second part of the interrupted quotation begins a new sentence, start it with a capital letter. Use a period after the speaker.

  "It's too late now," I said. "We'll have to come back later."

- If you are writing a conversation between two or more people, you are writing a **dialogue**. As the conversation goes back and forth, remember to identify which person is speaking each time. Start a new paragraph whenever there is a change of speakers.

Speak Up How would you punctuate these sentences? Which letters should be capitalized?

1. What time Tim asked does Mom's train arrive back home
2. Dad answered it will arrive at noon
3. I'm sure she missed the city Tim said
4. She'll have photographs replied Dad and probably videos
5. Maybe she'll have presents for us too said Tim we want to hear about her trip to the ranch

Summing Up

- Use **quotation marks** to set off a speaker's exact words from the rest of the sentence. In most cases place end punctuation inside the closing quotation marks.

- Begin the first word of a quotation with a capital letter.

- Use commas to separate most quotations from the rest of the sentence.

Write these sentences, using correct punctuation and capitalization.

Example: Little strokes Benjamin Franklin said fell great oaks.
  "Little strokes," Benjamin Franklin said, "fell great oaks."

6. Sherlock Holmes said it's elementary, my dear Watson.
7. The mere absence of war stated John F. Kennedy is not peace.
8. I have a dream exclaimed Martin Luther King Jr.
9. A poem said Robert Frost begins with a lump in the throat.
10. We need our heroes wrote Eleanor Roosevelt.
11. Of whom asked Emily Dickinson am I afraid?

more ▶

12. Walt Whitman said I hear America singing.
13. Where have all the flowers gone asked singer Pete Seeger.

14–26. This dialogue from a TV show has thirteen punctuation and capitalization errors. Write the dialogue correctly.

Example: Thoughts Thomas Mann said come clearly while one walks

> *"Thoughts," Thomas Mann said, "come clearly while one walks."*

Speak for Yourself

"Why are you always quoting famous people" asked Leah.

"Well," said Luke, "They say things much better than I do.

But your words should express your *own* ideas." Leah replied. "Sometimes that's more important."

Luke asked, "do you really think so"?

"Of course" Leah exclaimed. it's great to repeat famous quotations, but I want to hear *your* words too!"

"Well, Luke said with a smile, that's nice to know".

Writing Wrap-Up WRITING • THINKING • LISTENING • SPEAKING

EXPRESSING

Write Dialogue

Write a dialogue between you and a friend who disagrees with you about something, such as whether to go to a party, whom to vote for, whether to recycle, or which band is best. Make the dialogue sound real. State your opinion, and give reasons why you think that way. Ask two classmates to read your dialogue. Can they follow your punctuation cues?

8 Titles

One-Minute Warm-Up

Which is a book? Which is an article? How do you know?

"Making the Punishment Fit the Crime," by Watts E. Dunn

Legal Decisions, by Dolores Clear

- When you write the titles of books, magazines, newspapers, songs, and other works, you must treat them in special ways. Capitalize the nouns, verbs, and other important words in a title. Do not capitalize short words such as *a, an, the, and, or, at, to, up*, and *for* unless these words begin or end a title.

  "The Mouse That Won the Race"
  Where the Red Fern Grows
  The View from Saturday

- Titles of books, magazines, newspapers, and movies are underlined in writing. In print, such titles appear in slanted type called *italics*.

HELP ? Tip

Don't try handwriting a title in italics! Use underlining instead.

Titles of Major Works		
Publications	**In writing, underline the title.**	**In print, the title is in italics.**
books	Passage to Freedom	*Passage to Freedom*
magazines	Cricket	*Cricket*
newspapers	Grafton Press Herald	*Grafton Press Herald*
movies	National Velvet	*National Velvet*

In writing: She reads The Washington Post on the train.
In print: She reads *The Washington Post* on the train.

- Titles of short stories, articles, songs, book chapters, and most poems should be enclosed in quotation marks. The punctuation that follows a title should usually be placed inside the quotation marks.

Titles of Minor Works	
Publications	**Examples**
short stories	"Out There"
articles	"Endangered Lands"
songs	"Happy Birthday"
book chapters	"Pond Life"
most poems	"Ode to a Toaster"

The third chapter is called "Planting Your Garden."

My first song, "Butterflies in the Snow," was not published.

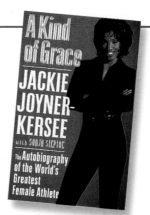

Try It Out

Speak Up How would you write these titles correctly?

1. the necklace (short story)
2. to be a clown (article)
3. a kind of grace (book)
4. the raven (poem)
5. travel news (magazine)
6. flying kites (book chapter)

How would you punctuate and capitalize the titles in these sentences?

7. A magazine for young writers, cricket, published my poem.
8. Readers of the new york times live all over the world.
9. I read an article called today's american family.
10. At the school festival, we sang moon river.

Summing Up

- Capitalize the first, last, and all important words in a title.
- Underline the titles of books, magazines, newspapers, and movies.
- Use quotation marks around titles of short stories, articles, songs, book chapters, and most poems. Punctuation that follows a title usually goes inside the quotation marks.

Write these sentences, correcting each title.

Example: A herald reporter wrote the article too few frogs.
      A Herald reporter wrote the article "Too Few Frogs."

11. Yes, the man without a country is definitely a short story.
12. The song in your eyes is based on the poem eyes of green.
13. The magazine newsweek printed the article ending hunger.
14. Today's globe has a review of the book countdown to noon.
15. The first chapter of the book birds and more is flying home.
16. Did the movie community unity win the Oscar?

17–24. This online calendar of library events has eight incorrect titles. Write the calendar correctly.

Example: "Journal" editor Pilar Lupo will discuss her book at the top.
      Journal editor Pilar Lupo will discuss her book At the Top.

Proofreading

	Web site	

Upcoming Events at the Milton Public Library

4/8   Poet Amy Cohen reads her work "Flowers alive."
4/22   T. Will tells how he researched his article "the Big Climb."
5/12   L. Ivo, a magazine editor, takes us behind the scene at Views.
5/19   Professor Jo Alba reviews the books "Red rain" and "Ivy."
5/28   Dr. Lila Evans leads us in songs such as "by the sea" and "Sigh".
6/4   Ben Vox, reviewer for the new york times, gives his opinion of the story Stardust.

Writing Wrap-Up WRITING • THINKING • LISTENING • SPEAKING

INFORMING

Write a Calendar of Events
What experts or celebrities would you like to have appear at your school? Write a calendar of events you might put together. List at least five speakers or performers, and include a title with each one. Find a partner, and read your lists to each other. Do you share any listings?

Enrichment

Telephone Talk

Write a telephone conversation between two friends who are talking about some exciting news. Write it as a dialogue, using quotation marks correctly. Include some introductory words, nouns of direct address, and interjections. Remember to punctuate them properly. Start a new paragraph each time the speaker changes.

"Hey, did you hear the news, Jenny?" asked Alex.

"Yes, Alex, I heard," said Jenny. "Wow! I can't believe it!"

Challenge Use your dialogue as a starting point for a very short story with a funny or surprising ending. Include at least one more section of dialogue.

Reading File

Get together with classmates and make a Recommended Reading file. First, think of five good books that you have read in the past year. Write the title and author of each book at the top of an index card. Below that, write a few sentences telling why you recommend the book. Include at least two compound sentences. Be sure to punctuate properly. Collect everyone's cards, and divide them by subject, such as science, biography, and history. Make a divider card for each subject (see the picture), and put the cards in a box for the class to use.

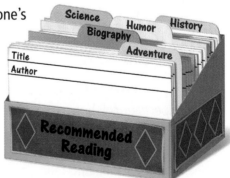

1 **Reviewing End Punctuation** *(p. 234)* Write these sentences. Add the correct end punctuation.

1. Stop at this campsite for the day
2. What a large bird that is
3. Is its nest near
4. Please carry the binoculars
5. I see different kinds of birds
6. Do you recognize these tracks

2 **Proper Nouns and Adjectives** *(p. 236)* Write each proper noun and proper adjective. Capitalize them correctly.

7. The capital of canada is ottawa.
8. It is on the ottawa river in the province of ontario.
9. Last july aunt rita and I visited the national gallery of canada.
10. It has european and canadian art.

3 **Interjections** *(p. 239)* Write each sentence. Add the punctuation that is missing.

11. Hey these are wonderful seats.
12. Well that was a funny play.
13. Oh we could not stop laughing!
14. Wow The actors were great.
15. Oh, my The audience cheered.

4 **Commas in a Series** *(p. 241)* Write the sentences. Add commas where needed.

16. Greg Bob and Cynthia visited me.
17. We took them to a museum a beach and a TV studio.
18. Greg took photographs wrote postcards and bought souvenirs.
19. Did he buy one two or three gifts?

5 **More Uses for Commas** *(p. 246)* Write the sentences. Add commas where needed.

20. Set a timer Ed to develop the film.
21. Well how much time do we need?
22. The directions call for two minutes but we will need six.
23. The developer this strong-smelling chemical is too cool now.
24. After Ed pours out the developer Kay will refill the tank with clean water.

6 **Abbreviations** *(p. 251)* Write the correct abbreviation for each of the following items.

25. The Goldenrod Company
26. 26 Fairfield Street
27. Post Office Box 542
28. Apartment 356
29. Buffalo, New York
30. 12 inches

7 **Quotations** *(p. 254)* Write each sentence below, punctuating and capitalizing the quotation correctly.

31. This train goes to the airport said the guard.
32. Which train asked the tourist do I take to the art museum?
33. Take the north train the conductor answered get off at the third stop.
34. The visitors exclaimed what a beautiful museum this is.
35. Where is the Greek sculpture they asked we want to go and see that.

8 **Titles** *(p. 257)* Write each sentence, correcting the title.

36. The book I am reading now is why the tides ebb and flow.
37. On our bus trip, the class sang the impossible dream.
38. My mom reads the magazine modern life every Saturday.
39. I've just finished reading the short story strangers that came to town.
40. The poem snow is very short.

Mixed Review 41–52. This Web site article has five capitalization errors and seven punctuation errors. Write the article correctly.

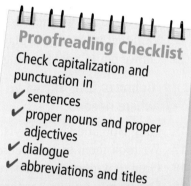

Proofreading Checklist

Check capitalization and punctuation in

✔ sentences
✔ proper nouns and proper adjectives
✔ dialogue
✔ abbreviations and titles

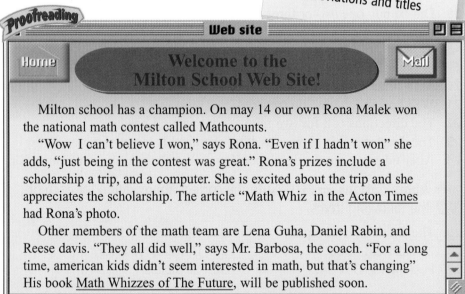

Web site

Home

Welcome to the Milton School Web Site!

Mail

Milton school has a champion. On may 14 our own Rona Malek won the national math contest called Mathcounts.

"Wow I can't believe I won," says Rona. "Even if I hadn't won" she adds, "just being in the contest was great." Rona's prizes include a scholarship a trip, and a computer. She is excited about the trip and she appreciates the scholarship. The article "Math Whiz in the <u>Acton Times</u> had Rona's photo.

Other members of the math team are Lena Guha, Daniel Rabin, and Reese davis. "They all did well," says Mr. Barbosa, the coach. "For a long time, american kids didn't seem interested in math, but that's changing" His book <u>Math Whizzes of The Future</u>, will be published soon.

Test Practice

Write the numbers 1–6 on your paper. Read the passage, and look at the numbered, underlined parts. Choose the correct way to capitalize and punctuate each underlined part. If it is already correct, choose "Correct as it is." Write the letter for the answer you choose.

"Leah," said Ali, "we must work on our video <u>for spanish class."</u>
<u>(1)</u> (2)
"I know," said Leah. "It's due on <u>Friday and we</u> don't have a script!"
(3)
Leah and Ali had planned a very complicated video. It involved

<u>animation puppets and live actors.</u> The girls' <u>teacher Mr. Ruiz had</u>
(4) (5)
taught them how to make a video. They even had an idea. Leah and Ali

would <u>retell the secret garden.</u> Now all they needed was a script.
(6)

---

1 A "Leah, said Ali, we
  B "Leah" said Ali, "we
  C "Leah", said Ali "we
  D Correct as it is

2 F for spanish class".
  G for Spanish Class."
  H for Spanish class."
  J Correct as it is

3 A Friday, and we
  B Friday! and we
  C Friday? and we
  D Correct as it is

4 F animation puppets, and live actors
  G animation, puppets, and live actors
  H animation, puppets, and, live actors
  J Correct as it is

5 A teacher Mr. Ruiz, had
  B teacher, Mr. Ruiz, had
  C teacher, Mr., Ruiz had
  D Correct as it is

6 F retell *The secret garden*
  G retell *the Secret Garden*
  H retell *The Secret Garden*
  J Correct as it is

✓ Test Practice *continued*

Write the numbers 7–10 on your paper. Read the passage all the way through once. Then look at the underlined parts. Decide if they need to be changed or if they are fine as they are. Choose the best answer from the choices given. Write the letter for each answer.

Claude Monet <u>was a french</u>
<u>(7)</u>
<u>artist. He</u> helped found a style of

painting that is known as impres-

sionism. The impressionists

thought that it was <u>more impor-</u>

<u>tanter for paintings</u> to show the
<u>(8)</u>
effects of light than to tell a story.

They worked outside instead of in

studios.

Monet loved to paint the same

scenes over and over. Some of the

objects he painted <u>frequent were</u>

<u>boats haystacks and flowers.</u>
<u>(9)</u>

Monet <u>didn't never tire of</u>
<u>(10)</u>
painting. When he was an old

man, he painted huge pictures of

his lovely water gardens.

7 A was a French artist? He
B was a french Artist. He
C was a French artist. He
D (No changes)

8 F more importantly for paintings
G more important for paintings
H most important for paintings
J (No changes)

9 A frequently were boats, haystacks, and flowers
B frequenter were boats, haystacks and flowers
C frequently were boats, haystacks, and, flowers
D (No changes)

10 F didnt ever tire
G didnt' ever tire
H didn't ever tire
J (No changes)

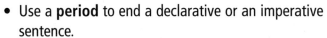
(pages 234–235)

1 Reviewing End Punctuation

Remember

- Use a **period** to end a declarative or an imperative sentence.
- Use a **question mark** to end an interrogative sentence.
- Use an **exclamation point** to end an exclamatory sentence.

● Write each sentence. Add the correct end punctuation.

Example: We sing a song about the flag of the United States
We sing a song about the flag of the United States.

1. Do you know the name of the song
2. Francis Scott Key wrote the song in 1814
3. The song is about a real flag
4. Go see it in a museum in Washington
5. What a big flag it is

▲ Write each sentence, using correct end punctuation. Label each sentence *declarative, interrogative, imperative,* or *exclamatory.*

Example: Nations have flags   *Nations have flags.   declarative*

6. Do you know about the state flags of the United States
7. Each state in the nation has its own flag
8. Look at this one from Texas
9. What a pretty flag it is
10. Why does it have only one star

■ Rewrite each sentence as a different kind of sentence. Use correct end punctuation. You may add or change some words.

Example: Flags were once used for weather forecasts.
Were flags once used for weather forecasts?

11. What a variety of flags the National Weather Bureau had!
12. A white flag meant clear weather.
13. Did a blue one mean rain or snow?
14. Please show me the warning flags.
15. A red flag with a black square meant that a storm was coming.

(pages 236–238)

2 Proper Nouns and Adjectives

- Capitalize proper nouns and proper adjectives.
- If a proper noun consists of more than one word, capitalize all the important words.

Remember

● Write the underlined proper nouns and adjectives. Capitalize them correctly.

Example: Many people are interested in egypt. *Egypt*

1. Egypt is on the african coast.
2. Each year people visit the great pyramid and the valley of the kings.
3. Many ancient tombs were discovered by british explorers.
4. Howard carter worked with the egyptian exploration fund.
5. One of the most famous egyptian kings was king tutankhamen.
6. Objects from his tomb are in the metropolitan museum of art.
7. Others are in the national museum at cairo.

▲ Write the proper nouns and proper adjectives. Capitalize them correctly.

Example: People from many countries have come to america. *America*

8. The british colonists were among the first settlers.
9. They started a colony in plymouth, massachusetts.
10. Many traders settled in what is now canadian territory.
11. Many european citizens left their native lands.
12. They came to ellis island in new york bay.
13. Many people in california have asian ancestors.

■ Write each sentence. Capitalize all the proper nouns and proper adjectives.

Example: Is james herriot a famous veterinarian?
Is James Herriot a famous veterinarian?

14. His books about life in yorkshire, england, are popular.
15. The doctor and his partner, siegfried, are likable.
16. They visit many farms in the english countryside.
17. Among their patients are german shepherds.
18. They also treat farm animals such as swiss cows.
19. Their more unusual patients include arabian horses.
20. Herriot's books appeal to people in big cities such as new york.

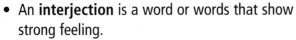

(pages 239–240)

③ Interjections

Remember

- An **interjection** is a word or words that show strong feeling.
- Use an exclamation point or a comma to set off an interjection.

● Write the interjection and the punctuation that follows it in each sentence.

Example: Oh, no! I forgot about the math quiz.   *Oh, no!*

1. Well, you don't have to worry.
2. Yes, I certainly do!
3. Wow! This test is so difficult.
4. Oh, Pete never has trouble with math.
5. Whew! I finished just before the final bell.
6. Oh, my! I'm glad that's over.
7. Hooray! I received a perfect score.

▲ Write each sentence, punctuating the interjection correctly.

Example: Oh, my It can't be you.   *Oh, my! It can't be you.*

8. Well it is.
9. Goodness You've really changed.
10. Oops I hope I didn't offend you.
11. Oh, no you couldn't ever do that.
12. Well how have you been?
13. Ah I have felt better.

■ Rewrite each sentence, using an interjection.

Example: What's all the excitement?   *Hey! What's all the excitement?*

14. My sister's hamster escaped from its cage.
15. Where can it be?
16. I'll help you find it.
17. We found the hamster in your room.
18. It was in your model race car.
19. How could it have climbed in there?
20. Don't let your hamster escape again.

(pages 241–243)

4 Commas in a Series

- Use a comma to separate items in a series. The commas tell your reader to pause between items.
- Use a comma before the conjunction that connects the items.

● Write each of the following sentences. Add commas where they are needed.

Example: Kate invited Mary Joe and me. *Kate invited Mary, Joe, and me.*

1. We went swimming bike riding and walking.
2. Kate brought food a blanket and a jug to the park.
3. She served chicken carrot sticks celery and rolls.
4. I brought apples juice and peanuts.
5. Kate Joe and I cleared away the picnic.
6. We put the paper plates cups and napkins into the trash barrel.
7. Then we played games jumped rope and walked home.

▲ Write a sentence with items in a series for each group of words. Separate the items in each series with commas.

Example: lamps—tables—vases *Are the lamps, the table, and the vases new?*

8. sheets—towels—blankets
9. dishes—glasses—silverware
10. washed—scraped—painted
11. paint—wallpaper—rugs—curtains
12. painting—calendar—poster—photograph
13. aunts—uncles—cousins

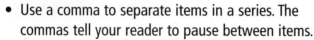

■ Use each pair of words in two sentences. In the first sentence, use the two words as one item. In the second sentence, use each word as part of a series of items. Underline the words, and punctuate the sentences correctly.

Example: gold rings *We found three <u>gold rings</u> buried in the garden. Silver, <u>gold</u>, <u>rings</u>, and bracelets were lost in the sunken ship.*

14. spinach salad
15. banana bread
16. paper bags
17. tomato soup
18. water pipes
19. glass jar
20. milk bottles
21. orange juice
22. sports news

(pages 246–248)

5 More Uses for Commas

Remember

- Use a comma to separate simple sentences in a compound sentence.
- Use commas to set off an appositive.
- Use a comma after introductory words such as *well*, *yes*, and *no*.
- Use commas to set off a noun in direct address.

● Each sentence contains a question mark in parentheses. Write *yes* if a comma belongs in that place. Write *no* if it does not.

Example: Jon (?) tell us about salmon. *yes*

1. Salmon, a kind of fish (?) is very special.
2. Salmon live in salt water (?) and they live in fresh water too.
3. Yes (?) it does sound strange.
4. Salmon eggs (?) hatch in streams.
5. The young fish swim to the sea (?) and they grow up there.

▲ Write each sentence, adding the missing commas.

Example: In 1931 a boat the *Baychimo* headed north.
　　　　　In 1931 a boat, the Baychimo, *headed north.*

6. A bad storm came and the boat was caught in ice.
7. John Cornwell the captain told the crew to leave.
8. During an awful storm a blizzard the boat disappeared.
9. Yes it floated off with no one on board.
10. That boat was spotted Carol as late as 1969.

■ Write each sentence, adding each missing comma. Then tell why the commas are needed.

Example: Tell us about swordfish Kim.
　　　　　Tell us about swordfish, Kim. direct address

11. Swordfish rapid and powerful swimmers like warm water.
12. They often swim fast but they move slowly in calm weather.
13. Are sailfish similar to swordfish Jim?
14. Yes they have the same long, sharp upper jaw.
15. Do you know Dave how much sailfish weigh?

(pages 251–253)

6 Abbreviations

- **Abbreviations** are shortened forms of words.
- Most abbreviations begin with capital letters and end with periods.

● Write the abbreviation from the word box for the underlined word or words.

Example: Police Department   *P.D.*

mph	Rd.
P.O.	P.D.
St.	NJ
R.N.	IN
ft	

1. Brook <u>Road</u>
2. Elm <u>Street</u>
3. <u>miles per hour</u>
4. <u>Registered Nurse</u>
5. <u>New Jersey</u>
6. <u>Post Office</u> Box 242
7. twenty <u>feet</u>
8. <u>Indiana</u>

▲ Write the following names and addresses, using abbreviations from the word box.

Example: Mount Rushmore   *Mt. Rushmore*

Co.	J.P.
in.	SC
SBA	Apt.
Pkwy.	Ltd.
FBI	Mt.
hp	

9. Webster Company
10. 111 Orchard Parkway
11. Barton and Jones, Limited
12. Columbia, South Carolina
13. Apartment 3
14. Avis Holmes, Justice of the Peace
15. Small Business Administration
16. sixty inches
17. Federal Bureau of Investigation
18. twenty horsepower

■ Rewrite the following items, using abbreviations.

Example: 1004 Halton Street   *1004 Halton St.*

19. Mount Washington
20. National Public Radio
21. Registered Nurse
22. Santa Fe, New Mexico
23. Route 66
24. Music Network, Incorporated
25. 55 miles per hour
26. the Southeast Expressway

(pages 254–256)

7 Quotations

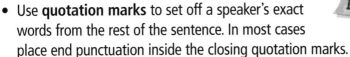Remember

- Use **quotation marks** to set off a speaker's exact words from the rest of the sentence. In most cases place end punctuation inside the closing quotation marks.
- Begin the first word of a quotation with a capital letter.
- Use commas to separate most quotations from the rest of the sentence.

● Write the following sentences. Add quotation marks where they are needed.

Example: Look at me! said Ben. *"Look at me!" said Ben.*

1. Ned asked, What are you doing?
2. Look quickly, said Ben, before I fall down!
3. Are you really standing on your hands? Ned said.
4. Yes, I am, said Ben. Do you want to try?
5. Will you hold my feet? Ned asked.

▲ Write the following sentences. Capitalize and punctuate them correctly.

Example: What are you writing asked Lara
"What are you writing?" asked Lara.

6. I am making a day book answered Kareem
7. A day book said Kareem is a book of quotations
8. Where do you get a quotation a day Lara asked
9. It's not hard said Kareem books have many quotations
10. Well Kareem suggested why don't you start a day book

■ Write each sentence below as dialogue. Put the authors' names in different places in your sentences. Use correct punctuation and capitalization.

Example: The impossible is often the untried. Jim Goodwin
"The impossible," said Jim Goodwin, "is often the untried."

11. We are tomorrow's past. Mary Webb
12. The pen is mightier than the sword. Edward Bulwer-Lytton
13. Nothing in life is to be feared. Marie Curie
14. I have not yet begun to fight. John Paul Jones
15. It takes all sorts of people to make a world. Douglas Jerrold
16. There is no substitute for hard work. Thomas Edison

(pages 257–259)

8 Titles

- Capitalize the first, last, and all important words in a title.
- Underline the titles of books, magazines, newspapers, and movies.
- Use quotation marks around titles of short stories, articles, songs, book chapters, and most poems. Punctuation that follows a title usually goes inside the quotation marks.

● Each title below should be underlined or enclosed in quotation marks. Write each title correctly.

Example: The Washington Post (newspaper)
The Washington Post

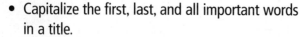

1. The Rush for Gold (article)
2. When You Talk to a Monkey (poem)
3. Penny Power (magazine)
4. The Lion and the Mouse (story)
5. Codes and Secret Writing (book)

▲ Write and punctuate each sentence correctly.

Example: Mollie Hunter wrote the book the haunted mountain.
Mollie Hunter wrote the book The Haunted Mountain.

6. Mollie Hunter also wrote the book the kelpie's pearls.
7. We laughed at the poem called what a funny bird the frog are.
8. My brother is a reporter for the daily news, our local newspaper.
9. Paul McCartney wrote the beautiful song yesterday.
10. I read the chapter called old two toes.

■ Complete the following sentences by adding titles.

Example: Kim enjoys reading books like _____. (book title)
Kim enjoys reading books like The Trumpet of the Swan.

11. She has a book called _____ that lists things. (book title)
12. She had read about the song in the _____. (newspaper title)
13. The name comes from the poem _____. (poem title)
14. An article called _____ will be in the next issue. (article title)

Artful carvings you'll find
All along the staircase.
They call you to climb
And to spiral through space.

Pronouns and Antecedents

The word *they* in the second half of this sentence refers to which word in the first half? How can you tell?

Once hurricanes form, they begin to travel.

—from *Storms,* by Seymour Simon

- You have already learned how to use nouns in sentences. A **pronoun** is a word that takes the place of one or more nouns. Pronouns keep us from having to repeat the same noun.

  James owns an ax, but James needs a log splitter.
  James owns an ax, but he needs a log splitter.

- Singular pronouns refer to one person or thing. Plural pronouns refer to more than one.

Singular Pronouns:	I	you	he	she	it
Plural Pronouns:	we	you	they		

- A pronoun takes its meaning from the noun it replaces. The noun that the pronoun refers to is called the **antecedent**. A pronoun must agree with its antecedent. That is, it must be the same in number (singular or plural) and gender as the noun it replaces.

  When George had enough money, he bought a bike.

  George left the bike out in the rain, and it rusted.

- Make sure that you have a clear antecedent for every pronoun. A pronoun can have more than one antecedent.

  After Brian and Carla had collected many recipes, they decided to write a cookbook.

- The antecedent does not have to be in the same sentence as the pronoun.

  Brian and Carla wrote the cookbook. It was illustrated by Carla.

Speak Up What pronoun would you use to replace the underlined part of each sentence?

1. Tom and Wendy walked home quickly.
2. Nancy walked fast too.
3. The streets were empty.
4. Bruce answered the door.
5. Ruth looked at the clear sky.
6. The friends went inside.
7. The rainstorm began suddenly.
8. The road was flooded.

Summing Up

- A **pronoun** is a word that takes the place of one or more nouns.
- The **antecedent** of a pronoun is the noun or nouns to which the pronoun refers.
- A pronoun must agree in number and gender with its antecedent.

On Your Own

Write each pronoun. Then write its antecedent.

Example: Are Dan and Rosa still here, or did they leave?
they   Dan, Rosa

9. The fans cheered when they saw the touchdown.
10. The seats were in the back, and they were uncomfortable.
11. The singer took a bow. Then he took another bow.
12. The musicians played the school song. Then they marched off the field.
13. Judy knew the melody, but she didn't know the words.
14. Angel held the football until it was stolen away.
15. The player of the game was Larry. Does he know yet?

more ▶

On Your Own continued

16–25. This editorial for an online school newspaper has ten incorrect pronouns. Write the editorial correctly.

Example: Ms. Angeli is our principal, and they supports the proposal.
Ms. Angeli is our principal, and she supports the proposal.

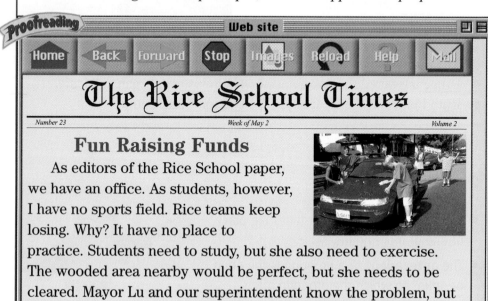

Proofreading

Web site

Home | Back | Forward | Stop | Images | Reload | Help | Mail

The Rice School Times

Number 23   Week of May 2   Volume 2

Fun Raising Funds

As editors of the Rice School paper, we have an office. As students, however, I have no sports field. Rice teams keep losing. Why? It have no place to practice. Students need to study, but she also need to exercise. The wooded area nearby would be perfect, but she needs to be cleared. Mayor Lu and our superintendent know the problem, but he have no funding. Our principal, Ms. Angeli, is in favor of the field, and he has made a suggestion. If students want a field, it can help raise the money. Car washes, bake sales, and shows can be fun, and it bring in cash. The town would probably help if he sees these efforts. Rice students, are she up to this challenge?

Writing Wrap-Up

WRITING • THINKING • LISTENING • SPEAKING

PERSUADING

Write an Editorial

How might you argue against the editorial above? Think about trees and wildlife, students' time, and other school needs. Write an editorial opposing the sports field, or choose an issue at your own school. Give strong reasons for your opinions. Use pronouns from this lesson. Then find a partner to listen as you read your editorial. Ask your partner to restate your main idea.

Writing with Pronouns

Writing Clearly with Pronouns When you use pronouns, make sure that your reader can tell whom or what they refer to. Replace a confusing pronoun with a noun or a noun phrase.

Confusing
It was their first year on the cheerleading squad.
They lifted them onto their shoulders.
Then they performed athletic back flips.

Clear
It was Karen and Jeff's first year on the cheerleading squad.
The experienced cheerleaders lifted their teammates onto their shoulders.
Then everyone performed athletic back flips.

Apply It

1–8. Eight pronouns in this news article are confusing. Rewrite the article, replacing pronouns with nouns or noun phrases as needed.

SPORTS CORNER **Middle School Cheerleaders Sweep Competition**

The Comets, our cheerleading team, beat fifteen other teams and won first place. They made amazing formations, such as the Heel Stretch Pyramid and the Scorpion. They are very difficult. They were steady and quick and beat them.

The team captain, Julie Lee, twisted her ankle last week. The coach, Ms. Desmond, wasn't sure she would get to the competition, but she surprised everyone when she did. Congratulations to her and them.

more

Avoiding Pronoun Overload If you repeat the same pronoun again and again, your writing will sound boring! To keep your writing lively, substitute nouns or noun phrases for some of the pronouns.

Droning Pronouns

The students started a pep club. They recruited club members, and they worked hard to increase school spirit. They organized homecoming events too. They want to support our terrific athletes!

Mix of Nouns and Pronouns

The students started a pep club. They recruited club members, and they worked hard to increase school spirit. The students organized homecoming events too. These hard workers want to support our terrific athletes!

Apply It

9–12. Rewrite this club's newsletter. For each of the four sections, replace one or more repeated pronouns with nouns or noun phrases.

Revising

M
Homecoming Activities

- There will be a pep rally today! It will take place in the stadium. The coaches will speak at it. It will be great!

- The club will hand out banners during lunch. Bring them to the rally, and paste them on your lockers. Wave them at Saturday's game too. Our club designed them!

- The club is selling T-shirts. A picture of our mascot is on them. They come in our school colors. You can buy them during homeroom.

- The members are organizing a food drive and collecting canned food in the cafeteria. Cans should be left in baskets next to the cashier. All of them will be donated to charity.

2 Subject and Object Pronouns

One-Minute Warm-Up

What's incorrect in this verse? Rewrite it so that it's correct and still rhymes.

Her shouted at I, "Look up at the sky!"
I saw an eagle, but did it see I?

- You know that nouns can be subjects or direct objects. A pronoun that replaces a subject is a **subject pronoun**.

  <u>Bob Phillips</u> hit the ball. <u>He</u> hit the ball.

- A pronoun that replaces a direct object is an **object pronoun**. An object pronoun receives the action of a verb. Object pronouns are also used after words such as *to, in, for,* and *at.*

  Dad knows <u>Sue Fox</u>. Dad knows <u>her</u>.
  Kevin threw the ball to <u>Joan</u>. Kevin threw the ball to <u>her</u>.

HELP
? Tip

Before you select a pronoun for your sentences, decide whether the pronoun will be used as a subject or an object.

The chart shows how singular and plural pronouns change their forms according to their use.

Subject Pronouns		Object Pronouns	
Singular	**Plural**	**Singular**	**Plural**
I	we	me	us
you	you	you	you
he, she, it	they	him, her, it	them

Try It Out

Speak Up Are the underlined pronouns subject or object pronouns?

1. <u>I</u> am learning about the eagle.
2. <u>It</u> is a very powerful and unusual bird.
3. The Great Seal of the United States displays <u>it</u>.

more ▶

4. Eagles are important to <u>us</u>.
5. Years ago people hunted <u>them</u>.
6. Pollution affects <u>them</u>.
7. Now <u>they</u> are protected by strict laws.
8. <u>They</u> live for as long as thirty years.
9. <u>We</u> can find eagles in the wilderness of the United States and Canada.
10. Elliot has seen <u>them</u> only in pictures.

Summing Up

- Use a **subject pronoun** to replace a noun used as a subject.

- Use an **object pronoun** to replace a noun used as a direct object and after words such as *to, in, for,* and *at.*

On Your Own

Write these sentences, choosing the correct pronouns in parentheses. Label each pronoun *subject* or *object.*

Example: (I, Me) saw some eagles in the mountains.
　　　　I saw some eagles in the mountains.　subject

11. (They, Them) soared high in the sky.
12. Allen spotted (they, them), and they amazed (he, him).
13. (I, Me) shouted, and the eagles stared fiercely at (we, us).
14. Ari stared back at (they, them), and (he, him) felt brave.
15. Tonia knows a lot about eagles, and (she, her) admires them.
16. (We, Us) can see many in Alaska, according to (she, her).
17. (They, Them) have wings that spread to seven feet.

more ▶

18–28. This part of an essay has eleven incorrect pronouns. Write the essay correctly.

Example: Is the eagle the right symbol for we?
Is the eagle the right symbol for us?

A Worthy National Symbol

In 1776 Ben Franklin and others tried to design a United States seal, but them failed. Then in 1782 William Barton tried again, and him succeeded. He drew a bald eagle, and because of he, the eagle became the national bird. Eagles are powerful hunters, and humans have admired they since ancient times. Today us still see eagles as proud and brave. Franklin did not approve of they, though. He preferred the peaceful, useful turkey. Me must agree with he. In the Roman Empire, eagles stood for war and the army. Do us really want such a symbol? Should a fierce creature represent we? For I, a strong but sociable animal would be better. I would prefer the smart wolf or the busy beaver.

Writing Wrap-Up
WRITING • THINKING • LISTENING • SPEAKING

EXPRESSING

Write an Essay
What animal, object, place, or person do you recommend as a new symbol for your school or city? Choose a symbol, and write an essay explaining why your choice is so fitting. You may wish to write from the point of view of the animal or the object. Use some subject and object pronouns. Compare your essay with others'. How are the symbols different? similar?

3 Possessive Pronouns

Which two words in this sentence show ownership? What other similar words do you know?

During my third year in Little Dribblers, our team qualified for the national championships.

—from *Bounce Back,* by Sheryl Swoopes

- You know that possessive nouns show ownership. A pronoun can replace a possessive noun. A pronoun that shows ownership is called a **possessive pronoun**.

  Daniel's mug is on the table.   His mug is on the table.

- Some possessive pronouns are always used with nouns. Other possessive pronouns always stand alone.

  Before nouns: Her *mug* is red.   Our *glasses* are clean.

  Stand alone: That mug is theirs.   This is mine, not hers.

- The pronouns *his* and *its* can be used with nouns or can stand alone.

Possessive Pronouns			
Used Before Nouns		**Used Alone**	
my	our	mine	ours
your	your	yours	yours
his, her, its	their	his, hers, its	theirs

- Do not confuse possessive pronouns with contractions. Possessive pronouns do not have apostrophes.

Possessive Pronouns		Contractions	
its	(belongs to it)	it's	(it is)
their	(belongs to them)	they're	(they are)
your	(belongs to you)	you're	(you are)

Speak Up Replace the underlined word or words with a possessive pronoun.

1. <u>Keith's</u> cat likes people.
2. The brown house is <u>Mr. and Mrs. Pratt's</u>.
3. I use <u>my family's</u> computer for homework assignments.
4. A <u>computer's</u> memory is in the hard drive.
5. <u>Aunt Eva's</u> computer has a calculator.
6. The guidance counselor used special software for <u>the students'</u> new September schedules.
7. The only Dalmation in the neighborhood is <u>my family's</u>.

Summing Up

- Use a **possessive pronoun** to show ownership, replacing a possessive noun.

- Some possessive pronouns are used with nouns, and some stand alone.

- Never use an apostrophe in a possessive pronoun.

Write each sentence, choosing the correct word in parentheses.

Example: The snake had already shed (it's, its) skin.
The snake had already shed its skin.

8. The poster on the bulletin board is (our, ours).
9. (Its, It's) colors are very bright.
10. (Their, They're) designing (their, they're) T-shirt logo.
11. (They're, Their) house is closer than (your's, yours).
12. (My, Mine) desk needs more work than (you're, your) desk.
13. (Your, You're) doing (your, you're) homework early.

more ▶

14. I'll paint (my, mine), and she'll paint (her, hers).
15. Is that desk really (their's, theirs)?
16. (Her, Hers) umbrella is so old that (it's, its) handle is broken.
17. (Your, You're) aunt is moving to (our, ours) neighborhood.

18–26. This set of instructions for an electronic bulletin board has nine incorrect pronouns. Write the instructions correctly.

Example: Never fly you're kite in a thunderstorm. You're not Ben Franklin.
Never fly your kite in a thunderstorm. You're not Ben Franklin.

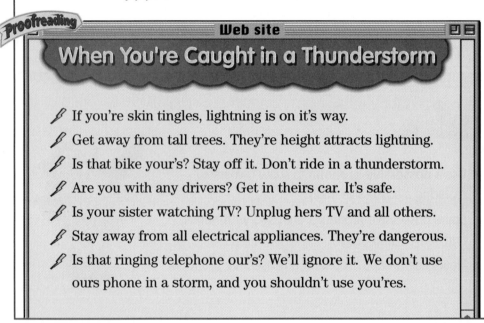

Proofreading

Web site

When You're Caught in a Thunderstorm

- If you're skin tingles, lightning is on it's way.
- Get away from tall trees. They're height attracts lightning.
- Is that bike your's? Stay off it. Don't ride in a thunderstorm.
- Are you with any drivers? Get in theirs car. It's safe.
- Is your sister watching TV? Unplug hers TV and all others.
- Stay away from all electrical appliances. They're dangerous.
- Is that ringing telephone our's? We'll ignore it. We don't use ours phone in a storm, and you shouldn't use you'res.

Writing Wrap-Up
WRITING • THINKING • LISTENING • SPEAKING

EXPLAINING

Write a Paragraph of Cause and Effect
What observations have you made of nature? Have you watched a plant grow from a seed? a bee sting someone? a storm approach? ants carry bits of food? Write a paragraph explaining the natural event and its effect on something or someone. Give complete details so that your reader can understand. Use at least four possessive pronouns. Read your work to a group. Does anyone have anything to add?

4 Pronouns After Linking Verbs

One-Minute Warm-Up

What's the confusion all about in this scene?

"Who is it?"

"It's Sy."

"Who's 'I'? I'm not opening this door until you tell me your name!"

- You have learned that a linking verb can join the subject of a sentence with a predicate noun. A pronoun can replace a predicate noun. Always use subject pronouns after linking verbs.

  The champions <u>were</u> they.   The team members <u>were</u> she and I.

- To check that the pronoun is correct, reverse the order of the sentence. *They were* is correct. *Them were* is not.

Try It Out

Speak Up Which pronoun is correct?

1. It was (they, them) who found the boat.
2. It was (I, me) who saw the wreck.
3. The owners of the boat are (they, them).
4. The rescuers were Jake and (we, us).
5. The bravest ones were (her, she) and (him, he).
6. Which of the experienced swimmers was (he, him)?
7. That is (he, him) in the life vest.
8. The photographers at the scene were (us, we).
9. The most grateful person at the dock must be (she, her).
10. The heroes are (they, them).

Summing Up

- A subject pronoun is used after a linking verb.

Write each sentence correctly.

Example: The woman with the prettiest garden is (her, she).
The woman with the prettiest garden is she.

11. It was (we, us) who planted the roses.
12. That is (he, him) now.
13. Our friends are (they, them).
14. The person in the sun hat is (I, me).
15. The gardeners with the best ideas are (him, he) and (her, she).

16–20. This dialogue has five incorrect pronouns. Write the dialogue correctly.

Example: The best local expert on flowers is (he, him).
The best local expert on flowers is he.

Proofreading

Tulip Treads

The owner of the trampled tulips is him.

He is furious. "Who stepped on my tulips? The guilty one must be he."

"No. The person in the garden was her, not me."

"There were two people. The tulip tramplers must be them."

"No, the careless person was me alone. I confess. It was I."

Writing Wrap-Up WRITING · THINKING · LISTENING · SPEAKING

NARRATING

Write a Dialogue
Think of a funny, sad, or touching moment you have been a part of or witnessed. Write the dialogue for the closing scene of a story based on that moment. Be sure to start a new paragraph each time the speaker changes. Give your audience enough details to convey your meaning and your feelings. Use some pronouns after linking verbs. Ask a classmate to read the dialogue aloud with you. Work together to check your pronouns.

5 Pronouns in Compounds

One-Minute Warm-Up

What's incorrect about this joke? How can you fix it?

Abe asked Hahn and I, "Can you tell me how fast light travels?"

"The same way that slow light travels!" Hahn and me answered.

- You know that two or more simple subjects joined by *and* or *or* make up a compound subject. Use subject pronouns in compound subjects. If you want to include yourself as part of the compound subject, use the subject pronoun *I*. It is polite to mention yourself last.

  She and he invited the parents.

  Pam or I will speak at the assembly.

- To check that the pronoun is correct, try using it alone as the subject. For example, drop the words *Pam or*. *I will speak at the assembly* is correct. *Me will speak at the assembly* is not correct.

- You know that an object pronoun is used in two ways. It receives the action of a verb, and it is used after words such as *to, in, for,* and *at.* Any pronoun in a compound object must be an object pronoun. Here, too, it is polite to mention yourself last.

  The principal congratulated Tom and me.

  The class invited her, him, and me.

  An award was given to Ana and me.

- To be sure that the pronoun is correct, ask yourself which pronoun fits when used alone as the object. For example, drop *Tom and.* The principal *congratulated me* is correct. The *principal congratulated I* is not correct.

Speak Up Which pronouns are correct?

1. You and (I, me) are studying the French Revolution.
2. Marie Antoinette and Louis XVI interest (me and you, you and me).
3. France was ruled by (she, her) and (he, him).
4. To the French people, (she, her) and he seemed cruel and unjust.
5. The people criticized the king and (she, her).
6. They asked (him and her, he and she) for better laws.
7. She and (he, him) lived a life of luxury.
8. (They, Them) and the people lived very different lives.
9. A huge gap separated the people and (they, them).

Summing Up

- Use subject pronouns in compound subjects.
- Use object pronouns in compound objects.
- When you use *I* in a compound subject or *me* in a compound object, mention yourself last.

Write the sentences, choosing the correct words in parentheses.

Example: My classmates and (I, me) have studied Nicholas and Alexandra.
My classmates and I have studied Nicholas and Alexandra.

10. (He and she, Him and her) ruled Russia before the revolution.
11. The people forced (him and her, he and she) off the throne.
12. We thought that (him, he) and Alexandra had fled Russia.
13. (He, Him) and his family never managed to escape.
14. This was a surprise to (me and the others, the others and me).
15. (Them and me, They and I) wanted to learn more.

more ▶

16. The librarian helped the others and (I, me) with our research.
17. (Me and her, She and I) found several interesting books.

18–26. This online project plan has nine incorrect pronoun compounds. Write the project plan correctly.

Example: Me and them made a plan for our project on Russia.
They and *I* made a plan for our project on Russia.

Proofreading

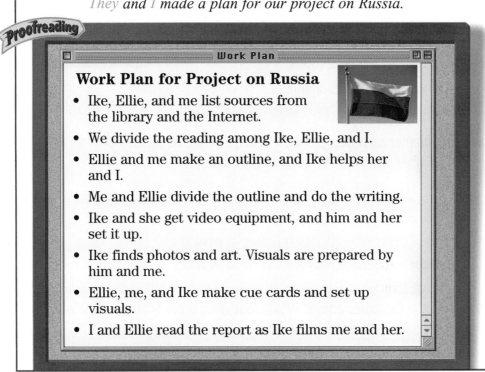

Work Plan

Work Plan for Project on Russia

- Ike, Ellie, and me list sources from the library and the Internet.
- We divide the reading among Ike, Ellie, and I.
- Ellie and me make an outline, and Ike helps her and I.
- Me and Ellie divide the outline and do the writing.
- Ike and she get video equipment, and him and her set it up.
- Ike finds photos and art. Visuals are prepared by him and me.
- Ellie, me, and Ike make cue cards and set up visuals.
- I and Ellie read the report as Ike films me and her.

Writing Wrap-Up   WRITING • THINKING • LISTENING • SPEAKING

EXPLAINING

Write a Journal Entry

Think of a group project you wish would happen. Is it renovating your room? organizing a community service project at your school? helping at a nursing home? Write a journal entry, explaining the project you want and why. Tell what part your friends or family will play. Use two or more compounds with pronouns. Read your entry to a small group. Have them question you about anything that is unclear and then find the compounds with pronouns.

For Extra Practice see page 311.

6 Using *who, whom, whose*

One-Minute Warm-Up

Whoooo is your candidate?

Whoooo will *you* vote for?

Which is the wiser owl? Why?

The words *who, whom,* and *whose* are forms of the pronoun *who.* They are often used to form questions.

- Use *who* as a subject pronoun.

  Who is running for office?   Who voted this morning?

- Use *whom* as an object pronoun. It can be used as the object of an action verb or after words such as *to, in, for,* and *at.*

  Whom do you believe? *(You do believe whom.)*

  Whom has Barry chosen? *(Barry has chosen whom.)*

  Whom is she waving to? *(She is waving to whom.)*

  To whom is she waving? *(She is waving to whom.)*

  To check that *whom* is correct, make a statement out of the question, as shown in the examples above. *Whom,* not *who,* is correct because it works as an object in each example.

- *Whose* is the possessive form of the pronoun *who.* You often use the pronoun *whose* when you ask questions about ownership.

  Whose vote will decide the election?

- Do not confuse *whose* and *who's. Whose* is a possessive pronoun. *Who's* is a contraction of the words *who is.* Remember that a possessive pronoun never has an apostrophe.

  Who's the best person for the job? *(contraction of* Who is*)*

  Whose sister is she?

HELP

? Tip

- Questions that begin with a preposition are formal. *To whom do I mail my job application?*
- It is also correct (but less formal) to end a question with a preposition. *Whom are you walking to school with?*

Speak Up Which form is correct?

1. (Who, Whom) did you see at the store?
2. (Who's, Whose) groceries are these?
3. (Who's, Whose) loading the produce?
4. For (who, whom) are you saving these tomatoes?
5. (Who, Whom) will she ask for the crates?
6. With (who, whom) are you working?
7. (Who, Whom) manages the store for Bobbie?
8. (Who, Whom) will you send this bill to?

Summing Up

- Use the pronoun *who* as a subject.
- Use the pronoun *whom* as a direct object or with words such as *to, in, for,* and *at.*
- Use the possessive pronoun *whose* to show ownership.
- Do not confuse *whose* with the contraction *who's.*

Write *who, whom,* or *whose* to complete each sentence.

Example: _____ turned out the light? *Who*

9. _____ did you like best?
10. _____ ordered the fishing pole from this catalog?
11 _____ book is on the floor?
12. _____ should I go to the movie with?
13. _____ can answer this question about water pollution?
14. For_____ is the gift with the big red bow?
15. _____ did you see at the gym yesterday?
16. To _____ are you giving your concert tickets?

more ▶

17–24. These phone survey questions have eight incorrect pronouns. Write the questions correctly.

Example: Who's radio is playing now?   *Whose radio is playing now?*

Tuning In to Listeners

- To who am I speaking?
- Who is in your household?
- Whom in your home has radios? How many are there?
- Who do you listen to most often on the radio?
- Who's programs do you like best?
- Who's listening to the radio now?
- Whom in the family listens to the radio most often?
- On your car radio, who do you usually choose for news?
- Do you listen in the shower? Whom are your favorite deejays?
- Who do you discuss music and radio stations with?
- On whom do you rely for weather reports?

Writing Wrap-Up   WRITING • THINKING • LISTENING • SPEAKING

Write Survey Questions

Write eight questions for a survey on students' reading habits, TV habits, or another topic. Use *who, whom,* or *whose* in five or more questions, making sure to use each pronoun at least once. Read your questions to a small group, and have group members write their responses. Then work together to check your pronouns.

Writing with Pronouns

Combining Sentences with Pronouns Readers get bored when you repeat the same noun too many times. When two sentences have the same subject, you can combine the sentences and replace one subject with a pronoun. Make sure that the pronoun has a clear antecedent.

Students and parents rely on radio announcements.

Students and parents need to know if school is closed.

Students and parents rely on radio announcements **because they** need to know if school is closed.

Because students and parents need to know if school is closed, **they** rely on radio announcements.

Apply It

1–4. Revise this radio commercial. Combine each pair of underlined sentences, replacing one sentence's subject with a pronoun. Connect the sentences with the subordinating conjunction in parentheses.

Revising

Dan: I'm Dan, and this is Dee.

Both: We're on WFUN—the BEST new station on the radio!

Dan: Country music is a pleasure to listen to. Country music is selected by our excellent staff. (when)

Dee: People of all ages listen to WFUN. People of all ages love to hear terrific music. (because)

Dan: Listeners find out how great we are. Listeners can't turn us off. (after)

Dee: Dan asks a trivia question. Dan gives the weather report. The first caller with the answer wins a prize! (before)

more

Combining Sentences with *who, whom,* and *whose* You know that a pronoun can replace a name. Sometimes you can join two sentences that repeat a name by replacing one name with *who, whom,* or *whose.* This will make your writing smoother.

Our class took a field trip with Mr. Shay. Mr. Shay is our English teacher.	Our class took a field trip with Mr. Shay, who is our English teacher.
Mr. Shay knows Dan, a radio disc jockey. He planned the field trip with Dan.	Mr. Shay knows Dan, a radio disc jockey with whom he planned the field trip.
I always listen to Dan. Dan's stories are funny.	I always listen to Dan, whose stories are funny.

Apply It

5–8. Rewrite this part of a field-trip report. Combine each pair of underlined sentences, using *who, whom,* or *whose.*

Revising

Our WFUN Field Trip

Going to WFUN was the best field trip I have ever taken. Our guide was Dan. Dan is on the morning show.

We met Becky Meyers. Becky Meyers's show was just starting. She works in a small booth. Becky took calls from listeners. She was always patient with the listeners. She was patient even when the callers rambled on. She introduced us to some of the news reporters. They work for her. They research, write, and read their own news stories. I learned about several different jobs in radio.

7 Using *we* and *us* with Nouns

What might these students be saying after their contest? Take turns making up sentences for the two teams. Use the words *we girls* and *us boys* in your sentences.

The pronouns *we* and *us* are often used before nouns for emphasis. Use the subject pronoun *we* with a subject or after a linking verb. Use the object pronoun *us* with a direct object or after words such as *to, in, for,* and *at.*

HELP

Tip

When in doubt, drop the noun and ask which pronoun fits.

With a subject:	We <u>girls</u> are the state champions.
After a linking verb:	The winning players <u>were</u> we boys.
With a direct object:	The team needs us <u>fans</u>.
After words like *to* and *in*:	The crowd cheers <u>for</u> us heroes.

Try It Out

Speak Up Which pronoun is correct?

1. (We, Us) students are learning about computers.
2. The learners are (we, us) sixth graders.
3. The most confused students were (we, us) beginners.
4. Our instructor talked to (we, us) students patiently.
5. Ms. Ide put (we, us) girls in front of the terminal.
6. (We, Us) students were surprised at its speed.
7. Anyone can ask for help from (we, us) experts.

Summing Up

- Use *we* with noun subjects or with nouns after linking verbs.
- Use *us* with nouns used as direct objects or with nouns after words such as *to, in, for,* and *at.*

Write the correct pronouns.

Example: The bus took (we, us) people to the San Diego Zoo.   *us*

8. (We, Us) shopkeepers saw the big tour group.
9. The toys impressed (we, us) children.
10. (We, Us) girls photographed the stuffed giraffe.
11. Our parents took (we, us) boys to a sea lion show.
12. The bus driver smiled at (we, us) visitors.
13. (We, Us) tourists loved the view from the safari bus.

14–18. This post card has five incorrect pronouns. Write the post card correctly.

Example: (We, Us) travelers have seen so much.
   We travelers have seen so much.

Proofreading

Statue of Liberty

June 7

   Here us vacationers are, at last,
in New York City. Today a boat took we
sightseers around the harbor. Then we
tourists stopped at the Statue of Liberty.
The statue looked huge to we tiny people
below! The guide led we sightseers up
to the crown. The most excited people in
the group were definitely us students.

Writing Wrap-Up   WRITING • THINKING • LISTENING • SPEAKING

EXPRESSING

Write a Post Card
   Write a post card to a friend. Tell something interesting you and
classmates or friends have done or seen. Use both *we* and *us* with
nouns at least once. Read your card to a partner. Then work together
to check that you both have used *we* and *us* with nouns correctly.

8 Indefinite Pronouns

What is the subject of the second sentence? Is it singular or plural? How can you tell?

There were eight regions in the state. Each was named for a major body of water that touched the counties within its boundary.

—from *The View from Saturday,* by E. L. Konigsburg

- You have learned that pronouns take the place of nouns. The nouns that they replace are called antecedents. However, pronouns called **indefinite pronouns** do not have definite antecedents. An indefinite pronoun does not refer to a specific person, place, or thing.

  Someone left a book on the desk.

  Does anybody need a pencil?

- Some indefinite pronouns are singular and always take a singular verb. Other indefinite pronouns are plural and always take a plural verb.

  Singular: Everybody is waiting for the teacher.

  Plural: Many are excited about the lesson.

  The chart shows the most common singular and plural indefinite pronouns.

Indefinite Pronouns		
Singular		**Plural**
anybody	everything	all
anyone	nobody	both
anything	nothing	few
each	somebody	many
everybody	someone	others
everyone	something	several
		some

Speak Up What is the indefinite pronoun in each sentence? Is it singular or plural?

1. Nobody is talking during the test.
2. Several have finished the test.
3. Others are still working.
4. Each of us needs help.
5. All of the students are hoping for a good grade.
6. Someone suddenly remembers an answer.
7. Does everyone know the first answer?

Summing Up

- **Indefinite pronouns** do not have definite antecedents.
- Indefinite pronouns can be singular or plural.
- A singular indefinite pronoun takes a singular verb. A plural indefinite pronoun takes a plural verb.

Write each indefinite pronoun. Then write the verb in parentheses that correctly completes each sentence.

Example: Everyone (is, are) in the auditorium.   *Everyone is*

8. All of us (is, are) learning about folk dancing.
9. Many of the dances (takes, take) practice.
10. Nobody (learns, learn) the dances quickly.
11. Few of the students (has, have) ever danced the Irish jig or the Highland fling.
12. Everybody (is, are) clapping to the music.
13. (Has, Have) anyone done these dances before?
14. Each (requires, require) a lot of energy.

more ▶

15. Some (is, are) really exhausting but fun anyway.
16. Several of the dancers (has, have) stopped for a rest.

17–26. This TV script has ten incorrect verb forms.
Write the script correctly.

Example: Now everyone are dancing.
Now everyone is dancing.

Proofreading

Dance on TV Without Hurting Your Set

We're joining a dance class tonight in Square
Dance City. Everybody in this class are a beginner.
We'll be watching the dancers as each try to whirl
around the floor in time to the caller's directions.
Several of the teachers is on the floor, waiting to
help. If someone don't listen to the caller, everyone
bump into each other. That is when some of these
expert teachers comes to the rescue. Once all of
the dancers is back in step, the dance continues.
When nobody are doing anything wrong, a square
dance makes several different patterns. Some is
complicated, others is easy, but all are fun!

Writing Wrap-Up   WRITING • THINKING • LISTENING • SPEAKING

DESCRIBING

Write an Announcement

Think of an upcoming event in your community. It could be a
dance class, a field day, a concert, a sports event, or a fundraiser.
Write an announcement for it that you could post on an
electronic bulletin board. Use some singular and plural indefinite
pronouns. Read your announcement to a group. Then ask your
listeners to question you about any part that is unclear.

Using Homophones Correctly

Homophones are words that sound the same but have different meanings and different spellings, like *he'll* and *heel*. Using the correct homophone in your writing clarifies the meaning of your sentence.

Buy
~~By~~ a raffle ticket ~~write~~ now!
right

Apply It

1–6. Rewrite the messages on the signs, correcting the homophones. Use the list of homophones and their definitions in the box to help you.

Revising

No food or drinks aloud.

Want to start a knew business?

Bye an add in hour newspaper! We charge by the line.

Welcome: Office of the Principle

Caution: Winding Rode Ahead

ad an advertisement
add to combine numbers
allowed permitted
aloud orally
knew recognized
new fresh or recent
by according to
bye good-bye
buy to purchase
hour 60 minutes
our belonging to us
principal head of a school
principle a basic truth or law
road a public way
rode carried in a vehicle

Enrichment

Pronouns!

PRONOUN CROSSWORD

Players: 2

Materials: graph paper, or regular paper divided into half-inch squares

To play: The first player writes a pronoun horizontally or vertically in the squares. The next player adds letters to form another pronoun. Each new pronoun must share a letter with a pronoun on the paper. Remember to use subject, object, possessive, and indefinite pronouns.

Scoring: Each letter in a pronoun earns one point.

Challenge After writing a pronoun, the player must use it correctly in a sentence in order to score.

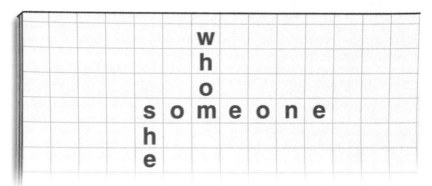

Order in the Court

You are a scriptwriter for a television show that dramatizes minor court cases. Develop part of a script about a trial involving a theft. Write a dialogue that occurs between a lawyer or judge and a witness. Use the pronouns *who, whom, whose,* and the contraction *who's* correctly. Underline these words in your script.

Whom did you see through the window?

1 **Pronouns and Antecedents** *(p. 274)* Write each pronoun and its antecedent. The antecedent may not be in the same sentence as the pronoun.

1. Rosa raises pigeons on the roof of the building where she lives.
2. They are specially trained to deliver messages.
3. Rosa rolls up the message that she has written.
4. Then she ties it to the leg of a pigeon.
5. She watches it fly sixty miles an hour to deliver the message safely.

2 **Subject and Object Pronouns** *(p. 279)* Write each pronoun in these sentences. Write *subject* if the pronoun is a subject and *object* if it is a direct object.

6. Today we cleaned the entire house.
7. I dusted the furniture.
8. Kay washed the curtains, and I hung them.
9. I washed the kitchen floor, and she waxed it.
10. Dad took us out for a hearty dinner afterward.

3 **Possessive Pronouns** *(p. 282)* Write the sentences, using the correct word in parentheses.

11. Let me use (your, you're) telescope.
12. (My, Mine) has lost (it's, its) cover.
13. Let's use (my, mine) telescope.
14. Liz will bring (her, hers) too.
15. Can I combine (their, they're) power?

4 **Pronouns After Linking Verbs** *(p. 285)* Write the sentences, using the pronoun in parentheses that is correct.

16. Our scorekeeper was (he, him).
17. That is (he, him) in the blue shirt.
18. My team is (she, her) and (I, me).
19. The winners were (us, we), not (they, them).

5 **Pronouns in Compounds** *(p. 287)* Write each sentence, using the compound subject or compound object that completes each sentence correctly.

20. Sue and (her, she) showed slides of London to Oscar and (I, me).
21. (He and I, Him and I) watched.
22. The Tower of London fascinated them and (I, me).
23. Big Ben impressed (him and me, me and him) too.

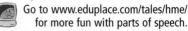

Go to www.eduplace.com/tales/hme/
for more fun with parts of speech.

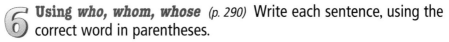

6 Using *who, whom, whose* (p. 290) Write each sentence, using the correct word in parentheses.

24. (Whose, Who's) at the party?
25. For (who, whom) is the card?
26. (Who, Whom) did you see?
27. (Whose, Who's) bracelet is this?
28. (Who, Whom) gave you the pen?
29. (Who, Whom) is he talking with?

7 Using *we* and *us* with Nouns (p. 295) Write each sentence, using the pronoun *we* or *us.*

30. Mrs. Jones allowed (we, us) players to rent her basketball court.
31. (We, Us) players raised money by washing cars.
32. Neighbors brought lunch for (we, us) workers.
33. The hardest workers were (we, us) teammates.

8 Indefinite Pronouns (p. 297) Write each sentence, using the correct verb in parentheses. Underline the indefinite pronouns.

34. Everyone (enjoys, enjoy) painting.
35. Somebody (has, have) blue paint.
36. Few (likes, like) to paint with brown.
37. All of them (is, are) on the table.

Mixed Review 38–45. This text for a museum plaque has six pronoun errors and two agreement errors. Write the text correctly.

Proofreading Checklist

Have you used these correctly?
- ✔ pronouns and their antecedents
- ✔ subject, object, possessive pronouns
- ✔ who, whom, whose
- ✔ verbs with indefinite pronouns

Proofreading

Jewelry in the Renaissance

Welcome to the exhibit. Everything here come from fifteenth- and sixteenth-century Europe. Who's jewelry is in the exhibit? Few of the owners are known, but all was wealthy. The jewelry may seem overdone to we today, but five hundred years ago jewelry was art. It's importance can be seen in paintings of the time. When men and women posed, they showed off they're riches. King Henry VIII and Queen Elizabeth I loved jewelry. Him and her are heavily jeweled in paintings of them.

Test Practice

Write the numbers 1–8 on a sheet of paper. Read each group of sentences. Choose the sentence that is written correctly. Write the letter for that answer.

1 A Everyone are coming to watch the fireworks.

  B Whom is in charge of safety during the display?

  C We kids like to lie down and stare up at the sky.

  D Them are the most beautiful things in the world.

2 F The skaters carefully lace up they're skates for the race.

  G I and Matt give each other high-fives.

  H Who's skates are those?

  J The announcer tells us skaters to get ready.

3 A Kate and me went to see some adorable river otters.

  B It was she who had the idea.

  C Her dad took we girls to the zoo to see the otters.

  D We watched a baby otter and it's mother playing together.

4 F You're the winner!

  G The runner-up is me!

  H Us boys guessed the number of jellybeans in the jar.

  J Everybody love a challenging contest like that.

5 A Selena and I joined the softball team this year.

  B Who has the coach chosen to play first base?

  C Who's mom is in charge of the equipment this week?

  D The person who hit the winning run was me!

6 F Did you get a splinter in you're toe?

  G Few knows what to do in a medical emergency.

  H The Bufords have a first-aid kit in there car.

  J Everybody practices calling 911 and giving information.

7 A Their going on a field trip to the Air and Space Museum.

  B Whom did Rory pick as his seatmate?

  C The driver ordered we kids to stop making noise.

  D Did you leave you're backpack in the luggage rack?

8 F The waiter brought him and I glasses of water.

  G Lola and her ordered salads.

  H Whose order included tacos?

  J Something spicy are in these eggs.

Now write the numbers 9–14 on your paper. Look at each underlined part of the paragraph. Find the correct way to write the underlined part in each numbered line. Write the letter for that answer. If the part is already correct, write the letter for the last answer, "Correct as it is."

> The Morrisons were driving from their home in Chicago to
> (9) their cousins home in Denver. The distance between the two
> (10) cities was 996 miles. It would be the most longerest road trip
> (11) the family had ever took they wanted it to be enjoyable. Mr.
> Morrison planned the event like a general planning an important
> (12) battle. He reminded the children to pack their favorite games.
> (13) He filled the cooler with fruit vegetables and cold drinks. He
> booked a motel with a pool for each stop along the route. He
> (14) ordered a book called *Wacky wonders of the road,* a guide to
> peculiar tourist sites they could stop to see along the way.

9 A their cousins's home
  B they cousins home
  C their cousins' home
  D Correct as it is

10 F most long
  G longerest
  H longest
  J Correct as it is

11 A had ever taken. They
  B had ever tooken. They
  C had ever taken, they
  D Correct as it is

12 F the childs to pack their
  G the children to pack they're
  H the children to pack there
  J Correct as it is

13 A with fruit, vegetables and cold drinks
  B with fruit, vegetables, and cold drinks
  C with fruit, vegetables and, cold drinks
  D Correct as it is

14 F "Wacky Wonders Of The Road" a guide
  G Wacky Wonders of the Road a guide
  H *Wacky Wonders of the Road,* a guide
  J Correct as it is

Now write the numbers 15–20 on your paper. Do this page the same way you did the page before. Find the correct way to write the underlined part in each numbered line. Write the letter for that answer. If the part is already correct, write the letter for the last answer, "Correct as it is."

---

(15) Margaret Bourke-White was <u>a photographer whom</u> showed the world that a woman could be a great photojournalist.

(16) <u>Photojournalists photographers who's work</u> tells a news story,

(17) often take <u>pictures of wars disasters and political events.</u>

(18) <u>Bourke-Whites photos told the storys</u> of poor American

(19) laborers and survivors of concentration camps. <u>She were the</u> first woman war correspondent for the U.S. Army. She

(20) photographed <u>both World War II and the Korean War.</u>

---

15 A an photographer whom
   B a photographer who
   C an photographer who
   D Correct as it is

16 F Photojournalists, photographers whose work
   G Photojournalists, photographers who's work
   H Photojournalists photographers whose work
   J Correct as it is

17 A Pictures of wars, disasters, and political events
   B pictures of wars, disasters and, political events
   C pictures of wars, disasters, and political events
   D Correct as it is

18 F Bourke-Whites' photos told the stories
   G Bourke-White's photos told the stories
   H Bourke-White's photos told the storys
   J Correct as it is

19 A She was the
   B She be the
   C She is the
   D Correct as it is

20 F both world war II and the korean war
   G both World war II and the Korean war
   H both World War II and the korean War
   J Correct as it is

(pages 274–276)

1 Pronouns and Antecedents

- A **pronoun** is a word that takes the place of one or more nouns.
- The **antecedent** of a pronoun is the noun or nouns to which the pronoun refers.
- A pronoun must agree in number and gender with its antecedent.

● Write each sentence and underline the pronoun.

Example: She is a good player.   *She is a good player.*

1. We can sit next to Nancy and Ben in the second row.
2. Where are they sitting?
3. He is wearing a red scarf and a dark blue sweater.
4. Do you have an extra ticket to the basketball game?
5. You will certainly enjoy the next basketball game.

▲ Write each pronoun and its antecedent.

Example: Soccer is a very big sport in Glen Falls.
It is more popular than baseball.   *It   Soccer*

6. Erin likes the two sports equally.
   She decided to play baseball and soccer.
7. Marty scored the winning goal on Saturday.
   He made a perfect shot over the goalie's head.
8. Edie and Lee were discussing a school project.
   They missed all the excitement.

■ Write pronouns to complete the sentences. Then write their antecedents.

Example: The girls on Fourth Avenue decided to publish a newspaper.
_____ had a meeting at Josie's house.   *They   girls*

9. Carla had the idea for the newspaper in the first place.
   _____ wanted the paper to have only two pages.
10. Her friends disagreed. _____ had many ideas for the paper.
11. Pamela wanted to write one story. _____ would be about sports.
12. Carla and Josie thought of a name for the newspaper.
    _____ named _____ the *Town Crier*.

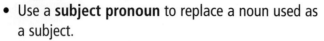

(pages 279–281)

2 Subject and Object Pronouns

Remember

- Use a **subject pronoun** to replace a noun used as a subject.
- Use an **object pronoun** to replace a noun used as a direct object and after words such as *to, in, for,* and *at.*

● Write each sentence. Label the underlined pronoun *subject* or *object.*

Example: I helped Grandmother plant a small garden.
   I helped Grandmother plant a small garden.   *subject*

1. Grandmother taught <u>me</u> a lot about gardening.
2. <u>She</u> prepared the soil.
3. Grandmother fertilized <u>it</u>.
4. <u>We</u> shopped for vegetable plants in the afternoon.
5. Mr. Hanscom sold <u>them</u> to Grandmother for half price.
6. He offered some good advice to <u>us</u>.

▲ Write these sentences, using the correct pronoun in parentheses.

Example: (They, Them) added a small greenhouse off the kitchen.
   They added a small greenhouse off the kitchen.

7. On Sunday (us, we) went to see the new addition.
8. Granddad showed hundreds of flower seedlings to (we, us).
9. Grandmother gave three seedlings to (I, me) to take home.
10. She always treated (they, them) with love.
11. (I, Me) will water (they, them) often.

■ Write a pronoun to fit each sentence. Label each pronoun *subject* or *object.*

Example: Dad drove _____ to the apple orchards.   *us*   *object*

12. _____ are near Lake Fairlee.
13. _____ climbed a ladder to pick the apples.
14. Two apples hit _____ on the shoulder.
15. _____ fell from the branches onto the ground.
16. I put _____ in a big wooden basket.
17. _____ will make applesauce with most of _____.
18. Dad and _____ worked side by side.

(pages 282–284)

3 Possessive Pronouns

Remember

- Use a **possessive pronoun** to show ownership, replacing a possessive noun.
- Some possessive pronouns are used with nouns, and some stand alone.
- Never use an apostrophe in a possessive pronoun.

● Write the possessive pronouns in these sentences. Remember that a possessive pronoun never has an apostrophe.

Example: Your coat is not in my locker. *Your   my*

1. Maybe it's in his locker.
2. Your coat is hanging over her chair.
3. They're cleaning out their desks now.
4. Lani put her red pen in her special blue folder.
5. Your book is newer and in better shape than mine.

▲ Write these sentences, using the correct word in parentheses.

Example: Did Mary leave (her, hers) bike on the Baileys' lawn?
Did Mary leave her bike on the Baileys' lawn?

6. (They're, Their) not going to be pleased.
7. Is it (your, you're) bike?
8. I don't think that the bike is (hers, her's).
9. Mrs. Bailey spends hours tending (her, hers) flowers.
10. (You're, Your) dog trampled (their, they're) roses.

■ Write the following sentences correctly. Then underline only the possessive pronouns in the corrected sentences.

Example: Their working together on they're models.
They're working together on <u>their</u> models.

11. You're projects should be on they're desks by Friday.
12. Our's needs it's final coat of black paint.
13. Her's has yellow blinking lights.
14. Its not mine; it's her.
15. They're model is stuffed with rags like my.

(pages 285–286)

4 Pronouns After Linking Verbs

- A subject pronoun is used after a linking verb.

Remember

● Write these sentences, and underline the pronouns that follow linking verbs.

Example: The first-place runner was she. *The first-place runner was <u>she</u>.*

1. The track-and-field judges were they.
2. The assistant coaches of the team were she and he.
3. The official starters for the games were he and I.
4. The stars of the afternoon were they.
5. The planners of the most difficult event were she and I.
6. The prize winners were he and she.
7. The one who handed out the prizes was he.

▲ Write the pronouns that complete the sentences correctly.

Example: It was (he, him) who jumped the longest distance.   *he*

8. The fans who cheered the loudest were (they, them).
9. The athletes who got sick were he and (I, me).
10. The gate attendants in the white caps were (they, them).
11. Was it (they, them) who recorded the scores?
12. The finalists were (she, her) and (I, me).
13. The band members with drums were (they, them) and (we, us).

■ Write these sentences. Complete each one by adding a subject pronoun.

Example: The woman who built the space rocket was _____.
   The woman who built the space rocket was she.

14. The astronauts who operate the controls are _____.
15. It was _____ who landed the craft safely.
16. The first reporter on the scene was _____.
17. The last people to leave the craft were _____ and _____.
18. It was _____ and _____ who made the final check.
19. The reporter who interviewed them was _____.
20. The astronaut who appeared in the photograph was _____.

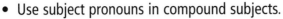

(pages 287–289)

5 Pronouns in Compounds

- Use subject pronouns in compound subjects.
- Use object pronouns in compound objects.
- When you use *I* in a compound subject or *me* in a compound object, mention yourself last.

Remember

● Write the compound subject or compound object in each sentence. Include the conjunction. Underline the pronouns.

Example: She and I walked on the nature trail. *She and I*

1. The bus left Lena and me by the entrance.
2. Mrs. Sanchez took George and me across the brook.
3. He or I can carry the camera.
4. The park ranger gave a reward to her and me.
5. Mrs. Sanchez and he took the bird to a safe place.

▲ Write each sentence, using the correct pronoun in parentheses.

Example: Carolyn and (I, me) stopped to eat lunch.
   Carolyn and I stopped to eat lunch.

6. We were joined by Ken and (he, him).
7. You and (me, I) will lead the others.
8. The snake did not scare Steve or (her, she).
9. The rain soaked Cora and (they, them).
10. Near Nicky and (me, I) was a huge oak tree.
11. The tree sheltered Nicky and (me, I).

■ Write each sentence, using a pronoun that completes each sentence correctly. Label each new pronoun *subject* or *object*.

Example: Juan and _____ hiked down the steep path.
   Juan and I hiked down the steep path. *subject*

12. _____ and I followed Luisa and Mark.
13. Mark cautioned Juan and _____ to be careful.
14. Luisa slipped toward Juan and _____.
15. Mark asked Juan and _____ if Cashman Falls was far away.
16. _____ and _____ were eager to see the waterfall.

(pages 290–292)

⑥ Using *who, whom, whose*

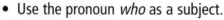

Remember

- Use the pronoun *who* as a subject.
- Use the pronoun *whom* as a direct object or with words such as *to, in, for,* and *at.*
- Use the possessive pronoun *whose* to show ownership.
- Do not confuse *whose* with the contraction *who's.*

● Write each sentence, using the correct word in parentheses.

Example: To (who, whom) did he speak? *To whom did he speak?*

1. (Who's, Whose) ice skates are in the hall closet?
2. For (who, whom) did you cheer at the game last night?
3. (Who, Whom) won the first two games of the season?
4. (Who's, Whose) that great goalie on our team?
5. (Who, Whom) do you know on the other team?
6. (Who, Whom) is the penalty on?

▲ Write *who, whom,* or *whose* to complete each sentence.

Example: _____ brought the basketball? *Who brought the basketball?*

7. _____ is the best guard on the high school team?
8. _____ did she replace?
9. _____ was the forward throwing that pass to?
10. _____ should we ask about the next game?
11. _____ volleyball net is this?
12. With _____ does she coach?

■ Write a question that each sentence below might answer. Use *who, whom,* or *whose* in each question.

Example: I would like to know. *Who would like to know?*

13. He may come with the Jackson brothers.
14. Ms. Greene is carrying the tickets.
15. This is Barry's newspaper story.
16. He called the editor of the sports page.
17. Grace asked for an autograph from Pete.
18. Dad bought her this gift.

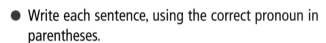

(pages 295–296)

7 Using *we* and *us* with Nouns

Remember

- Use *we* with noun subjects or with nouns after linking verbs.
- Use *us* with nouns used as direct objects or with nouns after words such as *to, in, for,* and *at.*

● Write each sentence, using the correct pronoun in parentheses.

Example: Mr. Dunn surprised (we, us) students.
Mr. Dunn surprised us students.

1. (We, Us) friends took a trip to New York.
2. The bus would not leave without (we, us) girls.
3. (We, Us) sixth-graders saw the Statue of Liberty.
4. The only group was (we, us) students.
5. The guide showed (we, us) visitors the museum.
6. (We, Us) students learned that the statue's full name is Liberty Enlightening the World.

▲ Write each sentence, using *we* or *us*.

Example: The Statue of Liberty was given to _____ Americans.
The Statue of Liberty was given to us Americans.

7. _____ French sent it as a gift.
8. The lucky ones were _____ citizens.
9. Were _____ children the most excited tourists?
10. _____ tourists see the face of the artist's mother.
11. The statue is a symbol of freedom to _____ immigrants.
12. The Statue of Liberty always welcomes _____ travelers home.

■ Write a complete sentence for each group of words.

Example: We singers *We singers in the band write our own songs.*

13. us experienced hikers
14. We artists and musicians
15. we athletes
16. from us newspaper reporters
17. We brave explorers
18. us volunteers

(pages 297–299)

⑧ Indefinite Pronouns

- **Indefinite pronouns** do not have definite antecedents.
- Indefinite pronouns can be singular or plural.
- A singular indefinite pronoun takes a singular verb. A plural indefinite pronoun takes a plural verb.

● Write each sentence. Underline each indefinite pronoun.

Example: Everyone in my class enjoys field trips.

Everyone in my class enjoys field trips.

1. Each of us has a memory of a favorite field trip.
2. Some like trips to museums best.
3. Others prefer trips to factories or office buildings.
4. Today all of us are going to a pet store and an animal hospital.
5. Everybody is getting on the school bus at nine o'clock.

▲ Write each indefinite pronoun. Then write the verb in parentheses that completes each sentence correctly.

Example: All of the campers (loves, love) Longacre Farm.   *All   love*

6. Many (comes, come) from faraway places every summer.
7. Some (gets, get) on the camp bus in New York City.
8. Something (is, are) always happening at Longacre Farm.
9. Today each of the campers (is, are) putting on a play.
10. Everybody (stays, stay) busy the whole day.

■ Complete each sentence by writing an indefinite pronoun that makes sense in the sentence and agrees with the verb.

Example: _____ of my friends have interesting hobbies.

Many of my friends have interesting hobbies.

11. _____ enjoy learning computer games.
12. _____ of these is an interesting hobby.
13. _____ collects postage stamps from around the world.
14. _____ of the stamps are colorful.
15. Has _____ in your neighborhood found an interesting hobby?

The Golden Gate Bridge in San Francisco sweeps gracefully over the bay.

Prepositional Phrases

Prepositions

Which group of words tells where he rolled his eyes? how he rolled his eyes? where the burden was?

> The Cowboys' little field-goal kicker rolled his eyes to the ceiling in mock alarm. He knew the burden on his shoulders.
>
> —from *Quarterback Walk-On*, by Thomas J. Dygard

- A word that shows the relationship between a noun or a pronoun and some other word in a sentence is a **preposition**.

  Andy kicked the ball <u>to</u> the goal post.

 Tip

Never use a subject pronoun (like *I* or *he*) after a preposition.

Common Prepositions					
about	around	beneath	during	of	to
above	as	beside	for	on	toward
across	at	between	from	over	under
after	before	beyond	in	past	until
against	behind	by	into	through	up
along	below	down	near	throughout	with

- The **object of a preposition** is the noun or the pronoun that follows a preposition. The preposition, its object, and any modifiers of the object make up a **prepositional phrase**.

      prep.   obj.
  I went to the football game.

- A prepositional phrase can have more than one object. If an object is a pronoun, it must be an object pronoun.

         prep. obj.   obj.
  Eva sat between Cal and Harry.

                   prep. obj.   obj.
  My friend explained the penalty to him and me.

Speak Up Find the preposition and the prepositional phrase in each sentence. What other word in the sentence does the phrase relate to?

1. Our trip began in Iowa.
2. We skated across the lake.
3. Others stood by the shore.
4. The moon shone in the sky.
5. At midnight everyone left.
6. Night on the lake was calm.

Summing Up

- A **preposition** is a word that shows the relationship between a noun or a pronoun and some other word in a sentence.

- A **prepositional phrase** includes the preposition, the **object of the preposition**, and the modifiers of the object.

- When the object of a preposition is a pronoun, it is always an object pronoun.

Write each prepositional phrase. Underline the objects of the preposition.

Example: Tyrone rode across town to the Science Museum.
　　　　　across <u>town</u>　　to the <u>Science Museum</u>

7. He waited for my brother and me.
8. Tyrone took a tour through the museum with us.
9. We studied a model of a dinosaur in one exhibit.

more ▶

10. It had been discovered by a scientist and a historian.
11. Then we went into a room with an unusual exhibit.
12. We watched a display of stars above our heads.
13. We also saw a show about thunder and lightning.
14. Lightning flashed across the dark ceiling.
15. A man explained lightning to the audience.

16–26. This part of an online science journal entry has eleven prepositional phrases. Write each prepositional phrase, and underline its object or objects.

Example: We wore protective glasses throughout the eclipse.
throughout the eclipse

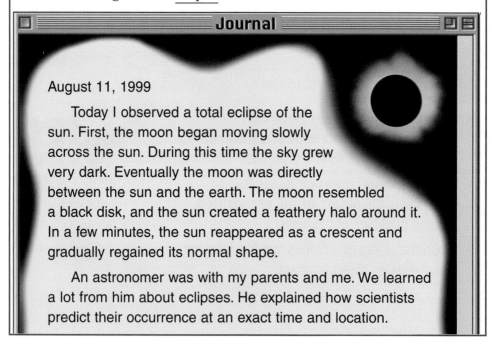

Journal

August 11, 1999

Today I observed a total eclipse of the sun. First, the moon began moving slowly across the sun. During this time the sky grew very dark. Eventually the moon was directly between the sun and the earth. The moon resembled a black disk, and the sun created a feathery halo around it. In a few minutes, the sun reappeared as a crescent and gradually regained its normal shape.

An astronomer was with my parents and me. We learned a lot from him about eclipses. He explained how scientists predict their occurrence at an exact time and location.

Writing Wrap-Up WRITING • THINKING • LISTENING • SPEAKING

DESCRIBING

Write a Scientific Observation

Have you ever observed a pigeon's behavior or the formation of icicles on a roof? Write a precise description of something you have observed in nature. Then find a partner, and read your descriptions to each other. Are any important details missing?

For Extra Practice see page 343.

2 Adjective Phrases

The prepositional phrase *with brass buttons* describes which noun in this passage? Does the phrase come before or after the word it modifies?

> The door opened, and a tall man came in. He wore a blue coat with brass buttons, and a cap, with CONDUCTOR in letters across its front.

—from *By the Shores of Silver Lake,* by Laura Ingalls Wilder

- An adjective describes a noun or a pronoun. Prepositional phrases can also describe nouns and pronouns. When they do, they are called **adjective phrases**. They can answer such questions as *what kind?* or *which one?*

  Everyone in the gym is cheering.

  The door to the building is locked.

- Unlike most adjectives, adjective phrases come after the words they modify.

One-Word Adjective	Prepositional Phrase
wild lion	lion in the wild
neighborhood dogs	dogs of the neighborhood

Try It Out

Speak Up The prepositional phrases that act as adjectives are underlined. What noun does each adjective phrase modify?

1. I built a model railroad with many cars.
2. A control panel in the center supplies the power.
3. Toy locomotives with electricity seem real.
4. The signal switches on the track are automatic.

more ▶

Identify the prepositional phrase in each sentence. What noun does each adjective phrase modify?

5. Our relatives from China hosted a party.
6. Many guests with international backgrounds attended.
7. We brought old snapshots of friends and family.
8. Some guests in traditional costume sang folk songs.

Summing Up

- A prepositional phrase can act as an adjective.

- **Adjective phrases** modify a noun or a pronoun and answer the question *what kind?* or *which one?*

On Your Own

Write the adjective phrase in each sentence. Then write the noun that it modifies.

Example: Several members of my music group play very well.
of my music group—members

9. We play classical music by many composers.
10. The girl with the silver flute is very talented.
11. Her lessons at the music school are helpful.
12. She will become a musician in an orchestra.
13. Our recent trip to a concert was very exciting.
14. A young man from Canada played a piano solo.
15. The conductor was a famous musician from Japan.
16. The music on the stage was played masterfully.
17. The musicians played lovely music by Handel.
18. I have studied the works of this composer.
19. Everyone in the audience applauded the musicians.

more ▶

20–30. This review of a concert has eleven adjective phrases. Write each adjective phrase. Then write the noun that it modifies.

Example: The song about cats was clever.   *about cats   song*

Midtown Sentinel

Sunday, June 3   *Volume 16, No. 22*

Zydeco Adds Zing to Concert

The summer's first concert in the park was a mixed bag. The first group sang songs for kids. The voices of the singers were not strong, and the woman with the worst voice sang loudest. The words to the songs were pretty babyish, so only kids under four or five really enjoyed them.

The performance after intermission was much better. A man with an accordion played and sang music from Louisiana called zydeco. The rhythms of the tunes were wonderfully lively and catchy. Many people at the concert started dancing!

Writing Wrap-Up

WRITING • THINKING • LISTENING • SPEAKING

COMPARING / CONTRASTING

Write a Review

Write a review comparing two concerts, songs, or other performances you have heard. How are the two similar? different? Which of the two did you like better? Why? Use adjective phrases. Find a partner, and take turns reading your reviews aloud. Have your partner tell you one memorable detail from your review.

3 Adverb Phrases

One-Minute Warm-Up

Play a game of "Preposition Charades." Write some prepositions from the chart on page 316 on scraps of paper. (Don't use *about, as, at, during, of,* or *until.*) Take turns picking a preposition, acting it out silently, and having others guess your preposition.

You know that a prepositional phrase can act as an adjective. A prepositional phrase can also work as an adverb. Like adverbs, **adverb phrases** modify verbs, adjectives, or other adverbs. They can tell *how, where,* or *when.*

HELP ? Tip

Look for adverb phrases everywhere in a sentence —the beginning, the middle, and the end!

Sue ran <u>toward the lake</u>. *(modifies verb)*

Ted was eager <u>for the race</u>. *(modifies adjective)*

Melanie swims early <u>in the morning</u>. *(modifies adverb)*

Try It Out

Speak Up Find the prepositional phrases that act as adverbs in the sentences below. What words do the adverb phrases modify?

1. On weekends my sister works until noon.
2. She works at a television station.
3. Animals perform for television audiences.
4. An eager dog leaped high over the boxes.
5. A frisky dog played beneath the hot studio lights.
6. The trainer spoke in a loud, clear voice.

more ▶

7. The dogs were ready for the program.
8. The children in the studio sat for an hour.
9. After the show my sister gave us a tour of the station.
10. Then later we waited patiently beside the entrance.

Summing Up

- A prepositional phrase can act as an adverb.
- **Adverb phrases** modify verbs, adjectives, or other adverbs, telling *how, where,* or *when.*

On Your Own

Write each adverb phrase. Then write the word or words that the phrase modifies.

Example: Sir Winston Churchill served Great Britain during World War II.
during World War II   served

11. Winston was born at Blenheim Palace.
12. Young Winston was not a good student and did poorly in school.
13. He spoke with a stutter.
14. He graduated from a military school and won many medals.
15. Churchill resigned from the army and became a reporter.
16. He was captured during the Boer War.
17. He slipped by the guards on duty and escaped.
18. Later he entered politics and served in Parliament.
19. He became Prime Minister of England in May 1940.
20. He became friendly with President Roosevelt.
21. They guided their countries through difficult times.
22. His speeches brought hope to the war-weary nation.
23. Churchill was knighted by Queen Elizabeth.
24. His remarkable career ended in 1955.
25. Churchill became a painter late in his life.

more ▶

26–36. This part of a biography for a history Web site has eleven adverb phrases. Write each adverb phrase. Then write and underline the word it modifies.

Example: Chisholm fought against inequality.
       against inequality *fought*

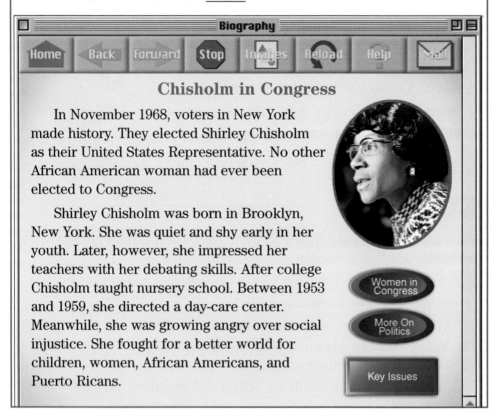

Biography

Chisholm in Congress

In November 1968, voters in New York made history. They elected Shirley Chisholm as their United States Representative. No other African American woman had ever been elected to Congress.

Shirley Chisholm was born in Brooklyn, New York. She was quiet and shy early in her youth. Later, however, she impressed her teachers with her debating skills. After college Chisholm taught nursery school. Between 1953 and 1959, she directed a day-care center. Meanwhile, she was growing angry over social injustice. She fought for a better world for children, women, African Americans, and Puerto Ricans.

Women in Congress

More On Politics

Key Issues

Writing Wrap-Up

WRITING • THINKING • LISTENING • SPEAKING

EXPRESSING

Write an Autobiography

In an autobiography, a writer tells the story of his or her own life. With a classmate or two, list some questions an autobiography might answer. Then write the opening paragraph of your own auto-biography. Which questions will you answer? How will you spark your readers' interest so that they will want to know more about you? Use adverb phrases in your paragraph.

Writing with Prepositional Phrases

Elaborating Sentences You can add information to your sentences by elaborating them with prepositional phrases.

Prime Minister Winston
Churchill led Great Britain.

> During the years of World War II,
> Prime Minister Winston Churchill
> led Great Britain through many hardships.

Place prepositional phrases so that you don't create silly sentences.

Silly Sentence
Churchill helped put out a fire
in a fire helmet and a coat.

Revised Sentence
In a fire helmet and coat,
Churchill helped put out a fire.

Apply It

1–5. Rewrite this part of a biography. Elaborate the underlined sentences with prepositional phrases. Use data from the student's notes.

Revising

Winston Churchill Education:

- Not a good student as a young boy
- Teen years interested in horses and the military
- Age thirteen went to new school
- 1893 started military school; successful
- Graduated twentieth of 130 students in his class

Winston Churchill was not a successful student. He was nervous when he talked and rather stubborn. He was an unhappy child.

Churchill developed new interests. He went to a new school and became a skilled horseback rider. Winston told his parents that he wanted to join the cavalry when he was old enough. He started military school. He became an excellent student. He graduated twentieth.

Combining Sentences Try combining the ideas in separate sentences by using prepositional phrases. This will smooth choppy writing and vary sentence length.

> After World War I, Winston Churchill spent much time writing and painting. Then World War II began.

> Between World War I and World War II, Winston Churchill spent much time writing and painting.

You may have to do some rewording to combine sentences. Make sure the new sentences make sense.

Apply It

6–10. Rewrite each set of underlined sentences in this part of a fact file. Use prepositional phrases to combine the sentences.

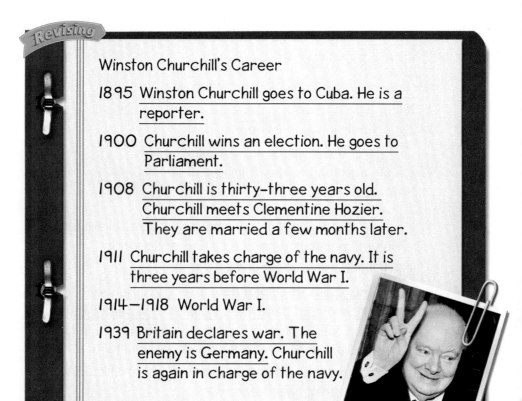

Revising

Winston Churchill's Career

1895 Winston Churchill goes to Cuba. He is a reporter.

1900 Churchill wins an election. He goes to Parliament.

1908 Churchill is thirty-three years old. Churchill meets Clementine Hozier. They are married a few months later.

1911 Churchill takes charge of the navy. It is three years before World War I.

1914–1918 World War I.

1939 Britain declares war. The enemy is Germany. Churchill is again in charge of the navy.

4 Preposition or Adverb?

Do not cut across.
Go around.

Both sentences on the sign end with an adverb. Change each adverb to a preposition by adding two words after each one.

Most words that are used as prepositions can also be used as adverbs. If the word stands alone, it is an adverb. If that same word begins a prepositional phrase, it is a preposition.

Adverb:	Susie invited me over.
Preposition:	I stepped over her dog.
Adverb:	No one was around.
Preposition:	We walked around the yard.

HELP ? Tip

A stand-alone adverb is not always the last word in the sentence.
Please come in, Jerry.

Try It Out

Speak Up Is the underlined word an adverb or a preposition?

1. Susie walked <u>by</u> the empty house.
2. She opened the front door and looked <u>inside</u>.
3. Susie went <u>inside</u> a quiet room.
4. I followed her <u>in</u>.
5. Old, broken furniture stood <u>in</u> every corner.

more ▶

Find the preposition or the adverb in each sentence. If the word is a preposition, what is the prepositional phrase?

6. A faded painting hung over the fireplace.
7. A huge dining room table was turned over.
8. A brass lamp had fallen down.
9. Spiders were climbing down the walls.
10. We heard a crash in the basement.

Summing Up

- Do not confuse adverbs with prepositions.
- An adverb stands alone.
- A preposition begins a prepositional phrase.

On Your Own

Write the adverb or the prepositional phrase in each sentence. Underline the preposition in each prepositional phrase.

Example: We heard more strange noises beneath us.   *beneath us*

11. Who else was in the old house?
12. We should have stayed outside!
13. Susie and I ran through the dark hall.
14. Something moved near the window.
15. Susie and I yelled and jumped back.
16. A sparrow flew in.
17. The bird landed on a chair.
18. It darted out.
19. We heard scratching and hissing noises below us.
20. Susie opened the basement door and looked down.
21. Five noisy cats ran by.
22. We laughed in relief.

more ▶

23–32. This part of a story has ten adverbs or prepositional phrases. If a sentence has an adverb, write the adverb. If a sentence has a prepositional phrase, write the whole phrase and underline the preposition.

Example: The floor creaked under our feet. *under our feet*

Deserted, Dark, and Dangerous

Celia and I wandered around the deserted house. We found a curving stairway and climbed up. On the second floor, several doors lined the hall. We opened a door near us and saw a large room. Celia walked in, and I followed. Heavy curtains covered the windows, so little light came through. We saw strange shapes through the dimness. I was wishing I had stayed behind. Then we heard something behind us. We whirled around.

Writing Wrap-Up

WRITING • THINKING • LISTENING • SPEAKING

NARRATING

Write a Story

Write the next paragraph of the story above. What was the sound that Celia and the narrator heard? Then what happened? Make your paragraph mysterious, scary, or comical. Use several adverbs and prepositions. Ask a classmate to listen to your paragraph. Then as you read it a second time, work with your partner to identify all of the adverbs and prepositions.

5 Using Prepositions Correctly

What's wrong with the bird's first sentence? How can you fix it?

Bird: You should of gone to the dance.
Butterfly: I couldn't.
Bird: Why not?
Butterfly: It was a moth ball.

- The prepositions *in* and *into* are often used incorrectly. When you are *in* a place, you are already there. When you go from the outside to the inside, you go *into* a place.

  We waited in the dark room.   The guide led us into the cave.

- Never use the preposition *of* as a helping verb.

  Incorrect: We <u>could of</u> seen more.

  Correct: We could have seen more.

Try It Out

Speak Up Which words are correct?

1. John James Audubon (must of, must have) been a genius.
2. Audubon painted birds (in, into) natural settings.
3. He would go (in, into) the woods to look for them.
4. He (must of, must have) been very interested in birds.
5. His pictures almost (could of, could have) come to life.
6. His drawings were printed (in, into) *Birds of America*.

more ▶

7. Rachel Carson was a serious student (in, into) school.
8. She hoped to study life (in, into) the ocean.
9. Rachel liked reaching (in, into) streams for creatures.
10. She also enjoyed spending time (in, into) the woods.
11. Rachel really believed that every living thing had a special place (in, into) nature.
12. She set free insects that wandered (in, into) her room.
13. As an adult, Rachel wrote books and went (in, into) classrooms to lecture.

Summing Up

- The preposition *in* means "located within."
- *Into* means "movement from the outside to the inside."
- Always use *of* as a preposition. It is not a helping verb.

On Your Own

Write each sentence, using the correct word or words in parentheses.

Example: Louis Agassiz (must of, must have) been a wonderful teacher.
    must have

14. He was a Swiss-born naturalist who (must of, must have) studied many different kinds of animals.
15. As a boy, Agassiz kept many pets (in, into) his room.
16. He put his pet mice (in, into) their cage when visitors came.
17. Wild birds perched on a pine branch (in, into) a corner of his bedroom.
18. His parents (could of, could have) been angry with their son's hobby.
19. They (must of, must have) enjoyed the surprises he carried home from the outdoors.
20. Louis brought home live fish to put (in, into) his own pond. more ▶

21. Visiting Louis's home (might of, might have) been like visiting a museum.
22. As an adult, he loved teaching (in, into) the great outdoors.
23. Agassiz's classes (would of, would have) been so interesting!

24–32. These two paragraphs from a letter contain nine prepositions that are used incorrectly. Write the paragraphs correctly.

Example: We dove in the lake. *We dove into the lake.*

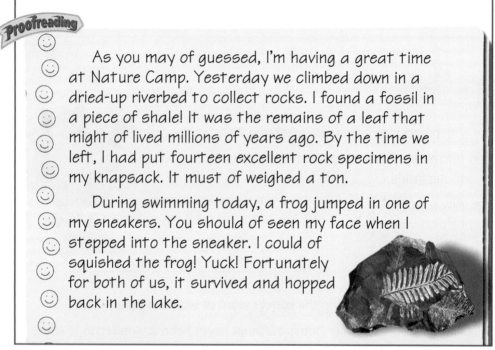

Proofreading

☺ ☺ ☺ ☺ ☺ ☺ ☺ ☺ ☺ ☺ ☺ ☺ ☺

As you may of guessed, I'm having a great time at Nature Camp. Yesterday we climbed down in a dried-up riverbed to collect rocks. I found a fossil in a piece of shale! It was the remains of a leaf that might of lived millions of years ago. By the time we left, I had put fourteen excellent rock specimens in my knapsack. It must of weighed a ton.

During swimming today, a frog jumped in one of my sneakers. You should of seen my face when I stepped into the sneaker. I could of squished the frog! Yuck! Fortunately for both of us, it survived and hopped back in the lake.

Writing Wrap-Up

WRITING • THINKING • LISTENING • SPEAKING

EXPRESSING

Write a Letter

Write a letter or an e-mail about an experience you had. It might be about an interesting project, a place you visited, or something funny that happened with friends. Use the prepositions *in* and *into* and verb forms such as *should have, could have,* and *would have*. With a partner take turns reading your letters. Then read them a second time to check that you both have used these words correctly.

 For Extra Practice see page 347.

Idioms

An **idiom** is a phrase that has a special meaning. That meaning is different from the meanings of the individual words in the phrase. For example, the idiom *in the doghouse* means "in trouble."

Apply It

1–8. Read the paragraphs, and match each underlined idiom with its meaning in the box. Then write each idiom and its meaning.

keep it a secret	thought it over carefully
spend too much	make a good impression
became very angry	make an embarrassing remark
go to bed	support

Revising

    I hit the roof when I found out that it would cost $500 to repair my car. I put on my thinking cap. I had to figure out how to get my car fixed for less. My friend, who is a mechanic, said he would go to bat for me. He looked at my car and told me how much the work should cost.

    When I got to the auto repair shop, I talked to the manager. I tried to put my best foot forward. I didn't want to put my foot in my mouth. I explained that I didn't want to pay through the nose. He said he would charge only $350, but he asked me to keep it under my hat. He didn't want anyone to know about our deal. By the end of the day, I was so tired I was ready to hit the sack.

Enrichment

Prepositional Phrases!

Limericks

A limerick is a humorous five-line poem. Lines one, two, and five rhyme with each other. Each of these lines has three strong beats. Lines three and four each have only two strong beats. These lines rhyme with each other but not with the other lines. Write your own limerick, following the form and the rhythm of the one below. Use several prepositional phrases in your limerick, and underline them.

A boy <u>on my street</u> is named Mike.

He rode <u>to the store</u> <u>on his bike</u>.

Then the tire <u>in the back</u>

Went <u>over a tack</u>,

And his ride <u>across town</u> was a hike.

Challenge Use at least two adjective phrases and two adverb phrases in your limerick. Underline the adjective phrases in red and the adverb phrases in blue.

Complaint Department

Think about a product you tried recently that disappointed you. Write a letter to the manufacturer, complaining about the product. Explain specifically why you were disappointed. (Remember to be polite!) Underline all the prepositional phrases.

Extra! Find the address of the manufacturer, and mail your letter.

1 **Prepositions** *(p. 316)* Write each prepositional phrase. Underline the object of each preposition.

1. Young people across the country earn money at unusual jobs.
2. Jobs of all kinds are open to you and me.
3. In Maine Leon catches lobsters in wooden traps.
4. During vacations from school, Linda baby-sits for lab mice.
5. Larry and some of his friends in the neighborhood raise worms.
6. They sell them by the handful.
7. Chris walks dogs to the city park before dinner.

2 **Adjective Phrases** *(p. 319)* Write each adjective phrase. Then write the noun it modifies.

8. A person with artistic ability can make masks of wet paper.
9. Make sure that the bag is the right size for your head.
10. Crumple the newspaper for your mask.
11. Features of your mask can be shaped.
12. Make strips of wet paper.
13. You can change the shape of any feature.
14. The mass of sticky paper will dry.
15. You can make a mask with colorful painted designs.

3 **Adverb Phrases** *(p. 322)* Write the adverb phrases. Then write the words that the phrases modify.

16. Nature makes bridges in many ways.
17. Often a log drops across a stream.
18. In early times people tied vines into rope bridges.
19. Later they built bridges from stronger materials.
20. Someone turned bricks on their ends and built an arch.
21. After several thousand years, that idea developed into arch bridges.
22. The Romans built their first bridge over the Tiber River.
23. A drawbridge was typical for a castle entrance.
24. The Brooklyn Bridge opened late in the nineteenth century.

4 **Preposition or Adverb?** *(p. 327)* Write each adverb and each prepositional phrase. If you write a phrase, underline the preposition.

25. Tim visits his aunt in the summer.
26. She invites him in.
27. Her house is by a pond.
28. He walks outside.
29. His aunt walks by.
30. They walk around the pond.
31. They sit near the weeds.
32. Tim's dog stays near.

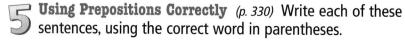

5 **Using Prepositions Correctly** *(p. 330)* Write each of these sentences, using the correct word in parentheses.

33. Val's friends put a windmill (in, into) their back yard.
34. The windmill was built (in, into) an open field.
35. They (could of, could have) built it on a hill.
36. Val's neighbors came (in, into) her yard to watch the windmill work.
37. Tourists coming (in, into) Charleston enjoy the sight too.
38. Windmills (must of, must have) been one of the earliest means of getting power from nature.
39. They (could of, could have) been used to pump water or grind grain.
40. The wind (must of, must have) turned the wheel.
41. What else (would have, would of) turned the wheel so fast?
42. Val's windmill (must of, must have) converted wind into electricity.
43. It (should of, should have) brought electricity (in, into) her house.
44. The electricity (might have, might of) been used to charge batteries.

Mixed Review 45–52. This part of a food magazine article has eight preposition errors. Write the article correctly.

Proofreading Checklist

Watch out for these errors.
✔ confusing *in* and *into*
✔ using *of* as a helping verb

My Comfort Food

Everyone has a "comfort food." That's a food, usually from childhood, that makes you feel warm, protected, and nourished. My favorite food in my childhood was mashed potatoes. I could of eaten them three times a day. Once in a while I must have actually done that. Cold, leftover mashed potatoes would of tasted delicious to me then.

Today mashed potatoes are still into my life. When I walk in a restaurant, I sniff the air. Is there a whiff of mashed potatoes in the air? If not, I feel unhappy. I should of gone to a different restaurant.

At home I always have potatoes into my refrigerator. When I am sick, I throw some potatoes into a pot and boil them. With mashed potatoes in my stomach, I always feel better. Sometimes I think I should of been a potato farmer. Then I could just pick as many potatoes into my fields as I liked. I certainly would have enjoyed that.

See www.eduplace.com/kids/hme/ for an online quiz.

Test Practice

Write the numbers 1–10 on your paper. Read each paragraph. Choose the line that shows the mistake. Write the letter for that answer. If there is no mistake, write the letter for the last answer.

1 A   We went in the cave.
  B A cheerful guard was beside
  C me. I was afraid of the dark.
  D (No mistakes)

2 F   Elena and I waited at
  G the deli counter. A long line
  H of people formed behind us.
  J (No mistakes)

3 A   You shouldn't of run
  B into the street. Traffic moves
  C quickly through this area.
  D (No mistakes)

4 F   Dad gave a list of
  G chores to my brother and I.
  H We worked until dusk!
  J (No mistakes)

5 A   The cat must have
  B devoured the salmon on the
  C counter. It's in big trouble!
  D (No mistakes)

6 F   Sign your name on the
  G dotted line. Then put the
  H completed form into the box.
  J (No mistakes)

7 A   Hannah and I went to
  B an afternoon movie. Mom
  C sat behind we in the theater.
  D (No mistakes)

8 F   Kyle flew into Miami
  G at night. He wished he
  H could of had a better view.
  J (No mistakes)

9 A   Put the dirty laundry
  B into the bin. Give the clean
  C towels to Jo and him to fold.
  D (No mistakes)

10 F   The blacksmith walked
  G into the barn. He showed how
  H to put a shoe on a horse.
  J (No mistakes)

Write the numbers 11–15 on a sheet of paper. Read the underlined sentences. Then find the answer that best combines them into one sentence. Write the letter for that answer.

11 <u>Greta scraped the scraps of food off the dishes.</u>
<u>Then she washed them.</u>

  A Greta scraped food off the dishes before she washed them.

  B Greta scraped food off the dishes, she washed them.

  C Greta washed the food off after scraping them.

  D Greta scraping food off the dishes and washing them.

12 <u>The man walked in the field.</u>
<u>The man was scattering seeds.</u>

  F The man walked in the field, he was scattering seeds.

  G The man walked in the field who was scattering seeds.

  H The man walked in the field and he was scattering seeds.

  J Scattering seeds, the man walked in the field.

13 <u>The ride was bumpy.</u>
<u>The ride was along a dirt road.</u>

  A The road was bumpy and it was along a dirt road.

  B The ride that was bumpy was also along a dirt road.

  C The ride along a dirt road was bumpy.

  D The ride was bumpy, and the road was dirty.

14 <u>I read about the movie star.</u>
<u>The movie star's new film is opening soon.</u>

  F I read about the movie star, but the star's new film is opening soon.

  G I read about the movie star whose new film is opening soon.

  H I read about the movie star although the new film is opening soon.

  J Opening soon, I read about the new film of the movie star.

15 <u>Sophie went to the park.</u>
<u>Sophie rode her skateboard.</u>

  F Sophie went to the park and rode her skateboard.

  G Sophie and she went to the park and rode her skateboard.

  H Sophie went to the park, and Sophie rode her skateboard.

  J Sophie went and rode her skateboard to the park.

Unit 1: The Sentence

Sentences, Subjects, and Predicates *(pp. 32, 35, 38)* Write each sentence with end punctuation. Write *declarative, interrogative, imperative,* or *exclamatory* to identify them. Write each simple subject and simple predicate.

1. Show me that photograph of the moon
2. How far away it is
3. What is on the moon's surface
4. The moon has dust and rocks
5. Has Pat seen a moon rock

Compound Subjects and Predicates *(pp. 44, 47)* Write the compound subjects and compound predicates. Label them *compound subject* or *compound predicate*.

6. I planted and watered the seeds.
7. Peas and beans grew quickly
8. Carl or Mo weeded the garden.
9. They grew herbs and cut some.
10. Fresh herbs or spices are good!

Unit 2: Nouns

Plural and Possessive Nouns *(pp. 92, 96)* Write the plural form of each noun. Then write the singular possessive and plural possessive forms of each one.

11. goose   12. life   13. county   14. radio   15. class   16. fish

Unit 3: Verbs

Action Verbs and Linking Verbs *(pp. 118, 129)* Write each sentence. Underline each verb and label it *action verb* or *linking verb*.

17. The Sahara is a large, dry desert.
18. Many animals live in the desert.
19. People ride camels across it.
20. Camels are good desert travelers.
21. Camels need very little water.

Verb Tenses, Irregular Verbs *(pp. 132, 139)* Write each verb and its present participle, past, and past participle forms.

22. fly   23. freeze   24. do   25. write   26. be   27. swim   28. see

sit, set; lie, lay; rise, raise *(p. 153)* Write the verb in parentheses that is correct in each sentence.

29. Fields (lie, lay) beyond the barn.
30. We (rise, raise) corn in one field.
31. (Sit, Set) your boots by the door.
32. Will you (rise, raise) early?

 See www.eduplace.com/kids/hme/ for a tricky usage or spelling question.

Unit 4: Modifiers

Adjectives and Adverbs *(pp. 180, 185, 197, 199)* Copy each sentence. Draw one line under each adjective, including the articles. Draw two lines under each adverb. Draw arrows to connect each modifier with the word it describes.

33. Joe plays a shiny trumpet in a thirty-member band.
34. He quickly learned difficult tunes.
35. Some very fast tunes are too difficult for most young musicians.
36. Joe practiced hard and soon mastered the hardest ones.

Comparing with Adjectives and Adverbs *(pp. 188, 191, 203)* Write the comparative and superlative forms.

37. proud   38. good   39. noisy   40. red   41. happily   42. fast

Adjective or Adverb? *(p. 209)* Write the correct adjective or adverb in parentheses for each sentence.

43. Becky plays soccer (good, well).   45. Becky learns (easy, easily).
44. She dribbles (careful, carefully).   46. She is a (good, well) listener.

Unit 5: Capitalization and Punctuation

End Punctuation *(p. 234)* Write each sentence, adding correct end punctuation.

47. Ride the elevator to the top of the building
48. Is that a water tower over there
49. How tiny the cars look from here
50. We can see far in every direction

Proper Nouns and Adjectives, Commas *(pp. 236, 241, 246)* Write each sentence. Add the necessary commas and capitalization.

51. My grandfather grandmother and father were all born in europe.
52. Do you still have relatives living there kate?
53. Yes my aunt elvira my mother's sister lives in a small italian village.
54. Kate did you enjoy italian french and greek food?

Interjections and Quotations *(pp. 239, 254)* Write each sentence, using the correct punctuation and capitalization.

55. What's your favorite holiday asked Lisa.
56. The Fourth of July is my favorite said Carlos.
57. Matthew exclaimed hey that's my favorite too!
58. If you would like said Carlos we could celebrate together this year.

Abbreviations *(p. 251)* Write these groups of words, using correct abbreviations.

59. Mount Hood
60. Hilton Road
61. Doctor Rome
62. Apartment 432
63. 12 feet
64. Polk Avenue

Titles *(p. 257)* Write each of the titles correctly.

65. I read an article by a new york times reporter.
66. The article writing for today's youth was in last Sunday's edition.
67. I read the book come sing, jimmy jo by Katherine Paterson.
68. Change is a poem that appears in a book of poetry for young people.
69. The magazine parents' choice has a book review column.

Unit 6: Pronouns

Antecedents *(p. 274)* Write the pronouns and their antecedents.

70. Rudy and Julie hike in Vermont. They are good hikers.
71. Some trails are steep. They are very tiring.
72. Rudy has hiked the Long Trail. It is over two thousand miles long.
73. Luis and I are learning to backpack. We carry extra clothing.

Subject and Object Pronouns *(p. 279)* Write each pronoun and label it *subject* or *object*.

74. Dad walked with us to the park.
75. My family and I flew kites.
76. We ran with the kites.
77. The wind carried them off.

Possessive Pronouns, Indefinite Pronouns *(pp. 282, 297)* Write the sentences, using the correct pronouns.

78. (Your, You're) glasses are here.
79. (Whose, Who's) glasses are these?
80. They are (my, mine).
81. Does (anyone, all) like vegetables?
82. (They're, Their) vitamins can improve (your, you're) vision.
83. (Everybody, Many) like carrots.

Pronouns After Linking Verbs; *we* and *us* *(pp. 285, 295)* Write these sentences with correct pronouns.

84. The team followed (we, us) captains onto the court.
85. The best players are (we, us) two.
86. (We, Us) players always score.
87. The coaches of our team are (he, him) and (she, her).
88. Soon the coach will be (I, me).

Pronouns in Compounds *(p. 287)* Write and label the correct compound subjects and compound objects.

89. (Juan and I, Juan and me) train animals for television.
90. Animal shelters work with (Juan and I, Juan and me).
91. (He and I, Him and me) take a van to the shelter.
92. The (caretaker and we, caretaker and us) choose the animals.
93. All the puppies liked the (caretaker and we, caretaker and us).

Unit 7: Prepositional Phrases

Prepositions *(p. 316)* Write each prepositional phrase. Underline each object of the preposition.

94. Look at the fish in that tank.
95. Bubbles float to the top.
96. Those fish belong to the aquarium.
97. Watch the fish with the red tail.
98. It swims around the other fish.

Adjective and Adverb Phrases *(pp. 319, 322)*
Write the prepositional phrases and the words they modify.

99. Mary Titcomb was a librarian from Maryland.
100. She invented the book wagon in the early 1900s.
101. At that time many people lived far from the town library.
102. Mary brought library books to them in a horse-drawn wagon.
103. Soon people on farms had books.

Preposition or Adverb? *(p. 327)* Write each adverb and prepositional phrase. Underline each preposition.

104. The young girl and her parents looked up.
105. The three boys walked in quickly.
106. The door in the next room shut.
107. The boys climbed up the stairs.

Using Prepositions Correctly *(p. 330)* Write the sentences, using the correct words in parentheses.

108. Steve's boat was coming (in, into) the harbor.
109. Steve knocked his fishing pole (in, into) the water.
110. He (must of, must have) slipped.
111. The tide (would of, would have) taken the fishing pole out to sea.
112. Steve reached (in, into) the water and grabbed his fishing pole.

(pages 316–318)

1 Prepositions

Remember

- A **preposition** is a word that shows the relation-ship between a noun or a pronoun and some other word in a sentence.
- A **prepositional phrase** includes the preposition, the **object of the preposition**, and the modifiers of the object.
- When the object of a preposition is a pronoun, it is always an object pronoun.

● Write the preposition in each sentence.

Example: The Sailors' Museum is near High Street. *near*

1. Parts of wrecked ships filled one room.
2. A museum guide spoke to us.
3. During a storm sailors work very hard.
4. David watched a film about clipper ships.
5. They were first made in the United States.
6. Clippers traded with China and Australia.

▲ Write the prepositional phrases. Underline each object of the preposition.

Example: The aquarium is beside the train station. *beside the train <u>station</u>*

7. A large holiday crowd moved through the ticket gate.
8. Sharks swam in their glass tank.
9. Stuart and I stopped at the fish pond and the tank.
10. Swordfish swam in the water beneath a small bridge.
11. We were fascinated by them.

■ Write the prepositional phrases in these sentences. Underline the prepositions once and the objects twice.

Example: On Monday, officials of the aquarium made an announcement.
  On <u>Monday</u>   of the <u>aquarium</u>

12. Happy, the seal that talked to people, had given birth.
13. The name of her new pup is Hoover.
14. Happy began talking after her third birthday.
15. The seal delighted us with her strange laugh and simple words.
16. The outdoor pool at the aquarium is home to her.

(pages 319–321)

2 Adjective Phrases

- A prepositional phrase can act as an adjective.
- **Adjective phrases** modify a noun or a pronoun and answer the question *what kind?* or *which one?*

Remember

● Write the nouns or pronouns that the underlined adjective phrases modify.

Example: The saxophone <u>in the black case</u> is mine.   *saxophone*

1. Everyone <u>in our school band</u> attended the tryouts.
2. The man <u>with the big smile</u> is our conductor.
3. The parade <u>for Founders' Day</u> is tomorrow.
4. Town Hall is the building <u>with the colorful flag.</u>
5. The library has many books <u>about John Philip Sousa.</u>
6. The band will play several songs <u>by this famous man.</u>

▲ Write each adjective phrase. Then write the noun that each one modifies.

Example: Jean composed a song about her summer vacation.
             about her summer vacation   song

7. Her uncle from New York encouraged her.
8. He is a teacher of music composition.
9. The school near the museum is his.
10. Students from many countries study there.
11. This piece of music is Jean's new song.
12. The title of the song is "Summer Skies."

■ Write an adjective phrase to modify each underlined noun.

Example: The <u>mayor</u> approved the music festival plans.
             The mayor of the town approved the music festival plans.

13. Many talented <u>performers</u> were invited.
14. The meeting place was the <u>park.</u>
15. Many <u>people</u> brought picnics.
16. The first group on the program sang a <u>song.</u>
17. <u>Sounds</u> filled the park and delighted the audience.
18. <u>People</u> clapped their hands and whistled.

(pages 322–324)

3 Adverb Phrases

- A prepositional phrase can work as an adverb.
- **Adverb phrases** modify verbs, adjectives, or other adverbs, telling *how, when,* or *where.*

Remember

● Write the adverb phrase that modifies the underlined word.

Example: He <u>spoke</u> with confidence.   *with confidence*

1. Mr. Garcia was <u>grateful</u> for the honor.
2. His daughter Susan <u>stood</u> beside him.
3. During his term, city workers <u>began</u> a strike.
4. Everyone worked <u>late</u> into the night.
5. Before dawn the workers <u>settled</u> the strike.
6. Mr. Garcia <u>spoke</u> calmly in some tense moments.

▲ Write the adverb phrases in these sentences. Then write the word that each adverb phrase modifies.

Example: Franklin Roosevelt became President in 1933.
     in 1933   became

7. He lived in the White House until 1945.
8. During law school he married his cousin Eleanor Roosevelt.
9. In 1920 he ran unsuccessfully for vice president.
10. He governed the country from a wheelchair.
11. At first few people knew about his illness.
12. He was dynamic in his national radio speeches.

■ For each of the following topics, write a sentence with a prepositional phrase that acts as an adverb. Underline the adverb phrase once and the word that it modifies twice.

Example: an adult member of your family
     My grandfather <u>ran</u> for City Council once.

13. your teacher
14. a celebrity
15. an athletic coach or a gym teacher
16. any historical figure famous for leadership qualities
17. a pet or your favorite animal
18. your closest friend

(pages 327–329)

4 Preposition or Adverb?

- Do not confuse adverbs with prepositions.
- An adverb stands alone.
- A preposition begins a prepositional phrase.

● Write each underlined word. Label it *adverb* or *preposition*.

Example: David introduced himself <u>before</u> dinner. *before preposition*

1. We had never met <u>before</u>.
2. He had a baseball cap <u>on</u>.
3. David put his cap <u>on</u> the doorknob.
4. It fell <u>off</u> the knob.
5. Perhaps his dog pulled it <u>off</u>.
6. The dog ran <u>across</u> the room.
7. He could have leaped <u>across</u>.
8. David raised his eyebrows <u>up</u>.
9. The dog dropped his head <u>down</u>.
10. He hid <u>under</u> a chair.

▲ Write the preposition or adverb in each sentence. If the word is a preposition, write the prepositional phrase.

Example: Kim and I walked along Little River. *along   along Little River*

11. Her dog tagged along.
12. Kim and I jumped in.
13. Kim lost her bracelet in the grass.
14. We looked around.
15. A chipmunk ran by.
16. Kim walked around our picnic area.
17. I searched beyond.
18. Kim stretched up.
19. She peeked inside a hollow tree.
20. Squirrels' nuts were hidden inside.
21. Kim found her bracelet near the tree.

■ Find the adverb or preposition in each sentence. If the word is an adverb, write a sentence using it as a preposition. If the word is a preposition, write a sentence using it as an adverb.

Example: Alex went fishing in a small rowboat. *He almost fell in.*

22. Seagulls circled the sky above him.
23. Alex's best fishing spot was beyond the marsh.
24. His grandfather had shown him the place a month before.
25. There were never any other people around.
26. Alex cast his line in and relaxed.
27. Below the water's surface, Alex spotted a turtle.
28. He watched a fiery sunset on the horizon.

(pages 330–332)

5 Using Prepositions Correctly

- The preposition *in* means "located within."
- *Into* means "movement from the outside to the inside."
- Always use *of* as a preposition. It is not a helping verb.

● Write the word or words that complete each sentence correctly.

Example: We went (in, into) the bus station. *into*

1. We (could have, could of) gone by train.
2. The bus (should have, should of) arrived earlier.
3. We arrived at the hotel and walked (in, into) the lobby.
4. The tour guide (might have, might of) stayed later.
5. We put our clothes (in, into) a drawer.
6. I followed Jay (in, into) the dining room.
7. They (should have, should of) served dinner by now.

▲ Write the word or words in parentheses that complete the sentences correctly.

Example: Did you put your camera (in, into) my bag? *into*

8. No, I put it (in, into) Yoko's backpack.
9. I (should have, should of) bought extra film.
10. The tour guide brought the visitors (in, into) the queen's bedroom.
11. Let's go (in, into) the gardens.
12. The king (might have, might of) walked here.
13. He (would have, would of) come here to think.

■ Write the following sentences correctly.

Example: There must of been fifty bedrooms in this castle.
There must have been fifty bedrooms in this castle.

14. It might of taken a week to make the beds.
15. The king's enemies could never get in the main tower.
16. It would of been impossible to open the main door.
17. You could of lived within the tower for weeks.
18. People carried food in the basement for emergencies.
19. The servants must of used the courtyard to prepare food.
20. I would of enjoyed living in a castle.

Part

2

Writing, Listening, Speaking, and Viewing

What You Will Find in This Part:

Expressing and Influencing

What You Will Find in This Section:

Getting Started

Listening to an Opinion

An **opinion** states someone's personal thoughts or feelings about a topic. Opinions cannot be proved true or false, but they can be backed up with reasons, facts, and examples. The main purposes for listening to an opinion are to learn what someone else thinks and to help yourself make up your own mind. Here are some guidelines to help you be a good listener.

Guidelines for Listening to an Opinion

► Identify the main topic. What is the author discussing?

► Listen for terms such as *I think, I believe, I love, good, bad, best, worst,* and *should.* They help to signal that an opinion is being stated.

► Listen for the opinion. What does the writer believe?

► Listen for reasons. Why does the author hold this opinion?

► Listen for details. What facts, examples, or anecdotes explain the reasons?

► Evaluate the reasons and details. Are the reasons strong? Do the details explain the reasons well?

► Consider the author's purpose. Why is the author expressing his or her opinion?

Try It Out Listen as your teacher reads aloud Virginia Hamilton's essay "Truck Farm–Plus in Yellow Springs." Take notes to help you answer the questions below.

- What is the topic?
- What is Virginia Hamilton's opinion about the topic?
- What reasons does the author give to back up her opinion?
- What details does she give to explain her reasons?
- Why do you think the author wants you to know her opinion?

📖 See page H33 for tips on taking notes while listening.

See www.eduplace.com/kids/ to learn about Virginia Hamilton.

Writing an Opinion Paragraph

A **paragraph** is a group of sentences that tell about one main idea. The first line is indented, or set in from the margin. A paragraph's **topic** is what the paragraph is about. The **main idea** is what the author wants to say about the topic. Every sentence is related to the main idea.

A paragraph that expresses a writer's thoughts or feelings is an **opinion paragraph**. Its main idea is the writer's opinion. What opinion is expressed in the paragraph below?

Indent ⌐

Opinion statement

Supporting sentences

Concluding sentence

> The new baseball diamond at Old Mill Park is a great addition to our town. Most important, kids now have a safe place to play. Two years ago a child playing baseball in the street was hit by a car; there have been no such accidents since the diamond was built. In addition, the new diamond gives the school's team a home field. When the team had to practice ten miles away in Danville, it won fewer than half its games. Now it has a new spirit and a better record. Finally, more fans can easily attend games. Last week over a hundred people turned out! Old Mill Park, always beautiful, is now wearing a valuable jewel that everyone can appreciate.

Opinion Statement

In the paragraph above, the topic is the baseball diamond. The main idea—the writer's opinion—is that the baseball diamond is a great addition to the town. Which sentence states the topic and the main idea?

Supporting Sentences

The labels show the three parts of an opinion paragraph.

Concluding Sentence

- The **opinion statement**, a kind of topic sentence, expresses the writer's opinion.
- The **supporting sentences** back up that opinion.
- The **concluding sentence** finishes the paragraph.

Think and Discuss Look again at the paragraph about the baseball diamond. What reasons are given in the supporting sentences?

The Opinion Statement

You have learned that in an opinion paragraph the **opinion statement** introduces the topic and states the writer's beliefs or feelings about it. The opinion statement usually begins the paragraph.

Topic ·   Main idea

Example: The new baseball diamond at Old Mill Park is a great addition to our town.

Main idea

Sometimes, however, the opinion statement is not the first sentence. It may come later in the paragraph. When it comes at the end, it takes the place of the concluding sentence.

Try It Out Read each paragraph below. On your own or with a partner, write the topic of each. Then write an opinion statement expressing the opinion that is the main idea for each paragraph.

1. _____*Opinion statement*_____. You can vary the great taste of pizza in so many ways. You can add mushrooms, onions, or olives—or anything else you like. Pizza is also not expensive, and it's a great food to share with friends. Four people can share one for only a few dollars each. In fact, I'm getting hungry for a slice of pizza right now.

2. When playing chess, you have to think ahead and plan several moves at one time. You also have to consider what your opponent might do to counter each of your possible moves. In addition, you have to be mentally flexible because the game doesn't always go the way you've planned. Your opponent's moves may force you to change your strategy several times during a game. _____*Opinion statement*_____.

Supporting Sentences

Supporting sentences usually follow the opinion statement in an opinion paragraph. They support the opinion with **reasons**, answering the question *Why?* about the writer's opinion. The reasons in turn are supported by details such as **facts** and **examples**. In the baseball diamond paragraph on page 353, the supporting sentences tell how things have improved since the field was built.

Reason: Now kids have a safe place to play.

Fact: When the team had to practice ten miles away in Danville, it won fewer than half its games.

Example: Last week over a hundred people turned out!

The paragraph below uses facts and examples in its supporting sentences.

The time kids spend watching television could be put to much better use. These days many kids spend more time watching TV than they do pursuing any other activity. You can learn a lot more from reading books or from visiting new places than from watching TV. A trip to the beach or a museum, for example, can be much more stimulating than mindless cartoons or sit-coms. In addition, you will be healthier if you play outside instead of sitting inertly for hours. Dedicated couch potatoes are often less healthy and more overweight than more active people. In fact, it's better even just to daydream than to watch TV. At least then you're using your imagination!

Think and Discuss Find two facts or examples mentioned in the paragraph above.

more ▶

Ordering Details Reasons in an opinion paragraph are usually arranged from least important to most important or from most important to least important. **Transitional words and phrases**, such as *first of all, moreover, furthermore, for example, finally,* and *most important,* connect the supporting details. In the baseball diamond paragraph, the most important reason is given first. What transitional words and phrases does the paragraph contain?

HELP ? See page 18 for more transitional words.

Try It Out On your own or with a partner, choose an opinion statement from those listed below. Write three sentences that support it with reasons and facts or examples. Add a transitional word or phrase to connect two of your sentences.

1. Dogs make better pets than cats.
2. Thanksgiving Day is the best of all holidays.
3. Winter is my favorite season.
4. Baseball is a thinking-person's sport to play or watch.

GRAMMAR TIP Watch out for run-on sentences!

The Concluding Sentence

The **concluding sentence** can restate the writer's opinion in a new and interesting way or make a final comment or observation. In the baseball diamond paragraph on page 353, it restates the writer's opinion in an interesting way. In the paragraph about kids and TV on page 355, it makes a final comment.

Try It Out Read the paragraph. On your own or with a partner, write two different concluding sentences for it.

Baby-sitting is a good way for a teenager to earn money. To begin with, you can choose the families you want to work for. What's more, the work itself is usually fun. For example, many children say and do really funny things. Perhaps most important, when the child is asleep, you can get your homework done, as most young children go to bed by about eight o'clock. *Concluding sentence* .

Write Your Own Opinion Paragraph

Now it's time for you to write your own opinion paragraph. First, think of a topic about which you have a strong opinion. Write it as an opinion statement. Then make a list of details, including reasons and facts or examples, that support your opinion. After you have discussed your opinion and supporting ideas with a partner, you are ready to write!

Checklist for My Paragraph

✔ My **opinion statement** introduces the topic and expresses my opinion about it.

✔ The **supporting sentences** give reasons for my opinion. Details such as facts and examples explain my reasons.

✔ My **concluding sentence** restates my opinion in a different way or makes a final comment or observation.

Looking Ahead

Now that you've written an opinion paragraph, you know the rules for writing an opinion essay—it's organized the same way. Here's a diagram that shows how the parts of an opinion paragraph do the same jobs as the parts of an opinion essay.

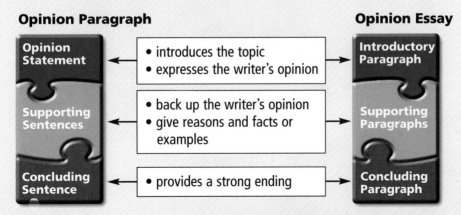

Opinion Paragraph

Opinion Essay

Opinion Statement	• introduces the topic • expresses the writer's opinion	Introductory Paragraph
Supporting Sentences	• back up the writer's opinion • give reasons and facts or examples	Supporting Paragraphs
Concluding Sentence	• provides a strong ending	Concluding Paragraph

Writing to Express an Opinion

The redwood, in all its awesome height and size, stands alone as my favorite tree.

Carla McQuillan tells why she believes that all children, including those who are blind, should be allowed to play sports. She presents many of her reasons in dialogue, as part of a true story about a girl named Jessica. How does Jessica's story help explain this opinion?

Skipping Stones
Vol. 10, No. 1   A Multicultural Children's Magazine   Display Until   May 31   US. $4.95 CAN. $5.25

Challenging Disability

Swing Wide the Doors of Diversity

What Do You Mean, She Can't Play Soccer?

by Carla McQuillan

Jessica's family has always been involved in sports, particularly soccer. When Jessica was in the second grade and wanted to play soccer, her family was delighted. The coach and team were glad to have her, but before she could play, she and her family had to determine how she would get around the field.

Jessica has been totally blind since birth. She uses a white cane to walk everywhere—but that could be a hazard for the other players on the soccer field. She tried playing without assistance, but didn't know which way to go and missed a lot of the game.

A teammate volunteered to hold Jessica's hand, giving verbal directions and a play-by-play description of the game. This worked beautifully. The coach was happy—the entire team was more attentive to the game. The parents of the other children were happy—their children learned new skills for working as a team. And Jessica was happy because she was able to play soccer with her friends.

When Jessica entered the third grade, she signed up for soccer again. Many teammates were the same kids Jessica had played with the year before, but the coach was different. The new coach refused to allow a blind child to play on *his* team.

The policy of the soccer organization is that everyone is permitted to play. There are no try-outs at this age level. But the new coach felt justified in saying, "Everybody plays, except *you*."

Jessica's mother contacted the National Federation of the Blind for help. It is an organization that works hard for all the blind people to be treated just like everybody else. They asked the coach why Jessica couldn't play and were told, "Because she's blind."

"But she played last year, and everyone had fun. Why can't she play this year?"

The coach said, "Because she might get hurt."

"But lots of children play soccer, and many do get hurt. Will you prevent a clumsy, sighted child from playing, just because he or she might get hurt?"

The coach said, "No."

"So why can't Jessica play?"

"Because the team will blame her when they lose," said the coach.

"At this age the most important thing is learning how to work and play as a team. Surely, you aren't saying any one child should be held responsible for the team winning or losing. Will you exclude sighted children who don't play well?"

"Of course not," said the coach.

"Then why can't Jessica play?"

The coach became angry and said, "You're acting as if it is normal for a blind child to play sports!"

It *should* be normal for a blind child to play sports, and for *every* child to be permitted to be a child, regardless of the physical challenges he or she experiences. All children should be permitted to play, to get hurt, to fail, and to succeed, without an adult asking them not to try.

Childhood is for exploring and falling down and getting back up again. This is true whether the child is blind or sighted, deaf or not, and whether he or she gets around on legs or wheels.

Jessica is in the third grade now—and she *is* playing soccer. And maybe the coach has learned a little more about teamwork in the process. Jessica and her mother spoke about their experience at the recent state convention. When she was asked how she plays soccer, Jessica said, "I was left-forward, and left-forward has to be out in front, scoring goals."

Jessica and her family know that in the future, there will be try-outs for positions on the team. They know at that time, she might not be able to play. They also know there will be other things she will never be able to do—such as driving a car. But they also know most things she wants to do in her life will be possible with a little creative adaptation.

Reading As a Writer

Think About the Opinion Essay

- In what way does Jessica's story help support the writer's opinion? What reasons does the writer give to support her opinion?
- Which sentence in the first paragraph on page 359 makes you curious? What does it make you ask?
- In which paragraph on page 360 does the writer state her opinion most clearly? Why do you think she does not give her opinion at the beginning?

Think About Writer's Craft

- How does the writer's use of dialogue make her opinion easier to understand?

Think About the Picture

- Look at the illustration on page 361. What part most draws your attention? Why do you think the artist made this part the main focus of the picture?

Responding

Write responses to these questions.

- **Personal Response** Do you think children who are blind should play sports? Which parts of the writer's essay did you find most convincing? Which parts had no effect on your opinion?
- **Critical Thinking** The author says that all children should be allowed to succeed and to fail. Do you agree? Why or why not? Use passages from this essay to support your opinion.

What Makes a Great Opinion Essay?

An **opinion essay** gives reasons and details to express how the writer thinks or feels.

When you write an opinion essay, remember these guidelines.

▶ Introduce your topic in a way that makes your readers curious about your opinion.

▶ Clearly state an opinion that matters to you.

▶ Give specific and interesting reasons to support your opinion.

▶ Use vivid details to elaborate, or explain, each reason.

▶ Organize your reasons from most to least important or from least to most important.

▶ Use expressive, engaging language that helps your readers understand your thoughts and feelings.

▶ Write a conclusion that leaves your readers thinking about your opinion.

GRAMMAR CHECK
Remember to use the correct forms of irregular verbs.

WORKING DRAFT

Tony Alonso loves baseball, and he wanted to explain why. Since he knows a great deal about this sport, he found plenty of good reasons to support his opinion. He wrote this draft of his opinion essay.

Tony Alonso

A Great Sport

To me, baseball is the best sport in the world. There are three good reasons backing up my claim. ~~Keep on reading to find out how baseball is the best sport in the world.~~

> Could you start with a detail you just love about baseball?

Baseball is a great sport because it has some of the best all-around athletes. If you've ever watched a ~~really great~~ championship team play, you know what I mean. Players on these teams are some of the ~~greatest~~ most skillful all-around athletes of all time. Football and soccer fans may disagree, but I think the skills needed to be a first-rate baseball player are tougher to master than those needed for other sports.

> How are they so skillful?

Playing baseball can teach you a lot about life. I can truly say that learning the game taught me about fair play and how to listen. To be a power hitter you must have a good stance, grip the bat properly, and keep your eye on the ball.

> Your reason is interesting. Does this detail really support it?

Then there is the fun factor. Watching a baseball game is suspenseful and exciting. Whenever I sit in the stands and watch a game, I always end up biting my nails from the tension. Who will win this one? Will my favorite team have a chance at the World Series this year? You never know which player is going to ~~hit~~ smash a homer, strike out, steal a base, or hit a foul that a fan can actually catch. One of the most ~~exciting~~ thrilling times in my life was catching a foul ball that came screaming straight for me. It ~~fell straight~~ smacked right into my outstretched hand—what a day!

This is such vivid language!

As you can see, baseball truly is a great sport. In my opinion, no true sports fan can turn down a chance to see—or play in—a game. "Batter up!" Oh, the game is starting again! I've got to go. See you at the ballpark!

This conclusion shows how much baseball means to you!

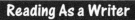

Reading As a Writer

- What did Joe think worked well in this opinion essay? What revisions might Tony want to make?
- What better details could Tony use to support his reason that baseball teaches about fair play and how to listen?
- How did Tony choose to organize his reasons?

FINAL COPY

Tony discussed his opinion essay with some classmates and then revised it. Read his final version to see what improvements he made.

Dialogue is a great way to start. I'm hooked!

Why I Love Baseball
by Tony Alonso

"Strike one...strike two...strike three! You're out of here!" Are you thrilled right at this moment? Are you in agony? It all depends. Were you in the batter's box or in the field? Was that hitter batting for your favorite team or against it? Whether you're playing or watching, winning or losing, baseball is a great sport.

You state your opinion so clearly!

The first reason that baseball is a great sport is because it has some of the best all-around athletes. If you've ever watched a championship team play, you know what I mean. Players on these teams run fast, hit with great power, and make acrobatic catches. They also use game strategy well, deciding when to hit and where to throw the ball in only a fraction of a second. Football and soccer fans may disagree, but I think the skills needed to be a first-rate baseball player are tougher to

Good! Transitional phrases now link your paragraphs.

master than those needed for other sports.

The second reason backing up my claim is that playing baseball can teach you a lot about life. I can truly say that learning the game taught me about fair play and how to listen. Our base coach is the one who helped me most with this. "Run to first!" he shouted to me during a game. I ran to third base instead and was tagged out before I even reached second base. That was my first lesson in listening to the base coach! He tells you when to go, stop, or steal. Now, of course, you don't steal in the real world; it's just a term used in baseball. However, baseball teaches you that it's hard to get away with stealing, no matter where you do it! It also teaches you how to play against a team without hating the other guys if they win instead of you.

Last but not least is baseball's fun factor. Watching a baseball game is suspenseful and exciting, like seeing an action movie for the first time or watching fireworks on the Fourth of July. Whenever I sit in the stands and watch a game, I

You offer strong examples. Now I understand your reason!

Wonderful! You've added two great similes!

always end up biting my nails from the tension. Who will win this one? Will my favorite team have a chance at the World Series this year? You never know which player is going to smash a homer, strike out, steal a base, or hit a foul that a fan can actually catch. One of the most thrilling times in my life was catching a foul ball that came screaming straight for me. It smacked right into my outstretched hand—what a day!

As you can see, baseball truly is a great sport. In my opinion, no true sports fan can turn down a chance to see—or play in—a game. "Batter up!" Oh, the game is starting again! I've got to go. See you at the ballpark!

Reading As a Writer

- What changes did Tony make to respond to Joe's comments?
- What details did Tony add to support his first reason? What examples did he add to support his second reason?
- Why did Tony delete the sentence in the third paragraph about learning to be a power hitter?

See www.eduplace.com/kids/hme/ for more examples of student writing.

Write an Opinion Essay

▶ Start Thinking

Make a writing folder for your opinion essay. Copy the questions in bold type, and put the paper in your folder. Write your answers as you think about and choose a topic.

- **What will be my purpose?** Will my opinion be serious or humorous? Will it be about an event? about a sport or hobby?
- **Who will be my audience?** Will it be classmates? people I don't know?
- **How will I publish or share my essay?** Will I publish it as a newspaper editorial or a book review? in a speech?

▶ Choose a Topic

HELP
?
Stuck for an Idea?

Complete these sentences.
- If I could be anyone, I would be…
- I think it's funny that…
- Every kid needs…

See page 381 for more ideas.

❶ **Make a list** of topics and opinions.

- List five topics that interest you. Don't list people.
- Write one or more opinions for each topic.
- Is any opinion too broad? Notice how Tony broke one big idea, *I love sports*, into smaller parts.

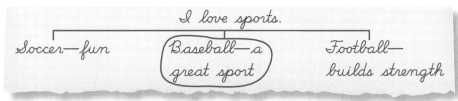

I love sports.

Soccer—fun   Baseball—a   Football—
                      great sport   builds strength

❷ **Discuss** each opinion with a partner. Can you state your opinion in one clear sentence? Do you have good reasons for this opinion? Can you support each reason with details?

❸ **Ask** yourself these questions about each opinion in your chart. Then circle the opinion you want to write about.

- Do I feel strongly about this opinion? Will I enjoy writing about it?
- Do I have enough to say about it? Can I make my thinking clear?
- Can I keep my audience interested?

Focus Skill

Supporting Your Opinion

Reasons explain why you think or feel the way you do.

Give real reasons. A reason that restates your opinion does not explain it. *I hate camping* does not explain the opinion *Camping is unpleasant.*

Give reasons that relate to your opinion. Stick to the point.

Opinion: *Camping is unpleasant.*

Doesn't Support Opinion	Supports Opinion
We drive too much on vacation.	I sleep really badly in a tent.

Give specific reasons. Don't be too general. Say exactly what you mean.

Opinion: *Immigrants have helped make America great.*

Vague Reason	Specific Reason
Immigrants have new ideas.	Many immigrants create new businesses.

Try It Out

- Working with a small group, think of two more strong reasons for one of the opinions shown above.

▶ Explore Your Opinion

Start an opinion map like the one Tony started, shown below. Write your opinion in one short sentence. Add three to five reasons to support it.

> *Opinion: Baseball is a great sport.*
>
> *Reason: has great athletes*   *Reason: suspenseful to watch*   *Reason: teaches about life*

HELP? See page 14 for other ideas for exploring your topic.

Elaborating Your Reasons

Don't leave your readers in the dark. Use descriptive details to light up your reasons. Make each reader say, "Oh, now I see!"

> Sometimes you need several details to elaborate a reason.

Elaborate with facts. Give names, dates, numbers, amounts, or other factual information that makes your reason clear.

Reason: *I sleep really badly in a tent.*

Weak Details: Too General	Strong Details: Vivid Fact
It's cold sleeping in a tent. It can also be wet.	The nylon walls of the tent don't keep you warm. If you roll against them during a rainstorm, you can also get wet.

Elaborate with examples. Tell events that happened to you or someone else.

Reason: *Many immigrants create new businesses.*

Weak Details: Too General	Strong Details: Vivid Example
They start large companies and small ones.	Mr. Lee, who gave money to our school, moved here from China twenty years ago and started a computer company.

Think and Discuss Look at Tony's final copy on pages 366–368.

- What details does Tony use to elaborate, or explain, his reason about baseball's fun factor?

▶ **Explore Your Reasons**

❶ Brainstorm details, such as facts and examples, to elaborate all your reasons.

HELP ? **Outside Help**

You may need to do research or interview people to get more facts and examples.

- Try to anticipate and then answer questions your readers might ask about each reason, such as *Why?* or *How do you know?*
- Is each detail vivid and specific?

❷ Add these details to your opinion map. If any reasons need more details, do some more brainstorming, perhaps with a partner.

Reason: has great athletes

Details:
- watching a championship team
- some of the most skillful all-around athletes
- skills—tougher to master than other sports

Reason: suspenseful to watch

Details:
- time I caught a foul ball in the stands
- never know what's next—homer, strike out, pop foul
- will my team make the World Series?

▲ **Part of Tony's map**

Make sure you have grouped your details with the reasons they elaborate.

HELP ? **Detail Drought?**

If you don't have any details to support a reason, try to think of another reason.

Organizing Your Reasons

Choose and order your reasons so your essay is easy to follow.

Choose your reasons. Your essay needs at least three strong reasons. Use Joe's questions to decide which ones you will include.

Plan your paragraphs. Each reason will be part of a different paragraph. Your details will be supporting sentences for the reason they elaborate.

> • Do you feel strongly about this reason?
> • Will this reason make sense to your readers?
> • Does this reason have enough details?

Arrange your reasons in order of importance. Start or end with the reason you feel most strongly about.

Use transitional words and phrases. Connect your paragraphs to show the order of your reasons. Link the supporting sentences within a paragraph.

Weak: Without Transitions	Strong: With Transitions
Immigrants make America better. They teach us new things. A friend from Cuba can help you improve your Spanish.	Immigrants **also** make America better **because** they teach us new things. **For example**, a friend from Cuba can help you improve your Spanish.

Think and Discuss Look at Tony's final copy on pages 366–368.

- Which transitional words and phrases did Tony use?
- List five other transitional words or phrases that he might have used.

▶ Plan Your Opinion Essay

❶ **Reread** your opinion pyramid.

❷ **Star** your strongest reasons. Delete any weak ones.

❸ **Number** your starred reasons from most to least important or from least to most important.

Focus Skill

Writing with Voice

Your voice—the way you sound when you write—can help your readers know the writer behind the opinion.

Express yourself. Use descriptive language and details to show your feelings about your opinion. Are you completely serious? half-joking? annoyed?

Weak: Unexpressive Voice	Strong: Expressive Voice
I don't like the food very much. It tastes really strange. It doesn't smell good either.	I can't stand the food. Our freeze-dried meals all taste like sawdust cooked in chicken soup, and the dried apricots smell like rubber.

Avoid overly difficult language. Let your voice come through by using familiar words that say just what you mean.

Weak: Too Many Difficult Words	Strong: Clear, Direct Words
Many immigrants made **arduous odysseys** across the ocean to **elude cataclysms** such as **destitution** and **military conflict**.	Many immigrants made **difficult trips** across the ocean to **escape** from **hardships** such as **poverty** or **war**.

Think and Discuss Compare the passages about camping food above.

- What makes the strong example strong?

▶ Draft Your Opinion Essay

❶ **Draft** your essay. Don't worry about mistakes. Just write.

❷ **Follow** your opinion map. State a reason in the topic sentence of each paragraph. Use the details to write supporting sentences for each reason.

❸ **Express** yourself in clear, descriptive language.

 HELP

Another Idea!

Neatness doesn't count in drafting, but ideas do. If you think of new reasons and details as you draft, add them!

Focus Skill

Introductions and Conclusions

Start your readers thinking.
Here are some ways to introduce your
topic and make your readers curious.

You can state
your opinion
first or later
in your essay.

Ask a question.	Would you like it if everyone were the same? New immigrants bring exciting differences to our society.
Describe a scene.	Picture Ellis Island, where immigrants once stepped off boats and onto the soil of this nation.
Give an example.	My best friends are Malaika and Manuel. I wouldn't even know them if their ancestors had not immigrated here from Kenya and Argentina.

Leave your readers thinking. Your conclusion can sum up your reasons or
make a final comment about your opinion.

Weak Conclusion	Strong Conclusion: Final Comment
So that is why I think camping is such a pain.	The only good part of camping is coming home. Does it have a switch? I turn it on—TV, radio, computer, whatever. Is it time for dinner? We'll have hot food and cold drinks, with no bugs! Now that's living!

Try It Out

- With a partner, write an introduction for the strong conclusion.

▶ Draft Your Introduction and Conclusion

Write two different introductions and conclusions for your essay. Choose
the ones that you prefer.

Evaluating Your Opinion Essay

► **Reread** your opinion essay. What do you need to do to make it better? Use this rubric to help you decide. Write the sentences that describe your essay.

Loud and Clear!

- ▦ The introduction will make my readers want to read on.
- ▦ My opinion is focused. I state it in one clear sentence.
- ▦ At least three specific reasons support my opinion.
- ▦ Thought-provoking details elaborate each reason.
- ▦ My reasons are in a clear order of importance.
- ▦ Engaging language expresses my thoughts and feelings.
- ▦ My conclusion wraps up my essay in an interesting way.
- ▦ *There are few mistakes in grammar, spelling, or punctuation.*

Sounding Stronger

- ▦ This introduction feels flat. It will be boring to read.
- ▦ My opinion is too broad. I need to narrow my focus.
- ▦ Some of my reasons don't support my opinion.
- ▦ Some details are too vague to explain my reasons.
- ▦ My ideas are in order but lack transitions.
- ▦ I sound confident, but some of my language is overblown.
- ▦ My conclusion just repeats everything I've already said.
- ▦ *Mistakes in grammar make my opinion confusing.*

Turn Up the Volume

- ☐ What introduction? I forgot to write one.
- ☐ I never clearly say how I think or feel.
- ☐ My reasons don't support my opinion.
- ☐ I need a lot more details to explain my reasons.
- ☐ The order of my reasons is confusing. I repeat myself.
- ☐ I can't hear myself in my writing.
- ☐ There is no conclusion. I just stopped writing.
- ▦ *Too many mistakes make the essay very hard to read.*

   See www.eduplace.com/kids/hme/ to interact with this rubric.

Revise Your Opinion Essay

❶ **Revise** your essay. Use the list of sentences you wrote from the rubric. Work on the parts that you described with sentences from "Sounding Stronger" and "Turn Up the Volume."

❷ **Have a writing conference.**

When You're the Writer Read your essay aloud to a partner. Ask questions about any problems you are having. Take notes.

When You're the Listener Say at least two things you like about the essay. Ask about parts that are unclear. The chart below can help.

Revising Tip

Check your support.
- Underline reasons in one color.
- Underline details in another color.

What should I say?

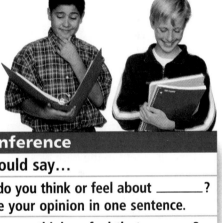

Writing Conference

If you're thinking...	You could say...
I don't understand the writer's opinion.	What do you think or feel about _____? Tell me your opinion in one sentence.
Where are the reasons?	Why do you think or feel that _____?
That reason doesn't exactly make sense.	What do you mean by _____? What details might help explain it?
What's that detail doing here?	Does that detail tell more about this particular reason?
Wait! Stop! I'm lost.	Does each paragraph explain one reason? What transitional words could you use?
I can't understand this overblown language.	What does the word _____ mean? Is there a clearer word you could use?
The beginning and the ending lack punch.	Can you start by asking a question? Can you end with a final comment?

❸ **Make** more revisions to your opinion essay. Use your conference notes and the Revising Strategies on the next page.

Revising Strategies

Elaborating: Word Choice Words that have almost the same meaning are **synonyms**. Choose synonyms to vary the words you use, but use a dictionary to make sure each word has the exact meaning you want.

Not Quite Right	Exactly Right
My flute is the possession most **celebrated** to me.	My flute is the possession most important to me.
Some athletes are more **important** than the President.	Some athletes are more celebrated than the President.

▶ Find two places in your essay where you can use synonyms.

📖 Use the Thesaurus Plus on page H96. See also page H14.

Elaborating: Details Add details to a sentence, or write more sentences.

Without Details	With Details
Setting up a tent in the dark was hard.	Setting up a tent in the dark was a nightmare. We tripped over rocks and couldn't see which poles went where.

▶ Find three places in your essay where you can add details.

Sentence Fluency Writing sentences of different lengths can make your writing read more clearly and flow more smoothly.

Simple sentences	We had oatmeal for breakfast. We had oatmeal for lunch. We had oatmeal for dinner. My parents had not packed enough food.
Complex sentences	We had oatmeal for breakfast, lunch, and dinner because my parents had not packed enough food.

▶ Experiment with a group of sentences in your essay. Combine them or break them apart. Which way says what you mean most clearly?

GRAMMAR LINK ▶ *See also page 60.*

▶ # Proofread Your Opinion Essay

Proofread your essay, using the Proofreading Checklist and the Grammar and Spelling Connections. Proofread for one skill at a time. Use a class dictionary to check spellings.

Proofreading Checklist

Did I

✔ indent all paragraphs?

✔ correct any sentence fragments and run-on sentences?

✔ use correct verb forms?

✔ capitalize proper nouns?

✔ correct any spelling errors?

📖 Use the Guide to Capitalization, Punctuation, and Usage on page H64.

Proofreading Marks

¶	Indent
∧	Add
⌿	Delete
≡	Capital letter
/	Small letter
⌄"⌄"	Add quotes
⋏	Add comma
⊙	Add period
∩	Transpose

HELP

Proofreading Tip

Read your paper aloud. You may notice mistakes when you hear them.

Grammar and Spelling Connections

Irregular Verbs Many commonly used verbs are irregular. Check to make sure you used the correct form.

Present Tense	Past Tense
The ball flies toward first base.	The bird flew through the open window.
Emily brings flowers to dinner.	Ted brought his sister to the dance.

GRAMMAR LINK *See also page 139.*

Spelling the Prefix *in-* The prefix *in-* is spelled *im* before the consonant *m* or *p*.

He was immensely impolite to involve himself in that conversation.

📖 See the Spelling Guide on page H80.

▶ Publish Your Opinion Essay

❶ Make a neat final copy of your essay. Be sure you fixed all errors.

❷ Title your essay. Choose an attention-getting title, such as "Are We Having Fun Yet?" rather than "Pros and Cons of Camping."

GRAMMAR TIP ▶ *Capitalize the first, the last, and each important word in a title.*

❸ Publish or share your essay in a way that fits your audience.

Tips for Giving a Speech

- Make a note card for each reason and the details that support it. Practice your speech beforehand.
- Speak more loudly and slowly to a large group in a large room than to a small group in a small room.
- Speak in a confident tone. Use gestures and facial expressions to show your thoughts and feelings.

📖 See also page H7.

Ideas for Sharing

Write It Down
- Publish an editorial or a review in your school newspaper.

Talk It Up
- Present your essay as a speech.
- Have a panel discussion. Read your essay aloud to begin the discussion. See page 391.

Show It Off
- Make a bulletin board display. Illustrate each reason.

▶ Reflect

Write about your writing experience. Use these questions to get started.

- What was difficult about writing an opinion essay? What was easy?
- Which part most clearly expresses how you think or feel? Why do you think this part works so well?
- How does this paper compare with other papers you have written?

Writing Prompts

Use these prompts as ideas for opinion essays or to practice for a test. Decide who your audience will be, and write your essay in a way that they will understand and enjoy.

1 What career will you choose? Use reasons and details to explain why you think this profession might be perfect for you.

2 Write about a sport or hobby that you enjoy. What makes it special for you? Look for reasons that might surprise your readers.

3 A sense of humor does more good than harm at school. Do you agree or disagree? Write an essay expressing your opinion.

4 What do you like or dislike about summer vacation? Write an essay expressing your thoughts and feelings about this time of year.

Writing Across the Curriculum

5 **FINE ART**
Many people spend weeks or even months preparing to march in a parade. Do you think that being part of a parade is worth the work involved? State your opinion. Support it with specific reasons and interesting details.

Hirshhorn Museum and Sculpture Garden
Smithsonian Institution
Gift of Joseph H. Hirshhorn, 1966

Parade, by Jacob Lawrence

Test Practice

This prompt to write an opinion essay is like ones you might find on a writing test. Read the prompt.

> **A sense of humor does more good than harm at school. Do you agree or disagree? Write an essay expressing your opinion.**

Here are some strategies to help you do a good job responding to a prompt for an opinion essay.

> Remember, an opinion essay gives reasons and details to express how the writer thinks or feels.

❶ Look for clue words that tell what to write about. What are the clue words in the prompt above?

❷ Choose a topic that fits the clue words. Write the clue words that identify your topic.

Clue Words	My Topic
A sense of humor does more good than harm at school. agree or disagree	A kid can't get through a day at school without a sense of humor.

❸ Plan your essay. Use an opinion map.

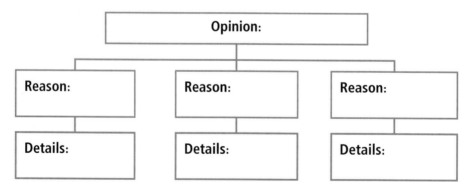

❹ You will get a good score if you remember what kind of opinion essay sounds loud and clear in the rubric on page 376.

See www.eduplace.com/kids/hme/ for graphic organizers.

Writing a Book Report

A **book report** provides information about the main events in a book and states the writer's opinion. Read Ron's report on *My Side of the Mountain.*

Title → ***My Side of the Mountain***

Author → by Jean Craighead George

Introduction —
Have you ever wondered what it would be like to live alone on your own? *My Side of the Mountain* is a story about a city teenager named Sam Gribley who decides to go live in the woods.

Description —
Sam's father has told him stories about his great-grandfather's life years ago on a farm in the Catskill Mountains. When Sam tells his family he wants to see what life would be like there, they laugh. They tell him to go ahead, thinking he'll be back home in a couple of hours. They are wrong.

Sam meets people as he takes the train and makes his way to the mountains. On his great-grandfather's land, he builds fires using just flint and steel, and learns how to fish for his food. Sam becomes friends with a falcon, which he names Frightful. Sam's family keeps thinking he will come back, but that is not in Sam's plan.

Opinion —
When I was asked to read *My Side of the Mountain*, I was a bit skeptical. Some of my friends said it was a good book, and some said it wasn't. I didn't know what to think. But from page one I loved the book. I thought the theme of someone trying to survive in the woods was great.

Conclusion —
The next time someone asks me for a good book to read, I will recommend *My Side of the Mountain*. Once you start reading about Sam's adventures you won't want to stop.

more ▶

See www.eduplace.com/kids/hme/ for more examples of book reports.

Reading As a Writer

- The **title** gives the name of the book.
  What is the title of the book?
- The **author** is the person who wrote the book.
  Who is the author?
- The **introduction** presents the subject of the report and captures the reader's interest. *How does Ron draw in his readers?*
- The **description** tells what the book is about.
  Who is the main character? What does he do?
- The **opinion** tells what the reader thought of the book.
  What does Ron like or dislike about this book?
- The **conclusion** sums up the report and leaves the reader with something to think about. *Does Ron recommend the book?*

How to Write a Book Report

1 **List** the title of the book and the author's name.

2 **Introduce** the book by asking a question or including a quotation that makes the reader curious. Be sure to make it clear whether the book is fiction or based on facts.

> What one event stands out? Is the story funny, sad, suspenseful, or frightening?

3 **Summarize** information about the plot, the characters, and the setting. Include at least one main event from the story.

4 **Give** your opinion. Tell what you thought about this book and why. Did the illustrations make the story clearer or more enjoyable?

5 **Write** a conclusion that sums up your book report. Would you recommend it to the reader?

6 **Revise and proofread** your report. Use the Proofreading Checklist on page 379. Use a dictionary to check your spelling.

7 **Display** a neat final copy of your book report for others to read. Place it in your classroom's reading center or in the school library.

Writing a Poem

Poets can share a whole experience in a descriptive poem. In a few well-chosen words, they can express what they saw, felt, tasted, heard, smelled, or imagined. By putting together sounds and rhythms, poets can also create a mood.

Read these descriptive poems to share an experience with each poet.

The City Dump

City asleep
City asleep
Papers fly at the garbage heap.
Refuse dumped and
The sea gulls reap
Grapefruit rinds
And coffee grinds
And apple peels.
The sea gull reels and
The field mouse steals
In for a bite
At the end of night
Of crusts and crumbs
And pits of plums.
The white eggshells
And the green-blue smells
And the gray gull's cry
And the red dawn sky. . . .
City asleep
City asleep
A carnival
On the garbage heap.

Felice Holman

At the Water's Edge

Hungry gulls
in the drizzle

white nothings
between grass and gray

white flight
with folded wings

hungry gulls
far-off on the meadow

Homero Aridjis

Translated by Eliot Weinberger

Circus Elephant

Does the elephant remember,
in the gray light before dawn,
the old noises of the jungle
in the mornings long gone?

Does the elephant remember
the cry of hungry beasts,
the tiger and the leopard
and the lion at its feasts?

Do his mighty ears listen
for the sound of thundering feet
of the buffalo and zebra
in the dark and dreadful heat?

Does his majesty remember,
does he stir himself and dream
of the long-forgotten music
of a long-forgotten stream?

Sarah Amaya,
Student Writer

Reading As a Writer

- What is the mood of each poem? Which words or rhythms help create the mood?

- In each poem, which words help you see, feel, taste, smell, or hear?

How to Write a Descriptive Poem

1 **Pick a topic** for your poem. Think of something interesting to describe, such as a place, a person, a scene you have imagined, or an animal. Here are ideas from the published models.

- Describe something that most people overlook, like the dump that Felice Holman described.
- Describe a scene, focusing on a few important details, as Homero Aridjis did.
- Describe something from an animal's point of view, as Sarah Amaya did.

2 **Brainstorm** ideas. On a word web like this one, include sensory details. If your poem will mention something that happens, note that too.

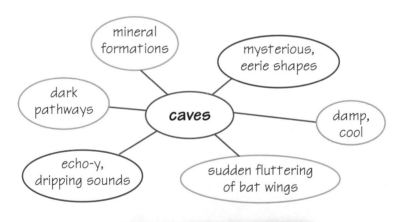

more ▶

❸ **Think** about mood. Add ideas to your web.

Create a Mood

Give your poem a special atmosphere. It can be peaceful, cheerful, mysterious, sad, or scary. Try these ideas to set a mood that your audience will remember.

- Use words with sounds that suit the poem. For a gentle or calm effect, consider smooth-sounding words such as *blue, away, pool, slumber,* and *lilting.* For a different effect, use hard or snapping consonants, such as *cackle, shock, brittle,* and *quirk.*
- Think about rhythm. Does a pounding beat or graceful rhythm fit your topic? The poem by Sarah Amaya has a gentle rhythm. The one by Felice Holman has a livelier beat.
- Once you've chosen a mood, stick with it. Don't jump from a sad, thoughtful mood to a silly or joking one.

4 **Write** your poem. Use ideas from your web, and try some of these tips.

- Use a pattern of stanzas and rhyme, as Sarah Amaya did.
- Use free verse, as Homero Aridjis did. Free verse allows the writer to use lines of any length. Free verse doesn't have a strict rhyming pattern, though it may include rhyme.
- For a lively, active poem, pile up interesting details.
- For a spare, stark effect, trim down the details to the most essential.
- Repeat words or whole lines if you want to show their importance.

5 **Reread** your poem. Does your word choice fit the mood? Are some parts too wordy? Have you painted a memorable picture for your reader? Make changes to improve your poem.

Read your poem aloud to a partner. Ask for feedback. Make more revisions if you need them.

6 **Proofread** your poem. Check your spelling in a class dictionary. Use punctuation and capitalization in a way that makes sense in your poem. Use the published models for ideas.

7 **Publish** your poem. Create a visual, such as a collage, a painting, or a clay sculpture, to go with it.

Give your poem an interesting title that fits its mood.

more ▶

Writing a Limerick

A limerick tells a funny story in just five lines.

- The first line names the topic of the poem.
- Lines 1, 2, and 5 rhyme. Each has three beats.
- Lines 3 and 4 rhyme. Each has two beats. Usually these lines are indented.
- The last line tells how things ended—the sillier, the better!

Read Arnold Lobel's limerick.

There was a sad pig with a tail
Not curly, but straight as a nail.
So he ate simply oodles
Of pretzels and noodles,
Which put a fine twist to his tail.

Arnold Lobel

Reading As a Writer

- What is the rhyme pattern in the limerick?
- Which lines have three strong beats? Which have two?

How to Write a Limerick

❶ Choose a topic, such as an imaginary person, a made-up creature with a strange name, or an animal.

❷ Decide what will happen to this character. Traveling somewhere, meeting someone, winning something, or solving a problem are just a few ideas.

❸ Think of rhyme words related to the character and to what happens.

❹ Write your limerick, following the guidelines above.

❺ Enjoy your limerick! Have a class limerick day, in which students dress as the person or creature they wrote about. Take turns reciting your limericks from memory.

Having a Panel Discussion

In a panel discussion, a group of people exchange ideas about a subject in front of an audience. Sometimes a panel discussion can provide a solution to a problem, or it can be used to help plan a course of action.

To organize a discussion, you'll need a topic, a group of panelists, and a moderator. The panelists take turns sharing their information and ideas. Each has a limited time period to speak. The moderator introduces the panelists and makes sure that the discussion goes smoothly and stays on time.

How a Panel Discussion Works	
Members of the Panel	**What They Do**
Panelists (at least three)	• give their opinion or a point of view on the subject • listen to other panelists • participate in the discussion • answer questions from the audience and each other
Moderator	• keeps panelists to a time limit • keeps panelists and audience focused on the topic • introduces and summarizes the discussion

more ▶

When you take part in a panel discussion, you are both a speaker and a listener. Here are some guidelines to help you.

Guidelines for Being a Panelist

When You Are Speaking
▶ Clearly state your opinion about the topic.
▶ Give reasons for your opinion. Support your reasons with facts.
▶ Speak loudly and clearly enough so that everyone can hear you.
▶ Be polite when you disagree with others.

When You Are Listening
▶ Listen carefully to the person who is speaking. Focus on the speaker's face and listen to his or her tone of voice.
▶ Listen for the speaker's point of view. What reasons, supporting facts, and examples does he or she give? Are the reasons based on fact or opinion?
▶ Don't interrupt another panelist. Ask questions after the speaker has finished.
▶ Pay attention to the nonverbal cues of the audience and of other panelists. Lack of eye contact or fidgeting, for example, may mean listeners have lost interest or are distracted.

 Read page 7 for more help on nonverbal cues.

Apply It

Choose a topic for a panel discussion. Research the topic and then write your opinion about it. Prepare notes. Use the Guidelines for Being a Panelist when you are speaking and listening. After the discussion, answer these questions.

● Which guidelines were difficult to follow? Why do you think so?
● Were your views supported more by facts or opinions?
● Did you find yourself changing your views based upon what other panelists had to say?

Identifying Points of View in Media

Images that you see in the media have a point of view, or viewpoint. A viewpoint is a way of feeling and thinking about a subject.

People who work in the media write and edit information as they prepare to publish or broadcast it. The kinds of articles, books, Internet sites, and TV or radio programs they create reflect their viewpoints. Their viewpoints can influence yours.

Channel A The camera focuses on a young Native American dancing at a powwow. A reporter interviews the young man about traditions, while the sound person records the drums and dance music.

Channel B The camera and sound people focus on the families attending the powwow. A reporter interviews a Native American dancer and finds out that she is studying mathematics at the local university.

Two Viewpoints, One Event

Look at the images and read the captions. The choices made by the media people at the powwow created two different versions of the same event. What information did Channel A leave out? What message did Channel B give about Native Americans?

Media people may rely on stereotypes to tell a story quickly. A stereotype is an overly simple picture or opinion of people, places, ideas, or things. Stereotypes usually give incomplete or misleading information.

more ▶

Seeing Is Believing—Or Is It?

Many people believe that what they see with their eyes is true. Because of this, they may think that what they see in photographs or news video footage is truthful and accurate. Photos may appear to be complete, but they cannot tell the whole story.

Photographers—including video photographers—shape images to express a viewpoint. For example, by cropping they can alter a picture to show only what they want the viewer to see. The photo on the right has been cropped. Find the cropped part that is shown in the photo on the left. The chart below lists other ways photographs can be altered.

Ways Photographers Can Alter Images	
Camera Technique	**Definition**
crop	including only part of a scene in the camera frame
long shot	shooting a subject from far away
close-up	shooting a subject from a very short distance
pan	moving the camera along the horizon to make the subject look wide or vast
fade-out	letting an image gradually disappear
bump to black	abruptly ending an image and letting the screen go black

When a photographer shoots a subject, he or she has a purpose. It may be to help the viewer understand written information. It may be to persuade someone to buy something. The purpose shapes the choices that media people make about what to shoot and how to do it.

Here are some ideas to help you identify the viewpoint in different media.

Guidelines for Identifying Points of View in Media

▶ Think about who created the photograph, video segment, or movie. Why are they publishing, showing, or broadcasting it?

▶ Find the purpose of the example. Decide whether it is intended to inform, persuade, advertise, or entertain.

▶ Consider whether any information is missing from the example.

▶ Notice the photographic techniques that are used to attract the viewer's attention. How does the information look and sound?

▶ Does the example seem to have a message? Decide what it is.

▶ Think about the group of people the message is meant to reach. Who do you think the audience is?

Apply It

Look at photographs in a news magazine. Choose two. Using the guidelines above to help you, describe a possible viewpoint for each photo. Then answer these questions.

● What camera techniques were used? Describe how the techniques could affect a viewer's response to the content of the photos.

● Was the viewpoint obvious in the photos? Explain why or why not.

Keep notes in a notebook for a week about different points of view in media. Use the guidelines and look at several kinds of media. Share your ideas with classmates.

Unit 9

Writing to Persuade

Our class should organize a car wash to raise funds for our year-end project.

Earth is getting warmer, but Samantha Bonar wrote an essay to persuade people to change that. What can we do to help keep Earth cool?

Forecast: Hot and Hotter

by Samantha Bonar, *originally published in Contact*

Imagine a baby covered in a snug blanket. If the blanket were too thick, the baby would get too hot. If the blanket were too thin, the baby would be cold. But the blanket is perfect, so the baby feels just right.

Earth is like a baby wrapped in a great blanket—the atmosphere. Made of gases and water vapor, our atmosphere is neither too thin nor too thick. It lets in just enough sunlight to warm the planet. And it filters out just enough sunlight so that Earth's climate stays comfortable. But over the past century, Earth's atmosphere has changed.

Earth's atmosphere from space

more ▶

Like an overwrapped baby, Earth may be growing too warm. Many scientists say this global warming is bad for our planet—and for the people, plants, and animals that inhabit it.

The Intergovernmental Panel on Climate Change (IPCC) is made up of climate experts from 60 countries. Last fall, it predicted that the overall global temperature may rise six degrees Fahrenheit by the year 2100. Big deal, huh?

It *is* a big deal. Especially if you consider that Earth's average temperature has not changed in 20,000 years. The last time Earth's temperature increased—by only nine degrees—the warming ended the Ice Age. That's when vast sheets of thick ice covered the earth.

Wild Weather!

People living in a cold climate might think global warming is a good idea! It's possible that winters would get warmer worldwide, but that may not be worth the tradeoff.

Plants and animals that can't adapt to the changing climate could become extinct. Densely populated lands could be flooded when seas rise, due to melting at the North and South Poles. Some islands might be completely covered by water. According to the IPCC, this flooding would submerge most of the beaches on the Atlantic coast of the United States.

Since climate affects weather, weather patterns could become more severe. That means broiling summers, winter blizzards, floods, droughts, tornadoes, and hurricanes. What's causing this warming trend? According to the IPCC, the answer is . . . humans! The trouble began in the mid-1700s, when people began using "fossil fuels," like coal, oil, and natural gas. Burning huge amounts of these substances releases an invisible gas in the air called carbon dioxide (CO_2). Since the 1880s, the amount of CO_2 in the air has risen more than 22 percent.

Some Like It Hot!

So what's the problem with carbon dioxide? Carbon dioxide acts like the glass in a greenhouse. It lets in the sun's warmth, but doesn't let it out. That's why this kind of warming is sometimes called the "greenhouse effect."

Now, at the end of the 20th century, global warming has become a hot issue. Sixty million tons of carbon dioxide are released into the atmosphere each day. The gas comes from steel mills, power plants, burning rain forests, and 500 million cars around the world.

There's Hope

There is hope for our planet. To lower global warming, the IPCC says we should switch from oil and coal to natural gas as an energy source. Natural gas is an invisible gas trapped under the earth. When burned, it produces much less CO_2. We should also turn to solar and wind power, stop burning rain forests, and drive less. Sounds cool!

◄ A solar-powered car

Modern windmills ►

more ▶

Reading As a Writer

Think About the Persuasive Essay

- What does Samantha Bonar want her audience to do?
- What reasons does the author give to support her goal?
- What possible objection does the author introduce in the fourth paragraph on page 398? How does she answer it?

Think About Writer's Craft

- To what does the author compare Earth and its atmosphere in the second paragraph on page 397? What qualities does this comparison suggest that Earth and a baby share?

Think About the Picture

- Look at the pictures on page 399. How do these pictures tell more about what we can do to keep Earth cool?

Responding

Write responses to these questions.

- **Personal Response** Which of your daily activities could you change in order to slow global warming? Why is it important to make such changes?
- **Critical Thinking** Why do you think the author waits until the end of her article to tell readers what she wants them to do?

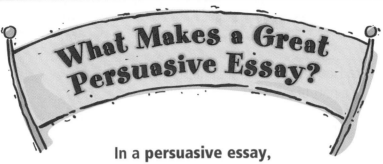

What Makes a Great Persuasive Essay?

In a **persuasive essay,**
the writer tries to convince an audience
to take a specific action.

When you write a persuasive essay, remember to follow these guidelines.

▶ Clearly state your goal, what you want your audience to do.

▶ Include at least three strong reasons to support your goal.

▶ Support, or elaborate, each reason with facts and examples.

▶ Use convincing language that is both positive and polite.

▶ Put your reasons in an order that works best to persuade your audience.

▶ Answer objections your audience might have.

▶ End by summarizing your reasons and calling your audience to action.

GRAMMAR CHECK

Use singular verbs for singular subjects and plural verbs for plural subjects.

WORKING DRAFT

Jessica Figueroa believes that music should be a part of everyone's life. Jessica knows many good reasons why her classmates should participate in music, so she wrote this draft of her persuasive essay.

Jessica Figueroa

What do you want your audience to do?

Music

~~I think~~ Music is a great thing! It amazes me how much music does for us. Lots of kids don't realize just how important music is.

Does this reason support your goal?

You could learn more about Louis Armstrong and other musicians. It's always good to know about famous musicians. Louis Armstrong traveled all over the world performing music until he died in 1971. ~~His nickname was "Satchmo."~~ He recorded a lot of records and appeared in many shows.

Have you ever been stressed out from school? Try listening to music. Put on your favorite CD, sit or lie down, close your eyes, and listen. Lose yourself in the music, and your stress will begin to go away. After a few minutes of listening to music, you'll feel better because music helps your mind let go of stress. Put a little rhythm into your relaxation!

What about TV? It's a great way to relax too.

Can you add examples to support your reason more clearly?

Have you noticed how some music makes you feel happy and other music makes you feel sad? The musicians who made that music were expressing their emotions and creativity. If you play an instrument, you will also be able to express yourself in such a way.

Have you ever caught yourself dancing to a good song on the radio? If you're out of shape but don't like to do sports, you can dance your way into good physical condition! Studies show that dancing makes you stronger and more coordinated. Certain dances even include jumping, which is great aerobic exercise according to the American Heart Association.

Music is more than just popping a CD into your stereo. Get involved in music! You'll be amazed too.

Reading As a Writer

- What did Joe think worked well in this essay? What revisions might Jessica make to address Joe's questions?
- Which of Jessica's reasons did you find the most convincing? Why?
- What facts does Jessica give to support her reason that music can help people stay in shape?
- Which sentences show Jessica's enthusiasm about her goal?

FINAL COPY

Jessica revised her persuasive essay after discussing it with a classmate. Read her final version to see how she improved it.

Music Will Amaze You!
by Jessica Figueroa

Music is a great thing! It amazes me how much music does for us. I strongly believe that more kids should get involved with music.

Have you ever been stressed out from school? Try listening to music. Some people think that plopping down in front of the TV is a good way to relax, but there is a better way. Put on your favorite CD, sit or lie down, close your eyes, and listen. Lose yourself in the music, and your stress will begin to go away. Watching TV may take no energy, but TV is way too busy to help you relax the way music can. After a few minutes of listening to music, you'll feel better because music helps your mind let go of what is stressing it out. Put a little rhythm into your relaxation!

Also, have you ever caught yourself dancing to a good song on the radio? If you're out of shape but don't like to do sports, you can dance your way into good physical condition! Studies show that dancing makes you stronger and more coordinated. Certain dances even include jumping, which is a great aerobic exercise according to the American Heart Association.

Most important, have you noticed how some music makes you feel happy and other music makes you feel sad? The musicians who made

> Your introduction is clearer now.

> I like the way you answered my objection.

> Smart! You put your most important reason last.

that music were expressing their emotions and creativity. If you play an instrument, you will also be able to express yourself in such a way. There are many instruments to choose from. Experiment by playing different ones or by thinking about different instruments you like to listen to. Then choose one to learn to play. I have been really happy and able to express myself since I learned to play the piano. Although it may take some time to learn to play an instrument well, in the end you will have a way to create your own beautiful music.

> This example really supports your reason!

As you can see, music is more than just popping a CD into your stereo. Just listening to music is a joy, but you can also use music to help you relax, to get exercise, and to express yourself. Get involved in music! You'll be amazed too.

> This is a clear and forceful ending.

Reading As a Writer

- How did Jessica respond to Joe's questions?
- What did Jessica say about TV to answer Joe's objection?
- What examples did Jessica add to her fourth paragraph?
- What did Jessica add to her conclusion?

 See www.eduplace.com/kids/hme/ for more examples of student writing.

Student Model   405

Write a Persuasive Essay

▶ Start Thinking

 Make a writing folder for your persuasive essay. Copy the questions in bold type, and put your paper in your folder. Write your answers as you choose and explore your topic.

- **What will be my purpose or goal?** What do I want my readers to do? Why should they take this action?
- **Who will be my audience?** Will I try to convince my fellow classmates? the principal? my parents?
- **How will I publish or share my essay?** Will I publish it on the Internet? as a newspaper editorial? as part of a debate?

▶ Choose Your Goal

❶ **List** five goals. Make a chart like the one below to help you think of ideas. For each goal, name the audience you want to take action.

Goal	Audience	Publishing
get after-school job	parents	speech
get involved in music	classmates	editorial for the paper
create new lunch menu	principal	letter

❷ **Talk** to a partner about each of your goals.

- Is each goal clear? Can your audience actually do what you suggest?
- Which goal does your partner think is the most interesting? Why?
- Can you support this goal with convincing reasons?

Don't choose a goal that everyone already agrees with.

❸ **Ask** yourself these questions about each goal. Then pick the one you want to write about.

- Do I feel strongly about this goal?
- Is this goal too large? too small?
- Do I have facts and examples to support each reason?

 See page 418 for more ideas for persuasive goals.

Focus Skill

Supporting Your Goal and Reasons

Think of strong reasons. Strong reasons tell your audience clearly and specifically why they should do what you suggest. Weak reasons are vague or unrelated to your goal.

Goal: to convince the principal to expand the arts program at school

Weak Reason	Strong Reason
Art is my favorite subject.	The arts give students multiple ways to express themselves.

Use facts and examples to elaborate, or support, your reasons. **Facts** are information that can be proved to be true. **Examples** are anecdotes or observations made about something.

Don't use opinions to support your reasons. Opinions state feelings or thoughts.

Reason: Uniforms help students concentrate on their studies.

Example	Fact
Students in our school report that they worry less about clothes and more about social studies.	At one school, test scores rose an average of 17 percent after uniforms were introduced.

Evaluate your reasons. Now that you've brainstormed reasons, facts, and examples, examine them. Ask yourself the questions below and on the next page.

- Do I have the right reasons for my audience? Reasons that make sense to a classmate might not make sense to an adult.

Goal: to persuade my audience to support school uniforms

Student Audience	Grown-Up Audience
It would be nice not to have to worry about the clothes you wear every day.	Students would spend less time competing over clothes and more time concentrating on school activities and getting along with one another.

more ▶

Focus Skill continued

- Do my reasons clearly support my goal? Good reasons do not exaggerate. They can be easily supported with facts and examples. *Our cafeteria serves poisonous food!* would never persuade the principal to adopt a new lunch menu.
- Are my facts and examples convincing? Look at the support for the reason below.

Reason: Our lunch menu has little variety.

Weak Example	**Strong Example**
For example, the same vegetables are served day after day.	For example, lima beans are usually served three times a week.

Think and Discuss

- Find three facts or examples in the published model on pages 397–399.
- Who is Jessica's audience in her final copy on pages 404–405? Which reasons might have changed if her audience were parents?

▶ Explore Your Goal and Reasons

❶ Make a diagram like the one shown here. Write your goal.

❷ Write all the reasons you can think of for your goal.

❸ Brainstorm facts and examples to support your reasons. Write them in boxes under your reasons.

❹ Look at the reasons on your diagram. Star the reasons that best support your goal. Star the facts or examples that best support each reason.

HELP
?
Stuck for Reasons?

If you can't think of three strong reasons, try a different topic.

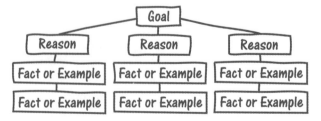

 See page 14 for other ideas on exploring a topic.

Focus Skill

Answering Objections

What might your audience say if they don't agree with you? Your reasons should show that you have thought about and can answer possible objections.

For example, what objection might other students have to the goal that your school should have uniforms? How might you answer that objection?

Possible Objection	Objection Answered
Uniforms make everybody look the same.	Some might worry that uniforms will make students lose their individuality. However, students can easily find more creative ways to express themselves.

Possible Objection	Objection Answered
Many people cannot afford uniforms.	Although uniforms can be more expensive, they last a lot longer than regular clothing and will save students and their families money.

Think and Discuss Work with a partner.

- Think of objections that your classmates might have to this goal: all students should participate in a school sport. Answer each objection.

▶ Explore Possible Objections

❶ **Ask a partner** to think of possible objections to your goal or reasons.

❷ **Answer** each objection with your partner. You may need to find new reasons or new facts and examples. Add each answer to your diagram.

Focus Skill

Organizing Your Argument

Your **argument** is your reasons, supported by facts and examples. An argument that is hard to follow will not convince anyone.

Order your reasons. Think about your audience, and choose the more convincing order.

- Going from your least important to your most important reason builds interest and leaves your audience thinking about your strongest argument.
- Going from your most important to your least important reason grabs your audience's attention right away.

Plan a separate paragraph for each reason. State the reason in the topic sentence. Then support your reason with facts and examples. Connect both your sentences and your paragraphs with transitional words and phrases.

Transitional Words	Transitional Phrases
first, second, then, next, finally, another, therefore, thus, although, also, similarly, too, furthermore, moreover	to begin with, first of all, in addition, most important, in conclusion, my third reason, last of all, in response to, for example, above all

GRAMMAR TIP   Always use a comma after order words such as **first, second, third.** Do not use the words **firstly, secondly,** or **thirdly.**

Keep to the topic. Make sure that all your facts and examples support your reasons and your goal.

. . . .

Think and Discuss Look at Jessica's final copy on pages 404–405.

- Did Jessica put her most important reason first or last?
- What transitional words and phrases did Jessica use? What others might she have used?

▶ **Plan Your Essay**

❶ **Reread** your diagram.

❷ **Number** your reasons in the order you want to write about them.

Focus Skill

Introductions and Conclusions

Make your introduction clear and interesting. Your introduction should grab your reader's attention and clearly state your goal.

- Begin with a question. Get your readers thinking.

Weak Introduction	Strong Introduction
I think kids should wear uniforms at our school.	Are you spending all of your money on clothes? This school should have uniforms. Then you could use your money for other things.

- Begin with a startling fact. Surprise your readers.

Weak Introduction	Strong Introduction
We need a bike path.	In this town, an average of seventeen bike riders are injured every month in accidents involving cars. A good bike path would end these accidents.

Make your conclusion forceful. Briefly review your reasons. Then ask for the action you want.

Weak Conclusion	Strong Conclusion
Wearing uniforms would make our school look modern. Blue would be the best color.	Having uniforms would help us to show unity when competing in sports and in academics. Uniforms can also express our sense of style. Choose uniforms for our school today!

Think and Discuss Compare the weak and strong examples above.

- What makes the second strong introduction better than the weak one?
- What makes the strong conclusion better than the weak one?

▶ Draft Your Introduction

Write one introduction that begins with a question and another that begins with a startling fact. Choose the one that suits your goal and audience.

Focus Skill

Writing with Voice

Your **voice** is the way you express your thoughts and feelings in writing. In a persuasive essay, your voice can help convince your audience.

Use words that fit your audience. Careful, precise language is called **formal language**. Casual speech, often used with friends or in relaxed settings, is called **informal language**.

Formal Language	Informal Language
This fall students at our school will be required to wear uniforms.	Listen up! Uniforms are headed our way.

Use persuasive language. Choose your words carefully, using a thesaurus when necessary. Use persuasive words and phrases such as *certainly, surely, without a doubt, of course,* and *definitely.*

Use a positive tone. Make your argument in a confident way. If you sound sarcastic, you may simply annoy your audience.

Weak: Negative Voice	Strong: Positive Voice
Only idiots spend hundreds of dollars on brand-name stuff when they can buy the same stuff, without the fancy names, a lot more cheaply.	Are you simply going for a famous name when you buy a brand-name item? Often the less expensive, no-name brand is just as good as the name brand.

Think and Discuss

- How did you feel when you read the example of negative voice?
- Which words make the two examples of voice sound different?

▶ Draft Your Essay

❶ **Write** the rest of your essay. Follow the order you marked on your diagram. Don't worry about mistakes.

❷ **Use** a voice that fits your audience.

❸ **Conclude** your essay by summarizing your reasons and your goal.

Evaluating Your Persuasive Essay

▶ Reread your persuasive essay. What do you need to do to make it better? Use this rubric to help you decide. Write the sentences that describe your essay.

Loud and Clear!

■ My introduction includes a clear statement of my goal.
■ I have at least three strong reasons to support my goal.
■ Facts and examples elaborate each reason.
■ The order of my reasons makes sense.
■ My voice sounds positive and fits my audience.
■ I have answered possible objections.
■ My conclusion forcefully presents my reasons and my goal.
■ *There are few mistakes in grammar, spelling, or punctuation.*

Sounding Stronger

■ My introduction does not clearly state my goal.
■ I have only one or two strong reasons to support my goal.
■ My reasons need more facts and examples.
■ I haven't ordered my reasons carefully.
■ My voice could fit my audience better.
■ I mention an objection but don't answer it.
■ My conclusion is not strong enough.
■ *I made at least one mistake in every paragraph.*

Turn Up the Volume

☐ I never stated my goal.
☐ My reasons are unclear.
☐ Every reason needs more facts and examples.
☐ The order of my reasons is confusing.
☐ My audience might not like the way I sound.
☐ I haven't answered possible objections.
☐ My conclusion does not sum up my reasons or restate my goal.
■ *Too many mistakes make my essay hard to understand.*

See www.eduplace.com/kids/hme/ to interact with this rubric.

▶ # Revise Your Persuasive Essay

HELP

Revising Tip

Underline all of your persuasive words. Have you varied them?

❶ Revise your essay. Use the list of sentences you wrote from the rubric. Work on the parts that you described with sentences from "Sounding Stronger" and "Turn Up the Volume."

❷ Have a writing conference.

When You're the Writer Read your essay to a partner. Mention any problems or questions you have. Take notes.

When You're the Listener Tell at least two things that you like about the essay. Ask questions about anything that is unclear. Use the chart below for help.

What should I say?

The Writing Conference

If you're thinking . . .	**You could ask . . .**
I don't understand the goal.	**What do you want your reader to do?**
Some of the reasons are not convincing.	**Are these the best reasons for your audience? Do you have any facts or examples to support these reasons?**
The voice is negative.	**Who is your audience? What kind of language fits them better?**
The order of the reasons doesn't seem right.	**Which reason is the most important? Should that reason be first or last?**
The audience might disagree.	**Someone might say _____. How would you answer this objection?**
The conclusion is weak.	**Tell me your reasons again. What could you say to make me excited about your goal?**

❸ Make more revisions to your persuasive essay. Use your conference notes and the Revising Strategies on the next page.

Revising Strategies

Elaborating: Word Choice The feelings that a word brings to mind are called its **connotations**. Connotations can be positive or negative. Use words with connotations that fit or support your argument.

Weak: Negative Connotations	Strong: Positive Connotations
scrawny, stubborn, aggressive, hazardous, nosy, rant, snoop	slim, determined, assertive, challenging, curious, speak, investigate

▶ Find at least two places in your essay where you can use another word with a connotation that will help convince your audience.

📖 Use the Thesaurus Plus on page H96. See also page H16.

Elaborating: Details Your examples and facts will be easier to picture and more persuasive if you use vivid language that appeals to the senses.

Few Details	Elaborated with Details
A park would give people somewhere to go and something to do.	Imagine families having picnics on a cool lawn, under shaded trees. The adults talk while the children chase soaring kites in the meadow.

▶ Find at least three places in your essay where you can add vivid details.

Sentence Fluency Avoid wordiness. Get straight to the point.

Weak: Too Wordy	Strong: Concise
By having a classroom pet and by taking care of it, all the students in the class would learn to be responsible for taking care of something.	By taking care of a classroom pet, students would learn responsibility.

▶ Rewrite three of your sentences, using fewer words. Which way is more effective?

▶ Proofread Your Persuasive Essay

Proofread your essay, using the Proofreading Checklist and the Grammar and Spelling Connections. Proofread for one skill at a time. Use a class dictionary to check spellings.

Proofreading Checklist

Did I
✔ indent all paragraphs?
✔ use commas correctly?
✔ make all subjects and verbs agree?
✔ use contractions and possessive pronouns correctly?
✔ correct any spelling errors?

📖 Use the Guide to Capitalization, Punctuation, and Usage on page H64.

Proofreading Marks

¶ Indent
∧ Add
⌿ Delete
≡ Capital letter
/ Small letter
ᐯᐯ Add quotes
⩘ Add comma
⊙ Add period
∼ Transpose

Tech Tip
Print out your essay to proofread it. Mistakes are easy to miss on screen.

Grammar and Spelling Connections

Subject-Verb Agreement Use singular verbs for singular subjects and plural verbs for plural subjects.

- **Singular** The boy catches every ball.
- **Plural** The boy and the girl catch every ball.

GRAMMAR LINK ▸ *See also page 144.*

Contractions and Possessive Pronouns Possessive pronouns do not have apostrophes. In a contraction the apostrophe stands for omitted letters: **its** and **it's** (it is); **their** and **they're** (they are); **your** and **you're** (you are).

GRAMMAR LINK ▸ *See also pages 150 and 282.*

Spelling Final Unstressed |ĭk| Sounds The final unstressed |ĭk| sounds are often spelled *ic:* fantastic, specific, terrific.

📖 See the Spelling Guide on page H80.

  See www.eduplace.com/kids/hme/ for proofreading practice.

▶ Publish Your Persuasive Essay

❶ Make a neat final copy of your essay. Be sure you fixed all mistakes.

❷ Title your essay. Choose an attention-grabbing title, such as "Uniforms Make Strong Schools" rather than "We Need School Uniforms."

❸ Publish or share your essay in a way that fits your audience and goal. See the Ideas for Sharing box.

Ideas for Sharing

Write It Down
- Publish your essay as an editorial in your school newspaper.

Talk It Up
- Hold a debate using persuasive essays with opposing goals.

Show It Off
- Create a poster that uses both words and pictures to show your goal and reasons.
- Make slides that illustrate your reasons. Read your essay as you show your slides. See page H29.

Tips for Holding a Debate
- Speak more loudly and slowly to a large group than to a small one.
- Listen carefully to your opponent.
- Respond to your opponent's points after he or she is done speaking.

 See page 428 for tips.

▶ Reflect

Write about your writing experience. Use these questions to get started.

- What was difficult about writing your essay? What was easy?
- What advice would you give someone who was going to write a persuasive essay for the first time?
- How does this paper compare with others you have written?

Writing Prompts

Use these prompts as ideas for writing a persuasive essay or to practice for a test. Some of them will fit other areas you study. Decide who your audience will be, and write your essay in a way that will appeal to them.

1 Choose a television program you think should be canceled. Write a letter to the television station telling why you think it should be taken off the air.

2 Choose something in your school that should be changed. Write a persuasive letter to your principal or your school board suggesting this change.

3 Write an editorial persuading your classmates to vote for a new after-school activity.

4 Your school board is considering making the school year longer. Write a letter persuading the board to vote for or against this proposal.

Writing Across the Curriculum

5 **SOCIAL STUDIES**
Should your town pass a law requiring people to recycle? Persuade adults in your town to accept or reject such a law.

6 **MATHEMATICS**
Should your allowance be raised? by how much? Persuade your parents to take action. Use math to support your reasons.

7 **SCIENCE**
Write a letter to a scientist convincing him or her to come speak to your class about science.

8 **ARTS**
Write a letter to your school board persuading them to expand the arts program in your school.

Test Practice

This prompt to write a persuasive essay is like one you might find on a writing test. Read the prompt.

> **Your school board is considering making the school year longer. Write a letter persuading the board to vote for or against this proposal.**

How can you do a good job? Here are some strategies to help you.

1 Look for clue words that tell what to write about. What are the clue words in the prompt above?

2 Choose a topic that fits the clue words. Write the clue words that tell your audience, your goal, and sometimes your format.

> Remember, in a persuasive essay, the writer tries to convince an audience to take a specific action.

Clue Words	My Topic
school board, making the school year longer, letter, for or against this proposal	I will write a letter persuading members of my school board to vote against a longer school year.

3 Plan your writing. Use a diagram.

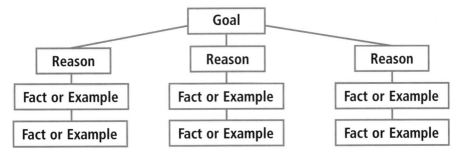

4 You will get a good score if you remember what kind of essay sounds loud and clear in the rubric on page 413.

See www.eduplace.com/kids/hme/ for graphic organizers.

Writing a Business Letter

A **business letter** is usually written to order a product, to apply for a job, to ask for information, or to persuade someone to do something. A business letter should be brief and to the point. The language should be formal and polite. Read Benny's business letter.

Heading ——
Tubman Middle School
1000 Granada Road
Riverdale, CA 93607
February 8, 2001

Inside address ——
Director of Educational Programs, NASA
Johnson Space Center
2101 NASA Road 1
Houston, TX 77058

Greeting — To whom it may concern:

I am a sixth grader at Tubman Middle School in Riverdale, California. My science class is required to write a research report on one part of the space program. I have chosen to find out what astronauts wear during their space flights.

Body —
Would you be able to send me information on the space suit used in space travel? Has it changed much over the years? Has the material of the suit become lighter or heavier? Has the amount of oxygen that a space suit carries changed?

I know that Senator John Glenn was an astronaut twice and that 36 years passed between his space flights. I would be grateful to get information on his two flights and other information you might have about the two space suits he wore.

Thank you for your help.

Closing ——➤ Sincerely,

Signature ——➤ *Benny Athwal*

Benny Athwal

- The **heading** contains the sender's address and the date.
  What is the date of Benny's letter?

- The **inside address** includes the name and complete address of the person, business, or organization who will receive the letter.
  Who is to receive Benny's letter?

- The **greeting** can give a person's name, or it can say *To whom it may concern.* It is followed by a colon.
  Why do you think Benny used To whom it may concern?

- The **body** tells the purpose of the letter. The information in the body should be written in a polite and formal way.
  Why is Benny writing his letter?

- The formal **closing** should be followed by a comma.
  How did Benny close his letter?

- The **signature** is written above the typed signature.
  Why is a handwritten signature important in a business letter?

How to Write a Business Letter

1 **Think** about what you want and from whom you should request it.

2 **Make notes** and organize them in a logical order.

3 **Write** the body of the letter. Tell who you are and why you are writing. Include all six parts of a business letter: heading, inside address, greeting, body, closing, and your signature.

4 **Use formal language.** Be polite and direct. If you are requesting information or help, be persuasive.

5 **Revise** your letter. Is it clear and businesslike?

6 **Proofread** your letter. Use the Proofreading Checklist on page 416. Use a dictionary to check your spelling.

7 **Mail** a neat final copy of your letter. Make sure that the addresses on the envelope match the addresses on the letter.

Listening for Persuasive Tactics

Many times a day you may be asked to do something. Sometimes you are given reasons or given time to think about it. Other times, the speaker may use tactics to persuade you. These tactics may tug on your feelings and keep you from thinking clearly. Look at the situations shown below.

Promises

Flattery

The speakers shown in the cartoons seem desperate. What emotions might this cause a listener to feel?

Sometimes a speaker may use the fact that he or she is older to convince you to do something. Other times, a speaker may use taunts or dares, claiming that you can't do something, just so that you will prove that you can. What other tactics are familiar to you?

Decide for Yourself

Think about what you hear. Then decide for yourself what to do.

- **Think about the goal.** What does the speaker want you to do? Why is this goal important to him or her?
- **Think about the reasons.** Why does the speaker think you should do this? Does each reason make sense to you? Do the reasons go against any rules you should obey?
- **Think about the explanation.** How does the speaker explain each reason? Does the speaker just repeat an opinion, or does he or she give facts and examples?

Guidelines for Listening for Persuasive Tactics

1. Listen for promises. Is the speaker claiming that something good will happen to you if you do what he or she asks? Do you think this promise will be kept? Why?

2. Listen for flattery. Is the speaker telling you how good or great you are? Does the speaker mean it? Is being "great" a good reason for doing what the speaker asks?

3. Listen for dares. Is the speaker asking you to prove you can do something? Is the speaker claiming you are afraid of doing something? Is what the speaker says fair?

Apply It

For a week, listen carefully when someone tries to talk you into doing something. Take notes on what you hear.

- What did each speaker want you to do?
- What reasons did each speaker give? What facts and examples did each speaker give?
- Did each speaker use any persuasive tactics? Which ones did he or she use?

Recognizing Persuasive Tactics

If asked, you could probably name several types of media. You might answer television, radio, the Internet, newspapers, and magazines. You'd be right, but media are also billboards, store displays, coupons, shopping malls, and amusement parks. Mass media are designed to deliver information to large numbers of people.

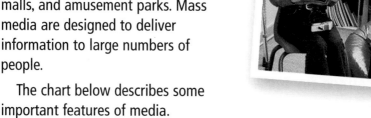

The chart below describes some important features of media.

About Media
• Media messages are constructed. This means that they are made by people to send a particular message.
• Media are kinds of communication that use verbal and visual language. Different media use their own languages and special ways of presenting a message. For example, a TV drama does not follow the same rules as a TV infomercial.
• Different people will not experience the same media message in the same way.

Advertising

What we experience through the media often happens so quickly that there is little time to think about it. Advertisements, for example, are short, and they are made to appeal to your emotions.

Businesses spend millions of dollars creating their ads. They choose images and words to appeal to the feelings of their "target" audiences. They choose music they think audiences will like. They may use bright colors and fast-action images. People in their ads are actors who may be asked to look happy, to look "cool," or to act out a funny role.

The purpose of ads is to persuade. Ads are made to get people to buy products, use services, or vote for candidates. Many ads use persuasive tactics, or methods, that don't tell the whole story. Look at the following examples.

Persuasive Tactics	
Bandwagon This tactic tries to make you feel that something is good because it is popular.	The ZOOM crowd. They're walking.
Testimonial This tactic involves paying a famous person to tell you that the product is great.	I've won every race in my ZOOM shoes.
Exaggeration This tactic "stretches" the truth or makes an unprovable claim.	ZOOM Best in the world!
Flattery This tactic compliments you. It may tell you how smart you are to have the product.	You're athletic. You're smart. You deserve ZOOMs.

Stop and Think

When you look at an advertisement, remember that you are seeing only what the people who made it want you to see. They often leave out facts, or they tell you only good opinions.

The words and images in ads are simple and appealing to the audience. Sometimes the words are meant to scare the audience into buying the product. Listen carefully to the words. What exactly do they tell you about the product?

more ▶

Some ads promise that their products solve a problem. Ask yourself whether the problem is truly a problem. These ads want you to feel insecure about something. You might buy the product to make yourself feel better. Look at the ad shown here. What information is left out? Do you think a persuasive tactic is used?

Before
the Very Best
Sneaker Cleaner

THE VERY BEST
SNEAKER
CLEANER

After
the Very Best
Sneaker Cleaner

Propaganda

Different forms of media are used to spread propaganda. Propaganda is slanted and false information that encourages support for a particular view or belief. Propaganda often uses stereotypes. A stereotype is a view of a group of people that is too simple and therefore unfair.

Don't let brawn bully brain!
Too many sports means
too few computers
at our school!

Think and Discuss

- How is the example slanted or exaggerated? What is the propaganda trying to make you believe?
- What prejudices are shown? What beliefs are supported?

Use the guidelines below for finding persuasive tactics in ads. Look for tactics that distract you from thinking about the quality of the product.

Guidelines for Looking at Media Advertisements

▶ Look carefully at the advertisement. Who made it? What does it want you to do?

▶ Study the images, music, and speech used. How do they make you feel?

▶ Read the text of the ad. Does the ad use facts or opinions? Does it tell you all there is to know? Do the words focus on the product or on a mood or an idea?

▶ Study the ad to see which persuasive tactics were used, if any. Why do you think the tactic was chosen?

▶ Ask yourself if the ad is fair and truthful.

▶ Ask yourself what the ad wants you to believe. Make up your own mind about what you see.

Apply It

Keep a notebook for a week in which you watch for persuasive tactics in advertisements. Use the guidelines above to help you. In which types of media did the ads appear? Describe the tactics used. Comment on how the ads appeal to your emotions.

● Videotape an hour's worth of television on a channel that has commercials. Play the tape and choose a commercial that interests you. Watch the commercial without sound. Then listen to it without watching the visuals. What do you notice in each case?

● Tape-record a radio commercial. Listen to the recording. What images come into your mind? What do you notice about the words used?

● Look at ads in teen magazines. Choose one and carefully examine the visuals and words. Is a product shown in the ad? If so, how?

Conducting a Debate

People debate when they disagree on a topic and want to explain their reasons why. In a formal debate, two teams of people disagree, but they follow a set of rules. The rules ensure that each team has a fair chance to express its views.

Before the debate, the teams are given a topic statement. One team will argue for it. The other team will argue against it. Team members on both sides organize their ideas and prepare a speech.

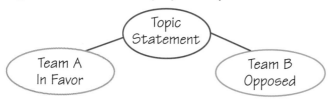

The chart below shows one way a debate can be organized. Each part of a debate has a time limit.

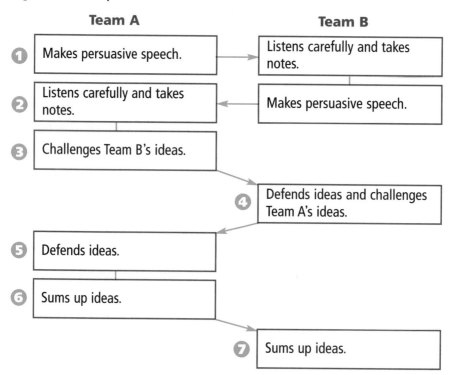

	Team A		Team B
1	Makes persuasive speech.	→	Listens carefully and takes notes.
2	Listens carefully and takes notes.	←	Makes persuasive speech.
3	Challenges Team B's ideas.		
4			Defends ideas and challenges Team A's ideas.
5	Defends ideas.		
6	Sums up ideas.		
7			Sums up ideas.

In a debate, good speaking and listening skills are important.

Guidelines for Speaking in a Debate

▶ Choose exact words that support your position.

▶ Try not to use slang. Formal language usually works better in a debate.

▶ Use persuasive words such as *plainly* or *definitely,* and speak in a persuasive but polite tone.

▶ Keep your voice low, calm, and confident. A high-pitched voice often sounds nervous.

▶ Speak slowly and clearly for a large audience in a large space. Pronounce each word carefully.

Guidelines for Listening in a Debate

▶ Think about the speaker's reasons. Do they support the speaker's argument? Are they vague or exaggerated?

▶ Think about each fact and example. Does it elaborate a specific reason? Is it accurate?

▶ Watch the speaker's gestures and expressions. Are they natural and relaxed or stiff?

▶ Listen to the tone of the speaker's voice. Does the speaker sound uncertain about any reason?

▶ Watch how audience members react to the speaker. Which reasons seem most convincing to them?

Apply It

Hold your own debate. Follow the guidelines above. Then answer these questions.

● Did each team argue well for its side of the debate? Give an example of what worked.

● Did the teams do enough research on the topic? Did they need more facts and examples?

● What would you plan differently for another debate? Explain why.

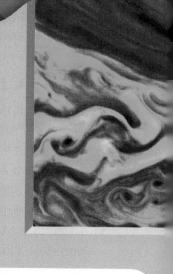

What You Will Find in This Section:

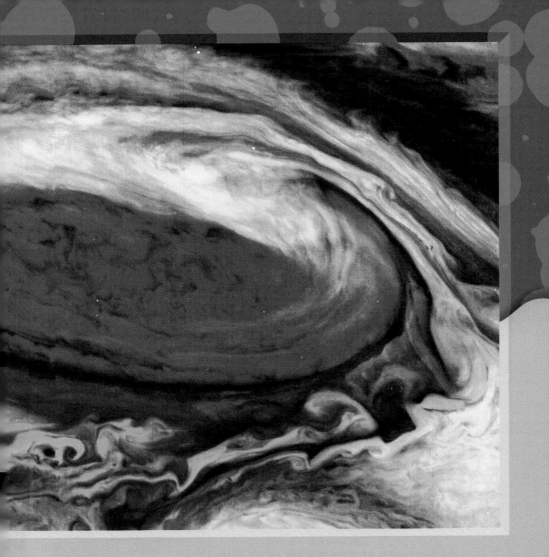

Listening for Information

Whether you're listening to a news report or to your teacher giving a math lesson, you're **listening for factual information**. **Facts** can be proved true. You can use them to make decisions, to solve problems, and to increase your knowledge. Here are some guidelines that will help you to listen successfully.

Guidelines for Listening for Information

▶ Listen for the topic. What is the general subject of the information you're hearing?

▶ Listen for the main idea. What does the author have to say about the topic?

▶ Listen for examples and specific facts, such as numbers. How do they elaborate the main idea?

▶ Listen for the sources of the information, if given. How well do you know the sources? Are they reliable?

▶ Listen for the author's purpose. Why is the author telling about this topic?

Try It Out Listen as your teacher reads from *What Does the Crow Know?* by Margery Facklam. Take notes to help you answer the questions below.

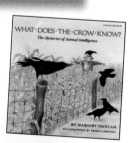

WHAT·DOES·THE·CROW·KNOW?
The Mysteries of Animal Intelligence

BY MARGERY FACKLAM
ILLUSTRATIONS BY PAMELA JOHNSON

- What is the topic of the expository piece?
- What is Margery Facklam's main idea?
- What facts and examples does the author include?
- Why do you think Margery Facklam wrote this piece?

📖 See page H33 for tips on taking notes while listening.

 See www.eduplace.com/kids/ to learn about Margery Facklam.

Writing Expository Paragraphs

An **expository paragraph** is full of facts. The writer's purpose is to share information about a topic he or she knows well. An expository paragraph has a topic and a main idea. The **topic** is the subject of the paragraph. The **main idea** is what the author has to say about the subject. What is the topic of the expository paragraph below? What is the main idea?

Remember, the first line of a paragraph is indented.

Indent

Topic sentence

Supporting sentences

Concluding sentence

Wolves are social animals. They live in groups called packs. Most wolf packs have between six and ten wolves in them. They include adult wolves and baby wolves, called pups.

All of the adult wolves help feed and care for the pups. If a mother wolf dies, her pups are cared for by another female in the pack. When the pups grow up, they start their own packs. Many people are surprised when they learn that wolves are such social, family-oriented animals!

Topic Sentence

The topic of the paragraph is wolves. The main idea is that wolves are social animals. Which sentence tells the topic and the main idea?

Supporting Sentences

The labels show the parts of an expository paragraph.

- The **topic sentence** states the topic and tells the writer's main idea.

- The **supporting sentences** give facts and examples that explain the main idea.

Concluding Sentence

- The **concluding sentence** finishes the paragraph.

Think and Discuss What facts are given in the wolf paragraph's supporting sentences?

The Topic Sentence

You've learned that in an expository paragraph, the **topic sentence** names the subject and tells what the writer wants to say about it. A good topic sentence will also make the reader want to continue reading.

     Topic   Main idea

Example: The Beatles were one of the most popular rock-and-roll groups ever.

In expository paragraphs the topic sentence is often the first sentence, as it is in the paragraph about wolves on page 433. Sometimes, though, the topic sentence comes at the end of the paragraph and takes the place of the concluding sentence. Which is the topic sentence in the paragraph below? Which are the supporting sentences?

> The Spaniard Hernando Cortez arrived in the Aztec Empire in 1519. While there, he watched Emperor Montezuma constantly refilling his golden goblet with a rich drink made from water, hot peppers, and small, bitter beans. After trying the spicy drink himself, Cortez brought several chests of the dark beans home to Queen Isabella. Soon, wealthy Spaniards were making the tasty drink. The Spaniards, however, added sugar instead of peppers. Cortez had begun a worldwide love for the Aztec treasure of chocolate.

Try It Out On your own or with a partner, write the topic and the main idea of the paragraph below. Then write two possible topic sentences for it.

> _____Topic sentence_____. Only one fact is known for certain. The Great Red Spot is a huge storm in Jupiter's atmosphere. However, to this day no one knows the cause of the storm or why it has lasted for so long. Just like the astronomers of centuries ago, scientists today look up at the Great Red Spot and wonder.

Supporting Sentences

In expository paragraphs, the **supporting sentences** use details such as **facts** and **examples** to explain the main idea. The supporting sentences can also include **sensory words** that describe how things look, smell, feel, taste, and sound.

Fact: The Spaniard Hernando Cortez arrived in the Aztec Empire in 1519.

Example: If a mother wolf dies, her pups are cared for by another female in the pack.

Sensory words: golden goblet; warm water; small, bitter beans; spicy drink

The *carnivorous*, or "meat-eating," Venus's-flytrap feeds itself as few other plants can. It attracts insects to its clamshell-shaped leaves with a sweet-scented nectar. As soon as an insect lands, thorny bristles trigger the hinged leaf to slam shut, trapping the prey. Then acidic fluids in the leaf's center begin to slowly dissolve and digest the soft parts of the insect's body. Within about two weeks, the efficient flytrap is ready for another meal.

Think and Discuss What facts and examples are in the paragraph above? What sensory words can you find?

Ordering Details Supporting sentences in an expository paragraph are organized in an order that's easy for the reader to follow. For example, details about a sequence of events are usually organized in time order. Other types of expository details might be arranged in order of importance or in some other order that makes sense. **Transitional words and phrases**, such as *first, then, as soon as, moreover,* and *most important*, help readers understand how these details are connected.

How are details arranged in the Venus's-flytrap paragraph above? in the paragraph about chocolate on the previous page? What transitional words and phrases are used in each?

 See page 16 for more on ordering details. See page 18 for more transitional words. **more ▶**

Try It Out On your own or with a partner, use the photograph below and the facts provided to write at least four supporting sentences for the topic sentence. Link your sentences with transitional words or phrases.

Topic sentence: An ambulance is like a mini-hospital on wheels.

Bandages for wrapping wounds

Splints for securing broken limbs

Highly trained paramedics

Oxygen masks for patients having difficulty breathing

Two-way radio for communicating with hospital and doctors

Stretcher for transporting patients

 GRAMMAR TIP ▶ A complete sentence has a subject and a predicate and tells a complete thought.

The Concluding Sentence

 The **concluding sentence** can restate the main idea in a new way or add a final comment or observation. For example, the wolf paragraph on page 433 ends with an interesting restatement of the main idea. The Venus's-flytrap paragraph on page 435 ends with a factual observation. The paragraph about Jupiter's Great Red Spot on page 434 ends with a final comment.

Try It Out Read the paragraph below. On your own or with a partner, write two different concluding sentences.

The Beatles were one of the most popular rock-and-roll groups ever. From 1960 to 1970, they wrote and recorded hundreds of hit songs. Between 1964 and 1969 alone, thirty of their hits made the Top Ten record charts. In 1994, some thirty years later, a collection of new and old Beatles songs sold out in two days. _____*Concluding sentence*_____ .

Paragraphs That Compare and Contrast

Some informational paragraphs compare and contrast two subjects, telling how they are similar and how they are different. A **paragraph that compares and contrasts** has a topic sentence that introduces the two subjects, supporting sentences that give examples of similarities and differences, and a concluding sentence. Transitional words and phrases, such as *on the other hand* or *in contrast,* connect the supporting sentences and help the reader keep track of the details.

> If two subjects are alike and different in many ways, one paragraph may compare them and another contrast them.

Which sentences compare and which ones contrast in the paragraph below? What transitional words and phrases do you find?

Topic sentence

Alligators and crocodiles are similar animals, but they have important differences. For example, alligators and crocodiles are both large reptiles that look like lizards. Each animal has a long tail and a large, powerful jaw with dangerously sharp teeth. Both

Supporting sentences

live in swamps. However, an alligator will rarely grow to be more than twelve feet long. A crocodile, on the other hand, can reach twenty-three feet in length. An alligator's snout is short and broad, while a crocodile's is long and thin. Whether you correctly identify them or not, the alligator and the crocodile are unusual, fearsome creatures.

Concluding sentence

Try It Out On your own or with a partner, choose one of the pairs listed below. Make a list of the items' similarities and differences. Then write at least three supporting sentences that compare and contrast the items.

1. two different games or sports
2. books and movies
3. rain and snow

Paragraphs That Show Cause and Effect

When one or more things make something else happen, we call it *cause and effect*. In an expository **paragraph that shows cause and effect**, the topic sentence introduces the cause, a result, or both. Supporting sentences give details about causes and effects. A concluding sentence wraps up the paragraph. Transitional words and phrases, such as *because, as a result,* and *for example,* link the supporting sentences.

Read the paragraph below. What is the cause? What are the effects?

Topic sentence

Supporting sentences

Concluding sentence

> The damage that an earthquake causes in a city partly depends upon how strong the earthquake is. Most earthquakes are mild. Windows may rattle, but the quake's vibrations only shake things a little. Some earthquakes, however, have serious effects. For example, people and animals can be injured. Buildings can lose bricks or completely fall apart. Severe quakes can also destroy roads, pull down electric lines, and burst gas mains. Fires may break out too. Whether an earthquake is mild or severe, it can shake your confidence in the ground you walk on.

Try It Out On your own or with a partner, choose one of the topic sentences below. Identify the cause stated in the topic sentence, and brainstorm a list of effects. Then use your list to write at least three sentences that explain the effects.

1. Saving money has several valuable benefits.
2. Driving too fast can have serious consequences.
3. When a pet becomes lost, several things happen as a result.
4. Christopher Columbus's journey in 1492 changed many people's lives.

Write Your Own Expository Paragraph

Now it's time for you to write your own expository paragraph. You may choose to write a paragraph that explains what something is or does, one that compares and contrasts, or one that shows cause and effect. First, think of a topic that interests you, such as computers or a current event. Then make a list of details to include. After you share your ideas with a partner, you're ready to write!

Checklist for My Paragraph

✔ I wrote a **topic sentence** that clearly tells the topic and the main idea.

✔ My **supporting sentences** give details, such as facts, examples, and sensory words, that elaborate the main idea.

✔ My **concluding sentence** restates the main idea in an interesting way or makes a final comment.

Looking Ahead

Now that you know how to write an expository paragraph, writing an expository essay will be easy! This diagram shows how the parts of an expository paragraph match the parts of a longer composition.

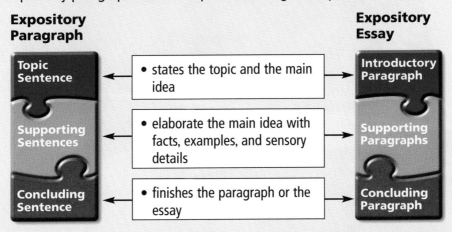

Expository Paragraph		Expository Essay
Topic Sentence	• states the topic and the main idea	Introductory Paragraph
Supporting Sentences	• elaborate the main idea with facts, examples, and sensory details	Supporting Paragraphs
Concluding Sentence	• finishes the paragraph or the essay	Concluding Paragraph

Writing to Compare and Contrast

What's the best way to travel—by tall ship or by rowboat? The two vessels are similar in some ways but very different in others.

Amphibians and reptiles are two different classes of animals. What is the author's purpose for comparing and contrasting them?

Cold-Blooded Reptiles

from *Snakes*, by Eric S. Grace

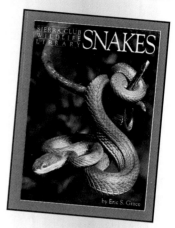

About six thousand different species of reptiles are living today, nearly half of which are snakes. But many other sorts of reptiles lived on Earth in the past. The most famous of these ancient reptiles are the dinosaurs, which first appeared just over 225 million years ago. The long period that began then is sometimes called the Age of Reptiles. During this period, dinosaurs lived in swamps, deserts, and forests around the world. Flying reptiles soared through the air, and whale-size reptiles hunted in lakes and oceans. Nearly all of these reptiles became extinct more than 65 million years ago. We know about them today only from some of their remains that were preserved as fossils.

Two important things helped reptiles become such a widespread group of animals for such a long time: their scaly skins and their eggs. To understand why these are important, compare reptiles with amphibians, such as frogs and newts.

Amphibians are a group of animals that evolved to live on land before reptiles did. Most amphibians have thin skin that easily dries out in the air. They usually lay their eggs in jellylike clusters in streams or ponds or under rotting logs. Because their thin skins and their eggs need to stay moist, most amphibians cannot live long far from water or damp soil.

Reptiles are better prepared to avoid dehydration than amphibians are. A reptile's scaly skin is waterproof, keeping its body from drying out. Most reptile eggs are large and yolky with leathery shells that help prevent them from losing moisture. Thanks to their scaly skins and large, tough-shelled eggs, reptiles can live in many different places on land far from water. Reptiles are at home in dry deserts and grasslands where most amphibians could not survive.

Reading As a Writer

Think About the Compare-Contrast Essay

- Why does the author compare reptiles to amphibians? Which sentence states his purpose for comparing?
- Which sentence tells the main idea of the last paragraph on page 442?
- How are reptiles and amphibians alike? How are they different?

Think About Writer's Craft

- What descriptive words help you to picture the eggs of amphibians? the eggs of reptiles?

Think About the Pictures

- What do the photographs of reptiles add to your understanding of information found in the text?

Responding

Write responses to these questions.

- **Personal Response** How would you feel about traveling back to the Age of Reptiles? Use information from the text to support your answers.

- **Critical Thinking** What would happen to a frog colony transplanted to the dry grasslands? Find information in the essay to support your answer.

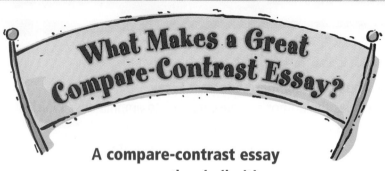

What Makes a Great Compare-Contrast Essay?

A **compare-contrast essay** compares the similarities and contrasts the differences between two subjects.

Remember these guidelines when you write a compare-contrast essay.

▶ Choose two subjects you can compare and contrast easily.

▶ Write an engaging introduction that names your two subjects.

▶ Compare and contrast corresponding details for each subject.

▶ Select a method of organization, and stick to it from beginning to end.

▶ Use topic sentences to state the main idea of paragraphs.

▶ Use transitional words and phrases to compare and contrast.

▶ Write a conclusion that sums up your main ideas in a satisfying way.

GRAMMAR CHECK

Remember to use correct comparative and superlative forms of adjectives and adverbs.

Kyle Colligan

WORKING DRAFT

When Kyle Colligan was asked to compare and contrast two subjects he knows a lot about, he immediately thought of ice cream and Mexican food, his two favorite foods. He wrote this draft to show how they are alike and how they are different.

I love your choice of subjects!

Working Draft

This essay is about ice cream and Mexican food. They are two of my favorite things to eat.

Even though it does not seem like ice cream and Mexican food are alike in any way, they have some surprising similarities. They are both visually appealing. When you look down at the flavors in the cooler at your favorite ice-cream shop, you see bright colors such as lemon yellow, bubble-gum pink, icy white, chocolate brown, vibrant orange, and lime green. As your plate of Mexican food is set in front of you, you also see bright colors. Mexican food can be an appetizer, a main course, or a dessert, while ice cream is only served as a dessert. Variety is another similarity. When choosing ice cream you can pick from dozens of flavors. When choosing Mexican food, you can decide among dozens of different dishes. (Are you feeling hungry yet?) The atmosphere where ice cream is sold resembles the atmosphere where Mexican food is sold. Most ice-cream shops and Mexican restaurants are comfortable places. Like ice-cream

Will this beginning draw your readers into your essay?

I can picture how the ice cream looks. Can you add details about the colors of Mexican food?

Does every sentence in this paragraph tell a similarity?

more

I can really hear your voice here. It sounds just like you!

shops, Mexican restaurants are rarely empty and, more often, are full of happy people! How can you be grumpy when you're licking a triple scoop of mint chocolate chip ice cream or sitting in front of a sizzling plate of chicken fajitas?

Can you add a topic sentence to this paragraph?

Ice cream is cold, smooth, creamy, and soothing. Mexican food is hot, crunchy, chunky, and spicy. Ice cream is most commonly served in cups, cones, or cakes. Mexican food is most commonly served on large, hot plates, often sizzling!

Reading As a Writer

- What questions did Joe have? What revisions might Kyle make?
- Where does Kyle describe differences? Where does he describe similarities?
- Which sentence needs to be moved? Where does it belong?
- What could Kyle do to make his essay feel less cut off at the end?

FINAL COPY

Kyle revised his compare-contrast essay after discussing it with his classmates. Read his final version to see what changes he made to improve it.

My Dream Diet
by Kyle Colligan

If I had my way, I would have ice cream and Mexican food every day! I would eat ice cream for breakfast, Mexican food for lunch, and both again for dinner. Ice cream and Mexican food are my two favorite things to eat. They simply taste great!

> Now your beginning is much more interesting!

Even though it does not seem like ice cream and Mexican food are alike in any way, they have some surprising similarities. For instance, they are both visually appealing. When you look down at the flavors in the cooler at your favorite ice-cream shop, you see bright colors such as lemon yellow, bubble-gum pink, icy white, chocolate brown, vibrant orange, and lime green. Likewise, as your plate of Mexican food is set in front of you, you see fresh green guacamole, creamy white sour cream, bright orange cheddar cheese, golden yellow rice, and coffee-colored frijoles (a kind of bean). Variety is another similarity. When choosing ice cream, you can pick from dozens of flavors, such as vanilla, chocolate, strawberry, rocky road, and sherbert. Similarly, when choosing Mexican food, you can decide among dozens of

> These new details make my mouth water! I can practically taste those frijoles!

more

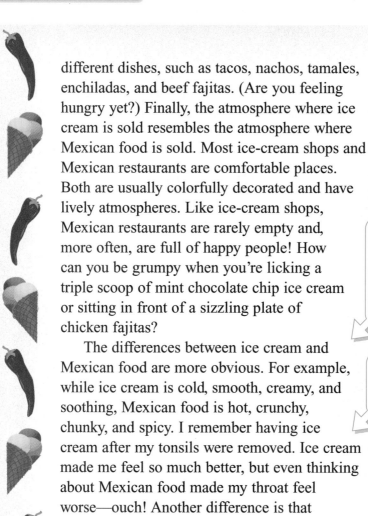

different dishes, such as tacos, nachos, tamales, enchiladas, and beef fajitas. (Are you feeling hungry yet?) Finally, the atmosphere where ice cream is sold resembles the atmosphere where Mexican food is sold. Most ice-cream shops and Mexican restaurants are comfortable places. Both are usually colorfully decorated and have lively atmospheres. Like ice-cream shops, Mexican restaurants are rarely empty and, more often, are full of happy people! How can you be grumpy when you're licking a triple scoop of mint chocolate chip ice cream or sitting in front of a sizzling plate of chicken fajitas?

This topic sentence helps readers know that you're now switching to differences.

The differences between ice cream and Mexican food are more obvious. For example, while ice cream is cold, smooth, creamy, and soothing, Mexican food is hot, crunchy, chunky, and spicy. I remember having ice cream after my tonsils were removed. Ice cream made me feel so much better, but even thinking about Mexican food made my throat feel worse—ouch! Another difference is that Mexican food can be an appetizer, a main course, or a dessert, while ice cream is only served as a dessert. Last but not least, ice cream is most commonly served in cups, cones, or cakes. However, Mexican food is most commonly served on large, hot plates, often

New details make the differences clearer.

sizzling! Can you imagine what would happen to your ice cream if it were served this way?

As you can see, ice cream and Mexican food have some interesting similarities as well as some obvious differences. I suppose I should be glad that they're not exactly alike. If I ever get my way and can eat only ice cream and Mexican food for the rest of my life, at least I won't get bored!

Reading As a Writer

- What changes did Kyle make to respond to Joe's questions?
- How did Kyle improve his introduction? his conclusion?
- What details did Kyle add to the second paragraph on page 447 to describe Mexican food and ice cream?
- What transitional words and phrases did Kyle add?

See www.eduplace.com/kids/hme/ for more examples of student writing.

Student Model   449

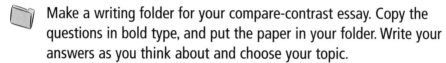
Write a Compare-Contrast Essay

▶ Start Thinking

Make a writing folder for your compare-contrast essay. Copy the questions in bold type, and put the paper in your folder. Write your answers as you think about and choose your topic.

- **Who will be my audience?** Will it be my friends? a teacher?
- **What will be my purpose?** Will it be to explain? to entertain? to inform?
- **How will I share or publish my essay?** Will I perform it as a choral reading with a partner? make a pop-up book? make an audiotape?

▶ Choose Your Subjects

❶ **List** five people, places, or things that interest you. For each, list one other person, place, or thing with which you can compare and contrast it.

❷ **Discuss** your ideas with a partner. Which pair of subjects does your partner find most interesting? Why? Which pair has enough details to compare and contrast?

❸ **Make notes** next to each pair of subjects, as Kyle did. Then circle the pair you will write about.

HELP
? *Stuck for a Topic?*

Choose two subjects from these subject pairs.
- two inventions
- a book and its movie version
- two games
- two animals

See page 461 for more ideas.

Make sure to choose subjects that have something in common.

floods and glaciers	know only a little about glaciers
bats and mice	won't enjoy writing about this topic
Mexican food and ice cream	unexpected similarities here

▶ Explore Your Subjects

❶ Think about your topic as a barbell. Close your eyes and imagine adding "weights"—details that describe your subjects—onto each end. Keep the barbell balanced! Don't add a detail for one subject if you can't add a corresponding detail for the other subject.

❷ Draw a Venn diagram. Use the diagram shown below as a model.

❸ List details about each subject in your Venn diagram. Write details that tell how the subjects are different in the outer circles. Write details that tell how they are alike in the space where the circles overlap. Keep the categories below in mind when you try to think of details to include.

- appearance
- special features
- behavior
- diet
- where found
- movement
- uses
- costs

❹ Connect or highlight in matching colors details that describe the same feature for both subjects. Cross out any details that you can't connect.

Look for interesting or unusual details that will keep your readers interested.

Sun	Both	Moon
93,000,000 miles from Earth	source of light	diameter ¼ size of Earth's
~~can burn your skin~~	affect Earth	238,860 miles from Earth
diameter over 100 times that of Earth	visible from Earth	reflects light from the sun
necessary to life on Earth		affects Earth's tides
source of heat		

 See page 14 for other ideas about exploring a topic.

 Go to www.eduplace.com/kids/hme/ for graphic organizers.

Focus Skill

Organizing Your Essay

Now that you've come up with some great ideas, how can you best present them? Pick one of the methods shown below. Stick with that type of organization throughout your essay.

Write about similarities, then differences. Write one or more paragraphs telling how your subjects are alike. Then write separate paragraphs telling how they are different. Here are parts of an essay that is organized this way.

Similarities

> The sun and the moon have some obvious similarities. Both are visible from Earth, and both give us light. Each has a powerful effect on Earth.

Differences

> The sun and the moon, however, have more differences than similarities. While the sun is a star around which Earth revolves, the moon is a satellite that revolves around Earth.

> Good ideas can come at any time! Add any more details you think of while organizing.

Focus Skill continued

Use feature-by-feature order.

Select two or three features your subjects share. Compare and contrast these features. Keep related sentences together. The following paragraphs use feature-by-feature order.

If you have several sentences that tell about one feature, you may want to group them together in their own paragraph.

Temperature

> Astronauts have actually measured the temperature of the moon, but scientists can only estimate the sun's temperature. The moon's temperature can climb as high as 260 degrees Fahrenheit, but scientists think the sun's core probably reaches temperatures close to 27,000,000 degrees. That's hot!

Measuring time

> In ancient times, people relied on both the sun and the moon to keep track of time. They watched the direction of the sun's shadow to track time during a single day, and they used the moon's changing shape to track days, weeks, and months.

Think and Discuss Look at Kyle's final copy on page 447.

- Which type of organization did Kyle choose for his essay? Did he stick to this organization from beginning to end?
- How else might Kyle have organized his essay?

▶ Plan Your Essay

❶ Decide which type of organization will work best for your essay: similarities and then differences or feature-by-feature order.

❷ Create an outline. Keep in mind the organization you have chosen as you order your details.

📖 See page H34 for information about outlining.

Focus Skill

Introductions and Conclusions

Write an introduction that hooks your readers. Find an interesting way to present your subjects. You might ask a question, tell a story, or state a startling fact.

> Don't just name your subjects, or you'll put us all to sleep!

Weak Introduction

In this compare-contrast essay, I will tell you how my identical twin and I are alike and how we are different.

Strong Introduction

Did your parents have to struggle to tell you apart from your brother? Mine did because I am an identical twin. My brother Jake and I look exactly alike, but our personalities couldn't be more different.

Write a memorable conclusion. Find a smooth, satisfying way to sum up your ideas or make a final comment to make your essay feel finished.

Weak Conclusion

As you can see, my brother and I are alike in some ways, but different in others. It's really annoying when people mix us up.

Strong Conclusion

The next time you meet twins, don't assume that because they look alike, they think, feel, and act alike too. Remember, the word *identical* is only skin-deep.

Try It Out

- Work with a partner. Find new ways to improve the weak introduction above. Try telling an incident or stating a startling fact.

▶ Draft Your Introduction

❶ **Write** two introductions that present your topic in an interesting way. Make sure they name the subjects you will compare and contrast.

❷ **Choose** one introduction, keeping in mind your purpose and audience.

Focus Skill

Topic Sentences

A **topic sentence** expresses a paragraph's main idea. In a compare-contrast essay, a good topic sentence lets the reader know whether the paragraph will tell about differences, similarities, or a particular feature. The topic sentence is usually first, but it may come later in the paragraph.

The topic sentences in the paragraphs below are underlined.

Similarities

> <u>High-protein diets and low-sugar diets have more in common than you might think.</u> Both require that you avoid certain types of food. Both claim to burn up stored fat. Finally, both promise that you will gain new muscle tissue and strength if you follow the diet strictly.

All about one feature

> <u>When it comes to danger, rock climbing and spelunking (exploring caves) have a lot in common.</u> Like rock climbers, spelunkers can be in trouble if weather conditions change unexpectedly. For rock climbers, a blizzard can be deadly. For spelunkers, flash floods can be just as deadly.

Think and Discuss Look back at Kyle's final copy on pages 447–449.

- Find the topic sentence in each of Kyle's first three paragraphs. What information does each topic sentence provide?

▶ Draft Your Essay

❶ **Write** a topic sentence for each paragraph. Add details that support each main idea.

❷ **Write** a strong conclusion that sums up your ideas.

HELP

? Transitional Words and Phrases

- To compare subjects: *in addition, besides which, likewise, furthermore, similarly*
- To contrast subjects: *on the other hand, however, unlike, but*

Evaluating Your Compare-Contrast Essay

▶ **Reread** your essay. What do you need to do to make it better? Use this rubric to help you decide. Copy the sentences that best describe your essay.

Loud and Clear!

- The introduction states my subjects and hooks my readers.
- I compare and contrast corresponding details for each subject.
- I use one method of organization throughout my essay.
- A topic sentence tells the main idea of each paragraph.
- Transitional words make similarities and differences clear.
- My conclusion sums up my ideas in a satisfying way.
- *There are few mistakes in grammar, spelling, or punctuation.*

Sounding Stronger

- The introduction states my subjects, but it's boring.
- I didn't always compare and contrast corresponding details.
- I bounce back and forth between two types of organization.
- Some paragraphs need topic sentences.
- More transitional words would sharpen the relationship between my subjects.
- My conclusion could be more memorable.
- *A number of mistakes make my essay hard to follow.*

Turn Up the Volume

- The introduction doesn't state my subjects.
- I often don't compare and contrast corresponding details about the other subject.
- I don't use either type of organization.
- None of my paragraphs have topic sentences.
- There are no transitional words.
- My essay stops short. There is no conclusion.
- *Too many mistakes make my essay hard to read.*

See www.eduplace.com/kids/hme/ to interact with this rubric.

▶ Revise Your Compare-Contrast Essay

❶ Revise your essay. Use the list of sentences you wrote from the rubric. Work on the parts that you described with sentences from "Sounding Stronger" and "Turn Up the Volume."

❷ Have a writing conference.

What should I say?

When You're the Writer Read your essay aloud to your partner. Ask for feedback about the essay's strengths and weaknesses. Take notes.

When You're the Listener Tell your partner at least two things you like about the essay. Ask questions about anything that seems unclear. Use the chart below to help you.

The Writing Conference

If you're thinking . . .	You could ask . . .
The beginning doesn't grab my attention.	**Could you start with a startling fact or a question?**
I'm lost! What's happening?	**What kind of organization are you using? Can you add transitional words?**
How do the details in this paragraph fit together?	**Can you write a topic sentence that states the main idea of the paragraph?**
I can't picture the similarities and differences.	**Can you add more details to tell how _____ is similar to _____?**
The essay seems cut off at the end.	**Could you summarize your ideas in the conclusion?**

❸ Make additional revisions to your essay. Use your conference notes and the Revising Strategies on the next page.

Tech Tip
Underline sentences that compare, and boldface sentences that contrast. Is every sentence in the right place?

Revising Strategies

Elaborating: Word Choice Use **antonyms**, or opposites, to clarify meaning or to sharpen the contrast between your two subjects.

General	Elaborated with Antonyms
Jim's nachos were zesty and crisp, but Maria's were **not**.	Jim's nachos were zesty and crisp, but Maria's were tasteless and soggy.

▶ Find one place in your essay where you can elaborate using antonyms.

📖 See also page H15.

Elaborating: Details Adding vivid details about your subjects can clarify the similarities and differences between them.

Not Elaborated	Elaborated with Details
Dogs and cats make great pets.	What can compare with the warmth of a shaggy dog on your feet in the winter or the purr of a contented and well-fed cat?

▶ Find three places to improve your essay by adding details.

Sentence Fluency Make your writing more interesting to your audience by varying the way your sentences begin. Read these sentences comparing juice and soda.

Similar Beginnings	Varied Beginnings
Juice and soda can quench your thirst. **Juice** and soda have sugar. **Juice** is more nutritious.	Juice and soda can quench your thirst. Both drinks have sugar, but juice is more nutritious.

▶ Vary sentence beginnings in at least two places. Read your essay aloud and decide if it sounds better.

GRAMMAR LINK *See also page 50.*

► Proofread Your Compare-Contrast Essay

Proofread your essay, using the Proofreading Checklist and the Grammar and Spelling Connections. Proofread for one skill at a time. Use a class dictionary to check spellings.

Proofreading Marks

¶	Indent
∧	Add
ℐ	Delete
≡	Capital letter
/	Small letter
ᵛ⁄ᵛ	Add quotes
⋀	Add comma
⊙	Add period
∿	Transpose

Proofreading Checklist

Did I
- ✔ indent all paragraphs?
- ✔ begin and end sentences correctly?
- ✔ use correct comparative and superlative forms?
- ✔ use apostrophes in possessives?
- ✔ spell all the words correctly?

📖 Use the Guide to Capitalization, Punctuation, and Usage on page H64.

Tech Tip
To make proofreading easier on the computer, increase your document's type size to 14 or 16 points.

Grammar and Spelling Connections

Comparative and Superlative Forms Use different forms of adjectives to compare and contrast two or more persons, places, or things.

Basic form	no comparison	My balance beam routine is tough.
Comparative	compares two	My floor routine is even tougher.
Superlative	compares three or more	My vault is by far the toughest.

 See also pages 188 and 191.

Changing Final *y* to *i* If a word ends in a consonant + *y*, the *y* changes to *i* when the ending *-es, -ed, -er,* or *-est* or the suffix *-ness, -ful,* or *-ly* is added.

berries hurried muddier funniest scaliness pitiful happily

📖 See the Spelling Guide on page H80.

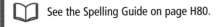

▶ Publish Your Compare-Contrast Essay

❶ Make a neat final copy of your essay. Be sure you've fixed all errors.

❷ Choose a title for your essay that states your topic and will make your readers curious. For example, "What Would Life Be Like Without the Sun and the Moon?" is more interesting than "The Sun and the Moon."

GRAMMAR TIP ▶ Capitalize the first, the last, and each important word in a title.

❸ Publish or share your essay. See the Ideas for Sharing box.

Ice cream and Mexican food are my two favorite things to eat.

Tips for Pop-up Illustrations

- Draw pictures or find photographs to illustrate each subject in your essay.
- Glue pictures or photographs on construction paper. Cut them out.
- Glue two strips of construction paper together to form an L. Fold one strip over the other again and again.
- Glue one end of the spring to the illustration and the other to the page. You can add background illustrations to the page.

Ideas for Sharing
Write It Down
- Send your essay in an e-mail. See page H44 for tips.
  Make it into a pop-up book for the Reading Center.

Talk It Up
- Tape record your essay. Add appropriate sound effects.
- Perform a choral reading with a partner.

Show It Off
  Create a poster. Compare and contrast your topics visually. Display it with your essay. See page H29 for tips.

▶ Reflect

Write about your writing experience. Use these questions to get started.

- What is your favorite part of your compare-contrast essay?
- What was easy and what was difficult about writing the essay?
- How does this paper compare with other papers you have written?

Writing Prompts

Use these prompts as ideas for compare-contrast essays or to practice for a test. Some of them may relate to other subjects you study. Consider your audience, and write your essay in a way they will understand.

1 Compare and contrast two people you know. How does each look and act? What does each like to do?

2 Write about the similarities and differences between two places you have visited or would like to visit.

3 Compare and contrast watching movies on television and watching them in the theater. Consider factors such as cost, environment, and comfort.

4 Compare and contrast two activities you do with your friends, such as participating in sports, studying, or going to the mall. What is special about each?

Writing Across the Curriculum

5 SCIENCE

Compare and contrast two vegetables. Include details about how and where they grow, their appearance, smell, texture, and taste.

6 SOCIAL STUDIES

Compare and contrast two famous people. Include information about their occupations and their personalities.

7 PHYSICAL EDUCATION

Compare and contrast games that involve throwing a ball and games that involve kicking a ball.

8 LITERATURE/READING

Compare and contrast yourself with a fictional character. Think about your ages, interests, friends, and families.

 See www.eduplace.com/kids/hme/ for more prompts.

Test Practice

Remember that a compare-contrast essay compares the similarities and contrasts the differences between two subjects.

Sometimes on a test you will be asked to write a paper in response to a picture prompt.

These pictures show a watch and a grandfather clock. Look carefully at each picture. Then write a short essay comparing and contrasting the watch and the clock.

 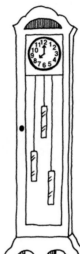

Here are some strategies to help you do a good job responding to a prompt like the one on this page.

❶ Look at each picture and answer these questions:
  - What objects are shown?
  - How are these objects alike? How are they different?

❷ Plan your writing. Use a Venn diagram like the one shown on page 451. Compare and contrast the two pictures.

❸ You will get a good score if you remember what kind of essay sounds loud and clear in the rubric on page 456.

Writing Instructions

Instructions explain how to make or do something. Read Clara's instructions on how to take care of tadpoles. Could you explain to someone else how to take care of them after reading these instructions?

Taking Care of Tadpoles

Introduction —

Do you want a pet that is easy to take care of and fun to watch? Then tadpoles are perfect for you! They'll turn into frogs right before your eyes. Here's all you need to do.

Materials —

You can catch your tadpoles in a pond or buy them in a pet store. You will need a glass, ceramic, or clear plastic container large enough to hold the tadpoles. For six or seven tadpoles, use a container that holds about ten gallons of water. Do not use a metal can! The materials in metal are harmful to tadpoles. Find a screen to cover the container and a rock that sticks up out of the water. You will also need water conditioner, a filter, ground-up rabbit pellets, and flaked fish food. You can get all of these at a pet store.

Order word

Steps —

Start by filling the container with water. Leave a few inches of air at the top. Be sure to use the water conditioner and the filter to remove the chlorine in the water. Next, put the tadpoles into your container with the clear water and the rock. You may wish to add some floating plants, such as elodea. The tadpoles will hide around the rock and plants. After their legs and lungs develop, the tadpoles will sometimes climb on the rock. They will need less water as they get older. Remember to keep the screen on the container, unless you want the tadpoles hopping everywhere. Put the container by a window so they can get light.

Once a day, feed each tadpole three to four ground-up rabbit pellets. Tadpoles also enjoy eating flaked fish food and small worms. You will want to check the water to see when it should be changed. If it turns yellow, change it. This will usually happen once a week if you have

more ▶

Steps — many tadpoles in the container. To change the water, first remove the rock and floating plants. Then carefully scoop out most of the water. Don't scoop up the tadpoles! Finally, put the rock and the floating plants back in with some fresh water. Remember to use the water conditioner.

Conclusion — It will be interesting for you to watch the tadpoles grow up. They go through stages gradually. After the tadpoles turn into frogs, take them back to the pond where you found them. In the meantime, take good care of your tadpoles if you want them to be healthy pets.

Reading As a Writer

- The **introduction** tells the purpose of the instructions and gives brief, interesting information about the subject.
  What interesting information about tadpoles does Clara include in her introduction?

- All **materials** are given, including sizes, correct amounts, and where to get them. *What materials does Clara list?*

- All the **steps** needed to perform the task are described clearly and in order. *What steps and details does Clara explain?*

- **Order words**, such as *first, next, finally, to begin, then,* and *later,* help the reader clearly understand the sequence of steps. *What order words does Clara use?*

- The **conclusion** completes the steps and may include additional interesting information about the topic.
  What final instructions does Clara give in her conclusion?

How to Write Instructions

❶ Choose a task that you can do well. As you think about the task, ask yourself these questions.

- Can I clearly and easily explain it in one or two pages?
- Can I explain it in words and sentences, without a demonstration or pictures?
- Who will be my audience?

❷ List all of the necessary materials; then list the steps to follow.

❸ Organize the steps in order. Make a chart or take notes on note cards. Include details that explain each step. Be specific. Ask yourself:

- Why is each step important?
- Are the steps in the correct order? Can any steps be taken out or combined?
- What details, reasons, facts, or examples do I need to give my readers? Keep in mind your audience and the purpose of your instructions.

 HELP

Stuck for an Idea?

Try these suggestions.
How to
- mix granola
- tie-dye a T-shirt
- make a terrarium
- create an exercise routine
- organize a yard sale
- program the speed dial on a phone

Steps	Details
1. Fill container with water.	Don't use metal containers—harmful!
2. Use water conditioner and a filter.	Keep the water clean.
3. Add rocks and floating plants.	Tadpoles will hide behind rocks and plants.
4. Put tadpoles in container.	Six or seven tadpoles to a container is best.

more ▶

4 **Write** a first draft of your instructions, using your notes or chart.

- Include an introduction that states your topic and purpose. You may want to start with a question, like Clara did. You could also start with a quotation from a book, a poem, or a speech that describes your topic. If you do start with a quotation, make sure that you include where you got it from or who said it.

> Try working through the steps in your mind to see if they are complete and in the proper order.

- Use exact words to make your instructions clear to the reader. Look at the exact words in this example.

> Once a day, feed each tadpole three to four ground-up rabbit pellets. Tadpoles also enjoy eating flaked fish food and small worms.

❺ Use order words and phrases to help the reader follow each step in sequence. You might want to underline the order words in your first draft so that you can quickly and easily check that your steps are arranged correctly.

Order Words		Order Phrases
first	later	at first
second	when	start by
before	while	soon after
after	finally	after a while
next	immediately	later in the day
now		in a few minutes
		in the meantime

❻ Write an interesting conclusion. You may want to tell how making or doing what you described can be rewarding and fun. Think of something to say that sums up the instructions and makes your audience want to follow them.

❼ Revise your draft. Use the Revising Checklist to help you evaluate and improve your instructions.

Revising Checklist
✔ What information did I include in my introduction to interest my readers?
✔ Have I included all the materials and provided any necessary details about them?
✔ Did I include all steps? What other details are needed?
✔ Are all the steps in order?
✔ Where do I need order words or phrases?

more ▶

8 **Have** a writing conference. Trade your instructions with a partner. These questions may help.

The Writing Conference	
If you're thinking . . .	**You could ask . . .**
This needs an introduction.	**Could you start with an interesting question or statement about your task?**
I can't follow this. These steps don't make any sense.	**Are all of the materials listed? Are all the steps given? Are they in the right order?**
I want to know more about this step.	**Could you give more details and exact information?**
Why is this step here?	**Is this step really important?**
Your instructions seem to just stop.	**Could you finish by telling why the task you've described is fun or worthwhile?**

9 **Proofread** your instructions, using the Proofreading Checklist on page 459. Use a dictionary to check spellings.

10 **Publish** or share a final copy of your instructions with your audience. Create illustrations for each step, and work with other writers to produce a class how-to book. Another idea would be to read your instructions while a classmate acts them out.

Taking Care of Tadpoles

Do you want a pet that is easy to take care of and fun to watch? Then tadpoles are perfect for you! They'll turn into frogs right before your eyes. Here's all you need to do.

You can catch your tadpole in a pond or buy them in a pet store. You will need a glass, ceramic, or clear plastic container large enough to hold the tadpoles. For six or seven tadpoles, use a container that holds about ten gallons of water. Do not use a metal can! The materials in metal are harmful to tadpoles. Find a screen to cover the container and a rock that sticks up out of the water. You will also need water conditioner, a filter, ground-up rabbit pellets, and flaked fish food. You can get all of these at a pet store.

Start by filling the container with water. Leave a few inches of air at the top. Be sure to use the water conditioner and the filter to remove the chlorine in the water. Next, put the tadpoles into your container with the clear water and the rock. You may wish to add some floating plants, such as elodea. The tadpoles will hide around the rock and plants. After their legs and lungs develop, the tadpoles will sometimes climb on the rock. They will need less water as they get older. Remember to keep the screen on the container, unless you want the tadpoles hopping everywhere. Put the container by a window so they can get light.

Once a day, feed each tadpole three to four ground-up rabbit pellets. Tadpoles also enjoy eating flaked fish food and small worms. You will want to check the water to see when it should be changed. If it turns yellow, change it. This will usually happen once a week if you have many tadpoles in the container. To change the water, first remove the rock and floating plants. Then carefully scoop out most of the water. Don't scoop up the tadpoles! Finally, put the rock and the floating plants back in with some fresh water. Remember to use the water conditioner.

It will be interesting for you to watch the tadpoles grow up. They go through stages gradually. After the tadpoles turn into frogs, take them back to the pond where you found them. In the meantime, take good care of your tadpoles if you want them to be healthy pets.

Comparing Meaning in Visuals

Visuals play an important role in shaping our sense of the world. They are full of information and different kinds of meaning.

To understand visuals, such as illustrations, political cartoons, and photographs, it helps to recognize their purpose. Think about who made or displayed them, and why.

Illustrations

Maps, diagrams, and drawings are types of illustrations. They are made to explain, or illustrate, written information.

An illustration gives an artist's sense of a subject. This means that different illustrators might portray the same subject very differently. Illustrations appear in newspapers, magazines, encyclopedias, textbooks, television news, and many other media. What examples can you think of?

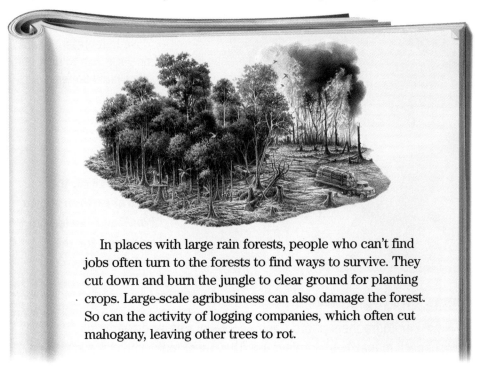

In places with large rain forests, people who can't find jobs often turn to the forests to find ways to survive. They cut down and burn the jungle to clear ground for planting crops. Large-scale agribusiness can also damage the forest. So can the activity of logging companies, which often cut mahogany, leaving other trees to rot.

Look at the illustration above from an article about rain forests. Does it make the written information easier to understand? Think of another way to illustrate this text.

more ▶

Political Cartoon

A political cartoon is drawn to give an opinion about a current issue or event. Political cartoons are almost always intended to persuade. They are often humorous, but can be critical or harsh as well. The artist may use caricatures or symbols to comment visually on the subject. You can find political cartoons on the editorial pages of major newspapers.

Look at the cartoon shown here. The cartoonist shows two world powers (Russia and the United States) "grabbing" for land or for world domination. What do you think is the cartoonist's opinion about the subject?

HELP ?

What Does It Mean?

- A **caricature** exaggerates physical features, for example, making big ears look huge or a hairstyle look ridiculous.
- A **symbol** is an image or object that stands for or suggests something else. Symbols in political cartoons can include a dove to represent peace or Uncle Sam to represent the United States.

◄ Drawn in 1873, this political cartoon shows "Ivan" and Uncle Sam competing for the Pacific Islands.

News Photography

News photographers photograph people, places, and events for newspapers, magazines, or television. They must make choices about what to include in their photos. These decisions may be influenced by the photographer's emotions or opinions, or by what newspapers or magazines want to show the public.

Suppose the two photos shown here depict the same rain forest region. Think of reasons why a news magazine might choose to publish only one of them in an article.

The guidelines below will help you understand visuals.

Guidelines for Understanding Visuals

▶ Decide on the purpose of the visual. Is it intended to inform, persuade, advertise, or entertain?

▶ Think about the story or message the artist or photographer is trying to communicate. Try to put it into words.

▶ Notice where the visual is placed. How is it used? Does it add information?

▶ Think about the mood of the picture. What techniques does the artist or photographer use to create the mood?

Apply It

Choose visuals from three different sections of the newspaper. Use the guidelines to compare them. Then answer the following questions.

● How is each visual used?

● If the visual is a photograph, could an illustration be used in its place? Why or why not?

Writing a Research Report

To prove their wealth and power, Egyptian pharaohs built gigantic tombs and statues. More than four thousand years later, the statues still command attention.

This article explains how one of the world's most famous monuments was built. In what order does the author arrange the facts to make them easy to follow?

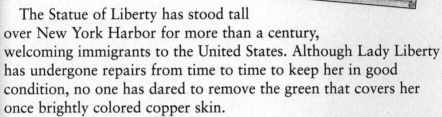

The Lady with the Green Skin

by Sylvia C. Montrone

The Statue of Liberty has stood tall over New York Harbor for more than a century, welcoming immigrants to the United States. Although Lady Liberty has undergone repairs from time to time to keep her in good condition, no one has dared to remove the green that covers her once brightly colored copper skin.

In 1871, a French sculptor, Frédéric Auguste Bartholdi, traveled to the United States to promote interest in a statue commemorating 100 years of American independence. Bartholdi and other French citizens were great admirers of American democracy and wanted to present the statue as a gift from the people of France to the people of the United States.

Just as his ship entered New York Harbor, Bartholdi had a vision of a grand monument with a glowing torch welcoming voyagers to America. Seven spokes in the lady's crown depicted the world's seven seas and continents.

Bartholdi planned to build Lady Liberty in Paris, France, then move her across the Atlantic Ocean to America. At that time large statues were constructed of stone, bronze, or cast iron, which made them too heavy to transport. So Bartholdi and the engineers working on the statue decided to give the lady a copper skin over an iron skeleton. They believed that the lightweight copper could withstand New York Harbor's harsh winds and salt sea air, as long as it was supported by a strong frame.

more ▶

In a specially built Paris workshop, artisans perfected the statue's form by making several plaster models from Bartholdi's sketches. Each plaster model was bigger than the last. The biggest was full-size: 151 feet, 1 inch tall. This model was divided into 300 sections. Carpenters made wooden molds from each section, and metal craftsmen hammered shiny copper sheets into the molds. The copper was the kind used today in craft projects, except the sheets were much larger and, at $\frac{3}{32}$ of an inch, about the thickness of a pizza crust. The artisans shaped the copper to create the folds of Lady Liberty's gown, her facial features, and even the law book inscribed *4 July 1776*.

Alexandre Gustave Eiffel, designer of the Eiffel Tower, engineered the statue's iron skeleton. Four iron posts formed the skeleton's center, with space inside for stairways. What looked like a spider web of iron bars, contoured to the statue's final form, hung around the center. After each piece of copper skin was hammered into shape, craftsmen attached it to the iron web. Shiny like a new penny, Lady Liberty steadily grew on a platform outside the workshop. She received visitors in Paris for almost a year before workers dismantled her, numbering each part. On the day she emigrated, a 70-car train carried 214 oddly shaped crates from Paris to a ship bound for America.

Reassembling Lady Liberty atop a 154-foot-high pedestal on Bedloe's Island in New York Harbor was like putting together a colossal jigsaw puzzle. Hundreds of thousands of rivets were needed to attach the 300 pieces of copper skin to the iron web. Asbestos insulation was placed between the skin and the iron ribs wherever

the two metals met. Eiffel feared that, without insulation, the statue might become a giant electric battery, shocking visitors!

In 1886, fifteen years after Bartholdi's first trip to the United States, President Cleveland unveiled the Statue of Liberty exactly where the sculptor had envisioned her. Mounted on her pedestal, she rose 305 feet above the harbor, nearly as high as a football field standing on end.

By that time, her shiny copper skin had turned the dull brown color of an old penny. At the turn of the century, her skin was streaked with black and green, which gradually changed to the blue-green patina she wears today. Patina is a crust that forms when a copper surface is attacked by elements in the atmosphere and combines with them. Metropolitan New York's humidity, snow, rain, and industrial pollution all reacted with the statue's skin. If you've ever uncovered a penny buried in the ground for a long time, you've probably noticed its crusty, pale green edges, or patina. Like the penny, Lady Liberty responded to the environment's bullying with a trick from

more ▶

Mother Nature. Once the patina had spread over her entire copper skin, she was protected from further environmental damage.

Between 1981 and 1986, Lady Liberty got a complete makeover. A new steel-alloy web replaced her badly corroded iron web. A glass elevator was installed. Electrical engineers even devised a new lighting system. However, polishing her skin to its original bright copper would have decreased its thickness and shortened her life. So, throughout restoration, Lady Liberty was allowed to keep her patina cloak. Now scientists expect she'll survive a thousand years.

Although many, many people worked to restore the statue to full glory, Lady Liberty today stands proudly protected in a green patina cloak—one she made all by herself.

Reading As a Writer

Think About the Article

- In what order is this article organized?
- What is the main topic of this article?
- In the first paragraph on page 474, which sentence tells what the paragraph is about? What are the supporting details?
- How does the conclusion relate to the introduction?

Think About Writer's Craft

- What is interesting about the title?
- What comparisons does the author make on pages 474 and 475?

Think About the Pictures

- Look closely at the photograph on page 476. Why is a picture taken from a distance better than a close-up for the conclusion of this article? Why is a picture in color better than one in black and white?

Responding

Write responses to these questions.

- **Personal Response** What meaning does the Statue of Liberty have for you? How did reading this article affect what you think of it?

- **Critical Thinking** Write your opinion about whether monuments like the Statue of Liberty should be preserved at great expense to the public. Use information from the article as support.

What Makes a Great Research Report?

A **research report** is a report on
factual information learned
through research.

When you write a research report, remember these points.

▶ Do thorough, well-organized research.

▶ Write an engaging introduction that tells the main idea.

▶ Create a paragraph for each main topic. Support each topic
sentence with at least two facts or examples.

▶ Write in the third person. Focus on facts, not opinions.

▶ Use your own words. *Don't plagiarize!*

▶ Show how your ideas are connected.

▶ Write a conclusion that sums up the main idea of
your report.

▶ Include an accurate list of sources.

GRAMMAR CHECK
Avoid using double
negatives.

Elizabeth Coultas

WORKING DRAFT

Elizabeth Coultas grew curious about the platypus after glimpsing it on a TV program about Australia. She thought it would make a perfect topic for her report. Here is her working draft.

> Your first sentence grabs me!

The Duckbilled Platypus

Have you ever seen an animal that looks like a beaver and a duck all in one? A platypus is just that! The platypus is so unusual that ~~a special scientific group~~ scientists created a special classification for this kind of mammal.

Platypuses have thick fur that varies in color from yellowish to dark brown. The platypus is weird-looking. It has a ducklike bill. It has webbed feet. It has paws with claws. It also has paddlelike limbs. It has a 14-inch barrel-shaped body. It has a beaverlike tail. Some people have even come to the conclusion that it is a crossed animal.

> Could you explain this point and vary the sentences in this paragraph?

more

A platypus is a strange sort of mammal. In fact, ~~platypuses are not crossbreeds. They have characteristics of both a mammal and a reptile.~~ They are one of the world's two monotremes. They are something like mammals and something like reptiles, but they are actually mammals. With their paddlelike limbs and their long tails, platypuses are also well equipped for swimming, as many reptiles are.

> Could you give some facts and examples to make this clear?

Platypuses live in eastern Australia and Tasmania in burrows near lakes and streams. They eat many things from the lakes and streams. They have an interesting way of getting their food. When the female is ready to lay her eggs, she makes a special burrow deep in a bank, creating an

> Should you move some information to the next paragraph?

underground tunnel. She lays from one to three eggs. Each measures about one half inch.

~~Platypuses get most of their food from the water~~ Platypuses eat insects, crayfish, worms, and mollusks. Platypuses cannot see when underwater. Their wide tails help them swim, and their ducklike bills help them gather their food. They usually feed during the early morning or the late evening. The mud and sand that platypuses end up eating along with their food help them break up their food. Platypuses don't have teeth. I think it would be fun to swim with a platypus.

Platypuses are now protected by law.

> Can you tell us why they can't see?

> Does this information fit the rest of your report? Can you summarize your main points instead?

> You've done fine research!

Reading As a Writer

- What did Joe like about Elizabeth's report? What suggestions did he make?
- Where did Elizabeth let her opinion slip in?
- What questions would you ask Elizabeth? What seems unclear to you about her report?

FINAL COPY

Elizabeth got helpful feedback from other students before she revised her report. Read the final copy to see what changes she made.

The Duckbilled Platypus
by Elizabeth Coultas

Have you ever seen an animal that looks like a beaver and a duck all in one? A platypus is just that! The platypus is so unusual that scientists created a special classification for this kind of mammal.

Platypuses have thick fur that varies in color from yellowish to dark brown. That's not so strange, but the platypus is a very weird-looking animal in other ways. This mammal has a ducklike bill, webbed feet, clawed paws, and paddlelike limbs. Its 14-inch barrel-shaped body ends with a beaverlike tail. Some early scientists believed that the platypus was a cross between a mammal and a duck or reptile.

In fact, platypuses are not crossbreeds. They are one of the world's two monotremes—a special class of mammals that have certain characteristics of reptiles. For example, a platypus has hair, as all

> Now your point is clear—and interesting too!

mammals do. Platypus mothers feed
their babies their own milk, as other
mammals do. Like reptiles, however,
platypus females lay leathery eggs. With
their paddlelike limbs and their long tails,
platypuses are also well equipped for
swimming, as many reptiles are. The
only other monotreme is Australia's
spiny anteater, or echidna.

You've added great details and examples!

Now this paragraph has one main topic.

Platypuses live in eastern Australia
and Tasmania in burrows near lakes
and streams. Most burrows are almost 25
feet long. When the female is ready to lay
her eggs, she makes a special burrow deep
in a bank, creating an underground
tunnel. She lays from one to three eggs.
Each measures about one half inch.

more

Platypuses eat crayfish, worms, and mollusks from lakes and streams. Platypuses cannot see when underwater because folds of skin cover their eyes, but their wide tails help them swim, and their ducklike bills help them gather their food. They usually feed during the early morning or the late evening. The mud and sand that platypuses end up eating along with their food help them break up their food. Platypuses don't have teeth.

> This report has a strong conclusion.

Platypuses are nearly unique animals that have adapted well to their surroundings. Although the creatures no longer baffle scientists, the study of the duckbilled platypus will surely continue for years to come.

Sources

Katz, Barbara. "Platypus." *Compton's Encyclopedia Online.* vers. 3.0. 1998. The Learning Company. America Online. 3 Oct. 2001.

"Platypus." *National Geographic Book of Mammals.* Vol. 2. Washington, DC: National Geographic, 1998.

Reilly, Pauline, and Will Rolland (illus.). *Platypus.* Kenthurst, Australia: Kangaroo Press, 1991.

Short, Joan, with Jack Green, Bettina Bird, and Andrew Wichlinski (illus.). *Platypus.* Greenvale, NY: Mondo Publishing, 1997.

> You included a list of sources. Well done!

Reading As a Writer

- What did Elizabeth do in response to Joe's comments?
- What did she do to improve the second paragraph?
- What is different about her revised conclusion?
- What does the list of sources tell you about her research?

 See www.eduplace.com/kids/hme/ for more examples of student writing.

Write a Research Report

▶ Start Thinking

 Make a writing folder for your research report. Copy the questions in bold type. Write your answers as you choose and explore your topic. Keep the paper in your folder.

- **Who will be my audience?** Will it be my classmates? readers of my school newspaper? online friends?
- **What will be the purpose of my report?** Will it be to answer a question that I have wondered about? to find out more about a topic?
- **How will I publish or share my report?** Will I put it in a class book? videotape my own "television special"? make a visual display?

▶ Choose Your Research Topic

1 **List** five topics you might like to write about. Topics that make you wonder will probably be interesting to others too.

2 **Discuss** your topic ideas with a partner.

- Which ideas interest your partner most? Why?
- Do you need to broaden or narrow any of your topic ideas?

3 **Ask** yourself these questions. Then create a short list of your three favorite ideas.

- Which topics interest me most?
- Which would my readers like?

4 **Circle** the topic you will write about. Keep your short list in case you can't find enough information.

> **HELP**
> **?**
> **Can't Think of a Topic?**
>
> - Find an encyclopedia volume that starts with your first initial. Browse through it to find interesting topics.
> - What do you like to do in your spare time? Learn more about one of your interests.
>
> See page 503 for more ideas.

> Writing a research report can make you an expert on just about anything that makes you curious.

▶ Explore Your Topic

❶ Narrow your topic if it's too broad to cover in a short report. Use an inverted triangle. Keep narrowing your topic until it's a manageable size.

Here is Elizabeth's triangle.

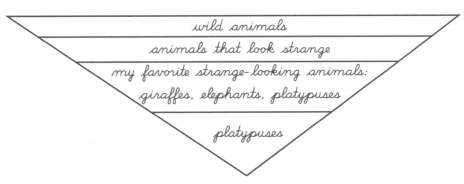

wild animals

animals that look strange

my favorite strange-looking animals: giraffes, elephants, platypuses

platypuses

❷ Make a K-W-S chart to help you find out about your topic. Fill in the first two columns.

Here is the chart Elizabeth made before beginning her research.

What I Know	What I Want to Learn	Possible Sources
They have fur and a funny bill. They can swim. They don't live in the United States.	Why do they look the way they do? How do they get their food? What do they eat? Where do they live?	

❸ Add more questions to your chart. What else do you want to know about your topic? Ask *Who? What? When? Where? Why? How?* Your questions will guide your research.

Think of your topic as a mystery you can solve by asking questions.

HELP? See page 16 for other ideas for exploring your topic.

Go to www.eduplace.com/kids/hme/ for graphic organizers.

Focus Skill

Finding the Best Information

Locating Information

Find answers to your research questions by gathering information.

Talk to people. Interviewing is a great way to do research. Do you know a local expert? Can you call a nearby organization to find one? You might speak with a museum staff person, an expert gardener, a pet shop owner, or a college professor.

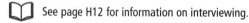 See page H12 for information on interviewing.

Look in print sources.

- Encyclopedias can give you a broad overview of a topic.
- Nonfiction books on your specific topic are a good source of in-depth information.
- Newspapers and magazines offer short articles. They're especially helpful when you need up-to-date information.

Use technology. Web sites, online encyclopedias, and reference works on CD-ROM provide information on many topics.

See pages H25 and H51 for information on using the library and the Internet.

Evaluating Information

Evaluate your sources. Ask these questions about each source of information you might use for your report.

- Is the information related to my topic?
- Is the author or expert dependable? Check for a special degree or years of experience in the field.
- Is information from the Internet created by a professional? Amateur sites often have errors. Look for sites created by schools, well-known publications, or respected organizations such as NASA.
- Is the source current? Check the copyright date. Use the most up-to-date information you can find.

Think and Discuss

- If you were writing a report on butterflies, what sources would you explore first?
- What organizations in your area might provide information on history topics? nature topics? career topics?

▶ Explore Your Sources

❶ Read a short encyclopedia entry on your topic, to get an overview.

❷ Find possible sources of information. Browse through your library. Write your ideas in the third column of your K-W-S chart.

❸ Evaluate these sources. Choose the four strongest ones. Only one should be a general encyclopedia.

❹ Set up an interview if you can.

> If you can't find good sources, choose a different topic from your short list.

▶ Research Your Topic

❶ Skim each source you have chosen, reading headings and the first sentence of some paragraphs. Scan the text for important words. Will it have answers to your questions?

📖 See page H35 for information on skimming and scanning.

❷ Take notes on note cards as you find answers to your questions.

- Keep a card listing your sources. Number each source.
- Write a question from your chart on a card. Write related facts from one source. Note the source number. You may have a number of cards for each question.
- Use your own words. Write in phrases or sentences.
- If you want to use a phrase or a sentence exactly as it appears in a source, copy the words, and enclose them in quotation marks.
- Write down facts, not opinions. Facts can be proved true. Opinions state feelings or thoughts.

> If you copy someone else's words without giving credit, you are plagiarizing.

Fact:	Butterflies' wings can have intricate, colorful patterns.
Opinion:	Butterflies have the most beautiful wings of any insect.

- Check the facts in the What I Know column of your chart. Put this information on cards if you plan to use it in your report.

Tech Tip If you have access to a laptop computer, you might use it for taking notes.

Here is some information that Elizabeth found in a print source and the notes she took.

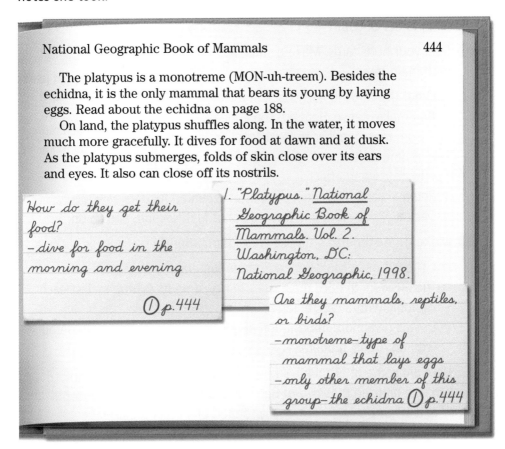

National Geographic Book of Mammals   444

The platypus is a monotreme (MON-uh-treem). Besides the echidna, it is the only mammal that bears its young by laying eggs. Read about the echidna on page 188.

On land, the platypus shuffles along. In the water, it moves much more gracefully. It dives for food at dawn and at dusk. As the platypus submerges, folds of skin close over its ears and eyes. It also can close off its nostrils.

How do they get their food?
—dive for food in the morning and evening
① p.444

1. "Platypus." *National Geographic Book of Mammals*. Vol. 2. Washington, DC: National Geographic, 1998.

Are they mammals, reptiles, or birds?
—monotreme—type of mammal that lays eggs
—only other member of this group—the echidna ① p.444

❸ **Look** at the questions on your K-W-S chart.

- You'll discover new things about your topic as you take notes. Add questions to your chart about new information you want to use.
- Delete questions that don't seem important anymore.
- Delete some questions if you're getting overloaded with information. Keep the most important ones.
- Find another information source if you haven't yet answered all the important questions.

Elizabeth added this new question to her K-W-S chart as she did her research: *Are they mammals, reptiles, or birds?*

▶ Plan Your Report

❶ Think about main topics. The main questions you answered are the main topics of your report.

❷ Sort your note cards. Make a stack for each main topic.

- Order the cards in each stack in a way that makes sense. Here are some ideas.
  - from most familiar to least familiar
  - in time order
  - by cause and effect
- Remove cards with unimportant or repeated facts.
- Decide which stack you'll write about first, second, and so on.

> **HELP**
> **?** **Enough Cards?**
> You should have at least two facts or examples to support each main topic. If you need more information, do more research.

❸ Make an outline to organize your information.

- List each main topic with a Roman numeral.
- The answers to each main question become its subtopics. List each subtopic with a capital letter.
- Details give more information about the subtopics. List each detail with an Arabic numeral.

Here are some of Elizabeth's notes and part of her outline. As she worked, she realized that two of her K-W-S questions (*How do they get their food?* and *What do they eat?*) really formed one main topic.

What do they eat?
–crayfish, worms, and mollusks
③ *p. 12*

How do they get their food?
–eat mud and sand with their food
–helps break up the food
③ *p. 13*

V. Feeding habits of platypuses
  A. What they eat: crayfish, worms, mollusks
  B. How they get food
    1. Can't see when under water
    2. Helped by tails and ducklike bills
    3. Feed at morning and at evening
    4. Eat mud and sand, which break up food

📖 See page H34 for more information on outlining.

Writing from an Outline

Write topic sentences. Write one for each main topic in your outline. State the idea clearly. Put each topic sentence on a note card or a separate piece of paper.

> If a main topic has lots of information, write two paragraphs for it. Give each a topic sentence!

Write paragraphs. Using subtopics and details from your outline, write a paragraph for each topic sentence. Write in the third person. These paragraphs will make up the body of your report.

GRAMMAR TIP ➤ Be sure to capitalize proper nouns and proper adjectives.

I. Life cycle of butterfly
    A. Starts as egg
    B. Hatches into caterpillar
    C. Forms shell called chrysalis
        1. Hangs from an object
        2. Spends from a few days to
           more than a year in chrysalis
    D. Emerges as a butterfly

    A butterfly's life has four stages. A butterfly first comes into the world as an egg. The egg hatches into a wormlike creature called a caterpillar. The caterpillar later forms a shell called a chrysalis and spends anywhere from a few days to over a year in it, depending on the species. Then it turns into a butterfly.

more ▶

Focus Skill continued

Use transitional words and phrases. They will make your report flow smoothly.

To introduce examples	for example, for instance, in fact, in one case, to begin with
To add another point	another, besides, also, in addition (to), furthermore
To show time relationships	after, before, next, eventually, since, finally, first, then, later, until, now
To show causes and effects	because (of), as a result, due to, therefore, thus
To compare and contrast	just as, like, similarly, on the other hand, in contrast, despite the fact that
To connect ideas	however, yet, so, though, moreover

Think and Discuss

Use the example paragraph on page 493 to answer these questions.

- What is the topic sentence?
- What transitional words does the writer use?

▶ Draft the Body of Your Report

❶ **Write** a topic sentence for each main topic on your outline.

❷ **Write** a paragraph for each topic sentence. Use vivid language, strong examples, and interesting details. Use a quotation if you have a really good one.

❸ **Break** a big main topic into more than one paragraph. Give each paragraph a topic sentence.

Focus Skill

Introductions and Conclusions

Write a focus statement. Look at what you've written so far. What main idea pulls it all together? Express that idea in one sentence.

> Write with style!
> Deliver the facts in your own personal voice.

Introduce your topic. Your first paragraph should express your main idea and get attention too. You might hint at the interesting information that will follow or give a surprising fact.

Weak Introduction	Strong Introduction
In December 1787 a ship set out for the South Pacific. It left England. It was called the *Bounty*. The crew had a long, long trip ahead.	In December 1787 the British ship *Bounty* set out for the South Pacific. Nobody knew that this trip would be its last.

Write a strong conclusion. In your closing paragraph, sum up the report's main idea in an interesting way. You might note how the information is useful, fascinating, or important to history.

Weak Conclusion	Strong Conclusion
These three kinds of clouds have similarities and differences. Scientists keep on studying them. This report has told you the basic information about them.	Anyone taking a trip to the beach should first look at the clouds. Are they cumulus? cirrostratus? cumulonimbus? Each kind gives a clue about the coming weather.

Think and Discuss Compare the introductions above.

- What makes the strong introduction more interesting?

▶ Draft Your Introduction and Conclusion

❶ **Write** a focus statement expressing the main idea of your report.

❷ **Write** an introduction and a conclusion.

❸ **Prepare** a list of sources as shown on page 485.

Evaluating Your Research Report

▶ **Reread** your report. Use this rubric to help you revise. Write the sentences that describe your report.

Loud and Clear!

- ▪ The report shows good research based on reliable sources.
- ▪ The introduction and conclusion present the main idea.
- ▪ The report is well organized. Smooth transitions connect ideas.
- ▪ Each paragraph has a topic sentence and supporting details.
- ▪ I have written in the third person and in my own words.
- ▪ My list of sources is accurate and complete.
- ▪ There are very few spelling or grammar mistakes.

Sounding Stronger

- ▪ Parts of the report are well researched, but others aren't.
- ▪ The introduction and conclusion are boring.
- ▪ I ordered the paragraphs well, but I need better transitions.
- ▪ Some paragraphs need topic sentences or more details.
- ▪ I give an opinion that should be deleted.
- ▪ I need to make sure that a quotation is written correctly.
- ▪ I have a list of sources, but it is incomplete.
- ▪ Mistakes make some sentences confusing.

Turn Up the Volume

- ☐ I have not done enough research.
- ☐ The report lacks an introduction and a conclusion.
- ☐ The paragraphs are not in an order that makes sense.
- ☐ I have few topic sentences and few supporting facts.
- ☐ The writing mixes opinions with facts.
- ☐ I have not quoted carefully. I may have plagiarized.
- ☐ I forgot to include a list of sources.
- ▪ Mistakes make the report hard to understand.

 See www.eduplace.com/kids/hme/ to interact with this rubric

Revise Your Research Report

❶ Revise your report. Use the list of sentences you wrote from the rubric. Work on the parts that you described with sentences from "Sounding Stronger" and "Turn Up the Volume."

HELP?

Revising Tip

Highlight your transitional words and phrases. Add more if you need them.

❷ Have a writing conference.

When You're the Writer Read your report aloud to your partner. Ask for feedback. Listen while your partner is talking, and take notes. Then decide which changes to make.

When You're the Listener Tell your partner at least two things you like about the report. Ask questions about anything that seemed confusing or seemed boring. Use the chart below for ideas.

What should I say?

The Writing Conference	
If you're thinking . . .	**You could ask . . .**
The introduction is dull.	**Could you begin with a surprising fact? a hint of what is to come?**
These facts seem unrelated.	**Could you put these ideas in a better order? Could you make better transitions?**
I don't understand what you mean.	**Could you explain the part about _____ more clearly? Could you use an example?**
This sentence doesn't sound like the writer.	**Did you make sure to use your own words?**
The report has no conclusion.	**Can you sum up your main idea at the end?**

❸ Make revisions, using your notes from the writing conference and the Revising Strategies on the next page.

Revising Strategies

Elaborating: Word Choice To prevent confusion, define words that your audience might not know.

No Definition	Definition Added
The club focused on preserving **wetlands**.	The club focused on preserving wetlands, low areas such as swamps and riverbanks that are often flooded.

▶ Find two places where you can define a term.

Elaborating: Details Make your reader say "Wow!" by adding unusual facts and fascinating details to your writing.

Few Details	High-Interest Details Added
Inca weavers made fine fabrics that are colorful and densely woven.	Inca weavers made fine fabrics, using simple wooden tools. The cloth was colored with vegetable dyes in red, blue, and gold hues. Densely woven, many fabrics have as many as 135 threads to the inch.

▶ Find three places in your report to add high-interest details.

Sentence Fluency Two related ideas in a sentence should be structured in a similar, or parallel, way. Often such ideas are linked with *and* or *or.*

Without Parallel Structure	With Parallel Structure
Vegetation keeps the soil from eroding, **protecting it from wind** and **to give it shade from the hot sun.**	Vegetation keeps the soil from eroding, protecting it from the wind and giving it shade from the hot sun.

▶ Find three sentences in your report with ideas joined by *and* or *or,* and check them for parallel structure.

GRAMMAR LINK ▶ *See also page 244.*

Adding Graphics and Visuals

Pictures, charts, maps, and other visual aids can make your report more interesting and informative. Put them on the cover, within the report, or in a special section at the end. However, not all reports lend themselves to visuals—don't force them in if they don't fit.

Include pictures of people, places, or things that are important to your topic. Draw your own, or use magazine clippings or photocopies. Credit the source if you use a copy.

Give every visual aid a caption or a title.

▶ Think about adding a picture to your report.

Draw a time line if your report discusses events that happen over a stretch of time. This one comes from a report on the early years of space exploration.

Early Space Vehicles Sent to the Moon

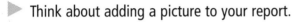

Russian Luna 2	Russian Luna 3	U.S. Ranger 7	U.S. Surveyor I
September 1959	October 1959	July 1964	May 30, 1966

▶ Include a time line in your report if it will help show a sequence of events.

Add a map, hand-drawn or photocopied, to your report. Label only the things that the reader needs to know. This one comes from a report on Portugal.

▶ If your readers need to know locations or the path of a journey, consider adding a map.

▲ A map of Portugal

more ▶

Use charts and graphs to organize information or to compare amounts. This chart adds interesting facts to a report on types of bridges.

The Longest Bridges in the United States		
Name	Location	Length in Feet
Verrazano-Narrows	Lower New York Bay	4,260
Golden Gate	San Francisco Bay	4,200
Mackinac Bridge	Mackinac Straits, Michigan	3,800
George Washington	Hudson River, New York City	3,500

▶ Use a chart or graph if it clarifies information you want to present.

Tech Tip
Your computer may have a program that makes charts and graphs.

Draw a diagram to show a step in a process or how something is put together. This diagram is from a report on the history of baseball.

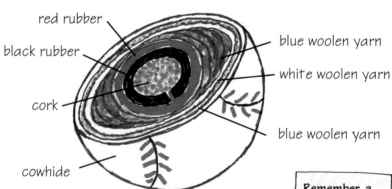

red rubber
black rubber
cork
cowhide
blue woolen yarn
white woolen yarn
blue woolen yarn

Figure 1. The structure of a baseball

Remember, a visual cannot take the place of text in your report.

▶ Put a diagram in your report if it fits.

▶ Proofread Your Research Report

Proofread your report, using the Proofreading Checklist and the Grammar and Spelling Connections. Proofread for one skill at a time.

HELP ?

Proofreading Tip

Circle any words that might be misspelled. Check spellings in a class dictionary.

Proofreading Checklist

Did I

✔ indent all paragraphs?
✔ begin and end sentences correctly?
✔ use negatives correctly?
✔ use commas in a series?
✔ spell all the words correctly?

📖 Use the Guide to Capitalization, Punctuation, and Usage on page H64.

Proofreading Marks

¶ Indent
∧ Add
⌐ Delete
≡ Capital letter
/ Small letter
˅˅ Add quotes
∧ Add comma
⊙ Add period
∿ Transpose

Grammar and Spelling Connections

Negatives Avoid using a double negative, that is, two negatives together.

Incorrect	Correct
This cactus **doesn't** have **no** flowers.	This cactus doesn't have any flowers.

GRAMMAR LINK *See also page 206.*

Commas Use commas to separate items in a series.

Langston Hughes wrote poems, stories, plays, songs, and novels.

GRAMMAR LINK *See also page 241.*

Spelling Words with *-ion* You can change many verbs into nouns by adding the suffix *-ion*.

elect election   discuss discussion   educate education

📖 See the Spelling Guide on page H80.

▶ Publish Your Research Report

❶ **Make a neat final copy** of your report. Did you correct all mistakes?

❷ **Title** your report to make it sound fascinating. Would you rather read "Alexander Selkirk" or "The Real Robinson Crusoe"?

❸ **Publish** or share your report in a way that suits your audience. See the Ideas for Sharing box.

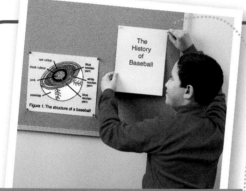

The History of Baseball

Figure 1. The structure of a baseball

Tips for Creating a Visual Display

- Create large visuals to enhance your report. Use nice lettering and art.
- Include quotations, a diorama, objects related to your topic, or a trivia game to test viewers' knowledge of the subject.
- Arrange your visuals on posterboard, on the bulletin board, or as a "museum exhibit" of objects and resources. Display your report with your visuals.

HELP? See page 512 for tips.

Ideas for Sharing

Write It Down
- With your classmates, collect your research reports in a class *Book of Knowledge.* Include a table of contents.
- Submit your report to the school newspaper.

Talk It Up
- Present your report orally. See page 512 for tips.
- In a small group, tape-record your reports as a radio show. Introduce each speaker as a specialist in the field.

Show It Off
- Create an electronic multimedia presentation. See page H53 for tips.
- ★ Make a visual display.

▶ Reflect

Write about your writing experience. Use these questions to get started.

- What did you find easy and difficult about writing a research report?
- What else would you like to learn about this topic or a related one?
- How does this report compare with other papers you have written?

Writing Prompts

Use these prompts as ideas for research reports. They relate to other subjects you study. Think of a topic your audience will find interesting, and write your report in a way that they will understand and enjoy.

Writing Across the Curriculum

1 SOCIAL STUDIES

Research a famous person you admire. Write about important accomplishments, struggles, and the person's influence on others.

2 ART

Research a building in your city. When was it built? Who was the architect? Include drawings.

3 MATHEMATICS

Research the history of mapmaking, the compass, or the sextant. Describe how it uses math concepts. Include diagrams.

4 SCIENCE

Nature is full of tiny life forms, such as the firefly or the inchworm. Write a report on the physical features and life cycle of one of them.

5 SOCIAL STUDIES

Which foreign country interests you most? Write a report on it. Focus on its people and culture, its history, its geography, or a particular area. Provide a map.

6 LITERATURE/READING

Write about the real-life place that is the setting of a favorite novel. Describe the landscape, the buildings, the people, and other unique features.

7 SCIENCE

Research a strange weather phenomenon. What causes a tornado? a huge snowstorm? lightning and thunder?

8 ART

Learn how to do a new craft, and report on it. You might try quilting, papier-mâché, candle making, or woodworking.

Writing to Solve a Problem

When you write to **solve a problem**, you define the problem, identify and consult resources to help you solve it, and explain your solution. Read how Henry solved his problem.

Problem: What kind of dog should we get?	Possible Sources of Information
Problems — • Mom wants a short-haired dog. • Dad wants a good watchdog. • Jimmy wants a gentle dog. • I want a playful friend.	• books about dogs • the Internet • Dr. Tull, veterinarian — Resources • friends who already own dogs • organizations of dog breeders

Summary —

    My problem was finding a breed of dog that made my entire family happy. Mom wanted a short-haired dog, so that it didn't shed much. Dad wanted a good watchdog. The dog also had to be gentle enough for my little brother, Jimmy, but frisky enough for me to have fun with too.

    I started by researching breeds at the public library and on the Internet. I made a list of breeds that I thought matched what we were looking for. Then I took my list to Dr. Tull, our veterinarian. She said that of all the dogs on my list, German shepherds, collies, and boxers were the best watchdogs. Collies, however, are out because they are long-haired.

    After visiting the vet, I talked to some friends who already own dogs. One who owns a German shepherd thought that it might play a bit too rough for Jimmy.

Solution
Finally, I decided to send for some information about boxers from the American Boxer Club. I learned that boxers have everything we want in a dog. Although they do shed, boxers have short hair. They are alert and brave watchdogs. They look fierce but are really kind and patient with kids. They do get a little large, almost two feet high, but we all like big dogs. Best of all, they love to run and even wrestle with their owners.

The information I sent for included a list of boxer rescue sites. We contacted several and soon found just the puppy we wanted. His name is Max. We all love him!

Our puppy, Max, a boxer

Reading As a Writer

- The **problem** is the situation you need to fix.
  What was Henry's problem?

- **Resources** can be people, places, and materials that provide information to solve the problem.
  What kinds of resources did Henry list?

- The **summary** restates the problem and explains the actions taken to solve the problem. *Which paragraph restates the problem?*

- The **solution** is the decision you make.
  What did Henry decide?

more ▶

How to Write to Solve a Problem

❶ State your problem in one clear sentence.

❷ Write a list of questions you want to answer. Identify sources of information.

❸ Research the answers to your questions. Organize your information and your sources in a chart.

Information	Source
Possible breeds: Welsh corgi, Airedale terrier, boxer, golden retriever, German shepherd, collie	library books, American Kennel Club Web site
Good watchdogs: German shepherds, boxers, collies,—collies long-haired	Dr. Tull, veterinarian
German shepherds may be too rough for Jimmy.	friends who have dogs
Boxers—short-haired, good watchdogs, gentle with kids, but very playful	American Boxer Club information

❹ Solve the problem, using the information you collected. Write a paragraph explaining your decision and why you made that choice.

Writing a Feature Article

A **feature article** is a newspaper or newsletter article that gives detailed information about a past event or an event planned for the near future. A feature article is different from a news article, which focuses on immediate news. Feature articles may or may not be written to be printed on a specific date. Read Yurico's article.

Headline ⟶ **Vista Verde Goes Hollywood**

Byline ⟶ by Yurico Tellez

Introduction or Lead paragraph — Friday morning something unexpected happened at Vista Verde Middle School. An unfamiliar voice made the 8:00 A.M. announcements, and then said, "Good morning, Vista Verde students. Would all of you please come to the auditorium at this time?"

Who belonged to this unknown voice? Students filed into the auditorium. Everyone was buzzing. What was this all about?

The auditorium lights went out and a spotlight lit up the podium on the stage. Then a woman walked out to the

Direct quotation — podium. She said, "Hello, students of Vista Verde. My name is Elisa Tomas, and I'm here because I want to make a movie about your school."

Tomas explained that she works for a film company called Western EdTex Films. The company plans to film a movie at Vista Verde for an educational conference in California next year.

Supporting details — The movie will show middle school students how to start recycling programs in their schools. The company chose

Vista Verde to film because the school has won awards for its recycling program.

"I'm looking forward to working with you," said Tomas. "This is your chance to show students in other schools what makes Vista Verde special."

Tomas is not actually the one who holds the camera. She will interview students. A special team will set up the lights and cameras and make sure the sound is recorded correctly. Filming begins Monday.

Students are excited about the movie. "I can't wait to e-mail my cousin in Sarasota and tell her!" exclaimed Karlee Dodds, age 12. Brian Herzl, 15, said, "Who ever thought we'd be in a movie?"

Conclusion

more ▶

- The **headline** grabs the reader's attention while introducing the main idea of the article. *What is the headline of the article?*

- The **byline** is the name of the person who wrote the article. *What is the byline of this article?*

- The **introduction** or **lead paragraph** may be written to make readers curious. It doesn't have to answer *Who? What? Where? When? Why?* and *How?* like a news article. *How does Yurico introduce the article?*

- The **supporting details** are facts reported in the body of the feature article. Remember that a fact can be proved true. It is not an opinion. *Name two facts given in Yurico's article.*

- A **direct quotation** provides the exact words people say about the event. *Who is quoted in Yurico's article?*

- The **conclusion** brings the article to a close with a fact, question, quotation, or light remark. *How does Yurico's article end?*

The chart below shows some ways that feature articles are similar to and different from news articles.

Feature Article	News Article
• does not need to answer *Who? What? Where? When? Why?* and *How?* in the lead paragraph	• answers *Who? What? Where? When? Why?* and *How?* in the lead paragraph
• uses facts, but can be written from one point of view • can include the writer's opinion and voice	• uses only verified facts • does not include any opinions • may include different points of view
• not necessarily written to be printed at a specific time	• very timely and immediate
• usually has a human-interest focus	• can be about anything considered "news"

How to Write a Feature Article

❶ Choose an event to report. Think about why your audience may want to know about it. Feature articles usually deal with human-interest topics, such as a student graduating without ever missing a day of school.

❷ Research your subject. Take careful notes about the event. Interview people who were at the event, or know about it, for direct quotations.

❸ Write your article. Feature writers usually describe events in chronological order, which is the order in which they happened.

❹ Think of a headline that states the article's main idea and gets your reader's attention.

❺ Revise your article. Check to see that each fact and quotation supports your point of view.

❻ Proofread your article, using a dictionary to check spellings. Check the spelling of each name you include.

❼ Publish your feature article in a class newsletter, or send it to the editor of your community newspaper.

When will the film be finished?

Why was Vista Verde chosen?

What do students think about the movie?

To get exact quotations when you interview people, use a cassette recorder.

Completing a Form

When an organization, a club, or a business needs to know specific information about someone, the person may be asked to **complete a form**. People fill out forms to join video rental clubs, to order items from businesses on the Internet, to get credit cards, or to open a bank account. Look at the example of a form below.

APPLICATION

Savings Account

Directions —

Please print the following information and complete all of the sections. Sign and date this application and return it to a bank representative.

Personal information —

Name: <u>Marcia Dena Alvarez</u>   Telephone: <u>509–555–2671</u>

Street: <u>2104 W. Woodbridge Street</u>

City: <u>Spokane</u>   State: <u>Washington</u>   Zip: <u>99228</u>

Date of Birth: <u>April 21, 1990</u>   Occupation: <u>Student</u>

Mother's Maiden Name: <u>Parker</u>

Account information —

Type of Savings Account (check one):   <u>X</u> Basic   ____ MultiService

ATM Card (check one):   ____ Yes   <u>X</u> No

I certify that the information given above is accurate and correct to the best of my knowledge.   Date

Signature —

<u>Marcia Dena Alvarez</u>   <u>January 30, 2001</u>
Signature of Applicant   Date

<u>T. Alvarez</u>   <u>January 30, 2001</u>
Signature of Parent/Guardian   Date

Signature of parent or guardian required if applicant is under 18 years of age.

- The **directions** explain how to complete the form. *What directions are given for completing this form?*

- The **personal information** often includes your name, address, and telephone number. Sometimes businesses request other information, such as your date of birth and social security number. *When was Marcia born?*

- The **account information** tells the bank what kind of service you are requesting. *What kind of savings account is Marcia applying for?*

- Many forms ask for your **signature** and that of a parent or guardian. By signing your name, you are saying that you understand the form. It also means that you have given correct information and that you agree to any rules or requirements stated. *Why did Marcia's parent have to sign the form?*

- The **date** is the month, day, and year on which you completed the form. *When did Marcia complete this form?*

How to Complete a Form

❶ **Read** the directions carefully. Then look over the whole form. Ask about any parts that you don't understand.

❷ **Complete** the form, writing neatly. Ask a family member to help you with any information that you don't know.

❸ **Sign** and date the form.

❹ **Proofread** your form for mistakes. Make certain that the information you have written is correct and that you have completed all of the areas on the form that apply to you.

❺ **Return** or mail your completed form to the place from which you received it.

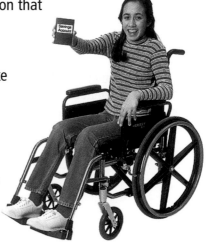

Giving an Oral Report

The goal of an oral report is to present information in a way that listeners can understand. You may need to do research to support your ideas and to present your information using multimedia. You'll need to speak clearly and use words that fit your topic and your audience.

Which Media?	
Models Models give a sense of scale. They show subjects in three dimensions.	• dioramas, collages, clay models, papier-mâché objects
Illustrations Organizing data or information into charts and drawings can help to explain your ideas.	• charts, graphs, diagrams, tables, fine art, cut-away diagrams 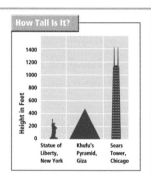
Photographs Photographs can show details and events or present different viewpoints.	• posters, slides; pictures from newspapers, magazines, books, coffee-table books
Technology Presenting ideas through music or by using computer technology can add important information to your report and interest your listeners.	• audiotapes, videotapes, CDs, DVDs, Internet, CD-ROMs, computer programs for tables and graphs, digital photography, and videotaping and recording systems 

 See pages H53–H56 in the Tools and Tips Handbook.

Getting Ready

Colorful maps and video clips will not hold your listeners' attention unless your report is well-organized and clearly presented.

- Write notes, or key words and phrases, on note cards.
- Put your notes in the order in which you want to present your ideas.
- Start with a beginning that will capture the attention of your audience.
- Record your talk, then listen to it. Identify parts that need more practice.

Use the guidelines below to help you use media aids.

> Make sure the models, charts, and graphs you show are large enough for everyone to see.

Guidelines for Giving an Oral Report with Media Aids

▶ Prepare your media ahead of time. If you plan to show an Internet site, bookmark the site, and have it on-screen and ready to go.

▶ Keep images simple. Use bright colors and clear print.

▶ When you make your own visuals using a computer, don't overdecorate them. Save and duplicate any electronic files you use.

▶ Be sure that maps, charts, and graphs are free of errors.

▶ Point to the area of the visual that you are talking about.

▶ Keep visuals covered, or turned off, until you are ready to show them.

Apply It

Choose a report you have already written and prepare media to use in presenting it orally. Use the guidelines above. After you give your report, answer these questions.

- Which media did you choose? Why?
- Did your report hold the attention of your audience? How do you know?
- If you could present your report again, what would you do differently?

Evaluating Mass Media

Newspapers, magazines, books, radio, television, and the Internet are types of mass media. They provide information to large numbers of people.

Many people get news about current events from the mass media. Depending on the type of media they use, they may get very different information about the same events.

Newspaper and Television News

Newspapers and network television news programs are two sources of media news. Usually, companies own and run these news sources for profit. Dozens, even hundreds, of people may help prepare the news. The people who prepare the news must make decisions about the length of their stories and the visuals and sound that go with them. Their decisions affect the accuracy and fairness of the news you receive.

News Stories in Two Media	
Newspapers	**Network Television News**
Readers read written stories that may include photographs or other visuals.	Viewers see and hear spoken stories that may include other sounds, video images, and other visuals.
Readers choose what to read.	Viewers watch what is shown.
Readers take time to read a news story.	Viewers can watch or listen to a TV news story while doing something else.
Readers can set their own pace.	Viewers get the news at the pace set by the TV workers.
Readers can go back to the story and reread it.	Viewers cannot go back to a story (unless they've taped the broadcast or can find it on the network's Internet site).
Readers often find information and details that aren't in broadcast stories.	Viewers sometimes see events "live" as they happen.

Look at the chart on page 514. What do you think is the main difference between reading and viewing the news? If you saw an event "live" on TV one evening, why might you still want to read about it in the paper the next day?

Use the guidelines below to help you evaluate the news in different media.

Guidelines for Evaluating News in Different Media

▶ List the news stories, in order of appearance, on a TV news program or in a newspaper. Which stories appeared first? Do you think they are the most important stories of the day?

▶ Notice how much time or space is devoted to the stories. What do you think limits the time or space given to the news?

▶ Look at how the lead, or beginning, story is presented. Does the newspaper include large headlines or photographs? Does the TV program use visuals, video footage, or maps?

▶ Notice whether any stories are biased. How can you tell?

▶ Think about the kinds of commercials shown during the news program. What kinds of advertisements are in the paper?

Laws Govern the Media

The Constitution of the United States guarantees freedom of speech and freedom of the press. Still, some types of expression are *not* legal:

• *Plagiarism* is the attempt to pass off someone's ideas or work as your own.
• *Libel* is a public statement that is unfair to a person's reputation.

Apply It

Compare a daily newspaper and a TV news program shown on the same day. Use the guidelines above to help you answer these questions.

● Which stories were covered in both media? Was the same information in both? How was it similar? How was it different?
● Why do you think some stories were left out of different media?
● Which medium do you think gave the best news coverage? Explain why.

Narrating and Entertaining

What You Will Find in This Section:

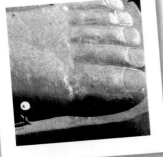

Listening to a Narrative

A **narrative** tells a story about real or made-up events and experiences. Listening to a narrative is different from listening to an opinion or a report. Although a narrative may have a moral or show the author's opinion, the main purpose for listening to a narrative is enjoyment. Here are some guidelines for being an effective listener.

Guidelines for Listening to a Narrative

▶ Listen for the main idea. What is the narrative about?
▶ Listen for the main events. What happens? in what order?
▶ Listen for details that help you picture what happened.
▶ Listen to find out who the most important people or characters are. What are they like? What do they want?
▶ Listen to find out when and where the story takes place.
▶ Listen for the author's purpose. Does the author want to scare you? make you laugh? teach a lesson?

Try It Out Listen as your teacher reads aloud from "The Raccoon Brigade," a true narrative by Pat Kertzman. Take notes to help you answer the questions below.

- Where and when does the narrative take place?
- Who are the most important people and animals in the narrative?
- What main events does Pat Kertzman describe? Tell them in order.
- What details help you picture how the raccoons looked and acted?
- What do you think is the author's purpose for telling this story?

📖 See page H33 for tips on taking notes while listening.

Writing a Narrative Paragraph

A paragraph that tells a real or imagined story is called a **narrative paragraph**. A narrative paragraph has a topic and a main idea. The **topic** is what the story is about. The **main idea** is what the writer has to say about the topic. What is the topic of the narrative paragraph below? What is the main idea?

> Remember, the first line of a paragraph is indented.

Indent —

Lead sentence —

    My dog, Romeo, does not want me to finish school. Last week I was using a calculator to do a difficult math problem. Just as I was finishing, Romeo jumped up on my desk and hit the calculator with his

Supporting sentences —

paw. I had to start all over again. That's not all. Yesterday morning I finished building a model of the Appalachian Mountains for my geography class. I was proud of the plaster-of-Paris range covered with green and brown paint and bits of spongy moss from our backyard.

Concluding sentence —

While I was getting dressed, Romeo chewed on the mountains until they looked like the Appalachian anthills. Maybe Romeo should be in school—dog training school!

The topic is the writer's dog, Romeo. The main idea is that Romeo interferes with the writer's schoolwork. Which sentence states the topic and the main idea?

The labels show the parts of a narrative paragraph.

Lead Sentence

Supporting Sentences

Concluding Sentence

- The **lead sentence** introduces the narrative and states or hints at the main idea.

- **Supporting sentences** follow the lead sentence and give details that tell what happens.

- The **concluding sentence** ends the paragraph and finishes the narrative.

Think and Discuss Look again at the paragraph above. What details does the writer include in the supporting sentences?

The Lead Sentence

A paragraph usually begins with a sentence that states the topic and the writer's main idea about the topic. In a narrative paragraph, the first sentence is called the **lead sentence**. It introduces the story and may give a hint about the main idea of the narrative or tell how the writer felt.

Topic	Main idea

Example: My dog, Romeo, does not want me to finish school.

What might narratives with these lead sentences be about?

- The rude buzz of my alarm clock at 6:00 A.M. was only the first insult of many in a terrible day.

- I was just walking to the store for some milk, I thought, but I walked into an adventure instead.

Try It Out Read each paragraph below. On your own or with a partner, write the topic and the main idea. Then write two different lead sentences for each paragraph.

1. _____*Lead sentence*_____ . First, Dad couldn't find the flashlight he'd left on the coffee table. Then Mom couldn't find her hairbrush, one slipper, and the remote control. Even a box of prunes was gone from the refrigerator! Two hours later we were still searching for our missing loot. Then my sister breezed in the front door carrying a large bag brimming with our stuff. "My team won the scavenger hunt!" she announced cheerily.

2. _____*Lead sentence*_____ . When the flight attendant asked if I wanted headphones, I answered her in Spanish instead of English. After we landed in Puerto Rico, I read the signs and proudly led my family to the baggage area. While we waited in a cafe for my grandparents, I ordered snacks for everyone. I'll admit that Dad helped when someone asked for the time, but, considering I was in my first year of Spanish, I'd say the trip was a great success!

Supporting Sentences

Supporting sentences follow the lead sentence and give details that support the main idea. **Factual** and **sensory details** may answer the questions *Who? What? Where? When? Why?* and *How?* They may also describe how things look, sound, taste, smell, or feel. In the paragraph about Romeo on page 519, the supporting sentences tell what the dog did to ruin the writer's homework.

Factual detail: Romeo hit the calculator with his paw.
Sensory detail: plaster-of-Paris range, green and brown paint, bits of spongy moss

Try It Out Choose one of the lead sentences below. List at least four details to support it. Then write at least three supporting sentences, using details from your list.

1. It was the worst summer vacation I ever had.
2. We had tied the score with only forty-two seconds left on the clock.

GRAMMAR TIP ▶ Use periods, commas, and apostrophes correctly in your sentences.

Keeping to the Main Idea All the supporting sentences should relate to the main idea. Unrelated details disrupt the flow of the paragraph.

Think and Discuss What is the main idea of the paragraph below? Which sentence does not keep to the main idea?

> My audition for the school musical today was a painful ordeal. First, I had to stand onstage and read from the script. My voice cracked so much, I sounded like a frog! Then I had to sing "America the Beautiful." The director stopped me before I got to *purple mountains' majesty*! I wish that song were our national anthem. Finally, I had to dance a waltz with Amy to show that I don't have two left feet. Two hours later, I'm still a wreck!

more ▶

Ordering Details Events in a narrative paragraph are usually told in the order they happened. **Time-clue words and phrases**, such as *before, later,* and *in the morning,* help the reader understand when events took place.

HELP ? See page 18 for more time-clue words.

Think and Discuss Which two sentences are out of order? Where do they belong? What time-clue phrases can you find?

    Yesterday was my most exciting day ever! Early in the morning, Dad and I lugged Grandpa's grungy old desk from the trunk of the car into the auditorium. When our turn came, she told us and the television audience that the desk was "quite valuable." We waited in line for over an hour to speak with the antiques expert. Even better, I knew that my friends were watching the program!

The Concluding Sentence

The **concluding sentence** can tell the narrative's last event, as in the scavenger hunt paragraph on page 520. It can explain what the writer thought or felt, as in the paragraph about Romeo on page 519, or it can repeat the main idea in a new way.

Try It Out Read the paragraph below. On your own or with a partner, write two different concluding sentences.

    Last Christmas Eve, I was trying to sneak my family's presents into the house when I accidentally locked myself out. Suddenly, I had a brilliant idea—I'd sneak in through the little doggie door in the back. I had wiggled about halfway through before I got stuck! After I yelled for help, my sister came running. When she found me, she began to laugh. First I was mad, but then I started laughing too. Eventually, she helped me get unstuck. _____*Concluding sentence*_____.

Write Your Own Narrative Paragraph

Now it's time to write a narrative paragraph about something that happened to you. Think of a time when you were happy, sad, excited, scared, or embarrassed. Then picture what happened and make a list of details. After you have practiced telling your narrative to a partner, you are ready to write!

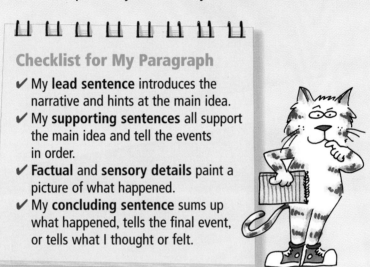

Checklist for My Paragraph

✔ My **lead sentence** introduces the narrative and hints at the main idea.

✔ My **supporting sentences** all support the main idea and tell the events in order.

✔ **Factual** and **sensory details** paint a picture of what happened.

✔ My **concluding sentence** sums up what happened, tells the final event, or tells what I thought or felt.

Looking Ahead

Writing a longer narrative is a lot like writing a narrative paragraph. Here's a diagram that shows how the parts of a narrative paragraph do the same jobs as the parts of a longer narrative.

Narrative Paragraph   **Longer Narrative**

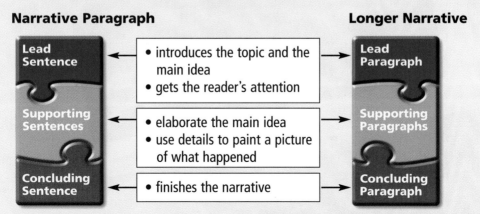

Lead Sentence	• introduces the topic and the main idea • gets the reader's attention	Lead Paragraph
Supporting Sentences	• elaborate the main idea • use details to paint a picture of what happened	Supporting Paragraphs
Concluding Sentence	• finishes the narrative	Concluding Paragraph

Writing a Personal Narrative

Last Saturday I nearly flew to the top during the final competition.

This personal narrative recaptures a childhood experience in vivid detail. Can you see, taste, smell, hear, and feel what happened during this storm?

Storm!

from *Under the Royal Palms: A Childhood in Cuba,*
by Alma Flor Ada

Every morning, when I was a very young child, my grandmother would come silently into my room while I was still sleeping. I would wake up in her arms, fragrant with ylang-ylang, which she gathered from a large tree by the entrance of the house and then dried to put in all her drawers. She would help me dress and then take me by the hand to go see the cows and to drink a glass of fresh and foamy milk.

The best cow, the one with the creamiest and most abundant milk, was called Lolita, just like my grandmother. No one considered this disrespectful. It was common to give a cow its owner's name.

But when I was seven years old and we moved to the city after my uncle's death, all the cows were sold. After living in the city for a few years, we returned to live in *La Quintica*, a very small house by the river, built by my father with his own hands. The big house was too large. Now that the family had dispersed we could not afford to keep it up on our own, so it was leased out to a trucking company. Then one of my mother's cousins who had a farm gave us a cow. The cow was allowed to roam freely in a pasture on the other side of the river. Once a day, a neighboring farmer milked her for us.

My mother named the cow Matilde, in honor of her cousin's wife. It was a black cow with white spots, and from the day she arrived we never lacked fresh milk. The milk was so rich, we saved the cream to make our own butter.

more ▶

See www.eduplace.com/kids/ for information about Alma Flor Ada.

A Published Model   525

Every day, I placed the cream in the refrigerator. Once a week, I gathered it in a bowl and stirred it over and over again with a wooden spoon. As it grew harder, I placed ice cubes in the bowl and continued to stir. Then I washed the hardened cream several times with cold water. The first few times the water was milky, but I kept on washing until the water was completely clear and the cool butter was resting on the bottom of the bowl, ready to be sprinkled with salt and spread on the freshly baked bread the baker had just brought in.

One reason the cow Matilde gave us so much milk was that she was going to have a calf. And we could not agree on what the calf's name would be. Felipe, after my mother's cousin? Lolita, after my grandmother's favorite cow?

One night we woke up, startled by the sound of thunder. Lightning had struck close to the house, which shook as if hit by an explosion. My father said he thought he heard the cow Matilde mooing in distress.

None of us heard anything except the cracks of thunder and the drumming rain. But my father, always proud of his good hearing, put on his overcoat and walked out into the torrent falling from the sky. The fading light from his lantern signaled to us that he had gone toward the wooden bridge. With the heavy rain, the river would be too full to ford at the crossing. My mother and I stayed up waiting for him. She warmed some milk on the stove and put some water to boil to make fresh coffee. Very soon, its strong aroma filled the house.

I accepted a cup of warm milk with some drops of heavy coffee and soon fell asleep on the couch. When the thunder woke me again, my mother was on the porch. I joined her just at the moment a gust of wind sent a sheet of rain against the house, soaking us. But my mother refused to go back in, searching in the darkness for some sign of my father.

All of a sudden, a flash of lightning outlined the shape of what looked to be a horrible monster. Although shorter than a man, it had a monstrous head that made me think of the Minotaur in one of my grandmother's books of mythology. I shook with fear.

My mother instead ran toward the shadowy figure that was approaching our porch. Not knowing very well what to do, I followed her. Right then, another flash of lightning illuminated the night. As though struck by the bolt, the monster seemed to split in two as my father took the newborn calf that he had been carrying on his shoulders and placed it on its wobbling legs. Matilde, who had followed my father and her calf through the storm, stood nearby.

"What about calling it *Temporal?*" my father asked as he shook out his jacket. My mother laughed. Unquestionably, *Temporal,* the Spanish word for "tropical storm," was a perfect name. She continued to laugh as she tried to dry the rainwater from my father's face. They both went in the house.

I stayed outside, soaking wet, watching Matilde lick her newborn calf as though the rain, which had become softer and softer, were not enough to clean him.

more ▶

Reading As a Writer

Think About the Personal Narrative

- Find examples of sensory details. What do they contribute to the narrative?
- How can you tell who is writing the narrative?
- What is the main event of the narrative? How does the writer build up to it?
- How does the beginning draw you in?

Think About Writer's Craft

- In the second paragraph on page 527, the writer compares the shape in the darkness to a creature from mythology. How does this comparison help you picture the scene?

Think About the Picture

- Look at the photo on page 526 of Alma Flor Ada as a young girl. In what way does this photo bring her narrative to life? Why is a photograph more effective than a drawing would be?

Responding

Write responses to these questions.

- **Personal Response** Have you ever had to wait in suspense, as the writer did while waiting for her father? Write about the feelings you experienced. In what ways were they similar to those of Alma Flor Ada? In what ways were they different?

- **Critical Thinking** Think about how the storm affects the personal narrative. How would the story be different if the events had taken place on a sunny day?

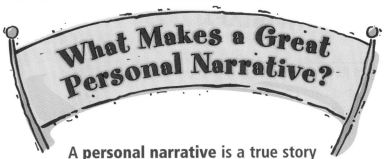

What Makes a Great Personal Narrative?

A personal narrative is a true story about something that happened to the person telling it.

Remember to follow these guidelines when you write a personal narrative.

▶ Grab your readers' attention right away.

▶ Use the pronoun *I*.

▶ Present the important events in time order.

▶ Use descriptive details to elaborate your narrative. Use dialogue, too, if it fits your story.

▶ Write the narrative using your personal voice and style.

▶ End the narrative in a satisfying way.

GRAMMAR CHECK

Be sure that each pronoun you use has a clear antecedent.

WORKING DRAFT

When Roy Kramka visited the emergency room, he met with one problem after another. Roy had such an unusual experience that he decided to write a personal narrative about it.

Roy Kramka

Waiting Room

It started on a nice sunny day—birds were chirping, dogs were barking, and I was yelling, "Ouch!" Out in the backyard I was playing with my dog, Clancy. ~~I was falling over because of that crazy dog. When he plays outdoors, he really gets excited. Usually that's fun, but he doesn't know his own strength. That's Clancy for you.~~ I was about to throw a tennis ball for him to fetch when he jumped on me, knocking me into a hole where there used to be a well.

The old well was filled with stuff. My arm landed right on the stump, and my body landed on top of my arm. It didn't hurt too much until I turned over to get up. My right elbow felt weird.

My mom was at work when this happened, so I asked a neighbor to call her at work. When she got in her car to drive home, the battery was dead because she had left the lights on. Then she had to borrow someone else's car.

As soon as my mom got home I jumped in the car. She helped me put on my seatbelt because I could barely move my arm. While she was buckling the seatbelt, her purse hit the button, making the seatbelt

> Your voice and your sense of humor come through right away.

> Could you add some details to explain "stuff" and "weird"?

snap back against my arm. Ouch! She felt really bad about that. She apologized to me. On the way, we had to pick up my sister at aftercare. My sister was really disappointed to leave because she was the caller for bingo that day.

When we finally got to the emergency room, we sat in the waiting room for thirty minutes. Then a nurse showed us to a room with a table, and I got to lie down on it. She asked if we wanted to watch a movie while we were waiting for a doctor. The choices were Barney, Lamb Chop, and Sesame Street. We said, "No, thanks."

Does this paragraph need more time order words?

We waited in the room for about two and a half hours. We were so bored, we wished we were watching Barney. My mom saw red dots appearing on my face. They were on my stomach, in my hair, and on my arms too. "Oh, no!" I thought, but I didn't say anything. A doctor came in. My mom asked him if the dots on my head were chicken pox. He said yes. He said that I was going to the x-ray room. He seemed to be in a big hurry.

What were your feelings?

A few minutes later, a nurse walked in with a wheelchair and one of those masks doctors use in the

more

E.R. When I finally got to the x-ray room, I had to put my arm between two pieces of metal so they could take pictures of it. I had to put on the mask and be rolled to the x-ray room in the wheelchair. Rolling down the hall was probably the worst part of my grand adventure. It was hard to breathe through the mask, and it smelled like ~~stuff you clean with~~ ammonia.

The x-ray technician bent my arm back until I thought it would snap. Ouch! After I got back to the E.R., the same doctor came in to tell us my arm was broken. He said I had a hairline fracture in my elbow, but a cast wouldn't help in the part of my arm that was hurt. He also said it wouldn't be fun anyway to have chicken pox under a cast. He put my arm in a sling and said we could go home. When we left the hospital, it was around 11:30 P.M. We just had one more stop, the pharmacy, to pick up a prescription for pain medicine. We got home after midnight.

Is there something out of order?

Could you add some dialogue?

Reading As a Writer

- What questions did Joe have? What revisions might Roy make?
- What did you enjoy most about Roy's narrative? Why?
- What extra information might you ask Roy to delete?
- Describe Roy's ending. How well did it tie up the narrative?

FINAL COPY

After discussing his narrative with his classmates, Roy revised his writing. Compare the final version with Roy's working draft to see how he improved his narrative.

You thought of a clever title!

B.R. (Bored Room)

by Roy Kramka

It started on a nice sunny morning—birds were chirping, dogs were barking, and I was yelling, "Ouch!" Out in the backyard, I was playing with my dog, Clancy. I was about to throw a tennis ball for him to fetch when he jumped on me, knocking me into a hole where there used to be a well.

The old well was filled with rocks, dirt, leaves, twigs, and a tree stump. My arm landed right on the stump, and my body landed on top of my arm. It didn't hurt too much until I turned over to get up. My right elbow felt cold and numb, and I knew right away that something was broken.

This paragraph is much clearer!

My mom was at work when this happened, so I asked a neighbor to call her at work. As soon as my mom got home, I jumped in the car. She helped me put on my seatbelt because I could barely move my arm. While she was buckling the seatbelt, her purse hit the button, making the seatbelt snap back against my arm. Ouch! She felt really bad about that. She apologized to me.

When we finally got to the emergency room, we sat in the waiting room for thirty minutes. Then a nurse showed us to a room with a table, and I got to lie down on it. She asked if we wanted to watch

more

a movie while we were waiting for a doctor. The choices were *Barney, Lamb Chop,* and *Sesame Street.* We said, "No, thanks."

We waited in the room for about two and a half hours. After a while, we were so bored, we wished we were watching *Barney.* Sometime during the long wait, my mom saw red dots appearing on my face. Soon they were on my stomach, my scalp, and my arms. "Oh, no!" I thought, but I didn't say anything. I felt a bit scared and worried that my body was falling apart on me. When a doctor *finally* came, my mom asked, "Are the dots on Roy's head chicken pox?"

Adding time-clue words helps a lot!

He answered, "Yes! That certainly does look like chicken pox." Then he said that I was going to the x-ray room. He seemed to be in a big hurry.

A few minutes later, a nurse walked in with a wheelchair and one of those masks doctors use in the E.R. I had to put on the mask and be rolled to the x-ray room in the wheelchair. Rolling down the hall was probably the worst part of my grand adventure. It was hard to breathe through the mask, and it smelled like ammonia.

The events are in time order now.

When I finally got to the x-ray room, I had to put my arm between two pieces of metal so they could take pictures of it. The x-ray technician bent my arm back until I thought it would snap. Ouch! After I got back to the E.R., the same doctor came in to tell us my arm was broken. "You have a hairline fracture in your elbow," he said. Then he added, "But a cast won't help in the part of your arm that was hurt. It wouldn't be fun anyway to have chicken pox under a cast."

It's nice to hear them talk!

He put my arm in a sling and said we could go home. When we left the hospital, it was around 11:30 P.M. We made just one more stop, the pharmacy, to pick up a prescription for pain medicine. By the time we got home after midnight, it had been over twelve hours since I had fallen into the hole.

Do good things come to those who wait? Just getting home was good enough for me. I felt relieved! Now I just had to wait out the chicken pox.

Reading As a Writer

- What changes did Roy make in response to Joe's comments?
- Which information did Roy delete? What effect does this have?
- Where did Roy add dialogue? How does it improve the narrative?
- What details did Roy add to elaborate his writing?
- What changes did Roy make in his ending? How well does it work?

See www.eduplace.com/kids/hme/ for more examples of student writing.

Student Model 535

Write a Personal Narrative

▶ Start Thinking

Make a writing folder for your personal narrative. Copy the questions in bold type. Write your answers as you think about and choose your topic. Keep the paper in your folder.

- **Who will be my audience?** Will it be family? classmates? fellow club or team members?
- **What will be my purpose?** Is it to share an experience that I have in common with others? to inform? to entertain?
- **How will I publish or share my narrative?** Will I put it in a classroom display? read it for parents' night? present it on videotape?

▶ Choose Your Topic

❶ List five experiences from your life that could be narrative topics.

❷ Discuss with a partner the important parts of each of your ideas.

- Which idea does your partner seem most interested in? Why?
- Do you and your partner think this idea could be narrowed? Look at how Roy broke one big idea into smaller parts. Each part could be a whole personal narrative.

HELP

Need a Topic?

Make a list of important people in your life. Then, next to each name, write experiences you have shared.

See page 547 for more ideas.

```
        ┌──────────────────────────────────────────────┐
        │  times that I went to the emergency room     │
        └──────────────────────────────────────────────┘
┌─────────────────────┐  ┌─────────────────────┐  ┌─────────────────────┐
│ fell and hurt my arm│  │ slipped on the ice  │  │ got hurt while playing│
│                     │  │                     │  │ soccer               │
└─────────────────────┘  └─────────────────────┘  └─────────────────────┘
```

❸ Ask yourself these questions about your ideas. Then decide on one to write about.

- Which experience do I remember most clearly?
- Which one will interest my readers most?
- Which one will I most enjoy writing about and sharing?

▶ Explore Your Topic

❶ Make a memory chart to explore your idea for a personal narrative.

How to Make a Memory Chart

1. Divide a sheet of paper in quarters. Label the four rectangles *Events, People, Places, Objects.*

2. Under each heading, note what you remember about your experience.

3. After five minutes of writing, read your notes. Put a check beside the information you may want to use in your personal narrative.

Here is part of Roy's memory chart.

EVENTS	PEOPLE
✓hurt my arm and called Mom ✓waited forever in E.R. ✓hard for Mom to get home ✓got chicken pox missed five days of school	my mom ✓ my sister ✓ the doctor✓ the nurse ✓
PLACES	OBJECTS

❷ Build up details. Ask yourself these questions about the main events.

- What did I do and say?
- What did other people do and say?
- What did I see, hear, and feel?

Add this information to your chart.

HELP ? **Memory Gridlock?**

Is your memory chart empty? Try a different topic.

❸ Focus your ideas.

- Do you still have too much information for one narrative? Try focusing on just one part.
- Circle the two or three main events. Cut details that are not related to them.

HELP ? See page 14 for more ideas on exploring a topic.

Focus Skill

Organizing Your Narrative

Use time order. Describe events as they happened, from beginning to end. Don't let events jump around.

Stick to the topic. Delete anything—people, objects, places—that is not important.

Use time-clue words. Time clues will help readers follow your story. Choose some from this chart, or use others.

Get right into the main events of your narrative. Don't give lots of boring background information.

Time-Clue Words	Time-Clue Phrases
before, after, next, first, second, last, yesterday, tomorrow, Monday, Tuesday, meanwhile, finally, eventually, suddenly	no sooner than, the next time, soon after, in the meantime, at the same time, not long after, several days later

Think and Discuss Look at Roy's final copy to answer these questions.

- Why didn't Roy start his narrative earlier, perhaps with breakfast?
- What time-clue words did Roy use?

▶ Plan Your Personal Narrative

❶ Reread your memory chart.

❷ Make an outline.

- List and number the main events. Leave room under each one.
- List the related details under each event. Take details from your memory chart, and add others.

> I. I fall in a hole and get hurt.
>   • Having fun with the dog
>   • Clancy knocks me down.
>   • The hole is full of stuff.
>   • My elbow feels weird.
>
> 2. My mother takes me to the E.R.
>   • I can hardly move my arm.
>   • We had to get my sister.

▲ **Part of Roy's story outline**

 Go to www.eduplace.com/kids/hme/ for graphic organizers.

Good Beginnings

A good beginning tells readers that your narrative will be exciting all the way through. Here are three ways to catch your readers' attention.

Use dialogue. Let your characters speak. Show their personalities.

Weak Beginning	Strong Beginning
It was my first year in junior high school. Mrs. Lee seemed to pick on me.	"You will be teacher for the day!" chirped Mrs. Lee. Silence engulfed the room, and I realized she was talking to me.

> **GRAMMAR TIP** In dialogue, place the end punctuation inside the closing quotation mark.

Use a teaser. Write a beginning that arouses curiosity.

Weak Beginning	Strong Beginning
I once had a spider. I also had a pet snake. I liked to hold them.	Snakes and spiders make cuddly pets. Doesn't everyone love them?

Describe the setting. Show readers where the action takes place.

Weak Beginning	Strong Beginning
I was in the audition room. I was nervous. I had to sing a song.	The audition room had gray walls and no windows. The listeners sat behind an old plaid blanket hung from the ceiling. They were silent, totally silent.

Try It Out

- With a partner, rewrite each beginning, using a different technique.

▶ Draft Your Beginning

❶ **Write** three beginnings for your narrative, using dialogue, a teaser, and a setting.

❷ **Select** a beginning that your readers will enjoy.

Focus Skill

Writing with Voice

Your voice puts a personal stamp on your writing. Express yourself by choosing just the right words. Note how these short, snappy sentences fit Cara's movements and the long, graceful ones fit the kite's movements.

Short and Snappy	Long and Graceful
Cara ran. Boy, did she run! Her feet hammered the pavement. Panting, panting, she made it!	Sam's purple kite looped slowly above the treetops, riding each change in the wind until it caught in a tall pine.

Compare these examples of weak and strong voice.

Weak Voice	Strong Voice
We got stuck in a storm. We saw lightning, and we ran for cover.	As we got near the summit, the sky turned an angry gray. Thunder rumbled. Rain shot down. "Jim!" I shouted. "Let's head for cover!" My heart was racing double-time as we darted along the ledge.

Think and Discuss

- How do sentence length and punctuation help express feelings in the strong example?
- Why is *My heart was racing double-time* more interesting than *I was scared*?

▶ ## Draft Your Personal Narrative

HELP **?**   **Talk It Out**

If your writing isn't flowing well, try telling your story on tape.

❶ **Write** your draft freely. Don't worry about making mistakes.

❷ **Follow** your outline, but add new ideas as they come to you. Use time-clue words to guide readers.

❸ **Start a new paragraph** when the speaker or the scene changes.

❹ **Let your voice** and style sing out!

Good Endings

A good ending puts the finishing touch on the good writing you've done. Here are two ways you might end your personal narrative.

Leave the reader with a feeling. Share your emotion about the experience.

Weak Ending	Strong Ending
That was my first day of work at Uncle Jason's apple farm. I ate dinner and went to bed.	Though I was still learning to use the ladder, I felt tired and satisfied after a good day of picking apples. The apple pie at dinner made me feel even better!

Show, rather than tell, the final event. Put your reader in the middle of your experience by showing what happened at the end. Include dialogue if people are speaking.

Weak Ending	Strong Ending
Maria came in and returned my notes. I had thought that she'd never give them back, but she did.	At last, Maria entered the library. She walked slowly over to my table and smiled. "Here are your notes," she said. "May I buy you an ice cream, to say thank you?"

Think and Discuss

- What makes each strong ending better than the weak one?
- What kind of ending did Roy use in his final copy? How is it better than the ending of his working draft?

▶ Draft Your Ending

❶ **Write** two endings for your narrative.

❷ **Choose** the better ending.

Evaluating Your Personal Narrative

▶ **Reread** your narrative. How can you improve it? Use this rubric to help you decide. Write the sentences that describe your narrative.

Loud and Clear!

- ■ I grab my readers' attention right away.
- ■ I present the main events in order, using time-clue words.
- ■ Interesting details make my story come alive.
- ■ My personal voice carries through from start to finish.
- ■ The strong ending tells a feeling, shows an action, or finishes in another way.
- ■ *I have made very few grammar or spelling mistakes.*

Sounding Stronger

- ■ My beginning needs more pizzazz.
- ■ Some events are not in order. I need more time-clue words.
- ■ I have too many details about unimportant things.
- ■ I need more details about important things.
- ■ My voice is clear in some places, but not everywhere.
- ■ My ending is not strong enough.
- ■ *My mistakes sometimes get in the way of telling the story.*

Turn Up the Volume

- ☐ My beginning is just too dull.
- ☐ The order of events is confusing.
- ☐ The action, the people, and the setting need details.
- ☐ My voice is flat. I don't sound like the person I am.
- ☐ I really don't have an ending yet.
- ■ *Lots of mistakes make the narrative hard to read.*

See www.eduplace.com/kids/hme/ to interact with this rubric.

▶ Revise Your Personal Narrative

❶ Revise your narrative. Use the list of sentences you wrote from the rubric. Work on the parts that you described with sentences from "Sounding Stronger" and "Turn Up the Volume."

❷ Get together with a partner for a writing conference.

When You're the Writer Read your narrative aloud to your partner. If any parts are giving you trouble, ask for feedback. Take notes.

What should I say?

When You're the Listener Tell at least two things that you like about the story. If you feel that some parts are unclear, ask questions.

The Writing Conference

If you're thinking . . .	You could ask . . .
The beginning doesn't grab me.	Could you think of a different way to start?
Where is the person behind the writing?	Could you show your personality in your writing?
The events are all over the place.	Are the events in time order? Could you add time-clue clues?
The writing is vague and general.	Could you give more details—what you heard, tasted, smelled, saw, or felt?
What does this part have to do with the story?	Could you leave out the part about _____?
The ending sort of stops.	Could you end with a feeling or an action?

❸ Make more revisions to your narrative. Use your conference notes and the Revising Strategies on the next page.

Tech Tip
To make revising easier, save each draft and give each one a different file name.

Revising Strategies

Elaborating: Word Choice Figurative language can make your writing more vivid. Use a **simile** to compare one thing to another, using *like* or *as*. Use a **metaphor** to say one thing "is" something else.

Unelaborated	Elaborated with Figurative Language
I hurried to the cafeteria.	**Simile**: Like a bolt of lightning, I hurried to the cafeteria. **Metaphor**: I was a bolt of lightning, hurrying to the cafeteria.

▶ Add one simile or one metaphor to your narrative.

   📖 See also page H13.

Elaborating: Details You can slip details into a sentence or add another sentence to provide details.

Unelaborated	Elaborated with Details
The music I heard during the concert made me want to dance.	The deep, rhythmic bass of the rock-and-roll music I heard during the concert in the park made me want to dance. I tapped my toes and swayed in my seat.

▶ Find three places to improve your narrative by adding details.

Sentence Fluency For variety, combine simple sentences in different ways.

I went to the beach. I played volleyball with friends.
- I went to the beach, and I played volleyball with friends.
- I went to the beach and played volleyball with friends.
- When I went to the beach, I played volleyball with friends.

▶ Rewrite two sets of sentences in your narrative, combining them in two different ways.

 See also pages 51, 60, and 249.

▶ Proofread Your Narrative

Proofread your story, using the Proofreading Checklist and the Grammar and Spelling Connections. Tackle one skill at a time. Check spellings in a class dictionary.

Proofreading Marks
- ¶   Indent
- ∧   Add
- ⟋   Delete
- ≡   Capital letter
- ⟋   Small letter
- ⱽⱽ   Add quotes
- ⋏   Add comma
- ⊙   Add period
- ∿   Transpose

Proofreading Checklist

Did I
- ✔ indent all paragraphs?
- ✔ use pronouns clearly?
- ✔ correct fragments and run-ons?
- ✔ begin and end sentences correctly?
- ✔ correct any spelling errors?

📖 Use the Guide to Capitalization, Punctuation, and Usage on page H64.

Tech Tip
A spelling tool cannot fix capitalization at the beginning of sentences.

Grammar and Spelling Connections

Clear Antecedents Make sure each pronoun has a clear antecedent. Replace a confusing pronoun with a noun in the correct form.

Unclear	Clear
Malcolm spoke to Ron. **He** looked uncomfortable.	Malcolm spoke to Ron. Malcolm looked uncomfortable.
Sarah caught up with Tina. **Her** face was glowing.	Sarah caught up with Tina. Tina's face was glowing.

GRAMMAR LINK ▶ *See also page 277.*

Spelling Compound Words A compound word may be spelled as one word, as a hyphenated word, or as two words. Check the dictionary.

When I baby-sat that night, I was doing my homework in the family room.

📖 See the Spelling Guide on page H80.

 Go to www.eduplace.com/kids/hme/ for proofreading practice.

▶ Publish Your Personal Narrative

❶ Prepare a neat final copy of your narrative. Fix any errors.

❷ Put a title on your narrative that will make your readers curious. "An Afternoon in the Kitchen" is less effective than "Dessert of Horrors."

> GRAMMAR TIP ▷ *Capitalize the first, the last, and each important word in the title.*

❸ Publish or share your narrative. Look at the Ideas for Sharing box.

Ideas for Sharing

Write It Down
- Make a class book of personal narratives.
- Mail or e-mail your narrative to a friend or a relative.

Talk It Up
- Tape-record your story, and pantomime it for the class.
- Read your narrative aloud on a video "broadcast."

Show It Off
- Create a collage to display with your narrative. Use photographs, post cards, or souvenirs.
- Draw a picture of your narrative's high point, and tack it with your narrative to the bulletin board.

Tips for Video Broadcasting
- Speak clearly. Don't rush.
- Make eye contact with the camera.
- Have the camera operator use different shots and angles.
- Use props related to your narrative.

▶ Reflect

Write about your writing experience. These questions will help you begin.

- Which part of the narrative did you enjoy writing most? least? Why?
- What will you do differently the next time you write a narrative?
- How does this paper compare with other writing you have done?

Writing Prompts

Use these prompts as topics for personal narratives or to practice for a test. Some of them relate to other subjects that you study. Decide who your audience will be, and write your narrative in a way that they will understand and enjoy.

1 Write about a time you found something new, such as an abandoned cat, a new friend, or a fascinating hobby. What did you do, and how did you feel?

2 Write about an adventure you had with friends or family. It might be building a snowman, hiking in a new place, or cleaning out the garage.

3 Write about a special event you shared with family or friends. Was it a family tradition or something new and unusual? Bring the people and the events to life.

4 Write about a time when someone taught you how to do something important. What did you learn? Why will you remember the person and the lesson?

Writing Across the Curriculum

5 **SOCIAL STUDIES**
Write about a time you worked on a project in community service, conservation, or health awareness. What did you learn?

6 **DRAMA**
Write about an experience in your life as if you were a character in a play. Write it as a monologue, with yourself as the only speaker.

7 **HISTORY**
Write about a time when a historical event came to life for you. Did you visit a museum or play the part of a historical character in a play? Give details.

8 **SCIENCE**
Write about an experience you had in the natural world. Was it watching birds hatch or experiencing a record-breaking storm? Describe the events, and tell your feelings.

✓ Test Practice

Here is a prompt to write a personal narrative. It is like the ones you might find on a writing test. Read the prompt.

> **Write about a time you found something new, such as an abandoned cat, a new friend, or a fascinating hobby. What did you do, and how did you feel?**

Use these strategies to help you do your best when responding to this kind of prompt.

> Remember that a personal narrative is a true story about something that happened to the person telling it.

1 Look for clue words that tell you what to write about. Identify the clue words in the prompt above.

2 Choose a topic suggested by the clue words. Write those clue words and your topic on a piece of paper.

Clue Words	My Topic
a time you found something new what did you do how did you feel	I will write about the day I first met Greg.

3 Plan your writing. Use a story outline.

> 1. First event
>   • Detail
>   • Detail
> 2. Second event
>   • Detail
>   • Detail
> 3. Third event
>   • Detail
>   • Detail

4 You will get a good score if you remember what kind of narrative sounds loud and clear in the rubric on page 542.

Go to www.eduplace.com/kids/hme/
for graphic organizers.

Writing a Friendly Letter

A **friendly letter** gives you a chance to share thoughts, news, and feelings with someone you know personally. Read Ben's letter.

Heading — 110 Maiden Lane
Belmont, MA 02178
July 2, 2001

Greeting → Dear Sofia,

Body —
    I would love for you to spend a month with my family as an exchange student. Remember you said you wanted to see the fun-filled state of Massachusetts?

    There are many interesting sights and sounds in the city of Boston. First, there's Fenway Park where the Red Sox play baseball. Many museums also add to the list of things to do. I like the Museum of Fine Arts and, best of all, the New England Aquarium. The Aquarium has one of the largest saltwater tanks in the world.

    I hope you decide to stay with our family. We'd really have a lot of fun together. ¡Hasta la vista!

Closing ——→ Regards,
Signature ——→ Ben

Reading As a Writer

- The **heading** contains the writer's address and the date. *What information does each line contain?*

- The **greeting** usually begins with *Dear* and the name of the person receiving the letter. *To whom is Ben writing?*

- The **body** is the letter's main part. *Why is Ben writing?*

- The **closing**, such as *Your friend* or *Sincerely,* completes the letter. It is followed by a comma. *What closing did Ben use?*

- The **signature** is the writer's name. *Where is Ben's signature?*

more ▶

How to Write a Friendly Letter

❶ **Plan** what you want to say.

❷ **Write** the letter. Include all five parts of a friendly letter.

❸ **Proofread** for mistakes. Use the Proofreading Checklist on page 545. Use a dictionary to check spellings.

❹ **Make** a neat final copy of your letter.

❺ **Address** the envelope. Put a stamp on the envelope and mail it.

Return address —
Ben Hursh
110 Maiden Lane
Belmont, MA 02178

USA

Mailing address —
Sofia Rodo
23 Calle Ocho
Lima 14
Peru

Types of Friendly Letters

Thank-you Letter Writing a thank-you letter is a way to express appreciation for something a person did or said.

> Dear Mr. Viscelli,
>
>   Thank you for being a great English teacher. Whenever I had any questions, you gave me the help I needed. Even though you gave a lot of homework, I didn't mind because the assignments were interesting. Thanks again for a wonderful year!
>
>   Sincerely,
>
>   Erin Watkins

Invitation An invitation asks someone to come to an event such as a concert or a party. Most invitations include the name of the event, the place, the date, the time, and any special information, such as what to wear or bring. Invitations often give a phone number to call to respond.

Writing a Story

Wearing a wide-brimmed hat and swinging a sturdy cane, he slowly walked the length of the giant foot. Surely, he thought, this mystery could be solved.

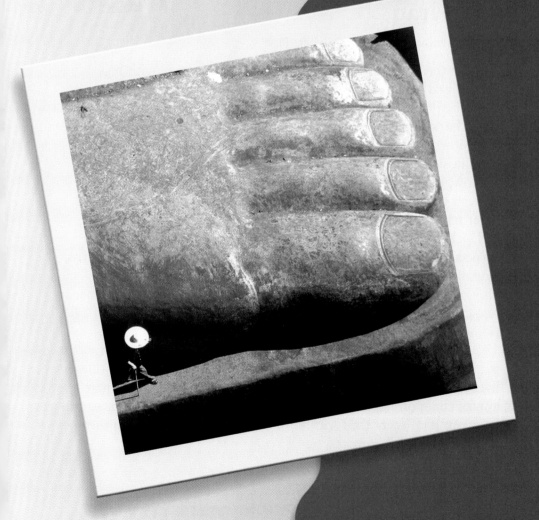

How many princes learn to weave carpets?
The prince in this story does, and his skill turns
out to be useful indeed. How does weaving save
his life?

The Weaving That Saved the Prince: A Folk Tale from Iraq

retold by Howard Schwartz and Barbara Rush

Once there was a prince who loved to play games with his
friends and dream of the day when he would rule the kingdom. But
his father, the king, insisted that the boy learn a trade as well. "My
son," he would often say, "you must be able to earn a living in
time of need or danger. Money may come and money may go, but
a profession lasts a lifetime."

Now, the boy did not fully understand the meaning of his
father's words, but he obeyed his wishes and began to study. And
what trade did the prince choose? Weaving carpets.

The boy was very clever and quickly learned how to weave
carpets of varied colors, decorated with letters and intricate patterns.
And after the prince had become a master weaver, his father, the
king, rewarded him with a precious gift—a noble horse. The prince
rejoiced greatly over this gift, and he began to study the skills of
riding until he became a rider whose ability was without equal.

One day, as the prince galloped on his horse into the desert
surrounding the kingdom, he stumbled upon a region where thieves
lived, hidden in caves. Now, when the thieves saw a young man
approaching on horseback, they went out and captured him. Afraid
he might give away the location of their caves, they decided they
would have to kill him.

The prince recognized from the first that he was in danger, and he knew he must keep his true identity a secret. It was then that he recalled the craft he had learned.

"Surely you can use more money," he told the thieves. "I am a skilled weaver, so I should be worth more to you alive than dead. For as long as you let me live, I will continue to weave beautiful carpets for you, carpets worthy of a king."

The thieves thought about this for a moment and then held a discussion among themselves. "If these carpets are really beautiful and fetch a good price," they whispered, "we will keep this boy here as our slave." Out loud they declared, "Very well, we will let you weave one carpet and we will see if what you say is true."

Meanwhile, the king and queen began to worry about their missing son, and when a day had passed with no word from him, they knew that the boy must be in danger. The king immediately sent a hundred of his troops to search for the prince, but all their efforts were in vain, for they knew nothing about the caves. Then the king proclaimed that a great reward would be given to whoever discovered what had happened to the prince or knew where he could be found. But days and weeks passed, and there was no clue to his fate.

more ▶

In the meantime, the prince told his captors to bring him a loom and silk threads of many colors, and he promised that within a month he would finish weaving a splendid carpet, worthy of the palace of the king. Thus the threads were brought, and the prince set to work. Hour after hour, day after day, the boy sat at the loom, weaving from dawn to dusk, with only pita and water to sustain him.

It was a very elaborate carpet he wove, with flowers and letters and patterns of all kinds. The clever prince also wove among its many decorations a crown, just like the one his father wore, and a hidden map, showing the location of the thieves' hideout.

The prince plied his craft with great speed, and when the carpet was completed, it astounded the thieves who beheld it. Never had they seen anything so magnificent, and they knew it would bring them a fortune. They planned to sell it in the marketplace, but the prince said, "Why not take it to the king's palace, for there you will surely receive the largest sum of money."

So two of the thieves hurried off to the king's palace. There the wondrous carpet was unrolled for the gatekeeper, who was dazzled by its beauty. Quickly he summoned the king's minister, who took the carpet straight to the king himself. The king, equally dazzled by the carpet's beauty, looked at it closely. As he did so, the crown, so like his own, caught his eye, and he knew that the carpet could have been woven only by the prince himself. Looking even more closely, he discovered the hidden map, and he knew what he must do.

The thieves were delighted, of course, when the king's minister returned to the gate and handed them a bag of gold. They thanked him and took their leave. But as soon as the men were gone, the king ordered his guards to set out for the caves to rescue the prince, using the map as their guide. As for the thieves, they were not expecting an attack and were quickly captured. At the same time, the prince was set free.

When he returned to the palace, the prince said to his father, "If not for your wisdom, my lord, I would never have lived to see this day. The trade I learned saved me from what would have been a bitter fate."

Reading As a Writer

Think About the Story

- What is the conflict, or problem, in this story? How is it resolved?
- What details show you what the prince is like?
- Where and when does this story take place? How do you know?

Think About Writer's Craft

- What if the authors were writing about a trip to a mall? Would they have used phrases such as *rewarded him with a precious gift* or *plied his craft with great speed*? Find three other phrases that would not belong in a story about life today.

Think About the Picture

- What does the king discover when he looks at the rug? What details in the picture on page 553 show his feelings about this discovery?

Responding

Write responses to these questions.

- **Personal Response** What piece of wisdom, or wise advice, has someone given you? Has this advice proven as helpful as the father's advice to his son in this story?
- **Critical Thinking** The prince is a resourceful person. If he hadn't known how to weave, he would have thought of another way to escape. Support this position with passages from the story.

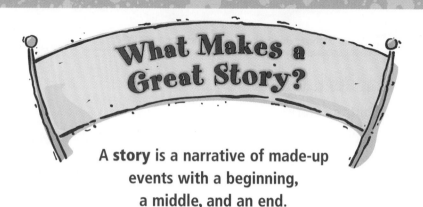

What Makes a Great Story?

A story is a narrative of made-up events with a beginning, a middle, and an end.

When you write a story, remember these guidelines.

▶ Create interesting, believable characters.

▶ Describe a setting by telling where and when the story takes place.

▶ Develop an engaging plot that includes a conflict and a resolution, as well as a climax, or high point.

▶ Tell the events in order, with a clear beginning, middle, and end.

▶ Include details and dialogue to bring characters, setting, and events to life.

▶ Use voice to create a mood, or emotion, for your story.

▶ Write an opening that introduces characters and setting.

▶ Write an ending that resolves the conflict and wraps up the story.

GRAMMAR CHECK

Put dialogue inside quotation marks. Use commas to separate most quotations from the rest of the sentence.

WORKING DRAFT

Dava Hollingsworth thought of a story with a surprise twist that would make her paper fun to read. She wrote this draft.

Dava Hollingsworth

Working Draft

Maggie's Birthday

Imaginary space creatures were Maggie's hobby, and she knew all about them. Suddenly, without warning, her computer flickered on all by itself.

> Where are we? I'm confused.

"What's going on?" Maggie shouted. She was so startled, she jumped up and ran away from it. Then just as suddenly, she felt herself begin moving toward the screen. It was almost as if a force were drawing her near.

The computer screen changed from bright green to bright purple. This frightened Maggie because her monitor had always been black and white. As Maggie stood there staring at the bright purple screen, a strange face appeared. "Who are you?" whispered Maggie, as if the face could hear her. It looked like the space creature in her comic book!

> What did the face look like?

Maggie began searching the house, but she could find no one. Her heart was pounding harder and harder. All she could think about was that strange face on her computer monitor. Her family wouldn't have left her alone, not on her birthday. Could they have seen the space creatures and run out? Could the space creatures be in the house even now?

more

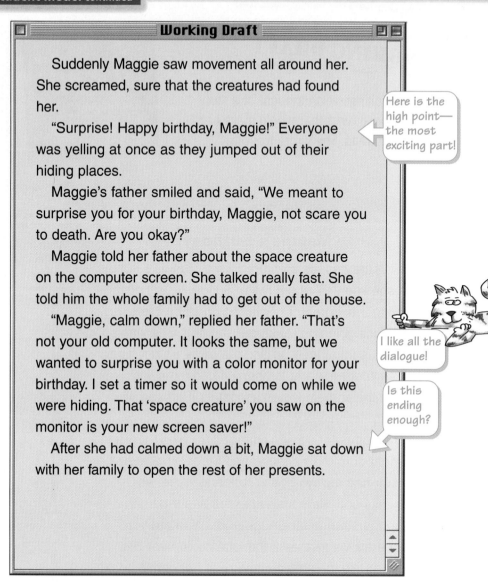

Working Draft

Suddenly Maggie saw movement all around her. She screamed, sure that the creatures had found her.

Here is the high point—the most exciting part!

"Surprise! Happy birthday, Maggie!" Everyone was yelling at once as they jumped out of their hiding places.

Maggie's father smiled and said, "We meant to surprise you for your birthday, Maggie, not scare you to death. Are you okay?"

Maggie told her father about the space creature on the computer screen. She talked really fast. She told him the whole family had to get out of the house.

"Maggie, calm down," replied her father. "That's not your old computer. It looks the same, but we wanted to surprise you with a color monitor for your birthday. I set a timer so it would come on while we were hiding. That 'space creature' you saw on the monitor is your new screen saver!"

After she had calmed down a bit, Maggie sat down with her family to open the rest of her presents.

I like all the dialogue!

Is this ending enough?

Reading As a Writer

- What questions did Joe have about this story? What revisions might Dava make?
- What conflict, or problem, does Maggie face? How is it resolved?
- What events lead up to the high point? What makes the high point the most exciting part of the story?

FINAL COPY

Dava revised her story after discussing it with a partner. Read her final version to see how she improved it.

Invasion!
by Dava Hollingsworth

It was Maggie's birthday, and she couldn't wait to see what the day had in store for her. She was sitting next to her computer in her bedroom, reading her newest comic book, *Invaders from Outer Space*. Imaginary space creatures were her hobby, and she knew all about them. Suddenly, without warning, the computer flickered on all by itself.

"What's going on?" Maggie shouted. She was so startled, she jumped up and ran away from it. Then, just as suddenly, she felt herself begin moving toward the screen. It was almost as if a force were drawing her near.

The computer screen changed from bright green to bright purple. This frightened Maggie because her monitor had always been black and white. As Maggie stood there staring at the bright purple screen, a strange face appeared. "Who are you?" whispered Maggie, as if the face could hear her. It looked like the space creature in her comic book! The face was silver, as though made entirely out of metal, and it had huge, saucer-shaped black eyes. The eyes never blinked. They just kept staring straight at her.

more

Frantically, Maggie began searching the house, but she could find no one. "Hello? Is anyone here? Where is everybody?" Her heart was pounding harder and harder. All she could think about was that strange face on her computer monitor. Her family wouldn't have left her alone, not on her birthday. Could they have seen the space creatures and run out? Could the space creatures be in the house even now?

Suddenly Maggie saw movement all around her. She screamed, sure that the creatures had found her.

"Surprise! Happy birthday, Maggie!" Everyone was yelling at once as they jumped out of their hiding places.

Maggie's father smiled and said gently, "We meant to surprise you for your birthday, Maggie, not scare you to death. Are you okay?"

"Dad, there's something wrong with my computer!" Maggie said breathlessly. "It came on all by itself!" The words came tumbling out as fast as she could say them. "And the screen turned purple! I saw a space creature on the screen! We've got to get out of here! Quickly!"

"Maggie, calm down," replied her father firmly. "That's not your old computer. It looks the same, but we wanted to surprise you with a color monitor for your birthday. I set a timer so it would come on while

Dialogue makes this scene more vivid.

we were hiding. That 'space creature' you saw on the monitor is your new screen saver!"

After she had calmed down a bit, Maggie sat down with her family to open the rest of her presents. One box was wrapped in blue paper with a shiny purple ribbon. As Maggie began to untie the ribbon, the box popped open! Maggie screamed again. It was a toy space creature!

Adding a second space creature is a great touch!

"This has certainly been a day full of excitement," said Maggie's mother.

"Maybe too exciting!" Maggie said with a grin. "I thought I was a goner! I know I've read enough space creature comic books for a while!"

Smart! You end by showing how she feels.

Reading As a Writer

- How did Dava respond to Joe's questions?
- What new details did Dava add to the beginning of her story? How do these details help her readers follow the plot?
- What did Dava add in the second half of her story to show how Maggie and her father thought, felt, and acted?

See www.eduplace.com/kids/hme/ for more examples of student writing.

Student Model **561**

Write a Story

▶ Start Thinking

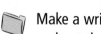 Make a writing folder for your story. Copy the questions in bold type, and put the paper in your folder. Write your answers as you think about and choose your topic.

- **Who will be my audience?** Will I write this story for my family? my classmates? my friends outside school?
- **What will be my purpose?** Do I want to puzzle my audience with a mystery? introduce them to a new experience?
- **How will I publish or share my story?** Will I make an illustrated book? do a dramatic presentation? record it on audiotape?

▶ Choose Your Story Idea

❶ **List** five story ideas. Use a chart like Dava's below to find ideas.

What If?	What Then?
A girl who loves to snowboard wants to learn to do a front flip.	She practices and practices and finally learns to do it.
A cabin boy on a sailing ship sees a floating island.	He lands on it and has many adventures with strange creatures.
The face of a space creature appears on a girl's computer.	She gets really scared and runs to find her family.

❷ **Talk** with a partner about each story idea.

- Which idea does your partner find most interesting? Why?
- Is any idea too big? Could you write about just one part of it?

❸ **Ask** yourself these questions about each story idea. Then decide which one you will write about.

- Which idea makes me most curious?
- Which one will I enjoy writing about?

> **HELP**
> **?** **Feeling Clueless?**
>
> Try one of these story ideas.
> - a wild horse lost in a city
> - a friend who moves away
> - a week-long blackout
> - a door that opens to another time
>
> See page 574 for more ideas.

▶ Explore Your Characters and Setting

❶ List lots of details about people or animals in your story. A good story has at least one main character.

Think About . . .	Ask Yourself . . .
Appearance	Does this character wear a hat? have red hair? move hurriedly?
Actions	Does this character eat chili for breakfast? ride a skateboard to school? hand in homework early?
Thoughts or feelings	Is this character nervous about school? happy alone in the woods at night? sad because a relative died?
Interests	Does this character scuba dive? play chess? sing?

❷ Develop the setting for your story. List specific details about where and when the story happens.

Think About . . .	Ask Yourself . . .
Place	Does this story happen on a clipper ship or a space ship? in my living room or on a mountaintop?
Time	Does this story happen last summer or next winter? a thousand years from now or the day after tomorrow?

Here is part of Dava's list.

Characters	Setting
Maggie—a kid my age	home
thinks a lot about space creatures	~~her school~~
draws them, reads about them	sitting at her computer
worries about them coming to Earth	weekend
	her birthday

HELP ? **Not Enough Details?**

If you can't think of enough specific details, try another story idea.

HELP ? For more exploring ideas, see page 14.

Developing Plot

What Is a Plot?

A plot is a series of made-up events with a beginning, a middle, and an end. Use these strategies to develop a plot.

Create a conflict. Look for a conflict, or problem, that your main characters must solve. Introduce the conflict near the beginning of the story.

Kinds of Conflicts	
Person against person	• Two boys compete to be starting quarterback. • Classmates make fun of a student for being different.
Person against nature	• A group of friends is caught at school during a flood. • A kid is baby-sitting during a blackout.
Person against self	• Someone can't decide between two groups of friends. • A student wants to act in a play but is afraid of crowds.

Increase the tension. Show your characters trying to solve the problem, but make your readers wonder whether they will succeed. Events should rise to a climax, or high point, near the middle or toward the end of the story.

Resolve the conflict. Show how the main characters solve their problem. The resolution should follow the climax. Answer any other questions your readers might have, and end your story soon after the resolution.

Plot Diagram: "The Weaving That Saved the Prince"

Climax King reads map.

Thieves bring the rug to the king.
Prince weaves a rug with a hidden map.

Guards use map to find prince.

Conflict Thieves capture prince and threaten to kill him.

Resolution Guards rescue prince.
Prince thanks king for his wisdom.

Think and Discuss Reread the *Kinds of Conflicts* chart above.

● Tell more about one conflict. How might the character resolve it?

Focus Skill   continued

What Makes a Strong Plot?

A strong plot includes a conflict that readers care about and want to see resolved. A weak plot has an uninteresting conflict or no conflict at all. Here are some strategies for creating a strong plot.

Make trouble for your main character. Do not make the conflict—what stands between your character and what your character wants—too easy to overcome.

Create suspense by revealing information gradually.

Show your main character resolving the conflict. Other people can help, but don't let someone else solve the problem.

Weak Plot	Strong Plot
Conflict Lost in the woods, a girl eats berries.	**Conflict** Lost in the woods, a girl breaks her leg.
Climax Girl meets a hiker who leads her out of the woods.	**Climax** Girl painfully gathers firewood to signal for help. Hearing a helicopter, she gets the fire going just in time and signals it.
Resolution Girl goes home.	**Resolution** Helicopter rescues girl.

Think and Discuss

● What makes the strong example above better than the weak one?

▶ ## Explore and Plan Your Story

Create a story map like the one shown.

● Plan the beginning. Tell important details about characters and setting, and introduce the conflict.
● Plan the middle. Show the characters trying to deal with the conflict.
● Plan the end. Show how the conflict is resolved.

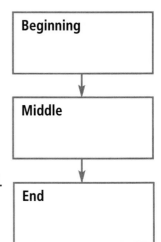

Beginning

Middle

End

 Go to www.eduplace.com/kids/hme/ for graphic organizers.

Focus Skill

Dialogue

Let your readers listen to what your characters say.

Show a character's personality.

- Use dialogue to tell a character's feelings in a certain situation.

Telling, Without Dialogue	Showing, With Dialogue
Sandra was afraid to snowboard over the big jump. She had an excuse, but her friends saw through it.	"Take the jump!" Alexa shouted. "I don't have the right gloves." "Gloves? You're just scared, Sandra."

GRAMMAR TIP ▶ Begin a new paragraph of dialogue each time the speaker changes.

- Use dialogue to show what a character is like.

Without Dialogue	With Dialogue
Aunt Macy still talked to us as if we were five years old.	"No playground voices, boys!" Aunt Macy said sweetly. "Indoor voices only."

GRAMMAR TIP ▶ Use adverbs to show how a character speaks.

- Capture the way people really speak. Does Aunt Macy say, "Silence, if you please!" or "Hey, cool it!"? Choose formal or informal language to tell more about each character.

Show actions. Sometimes you simply tell your readers what happens next. At other times, you can let your characters tell events in your story: "I found the key!" shouted Aja. "It was almost buried in the sand."

Think and Discuss

- When might a character use formal language? informal language?

▶ Draft Some Dialogue

Draft some dialogue for your main character.

Focus Skill

Narrating Your Story

Choosing a Point of View

Decide who your narrator, or storyteller, will be.

First-Person Point of View If you choose one of your characters to narrate the story, you have taken the first-person point of view. A first-person narrator can tell only what he or she sees, thinks, and feels.

Stay with just one point of view as you draft.

 GRAMMAR TIP ▶ Use first-person pronouns, such as **I**, **me**, **us**, and **we**.

Third-Person Point of View If your narrator is not a character, you have taken the third-person point of view. A third-person narrator can tell what one or more characters see, think, and feel.

GRAMMAR TIP ▶ Use third-person pronouns, such as **he**, **she**, **they**, and **their**.

Here is the same event told from two different points of view.

First-Person Point of View	Third-Person Point of View
I could hear a low roar coming from far away. I ran to the window. I wondered why the birds weren't singing. "Do they know a tornado is coming?" I thought. Behind me, I heard my mother come into the room. She looked worried. "Adam," she said in a steady voice, "get away from that window right now."	Adam could hear a low roar coming from far away. He ran to the window. He wondered why the birds weren't singing. "Do they know a tornado is coming?" he thought. Adam's mother came into the room. She was frightened. She knew very well the damage that tornadoes could cause. "Adam," she said, trying to keep her voice steady, "get away from that window right now."

Think and Discuss

● What does the third-person example above tell that the first-person example cannot?

more ▶

Focus Skill continued

Voice and Mood

Your voice is the way you sound when you write. Your story's narrative voice is the way your narrator sounds. It creates your story's mood, or emotional effect—frightening or funny, peaceful or angry.

Set the mood at the beginning. Use exact words and build sentences— long or short, simple or complex—to create the feeling you want. The two beginnings below describe the same scene but create different moods.

First Mood	Second Mood
My father shoved open the heavy, creaking door to our new house. The dirty windows blocked most of the sunlight. We saw empty floors. We saw bare, stained walls. Ahead of us lay months of cleaning and painting. We felt trapped in the gloom already.	My father flung open the oak door to show us our new house. Sunlight streamed through the tall windows. The waxed floors gleamed, just waiting for us to fill them with furniture. The empty walls begged us to decorate them. Anything could be done here.
A faded ribbon lay in one window. "Look at that scrap of old ribbon," said my mother quietly. "It looks used up and forgotten, just like this house."	In one window was a pink ribbon. "Look at that birthday ribbon!" my mother cried excitedly. "Doesn't it make our house seem like a gift?"

Think and Discuss

- What is the mood in each passage above? Which words, phrases, and sentences establish each mood?

▶ Draft Your Story

❶ **Choose** a point of view for your story.

❷ **Draft** two possible beginnings, each with a different mood. Choose the one that fits your story.

❸ **Draft** the rest of your story. Follow your story map. Use the dialogue you drafted if it still works. Include an ending that resolves the conflict and wraps up the plot.

HELP ? **Ways to Begin**

- Describe the setting.
- Use dialogue.
- Describe an exciting action.

Evaluating Your Story

▶ **Reread** your story. What do you need to do to make it better? Use this rubric to help you decide. Write the sentences that describe your narrative.

Loud and Clear!

- ■ Dialogue makes my characters seem real.
- ■ Details show when and where the story takes place.
- ■ The plot has a conflict, a climax, and a resolution.
- ■ My language creates a definite mood that suits my story.
- ■ I chose one point of view and stayed with it.
- ■ The opening introduces my characters and setting. The ending shows how the conflict is resolved.
- ■ There are very few mistakes in grammar, spelling, or punctuation.

Sounding Stronger

- ■ I need more dialogue to show how my characters think and feel.
- ■ Specific details would make the setting clearer.
- ■ Some events are unrelated to the conflict.
- ■ My voice is not strong, and so the mood is not clear.
- ■ I change point of view once or twice.
- ■ My beginning introduces setting and characters but could be more interesting. The ending is too abrupt.
- ■ Mistakes sometimes make the story hard to read.

Turn Up the Volume

- ☐ The characters don't seem real. There isn't any dialogue.
- ☐ My story has no clear setting.
- ☐ What's the conflict? Many events are unnecessary.
- ☐ The story has no emotional effect at all.
- ☐ The point of view wanders, making the story hard to follow.
- ☐ The beginning is confusing. It's not clear what happens at the end.
- ■ Many mistakes make the story very difficult to read.

▶ Revise Your Story

1 **Revise** your story. Use the list of sentences you wrote from the rubric. Work on the parts that you described with sentences from "Sounding Stronger" and "Turn Up the Volume."

2 **Have a writing conference.**

When You're the Writer Read your story aloud to a partner. Ask questions about any problems. Take notes.

When You're the Listener Say at least two things you like about the story. Ask questions about any parts that are unclear. Use the chart below for help.

HELP ?

Paragraphing Tip

- Find paragraphs that tell about too many events.
- Start a new paragraph for each new event.

What should I say?

The Writing Conference

If you're thinking . . .	**You could say . . .**
The story just began, and already I'm losing interest.	**How about starting with a surprising action? some dialogue?**
This character doesn't seem real.	**Would _____ really act like that? Would _____ really talk like that?**
I can't picture where this is happening.	**Tell me more about the setting.**
What's this story about?	**What is the conflict? Could you make this a problem for your main character?**
I'm having trouble following the plot.	**Tell me more about what happens. Are the events in the right order?**
The story ends too quickly.	**How is the problem solved? What happens to the characters?**

3 **Make more revisions.** Use your conference notes and the Revising Strategies on the next page.

Tech Tip

Use the Replace function to change a name throughout your story.

Revising Strategies

Elaborating: Word Choice Choosing exact nouns, verbs, adjectives, and adverbs will make your writing clearer.

Without Exact Words	With Exact Words
Angela **looked** back at the **tall girl moving** up the court. Then **another player ran** to the basket.	Angela glanced back at the giant center charging up the court. Then the forward darted to the basket.

▶ Find at least two places where you can use more exact words.

📖 Use the Thesaurus Plus on page H96.

Elaborating: Details Use adverbs and prepositional phrases to add details that tell *where, when, why,* and *how*.

Few Details	Elaborated with Details
An old man was walking. He looked up. "Where are the clouds?" he asked. Tonight would be too bright.	After sunset, an old man was walking down the road. He looked up at the rising moon. "Where are the clouds?" he asked bitterly. Tonight would be too bright for cattle rustling.

▶ Find at least two places in your story where you can add details using adverbs or prepositional phrases.

 See also page 201 and page 325.

Sentence Fluency Avoid loading up your sentences with too many clauses and phrases. Stringy sentences make your writing difficult to follow.

Stringy Sentences	Smooth Sentences
Band practice was now Thursdays, and this was when Sarah had to help her sick grandfather, and she couldn't make it to practice once.	Band practice was now Thursdays. Because this was when Sarah had to help her sick grandfather, she couldn't make it to practice once.

▶ Rewrite any sentences that have too many clauses and phrases.

▶ Proofread Your Story

Proofread your story, using the Proofreading Checklist and the Grammar and Spelling Connections. Proofread for one skill at a time. Use a class dictionary to check spellings.

HELP ?

Proofreading Tip

Read your paper aloud. You may notice mistakes when you hear them.

Proofreading Checklist

Did I
- ✔ indent all paragraphs?
- ✔ begin and end each sentence correctly?
- ✔ capitalize proper nouns?
- ✔ use correct subject and object pronouns?
- ✔ punctuate correctly with quotation marks?
- ✔ correct any spelling errors?

📖 Use the Guide to Capitalization, Punctuation, and Usage on page H64.

Proofreading Marks
- ¶ Indent
- ∧ Add
- ℛ Delete
- ≡ Capital letter
- / Small letter
- ⌄" ⌄" Add quotes
- ⋏ Add comma
- ⊙ Add period
- ∩ Transpose

Grammar and Spelling Connections

Subject and Object Pronouns Use a subject pronoun to replace a noun used as a subject. Use an object pronoun to replace a noun used as a direct object or a noun that follows prepositions such as *to, in, for,* and *at.*

GRAMMAR LINK See page 279.

Punctuating Dialogue Put a quotation mark around a speaker's exact words. Put the end punctuation inside the quotation marks.

"Don't touch that phone!" shrieked my sister.

GRAMMAR LINK See page 254.

Spelling the Prefix *ad-* The prefix *ad-* may be spelled *af, ac, ap,* or *as.*

accurate   assemble
approach   affair

📖 See the Spelling Guide on page H80.

▶ Publish Your Story

❶ Make a neat final copy of your story. Be sure you fixed all mistakes.

❷ Title your story. Make your readers curious. "Wrong Time to Slip on a Banana Peel" is a better title than "Ed's Accident."

❸ Publish or share your story. Consider your audience and purpose. See the Ideas for Sharing box.

Tips for Dramatizing

- Work with classmates. Each person takes the part of a different character or the narrator in your story.
- Discuss what the characters think and feel.
- Use gestures, facial expressions, and the sound of your voice to show your character's thoughts and emotions.
- Speak loudly and slowly enough to be heard by your audience.

 See page 582.

Ideas for Sharing

Write It Down
- Make your story into a booklet for the class reading center.

Talk It Up
- Read it aloud as a dramatic presentation.

Show It Off
- Illustrate your story with pictures of characters or events.

▶ Reflect

Write about your writing experience. Use these questions as a guide.

- What was difficult about writing a story? What was easy?
- What is your favorite part of your story?
- What could you do to improve your writing the next time?

- How does this paper compare with other papers you have written?

Writing Prompts

Use these prompts as ideas for stories or to practice for a test. Decide who your audience will be, and write your story in a way that they will understand and enjoy.

1 What if you woke up and discovered that you were only six inches tall? What would happen then? Write a story about your day.

2 Write a story that begins with the sentence *If I only had read that letter yesterday.* Who wrote the letter? What might it have prevented—or made happen?

3 You are suddenly whisked back in time holding one modern invention. What would that invention be? Write a story about how it helps or hurts you in an earlier time.

4 Write a story about a search for treasure. Who is searching for it? Where are they searching? Tell what happens.

Writing Across the Curriculum

5 **FINE ART**

The village looks so peaceful under the volcano. What could ever happen? Write a story about the next twenty-four hours. Use details from the painting. Include a conflict and a resolution.

Village with Volcano, by Susana Gonzalez-Pagliere

  See www.eduplace.com/kids/hme/ for more prompts.

Test Practice

This prompt to write a story is like ones you might find on a writing test. Read the prompt.

> **Write a story about a search for treasure. Who is searching for it? Where are they searching? Tell what happens.**

How can you do a good job? Here are some strategies.

Remember, a story is a narrative of made-up events with a beginning, a middle, and an end.

❶ Look for clue words that tell exactly what to write about.

❷ Choose a story that fits the clue words.

Clue Words	My Topic
search for treasure, who, where, what happens	Two brothers are hunting for a lost shipment of gold in a South American rain forest.

❸ Plan your writing. Use a story map to organize your plot.

> **Beginning**
> Introduce characters and setting.
> Introduce conflict.

> **Middle**
> Show characters dealing with conflict.
> Show events rising to a climax.

> **End**
> Resolve the conflict.

❹ You will get a good score if you remember what kind of story sounds loud and clear in the rubric on page 569.

Writing a Play

A **play** is a story that is acted out on a stage. The playwright tells the story through the actions of the characters and their dialogue. As in a story, a play may include more than one setting. Ximena is the playwright of *Alysson's Party*. Read her play to yourself or aloud with classmates.

Alysson's Party

Characters

ALYSSON, 13-year-old birthday girl

BRIDGET, Alysson's 15-year-old sister

ARTURO, Alysson's friend, age 12

LUKE, Alysson and Bridget's next-door neighbor, age 9

BILLY, Luke's brother, age 14

CHRISSY, Alysson's best friend, age 13

MARIKO, Alysson's friend, age 12

Props

Streamers

Balloons

Board games

Gift-wrapped packages

A cake with a Happy Birthday message

Setting

(Saturday evening at the home of two sisters, ALYSSON and BRIDGET. The stage is divided into two rooms: a living room with a couch, and a den with a couch, a small table, and a window with a curtain.)

Stage directions

(LUKE is in the corner of the den, looking upset. CHRISSY is sitting on the couch, arms crossed over her chest. ARTURO, BILLY, and MARIKO are decorating the den with party decorations. There is a small pile of gifts in one corner and a small pile of board games in another corner.)

BRIDGET: *(Entering den)* Okay, everyone! Are you almost done with the decorations?

BILLY: Yeah, we're just about set.

BRIDGET: Great! Then I'll go put the candles on the cake. *(Exits, calling back to CHRISSY)* Hey, Chrissy, do you want to help?

CHRISSY: *(Frowns as she gets up from the couch)* Okay, but wait'll Bridget finds out that Alysson knows about the party.

ARTURO: *(Raising his eyebrows)* Alysson knows?

CHRISSY: Yeah. Luke opened his big mouth.

MARIKO: *(Smiling)* Come on, Chrissy! Cheer up! It's still going to be great!

BILLY: *(Glaring at LUKE)* Too bad someone couldn't keep a secret!

LUKE: But Billy, I told you I didn't know it was a surprise!

ARTURO: Hey! Mariko's right. It'll still be a great party. *(Continues hanging decorations)*

MARIKO: I'll go tell Bridget. *(Exits)*

(All in room continue hanging decorations.)

LUKE: *(Speaking to no one in particular)* I said I was sorry!

(BRIDGET and MARIKO enter.)

BRIDGET: *(Carrying the cake, sets it on table)* Okay, Mariko's just filled me in. Now we know it was . . .

LUKE: *(Interrupting)* It was me! I'm sorry, Bridget! I didn't know it was a secret!

BRIDGET: I know, Luke, I know. What I was trying to say is that we know it was a mistake. Now, let's see how we can fix it. Any ideas?

(All in room pause, thinking.)

Dialogue

more ▶

BILLY: *(To BRIDGET)* What if Luke and I pretend to just be at your house, like always? We could be playing a game or something. Everyone else could be hiding in the den.

BRIDGET: Hey, that's good! Then when Alysson walks in . . .

LUKE: *(Finishes BRIDGET's sentence)* . . . we'll pretend it was all a big joke!

MARIKO and ARTURO: Oh, will Alysson ever be . . .

CHRISSY: *(Peeking out the window, shushing everyone)* Guys, Alysson's coming!

BRIDGET: Quick everyone! Hide! Luke, go grab one of the board games!

(ARTURO, MARIKO, and CHRISSY hide; CHRISSY turns off the den light; BILLY, LUKE, and BRIDGET lay out the board game in the living room and are setting it up to play.)

ALYSSON: *(Enters the living room)* Hey, guys! What's up?

BRIDGET: Nothing. *(Pretends to play game)*

ALYSSON: *(To LUKE)* Hey, Luke, I thought you said there was a surprise for me?

LUKE: Oh . . . that. Nope, sorry.

BILLY: Luke was just pulling your chain.

ALYSSON: *(Frowning, stares at the three around the game board)* Wow. Some joke.

BRIDGET: Hey, Alysson, could you go grab the score pad from the den? I forgot it.

ALYSSON: *(Still frowning)* Sure, why not?

(ALYSSON *crosses to the den and reaches for the light switch. As she does,* CHRISSY, MARIKO, *and* ARTURO *jump out from behind the couch.* BRIDGET, BILLY, *and* LUKE *jump up behind* ALYSSON.)

ALL: (*Except* ALYSSON) SURPRISE!!

CURTAIN

Reading As a Writer

- The list of **characters** at the beginning of the play sometimes includes a brief description of the characters.
  How many characters are in Ximena's play?

- The **props** are the items the characters will use in the play.
  What props are used in Ximena's play?

- The **setting** tells the specific place and time of the action.
  Where and when is Ximena's play set?

- The **stage directions** tell what the characters are doing and how they are doing it.
  Which stage directions does Ximena use to reveal how the characters think or feel?

- **Dialogue** is the conversation between characters. It moves the story along and can reveal how the characters feel.
  How does Ximena show that the characters are excited or upset?

more ▶

How to Write a Play

❶ Choose a story idea for a short play. Choose a topic that suits your purpose and will interest your audience. Use only a few characters and one or two settings. When choosing, think about these points.

- What is the problem or conflict?
- What is the play's setting? Is it appropriate for the problem or conflict?

❷ Plan your play. Use the story map below to help you. Add details about your characters, setting, and plot as you plan.

>
> **HELP**
> **?** ***Stuck for an Idea?***
>
> You could use
> - a story you have written,
> - a story from a book you have read, or
> - an experience of a friend or family member.

Characters	Setting	Plot
• Osamu, a know-it-all • Yuka, his frustrated friend • Ms. Takahashi, the art teacher	• classroom • museum room where Yuka's art is on the walls	**Beginning** Osamu changes Yuka's paintings. **Middle** They enter an art contest. **End** Yuka wins because she stayed true to herself.

❸ Draft your play.

- List your characters and describe the setting. Write stage directions that tell what the characters should say and do as the play starts.
- Write the dialogue and any stage directions. Put the stage directions in parentheses.
- If the action moves from one place to another, begin a new scene. Indicate the setting and stage directions for each new scene.
- End by resolving the central conflict. Do the characters get what they need or want? Why or why not? When you have finished, write CURTAIN or BLACKOUT.

Tech Tip
Use Caps Lock to type proper names in all capital letters.

4 **Read** it aloud to yourself or with one or more partners.

- Read the dialogue with expression. Does the dialogue sound natural? Does it reflect the characters' personalities? Is it appropriate for your purpose and audience?
- Walk through the action. Are the stage directions appropriate? Are any other directions needed?
- Is more dialogue or action needed to make the story problem and its resolution clear? Should anything be taken out?

> Record your dialogue on audio-tape. Does it sound natural?

5 **Revise** your play.

- Is the plot clear?
- Is the play too short? Is it too long?
- Should any characters be taken out or added?
- Are any of the parts uninteresting or unclear?
- Do the final events make the play feel finished?

6 **Proofread** your play. Did you spell the characters' names consistently? Is the end punctuation accurate for the expression you want in the dialogue? Use a dictionary to check the meanings and spellings of any words you aren't sure of.

7 **Perform** your play for an audience, such as your class, your school, or a community group.

HELP ? See pages 582–583 for dramatizing tips.

Here are some other suggestions:

- Conduct a readers' theater, or staged reading. There's no need to memorize the dialogue, but everyone should read with feeling.
- Videotape your play. Send it to a friend or family member.

Dramatizing

To bring a story to life, storytellers dramatize, or act out, the story's characters and events. They speak and move as the characters would and use their voices to keep listeners interested.

Good storytellers listen for clues in a story to understand how the characters would behave and what their feelings might be. Like actors, storytellers choose which words to stress. They think about how to use their speaking voices to show emotions and to change the mood of a story.

The beginning of an African folktale is given below. As you read it, think about the ways you would change your voice in a dramatic presentation.

Ananse the Spider in Search of a Fool

We do not mean, we do not really mean, that what we are going to say is true.

Hear my account of Spider Ananse and the fish traps.

Spider Ananse once lived by the sea. There were plenty of fish in those waters. Yes, there were fish to be caught for those who had traps made and set. But Ananse was not one to be working like that.

"I'd like to catch and sell fish," he thought, "the regular type and the shellfish, too. But if I'm to do that, I must hire a fool to make, set, and pull the traps. . . ."

So Spider Ananse set out to find a fool. He walked about the fishing village, calling, "I want a fool. I want a fool."

He saw a woman cooking. "I am looking for a fool," he said.

"A fool," she said, mocking him and shaking her wooden spoon. Spider ran off to the shore, where on the beach, he saw a busy fisherman.

"I am looking for a fool," said Spider.

"A pool?" asked the fisherman.

"No! A fool," said Spider.

"A tool?" asked the fisherman.

"A fool. A fool," howled Spider as he hurried off. . . .

Think About the Context

To dramatize a folktale, find out about the culture it is from. What are the people's traditions or beliefs that they have passed along through stories? Many West African tales are humorous and contain plays on words. Some feature a trickster animal, like Ananse, who is smart, but lazy, and who tries to trick other animals into doing his work.

Use the guidelines below to help you dramatize a folktale, a play, a poem, or a story of your own.

Guidelines for Dramatizing

▶ Look closely at the story and take notes about the characters. Are they angry, timid, or confident? Find words and phrases that give clues to how the characters would speak and act in each situation.

▶ Decide where you need to pause or slow down. Practice with a partner or make a tape recording so that you can make improvements.

▶ To keep your audience interested, avoid talking in the same tone of voice. Change the volume and pitch (high to low, or deep) of your voice to show changes in the story's events.

▶ Use facial expressions and gestures. These nonverbal cues will help your listeners understand the feelings of the characters.

▶ Speak clearly so that all of your listeners can hear and understand you.

Apply It

Choose part of a folktale to dramatize. Perform for a small group or the class. Use the guidelines above to help you. Then answer these questions.

● Describe the main character. In what ways did you change your voice or use gestures to show what the character is like?

● If you were to perform the tale again, in what ways would you dramatize it differently? Explain.

Comparing Stories in Print and on Film

Have you ever seen the movie version of a favorite book? You probably noticed that the story in the movie was different from the story in the book. Maybe a character was dropped or the ending was changed. Filmmakers make changes because stories are told differently in film. The following chart lists some of the differences.

Stories in Print	Stories in Film
Authorship Writers decide how to tell their stories. They use written language to create the characters, the setting, the plot, the dialogue, and the action.	**Authorship** Directors, producers, screenwriters, special-effects people, and actors decide how a story will be told. They may use film sets, cameras, music, and computers to tell the story.
Audience • Readers use the author's words and their own imaginations to form mental pictures of the setting, the mood, and the characters. • Readers can read the story as slowly or as quickly as they like. They can also reread or skip parts.	**Audience** • Moviegoers are shown the setting and the characters on screen. Changing images, recorded speech, and sound effects tell the story and set the mood. • Moviegoers cannot change the rate at which the story is told.
Length Authors can tell their stories in a few pages or a few thousand pages.	**Length** Filmmakers usually limit the time it takes to tell their stories. Most movies are about two hours long.
Cost Books and magazines are expensive to print, but they still cost less to produce than most films.	**Cost** Most movies cost thousands, even millions, of dollars to produce. Filmmakers hire a staff and actors, and they must pay for props, costumes, special effects, and filming in studios or on location.

The use of technology can change the movie version of a story. Special effects, sound effects, music, and computer-generated graphics provide new details and mood. These may be different from what you or the author imagined. In fact, a movie is a new way of experiencing the story.

Use these guidelines to compare a story in print to a story in a movie.

Guidelines for Evaluating a Movie Based on a Book

❶	**Plot**	● Which scenes or events in the book were added, dropped, or changed?
		● How did these changes affect the story? Why do you think they were made?
❷	**Characters**	● Were characters added, dropped, or changed?
		● Do they look and sound the way you imagined while reading the story?
		● How do these changes affect the story? Why do you think they were made?
❸	**Setting and Mood**	● Are the movie's setting and mood the same as in the book? If not, how are they different?
❹	**Technical Features**	● In what ways do camera angles, music, special effects, and lighting add to or change the story?

Apply It

Watch a movie based on a story you have read. Take notes while you watch. Then, using the guidelines above and these questions, write a review of the movie.

- Which version did you like better—the book or the movie? Why?
- What were the main differences between the book and the movie?
- As a reviewer, explain the movie's weaknesses. Make suggestions for ways to improve the story.

Books with Movie Versions

- *The Yearling*
- *Little Women*
- *To Kill a Mockingbird*
- *The Red Badge of Courage*
- *Frankenstein*

3

Tools
and
Tips

What You Will Find in This Part:

Giving and Following Directions

Directions, or instructions, tell listeners how to do or how to make something. These guidelines will help you give good directions.

Guidelines for Giving Directions

1. Consider your audience. Use words a child younger than you is able to understand. Learn whether or not the person speaks English fluently or has a hearing problem.

2. Make the purpose of the directions clear.

3. Speak slowly so that your directions can be understood.

4. Give the directions in the correct order, step by step. Use words that signal this order, such as *first, second, next, then, now,* and *finally.*

5. Include all necessary details, such as materials, sizes, and amounts.

6. Use gestures, such as pointing, to support the directions, if appropriate.

It is also important to be able to understand directions when they are given to you. The following guidelines will help you to follow directions.

Guidelines for Following Directions

1. Listen for each step. Try to picture what to do.

2. Listen for order words, such as *first, next, after, when,* and *finally.*

3. Ask questions if any part of the directions is not absolutely clear.

4. Repeat the steps out loud so that the person giving the directions can correct any misunderstanding.

Apply It

Tell a classmate how to perform a skill. Have the classmate actually follow your directions. Adjust the directions until the classmate is successful. Then switch roles.

Resolving Problems

In the cartoon above, why did the discussion turn into an argument? What could the boy and girl have done to resolve the problem calmly?

Think about what pushes your anger button during a disagreement. If you follow the tips and guidelines here, you may find that instead of quarrels, you can resolve problems and have productive discussions.

Avoiding an Argument You don't have to get into an argument every time you disagree with someone. Check out a fact before you argue. Ask yourself if the disagreement really matters, and change the subject, if necessary. Don't take sides in other people's quarrels.

When you disagree with someone, choose your words carefully. Use words that show you are open-minded and willing to listen to another point of view.

Language to Use During a Discussion	Language to Avoid During a Discussion
Perhaps . . .	You're wrong!
I wonder if . . .	That's stupid.
May I suggest . . .	I'm positive . . .
Let's consider . . .	There's no way . . .
It occurs to me . . .	Definitely not!
I believe . . .	Forget it!
That's true, but . . .	That's impossible.

more ▶

Resolving Problems **H5**

Resolving Problems *continued*

Settling an Argument If an argument does begin, there doesn't always have to be a "winner" for it to be settled. You and the other person can reach a **compromise**, a settlement in which each of you gives up some of your ideas or wishes. If you keep an open mind, you may even realize that you are both right! If you follow the guidelines below and you don't insult each other personally, you will still be friends.

Guidelines for Resolving Problems

DO try to understand the other person's point of view.

DO express opinions in a way that suggests possibility rather than certainty.

DO point out the part of the other person's argument that you agree with.

DO give valid reasons for your point of view, and always offer alternatives.

DO stay calm.

DO try to be fair.

DON'T shout.

DON'T make personal remarks.

DON'T dismiss someone's ideas.

DON'T close your mind to compromise.

DON'T make statements that do nothing but express your anger or contempt.

DON'T act like a know-it-all.

Apply It

With a partner, role-play one of the situations below, or create one of your own. Follow the guidelines. Perform the scene in front of a group of classmates. Discuss how you handled the disagreement.

- You go to the movies with a friend and can't agree where to sit.
- You and your sister or brother disagree about which TV program to watch.
- You are doing math homework with a friend. You disagree with his method for solving one of the problems.

Giving a Speech

To give a good speech, you must know your subject and audience, organize your thoughts, and rehearse the performance until it is smooth.

Guidelines for Giving a Speech

1 **Plan** your speech.
- Think about what your listeners know about your topic.
- Decide if the purpose of your talk will be to inform, to persuade, or to entertain.

2 **Prepare** your speech.
- Research your topic and find the information you need.
- Gather any graphics or visuals, such as maps or pictures, to display.
- Write notes on note cards to use as reminders while you speak. Use words and ideas that are appropriate for your audience.
- Be sure your talk has a beginning, a middle, and an end. Put your notes in the correct order, and highlight key words.

3 **Practice** your speech.
- Study your notes until you have them almost memorized.
- Rehearse in front of a mirror using your notes and visual aids. Practice gestures until they are smooth and natural.
- Practice how you say your words. Think about the rate, volume, pitch, and tone of your voice.
- Time your speech as you practice in front of family or friends. Make revisions if necessary after listening to their comments.

4 **Present** your speech.
- Use your voice and visual aids in the same way that you practiced.
- Stand in a comfortable position with your weight on both feet and your head up.
- Speak slowly, clearly, and loudly enough for everyone to hear you. Remember to adjust the volume of your voice to the size of the room.
- Avoid saying *um, ah,* and *well.*
- Make eye contact with people in the audience.
- Speak with expression. See the next two pages for tips.

more ▶

Giving a Speech *continued*

How to Speak Expressively

When you write, punctuation marks help you express your meaning. When you speak, you have several different ways to express your meaning. These are pitch, stress, volume, rate, gestures, and juncture.

Pitch You can change the meaning of words by letting your voice go up and down. Say these three sentences, and notice how their meanings change as your voice rises and falls according to the punctuation.

Look at the moon.   Look at the moon!   Look at the moon?

Stress Giving emphasis to different words can also change a sentence. These three sentences change in meaning when a speaker puts emphasis on different words.

Maria will sing.   Maria **will** sing.   Maria will **sing.**

Volume You can make an important point by speaking loudly or softly. If you have been speaking in a level tone of voice, a change in volume (louder or softer) signals to the audience that you are saying something important.

Rate Slowing your rate of speaking will also help you make an important point. Quickening your rate occasionally will add excitement to your speech.

Gestures An appropriate gesture, or movement, will not only make your meaning clearer, it will add a little drama to what you say. Try saying, "There's a car" as a statement, an exclamation, and a question. In each case, add a gesture. Notice that the meaning is now much clearer and stronger. You can learn more about movements, or nonverbal cues, on pages H10–H11.

Juncture This term refers to pauses in speech. You pause when one thought ends and another begins. Repeat the following sentences.

Robert put the dog in its pen.   Robert, put the dog in its pen.

What changes the meaning in the written sentences? the spoken sentences?

Remember these guidelines for speaking expressively.

Guidelines for Speaking Expressively

1. Vary the pitch of your voice when you make a statement, make an exclamation, or ask a question.

2. Put stress on the most important words in the sentence.

3. Vary the volume of your voice to emphasize important points.

4. Change your rate of speech to draw attention to special ideas.

5. Use movements and gestures to clarify your meaning and make your speech more dramatic.

6. Use juncture, or pauses, in speaking for the same reasons that commas and other punctuation marks are used in writing.

Try It Out Here are some suggestions for speaking expressively.

A. Work with a partner. Say the following sentence as a statement, an exclamation, and a question. *There's a raccoon in the bushes.* Listen for, and discuss, the changes in pitch.

B. With your partner, practice saying the following sentences two ways by changing the juncture. Discuss the changes in meaning.
   1. Jennie let the baby crawl across the room.
   2. Can you hear Alfredo?

C. Repeat each sentence to a partner. Stress a different word each time. Then discuss the changes in meaning.
   3. I must finish this work.
   4. He decided not to go.
   5. Tasha will finish the report.

Apply It

Prepare a talk about a recent concert, magazine article, or topic of your choice. Practice different methods of speaking expressively. Have a partner listen as you say sentences with different pitch, stress, volume, and rate. Ask for feedback until you develop the most effective delivery for your speech.

Understanding Nonverbal Cues

Using Nonverbal Cues

Just like words, the nonverbal cues of facial expressions, body language, and gestures can convey what you think or how you feel.

Facial Expressions Your face can reflect or strengthen such strong emotions as anger and excitement; signal attitudes, such as boredom, disagreement, or approval; or convey tone, such as humor or seriousness.

Body Language Your body movements can send unspoken messages.

- Good posture, making eye contact, and using controlled movements show confidence. Slouching, looking at the floor or over someone's shoulder, shuffling, or fidgeting tend to signal nervousness, boredom, or lack of confidence.

Gestures Your hand motions can add to or distract from your message.

- You can use your hands to clarify a message, such as to point out something, to represent size or shape, or to demonstrate a task.

- You can use your hands for emphasis. For example, you could hold up three fingers to emphasize that you have three main points.

- Avoid using meaningless gestures.

    Warning! Keep in mind that your nonverbal cues may show feelings or thoughts that you don't want to share.

Listening and Speaking Strategies

Interpreting Nonverbal Cues

You need to interpret a speaker's nonverbal cues in order to understand the complete message and to recognize the most important ideas.

Interpreting others' nonverbal cues will also help you to be sensitive to their feelings. A pained look may indicate someone's feelings have been hurt. A look of confusion may indicate a need for more explanation. A bored look may mean you need to change the subject or not talk so much!

Remember these guidelines for understanding nonverbal cues.

Guidelines for Understanding Nonverbal Cues

- ▶ Avoid unnecessary or distracting nonverbal cues.
- ▶ Use facial expressions, gestures, and other body language to support your spoken messages or to communicate nonverbally.
- ▶ Be aware of the nonverbal cues you are sending.
- ▶ Interpret speakers' nonverbal cues to understand their ideas fully.
- ▶ Use others' nonverbal cues to guide your actions.

Apply It

A. With your class or a small group, take turns pantomiming and interpreting nonverbal cues to show different emotions or feelings.

B. Prepare a thirty-second message, such as giving directions, making an announcement, relating information, or describing an incident. Use nonverbal cues. Present your message to classmates, and ask for feedback about the effectiveness of your nonverbal cues.

Interviewing

Interviews with people knowledgeable about a particular subject are good sources of information. You can use interviews to gather information for a research paper, a news article, a persuasive argument, or just to satisfy your curiosity about a topic! These guidelines will help you be a good interviewer.

Guidelines for Interviewing

Planning the Interview

1. Brainstorm questions to ask. Use the five *W's*—*who, what, where, when, why*—and *how*. Avoid questions that can be answered with *yes* or *no*.

2. List your questions on paper in a sensible order. Leave space between questions so that you can fill in the answers.

3. Make an appointment for the interview. Be on time.

Conducting an Interview

4. State your purpose at the beginning of the interview.

5. Be courteous. If the person drifts away from your main purpose, bring the interview back in line tactfully.

6. Ask follow-up questions that show you are listening carefully. Don't be afraid to ask for an example or for a clearer explanation.

7. Take accurate notes. You may want to use a tape recorder instead.

8. You may want to quote important facts or comments. Ask the person's permission to use a quotation. Then write the quotation exactly and use quotation marks. Don't paraphrase.

9. Thank the person for his or her time and information. Send a follow-up thank-you note as well.

10. After the interview, review the notes to be sure they are clear.

Apply It

Write six questions for interviewing classmates about their first memory. Conduct two or three interviews and record the answers your classmates give you.

Similes and Metaphors

Writers often help their readers imagine something by comparing it to something else. In the first sentence below, the writer uses the word *like* to compare the farmland to a quilt. In the second sentence, *as* is used to compare music to a shower. A comparison that uses the word *like* or *as* is called a **simile**.

The music was as refreshing as a cool shower on a hot day.

The farmland looks like a huge quilt of green, yellow, and brown patches.

A **metaphor** is a comparison that says that one thing is another. It does not use *like* or *as*.

The moon was a white globe.

The farmland is a huge quilt of green, yellow and brown patches.

How do similes and metaphors help a reader picture what is being described?

Apply It

Complete each sentence with a simile or a metaphor. Write the kind of comparison shown in parentheses.

1. The old dog's fur was _____. (simile)
2. Philip leaped the enormous puddle _____. (simile)
3. The colorful umbrellas were _____. (metaphor)
4. The reflections on the water were _____. (metaphor)
5. The polished stone felt _____. (simile)
6. The sky at sunset was _____. (metaphor)

Synonyms

Words that have almost the same meanings are called **synonyms**. You can use synonyms to add variety to your writing. Notice how this writer used two different words for *looked*.

Eliza peered into the darkness. A pair of gleaming eyes stared back at her.

Here are some other synonyms for *looked*.

glared   glanced   gazed   peeked

Synonyms help you avoid using the same words over and over. They can also help you say exactly what you mean. When you write, use a synonym dictionary, or **thesaurus**, such as the Thesaurus Plus at the end of the Tools and Tips section. If the word processing program on your computer has an electronic thesaurus, use it as a handy tool for finding synonyms.

Apply It

Write each sentence, replacing the underlined word with its synonym from the word box. You may use a dictionary.

1. An odd <u>noise</u> woke me in the middle of the night.
2. <u>Shaking</u>, I went to my window.
3. I looked around <u>cautiously</u>.
4. A raccoon was <u>clumsily</u> dancing with our trash can.
5. The can tipped over, and all the garbage <u>fell</u> out.
6. The raccoon helped itself to a <u>crushed</u> sandwich half.
7. Then it <u>suddenly</u> stopped nibbling and looked up.
8. The raccoon dropped its dinner and <u>hurried</u> into the shadows.

quivering
abruptly
bustled
tumbled
smashed
warily
awkwardly
rattle

Antonyms

Antonyms are words that have opposite meanings. You can use antonyms to show how things contrast or differ from each other.

Jimmy waded cautiously into the water, but Daniel dove fearlessly into the rough waves.

Male birds can be identified by their brilliant colors. The drab plumage of baby birds helps to protect them from predators.

Often you can change a word into its antonym simply by adding the prefix *un-* or *non-*.

WORD:	known	resident	flammable
ANTONYM:	unknown	nonresident	nonflammable

Many words do not have opposites. *Wet* and *dry* are antonyms, but there is no antonym for *water*.

Apply It

One of the two words following each sentence is an antonym for the underlined word in the sentence. Write each sentence, using the antonym to fill in the blank. You may use a dictionary.

1. The moon underline{appeared} briefly from behind the clouds and then _____ again. (emerged, vanished)
2. Most of the paintings were underline{ordinary}, but a few were _____. (unique, common)
3. Years of use will cause underline{sharp} scissors to grow _____. (keen, dull)
4. Megan feels underline{nervous} before performing, but she becomes _____ once the concert begins. (jittery, serene)
5. The dollhouse was a _____ version of an underline{enormous} house. (miniature, gigantic)
6. The garden had once received much underline{care}, but now it suffered from _____. (attention, neglect)
7. A good detective will underline{examine} details that others might _____. (investigate, ignore)
8. A helmet is important underline{protection} against the _____ of bike injuries. (hazard, defense)

Antonyms **H15**

Connotations

The words you use can often create feelings and reactions. The associations that a word brings to mind are called its **connotations**. Read the sentences below.

Since a storm was approaching, the cautious fisherman decided to return to the harbor.

Although the water was calm, the timid boater stayed close to shore.

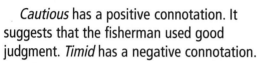

Cautious has a positive connotation. It suggests that the fisherman used good judgment. *Timid* has a negative connotation. *Timid* suggests that the boater was easily frightened. In order to convey the meaning you intend, it is important to know the connotations of the words you use. Look at the following examples.

Connotations	
Positive	**Negative**
hold	confine
amazed	shocked
relaxing	loafing

Apply It

Complete each sentence with one of the two words that follow it. Write the sentence. Then write whether the word you chose has a positive or a negative connotation.

1. Since he was always _____, he easily saved enough money for a new bicycle. (cheap, thrifty)
2. Her grandparents gave them a lot of _____ furniture. (old-fashioned, antique)
3. The _____ moved together across the street. (crowd, mob)
4. The candle provided _____ lighting in the dining room. (soft, dull)
5. The military school had a _____ student policy. (firm, rigid)

Prefixes and Suffixes

A **prefix** is a word part that is added to the beginning of a word. A **suffix** is a word part that is added to the end of a word. Prefixes and suffixes have meanings of their own.

The scientist was working in the lab.

He didn't leave until after midnight.

When the suffix *-ist,* "one that does," is added to *science,* the word's meaning changes to "one who does science." When the prefix *mid-,* "middle," is added to the base word *night,* the word's meaning changes to "middle of the night."

Word Part	Meaning	Example	Meaning
Prefixes			
pre-	before	precook	to cook before
un-	not, opposite of	uncommon	not common
dis-	not	disagree	to not agree
Suffixes			
-less	without	senseless	without sense
-able	able to	readable	able to be read
-ible	capable of	visible	can be seen

Words such as *repayable,* meaning "able to be payed back," have both a prefix and a suffix.

Apply It

Add a prefix, a suffix, or both to each of these words. Check your words in a dictionary. Then use each word in a sentence.

1. view
2. comfort
3. courage
4. breath
5. gain
6. command
7. count
8. connect

Word Roots

One way to add words to your vocabulary is to learn the meanings of common word parts, such as prefixes, suffixes, and word roots. A **word root** is the main part of a word. This same word root can be a part of many other words. It has a special meaning, but it is not a complete word. A prefix, a suffix, or both must be added to the word root to form a complete word. Knowing the meanings of word roots can help you learn and remember new words.

Word Root	Meaning	Example
tract	to pull or draw	tractor
vis	to see	vision
dict	to speak	predict
script, scrib	to write	prescription
struct	to build	structure
audi	to hear	audience
equ	even	equal

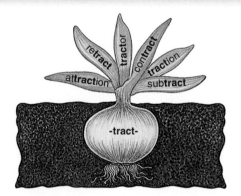

Apply It

Write the word root in each word. Then look up the word in a dictionary. Write its meaning, and use it in a sentence.

1. audible
2. audition
3. dictate
4. diction
5. envision
6. equate
7. equidistant
8. inscribe
9. obstruct
10. prescribe
11. retract
12. visor

Borrowed Words

The English language contains words borrowed from almost every language.

Keesha and her friends were all wearing baseball caps, big T-shirts, and dungarees.

The word *dungarees* is borrowed from the Hindi word meaning "trousers made of coarse cotton cloth."

British explorers and traders brought back to England words from around the globe. Early settlers in the United States borrowed words from the Native Americans. Later the language of the Spanish settlers mixed with that of the English settlers. We still add new words to English today.

Word	Origin
sofa	Arabic
ranch	Spanish
chipmunk	Ojibwa
garage	French
piano	Italian
tulip	Turkish

Apply It

Look up each of the following words in a dictionary. Write a definition of the word and the language from which it originated.

1. bagel
2. bouillon
3. caribou
4. kayak
5. lariat
6. luau
7. mesa
8. fragile
9. portfolio
10. soy
11. staccato
12. typhoon

Word Histories

Our language is always changing. Often we borrow words from other languages. We make up new words from old words and word parts. We give new meanings to old words. Therefore, languages and their individual words have histories. The history of a word is called its **etymology**.

Etymology can tell us many interesting and surprising facts about words and language. The word *eleven*, for example, originally meant "one left over after counting to ten." *Cow* and *beef,* oddly enough, both developed from the same word root, *bos. Catch* and *chase* were once synonyms meaning "to chase."

Many dictionaries give complete or partial etymologies. There are also special dictionaries of etymologies. Knowing the history of language can give you a fuller understanding of English vocabulary.

Apply It

Below are parts of six etymologies. Write a word from the word box to match each etymology. You may use a dictionary.

1. This word comes from a Latin word meaning "winter."
2. This word comes from a French phrase meaning "spiny pig."
3. Long ago, this word meant "any food in general."
4. This word was named after the city of Tangier, Morocco.
5. This word and *Thursday* are both related to Thor, a god in Old Norse mythology.
6. This word comes from the same word root as *annual*.

> meat
> thunder
> hibernate
> anniversary
> porcupine
> tangerine

Regional and Cultural Vocabulary

In different parts of the country, people sometimes use different words to name the same thing. Using language that reflects local speech can make your writing more interesting to read. It can also make it sound more authentic if you are writing about a particular area.

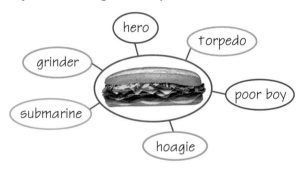

Let's say you are writing about a character who wants to buy a long sandwich filled with a variety of ingredients, such as meat, cheese, and vegetables. There are many names for this sandwich. If your story takes place in Philadelphia, it would be called a hoagie or grinder. But if the story takes place in New York or Los Angeles, the sandwich would be called a hero or submarine.

Language can also reflect a culture. For example, in a Spanish-speaking family a pudding might be called flan. In a Jewish family it might be called kugel. What we call an elevator in the United States is called a lift in England.

Apply It

The words in each group below are used by different regions and cultures to mean similar things. Choose the word that is the most familiar to you, and use it in a sentence. Afterwards, compare chosen words and sentences with your classmates. What is the effect of the different words?

1. firefly, glow worm, lightning bug
2. soda, pop, tonic, phosphate
3. won ton, ravioli, kreplach, pelmeny
4. faucet, spigot, spicket, tap
5. expressway, freeway, motorway
6. crepes, palacsintas, dosai, tortillas, blini

Using a Dictionary

Your dictionary contains a lot of information. Learning to use it efficiently will help you to find facts quickly.

Guide Words At the top of each dictionary page, you will find the first and last words that are on that page. These guide words will help you to locate an **entry word**, such as the following entry for *forecast,* more quickly.

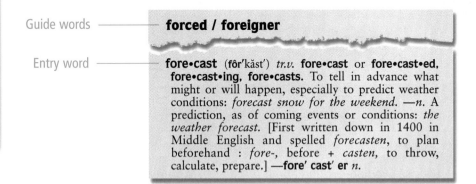

Guide words —— **forced / foreigner**

Entry word —— **fore•cast** (fôr′kăst′) *tr.v.* **fore•cast** or **fore•cast•ed, fore•cast•ing, fore•casts.** To tell in advance what might or will happen, especially to predict weather conditions: *forecast snow for the weekend.* —*n.* A prediction, as of coming events or conditions: *the weather forecast.* [First written down in 1400 in Middle English and spelled *forecasten*, to plan beforehand : *fore-*, before + *casten*, to throw, calculate, prepare.] —**fore′ cast′ er** *n.*

Syllabication Entry words are divided into syllables, which are separated by dots.

Phonetic Respelling To help you to pronounce an entry word, its phonetic respelling is given. Accent marks show where a word has primary (′) and secondary (′) stress. A **pronunciation key** at the foot of each or every other page explains the phonetic symbols. Check the pronunciation key for examples of the sounds shown in the respelling.

ă	pat	oi	boy
ā	pay	ou	out
âr	care	ŏŏ	took
ä	father	ōō	boot
ĕ	pet	ŭ	cut
ē	be	ûr	urge
ĭ	pit	th	thin
ī	pie	*th*	this
îr	pier	hw	whoop
ŏ	pot	zh	vision
ō	toe	ə	about
ô	paw	N	*French* bon

Parts of Speech The part of speech of the entry word is often abbreviated *n., v., adj., adv.,* or *prep.* This label can be a clue to choosing a definition that you need. Notice how the word *groom* is used in the sentence *Mr. Apple will groom Brian to be a salesperson. Groom* is used as a verb. Now check the verb definitions in the entry below. Definition 3 fits the sentence above.

groom (grōōm *or* grŏŏm) *n.* **1.** A person employed to take care of horses. **2.** A bridegroom. —*tr.v.* **groomed, groom•ing, grooms. 1.** To make neat and trim especially in personal appearance: *groomed themselves in front of the mirror before going to the party.* **2.** To clean and brush (an animal). **3.** To train (a person), as for a certain job or position: *groom a successor to the manager.*

Parts of speech

Definitions The meanings of a word form the main part of a dictionary entry. If there is more than one definition, each one is numbered.

Etymology The history or origin of a word—its *etymology*—often appears in brackets at the end of a definition. The definition of *gargoyle* below shows that the word comes from Middle English and Old French.

Part of speech

Definition

Etymology

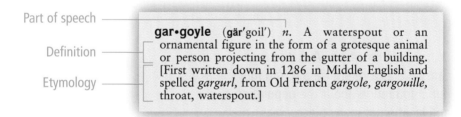

gar•goyle (gär′goil′) *n.* A waterspout or an ornamental figure in the form of a grotesque animal or person projecting from the gutter of a building. [First written down in 1286 in Middle English and spelled *gargurl,* from Old French *gargole, gargouille,* throat, waterspout.]

Shown below is the entry for *insulate,* which comes from *insula,* the Latin word for "island." The present meaning of *insulate* is related to the Latin word because an island is land that is isolated or detached.

in•su•late (ĭn′ sə lāt′) *tr.v.* **in•su•lat•ed, in•su•lat• ing, in•su•lates. 1.** To cover or surround with a material that prevents the passage of heat, electricity, or sound into or out of: *We insulated our attic to keep out the cold.* **2.** To detach; isolate: *The mountain valley is insulated from outside influences.* [First written down in 1538 in Modern English, from Latin *īnsula,* island.]

Etymology

more ▶

Using a Dictionary *continued*

Homographs Some words have the same spellings but different meanings and origins. These words are listed as separate entries. In the following homographs, you can see that *sash*¹ and *sash*² have different origins. Notice that *sash*¹ comes from Arabic, and *sash*² comes from French.

Raised number

First homograph

Second homograph

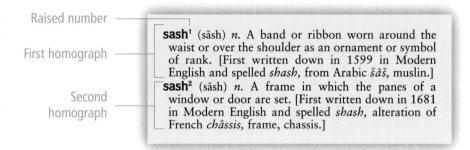

sash¹ (săsh) *n.* A band or ribbon worn around the waist or over the shoulder as an ornament or symbol of rank. [First written down in 1599 in Modern English and spelled *shash,* from Arabic *šăš,* muslin.]

sash² (săsh) *n.* A frame in which the panes of a window or door are set. [First written down in 1681 in Modern English and spelled *shash,* alteration of French *châssis,* frame, chassis.]

Usage Labels The label *Informal* is used to identify words not suitable for formal writing but frequently used in conversation and ordinary writing. The label *Slang* identifies words appropriate only in casual speech.

sa•shay (să shāy′) *intr. v. Informal.* To strut or flounce. [Var. of French *chassé,* a dance step.]

Other Information A dictionary also can serve as a reference aid. You may find information about the population and location of many places. Maps may be included. Entries for famous people may include dates of birth and death, nationalities, and important accomplishments. Significant events, such as holidays and wars, may be listed as well. Various tables may show an alphabet such as Braille, the metric system, Morse code, and proofreading marks. Check the table of contents to see what other information your dictionary offers.

The Braille Alphabet

a	b	c	d	e	f	g	h

i	j	k	l	m	n	o	p

q	r	s	t	u	v	x	y

z	and	for	of	the	with	ch	gh

sh	th	wh	ed	er	ou	ow	w

Using the Library

Classification Systems

Most libraries have a systematic arrangement that makes it possible to locate any book in the collection. Fiction books are shelved by the last names of the authors. Nonfiction works are organized by the Dewey decimal system or the Library of Congress system. Most libraries use the Dewey decimal system.

Dewey Decimal System In this system, books are grouped into ten major categories. Each category includes a range of numbers, and every book in the category has its own number within that range. Decimals are used to indicate the smallest subdivisions. One history book might have the number 942.16, and another might be numbered 981.73. The number assigned to a particular book is its **call number.** The following table gives the numbers of the major categories and some of their subcategories in the Dewey decimal system.

000–099 **General Works** (reference materials)

100–199 **Philosophy** (psychology and ethics)

200–299 **Religion** (mythology)

300–399 **Social Sciences** (communication, economics, education, government)

400–499 **Language** (grammar books, dictionaries)

500–599 **Science** (biology, chemistry, mathematics)

600–699 **Technology** (engineering, medicine)

700–799 **The Arts** (music, painting, photography, sports)

800–899 **Literature** (essays, plays, poetry)

900–999 **History** (biography, geography, travel)

Call numbers

Indicates a reference book

more ▶

Using the Library *continued*

In addition to the call number of a book, you also need to know how the library arranges its books. Often, a sign at the end of each shelf shows the range of call numbers of the nonfiction books stored there.

The fiction books in a library are usually placed in a separate section and are arranged alphabetically by the authors' last names. Some libraries group autobiographies and biographies in a separate section. Although biographies are nonfiction, they are shelved alphabetically by the name of the person who is the subject, not by the name of the author.

The section of reference books, which cannot be checked out of the library, includes atlases, encyclopedias, dictionaries, and almanacs.

Library Catalogs

Using an electronic or traditional card catalog will enable you to find any book a library owns when you know the title or author. It will also help you find a selection of books when you just have a subject in mind.

Electronic Catalogs Many libraries use a computerized, or electronic, catalog that serves just the library itself, or it may be connected to a network of libraries. The World Wide Web is also a source of many library catalogs.

To search for a book using a computer, enter either the book's title, the author's name, a keyword, or the subject of the book. Do not enter the words *A, An,* or *The* at the beginning of a title.

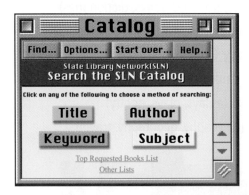

The computer will search its database of materials in the library's system for your request. If you enter an author's name, the computer will provide you with a list of all books written by that author. If you enter a subject or keyword, such as *bicycle touring,* the computer will provide a list of books on that particular subject.

From either of these lists, you can choose the title of a particular book and get more information. If an *R* or *Ref* appears with the call number, this indicates that the book is a reference work. Although libraries let you borrow other kinds of books, most libraries do not allow you to check out reference materials.

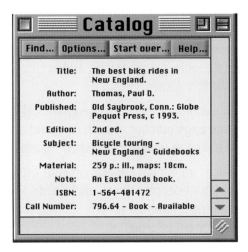

Card Catalogs If your library uses a card catalog in long wooden drawers, you will find title, author, and subject cards for every book in the library. Here are examples of each kind of card.

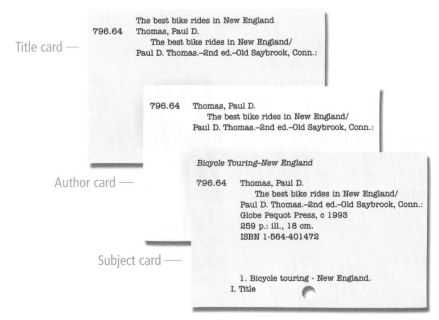

Title card —

Author card —

Subject card —

more ▶

Reference Materials

Reference materials in a library are full of information to help you write a research report or answer just about any question you may have. Most libraries devote an entire section to reference materials, such as the following sources.

See also "The Internet" on pages H51–H52 to read about using computers and the Internet to help you do research.

Encyclopedia An encyclopedia, which is a source of general information, contains articles about people, places, things, and events. The articles are arranged alphabetically in volumes.

Atlas An atlas is a collection of maps and geographical information. The atlas index provides the page number of each map and also gives the exact location of cities and towns as well as population information.

Almanac An almanac is an annual publication with lists, charts, and tables of information on important people, places, and events. The index in the front of an almanac gives all the references for any subject. The most recent almanac has the most current information.

Thesaurus A thesaurus is a reference book that lists synonyms and antonyms for each entry word. Some thesauruses have an index to locate entry words, and others are arranged alphabetically.

More Dictionaries In addition to the traditional dictionary, there are dictionaries that deal with specific topics. For example, there are dictionaries of geography, biographies, and even Native American tribes of North America.

Microforms Many libraries save space by storing some materials, such as newspapers, on pieces of film called microforms. If the film comes in rolled strips, it is called microfilm. If the film comes in cards, it is called microfiche. Special machines must be used to read microforms.

Using Visuals

Many articles and books include lists and drawings that present complex information in an easy-to-read form. These visuals show how things relate to each other and can be understood at a glance.

Tables

Facts and figures can be displayed in an organized way on tables. The vertical lines of information are called **columns**, and the horizontal lines are referred to as **rows**.

The table below lists the largest U.S. national parks in order of their size. The title tells you that only those parks with over one million acres are listed. Notice that each of the four columns is labeled with a caption, such as *Year Established.* Each row is labeled with the name of a national park. To find facts about Denali National Park, read down Column 1 until you find the name *Denali;* then read across Row 3 to get the information you need.

U.S. National Parks over 1 Million Acres			
Name	**State**	**Year Established**	**Number of Acres**
Wrangell-St. Elias	Alaska	1980	8,323,618
Gates of the Arctic	Alaska	1980	7,523,888
Denali	Alaska	1917	4,741,910
Katmai	Alaska	1980	3,674,541
Glacier Bay	Alaska	1980	3,225,284
Lake Clark	Alaska	1980	2,636,839
Yellowstone	Wyoming-Idaho-Montana	1872	2,219,791
Kobuk Valley	Alaska	1980	1,750,737
Everglades	Florida	1934	1,507,850
Grand Canyon	Arizona	1919	1,217,158
Glacier	Montana	1910	1,013,572

more ▶

Graphs

Drawings that show numerical information are called **graphs**. There are several types: picture graphs, bar graphs, line graphs, and circle graphs. On a circle graph, or pie graph, a circle is divided like a pie into sections that represent a percentage of the whole circle. Usually each section is shown in a different color or a different pattern to make it easier to read.

Look at the circle graph below that shows water use in the United States in 1997. Notice that the sections are different in size. Each section represents a different type of water use.

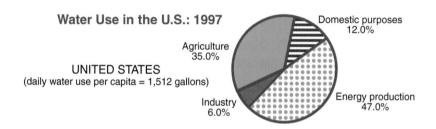

Water Use in the U.S.: 1997

Domestic purposes
12.0%

Agriculture
35.0%

UNITED STATES
(daily water use per capita = 1,512 gallons)

Energy production
47.0%

Industry
6.0%

Diagrams

Diagrams can be useful in helping you to visualize parts of something. A **picture diagram** is a drawing that shows how something is put together, how the parts relate to one another, or how the thing works. To understand a picture diagram, read each label and follow the lines to the parts being shown. Examine each part carefully.

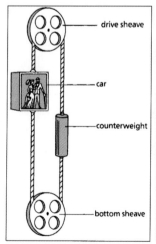

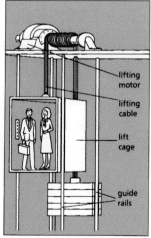

drive sheave

car

counterweight

bottom sheave

lifting motor

lifting cable

lift cage

guide rails

Fig.1 An early elevator   Fig.2 A modern elevator

Research and Study Strategies

Maps

Look at the map of Albuquerque, New Mexico. It shows streets, highways, and important places.

Legend A box printed on a map that explains important marks and symbols is called a **legend** or **key**.

The legend below has symbols that explain various types of highways. You can see that the interstate highways are represented by dark yellow lines. All of the other highways and city streets are shown with white lines. Other symbols tell you whether a highway is an interstate, federal, or state route.

Compass Rose The directions *north, south, east,* and *west* are shown on a compass rose. Use the direction arrows to figure out how one place is related to another. For example, the Albuquerque airport is in the southern part of the city.

Scale You can determine the distance from one place to another by using the scale of distance. Scales differ from map to map, so be sure to refer to the scale on the map you are using. Use a piece of paper to mark the space between two places on the map, and then use the scale of distance to determine the actual distance.

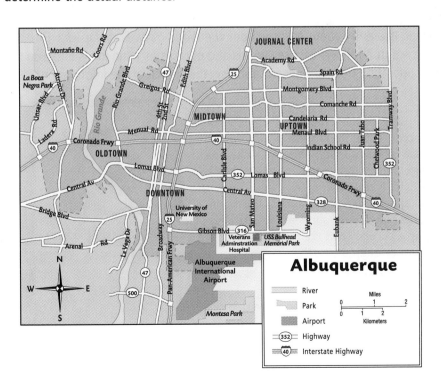

Research and Study Skills

Taking Notes

Whether you are reading, listening to a speaker, or watching a movie, taking good notes will help you recall what you read, hear, or see. Effective notes will help you remember much more than what you actually write down. These guidelines list important things to remember while taking notes.

Guidelines for Taking Notes

1. Don't copy material. Restate main ideas in your own words.
2. If you must use someone's exact words, use quotation marks and give him or her proper credit.
3. Write only key words and phrases, not entire sentences.
4. Following each main idea, list the details that support it.
5. Keep careful records of the sources you use.

Read this entry about eclipses from *The World Book Encyclopedia*. The note card that follows lists key words and phrases as main ideas and also lists supporting details. The card also lists the source of the information.

Eclipse is the darkening of a heavenly body. It occurs when the shadow of one object in space falls on another object or when one object moves in front of another to block its light. A solar eclipse takes place when the sun appears to become dark as the moon passes between the sun and the earth. A lunar eclipse occurs when the moon darkens as it passes through the earth's shadow. ———— Encyclopedia entry

Types of eclipses ———— Main idea
   –Solar eclipses
     sun appears to become dark
   –Lunar eclipses   Supporting details
     moon darkens
The World Book Encyclopedia, ———— Source
Volume 6, 1999 edition, page 51

Taking Notes While Listening If you are reading, you can look back and reread a section to check facts or recall information. But when listening to a speaker, it is important to take good notes, since you will not remember every word. Use the following guidelines to help you.

Guidelines for Taking Notes While Listening

1. Focus on the information presented. Don't let your mind wander. Shut out or move away from noises or other distractions.

2. Pay careful attention to the speaker's introduction and conclusion. A good speaker will outline the speech in an introduction and sum up the main points in the conclusion.

3. Listen for cue words, such as *first, the main point, most important,* or *in conclusion,* that signal important information.

4. Don't try to write everything you hear. Listen for important details, and write only key words or phrases. Read over your notes as soon as possible after the speech, and fill in missing details.

5. Record the speaker's name, the location, and the date.

Taking Notes While Viewing Taking notes while watching a film or event is more difficult than taking notes while listening or reading. Unless you are watching a video, there is no way to stop the action and see a section of the film again. Preparation is the key. In addition to the preceding guidelines for taking notes, the following guidelines will help you take good notes and still enjoy the viewing experience.

Guidelines for Taking Notes While Viewing

1. Prepare for the film or event by reading any related material ahead of time.

2. Listen to the dialogue or narrator even while you are taking notes.

3. Be aware of visual information, such as setting, body language, and facial expressions that add to your understanding of the film.

4. Check the credits at the end of the film for interesting information about the film's production.

5. Record the title of the film.

more ▶

Research and Study Skills *continued*

Outlining

After taking notes, the next step in organizing your thoughts is to write an outline. You can use a **sentence outline**, which uses a complete sentence for each heading and subheading, or a **topic outline**, which uses phrases.

To make an outline, decide which kind of order will be most useful in organizing your facts. Chronological order tells the order in which events happen. Spatial order describes the location of things in a place. Logical order groups together related ideas, such as details, in order of importance.

An outline has a title, main topics, subtopics, and details.

- A main topic tells the main idea. It is set off by a Roman numeral followed by a period.
- Subtopics give supporting facts. A subtopic is set off by a capital letter followed by a period.
- Details give more information about a subtopic. A detail is set off by a number followed by a period. More precise details may follow.

Never use a single subheading. If an idea cannot be separated into two ideas, do not separate it at all.

Look at the following example of a topic outline.

Knots
  I. History of Knots ———————————— Main topic
    A. One of the oldest inventions ———— Subtopic
      1. Used with bows and arrowheads ⎤
      2. Used for clothing and shelter ⎦— Details
    B. Famous Gordian knot
  II. Tying Knots
    A. Language of knots to name parts of a rope
    B. Preparing rope for knots
      1. Work the rope to take out stiffness
      2. Whip the ends so rope doesn't unravel
    C. Useful knots
      1. Square knot
      2. Bowline
      3. Two half hitches

Skimming and Scanning

You do not always need to read every word of a nonfiction article. Depending on your purpose for reading, you can skim or scan to quickly find the information you need.

Skimming When you want just an overview, or a general idea, skim a selection. Follow these steps to skim effectively.

Strategies for Skimming

1. Read the title and any headings.
2. Read all of the first two paragraphs.
3. Read the first sentence or two and the last sentence of the other paragraphs. Look for key words.
4. Look at any illustrations, and read the captions.
5. Read all of the last two paragraphs of the article. These may provide a summary.

Scanning When you need to find specific information, scan a selection. To scan quickly, follow these suggestions.

Strategies for Scanning

1. Look for a key word or words that will help you to find the facts you need. For example, to answer a question about marine life, look for related terms, such as *ocean*.
2. Next, look for typographic aids, such as numerals, capitalized words, and words in bold or italic type.
3. When you think you have found the facts you need, read that section slowly and carefully.

Remember these two ways of reading when you want to locate information quickly. Skim to get an overview or the main idea. Scan to get specific facts.

more ▶

Research and Study Skills *continued*

Summarizing

A **summary** is a shortened form of a longer article or story. By writing a summary, you can better understand fiction and nonfiction that you read.

Summarizing a Story Below is a summary of "The Weaving That Saved the Prince" on pages 552–555 of this book. Read, or reread, the story. Then read this summary. Notice how the writer was able to retell the story briefly.

> A king wants his son, the prince, to master a skill. The king reminds him that even a prince might need to work some day. After becoming an expert rug weaver, the prince goes out riding one day. Thieves capture him and want to kill him. He convinces the thieves that he can make them rich by weaving a beautiful rug that they can sell to the king for a fortune. Within the rug's design, the prince weaves a hidden map only his father will see. The thieves take the rug to the king, who immediately notices the map. He finds his son, using the map as a guide.

Read a story carefully before you write a summary. Follow these guidelines for summarizing a fictional work.

Guidelines for Summarizing a Story

1. Identify the major characters and events. Decide what aspects of the story to emphasize. In "The Weaving That Saved the Prince," the plot is very important. For another story you might stress the development of the characters.

2. Write clearly and briefly, but be certain that you tell enough about the plot to make the story easy for your reader to understand.

3. Include important names, dates, and places. The setting may be especially important in historical stories.

4. If possible, include information that captures the tone or the mood of the story. If you wish to quote a sentence or a phrase from the story, enclose it in quotation marks.

Summarizing an Article A summary helps you remember the most important facts and ideas. Here is a summary of the article, "The Lady with the Green Skin," on pages 473–477. Notice how it includes the major points of the article and how it is written in the writer's own words.

Frederic Bartholdi, a French sculptor, designed the Statue of Liberty in the late 1800s to honor American independence. To be lightweight and durable, the outside layer was made of copper, and a skeleton was made of iron. These materials would be able to withstand a harsh environment, but they were light enough so the statue could be transported to America. The statue was shipped to America in pieces and assembled on Bedloe's Island in New York Harbor. Because of corrosion by natural elements and pollution, the statue's skin has changed over the years to the blue-green color we see today. In the early 1980s, her rusting iron skeleton was replaced. Her copper skin was left unpolished because the patina that has developed protects her skin from further damage.

These guidelines will help you summarize a nonfiction article.

Guidelines for Summarizing an Article

1 Begin with a clear, brief statement of the main idea of the article.

2 Give details that support the main idea. It may help you to write down the sentences that state the main idea of each paragraph in the article. Then you can combine and restate those sentences in shortened form.

3 Include important names, dates, numbers, and places.

4 List any events or steps in the correct order.

5 As briefly as possible, put the facts into your own words. Be careful not to change the meaning of what you have read.

Word Analogies

Many tests ask you to complete word analogies. **Word analogies** compare two pairs of words in a special form using colons. In the example below, *near* and *far* are antonyms. *Polite* completes the analogy correctly because it is an antonym of *rude*. Both pairs of words now show antonyms.

near : far :: rude : *polite*

It is easier to complete a word analogy if you think of it as a sentence.

Near is to *far* as *rude* is to *polite*.

This chart shows some ways words can be related.

Word Relationship	Example
Word to its synonym	hide : conceal :: close : shut
Word to its antonym	rough : smooth :: persist : quit
Part to its whole	page : book :: tree : forest
Category to its member	fish : trout :: insect : ant
Object to its characteristic	whale : large :: guppy : small
Object to its use	pencil : write :: knife : cut
Person to his/her occupation	dancer : dancing :: pilot : flying
Worker to his/her tool	teacher : chalk :: dentist : drill
Worker to his/her product	gardener : flowers :: singer : song

Use these guidelines to help you complete word analogies.

Guidelines for Completing Word Analogies

1. Figure out the relationship between the first two words.

2. If you are asked to choose the second pair of words from a list, choose the pair that has the same relationship as the first pair.

3. If you are asked to choose the last word only, look at the first word in the second pair. Then try each of the possible answers in the blank. Decide which word creates the same relationship in the second pair as the relationship you identified in the first pair.

4. Double-check your answer. Say the completed analogy to yourself, substituting for the colons the words that explain the relationship.

A. Choose the pair of words that best completes each word analogy.

1. small : tiny ::
   a eager : bored
   b green : grass
   c frightened : scared
   d happy : angry

2. tailor : needle ::
   a baker : bread
   b farmer : plow
   c bone : dog
   d runner : running

3. knob : door ::
   a ocean : sand
   b hour : minute
   c willow : tree
   d wheel : car

4. potatoes : stew ::
   a lettuce : salad
   b ice cream : milk
   c warm : hot
   d car : automobile

5. sleepy : alert ::
   a happy : glad
   b tall : wide
   c willow : tree
   d timid : fierce

6. fast : swift ::
   a music : jazz
   b strong : powerful
   c sharp : dull
   d speed : runner

B. Write the word that best completes each analogy.

7. wool : scratchy ::
   satin : _____
   a cloth   **c** smooth
   b light   **d** sew

8. chef : meal ::
   poet : _____
   a pencil   **c** writes
   b magazine   **d** poem

9. apatosaurus : dinosaur ::
   Mars : _____
   a Pluto   **c** planet
   b planetarium **d** rocket

10. game : baseball ::
    color : _____
    a paint   **c** red
    b picture   **d** artist

11. broom : sweep ::
    stove :_____
    a hot   **c** kitchen
    b cook   **d** pot

12. barber : scissors ::
    gardener : _____
    a sunshine   **c** forest
    b shovel   **d** flowers

13. shirt : clothing ::
    typhoon : _____
    a windy   **c** blizzard
    b raincoat   **d** storm

14. star : constellation ::
    ship : _____
    a fleet   **c** engine
    b boat   **d** train

Test-Taking Strategies

Word Analogies   **H39**

Open-Response Questions

On some tests you are asked to read a passage and write answers to questions about it. Use these guidelines to help you write a good answer.

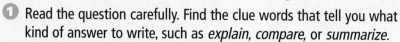

Guidelines for Answering an Essay Question

1. Read the question carefully. Find the clue words that tell you what kind of answer to write, such as *explain, compare,* or *summarize.*

2. Look for clue words that tell what the answer should be about.

3. Write a topic sentence using words from the question. The rest of your sentences should give details to support the topic sentence.

4. Answer only the question that is asked.

Read the following passage and the question at the end.

The Modern Zoo

The word *zoo* is from the Greek word *zoion* meaning "animal." Zoos were originally owned by emperors or private citizens, and the animals were displayed and used to stage fights. It has been a long time since zoo animals were used for fighting, but other changes in zoos have come more recently.

In this country, zoos were once parks with fenced enclosures and buildings that contained caged animals. The animals were grouped by category, such as cats, monkeys, and birds. Often the cages were too small to accommodate the animals, and the lack of natural settings made it difficult for them to thrive. Now, however, animals are usually grouped by natural habitat, giving them adequate living space and allowing them more freedom and the chance to interact naturally with their surroundings.

The methods zoos use to get animals have also changed. Zoo directors used to buy animals from dealers who captured them in the wild. Today, however, with the threat of many animals becoming extinct, most zoo animals are bred in zoos.

Zoos are no longer just a place for people to learn about animals. Zoo workers want to save animals from extinction, so they breed animals for other zoos. They also breed animals so that they can be released into their native habitats.

All these changes have not only made zoo life better for the animals, they have made viewing the animals a more natural and educational experience for human visitors as well.

Summarize the changes in American zoos.

Read these two answers to the question. Which one is a better answer?

People used to capture animals and put them in cages. The cages were really small, and the animals didn't do well in them. It doesn't really seem right for people to catch animals and put them someplace where they don't belong. Do you think it would be comfortable to live in a cage? An animal in a cage can't be with any other animals. It can't roam around and get the food it wants. Worst of all, it can't run and play. People should leave animals where they find them.

There have been important changes in American zoos. Animals used to be in cages and kept separate from one another. Now they are placed in natural settings that allow them more freedom. Zoos used to buy captured animals, but now most animals in zoos are bred there. Sometimes they are even released into the wild. Modern zoos are not only places where people can come to see animals but also places that try to make sure that animals do not become extinct.

The first answer doesn't mention any of the changes that have taken place in American zoos. The essay tells about animals being captured and put in cages, but doesn't even mention that this is how they once lived in zoos. It merely gives the writer's personal opinion about keeping animals in cages.

The second answer does a better job of answering the question. It uses words from the question in the topic sentence, and the supporting sentences summarize the main points. The answer gives only the information asked for.

Technology Terms

Computer Terms

Your school may be equipped with computers, or you may have one of your own. Try to become familiar with the following terms to understand how the computer works.

Monitor

Keyboard

Floppy disk

Disk drive

Hard copy

Printer

CD-ROM	A flat round piece of plastic on which computer data or music can be stored and read with a laser; many computers come with built-in CD-ROM drives.
cursor	The blinking square, dot, or bar on a computer screen that shows where the next typed character will appear.
disk drive	A device in a computer that can read information from a disk or write information onto a disk; you insert a disk into a disk drive through a thin slot.
document	A written or printed piece of writing.
floppy disk	A somewhat flexible plastic disk coated with magnetic material and used to store computer data.
font	Any one of various styles of letters in which computer type can appear.
hard copy	A computer document that is printed on paper.
hard drive	A computer disk that cannot be removed from the computer; hard disks hold more data and run faster than floppy disks.
hardware	The parts of a computer system, including the keyboard, monitor, memory storage devices, and printer.
keyboard	A part of the computer containing a set of keys.
menu	A list of commands and other items shown on a monitor.

modem	A machine that allows computers to communicate with other computers over telephone lines. It can be inside the computer or an external machine.
monitor	A part of a computer system that shows information on a screen.
printer	A part of a computer system that produces printed material.
software	Programs that are used to operate computers.

Word Processing Commands

These commands are often used in word processing. You can give each command by typing a key or a series of keys or selecting it from a menu.

Close	Closes the displayed document.
Copy	Copies selected, or highlighted, text.
Cut	Removes selected, or highlighted, text.
delete	Removes selected, or highlighted, text.
Find	Locates specific words or phrases in a document.
New	Opens a blank document.
Open	Displays a selected document.
Paste	Inserts copied or cut text in a new location in the same or another document.
Print	Prints the displayed document.
Quit	Leaves the program.
return	Moves the cursor to the beginning of the next line.
Save	Stores a document for later use.
shift	Allows you to type a capital letter or a new character.
Spelling	Activates the spelling tool.
tab	Indents the cursor to the right.

Using E-mail, Voice Mail, and Faxes

E-mail

Writing an e-mail is different from writing a letter or talking on the phone. Follow these guidelines to write good e-mail messages.

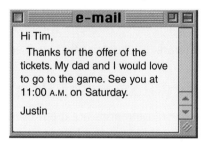

e-mail

Hi Tim,

Thanks for the offer of the tickets. My dad and I would love to go to the game. See you at 11:00 A.M. on Saturday.

Justin

Guidelines for Using E-mail Effectively

1. Give your message a specific title in the subject line. The recipient should know the subject before opening the e-mail.

2. Keep your paragraphs short. Long paragraphs are difficult to read on-screen.

3. Skip a line instead of indenting when you begin a new paragraph. Your message will be easier to read on-screen.

4. Remember that special type, such as italics or underlining, may not show up on the recipient's screen.

5. Be careful how you use humor. The other person can't hear your tone of voice and may not be able to tell when you're joking.

6. Follow the rules of good writing. An e-mail may seem more casual than a letter, but what and how you write reflects on *you*.

7. Proofread your messages, and fix all capitalization, punctuation, usage, and spelling mistakes.

8. Be sure that an e-mail is the best way to send your message. Sometimes a phone call or a letter is better.

Voice Mail

Voice mail is an alternative to e-mail. Follow these guidelines for recording a message, which you leave for someone else, and a greeting, which you record to answer incoming calls.

Guidelines for Recording a Message

1. Make notes or mentally plan what you want to say beforehand.
2. Speak clearly when giving important information such as phone numbers or addresses.
3. Be concise.
4. Sign off in a pleasant manner.

Guidelines for Recording a Greeting

1. Speak clearly.
2. Record your greeting in a quiet place with no background noise.
3. Make your greeting short. Don't make your caller wait!
4. Tell the caller how to respond. For example, you can ask for the caller's name, the time of the call, a brief message, and a phone number where the caller can be reached.

Faxes

When you want to send a paper document or a document with complex graphics, a fax (short for *facsimile*) may be the best option. Follow these guidelines for sending a fax.

Guidelines for Sending a Fax

1. Make sure that the font used in your document is large enough to be read easily.
2. Use dark ink for any handwriting. Pencil does not show up well.
3. Fill out a cover sheet or label, including the total number of pages, the recipient's name and fax number, your name, and your phone number.
4. Call the recipient to make sure the fax has arrived.

Using a Spelling Tool

Your computer's spelling tool can help you proofread your writing. Having a spelling tool on your computer doesn't mean you don't have to know how to spell, though.

Look at this letter. Do you see any misspelled words? If you do, you're smarter than a spelling tool because it didn't find any of the mistakes.

A spelling tool can't find a misspelled word that is the correct spelling of another word.

A spelling tool can't tell the difference between homophones.

A spelling tool doesn't know whether two words are supposed to be one word.

Letter

Dear Amy,

How our you? Its Tuesday night, and I kneed to write a science report, but I wanted to say hi to you first. I'm going to try out for a singing role in the school musical. Auditions are to day at four o'clock. I'll tell you what happens!

Your friend,
Aja

Be careful of troublesome homophones that you use every day, such as *it's* and *its*, *your* and *you're*, and *they're*, *there*, and *their*.

Think of a spelling tool as a proofreading partner. The spelling tool can help you find mistakes in your writing, but you still need to proofread to make sure the spelling tool didn't miss anything.

Computers and the Writing Process

Computers can help you plan, draft, revise, proofread, and publish your writing more efficiently. Here are some ideas for using a computer in the writing process.

PREWRITING

Type your thoughts as you think of them. Don't worry about completing your sentences or grouping ideas together. You can use the Cut and Paste commands to make changes later.

Dim the screen to help you concentrate on your thoughts rather than on correctness.

Create outlines, charts, or other graphic organizers to help you plan your writing. **Tip:** Some writing programs have ready-to-use graphic organizers that you just fill in.

Life in Space

I. Effects of weightlessness
    A. Changes in body features
        1. Wrinkles eliminated
        2. Foot size reduced
        3. One or two inches added
           to body height
    B. Changes in posture
        1. Slight crouch when standing
        2. Backward lean when sitting

DRAFTING

Save your prewriting notes and ideas under a new name, and then expand a list or an outline into a draft.

Boldface or underline words you may want to change later.

Double-space your draft so that you can write revisions on your printout.

Save early and often!

more ▶

Computers and the Writing Process *continued*

REVISING

Save a copy of your file under a new name before you begin making changes.

Conference with a partner right at the computer. Read your draft aloud and discuss any questions or problems you have. Then insert your partner's comments in capital letters. Later you can decide which comments you agree with.

Use the Cut and Paste commands to make changes. Move or delete words, sentences, or paragraphs with just a few clicks. **Tip:** If you're unsure about cutting something, just move text to the end of your document. You can always cut those "throwaways" later.

Rewrite problematic sentences or paragraphs under your original text. Boldface your new text and compare the different versions. Delete the version you don't want.

Use the Find and Replace commands to check for overused words. Enter words such as *and, then, pretty,* or *nice* in the Find function. When the word is found, click Replace and type in your change. You can also simply boldface the word and revise it later.

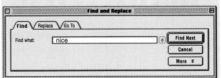

Use the electronic thesaurus in your word-processing program to find synonyms. Be careful to choose a synonym that has the meaning you want.

```
Thesaurus: English (US)
Looked Up:              Replace with Synonym:
nice                    pleasant
Meanings:               agreeable
pleasant                likeable
friendly                delightful
                        superior
                        good
                        admirable
                        pleasing
          Insert   Look Up   Cancel   Previous
```

PROOFREADING

Use your word processor's spelling tool. Then check for errors a spelling tool won't catch! See "Using a Spelling Tool" on page H46.

Turn your sentences into a list. Place the cursor after each end punctuation mark, and press Return. Now you can easily spot sentences that are too long or too short, run-on sentences, and fragments. You can also make sure that each sentence begins with a capital letter. When you're finished proofreading, simply delete the extra returns.

Computers make publishing your writing a snap. Here's how you can create professional-looking final products.

Choose your fonts carefully. Designers suggest using no more than three fonts per page.

Times Century

Helvetica

Choose a type size that can be read easily, but remember, type that is too big can look silly. Twelve-point type is usually a good choice.

10 point Times

12 point Times

14 point Times

Use bullets to separate the items in a list or to highlight a passage. On many computers, typing Option + 8 will produce a bullet (•).

Use other Option key combinations to make special pictures and symbols called *dingbats*. Many math and language symbols are included.

Design your title by changing the type size or font. Make a separate title page, if you like, and use your word processor's Borders and Shading functions to make the page fancy.

Add art to your paper or report.

- Use the computer's Paint or Draw functions to create your own picture.
- Cut and paste "clip art," which comes in a file on most computers.
- Use a scanner to copy images such as photographs onto your computer. You can then insert them electronically into your document.

If you don't have the equipment to create electronic art, simply leave a space in your document, print out a hard copy, and draw or paste in a picture.

more ▶

Computers and the Writing Process *continued*

PUBLISHING

Create tables, charts, or graphs to accompany your writing. For example, you can chart or graph the population growth in your town and include your findings in a research report.

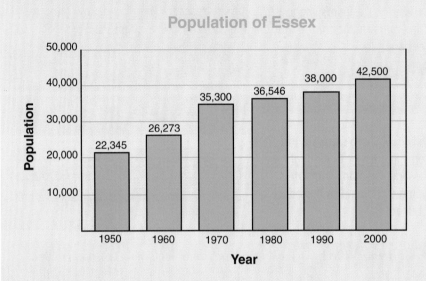

Population of Essex

Create newsletters, magazines, or brochures using word processing templates. Look at examples of real newspapers and magazines to see what kind of type to use, how big to make titles, and where to put pictures. Try combining electronic files to create a class newsletter that contains articles written by each of your classmates.

Choose your paper. White paper is always fine, but sometimes you may want to experiment with colored paper or stationery with borders or pictures. **Tip:** Check with an adult before changing the printer paper. Paper that is too thick or heavy can jam your printer.

Organize your writing in electronic folders. Create separate folders to store poems, stories, research reports, and letters. You can also make a folder for unfinished pieces.

Start an electronic portfolio for special pieces of your writing. You can create a portfolio folder on your hard drive or copy your files onto a floppy disk. Add pieces you choose throughout the year.

Using Technology

The Internet

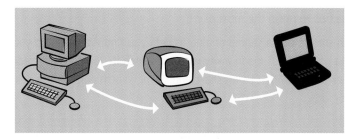

The **Internet** is a network of computers that connects people, businesses, and institutions all over the world. It lets computer users communicate with other computer users quickly and easily. Here are some of the many things you can do on the Internet.

- Do research on Web sites. You can watch a past president give a speech, take a tour of the White House, or hear music from the Great Depression. You can also search for current articles or historical documents.

- Visit an electronic bulletin board or chat room, where users "meet" to discuss specific topics. Here you can join an online book club, chat with other students who enjoy baseball, or debate current events.

- Send e-mail to your friends and family. Anyone who is online is reachable. See "Using E-mail, Voice Mail, and Faxes" on pages H44–H45.

- Use special software to create your own Web site. You design the page, write the text, and choose links to other sites. Your school may also have its own Web site where you can publish your work.

Tech Tip Visit Education Place at www.eduplace.com/kids/hme/ for fun activities and interesting information.

more ▶

The Internet *continued*

Tips for Using the Internet

Although the Internet can be a great way to get information, it can be confusing. Use these tips to make the most of it!

- Search smart! Use a search engine to help you find Web sites on your topic or area of interest. Type in a key word or search by topics. Many search engines also provide tips on searching. Some search engines are designed just for kids.

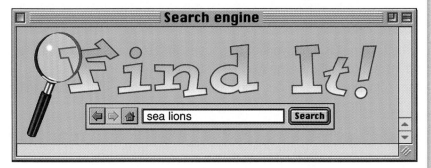

- Use quotation marks and words such as AND and OR to narrow your searches. Putting words in quotation marks tells the search engine to list only sites that contain those words in that order. Typing AND between words will bring up sites that contain all of those words. Typing OR between words will bring up sites that contain at least one of the words.

- Remember to write down the source of any information you find on the Internet just as you would do for a book. Along with the author, title, date of the material, and online address (URL), make sure you include the day you found the information. Information on the Internet can change daily.

- Check your sources carefully. The Internet is full of information, but not all of it is reliable. Web sites published by well-known organizations may be more trustworthy than those published by individuals.

- Protect your privacy. Never give your full name or address in a chat room.

Creating an Electronic Multimedia Presentation

An electronic multimedia presentation is a combination of text, images, and sound created on a computer. It lets you express much more than you could with just words. For example, an electronic multimedia presentation on volcanoes could contain a description of and animation showing the formation of a volcano, a recording of an interview with a geologist, photographs of Mount St. Helens and other volcanoes, and a video of an eruption.

Equipment

Here is what you need.

- a personal computer with a large memory
- high quality video and audio systems
- a CD-ROM drive
- a multimedia software program

Check with your school librarian or media specialist to find out what equipment is available.

Elements of an Electronic Multimedia Presentation

An electronic multimedia presentation may include text, photos and video, sound, and animation. Once you have created and selected the elements, an electronic multimedia authoring program lets you combine them.

Text The text of your presentation may include informative summaries, descriptions, directions, or photo captions. How the text appears on-screen is also important. You can adjust the font, size, and color of your text. **Tip:** Don't make your letters too small or put too many words on a single screen. Text should be easy to see and to read.

more ▶

Using Technology

Creating an Electronic Multimedia Presentation *continued*

Photos and Videos Images can be powerful, so choose them carefully. Here are some ways you can include pictures.

- Include a video that you film yourself.
- Scan in photos or artwork.
- Generate your own computer artwork.

Animation Computer animation lets you create objects and then bring them to life.

Two-dimensional animation lets you
- tell a story with animated figures,
- show an experiment being performed, or
- track changes in a chart or graph.

Three-dimensional animation lets you

- show how something is put together,
- show how something grows, or
- display an object from all sides.

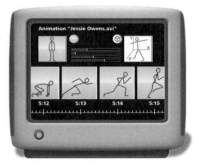

Sound Sound can help make an image or text come alive. Imagine viewing a video of track star Jesse Owens. Then imagine viewing the same video while listening to the cheers of the crowd and the crackle of the announcer's voice. You're practically in the stands! Here are some suggestions for using sound in your electronic multimedia presentation.

- Add appropriate background sounds— birds calling, water dripping, bells ringing.
- Use music to set a mood or emotion.
- Include songs that represent a time in history or emphasize a theme.
- Include a button to let users hear the text read aloud.
- Include audio to accompany video clips.

Using Technology

Designing an Electronic Multimedia Presentation

The process of designing an electronic multimedia presentation is similar to that of creating a piece of writing, but here are some additional things to consider.

Types of Media If you are planning a presentation on Mars, you might come up with the following list:

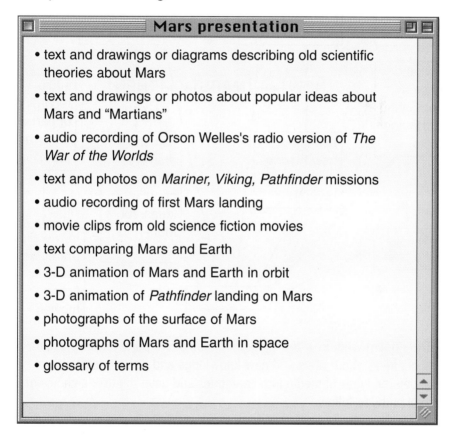

Mars presentation

- text and drawings or diagrams describing old scientific theories about Mars
- text and drawings or photos about popular ideas about Mars and "Martians"
- audio recording of Orson Welles's radio version of *The War of the Worlds*
- text and photos on *Mariner, Viking, Pathfinder* missions
- audio recording of first Mars landing
- movie clips from old science fiction movies
- text comparing Mars and Earth
- 3-D animation of Mars and Earth in orbit
- 3-D animation of *Pathfinder* landing on Mars
- photographs of the surface of Mars
- photographs of Mars and Earth in space
- glossary of terms

more ▶

Creating an Electronic Multimedia Presentation *continued*

Sequence Will the presentation have a specific order, or will you allow the user to choose his or her own path? A diagram, such as the one below, will help you plan.

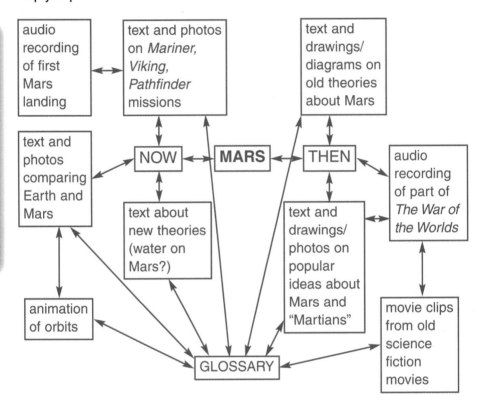

The student who drew this diagram planned two parts for his presentation: old ideas about Mars and new knowledge and discoveries. He then arranged the types of media into categories and gave the user a choice of several paths to follow.

Designing and creating an electronic multimedia presentation can be challenging and fun! **Tip:** As always, list your sources and write text in your own words. See the "Guide to Capitalization, Punctuation, and Usage" on pages H66–H67 for information on listing sources.

Keeping a Learning Log

A **learning log** is a notebook for recording what you learn in any of your subjects. It is a place to write facts and your thoughts about each subject.

Getting Started Write the date at the top of the page. Then use words, charts, or pictures—just get it all down on paper! Here's an example from one student's learning log.

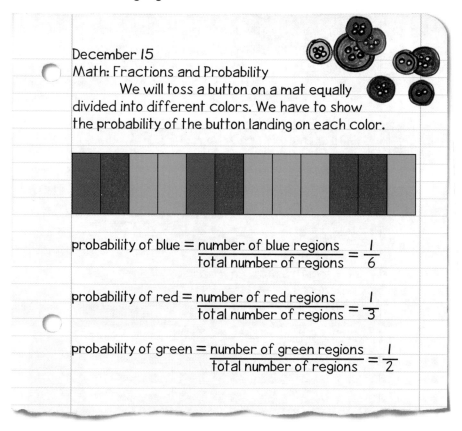

December 15
Math: Fractions and Probability
    We will toss a button on a mat equally divided into different colors. We have to show the probability of the button landing on each color.

probability of blue = $\dfrac{\text{number of blue regions}}{\text{total number of regions}} = \dfrac{1}{6}$

probability of red = $\dfrac{\text{number of red regions}}{\text{total number of regions}} = \dfrac{1}{3}$

probability of green = $\dfrac{\text{number of green regions}}{\text{total number of regions}} = \dfrac{1}{2}$

Try It Out Here are some suggestions for keeping a learning log.

- Make a vocabulary list for one subject. Include definitions.
- Work with classmates to record the results of a science experiment.
- Explain how fractions are similar to decimals. How are they different?
- Record your observations during a trip to a museum.
- Choose a country. Describe what it might be like to live there.
- Summarize what you have learned in a lesson in school.

Keeping a Writer's Notebook

A **writer's notebook** is a notebook you can keep just for writing. Make notes about ideas for stories, essays, or poems. List vivid words, record snippets of dialogue, or comment on authors you admire. Think of it as an artist's sketchbook. Write down whatever catches your eye.

When Do I Use It? Flip through your writer's notebook whenever you have a writing assignment. It can help you think of topic ideas, find exact words, recall details or dialogue, and develop support for a goal or an opinion. Parts of pages from one student's notebook are shown below.

Great Words

skewer   Tom skewered the paper with his pencil and spun it around.

befuddle I woke up befuddled and ate breakfast in the middle of the night.

On the Way to Aunt Susan's

We are in the car. We can't find Aunt Susan's new house.

"I can't read this map," my dad says. "This is a terrible map."

"Why don't you drive, Dad? Let Mom read the map," my sister says.

"I like to complain. What would I complain about if I were driving?"

Try It Out Start your own writer's notebook. Try some of these suggestions.

- Write about something your school needs.
- Copy examples of effective writing from a book or an article.
- Describe a surprising, frightening, or funny experience.
- List descriptive words. Then write a sentence to show how each one can be used.
- Describe certain sounds, such as a faucet dripping into a pan of water.
- List reasons why you like a sport or other activity.

Graphic Organizers

Are you stuck for an idea to write about? Are you confused about how to organize your ideas? Try using these graphic organizers to help you explore and plan your ideas.

Clusters or webs are good for brainstorming topics, exploring ideas, or organizing information. Write your topic in a center circle. Write details about your topic, circle them, and connect them to the center circle. Add more details to each circle.

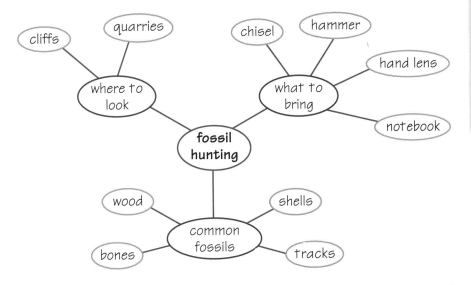

Inverted triangles can help you narrow topics that are too big. Write a broad topic in the first section of the triangle. Then write one part of that topic below it. Then write one part of the second topic. Keep going until you get a focused topic.

You can also use an inverted triangle to organize your details from most to least important.

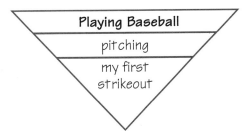

more ▶

Graphic Organizers *continued*

Planning charts help you organize your thinking about your purpose, your goals, and your audience before you begin to write.

My Topic _____

My Purpose	My Goals	My Audience
Circle one or more.	*Name at least one.*	*Answer these questions.*
• to tell a story • to explain • to persuade • to share • to plan • to learn • other _____		1. Who is my audience? 2. What do they know about my topic? 3. What do I want them to know? 4. What part would interest them most?

Time order charts are planning tools. They can be used after you have explored your topic by freewriting, listing, or using a cluster. Transfer the information from your brainstorming session into the boxes. Add more information where you see gaps.

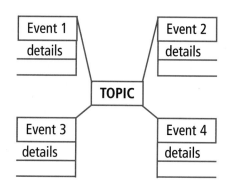

Story maps help you to gather details about setting, characters, and plot. Write notes in each section.

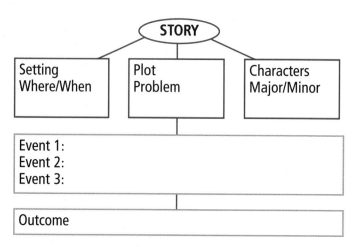

Observation charts organize details gathered through your five senses. Use them to add details to your writing. List details for your senses in separate columns. Depending on your topic, you may have more details in one column than another or no details at all.

Rainy Bus Ride				
sight	**sound**	**touch**	**taste**	**smell**
foggy windows yellow slickers water dripping wet hair	windshield wipers slapping wheels splashing	soggy lunch bag		wet clothes stuffy air

Writer's Tools

T-charts organize information into two groups. Use T-charts to lists details about two people, places, or things. They are also helpful for exploring two sides of an argument, showing likenesses and differences, or showing two points of view.

Draw a large T. Write your subjects at the top. Write details about each subject in the column below it. You may want to match the information in the columns.

me	my parents
listen to hip hop	listen to jazz
sleep late on weekends	get up early
always order French fries	ask for rice or baked potatoes

Step-by-step charts help you to plan your instructions. List the materials that are needed to follow your instructions. Then write each step in order. Include details your audience needs to know to complete each step.

Materials _____	
Steps	**Details**
Step 1 _____	_____
Step 2 _____	_____
Step 3 _____	_____

more ▶

Graphic Organizers *continued*

Venn diagrams are used to compare and contrast two subjects. Write details that tell how the subjects are different in the outer circles. Write details that tell how the subjects are alike where the circles overlap.

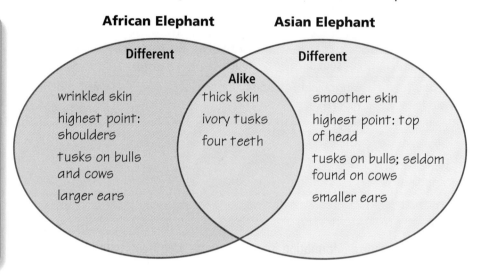

African Elephant   **Asian Elephant**

Different   **Alike**   **Different**

African Elephant (Different)	Alike	Asian Elephant (Different)
wrinkled skin	thick skin	smoother skin
highest point: shoulders	ivory tusks	highest point: top of head
tusks on bulls and cows	four teeth	tusks on bulls; seldom found on cows
larger ears		smaller ears

Persuasion maps can help you plan convincing arguments. Begin by stating your goal, a specific action you want a specific audience to take. Then write at least three reasons why your audience should do what you're suggesting. List facts and examples that elaborate your reasons.

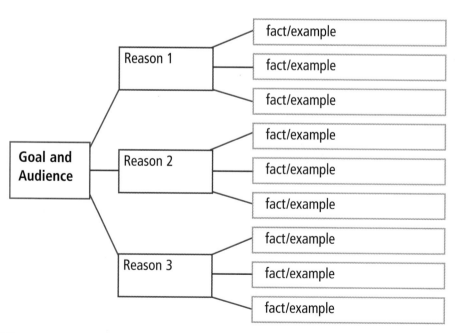

Writer's Tools

KWL charts show what you already **know** about a topic, what you **want** to know about it, and what you **learn** after doing research.

Mount Vesuvius		
What I Know	**What I Want to Know**	**What I Learned**
It's a volcano in Italy. It destroyed Pompeii.	Is this volcano still active? Do people live nearby?	The volcano is still active. Two million people live nearby.

ISP charts show **information (I)**, **sources (S)**, and, if appropriate, the **page references (P)** where you found the information.

Elephants		
I	**S**	**P**
largest teeth on the planet	Knowitall Encyclopedia	50
can weigh up to 7 tons	from the same source	102
don't drink through their trunks	zookeeper, Stone Zoo	

Time lines show events in order and tell when they happened. Draw an arrow, and write or draw events along it in order from left to right. Specify when each event took place.

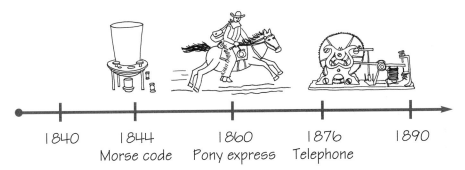

1840   1844   1860   1876   1890
        Morse code   Pony express Telephone

Abbreviations

Abbreviations are shortened forms of words. Most abbreviations begin with a capital letter and end with a period.

Titles	Mr. *(Mister)* Dr. *(Doctor)* Mrs. *(married woman)* Sr. *(Senior)* Ms. *(any woman)* Jr. *(Junior)* NOTE: *Miss* is not an abbreviation and does not end with a period.
Initials	John F. Kennedy *(John Fitzgerald Kennedy)* E. M. Forster *(Edward Morgan Forster)*
Days of the week	Sun. *(Sunday)* Thur. *(Thursday)* Mon. *(Monday)* Fri. *(Friday)* Tues. *(Tuesday)* Sat. *(Saturday)* Wed. *(Wednesday)*
Months of the year	Feb. *(February)* Sept. *(September)* NOTE: Do not abbreviate *May, June,* and *July.*
Time	A.M. *(midnight to noon)* P.M. *(noon to midnight)*
Words used in addresses	St. *(Street)* Rte. *(Route)* Rd. *(Road)* Apt. *(Apartment)* Ave. *(Avenue)* Pkwy. *(Parkway)* Dr. *(Drive)* Mt. *(Mount or Mountain)* Blvd. *(Boulevard)* Expy. *(Expressway)*
Words used in business	Co. *(Company)* Corp. *(Corporation)* Inc. *(Incorporated)* Ltd. *(Limited)*
Other abbreviations	**Some abbreviations are all capital letters, with a letter standing for each important word.** P.D. *(Police Department)* P.O. *(Post Office)* R.N. *(Registered Nurse)* M.A. *(Master of Arts)* **Abbreviations for units of measure use neither capital letters nor periods. The only exception is the abbreviation for** *inch.* mph *(miles per hour)* in. *(inch)* l *(liter)* **Abbreviations of government agencies or national organizations do not usually have periods.** PBS *(Public Broadcasting Service)* NATO *(North Atlantic Treaty Organization)*

States	The United States Postal Service uses two capital letters and no period in each of its state abbreviations.
	AL *(Alabama)* LA *(Louisiana)* OH *(Ohio)*
	AK *(Alaska)* ME *(Maine)* OK *(Oklahoma)*
	AZ *(Arizona)* MD *(Maryland)* OR *(Oregon)*
	AR *(Arkansas)* MA *(Massachusetts)* PA *(Pennsylvania)*
	CA *(California)* MI *(Michigan)* RI *(Rhode Island)*
	CO *(Colorado)* MN *(Minnesota)* SC *(South Carolina)*
	CT *(Connecticut)* MS *(Mississippi)* SD *(South Dakota)*
	DE *(Delaware)* MO *(Missouri)* TN *(Tennessee)*
	FL *(Florida)* MT *(Montana)* TX *(Texas)*
	GA *(Georgia)* NE *(Nebraska)* UT *(Utah)*
	HI *(Hawaii)* NV *(Nevada)* VT *(Vermont)*
	ID *(Idaho)* NH *(New Hampshire)* VA *(Virginia)*
	IL *(Illinois)* NJ *(New Jersey)* WA *(Washington)*
	IN *(Indiana)* NM *(New Mexico)* WV *(West Virginia)*
	IA *(Iowa)* NY *(New York)* WI *(Wisconsin)*
	KS *(Kansas)* NC *(North Carolina)* WY *(Wyoming)*
	KY *(Kentucky)* ND *(North Dakota)*
Numbers	**Spell out numbers under one hundred and numbers at the beginning of a sentence. Use numerals for numbers over one hundred.**
	My team has twenty-five players.
	Two hundred sixty people were in the audience.
	There are 174 apartments in my building.

Titles

Italicizing	**Titles of books, magazines, newspapers, long musical works, plays, works of art, movies, and TV series are italicized. The important words and the first and last words are capitalized.**
	In a Pickle (book) *As You Like It (play)*
	Miami Herald (newspaper) *Mona Lisa (painting)*
	Requiem (musical work) *Nature (TV series)*
Quotation marks	**Titles of short stories, articles, songs, poems, and book chapters are enclosed in quotation marks.**
	"The Party" *(short story)* "If" *(poem)*
	"Crewelwork" *(article)* "Saxon Art" *(chapter)*
	"America" *(song)*

more ▶

Capitalization / Punctuation / Usage

Guide to Capitalization, Punctuation, and Usage *continued*

Quotations

Quotation marks with commas and periods	Quotation marks are used to set a speaker's exact words apart from the rest of the sentence. The first word of a direct quotation begins with a capital letter. Question marks and exclamation points that belong to the quotation are placed inside the quotation marks. Question marks and exclamation points that do not belong to the quotation are placed outside the quotation marks. Commas separate a quotation from the rest of the sentence. Always place periods and commas inside quotation marks.
	"Where," Saul asked, "did I leave my keys?"
	Did Joe say, "I am going to Miami on my vacation"?
	Linda replied, "I don't know what time it is."

List of Sources/Bibliography

The basic organization of a list of sources is alphabetical. If the author's name is not given, list the title first, and alphabetize it by the first important word of the title.

NOTE: Most online and CD-ROM references will not come with all bibliographical information, especially author names. In these cases, students should simply cite the information that is available.

Books	List the author's name (last name first), the book title, the city where the publisher is located, the publisher's name, and the year of publication. Note the punctuation.
	Sbordoni, Valerio, and Forestiero, Saverio. *Butterflies of the World.* Buffalo, NY: Firefly Books, 1998.
CD-ROM	Citations for entire CD-ROMs are similar to those used for print sources. For a complete publication on a CD-ROM, list the author/editor (if available), the title of the work (italicized), the electronic medium, version, place of publication, publisher, and date.
	Ancient Lands. CD-ROM. Vers. 1.0. Redmond, WA: Microsoft, 1994.
	For part of a publication on a CD-ROM, add the title of the part (in quotation marks) before the title of the work.
	Hoyt, Reginald A. "Zebra." *World Book Multimedia Encyclopedia.* 1998 ed. CD-ROM. Chicago: World Book, Inc., 1998.

Encyclopedia article	List the author's name (last name first), then the title of the article (in quotation marks). Next, give the title of the encyclopedia (italicized) and the year of publication of the edition you are using. Note the punctuation. Ferrell, Keith. "Personal Computer." *The World Book Encyclopedia.* 1997 ed.
	If the author of the article is not given, begin your listing with the title of the article. "Charles River." *Collier's Encyclopedia.* 1997 ed.
Internet	For information found on a Web site, list the author/editor, the part title (in quotation marks), the source (italicized), location of the source, the date of the material (*n.d.* indicates no date of publication given), and the edition. Next, list the publication information: medium (e.g., Online), the electronic address, or URL, and the date of access. Kientz, Sue. "What Is It Like on Saturn and What Are the Rings Made Of?" *NASA Kids Corner* Washington, DC: NASA, n.d. Online. http://www.jpl.nasa.gov/cassini/kids/kidscorner.html. 27 Sept. 1999.
	For a magazine or newspaper article found on a Web site, list the author, article title (in quotation marks), the magazine or newspaper title (italicized), the date, edition, pages or paragraphs, medium, the URL, and the date of access. "The Kosovo Conflict." *New York Times* 19 May 1999: 9 pars. Online. http://www.nytimes.com/learning/students/writing/articles/april99b.html. 28 Sept. 1999.
Interview	To cite an interview, list the name of the person interviewed, the kind of interview (personal interview, telephone interview), and the date. Perez, Lucinda. Personal interview. 23 July 2000.
Magazine or newspaper article	Study these examples carefully. Note the order and the punctuation. **MAGAZINE:** Lemonick, Michael D. "A Very Close Call." *Time* Sept. 27, 1999: 34–37. **NEWSPAPER:** Lilley, Ray. "Airlift Rescues Ailing Doctor at South Pole." *Chicago Tribune* 16 Oct.1999, sec. News: 1, N. **NEWSPAPER:** (no author) "Habitat for Humanity to Dedicate Home." *South Bend Tribune* 9 Oct.1999, sec.Local/Area: a4.

more ▶

Guide to Capitalization, Punctuation, and Usage *continued*

Capitalization

Rules for capitalization	Capitalize geographical names such as cities, states, countries, continents, bodies of water, geographical features, and geographical areas. Do not capitalize small words like *the* and *of*.
	Paris Eastern Europe Asia Brazil Rock of Gibraltar Rio Grande Vermont the Northeast Yangtze River
	Do not capitalize directions. We live ten miles east of Philadelphia.
	Capitalize titles or their abbreviations when used with a person's name. Governor Bradford Senator Smith Dr. Lin
	Capitalize proper adjectives. We ate at a Hungarian restaurant. She is French.
	Capitalize the names of months and days. My birthday is on the last Monday in March.
	Capitalize the names of organizations, businesses, institutions, and agencies. National Hockey League The Status Company Franklin Mint Federal Aviation Administration
	Capitalize names of holidays and other special events, streets, highways, buildings, bridges, monuments, historical events, periods of time, and documents. Veterans Day World Trade Center Lincoln Memorial Jazz Age Route 9 Golden Gate Bridge French Revolution Bill of Rights
	Capitalize the first and last words and all important words in the titles of books, newspapers, stories, songs, poems, reports, and outlines. (Articles, short conjunctions, and short prepositions are not capitalized unless they are the first or last word.) *Julie of the Wolves* "The Necklace" "The Road Not Taken" "The Exports of Italy" *The New York Times* "Over the Rainbow" "Canadian National Parks"

Rules for capitalization *(continued)*	**Capitalize the first word of each main topic and subtopic in an outline.**
	
	I. Types of libraries
	   A. Large public library
	   B. Bookmobile
	   C. School library
	II. Library services

	Capitalize the first word in the greeting and closing of a letter. Dear Marcia, Dear Ms. Olsen: Your friend, Yours truly,
	Capitalize nationalities, races, languages, religions, religious terms, and specific school subjects followed by a number. Canadian Koran Buddhism Torah Old English Caucasian Spanish Geography 101

Punctuation

End marks	**A *period* (.) ends a declarative or imperative sentence. A *question mark* (?) follows an interrogative sentence. An *exclamation point* (!) is used after an exclamatory sentence and after an interjection that expresses strong feeling.** The scissors are on my desk. (declarative) Look up the spelling of that word. (imperative) How is the word spelled? (interrogative) This is your best poem so far! (exclamatory) Wow! (interjection) We've just won the essay prize.
Apostrophe	**To form the possessive of a singular noun, add an apostrophe and *s*.** sister-in-law's family's Agnes's
	To form the possessive of a plural noun that ends in s, add an apostrophe only. sisters' families' Joneses'
	For a plural noun that does not end in *s*, add an apostrophe and *s*. women's mice's sisters-in-law's

Capitalization / Punctuation / Usage

more ▶

Guide to Capitalization, Punctuation, and Usage *continued*

Punctuation *continued*

Apostrophe *(continued)*	**Use an apostrophe and *s* to form the plural of letters, numerals, symbols, and words that are used as words.** *s*'s *i*'s *2*'s ***'s Fill in the questionnaire with *yes*'s and *no*'s.
	Use an apostrophe in contractions in place of dropped letters. Do not use contractions in formal writing. isn't *(is not)* they've *(they have)* it's *(it is)*
Colon	**Use a colon to separate the hour from the minute.** 7:30 P.M. 8:15 A.M.
	Use a colon after the greeting in a business letter. Dear Mrs. Trimby: Dear Realty Homes:
	Use a colon before a list introduced by words like *the following* or *these*. Do not use a colon after a verb or a preposition. Call the following: Hester, Wanda, Doyle, and Carl. Next year I am taking English, history, and math. He arrived with a suitcase, a coat, and an umbrella.
Comma	**Use commas to separate words in a series.** Clyde asked if we had any apples, peaches, or grapes.
	Use commas between two or more adjectives that come before a noun. Do not use a comma if the adjectives are used together to express a single idea. Her shrill, urgent cry was alarming. The tired British tourists decided to rest.
	Use a comma to separate the simple sentences in a compound sentence. Some students were at lunch, but others were studying.
	Use commas after words, phrases, and clauses that come at the beginning of sentences. No, you cannot avoid the deadline. Following the applause, the speaker continued. When you are in doubt, ask for advice.
	Use commas to separate interrupters such as *of course, however,* and *by the way* from the rest of the sentence. Maureen, of course, was late for the bus again. The driver, however, had forgotten the directions.

Comma *(continued)*	**Use commas to set off an appositive from the rest of the sentence when the appositive is not necessary to the meaning of the sentence.** The writer Charles Dickens created complex plots. *(The appositive is necessary to the meaning.)* Texas, the Lone Star State, borders Mexico. *(The appositive is extra, not needed for meaning.)*
	Use a comma to separate a noun in direct address. Joe, help me fix this. How was your trip, Pa?
	Use a comma to separate the month and day from the year. Use a comma to separate the year from the rest of the sentence. Do not use commas if a specific day is not included. January 12, 1987, is the date of the banquet. Halley's Comet appeared during April 1986.
	Use a comma after an interjection that expresses mild emotion. Gee, I hope the bus comes soon.
	Use a comma between the names of a city and a state in an address. If the address is within a sentence, also use a comma after the name of the state. Do not use a comma before the ZIP code. Does Chicago, Illinois, have the world's tallest building? Denise lives at 10 Palm Court, Lima, OH 45807.
	Use a comma after the greeting in a friendly letter and after the closing in all letters. Dear Deena, Sincerely yours,
	Use commas to set off a nonessential phrase or clause, which adds optional information not necessary to the meaning of the sentence. If a phrase or clause is essential, do not use commas. Emily Dickinson, who was born in 1830, was a poet. *(The clause is not necessary to the meaning.)* The man who read the poem is my father. *(The clause is necessary to the meaning.)*

more ▶

Punctuation *continued*

Semicolon	**Use a semicolon to connect independent clauses that are closely related in thought or that have commas within them.**
	There were five movie tickets left; Ed needed six. He bought nuts, dates, and figs; we ate them all.
	Use a semicolon to join two independent clauses when the second clause begins with an adverb such as *however, therefore,* or *consequently*.
	It was growing dark; however, there were no clouds.
Hyphens, Dashes, Parentheses, Ellipses	**Use a hyphen to join the parts of compound numbers, inclusive numbering, to join two or more words that work together as one adjective before a noun, or to divide a word at the end of a line. Hyphens are also used in some compounds with *semi-, half-,* and *ex-*.**
	thirty-two long-range plans
	Raphael is known as one of Italy's many magnif-icent painters.
	semi-sweet half-mast ex-president
	Use dashes to show a sudden change of thought.
	The sky grew dark—it could mean snow.
	Use parentheses to enclose unnecessary information.
	Geraldine was reelected (once more) as treasurer.
	Use ellipses (three periods) to show omitted words or sentences.
	(Complete quote) "That is the last thing I remember about my walk last night. Then I woke up here."
	(Shortened quote) "That is the last thing I remember. . . . Then I woke up here." *(A period is added to the shortened sentence as well as ellipses.)*

Problem Words

Words	Rules	Examples
a, an	The indefinite articles *a* and *an* refer to any person, place, or thing. Use *a* before a word that begins with a consonant sound. Use *an* before a word that begins with a vowel sound.	a banana an apple

Words	Rules	Examples
the	The definite article *the* points out a specific noun or pronoun. Use *the* with both singular and plural nouns.	the apple the apples The books I like are long.
accept	The verb *accept* means "to receive."	The club accepted her.
except	The preposition *except* means "excluding."	They all went except James.
affect	The verb *affect* means "to influence."	The rain affected my plans.
effect	The verb *effect* means "to cause to happen."	They effected many changes.
	The noun *effect* means "result."	What effect has Sara had?
bad	*Bad* is an adjective. It can be used after linking verbs like *look* and *feel*.	This was a bad day. I feel bad.
badly	*Badly* is an adverb.	I play badly.
beside	*Beside* means "next to."	He is sitting beside me.
besides	*Besides* means "in addition to."	Who, besides Al, is going?
between	*Between* refers to two people or things.	I sat between Kyle and Pam.
among	*Among* refers to three or more people or things.	Talk among the four of you.
farther	Use *farther* to refer to physical distance.	Which town is farther away?
further	Use *further* in all other cases.	Please read further by tomorrow.
fewer	Use *fewer* or *fewest* with plural nouns.	Fewer boys are here today.
less	Use *less* or *least* with singular nouns.	I have the least money.
good	*Good* is an adjective.	The weather looks good.
well	*Well* is usually an adverb. It is used as an adjective only when it means "healthy."	She swims well. Do you feel well?
its	*Its* is a possessive pronoun.	The dog wagged its tail.
it's	*It's* is a contraction of *it is*.	It's cold today.

Capitalization / Punctuation / Usage

more ▶

Guide to Capitalization, Punctuation, and Usage   **H73**

Problem Words *continued*

Capitalization / Punctuation / Usage

Words	Rules	Examples
lie	*Lie* means "to rest, recline, or remain in one place."	The dog lies in its bed.
lay	*Lay* means "to put or place something."	Please lay the books here.
raise	*Raise* means "to move something up," "to increase something," or "to grow something."	Please raise the window. The store raised its prices. Maggie raises sunflowers.
rise	*Rise* means "to get up or go up."	The elevator rises slowly.
shall	*Shall* is used with *I* and *we* in formal English.	We shall be there today.
will	*Will* is used in all other cases.	He will go tomorrow.
their	*Their* is a possessive pronoun.	Their coats are on the bed.
there	*There* is an adverb. It may be used to begin a sentence.	Is Carlos there? There is my book.
they're	*They're* is a contraction of *they are*.	They're going to the store.
theirs	*Theirs* is a possessive pronoun.	This dog is theirs.
there's	*There's* is a contraction of *there is*.	There's his tag.
them	*Them* is not a demonstrative pronoun.	These (not Them) are mine.
to	*To* used as a preposition means "in the direction of."	They are going to the city.
	To can be used to form an infinitive.	Now is the time to leave.
too	*Too* is an adverb that means "more than enough" and "also."	She ate too many grapes. Can my sister go too?
two	*Two* used as an adjective is a number.	I have two notebooks.
whose	*Whose* is an interrogative pronoun.	Whose tickets are these?
	Whose is also a possessive pronoun.	Jan, whose book I borrowed, is here today.
who's	*Who's* is a contraction of *who is*.	Who's that woman?
your	*Your* is a possessive pronoun.	Are these your glasses?
you're	*You're* is a contraction of *you are*.	You're late again!

Comparing	**To compare two things, add -er to one-syllable adjectives and adverbs or use the word more.** This lily is taller than that one. It grew more quickly.
	To compare three or more things, add -est or use the word most. This lily is the tallest of all. It grew most quickly.
	Add -er or -est to short adjectives or adverbs. Use more or most and less or least with most modifiers of two or more syllables. thinner fastest less colorful most easily
Double comparisons	**Avoid double comparisons.** She is a better (not more better) skier than he. This is the deepest (not most deepest) snow ever!
Irregular comparisons	**Some adjectives and adverbs have special forms for making comparisons.**

Adjectives

good	better	best
bad	worse	worst
many	more	most
little	less	least
far	farther	farthest

Adverbs

well	better	best
badly	worse	worst
far	further	furthest

Position of adverbs	**An adverb such as *almost, even, hardly, just, nearly, merely, only,* or *scarcely* should be placed as close as possible to the word that it modifies.** Just Mark wants to come to the library. (Mark is the only person who wants to come.) Mark wants to come just to the library. (Mark wants to come to the library and nowhere else.)
fewer, less, much, many	**Use *little, less,* and *least* with things that cannot be counted. Use *few, fewer,* and *fewest* with countable things. Use *much* with uncountable things. Use *many* with countable things.** Is there less interest in Sullivan than in Wright? Are fewer skyscrapers being built now? The Hancock Building caused much trouble. Many windows fell out onto the street.

Capitalization / Punctuation / Usage

more ▶

Guide to Capitalization, Punctuation, and Usage *continued*

Adjective and Adverb Usage *continued*

real, really, sure, surely	*Real* and *sure* are adjectives. *Really* and *surely* are adverbs.
	This ring is made of real gold. Pat was sure of her answer.
	He is a really good skater. He surely is an excellent cook!

Negatives

Negatives	A double negative is the use of two negative words to express one negative idea. Avoid double negatives. *Barely, hardly,* and *scarcely* are considered negative words.
	INCORRECT: I didn't hardly have enough time.
	CORRECT: I hardly had enough time.

Pronoun Usage

Agreement	A pronoun must agree with the antecedent to which it refers.
	Kee bought a newspaper, but Mary read it first.
	Jeff and Cindy came to dinner. They enjoyed the meal.
Indefinite pronouns	An indefinite pronoun does not refer to a specific person or thing. When you use an indefinite pronoun as a subject, the verb must agree with it.
	Everyone is out. *(sing.)* Several were out. *(pl.)*
	Neither is here. *(sing.)* Many are here. *(pl.)*
	Pronouns must agree with indefinite pronouns used as antecedents.
	Each has its own name. Others forgot their books.
	Everyone should bring her own pencil.
Subject and object pronouns	A pronoun used as a subject or as a predicate pronoun (after a linking verb) is called a *subject pronoun*. It is in the *nominative case*.
	He composed many works for the piano.
	The writer was she.
	A pronoun used as an object is called an *object pronoun*. It is in the *objective case*.
	Clyde collected old coins and sold them. *(direct object)*
	Let's share these bananas with her. *(object of prep.)*
	She gave him a choice. *(indirect object)*

Compound subjects and objects	**To choose the correct pronoun in a compound subject or a compound object, say the sentence with the pronoun alone.** Pedro and I went hiking. (I went hiking.) Sara is visiting Al and me. (Sara is visiting me.)
Demonstrative pronouns this, that, these, those	**Do not use *this here, that there, these here,* or *those there.*** That (*not* That there) is a cute animal.
Incomplete comparisons	**To decide which pronoun form to use in an incomplete comparison, add the missing words.** Ben goes hiking more often than I (do). Lane gives him more help than (he gives) me.
Reflexive and intensive pronouns	**Do not use reflexive or intensive pronoun forms in place of personal pronouns.** INCORRECT: Ron and myself repaired the lamp. CORRECT: Ron and I repaired the lamp.
	Do not use *hisself* or *theirselves*. INCORRECT: Adam will do that hisself. CORRECT: Adam will do that himself. INCORRECT: They gave theirselves a head start. CORRECT: They gave themselves a head start.
I, me	***I* is used as a subject. *Me* is used as an object.** Jan and I are going to the show She is taking me.
	When using *I* or *me* with other nouns or pronouns, name yourself last. Beth and I will leave. Give the papers to Ron and me.
we, us	**Use the pronoun *we* with a noun that is the subject of the sentence or that follows a linking verb. Use the pronoun *us* with a noun that is an object.** We fans are proud. They saw us boys. It is we aunts again. He gave us girls a card.
who, whom	**Use the pronoun *who* as a subject. Use the pronoun *whom* as a direct object or object of a preposition.** Who was the surprise guest? *(subject)* Whom did you ask? (Did you ask whom?) *(direct object)* To whom did you speak? *(object of a preposition)*

more ▶

Capitalization / Punctuation / Usage

Pronoun Usage *continued*

who, whoever, whom, whomever	**The relative pronoun *who* or *whoever* can be used as the subject of a noun clause. The relative pronoun *whom* or *whomever* can be used as the object of a noun clause.**
	Whoever calls can talk to me. I'll give the message I know who is calling. to whomever it was Whom you meant is not clear. meant for.
who, whom, whose	**When the relative pronoun is the subject of an adjective clause, use *who*. When the relative pronoun is the object of a verb or a preposition in the relative clause, use *whom*. When the relative pronoun is possessive, use *whose*.**
	Jan is the student who has contributed the most. Jan is the writer whom we should all thank. Jan, whose stories are funny, will be our editor.

Verb Usage

Active and passive voice	**Use the passive voice when the doer of the action is unknown or unimportant. Use the active voice for direct, forceful sentences.**
	I baked the bread. (*not* The bread was baked by me.) The Erie Canal was completed in 1825.
Agreement: compound subjects	**A compound subject with *and* takes a plural verb.**
	Jason, Kelly, and Wanda have new dictionaries.
	A compound subject with *or* or *nor* takes a verb that agrees with the nearer subject.
	She or her cousins are ready to help. Her cousins or Paula is ready to help.
Agreement: titles, names, collective nouns, plural forms	**A title or name of a single thing takes a singular verb.**
	McNally, Doyle, and Hennessey is a law firm. *Journey Through Bookland* was Sophie's favorite book.
	A collective noun takes a singular verb unless the group's members are referred to.
	The committee is meeting at eight o'clock. The committee have different opinions about that issue.
	A noun with a plural form that names a single amount or item takes a singular verb.
	Ten dollars is too much to pay. (the whole amount)

Agreement: inverted and interrupted order	**Subject and verb must agree, no matter where the subject is.** In the pond were several frogs. The show of photographs is now open.		
Possessives with gerunds	**Use a possessive noun or a possessive pronoun before a gerund.** David's traveling took place on weekends. Their singing made the choir remarkable.		
Tenses	**Avoid unnecessary shifts in tense.** The sun came out, and we were (*not* are) surprised.		
	When a sentence describes actions that took place at two different times, use the past perfect for the earlier action and the past tense for the later action. Bob had trained hard, but he lost the match anyway.		
	When a sentence describes two actions in the future, use the future perfect for the earlier action and the present for the later action. I will have left for practice before the sun rises.		
	Use the present perfect for an action that occurred at an unspecified time in the past. She has ridden a horse only once.		
Irregular verbs	**Irregular verbs do not add -ed or -d to form the past participle. Their forms must be memorized. Use a form of *have* with the past participle.**		
	Verb	**Past**	**Past Participle**
	be	was	been
	choose	chose	chosen
	do	did	done
	eat	ate	eaten
	go	went	gone
	lay	laid	laid
	lie	lay	lain
	shine	shone	shone
	steal	stole	stolen
	tear	tore	torn
	throw	threw	thrown
	wear	wore	worn

Words Often Misspelled

You probably use many of the words on this list when you write. If you cannot think of the spelling of a word, you can always check this list. The words are in alphabetical order.

A

acquaintance
again
all right
a lot
always
anxious
anyone

B

basketball
beautiful
because
before
beige
believe
biscuit
brought
bureau

C

campaign
cannot
can't
captain
caught
clothes
colossal
coming
cousin

D

didn't
different
don't

E

eighth
enough
everyone
everything

F

family
favorite
field
finally
friend

G

getting
going
guarantee
guess
guy

H

happened
happily
haven't
heard
here

I

instead
its
it's

K

knew
know

M

might
millimeter
minuscule

N

nuisance

O

o'clock
once
outrageous

P

people
playwright
probably

R

really
received
right

S

someone
stopped
stretch
suppose
swimming

T

their
there
there's
they
they're
thought
through
to
tongue
tonight
too
two

U

usually

V

vacuum

W

weird
we're
whole
wouldn't
write

Y

your
you're

Spelling Guidelines

1. Short vowel sounds are usually spelled with just one vowel in one- or two-syllable words. Long vowel sounds are usually spelled vowel-consonant-*e* or with two vowel letters in one- or two-syllable words.

craft	passion	filter	raven	preach	deceit	donor
strict	meddle	option	theme	raisin	climax	unit
scrub	pennant	luster	roam	legion	triumph	

2. The |ô|, |îr|, |oi|, |ou|, |o͞o|, |o͝o|, |yo͞o|, |är|, |î|, |ôr|, and |ûr| sounds in words of two or more syllables are usually spelled the same as in one-syllable words.

haughty	noisy	flounder	intrude	booster	dilute	commute
merely	fully	wooden	frontier	superb	carton	cordial

3. If a word ends with **e**, the **e** is usually dropped before a suffix beginning with a vowel, such as **-ed** or **-ing**. If a word ends with a vowel and a single consonant and the final syllable is stressed, double the final consonant before adding **-ed** or **-ing**. If the suffix begins with a consonant, the final **e** is usually kept.

bubbling	donating	propelling	amusement
separating	occurred	regretted	scarcely

4. Spellings of final unstressed vowel sounds with **l**, **r**, or **n** must be remembered.

sample	rural	grammar	gallon
channel	error	litter	kitchen

5. The pronunciation of an unstressed final ending does not always give a clue to its spelling.

storage	image	relative	recognize	generous
sausage	positive	organize	exercise	

dairies	applied	sunnier	heaviest	dizziness	merciful

more ▶

Spelling Guidelines *continued*

6. If a word ends in a consonant + **y,** the **y** changes to **i** when the ending -**es, -ed, -er,** or -**est,** or the suffix -**ness, -ful,** or -**ly** is added.

dair**ies**	appl**ied**	sunn**ier**	heav**iest**	dizz**iness**	merc**iful**

7. Some words have unusual consonant spellings. Double consonant spellings often occur when prefixes or suffixes are added to a word or word root and when two words are joined to make a compound word.

she**ph**erd	a**ff**ectionate	sta**rr**y	ove**rr**ate
wrestle	a**gg**ravate	forbi**dd**en	u**nn**atural
de**bt**or	a**cc**ompany	contro**ll**er	mi**dd**ay
ras**pb**erry	fu**nn**y	tonsi**ll**itis	**irr**egular

8. The vowel + **r** sounds can be spelled in different ways.

y**ar**n	**ear**th	sk**ir**t	p**ier**ce	th**or**n	**ur**ge

9. Compound words may be spelled as one word, as a hyphenated word, or as two separate words.

newsstand	long-lived	cold front

10. To find the syllables of most VCCV words, divide the word between the consonants.

shou<u>l</u>der	bar<u>r</u>el	traf<u>f</u>ic	pat<u>t</u>ern	es<u>s</u>ay	sin<u>c</u>ere

11. When two different consonants in a VCCCV word spell one sound or form a cluster, divide the word into syllables before or after those two consonants.

laun<u>d</u>ry	mis<u>ch</u>ief	al<u>th</u>ough	com<u>pl</u>ex	func<u>t</u>ion	ex<u>tr</u>eme

12. To find the syllables of a VCV word, divide the word before or after the consonant.

ro<u>b</u>ot	clo<u>s</u>et	pre<u>f</u>er	re<u>p</u>eat	lo<u>g</u>ic	la<u>s</u>er

13. The |sh| sound is spelled **sh, ss, ci,** or **ti.**

cu**sh**ion	se**ss**ion	pre**ss**ure	an**ci**ent	par**ti**al	men**ti**on

14. The final unstressed |ĭk| sounds are often spelled **ic**. The final |əs| sounds are often spelled **ous**. The |chər| sounds are often spelled **ture**.

fantast**ic**	specif**ic**	curi**ous**	jeal**ous**	tor**ture**

15. The final unstressed |əns| or |ns| sounds in some words are spelled **ance** or **ence**. The final |āt| or |ĭt| sounds are spelled **ate**.

entr**ance**	influ**ence**	viol**ence**	fortun**ate**	separ**ate**
allow**ance**	sent**ence**	abs**ence**	associ**ate**	desper**ate**
inst**ance**	sil**ence**	audi**ence**	celebr**ate**	appreci**ate**

16. Final |īz| sounds can be spelled **-ise**, **-ize**, or **-yze**.

desp**ise**	ana**lyze**	memor**ize**	para**lyze**

17. The rule "Use **i** before **e** except after **c** or when sounded as |ā|, as in **neighbor** or **weigh**" has exceptions.

bel**ie**f	f**ie**ry	y**ie**ld	d**ie**sel	rec**ei**pt	for**ei**gn
spec**ie**s	rev**ie**w	th**ie**f	dec**ei**ve	fr**ei**ght	l**ei**sure

18. The prefix **con-** is spelled **com** before the consonant **m** or **p**.

confirm	**com**ment	**com**plicate
contest	**com**motion	**com**plete

19. The Latin prefixes **pre-**, **pro-**, **post-**, **ab-**, and **ad-**, and the Greek word part **anti-** bring meaning to words and word roots. The prefix **ab-** is spelled **abs-** before a root that begins with **c** or **t**.

prejudge	**anti**social	**pro**pel	**abs**cess	**post**pone	**ad**journ

20. The prefixes **dis-**, **ex-**, **inter-**, **de-**, **ob-**, **per-**, **pre-**, and **pro-** begin many words. The prefix **ob-** is spelled **oc** when followed by **c**.

disappear	**ex**perience	**de**bate	**ob**lige	**pro**cess
discovery	**inter**fere	**de**velop	**per**suade	**oc**cupy
exclaim	**inter**view	**ob**serve	**pre**paid	**oc**casion

21. The Latin prefix **ad-** may be spelled **af**, **ac**, **ap**, or **as**.

addition	**af**fair	**ac**count	**ap**prove	**as**sist	**as**sume

more ▶

22. The prefixes **in-**, **un-**, and **non-** may mean "not." Sometimes **in-** is changed to **ir-**, **il-**, or **im-** to match the spelling of the following consonant. Sometimes the prefixes **ad-** and **con-** also change their spelling to match the following consonant.

inaccurate	**ir**regular	**ap**petite	**com**municate
uncertain	**il**legal	**ac**cessory	**col**laborate
nonsense	**im**mature	**al**legiance	**cor**rupt

23. Combining **uni-**, **bi-**, **tri-**, and **semi-** with a word usually does not affect the spelling of the prefix.

universe	**uni**fy	**bi**cycle	**tri**color	**semi**circle	**semi**final

24. The suffix **-ion** can change verbs to nouns.

except	excep**tion**	situate	situa**tion**	conclude	conclus**ion**

25. The suffixes **-ure**, **-age**, **-ion**, **-ment**, **-or**, and **-er** can affect the spelling of words or word roots.

tex**ture**	bond**age**	orna**ment**	opin**ion**	modera**tor** lectur**er**

26. The suffixes **-ent**, **-ant**, **-ious**, **-ous**, **-able**, **-ible**, **-ile**, **-ial**, and **-al** form adjectives.

excell**ent**	prec**ious**	prob**able**	frag**ile**	artific**ial**
hesit**ant**	marvel**ous**	tang**ible**	fac**ial**	man**ual**

27. The noun suffixes **-ness**, **-dom**, **-ment**, and **-ian** sometimes affect the spelling of base words.

aware**ness**	free**dom**	king**dom**	argu**ment**	equip**ment**	comed**ian**

28. The suffix **-able** is usually added to base words. The suffix **-ible** is usually added to word roots.

desir**able**	reli**able**	allow**able**	leg**ible**	divis**ible**	aud**ible**

29. The suffixes **-ory**, **-ary**, and **-ery** are often joined to word roots. When the sound is not clear, the spelling must be remembered.

laborat**ory**	ordin**ary**	myst**ery**

30. Think of a related word before spelling the suffixes **-ant**, **-ance**, **-ent**, and **-ence**.

significant significance   intelligent intelligence   assistant assistance

31. The Latin prefixes **trans-** and **sub-** appear in many words. When **sub-** is added to a word or root beginning with **p,** the prefix becomes **sup-**.

transaction	**trans**fuse	**sub**merge	**sup**posedly
translate	**sub**urban	**sup**plement	**sup**ply

32. The Greek suffix **-logy** means "study of." It is often used with Greek roots.

socio**logy**	zoo**logy**	psycho**logy**
geo**logy**	mytho**logy**	anthropo**logy**

33. Words that are related in spelling and meaning are easier to remember in pairs.

severe   severity   excel   excellence   assume   assumption

34. Many English words came from ancient Greek, French, Spanish, and other languages. These words often have unusual spellings.

sphinx	fillet	lariat	kayak
pharmacy	brunette	sierra	ukulele

35. Some English words are formed from the names of people or places. Many of these words are no longer capitalized.

Braille	sequoia	cologne	cheddar
tuxedo	pasteurize	silhouette	Olympic

36. Some spelling problems can be solved through careful pronunciation.

chimney	governor	probably	temperament

37. The spelling of similar words is often confused. Note their sound, spelling, and meaning.

access   excess   dessert   desert   coma   comma

Diagramming Guide

When you diagram a sentence, you show the relationships among all its different parts. These lessons are designed to lead you through the diagramming process. In the first lessons, you will diagram only the basic parts of the sentence. In these first lessons, you will find certain structures that you do not yet know how to diagram. Do not be concerned. Diagram only those words for which you have directions. As you progress, you will eventually learn to diagram all the given constructions.

Subjects and Predicates

The two main parts of the sentence are the subject and the predicate. In a diagram the simple subject and the simple predicate are placed on a horizontal line called the **base line**. The simple subject is separated from the simple predicate by a vertical line that cuts through the base line.

Each child wore a different costume.

child	wore

In an imperative sentence, a sentence that gives a command, the subject is understood to be "you." Notice how the simple subject and the simple predicate are diagrammed.

Look at the knight's armor.

(you)	Look

Practice

Diagram each simple subject and simple predicate.

1. Mr. Antonavich designed the gorilla suit.
2. Gus fanned his peacock feathers proudly.
3. Listen to the guitar music.
4. First prize went to the child inside the papier-mâché guitar.
5. Many costumes imitated the movie stars' clothes.

Compound Subjects and Predicates

The parts of a compound subject or compound predicate are written on separate horizontal lines. The conjunction is written on a vertical dotted line joining the horizontal lines. Study the example at the top of the next page.

Charlie Chaplin, Ike, and Napoleon chatted and laughed together.

Practice

Diagram the simple or compound subject and the simple or compound predicate in each sentence.

1. Masks, makeup, and hats were popular disguises.
2. Babe Ruth and Eleanor Roosevelt wore authentic costumes.
3. Parents and teachers watched and enjoyed each child's act.
4. A clown, a giraffe, and a helicopter led the costume parade.

Predicate Nouns

Diagram predicate nouns by writing them on the base line after the verb. Between the verb and the predicate noun, draw a line slanting toward the subject to show that the subject and the predicate noun refer to the same thing. Study this example.

The automobile is a modern invention.

Notice how you diagram a sentence with a compound predicate noun.

The windshield is a protective barrier and a window.

Practice

Diagram the subjects, the verbs, and the predicate nouns in the following sentences.

1. Oliver Evans was an inventor and a steam engine designer.
2. Steam automobiles became the closest rival of the railroad.
3. Gottlieb Daimler and Karl Benz were the developers of the gasoline engine.
4. The trunk of a car was a large metal box originally.

more ▶

Predicate Adjectives

Diagram a predicate adjective on the base line after the verb. Draw a line slanting back toward the subject to show that the predicate adjective modifies the subject.

Study these diagrams of predicate adjectives.

In the late 1890s, the electric car was popular.

Steam cars had been impractical, noisy, and smelly.

Practice

Diagram the subjects, verbs, and predicate adjectives.

1. The world's first gasoline-powered vehicle was clumsy.
2. These carriages were horseless.
3. In the 1900s a muddy road could be messy and dangerous.
4. By 1908 the parts for cars of the same model were interchangeable.

Direct Objects

Diagram a direct object by writing it on the base line after the verb. Separate the direct object from the verb by a vertical line, but do not let the line cut through the base line.

Tom and Diane designed their new kitchen together.

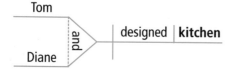

Study the diagram of a compound direct object.

They selected new appliances, cabinets, and fixtures.

Diagram each subject, verb, and direct object.

1. A carpenter and a plumber prepared the room for renovations.
2. Tom borrowed two ladders and some old canvas.
3. Tom, Diane, and her mother selected curtains for the windows.

Indirect Objects

Diagram an indirect object on a horizontal line below the base line. Draw a slanting line to connect it to the verb.

Mr. Talbot made us salads for lunch.

Mr. Talbot	made	salads

us

Diagram the following sentences, showing the subjects, the verbs, the direct objects, and the indirect objects.

1. Catherine baked us a loaf of French bread.
2. I offered Dad a piece.
3. Dad told us a story about a Paris restaurant.

Adjectives

Diagram an adjective or any of the articles *a, an,* or *the* by placing it on a slanting line under the word it modifies. Join a series of adjectives with a dotted line parallel to the base line. Note where *and* is placed.

Most supermarkets carry fresh, frozen, and canned foods.

Diagram all of the words in the following sentences.

1. The produce section contains fresh fruit.
2. Broccoli and peas are nutritious green foods.
3. A tall, thin, blond man bought some green seedless grapes.

more ▶

Adverbs

Diagram an adverb by placing it on a slanting line under the word that it modifies. Write the conjunction joining two or more adverbs on a dotted line between them.

The rather large wedding was planned quickly but carefully.

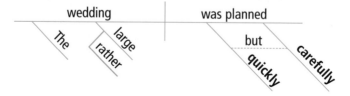

Practice

Diagram all of the words in the following sentences.

1. Some very traditional music was chosen finally.
2. The bride and groom made a relatively long guest list.
3. They discussed their rather complex plans frequently and happily.
4. Fortunately they found an outstandingly creative caterer.

Prepositional Phrases

Diagram a prepositional phrase by writing it under the word it modifies. Place the preposition on a line slanting from the base line. Place the object of the preposition on a horizontal line. Diagram its modifiers in the usual way.

The fancy lettering was done by the hand of a calligrapher.

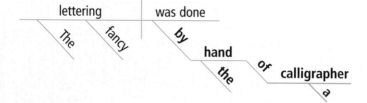

Practice

Diagram all of the words in the following sentences.

1. Calligraphers hold their pens at a certain angle.
2. The tip of the pen is selected for its width.
3. This nib is attached to an ink pen.
4. Calligraphers paint decorations in the margins of their parchments.

Participles and Participial Phrases

Diagram a participle like a prepositional phrase. In a participial phrase, the participle is followed by the word that completes the phrase.

Applauding the superstar wildly, they watched his hurried arrival.

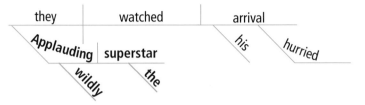

Practice

Diagram all of the words in the following sentences.

1. Happily, they saw him descending the airplane steps.
2. Shouting his name repeatedly, the crowd followed his every move.
3. The smiling film idol loved their totally unquestioning approval.

Gerunds and Gerund Phrases

Before you diagram a gerund, first write the other parts of the sentence on the base line. Then add the standard, or pedestal, for the gerund or the gerund phrase. Each gerund curves down "steps" in the standard, as shown in the example.

The key to managing Katie's puppy is daily training.

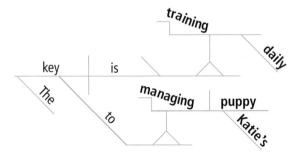

Practice

Diagram all of the words in the following sentences.

1. Developing good habits in her puppy was Katie's goal.
2. Repeating Daffy's name with each command was important.
3. Another important factor in pet rearing is being consistent.

more ▶

Diagramming Guide *continued*

Infinitives and Infinitive Phrases

When an infinitive or an infinitive phrase is used as a subject, a direct object, or a predicate noun, place it on a standard. If an infinitive is used as a modifier, diagram it as you would a prepositional phrase.

To publish a cookbook was hard to accomplish.

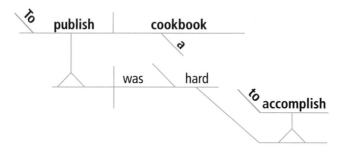

Practice

Diagram the following sentences completely.

1. To organize the recipes into categories seemed more logical to others.
2. To find a chicken recipe meant looking in the poultry section.
3. The reader uses an alphabetical index to locate each recipe.
4. The cookbooks to be sold at the bazaar will raise funds for the needy.

Appositives

Diagram an appositive by enclosing it in parentheses after the noun or the pronoun that it explains. Find the appositive in the sentence at the top of the next page. Then study how the appositive and its modifiers are diagrammed.

Dr. Carl Cohen, my periodontist, specializes in gum diseases.

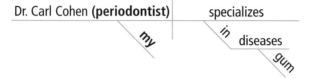

Practice

Diagram all of the words in the following sentences.

1. Debbie Carleton, a dental hygienist, taught me to floss correctly.
2. Gingivitis, a common periodontal disease, inflames the gum tissue.
3. Gums can be irritated by plaque, a sticky form of bacteria.

Compound Sentences

Diagram each clause of a compound sentence as if it were a separate sentence. Place the conjunction joining the clauses on a horizontal line to connect the verbs in the clauses.

William Shakespeare lived in Stratford-upon-Avon, but Anne Hathaway, his wife, grew up in Shottery.

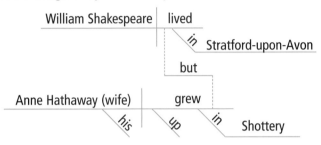

Practice

Diagram the following sentences.

1. Shakespeare began his career as an actor, but he earned his fame as a playwright.
2. His birthplace is on Henley Street, and many tourists visit it each day.
3. John Shakespeare, the writer's father, was a glovemaker, but he became mayor of Stratford-upon-Avon in 1568.

Complex Sentences: Adverb Clauses

Place an adverb clause below the word that it modifies in the main clause, and diagram it as if it were a separate sentence. Place the subordinating conjunction on a dotted line to connect the verb in the clause with the word that the clause modifies. Study the example below.

If the bus fare increases, some commuters will form a car pool.

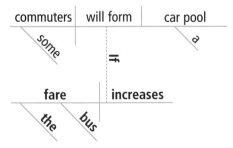

more ▶

Diagramming Guide *continued*

Practice

Diagram the following sentences.

1. Because they travel to the office on weekdays, they need five passengers.
2. Although the driving schedule is flexible, each person is responsible for one day of every week.
3. After the car pool was organized, Dave's day to drive was Thursday.
4. While some passengers nap during the commute, others read.

Complex Sentences: Adjective Clauses

Place an adjective clause below the noun or pronoun that it modifies in the main clause, and diagram it as if it were a separate sentence. Draw a dotted line to connect the relative pronoun in the clause with the noun or pronoun that the clause modifies. Study the example below.

Students who are going to the concert will be excused early.

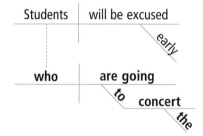

Practice

Diagram the following sentences.

1. The teachers who went on the field trip enjoyed themselves.
2. They all brought shoes that had extra support for walking.
3. The trip, which was paid for by the school, was very educational.
4. One museum that they planned to visit was closed.

Noun Clauses

A noun clause is diagrammed on a standard. First, write the other parts of the sentence on the base line, and then add the standard. Where you place the standard will depend on whether the noun clause is used as a subject, a direct object, an indirect object, an object of a preposition, or a predicate noun. In the following example, the noun clause is used as a direct object.

That girl always says whatever comes into her mind.

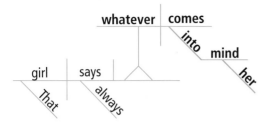

Practice

Diagram the following sentences.

1. The science class is what Roger likes best.
2. Students are often influenced by what they learn in class.
3. That Julianna is a good student is obvious to everyone.
4. Give whoever missed class the homework assignment.
5. Do you know why we are having a test tomorrow?

Nouns in Direct Address

A noun in direct address is diagrammed on a short line above and a bit to the left of the base line. This is its position no matter where the noun in direct address appears in the sentence.

Think, everyone, about our recent discussion and then try again.

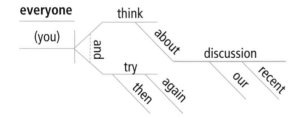

Practice

Diagram all of the words in these sentences.

1. Do you have any notes, Marcy?
2. I do not, sir.
3. She was sick, teacher, with the flu.
4. Now, George, I remember.
5. Children, form small groups and compare your notes.

Thesaurus Plus

How to Use This Thesaurus

When do you use a thesaurus? You use one when you want to make your writing more exact or more interesting. Suppose you wrote the following sentence:

After Ted cleaned the dirty window, it was clear.

Is *clear* the most exact word you can use? To find out, use your Thesaurus Plus.

Look up Your Word Turn to the Thesaurus Plus Index on page H98. You will find this entry.

clear, *adj.*

Entry words are in blue type. Because *clear* is blue, you can look up *clear* in the Thesaurus Plus.

Use Your Thesaurus The main entries in the Thesaurus Plus are listed in alphabetical order. Turn to *clear*. You will find the following entry.

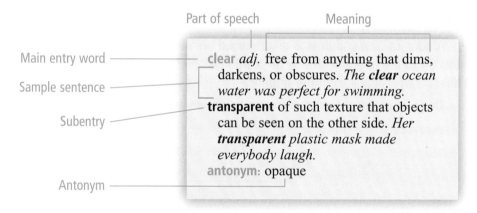

Part of speech

Meaning

Main entry word

Sample sentence

Subentry

Antonym

clear *adj.* free from anything that dims, darkens, or obscures. *The clear ocean water was perfect for swimming.*
transparent of such texture that objects can be seen on the other side. *Her transparent plastic mask made everybody laugh.*
antonym: opaque

Other Index Entries There are two other types of entries in your Thesaurus Plus Index.

1. The slanted type means that *convey* is a synonym of *move*.

2. The regular type tells you that *corrupt* is the opposite of *good*.

convey move, *v.*
convince persuade, *v.*
cool cold, *adj.*

corrupt good, *adj.*

A. Use your Thesaurus Plus Index to answer these questions.

1. Is *trait* a main word or a subentry word?
2. What part of speech is *amble*?
3. What is the main entry word for *rugged*?
4. Is *support* a subentry word or an antonym?

B. Use your Thesaurus Plus Index and Thesaurus Plus to answer these questions.

5. What antonyms are listed for *dark*?
6. How many subentries are listed for *reason*?
7. What does *relocate* mean?
8. How many antonyms are listed for *exciting*?
9. What part of speech is *scrumptious*?
10. What does *undisturbed* mean?
11. What is an antonym for *tired*?
12. What color is *vermilion*?
13. What subentries are listed for *rely*?
14. What is an antonym for *sudden*?

C. Use your Thesaurus Plus Index to find the entry for each underlined word. Then use the Thesaurus Plus to rewrite each sentence, using a more exact or interesting word.

15. Because of the American Revolution, the United States is not a part of the British Commonwealth.
16. The Boston Tea Party occurred before the Revolution.
17. Angry colonists boarded British ships and threw chests of tea into Boston Harbor.
18. They were expressing their objections to British rule.
19. The argument was about the British tax on tea.
20. It was the colonists' belief that the tax was unfair.
21. Rapidly they banded together to rebel.
22. Only a small quantity of colonists were pro-British.
23. The Declaration of Independence was an effect of the colonists' dissatisfaction with England.
24. On July 4, 1776, the Declaration of Independence said that the colonies should be self-governing.
25. The Treaty of Paris of 1783 brought an end to the war.
26. This was no little achievement for the colonists.

Thesaurus Plus

Thesaurus Plus Index

conscientious good, *adj.*
consent refuse, *v.*
consequence, *n.*
consider think, *v.*
contaminated bad, *adj.*
continue persist, *v.*
contract, *v.*
contrast, *v.*
converse talk, *v.*
convert change, *v.*
convey move, *v.*
convince persuade, *v.*
cool cold, *adj.*
corrupt bad, *adj.*
corrupt good, *adj.*
courageous brave, *adj.*
cowardly brave, *adj.*
crawl hurry, *v.*
creep hurry, *v.*
cried said, *v.*
crimson red, *adj.*
crisp cold, *adj.*
cunning sharp, *adj.*
current ancient, *adj.*

D

damage fix, *v.*
damage harm, *v.*
damp, *adj.*
dark, *adj.*
dark bright, *adj.*
dash hurry, *v.*
dawdle hurry, *v.*
dazzling bright, *adj.*
dazzling exciting, *adj.*
decadent good, *adj.*
declared said, *v.*
decline refuse, *v.*
decline reject, *v.*
definite sharp, *adj.*
delay hurry, *v.*
delectable good, *adj.*
delicious good, *adj.*
delightful bad, *adj.*
deny refuse, *v.*

depart move, *v.*
depend rely, *v.*
depressed happy, *adj.*
deprived rich, *adj.*
destroy, *v.*
detail, *n.*
dewy damp, *adj.*
dexterous good, *adj.*
difference likeness, *n.*
different alike, *adj.*
differentiate contrast, *v.*
difficult easy, *adj.*
dim bright, *adj.*
dim dark, *adj.*
diminish increase, *v.*
dire bad, *adj.*
disagreeable bad, *adj.*
discuss talk, *v.*
disobedient bad, *adj.*
distinct sharp, *adj.*
distinguish contrast, *v.*
divide mix, *v.*
doubt objection, *n.*
drag pull, *v.*
dreadful bad, *adj.*
dry damp, *adj.*
dull boring, *adj.*
dull colorless, *adj.*
dull exciting, *adj.*
dull interesting, *adj.*
dusky dark, *adj.*

E

earlier after, *adv.*
earlier before, *adv.*
earnest serious, *adj.*
easy, *adj.*
edge, *n.*
effect consequence, *n.*
effortless easy, *adj.*
electrifying exciting, *adj.*
emerald green, *adj.*
enchanting exciting, *adj.*
end conclusion, *n.*

energetic tired, *adj.*
engrossing exciting, *adj.*
enigmatic confusing, *adj.*
enlarge increase, *v.*
entertaining interesting, *adj.*
enticing exciting, *adj.*
entreated said, *v.*
equivalent alike, *adj.*
ethical good, *adj.*
evacuate move, *v.*
even rough, *adj.*
even smooth, *adj.*
evidence detail, *n.*
evil good, *adj.*
examine, *v.*
example, *n.*
exceedingly very, *adv.*
excellent bad, *adj.*
exceptionally very, *adv.*
exciting, *adj.*
exciting boring, *adj.*
exclaimed said, *v.*
expand contract, *v.*
expedition trip, *n.*
experience, *v.*
expert, *n.*
expert good, *adj.*
expose, *v.*

F

fact detail, *n.*
faded colorless, *adj.*
faint colorless, *adj.*
fascinating exciting, *adj.*
fascinating interesting, *adj.*

more ▶

Thesaurus Plus

law-abiding good, *adj.*
lead guide, *v.*
leading figure expert, *n.*
level rough, *adj.*
level smooth, *adj.*
light dark, *adj.*
light easy, *adj.*
light heavy, *adj.*
liken contrast, *v.*
likeness, *n.*
little small, *adj.*
long ago before, *adv.*
lug move, *v.*
lukewarm cold, *adj.*
lumpy smooth, *adj.*
luscious good, *adj.*

magenta red, *adj.*
main, *adj.*
mar harm, *v.*
maroon red, *adj.*
masterful good, *adj.*
meager small, *adj.*
melancholy sad, *adj.*
mend fix, *v.*
mesmerizing exciting, *adj.*
middle edge, *n.*
migrate move, *v.*
mingle mix, *v.*
minute small, *adj.*
misgiving objection, *n.*
mix, *v.*
moaned said, *v.*
modest shy, *adj.*
moist damp, *adj.*
monotonous boring, *adj.*

monotonous exciting, *adj.*
morose happy, *adj.*
motivate move, *v.*
motive reason, *n.*
mouth-watering good, *adj.*
move, *v.*
muggy damp, *adj.*
mumbled said, *v.*
murky confusing, *adj.*
murmured said, *v.*
muttered said, *v.*

N

naughty bad, *adj.*
needy rich, *adj.*
negligent careful, *adj.*
nippy cold, *adj.*
noble good, *adj.*
notable important, *adj.*
noted author expert, *n.*
notice see, *v.*
nubbly smooth, *adj.*

O

objection, *n.*
observe examine, *v.*
ominous bad, *adj.*
on account of because of, *prep.*
once after, *adv.*
once before, *adv.*
opaque clear, *adj.*
opinion, *n.*
opposite alike, *adj.*
opposition objection, *n.*
outcome consequence, *n.*
outgoing shy, *adj.*

P

paltry small, *adj.*
pass move, *v.*
patch fix, *v.*
peaceful smooth, *adj.*
penetrating sharp, *adj.*
pensive serious, *adj.*
perceive see, *v.*
perceptive sharp, *adj.*
persist, *v.*
persuade, *v.*
petite small, *adj.*
piercing sharp, *adj.*
pleasant bad, *adj.*
plod hurry, *v.*
point of view opinion, *n.*
poisoned bad, *adj.*
polished good, *adj.*
polished smooth, *adj.*
poor bad, *adj.*
poor rich, *adj.*
position argument, *n..*
preserve change, *v.*
previously after, *adv.*
previously before, *adv.*
primary main, *adj.*
primitive ancient, *adj.*
principal main, *adj.*
principled good, *adj.*
prior to after, *adv.*
prior to before, *adv.*
proclaimed said, *v.*
proficient good, *adj.*
pronounced said, *v.*
proof detail, *n.*
proper bad, *adj.*
provocative exciting, *adj.*
prudent careful, *adj.*
pull, *v.*
push pull, *v.*
pushiness spunk, *n.*
puzzling confusing, *adj.*

more ▶

Thesaurus Plus

stabbing sharp, *adj.*
stammered said, *v.*
stand argument, *n.*
stand rise, *v.*
start conclusion, *n.*
stated said, *v.*
steaming cold, *adj.*
steer guide, *v.*
stirring exciting, *adj.*
streaked, *adj.*
striped streaked, *adj.*
study examine, *v.*
stuttered said, *v.*
subsequently after, *adv.*
subsequently before,
   adv.
sudden, *adj.*
superior bad, *adj.*
support objection, *n.*
sweltering cold, *adj.*
swiftly quickly, *adv.*

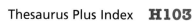

tainted bad, *adj.*
talented good, *adj.*
talk, *v.*
tall, *adj.*
teasing serious, *adj.*
tedious boring, *adj.*
tedious exciting, *adj.*
tepid cold, *adj.*
termination
   conclusion, *n.*
then after, *adv.*
thereafter after, *adv.*
therefore, *adv.*
think, *v.*
throw, *v.*
thus therefore, *adv.*
tiny small, *adj.*
tired, *adj.*
tiresome exciting, *adj.*

tiresome interesting,
   adj.
toasty cold, *adj.*
toss throw, *v.*
tote move, *v.*
touch move, *v.*
tour trip, *n.*
tow pull, *v.*
towering tall, *adj.*
trait characteristic, *n.*
tranquil smooth, *adj.*
transfer move, *v.*
transform change, *v.*
transparent clear, *adj.*
transport move, *v.*
trip, *n.*
trivial important, *adj.*
trust rely, *v.*
trustworthy good, *adj.*
tug pull, *v.*
turbulent smooth, *adj.*
turn down reject, *v.*

uncomplicated easy,
   adj.
undisturbed smooth,
   adj.
unfavorable bad, *adj.*
unimportant main, *adj.*
unmistakable sharp, *adj.*
unpleasant bad, *adj.*
unruffled angry, *adj.*
until now before, *adv.*
untroubled smooth, *adj.*
unwell healthy, *adj.*
unwrinkled smooth, *adj.*
upright good, *adj.*
upshot conclusion, *n.*
upstanding good, *adj.*

vacate move, *v.*
valiant brave, *adj.*
vast small, *adj.*
vermilion red, *adj.*
very, *adv.*
virtuous bad, *adj.*
virtuous good, *adj.*
vivid colorless, *adj.*

warm cold, *adj.*
watchful careful, *adj.*
weak healthy, *adj.*
wealthy rich, *adj.*
weary tired, *adj.*
weighty heavy, *adj.*
well healthy, *adj.*
well-behaved bad, *adj.*
well-defined sharp, *adj.*
well-to-do rich, *adj.*
whined said, *v.*
whispered said, *v.*
wicked bad, *adj.*
wicked good, *adj.*
win over persuade, *v.*
wintry cold, *adj.*
wreck destroy, *v.*
wretched sad, *adj.*
wrinkly rough, *adj.*

yelled said, *v.*
yummy good, *adj.*

Thesaurus Plus

Thesaurus Plus

after *adv.* behind in place or order. *You go ahead, and we'll come along after.*

subsequently following in time. *Sue started out taking French but subsequently dropped it.*

later after a particular time or event. *Let's eat now and hike later.*

once immediately after. *Once Michelle arrives, we can begin.*

thereafter from then on. *Jill learned to sew and thereafter made all her own clothes.*

then afterward. *I went to Paris and then London.*

antonyms: before, earlier, previously, prior to

alike *adj.* exactly or almost exactly the same. *His twin sisters look very much alike.*

similar related in appearance or nature; somewhat alike but not the same. *Your coat is similar to mine.*

comparable capable of being compared; having like traits. *A parakeet and a canary are comparable in size.*

equivalent equal in amount, value, meaning, force, measure. *A dime is equivalent to ten pennies.*

antonyms: different, opposite

ancient *adj.* very old, aged. *The abandoned house looks ancient.*

primitive of or in an early stage of development. *This museum has a collection of primitive sculpture.*

antonym: current

angry *adj.* feeling or showing ill temper. *The angry customer demanded a refund.*

furious full of extreme anger. *Lisa was furious when someone dented her new car.*

irritated annoyed; bothered. *Joel gets irritated when I call him Joe.*

seething violently agitated, disturbed, or annoyed. *Seething with anger, he stormed away.*

inflamed aroused by anger or other strong emotion. *The audience was inflamed by his unfair remarks.*

antonyms: calm, unruffled

argument *n.* a statement in support of a point of view; a reason. *The editorial listed several arguments against the proposed law.*

case a set of reasons offered in support of something. *She presented a strong case for buying a new bus.*

position a point of view or an attitude on a certain question. *The candidate's position on new taxes is well known.*

stand an opinion on an issue or question that one is prepared to defend. *The mayor took a strong stand against closing the school.*

issue a subject being discussed or disputed. *The new dress code is a hotly debated issue.*

ask *v.* to seek an answer to. *Ask Mrs. Jurigian if she saw anyone unusual outside her house.*

interrogate to question closely. *The police interrogated a suspect.*

inquire to seek information from. *They inquired about her job.*

query to question. *Officer Gould queried them about their whereabouts on June 10.*

antonyms: answer, reply, inform

Shades of Meaning

bad *adj.*

1. not good:
   *poor, foul, inferior,
   unpleasant, disagreeable*

2. morally evil:
   wicked, sinister, corrupt

3. causing distress:
   *dreadful, unfavorable,
   ominous, dire*

4. not behaving properly:
   *disobedient, naughty,
   improper, insubordinate*

5. diseased:
   *infected, contaminated,
   tainted, poisoned*

antonyms: good, pleasant,
virtuous, excellent, superior,
delightful, well-behaved, proper

because of *prep.* being brought on
or made possible by. ***Because of***
her strong will, she succeeded.

on account of due to. ***On account***
of *rain, the band concert was
postponed.*

as a result of being an outcome of.
*She fell **as a result of** fainting.*

Word Bank

before *adv.* at an earlier time.

at one time	formerly
earlier	some time back
in the past	previously
back then	prior to
once	
long ago	
until now	

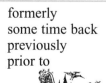

antonyms: after, afterward,
subsequently, later

boring *adj.* not interesting. *The TV
program was so **boring** that I fell
asleep.*

dull lacking excitement. *Not one
player scored during the **dull**
soccer match.*

monotonous not interesting because
of being always the same. *That
very **monotonous** song just
repeated the same words over
and over.*

tedious tiresome because of
slowness or length. *Copying
my lengthy term paper was a
tedious job.*

antonyms: exciting, interesting

brave *adj.* able to face danger or
pain without showing fear. *The
brave firefighter went calmly into
the burning house to look for the
family's pet.*

valiant showing great courage. *The
emergency team made a **valiant**
rescue in the blizzard.*

courageous able to face great
challenges without showing fear.
*The **courageous** knights protected
the king.*

antonyms: afraid, cowardly

bright *adj.* radiant with light or
color. ***Bright** umbrellas make
a rainy day more cheerful.*

shining giving off or reflecting a
steady light. *A **shining** lantern
lit the path.*

brilliant glittering; sparkling with
light. *The costume was **brilliant**
with sequins.*

dazzling so bright as to be blinding;
blazing with light. *The lifeguard
squinted in the **dazzling** sunlight.*

antonyms: dark, dim

more ▶

Thesaurus Plus

Shades of Brown

brown *adj.* having the color of most kinds of soil.

beige:	a very pale brown, like that of sand
fawn:	a light, yellowish-brown, like a young deer
khaki:	a dull, yellowish-brown, like a soldier's uniform
bronze:	an olive-brown, like the metal bronze
russet:	a dark, reddish-brown, like a dark-colored apple
sepia:	a grayish-brown, like the color of an antique photograph

C

careful *adj.* using caution or care. *Looking for clues, the detective made a **careful** search.*

cautious not taking chances. *Kim is too **cautious** to try the difficult climb to the top.*

prudent having or showing good judgement; sensible. *We made a **prudent** decision to save our money for college.*

watchful being alert to trouble or danger. *The **watchful** German shepherd barked at every passerby.*

antonyms: casual, reckless, negligent

change *v.* to make or become different. *The new owners of the house **changed** the color from pink to yellow.*

transform to make very different in form or appearance. *The decorations **transformed** the gym into a colorful dance floor.*

alter to make somewhat different. *Al must **alter** his report to make it shorter.*

convert to make or be made into something different. *We **converted** the barn into a guest house.*

antonyms: keep, preserve

characteristic *n.* something that makes one person, group, or thing different from others. *One **characteristic** of racing cars is a streamlined shape.*

trait a distinguishing aspect, as of a person or an animal. *Eye color is an inherited **trait**.*

quality a general tendency or effect. *Many folk songs have a sad **quality** to them.*

feature a noticeable part or aspect. *An important **feature** of this radio is its small size.*

clear *adj.* free from anything that dims, darkens, or obscures. *The **clear** ocean water was perfect for swimming.*

transparent of such texture that objects can be seen on the other side. *Her **transparent** plastic mask made everybody laugh.*

antonym: opaque

How Cold Was It?

cold *adj.* having a low temperature.

1. slightly cold:
   cool, fresh, bracing, brisk, crisp

2. quite cold:
   nippy, wintry, chilly, frosty

3. extremely cold:
   icy, frozen, frigid, freezing, bone-chilling

antonyms: hot, tepid, lukewarm, warm, toasty, sweltering, broiling, roasting, steaming

colorless *adj.* without a distinct hue. *The moon's landscape is* **colorless**.

faint not clearly seen; dim. *A* **faint** *light flickered in the distance.*

faded without brightness, owing to gradual changes. *The old curtains were* **faded** *from the sunlight.*

dull drab. *The desert's* **dull** *colors change with spring rains.*

indistinct not clear or well-defined; fuzzy. *The boat was* **indistinct** *in the fog.*

antonym: vivid

conclusion *n.* the last part of something. *The* **conclusion** *of her speech made us cheer.*

end the final part or limit of something. *Labor Day marks the* **end** *of summer.*

close an ending or finish. *Her home run brought the game to a* **close**.

termination a formal or official ending. *His failure to pay his dues led to the* **termination** *of his club membership.*

upshot the final result; outcome. *The* **upshot** *of her efforts was a raise.*

finish a stopping point or end. *The race was thrilling from the start to the* **finish**.

antonyms: beginning, start

confusing *adj.* causing misunderstanding. *These* **confusing** *instructions won't help us learn how to wallpaper.*

murky vague; difficult to understand. *Her* **murky** *explanation was impossible to follow.*

puzzling hard to figure out. *The disappearance of the money is very* **puzzling**.

enigmatic not clear in meaning; mysterious. *We wondered how to interpret his* **enigmatic** *message.*

antonym: clear

consequence *n.* something that follows from an action or condition. *One* **consequence** *of the construction was traffic delays.*

effect something that has happened in response or reaction to something else. *Sunshine and a cool breeze always has the* **effect** *of making me feel energetic.*

result the outgrowth of a particular action, operation, or cause. *He slept late and, as a* **result**, *missed the bus.*

outcome a final product. *To most people, the* **outcome** *of the election was no surprise.*

solution the successful outcome of a problem. *Moving to a dry climate was the* **solution** *to my cousin's health problems.*

antonym: cause

contract *v.* to draw together; make or become smaller in length. *She* **contracted** *her muscles to swing the baseball bat.*

compress to put pressure on something so as to reduce the space it takes up. *Everyone* **compressed** *their clothes to fit into their backpacks.*

antonym: expand

contrast *v.* to compare in order to reveal differences. *The reviewer* **contrasted** *two modern films with two silent movies.*

distinguish to recognize differences. *Some people cannot* **distinguish** *between red and green.*

differentiate to understand or show the differences between. *Alison* **differentiates** *between spiders and true insects in her science report.*

antonym: liken

more ▶

Thesaurus Plus

D

damp *adj.* slightly wet. *Our bathing suits are still **damp**.*

humid having a large amount of water vapor. *The rain shower made the air **humid**.*

moist slightly wet with water spread thinly over a surface. ***Moist** leaves clung to the windows.*

muggy unpleasantly warm and humid, with little or no breeze. *The **muggy** summer made us wish for a cold fall.*

soggy softened with moisture. *Our heels sank into the **soggy** earth.*

dewy slightly wet with water droplets. ***Dewy** spider webs glistened in the morning sun.*

antonym: dry

dark *adj.* without light or with very little light. *He felt his way across the **dark** cellar.*

shaded screened from light. *Most frogs like **shaded** places.*

dim faintly lighted. *A **dim** shape appeared across the field.*

shadowy having scattered areas of shade. *A **shadowy** path led through the woods.*

dusky tending to darkness, as from the approach of night. *She lit a lamp in the **dusky** room.*

antonyms: bright, light

destroy *v.* to wipe out or demolish. *The tornado **destroyed** the town.*

ruin to damage beyond repair. *Her shoes were **ruined** in the rain.*

wreck to cause to break up. *Using heavy-duty equipment, the crew **wrecked** the old convention hall.*

antonyms: repair, restore

detail *n.* a part of a report or other composition that supports the main idea; an individual or specific item. *Adding more **details** will help your story.*

fact something real or known with certainty. *Pamela couldn't find the **facts** to back up her idea.*

evidence something that serves as proof. *The author presented little **evidence** of an unhappy childhood.*

reason a fact or cause that explains why something should or does exist. *The major stressed safety as a **reason** for widening the road.*

proof demonstration of the truth of something. *Our success is **proof** that the plan works!*

information facts about a certain subject. *This textbook on intelligence contains much **information** about the brain.*

E

easy *adj.* not difficult. *Tad solved the **easy** puzzle quickly.*

uncomplicated not hard to understand, deal with, or solve. *We followed Dad's **uncomplicated** directions without any problem.*

effortless easily done. *The athlete made weightlifting seem **effortless**.*

light needing little effort. *Because I am tired, I will just do **light** work.*

simple not complicated. *This game is **simple** enough for a young child.*

antonyms: complex, difficult

edge *n.* the line where an object or area ends. *The fence at the **edge** of the canyon prevents accidents.*

border the boundary where one thing ends and another begins. *The river forms the **border** of the land.*

rim the outside line or margin of something. *The cup's **rim** is chipped.*

antonyms: center, middle

Thesaurus Plus

examine *v.* to look at carefully. *The child **examined** the new toy.*

inspect to look at carefully in order to detect flaws. *You should **inspect** a used car before you buy it.*

study to look at closely in order to find out something. *He **studied** her face to see how she really felt.*

observe to watch with attention. *The bird watchers **observed** the eagles.*

example *n.* one item that is typical of a whole class or category. *The Irish setter is an **example** of an excellent hunting dog.*

case a particular condition or occurrence. *Sometimes you get a busy signal, in which **case** you can phone again later.*

instance an action or occurrence that is representative of a general subject. *Interrupting was just one **instance** of her rudeness.*

illustration something that serves as an example or demonstration. *A falling rock is an **illustration** of the effect of gravity.*

Word Bank

exciting *adj.* arousing, stimulating.

stirring	captivating
rousing	fascinating
inspiring	intriguing
gripping	mesmerizing
enticing	spine-tingling
riveting	breathtaking
engrossing	electrifying
absorbing	sensational
dazzling	provocative
alluring	compelling
enchanting	hair-raising

antonyms: boring, bland, dull, tedious, tiresome, insipid, colorless, monotonous, humdrum

experience *v.* to take part in; live through. *Almost everyone **experiences** failure at times.*

feel to experience physically or emotionally. *He **felt** anxious alone in the house.*

sense to become aware of by instinct. *The animals **sensed** the approaching storm.*

go through to experience with pain or displeasure. *I hope you didn't **go through** much difficulty.*

expert *n.* a person with great knowledge in a particular field. *Dr. Lee is an **expert** on animal behavior.*

source a person who supplies information. *In describing the accident, the reporter used a witness as her **source** of information.*

leading figure a very important person in a certain field. *Her great talent made her a **leading figure** among painters.*

noted author a well-known writer. *A book by a **noted author** draws great interest.*

researcher a person who studies a subject in order to contribute new knowledge. *Medical **researchers** have developed cures for many different illnesses.*

spokesperson a person who speaks as a representative for others. *The **spokesperson** announced that the governor would hold a press conference tomorrow.*

authority an accepted source of knowledge or advice. *Her mother is an **authority** on gardening.*

scientist a person who studies the laws of nature. *Newton was the **scientist** who discovered the laws of gravity.*

antonym: amateur

more ▶

Thesaurus Plus

expose *v.* to uncover; lay bare. *I **exposed** my back to the sun.*

show to make visible. *They **showed** us the way out of the jungle.*

reveal to make known; disclose. *The magician **revealed** her secrets.*

● ———————— F ———————— ●

fix *v.* to set right. *This word processing program will **fix** the misspellings in my document.*

repair to put back in useful condition after damage, injury, or wear. *My uncle **repairs** old lawnmowers.*

mend to repair by joining torn, frayed, or broken parts. *Can you please **mend** this torn sleeve on my jacket?*

patch to cover a hole, rip, or torn place with a small piece of material. *She **patched** the nail hole in the bicycle tire.*

restore to bring back to an original condition. *The owner is **restoring** this historic house.*

antonyms: break, damage

funny *adj.* arousing laughter or amusement. *Rosa thinks that her practical jokes are **funny**.*

hilarious causing a great deal of laughter. *The cartoon had a **hilarious** scene with a silly pig in the mud.*

comical humorous. *The monkey's **comical** tricks made us laugh.*

antonyms: serious, solemn

● ———————— G ———————— ●

Shades of Meaning

good *adj.*

1. of high moral quality: *honorable, ethical, noble, law-abiding, upstanding, conscientious, virtuous, principled, upright, trustworthy, scrupulous, respectable, righteous*

2. having much ability: *skilled, proficient, gifted, qualified, accomplished, adept, talented, polished, expert, dexterous, masterful*

3. pleasant-tasting: *delicious, scrumptious, mouthwatering, delectable, appetizing, yummy, flavorful, savory, luscious*

antonyms: wicked, evil, immoral, decadent, corrupt

green *adj.* having the color of most plant leaves and growing grass. *The fields turned **green** with the spring rains.*

chartreuse of a light yellowish green. *Most new fire engines are **chartreuse** instead of red.*

emerald of a dark yellowish green. *The cat's **emerald** eyes shone against its white fur.*

guide *v.* to direct the course of. *Our counselor **guided** us on our hike.*

lead to show the way by going ahead. *The captain always **leads** the team onto the field.*

steer to physically control the course of a vehicle, ship, or plane. *It is difficult to **steer** a truck on this winding road.*

H

happy *adj.* feeling satisfaction and pleasure. *She was very **happy** when the gift arrived.*

joyful feeling great happiness. *Their wedding anniversary was a **joyful** occasion.*

radiant glowing or beaming with happiness. *Her **radiant** face told us that she had won.*

blissful full of calm contentment. *He spent a **blissful** afternoon sailing.*

antonyms: depressed, glum, morose, sad, sorrowful

harm *v.* to injure; hurt. *Looking directly at the sun can **harm** a person's eyes.*

damage to injure something so that it is less valuable or useful. *Frost **damaged** the orange crop.*

mar to spoil the surface or appearance of. *Those rough crates **marred** the table top.*

healthy *adj.* free from disease or injury. *The **healthy** plants grew strong and tall.*

fit being in good physical shape. *Drew exercises and feels **fit**.*

sound having no damage or weakness. *Surprisingly, the shabby old house still had a **sound** frame.*

well not sick. *Even during the flu season, he stayed **well**.*

antonyms: ill, weak, unwell

heavy *adj.* having relatively great weight. *The rocks are very **heavy**.*

weighty having great weight. *This package is too **weighty** to carry.*

antonym: light

hurry *v.* to move or act with haste. *The students **hurried** to their seats.*

dash to race with sudden speed. *He **dashed** through the closing doors.*

rush to move or act with great haste. *The ambulance **rushed** to the accident scene.*

scramble to move quickly in a disorganized manner. *The players **scrambled** for the loose ball.*

fly to move swiftly. *The horses **flew** by in a cloud of dust.*

antonyms: amble, crawl, creep, plod, dawdle, delay

I

important *adj.* able to determine or change things. *Gettysburg was the site of an **important** Civil War battle.*

serious worthy of concern. *A **serious** engine problem prevented the car from starting.*

significant full of meaning. *The footprints are a **significant** clue.*

notable worthy of notice or comment. *There is only one **notable** exception to the rule.*

antonyms: frivolous, trivial

increase *v.* to make or become greater or larger. *The **increase** in pollution is dangerous to us.*

enlarge to make or become larger. *We had our photographs **enlarged**.*

antonym: diminish

interesting *adj.* arousing and holding attention. *I read **interesting** books quickly.*

intriguing arousing one's curiosity. *The disappearance of the rake is an **intriguing** puzzle.*

entertaining pleasing and enjoyable. *His **entertaining** stories kept us amused.*

fascinating extremely interesting. *Visiting my foreign relatives is always **fascinating**.*

antonyms: boring, dull, tiresome

more ▶

Thesaurus Plus

L

likeness *n.* a way in which things are the same. *I see a real **likeness** between the plots of those two mystery stories.*

similarity the quality of being alike but not identical. *The **similarity** among the three sisters was startling.*

resemblance a closeness in appearance. *There is a strong **resemblance** between those twins.*

antonym: difference

M

main *adj.* most important; major. *The **main** ride in the park is a water slide.*

principal first in rank or importance. *Willa is the **principal** soloist in the chorus.*

central having the most influence or control. *All orders come from the **central** headquarters.*

primary first or best; chief. *Her **primary** goal is to get into a good college.*

antonym: unimportant

mix *v.* to blend into a single substance. *We **mixed** blue paint with white paint to make light blue.*

blend to unite or join completely. *The two sounds of the instruments **blended** into one.*

mingle to join in with others. *We **mingled** with the crowd during intermission.*

antonyms: divide, separate

Shades of Meaning

move *v.*

1. to take something from one place to another:
transport, carry, shift, transfer, convey, conduct, pass, bear, cart, haul, lug, tote

2. to leave one's location:
depart, relocate, quit, vacate, migrate, evacuate

3. to cause an emotion or change of feeling:
affect, arouse, touch, inspire, impress, motivate, influence

O

objection *n.* the expression of an opposing view or argument. *The committee explained their **objection** to the higher taxes.*

opposition the act of resisting or being in conflict. *The mayor's decision met with **opposition**.*

doubt worry; concern. *Mai had serious **doubts** about our plans.*

misgiving uncertainty about the wisdom of an action. *Leon now has **misgivings** about buying that used compact disc player.*

antonyms: agreement, support

opinion *n.* a belief not based on positive knowledge. *I don't agree with your **opinion** of the movie.*

belief something thought to be true. *The coach has **belief** in the team.*

point of view the position from which something is considered. *From this **point of view**, the decision was unfair.*

attitude a state of mind regarding someone or something. *Jeff has a positive attitude toward his job.*

feeling a belief based on emotion or instinct. *She had a strong feeling that we would succeed.*

judgment a decision reached after careful weighing of evidence. *The skipper's judgment was that the seas were too rough to sail.*

persist *v.* to insist or repeat obstinately. *She persists in practicing her saxophone.*

continue to keep on. *Even in snow or sleet, the mail carrier continues to work.*

antonym: quit

persuade *v.* to cause someone to do or believe something by arguing, pleading, or reasoning. *He persuaded us to wait another day.*

convince to cause someone to feel certain. *The lawyer had convinced the jury of her client's innocence.*

win over to appeal successfully to someone's emotions or sense of values. *His enthusiasm for the project won over the committee.*

influence to have an effect or impact on. *Our friendship did not influence my decision.*

pull *v.* to draw something forward. *I pulled a shirt from the closet.*

haul to draw or carry with effort. *The horses hauled the heavy load.*

tug to pull sharply. *A large fish tugged at the fish line.*

drag to draw or haul along the ground. *The dog dragged the branch across the yard.*

tow to draw along behind with a chain or rope. *A neighbor towed our car home after it broke down.*

antonyms: push, shove

quickly *adv.* with speed; right away. *The teller quickly counted the coins accurately.*

swiftly with great speed and smoothness. *The relay runner swiftly passed the baton to his teammate.*

rapidly in very fast sequence. *A hummingbird's wings beat so rapidly that you see only a blur.*

instantaneously immediately. *We instantaneously recognized the man in the photograph.*

antonym: slowly

reason *n.* a statement or fact that explains why something exists or occurs. *Do you have a good reason for being late to this meeting?*

cause a person, thing, condition, or action that makes something happen. *The cause of the fire was faulty wiring.*

grounds the foundation for a belief or an action. *They have no grounds for claiming that we are responsible for the horrible mistake.*

basis an underlying cause, idea, or fact. *Belief in freedom is the basis of the Constitution of the United States.*

motive an emotion or desire that causes someone to act in a certain way. *His motive for working was to make money for a summer sports camp.*

more ▶

Thesaurus Plus **H113**

Thesaurus Plus

Shades of Red	
red adj. the color of ripe cherries.	
rose:	a deep pinkish-red
scarlet:	a bright orange-red
burgundy:	a dark reddish-brown
vermilion:	a bright red
cerise:	a dark red
ruby:	a very deep red
crimson:	a vivid purplish-red
maroon:	a dark purplish-red
carmine:	a deep purplish-red
magenta:	a strong reddish-purple

refuse *v.* to be unwilling to accept or agree to. *Sam was so tired that he refused to shovel more snow.*

deny to withhold or keep back. *The guard denied us permission to photograph the paintings.*

decline to refuse politely. *I invited her to dinner, but she declined.*

reject to refuse to recognize or accept. *The voters rejected the proposal for a new gymnasium.*

antonyms: agree, consent, grant

reject *v.* to refuse to accept, use, grant, consider. *My parents rejected my idea of a pet monkey.*

decline to refuse to accept or do. *He declined my offer to help him.*

turn down to refuse to accept. *The faculty turned down the principal's plan.*

rely *v.* to count on the ability or willingness of someone or something. *I'll rely on you to do the job.*

depend to count on for support or help. *You can depend on a friend.*

trust to have confidence in the soundness or honesty of. *I trust you because you tell me the truth.*

remember *v.* to think of again. *I just remembered to turn left.*

bring to mind to cause to think of. *Your dog brings to mind one that I had years ago.*

recollect to remember through deliberate effort. *I cannot recollect where I left my key.*

recall to bring back to memory. *Can you recall the names of all the Great Lakes?*

antonym: forget

rich *adj.* having much money, goods, land, or other valuables. *If I were rich, I'd travel all over the world.*

wealthy having a great quantity of money, valuable possessions, or resources. *The United States is a wealthy nation.*

affluent having plenty of money. *Large, beautiful houses can be the mark of an affluent community.*

well-to-do well-off; enjoying wealth or profit. *Their successful business has made them well-to-do.*

antonyms: deprived, needy, poor

rise *v.* to go up; ascend. *The moon rises quickly.*

stand to take or maintain an upright position on the feet. *I don't like to stand in lines.*

antonym: sit

rough *adj.* having an irregular surface. *The ocean looks rough on a windy day.*

bumpy full of lumps. *We laughed as we drove down the bumpy road.*

coarse not smooth or fine. *The coarse sand hurt our feet.*

rocky full of lumps from or as if from rocks. *It was hard to walk on the rocky path.*

rugged having an uneven surface or jagged outline. *Four-wheel drive vehicles can drive over rugged terrain.*

shaggy having long, rough hair, wool, or fibers. *The animals still had their* **shaggy** *winter coats.*

wrinkly puckered or creased. *An elephant's skin is* **wrinkly**.
antonyms: even, level, smooth

run *v.* to move on foot at a pace faster than a walk. *The hitter* **ran** *to first base.*

gallop to run at a fast, rhythmic pace. *We heard the mustangs* **galloping** *toward us.*

shoot to move swiftly and smoothly. *A meteor* **shot** *across the sky.*

sad *adj.* showing, filled with, or expressing sorrow or regret. *The losing team members had* **sad** *faces.*

forlorn pitiful in appearance or condition. *The* **forlorn** *kitten cried for its mother.*

wretched full of misery or woe. *Brad felt* **wretched** *when he lost the club's money.*

melancholy gloomy; depressed. *Long periods of rain make many people feel* **melancholy**.
antonyms: glad, happy, joyful

Shades of Meaning

said *v.* spoke aloud.

1. said quietly or unclearly:
   whispered, murmured, mumbled, muttered, grunted

2. said openly and clearly:
   stated, announced, declared, articulated, pronounced, asserted, remarked, proclaimed

3. asked:
   questioned, queried, inquired, requested, interrogated

Shades of Meaning (cont.)

4. answered:
   replied, responded, retorted, returned

5. said in a complaining way:
   whined, moaned, groaned, grumbled, griped

6. said in an angry way:
   snarled, growled, snapped, hissed

7. said loudly:
   yelled, screamed, shrieked, bellowed, hollered, roared, shouted

8. said in an excited or nervous way:
   exclaimed, cried, stuttered, stammered

9. said in a pleading way:
   begged, implored, entreated, beseeched

see *v.* to become aware of by sight. *In the distance, he* **saw** *clouds of black smoke.*

spot to detect; recognize; locate. *We* **spotted** *a fawn under the bush.*

notice to become aware of casually or by chance. *On my way home, I* **noticed** *a hat on a park bench.*

perceive to recognize or understand information gathered through any of the senses. *He said he was fine, but I* **perceived** *he was very upset.*

serious *adj.* not joking or speaking casually. *Are you* **serious** *about moving to Chicago?*

earnest showing or expressing deep, sincere feeling. *The police chief made an* **earnest** *plea for help.*

more ▶

Thesaurus Plus

Thesaurus Plus

grave extremely serious; solemn. *The doctor's face was **grave** as she gave them the bad news.*

pensive in a thoughtful mood. *Jan was not unhappy, but she was quite **pensive**.*

antonyms: fooling, teasing

Shades of Meaning

sharp *adj.*

1. clearly outlined:
   clear, distinct, unmistakable, in focus, well-defined, definite

2. able to think quickly and well:
   intelligent, smart, bright, astute, shrewd, clever, canny, perceptive, cunning, alert, quick-witted

3. felt suddenly and strongly:
   piercing, penetrating, keen, acute, stabbing, intense

antonyms: blurry, fuzzy, foggy, hazy

---

shy *adj.* quiet and withdrawn in manner. *He was too **shy** to speak.*

bashful timid and embarrassed. *Sam felt **bashful** when he suddenly became the center of attention.*

modest tending to play down one's own talents, abilities, or accomplishments. *The concert pianist was **modest** about her talent.*

antonyms: bold, outgoing

small *adj.* slight in size, number, quantity, extent, volume, or importance. *Kate's room is too **small** for two people.*

little below average in size, quantity, or degree. *They have **little** faith in his promise.*

tiny extremely small. *The **tiny** ant looked like a speck.*

petite small and dainty. *One girl is tall, while the other is **petite**.*

paltry insignificant; small in power or value. *He earned a **paltry** sum.*

meager lacking in quantity or richness; scanty. *We looked for beans, but the crop was **meager**.*

minute exceptionally small. ***Minute** flecks of gold glittered in the sun.*

antonyms: big, great, huge, large, vast

Shades of Meaning

smooth *adj.*

1. flat:
   even, level, unwrinkled

2. having a fine-textured surface:
   sleek, slick, satiny, silky, slippery, glossy, glassy, polished

3. calm:
   undisturbed, untroubled, peaceful, serene, tranquil

antonyms: hilly, coarse, bumpy, rough, grainy, nubbly, lumpy, turbulent

---

spunk *n.* spirit; courage. *My friend showed real **spunk** by calling for help when I broke my arm.*

pushiness aggressiveness. *Your brother's **pushiness** is annoying.*

streaked *adj.* marked with irregular lines of color. *The sky was **streaked** with long, pink clouds.*

striped marked with straight, even lines of color. *His tie had a simple **striped** pattern.*

smeared marked with messy-looking streaks. *His apron was **smeared** with spaghetti sauce.*

sudden *adj.* happening without warning. *The rainstorm was surprisingly **sudden**.*

abrupt unexpected. *Later, we made an **abrupt** change of plans.*
antonym: gradual

---

talk *v.* to have a conversation. *At dinner Jill and Ray **talked** about the day's events.*

chatter to speak rapidly and without much purpose; jabber. *A noisy parrot **chattered** in a cage.*

gossip to start or spread rumors. *Mary **gossiped** about the mysterious visitor.*

discuss to speak together about. *We can **discuss** the issue at dinner.*

converse to speak informally with others. *Mark, who reads a lot, can **converse** on many subjects.*

tall *adj.* of greater than average height. *The redwood is one of the **tallest** trees in the world.*

colossal extreme in size, extent, or degree; enormous; gigantic. *From a distance, the people climbing the **colossal** pyramid looked like ants.*

rangy long-legged and thin. *The **rangy** girl stepped over the fence with ease.*

towering of impressive height; very tall. ***Towering** trees hid the sun.*
antonym: short

therefore *adv.* for that reason. *He was sleepy and **therefore** took a long nap.*

thus consequently; as a result. *They broke the tie, and **thus** they won the game.*

hence thereby. *This necklace is gold; **hence**, it is expensive.*

think *v.* to form an idea in one's mind. ***Think** about your purpose before you start writing.*

believe to suppose or to expect. *I **believe** that it will rain later today.*

consider to think over carefully. *She **considered** moving to Chicago.*

imagine to form a mental picture, idea, or impression of. *Can you **imagine** the world without colors?*

reason to think clearly and logically. *Try to **reason** out what must have really happened.*

speculate to think deeply on a particular subject; to ponder. *Scientists have **speculated** about why dinosaurs died out.*

throw *v.* to send something through the air with a swift motion of the arm. *The catcher **threw** the ball.*

hurl to throw with great force. *She **hurled** the javelin a long distance.*

toss to throw lightly. *He **tossed** the keys onto the desk.*

tired *adj.* having little physical or mental energy. *The **tired** dog paddled slowly to shore.*

weary feeling worn out. *We were **weary** after the long drive.*
antonyms: energetic, rested

trip *n.* a journey from one place to another. *We took a **trip** to Ohio.*

expedition a trip made by an organized group for a definite purpose. *The scientists made an **expedition** to study the eclipse.*

tour a trip to or through a place for the purpose of seeing it. *The geologist provides guided **tours**.*

---

very *adv.* to a high degree. *A chimpanzee is a **very** unusual pet.*

exceedingly to an extreme degree. *Computers can do mathematics **exceedingly** quickly.*

exceptionally to an unusual degree. *Jo is an **exceptionally** fine singer.*

Glossary of Language Arts Terms

abbreviation   the shortened form of a word.

active voice   when the subject of a verb is the doer of the action.

adjective   a word that describes a noun or a pronoun.

adjective phrase   a prepositional phrase that modifies a noun or a pronoun.

adverb   modifies a verb, an adjective, or another adverb. It tells how, when, where, or to what extent.

adverb phrase   a prepositional phrase that modifies a verb, an adjective, or an adverb.

agreement   the use of a singular verb with a singular subject and a plural verb with a plural subject.

antecedent   the noun that a pronoun replaces.

apostrophe   a punctuation mark (') used to form a possessive noun or to take the place of missing letters in a contraction.

appositive   a noun or a noun phrase that directly follows another noun and explains or identifies it.

articles   the special adjectives *a, an,* and *the.*

audience   the person or people who read or listen to something.

auxiliary verb   a helping verb used with a main verb to form a verb phrase.

brainstorm   to think of different ideas.

clause   a group of words that contains both a subject and a predicate.

cluster   See **web.**

collective noun   a word that names persons, animals, or things that act together as a group.

colon   a punctuation mark (:) used between hours and minutes in the time of day, after the greeting in a business letter, or before lists in sentences.

comma   a punctuation mark (,) used to separate the parts of a compound sentence, to separate three or more items in a series, or to set off introductory words or interrupters in sentences.

common noun   names any person, place, thing, or idea.

comparative degree of an adjective   used to compare two things. Add *-er* or *more* to the adjective.

comparative degree of an adverb   used to compare two actions or qualities. Add *-er* or *more* to the adverb.

complete predicate   includes all the words in the predicate.

complete subject   includes all the words in the subject.

complex sentence   includes at least one subordinate clause combined with one complete sentence.

compound noun   made up of two or more words that act as a single noun. A compound noun is written as one word, as separate words, or as hyphenated words.

compound predicate   formed by combining the predicates of two or more simple sentences with the same subject.

compound sentence   two or more independent clauses with related ideas joined by a comma and a conjunction.

Glossary

compound subject   formed by combining the subjects of two or more simple sentences with the same predicate.

conjunction   a word used to connect words or groups of words.

contraction   a word formed by combining two words and replacing one or more letters with an apostrophe.

conventions   the standard rules of spelling, grammar, usage, capitalization, and punctuation.

coordinating conjunction   connects words or groups of words of equal importance (*and, but, or*).

correlative conjunctions   used in pairs, such as *either/or*.

declarative sentence   a statement that ends with a period.

demonstrative pronoun   points out particular persons and things (*this, that, these, those*).

details   exact facts or information about a topic.

direct object   the noun or pronoun that receives the action of a transitive verb.

direct quotation   a speaker's exact words enclosed in quotation marks.

double negative   the incorrect use of two negative words for one idea.

drafting   the part of the writing process when the writer first attempts to put his or her ideas on paper in the form of a composition.

elaborate   to give more details or information.

exclamatory sentence   expresses strong feeling and ends with an exclamation point.

freewriting   a prewriting strategy that involves jotting down any words, phrases, or sentences that come to mind as a way of generating topics and details.

future perfect tense   used for an action that will be completed before another future action.

future tense   shows something that will happen later.

helping verb   an auxiliary verb used with the main verb to form a verb phrase.

ideas   thoughts that form the main points of a composition.

imperative sentence   gives a command or makes a request and ends with a period.

indent   to begin the first line of a sentence a few spaces in from the margin.

indirect object   tells who or what was affected by the action of a transitive verb.

indirect quotation   what a person says without using the person's exact words.

interjection   a word or a group of words that expresses feeling. It is followed by a comma or an exclamation point.

interrogative pronoun   used in questions (*what, which, who, whom,* and *whose*).

interrogative sentence   asks a question and ends with a question mark.

interrupted order   when other words come between the subject and the verb of a sentence.

intransitive verb   does not have an object.

irregular verb   a verb in which the past and past participle forms do not end with *-ed*.

linking verb   links the subject with a noun or an adjective in the predicate that names or describes the subject.

main idea   the most important thought or point.

more ▶

main verb in a verb phrase expresses the action or the state of being.

modifier a word that describes other words.

negative a word that means "no" or "not."

noun a word that names a person, place, thing, or idea.

object of the preposition the noun or pronoun that follows the preposition.

object pronoun used as a direct or indirect object.

order words words that signal sequence, such as *first, next,* and *finally.*

organization the structure of a composition.

paragraph a group of sentences that work together to express one main idea.

past perfect tense used for an action that was completed before another past action.

past tense used to show something that already happened.

perfect tense made up of a form of *have* and the past participle.

phrase a group of words that does not contain a subject and a predicate.

plural referring to more than one.

possessive noun a noun that shows ownership.

possessive pronoun replaces a possessive noun.

predicate tells what the subject is, has, does, or feels.

predicate adjective follows a linking verb and describes the subject.

predicate noun follows a linking verb and identifies or renames the subject.

preposition relates a noun or a pronoun to another word in the sentence.

prepositional phrase begins with a preposition, ends with the object of the preposition, and includes any words that modify the object.

present perfect tense used to show action that took place at an indefinite time in the past.

present tense used to show something happening now.

presentation the way in which writers show and share their compositions with their audience.

prewriting the part of the writing process when the writer chooses a topic and plans the composition.

principal parts the verb, the present participle, the past, and the past participle.

pronoun a word that takes the place of one or more nouns.

proofreading the part of the writing process when the writing is checked for errors in grammar, usage, mechanics, and spelling.

proper adjective formed from a proper noun and capitalized.

proper noun names a particular person, place, thing, or idea.

publish the part of the writing process when writers make a final copy of their composition.

purpose the goal of a composition.

regular verb a verb in which the past and past participle forms end with *-ed.*

revising the part of the writing process when the writer tries to improve the working draft by adding, deleting, reorganizing, and rewriting.

run-on sentence expresses too many thoughts without correct punctuation.

sensory words words that describe how something looks, sounds, feels, tastes, or smells.

Glossary

sentence   a group of words that expresses a complete thought.

sentence fluency   the structure and order of sentences so that a composition reads smoothly.

sentence fragment   a group of words that does not express a complete thought.

series   three or more items listed together in a sentence.

simple predicate   the key word or words in the complete predicate. It is always a verb.

simple sentence   an independent clause that stands by itself.

simple subject   the key word or words in the complete subject. It is usually a noun or a pronoun.

singular   referring to one.

subject   tells whom or what the sentence is about.

subject pronoun   used as a subject or a predicate pronoun.

subordinating conjunction   a word such as *before, when*, or *because* that is used to introduce some subordinate clauses.

superlative degree of an adjective used to compare three or more things. Add *-est* or *most* to the adjective.

superlative degree of an adverb used to compare three or more actions or qualities. Add *-est* or *most* to the adverb.

supporting sentences   sentences that tell more details or information about a main idea.

tense   of a verb tells when the action or the state of being occurs.

topic   the subject of discussion or composition.

topic sentence   a sentence that states a main idea about a subject.

transitional words   words that connect sentences or ideas, such as *also, however, for example,* and *more important.*

transitive verb   expresses action that is received by a noun or a pronoun in the predicate.

verb   expresses physical action, mental action, or a state of being.

verb phrase   a group of words functioning as a single verb; consists of a helping or auxiliary verb and a main verb.

voice   in writing, the personality of the writer conveyed through the written words.

web   words in connected circles that show how ideas are related.

word choice   the selection of interesting, exact words.

working draft   a composition that is still being revised or proofread and is not final.

writing conference   a discussion between a writer and a reader about the writer's composition.

writing process   a series of steps (prewriting, drafting, revising, proofreading, publishing) that a writer follows to write a composition.

Index

55–56, 57–59
coordinating, 57–59,
  60–61, 68, 77–79,
  80, 110, 268
subordinating, 57–59,
  60–61, 68, 80–81,
  246–248, 293–294
Connotation, 415, H16
Content areas, writing in
  art, 381, 418, 503, 574
  drama, 547
  literature, 461, 503
  math, 418, 503
  physical education,
    461
  science, 418, 461,
    503, 547
  social studies, 418,
    461, 503, 547
Contractions, 150–152,
  162, 176, 221, 416
Contrast. *See*
  Comparison and
  contrast
Conventions
  grammar, 32–49,
    52–59, 84–89,
    92–98, 101–103,
    118–134, 150–152,
    180–182, 185–200,
    203–205, 274–276,
    279–292, 295, 296,
    316–324, 327–329
  mechanics, 32–34,
    52–54, 57–59,
    62–65, 87–89,
    96–98, 101–103,
    150–152, 194–196,
    234–243, 246–248,
    251–259
  spelling, 92–95, 114,
    132–134, 139–141,
    218, 379, 416, 501,
    H80, H81–H85

usage, 62–65, 92–95,
  135–141, 144–149,
  153–158, 188–193,
  203–211, 274–276,
  279–292, 295–299,
  330–332
Creative activities, 34,
  128, 196, 213
Creative writing, 95,
  103, 141, 213, 528
Critical thinking, 362,
  400, 443, 477, 555

D
Debating, 428–429
Descriptions
  descriptive poems,
    385–389
  exact words, using 17
  the writing process
    and, 12–27
  See also Composition,
    types, description
Details
  elaborating with, 15,
    21, 378, 415, 458,
    498, 544, 571
  listening for, 432, 518
  sensory, 15, 387, 435,
    521
  using, 15, 17,
    371–372, 374, 415,
    455, 492–493, 563
Diagramming,
  H86–H95
Diagrams, 408, 500, H30
Dialogue. *See* Literary
  terms
Dictionary, using
  definitions, H22
  entry words, H22
  guide words, H22
  pronunciation key,
    H22

syllabication, H22
Direct objects. *See*
  Objects, direct
Directions. *See*
  Instructions
Discussions
  group, 3–5, 391–392
  how to conduct, 3–5,
    391–392
  panel, 391–392
Double negatives,
  avoiding, 206–208,
  215, 222, 231
Drafting, 18–19,
  374–375, 411–412,
  454–455, 493–495,
  539–541, 566–568
Drafts, revising
  by adding details,
    544
  for audience, 498
  for coherence, 60–61,
    571
  by combining, 50–51,
    60–61, 99–100,
    184, 202, 244–245,
    293–294, 326
  by deleting, 20, 415
  by elaborating, 21,
    183, 201–202, 325,
    378, 415, 458, 498,
    544, 571
  for sentence fluency,
    50–51, 60–61,
    99–100, 142–143,
    183, 244–245,
    277–278, 293–294,
    378, 415, 458, 498,
    544, 571
  for word choice, 183,
    212, 378, 415, 458,
    498, 544, 571
  See also Revising

Index

Index

Index

Writing process. *See*
Composition, steps
in writing

Writing prompts,
381–382, 418–419,
461–462, 503,
547–548, 574–575

Acknowledgments *continued*

"The Lady with the Green Skin" by Sylvia C. Montrone from *Cricket* Magazine, July 1998 issue, Volume 25, Number 11. Text copyright ©1998 by Sylvia C. Montrone. Cover copyright ©1998 by Carus Publishing Company. Reprinted by permission of the author and *Cricket* Magazine.

"The Lightwell" by Laurence Yep from *Home: A Collaboration of Thirty Distinguished Authors and Illustrators of Children's Books to Aid the Homeless.* Text copyright ©1992 by Laurence Yep. Cover copyright ©1992 by Leo & Diane Dillon. Reprinted by permission of Curtis Brown Ltd. on behalf of the author for the text and HarperCollins Children's Books for the cover.

From "Platypus" from *National Geographic Book Of Mammals.* Copyright ©1981, 1998 by National Geographic Society. Reproduced by permission of National Geographic Society, 1145 17th Street, N.W., Washington, D.C. 20036.

"Storm!" from *Under the Royal Palms: A Childhood in Cuba* by Alma Flor Ada. Text and photographs copyright ©1998 by Alma Flor Ada. Text reprinted with the permission of Atheneum Books for Young Readers, an imprint of Simon & Schuster Children's Publishing Division. Photographs used with permission of the Author and BookStop Literary Agency. All rights reserved.

"The Weaving That Saved the Prince" retold by Howard Schwartz and Barbara Rush, illustrated by Brett Helquist from *Cricket* Magazine, August 1998 issue, Volume 25, Number 12. Text copyright ©1998 by Howard Schwartz and Barbara Rush. Illustration copyright ©1998 by Brett Helquist. Cover copyright ©1998 by Carus Publishing Company. Reprinted by permission of the authors, the illustrator, and *Cricket* Magazine.

"What Do You Mean She Can't Play Soccer?" by Carla McQuillan, President, National Federation of the Blind of Oregon from *Skipping Stones* Magazine, January-February 1998 issue. Copyright ©1998 by Skipping Stones. Reprinted with permission from *Skipping Stones.*

Poetry
"At the Water's Edge" originally published as "A la orilla del agua" by Homero Aridjis from *Antologia Poetica,* published by Fondo de Cultura Economica, Mexico, 1994. Copyright © Homero Aridjis. English translation copyright ©1981 by Eliot Weinberger. Reprinted by permission of the author and translator.

"The City Dump" from *At the Top of My Voice and Other Poems* by Felice Holman. Published by Charles Scribner's Sons. Copyright ©1970 by Felice Holman. By permission of the author.

"There Was a Sad Pig with a Tail" from *The Book of Pigericks: Pig Limericks* by Arnold Lobel. Copyright ©1983 by Arnold Lobel. Used by permission of HarperCollins Publishers.

Book Report
My Side of the Mountain written and illustrated by Jean Craighead George. Artwork ©1990 by Michael Garland. Used by permission of Dutton Children's Books.

Acknowledgments

Student Handbook

Definitions of "forecast," "gargoyle," "insulate" and "sash" from *The American Heritage® Student Dictionary.* Copyright ©1998 by Houghton Mifflin Company. Reproduced by permission of *The American Heritage® Student Dictionary.*

"Eclipse" excerpt from *The World Book Encyclopedia,* Volume 6. Copyright ©2000 by World Book, Inc. By permission of the publisher. www.worldbook.com.

Pronunciation key on page 399 from *The American Heritage® Student Dictionary.* Copyright ©1998 by Houghton Mifflin Company. Reproduced by permission of *The American Heritage® Student Dictionary.*

"Water Use in the U.S." from *World Eagle,* September 1999 issue. Copyright ©1999 by World Eagle/IBA, Inc. Reprinted with permission from World Eagle, 111 King Street, Littleton, MA 01460 U.S.A. 1-800-854-8273. All rights reserved.

Getting Started: Listening

Cricket Magazine, May 1999 issue, Volume 26, Number 9. Copyright ©1999 by Carus Publishing Company. Reprinted by permission of *Cricket* Magazine.

What Does the Crow Know?: The Mysteries of Animal Intelligence by Margery Facklam, illustrated by Pamela Johnson. Illustrations copyright ©1994 by Pamela Johnson. Reprinted by permission of Sierra Club Books for Children.

One Minute Warm-up

6/1 *Discovering the Inca Ice Maiden: My Adventures on Ampato* by Johan Reinhard, published by National Geographic Society, 1998. Used by permission.

6/1 *Mama, I Want to Sing* by Vy Higginsen with Tonya Bolden. Illustration copyright ©1992 by Scholastic Inc. Used by permission.

6/1 *Mama's Gonna Buy You a Mockingbird* by Jean Little, published by Puffin Books, 1984. Used by permission.

6/2 *A Young Painter: The Life and Painting of Wang Yani, China's Extraordinary Artist* by Zhensun Zheng and Alice Low, published by Byron Preiss Visual Publications, 1991. Used by permission.

6/2 *Standing Tall: The Story of Ten Hispanic Americans* by Argentina Palacios, published by Scholastic Inc., 1994. Used by permission.

6/2 *The Wright Brothers: How They Invented the Airplane* by Russell Freedman, original photographs by Wilbur & Orville Wright, published by Holiday House, 1991. Used by permission.

6/3 *A Kind of Grace: The Autobiography of the World's Greatest Female Athlete* by Jackie Joyner-Kersey with Sonja Steptoe, published by Warner Books, 1997. Used by permission.

6/3 *Birthday Surprises: Ten Great Stories to Unwrap* edited by Johanna Hurwitz, published by Morrow Junior Books, 1995. Used by permission.

6/3 *Eyewitness Books: Shell* by Alex Arthur. Copyright ©1989 by Dorling Kindersley, Ltd. Reprinted by permission of Random House Children's Books, a division of Random House, Inc.

Acknowledgments *continued*

6/3 *Geology Crafts for Kids* by Alan Anderson, Gwen Diehn and Terry Krautwurst, published by Sterling Publishing Co., Inc., 1996. Used by permission.

6/4 *Black Artists in Photography, 1840–1940* by George Sullivan, published by Cobblehill Books, 1996. Used by permission.

6/4 *Hatchet* by Gary Paulsen. Text copyright ©1987 by Gary Paulsen. Cover illustration copyright ©1987 by Neil Waldman. Reprinted with the permission of Simon & Schuster Books for Young Readers, an imprint of Simon & Schuster Children's Publishing Division and Neil Waldman.

6/4 *Talking with Adventurers* compiled and edited by Pat Cummings & Linda Cummings, Ph.D., published by National Geographic Society, 1998. Used by permission.

6/4 *The Wind at Work: An Activity Guide to Windmills* by Gretchen Woelfle. Copyright ©1997 by Gretchen Woelfle. Published by Chicago Review Press, Incorporated, 814 North Franklin Street, Chicago, Illinois 60610, ISBN 1-55652-308-4. Used by permission.

6/5 *Baseball in April and Other Stories* by Gary Soto, published by Harcourt Brace & Company, 1990. Used by permission.

6/5 *One-Man Team* by Dean Hughes, cover illustration by Dennis Lyall. Cover illustration copyright ©1994 by Dennis Lyall. Reprinted by permission of Random House Children's Books, a division of Random House, Inc.

6/5 *Sally Ride: A Space Biography* by Barbara Kramer, published by Enslow Publishers, Inc., 1998. Used by permission.

6/5 *The Workers' Detective: A Story About Dr. Alice Hamilton* by Stephanie Sammartino McPherson, illustrated by Janet Schulz, published by Carolrhoda Books, Inc., 1992. Used by permission.

6/6 *Bounce Back* by Sheryl Swoopes with Greg Brown, illustrated by Doug Keith, published by Taylor Publishing Company, Dallas, Texas, 1996. Used by permission.

6/6 *Storms* by Seymour Simon, published by Morrow Junior Books, 1989. Used by permission.

6/6 *The View from Saturday* by E. L. Konigsburg. Copyright ©1996 by E. L. Konigsburg. Jacket illustration copyright ©1996 by E. L. Konigsburg. Reprinted with the permission of Atheneum Books for Young Readers, an imprint of Simon & Schuster Children's Publishing Division.

6/7 *By the Shores of Silver Lake* by Laura Ingalls Wilder, illustrated by Garth Williams, published by HarperCollins Publishers, 1953. Used by permission.

6/7 *Quarterback Walk-On* by Thomas J. Dygard, published by William Morrow & Company, 1982. Used by permission.

Student Writing Model Contributors
Hector Alonso, Sarah Amaya, Binay Paul Singh Athwal, Kyle Colligan, Elizabeth Coultas, Jessica Figueroa, James Glover, Ron Golan, Ben Gross, Dava Hollingsworth, Clara Kraft, Roy Kramka, Yurico Tellex, Ximena Vengoechea

Acknowledgments

Every effort has been made to contact the student Sarah Amaya for permission to reprint her poem "Circus Elephant." Address any information regarding her present address to School Permissions, Houghton Mifflin Company, 222 Berkeley Street, Boston, Massachusetts 02116.

Credits

Illustrations

Special Characters illustrated by: Joe, the Writing Pro by Rick Stromoski; Pencil Dog by Jennifer Beck Harris; Enrichment Animals by Scott Matthews.
John Bendall-Brunello: 35, 55, 120, 283, 295, 322 (top)
Ann Bissett: H30 (left)
Randy Chewning: 244
Chris Demarest: 234 (top), 254, 300, 355, 520-522
Eldon Doty: 197 (top), 287
Cynthia Fisher: 105 (bottom), 301 (bottom), 334 (bottom)
Kate Flanagan: 189, 322 (bottom)
Bonnie Gee: H18
Jennifer Harris: 191 (top)
Marian Heibel: 32, 181
Betsy James: 361
John Jones: 1-4, 6-8
True Kelley: 47, 191 (bottom), 285, 329
Victor Kennedy: 92
Jared Lee: 188
Andy Levine: 141, 197 (center)
Brian Lies: 385, 386, 390
Patrick Merrell: 86, 144, 147, 246, 330
Laurie Newton-King: 38
Tim Nihoff: 84
Beth Peck: 10
Trevor Pye: 234 (center)
Michael Reid: 23
Tim Robinson: 154
Claudia Sargent: H20, H105, H106 (top), H112-H116
Ellen Sasaki: 422

Lauren Scheuer: 104, 159, 212, 260 (center), 333, 334 (center), 451, 563, 564
Rémy Simard: 62, 126, 192
Michael Sloan: 41, 57
Jim Stout: H30 (right)
George Ulrich: 203, 206, 290, H106 (bottom)
Matt Wawiorka: 91, 153, 487
Bill Whitney: 249
Amy L. Young: 255, 279

Maps

Ortelius: 499, H31

Photographs

iv © Index Stock Photography, Inc. vi © Ron Sherman/Tony Stone Images. vii © Paul Chesley/National Geographic Image Collection. ix © Jeff Greenberg/PhotoEdit. xi Courtesy NASA. xii © Tim Wright/CORBIS. xiii © John Martin/The Stock Market. 31 © Tim Davis/The Stock Market. 34 © PhotoDisc, Inc. 35 © Mark Richards/PhotoEdit. 38 © Jonathan Blair/CORBIS. 40 © Culver Pictures. 41 © Jim Pickerell/Stock Connection/Picture Quest. 44 © Will & Deni McIntyre/Tony Stone Images. 47 © Paul Conklin/PhotoEdit. 48 © Chris Cheadle/Tony Stone Images. 50 (t) © CORBIS. (b) © PhotoDisc, Inc. 51 © PhotoDisc, Inc. 53 © Alejandro Balaguer/Tony Stone Images. 54 © PhotoDisc, Inc. 55 © Mark E. Gibson/Visuals Unlimited. 58 © Jeremy Woodhouse/PhotoDisc, Inc. 60 ©

PhotoDisc, Inc. **61** © James Gritz/PhotoDisc, Inc. **63** © David Madison/Tony Stone Images. **64** © Sandy Felsenthal/CORBIS. **65** © SuperStock, Inc. **69** © PhotoDisc, Inc. **73** © PhotoDisc, Inc. **75** © Bob Daemmrich/Stock Boston. **77** © PhotoDisc, Inc. **78** © C Squared Studios/PhotoDisc, Inc. **81** © Renee Stockdale/Animals Animals. **82** Image provided by MetaTools. **83** © Index Stock Photography, Inc. **84** © Jeff Greenberg/Visuals Unlimited. **88** © The Granger Collection, New York. **89** Courtesy of NASA. **90** © Richard Cummins/CORBIS. **93** © Frank Siteman/PhotoEdit. **94** © Bill Ivy/Tony Stone Images. **97** © Eastcott/Momatiuk/Tony Stone Images. **98** © Schomburg Center for Research in Black Culture. **99** © C Squared Studios/PhotoDisc, Inc. **100** © Bettmann/CORBIS. **102** © Art Wolfe/Tony Stone Images. **107** © Ariel Skelley/The Stock Market. **110** © PhotoDisc, Inc. **111** © Richard Laird/FPG International. **113** © Telegraph Colour Library/FPG International. **115** © PhotoDisc, Inc. **117** © Index Stock Photography, Inc. **118** © D. Cavagnaro/Visuals Unlimited. **119** © PhotoDisc, Inc. **121** © The Granger Collection, New York. **123** © SuperStock, Inc. **124** © Rudi Von Briel/PhotoEdit. **129** © Pete Saloutos/The Stock Market. **130** © Jack M. Bostrack/Visuals Unlimited. **133** © David Taylor/Allsport. **134** © Reuters Newmedia, Inc./CORBIS. **135** © Bob Daemmrich/The Image Works. **137** © Jim Whitmer. **140** © Tom Prettyman/PhotoEdit. **142** (l) © Spencer Grant/PhotoEdit. (r) © David Young-Wolff/PhotoEdit. **143** © National Gallery of Art, Washington, D.C./SuperStock, Inc. **145** © Ted Wood/Tony Stone Images. **148** ©

Jon Riley/Tony Stone Images. **151** © Rich Frishman/Tony Stone Images. **152** © InterNetwork Media/PhotoDisc, Inc. **155** © PhotoDisc, Inc. **156** © PhotoMondo/FPG International. **166** © Don Brown/Animals Animals. **167** © Bob Thomason/Tony Stone Images. **168** © SuperStock, Inc. **169** © David Young-Wolff/PhotoEdit. **170** © Charles Philip/Visuals Unlimited. **171** © Robert Brenner/PhotoEdit. **173** © PhotoDisc, Inc. **174** © Ralph Reinhold/Animals Animals. **176** © Clayton J. Price/The Stock Market. **178** © Walter Hodges/Tony Stone Images. **179** © Peter Cade/Tony Stone Images. **183** Courtesy Schwinn Cycling and Fitness, Inc. **184** © Joe Atlas/Artville. **186** © Ned Therrien/Visuals Unlimited. **187** (t) © Lee Foster/Words & Pictures/Picture Quest. (b) © Adalberto Rios Szalay/Sexto Sol/PhotoDisc, Inc. **195** © Robert Frerck/Tony Stone Images. **196** (t) © Stockbyte. (b) © Comstock, Inc. **198** © Chuck Fishman/Contact Press Images/Picture Quest. **199** © Michael Newman/PhotoEdit. **200** © Peter Cade/Tony Stone Images. **201** (tl) © American Images/FPG International/Picture Quest. (tr) © Tony Freeman/PhotoEdit. (br) © Andrea Booher/Tony Stone Images. (bl) © Kindra Clineff/AllStock/Picture Quest. **202** © Gabe Palmer/The Stock Market. **204** © John Darling/Tony Stone Images. **205** © Corel Corporation. **207** © David Young-Wolff/PhotoEdit. **209** © Mary Steinbacher/PhotoEdit. **210** © A. Ramey/PhotoEdit. **211** © CORBIS. **212** © CORBIS. **213** © Sven Martson/The Image Works. **219** © Walter Hodges/Tony Stone Images. **220** (t) © Antonio M.

Rosario/The Image Bank. (b) © Chuck Mason/International Stock Photo. **221** © PhotoDisc, Inc. **222** © Jean Kugler/FPG International. **223** © Myrleen Ferguson/PhotoEdit. **224** © J. Marshall/The Image Works. **225** © Jerry Driendl/FPG International. **227** (t) © PhotoDisc, Inc. (b) © Comstock, Inc. **228** © Comstock, Inc. **229** © Amos Nachoum/CORBIS. **231** © Newberry Library, Chicago/SuperStock, Inc. **233** © Ron Sherman/Tony Stone Images. **237** © The Granger Collection, New York. Frame provided by MetaTools. **238** © Bettmann/CORBIS. **240** © PhotoDisc, Inc. **241** © Barbara Filet/Tony Stone Images. **243** © PhotoDisc, Inc. **247** © The Granger Collection, New York. **248** © MetaCreations. **250** © PhotoDisc, Inc. **252** © Rich Iwasaki/AllStock/Picture Quest. **256** © Scott Barrow/International Stock Photo. **265** © PhotoDisc, Inc. **267** © Renee Stockdale/Animals Animals. **268** © PhotoDisc, Inc. **269** © Comstock, Inc. **271** © Tom & DeeAnn McCarthy/The Stock Market. **272** Image provided by MetaTools. **273** © Paul Chesley/National Geographic Image Collection. **275** © Dennis O'Clair/Tony Stone Images. **276** © Tony Freeman/PhotoEdit. **277** © Coco McCoy/Rainbow/Picture Quest. **279** © The Granger Collection, New York. **280** © David Myers/Tony Stone Images. **285** © Jeff Greenberg/Stock Boston. **287** © Charles Gupton/Stock Boston. **288** © The Granger Collection, New York. **289** © CORBIS. **291** © Paul Conklin/PhotoEdit. **292** © Corel Corporation. **294** © Jon Feingersh/The Stock Market. **295** © Hunter Freeman/Tony Stone Images. **296** © PhotoDisc, Inc. **298** © Tony Freeman/PhotoEdit/Picture Quest. **299** © David Young-Wolff/PhotoEdit. **307** © Joe Patronite/The Image Bank. **309** © Artville. **311** © PhotoDisc, Inc. **312** © PhotoDisc, Inc. **313** © CORBIS. **315** © Ed Pritchard/Tony Stone Images. **317** © Caroline Wood/AllStock/Picture Quest. **318** Courtesy of NASA. **319** © Robert Holmes/CORBIS. **321** © Kevin Jacobus/The Image Works. **324** © Ted Streshinsky/CORBIS. **326** © Bettmann/CORBIS. **327** © N. P. Alexander/Visuals Unlimited. **330** © SuperStock, Inc. **330** Frame provided by MetaTools. **332** © Breck P. Kent/Earth Scenes. **336** © Victor Scocozza/FPG International. **339** © PhotoDisc, Inc. **340** © CORBIS. **342** © M. Gibbs/Animals Animals. **343** © SuperStock, Inc. **344** © PhotoDisc, Inc. **345** © CORBIS. **347** © Robert Frerck/Woodfin Camp & Associates. **350** © Ken Biggs/Tony Stone Images. **350-51** © Jeff Greenberg/PhotoEdit. **351** (b) © Paul Barton/The Stock Market. **352** © Jim Callaway (used by permission of Virginia Hamilton). **356** © Renee Lynn/Tony Stone Images. **358** © Ken Biggs/Tony Stone Images. **368** (l) © StockTrek/PhotoDisc, Inc. (r) © Ed Bock/The Stock Market. **371** © Joe Atlas/Artville. **381** © Hirshhorn Museum and Sculpture Garden, Smithsonian Institution, Gift of Joseph H. Hirshhorn, 1966. Photo by Lee Stalsworth. **387** © David Muench/CORBIS. **388** © Kevin R. Morris/CORBIS. **393** (l) © Samuel Hoffman/*Fort Wayne Journal Gazette*. (r) © Ivan Strass. **394** © Dave G. Houser/CORBIS. **396** © Paul Barton/The Stock Market. **397** © NASA/Roger Ressmeyer/CORBIS. **399** (t) © Joseph Sohm/ChromoSohm, Inc./CORBIS.

Acknowledgments *continued*

(b) © Richard Hamilton Smith/CORBIS. **403** © PhotoDisc, Inc. **420** Courtesy NASA. **423** © PhotoDisc, Inc. **430** © Michael S. Yamashita/CORBIS. **430-1** Courtesy NASA. **431** © Werner Otto/Tony Stone Images. **432** © Wolfgang Kaehler/CORBIS. **433** © Peter Weimann/Animals Animals. **434** © Liane Enkelis/Stock Boston/Picture Quest. **435** © David Sieren/Visuals Unlimited. **436** © CORBIS. **437** (t) © Joe McDonald/CORBIS. (b) © Buddy Mays/CORBIS. **438** © Myrleen Ferguson/PhotoEdit. **440** © Michael S. Yamashita/CORBIS. **441** © R.W. Murphy. **442** © Kerry T. Givens/Tom Stack. **452** (t) © PhotoDisc, Inc. (b) © Gunter Marx/CORBIS. **470** © Bettmann/CORBIS. **471** (l) © M. Wendler/Okapia/Photo Researchers, Inc. (r) © Beth Wald/Network Aspen. **472** © Werner Otto/Tony Stone Images. **474** Courtesy Miriam and Ira D. Wallach Division of Art, Prints & Photographs. The New York Public Library. Astor, Lenox and Tilden Foundations. **475** Courtesy Library of Congress, neg. #62-14736. **476** © Ron Chapple/FPG International. **480** (l) © Joe McDonald/CORBIS. (c) © Fritz Prenzel/Animals Animals. (r) © Alan Root/Okapia/Photo Researchers, Inc. **483** (r) © Alan Root/Okapia/Photo Researchers, Inc. **484** © Fritz Prenzel/Animals Animals. **488** © Michael Krasowitz/FPG International. **493** (t) © Donald Specker/Animals Animals. (ct) © Robert Western/Tony Stone Images. (cb) © Bill Ivy/Tony Stone Images. (b) © James Gritz/PhotoDisc, Inc. **494** © Arthur Tilley/FPG International/Picture Quest. **500** © CORBIS. **505** © G.K. & Vikki Hart/The Image Bank/Picture Quest.

507 © Fisher/Thatcher/Tony Stone Images. **512** (t) © PhotoDisc, Inc. (b) © Boltin Picture Library. **514** © Ted Horowitz/The Stock Market. **516** © Tim Wright/CORBIS. **516-7** © John Martin/The Stock Market. **517** © Jodi Cobb/National Geographic Image Collection. **518** © W. Perry Conway/CORBIS. **519** © Chris Jones/The Stock Market. **524** © Tim Wright/CORBIS. **526** Courtesy Alma Flor Ada. **541** © Ariel Skelley/The Stock Market. **551** © Jodi Cobb/National Geographic Image Collection. **563** © Russell Illig/PhotoDisc, Inc. **566** © Alan Becker/The Image Bank. **567** © Warren Faidley/International Stock. **574** © Kactus Foto, Santiago, Chile/Kactus Foto/SuperStock, Inc. **583** © David Young-Wolff/PhotoEdit. **H8** © Greg Kuchik/PhotoDisc, Inc. **H13** © Bob Rowan/Progressive Image/CORBIS. **H16** © SuperStock, Inc. **H21** © PhotoDisc, Inc. **H28** © David Burnett/Contact Press Images/Picture Quest. **H32** Courtesy NASA. **H35** © Jeff Zaruba/The Stock Market. **H54** (t) © Bettmann/CORBIS. (b) © Brown Brothers.

Cover Photograph

© John Martin/The Stock Market.